Advances in Machine Learning Applications in Software Engineering

Du Zhang
California State University, USA

Jeffrey J.P. Tsai
University of Illinois at Chicago, USA

IDEA GROUP PUBLISHING

Hershey • London • Melbourne • Singapore

Acquisitions Editor:	Kristin Klinger
Development Editor:	Kristin Roth
Senior Managing Editor:	Jennifer Neidig
Managing Editor:	Sara Reed
Assistant Managing Editor:	Sharon Berger
Copy Editor:	Amanda Appicello
Typesetter:	Amanda Appicello
Cover Design:	Lisa Tosheff
Printed at:	Integrated Book Technology

Published in the United States of America by
 Idea Group Publishing (an imprint of Idea Group Inc.)
 701 E. Chocolate Avenue
 Hershey PA 17033
 Tel: 717-533-8845
 Fax: 717-533-8661
 E-mail: cust@idea-group.com
 Web site: http://www.idea-group.com

and in the United Kingdom by
 Idea Group Publishing (an imprint of Idea Group Inc.)
 3 Henrietta Street
 Covent Garden
 London WC2E 8LU
 Tel: 44 20 7240 0856
 Fax: 44 20 7379 0609
 Web site: http://www.eurospanonline.com

Library of Congress Cataloging-in-Publication Data

Advances in machine learning applications in software engineering / Du Zhang and Jeffrey J.P. Tsai, editors.
 p. cm.
 Summary: "This book provides analysis, characterization and refinement of software engineering data in terms of machine learning methods. It depicts applications of several machine learning approaches in software systems development and deployment, and the use of machine learning methods to establish predictive models for software quality while offering readers suggestions by proposing future work in this emerging research field"--Provided by publisher.
 Includes bibliographical references and index.
 ISBN 1-59140-941-1 (hardcover) -- ISBN 1-59140-942-X (softcover) -- ISBN 1-59140-943-8 (ebook)
 1. Software engineering. 2. Self-adaptive software. 3. Application software. 4. Machine learning. I. Zhang, Du. II. Tsai, Jeffrey J.-P.
 QA76.758.A375 2007
 005.1--dc22
       2006031366

British Cataloguing in Publication Data
A Cataloguing in Publication record for this book is available from the British Library.

Advances in Machine Learning Applications in Software Engineering

Table of Contents

Preface.. vi

Section I: Data Analysis and Refinement

Chapter I
A Two-Stage Zone Regression Method for Global Characterization of a Project
Database.. 1
    J. J. Dolado, University of the Basque Country, Spain
    D. Rodríguez, University of Reading, UK
    J. Riquelme, University of Seville, Spain
    F. Ferrer-Troyano, University of Seville, Spain
    J. J. Cuadrado, University of Alcalá de Henares, Spain

Chapter II
Intelligent Analysis of Software Maintenance Data................................ 14
    Marek Reformat, University of Alberta, Canada
    Petr Musilek, University of Alberta, Canada
    Efe Igbide, University of Alberta, Canada

Chapter III
Improving Credibility of Machine Learner Models in Software Engineering...... 52
    Gary D. Boetticher, University of Houston – Clear Lake, USA

Section II: Applications to Software Development

Chapter IV
ILP Applications to Software Engineering 74
    Daniele Gunetti, Università degli Studi di Torino, Italy

Chapter V
MMIR: An Advanced Content-Based Image Retrieval System Using a
Hierarchical Learning Framework 103
    Min Chen, Florida International University, USA
    Shu-Ching Chen, Florida International University, USA

Chapter VI
A Genetic Algorithm-Based QoS Analysis Tool for Reconfigurable
Service-Oriented Systems 121
    I-Ling Yen, University of Texas at Dallas, USA
    Tong Gao, University of Texas at Dallas, USA
    Hui Ma, University of Texas at Dallas, USA

Section III: Predictive Models for Software Quality and Relevancy

Chapter VII
Fuzzy Logic Classifiers and Models in Quantitative Software Engineering 148
    Witold Pedrycz, University of Alberta, Canada
    Giancarlo Succi, Free University of Bolzano, Italy

Chapter VIII
Modeling Relevance Relations Using Machine Learning Techniques 168
    Jelber Sayyad Shirabad, University of Ottawa, Canada
    Timothy C. Lethbridge, University of Ottawa, Canada
    Stan Matwin, University of Ottawa, Canada

Chapter IX
A Practical Software Quality Classification Model Using Genetic
Programming 208
    Yi Liu, Georgia College & State University, USA
    Taghi M. Khoshgoftaar, Florida Atlantic University, USA

Chapter X
A Statistical Framework for the Prediction of Fault-Proneness 237
    Yan Ma, West Virginia University, USA
    Lan Guo, West Virginia University, USA
    Bojan Cukic, West Virginia University, USA

Section IV: State-of-the-Practice

Chapter XI
Applying Rule Induction in Software Prediction 265
    Bhekisipho Twala, Brunel University, UK
    Michelle Cartwright, Brunel University, UK
    Martin Shepperd, Brunel University, UK

Chapter XII
Application of Genetic Algorithms in Software Testing 287
    Baowen Xu, Southeast University & Jiangsu Institute of Software Quality,
      China
    Xiaoyuan Xie, Southeast University & Jiangsu Institute of Software Quality,
      China
    Liang Shi, Southeast University & Jiangsu Institute of Software Quality,
      China
    Changhai Nie, Southeast University & Jiangsu Institute of Software Quality,
      China

Section V: Areas of Future Work

Chapter XIII
Formal Methods for Specifying and Analyzing Complex Software Systems 319
    Xudong He, Florida International University, USA
    Huiqun Yu, East China University of Science and Technology, China
    Yi Deng, Florida International University, USA

Chapter XIV
Practical Considerations in Automatic Code Generation 346
    Paul Dietz, Motorola, USA
    Aswin van den Berg, Motorola, USA
    Kevin Marth, Motorola, USA
    Thomas Weigert, Motorola, USA
    Frank Weil, Motorola, USA

Chapter XV
DPSSEE: A Distributed Proactive Semantic Software Engineering
Environment 409
    Donghua Deng, University of California, Irvine, USA
    Phillip C.-Y. Sheu, University of California, Irvine, USA

Chapter XVI
Adding Context into an Access Control Model for Computer Security Policy ... 439
    Shangping Ren, Illinois Institute of Technology, USA
    Jeffrey J.P. Tsai, University of Illinois at Chicago, USA
    Ophir Frieder, Illinois Institute of Technology, USA

About the Editors 457

About the Authors 458

Index 467

Preface

Machine learning is the study of how to build computer programs that improve their performance at some task through experience. The hallmark of machine learning is that it results in an improved ability to make better decisions. Machine learning algorithms have proven to be of great practical value in a variety of application domains. Not surprisingly, the field of software engineering turns out to be a fertile ground where many software development and maintenance tasks could be formulated as learning problems and approached in terms of learning algorithms.

To meet the challenge of developing and maintaining large and complex software systems in a dynamic and changing environment, machine learning methods have been playing an increasingly important role in many software development and maintenance tasks. The past two decades have witnessed an increasing interest, and some encouraging results and publications in machine learning application to software engineering. As a result, a crosscutting niche area emerges. Currently, there are efforts to raise the awareness and profile of this crosscutting, emerging area, and to systematically study various issues in it. It is our intention to capture, in this book, some of the latest advances in this emerging niche area.

Machine Learning Methods

Machine learning methods fall into the following broad categories: *supervised* learning, *unsupervised* learning, *semi-supervised* learning, *analytical* learning, and *reinforcement* learning. Supervised learning deals with learning a target function from labeled examples. Unsupervised learning attempts to learn patterns and associations from a set of objects that do not have attached class labels. Semi-supervised learning is learning from a combination of labeled and unlabeled examples. Analytical learning relies on domain theory or background knowledge, instead of labeled examples, to learn a target function. Reinforcement learning is concerned with learning a control policy through reinforcement from an environment.

There are a number of important issues in machine learning:

- How is a target function represented and specified (based on the formalism used to represent a target function, there are different machine learning approaches)? What are the interpretability, complexity, and properties of a target function? How does it generalize?
- What is the hypothesis space (the search space)? What are its properties?
- What are the issues in the search process for a target function? What are heuristics and bias utilized in searching for a target function?
- Is there any background knowledge or domain theory available for the learning process?
- What properties do the training data have?
- What are the theoretical underpinnings and practical issues in the learning process?

The following are some frequently-used machine learning methods in the aforementioned categories.

In concept learning, a target function is represented as a conjunction of constraints on attributes. The hypothesis space H consists of a lattice of possible conjunctions of attribute constraints for a given problem domain. A least-commitment search strategy is adopted to eliminate hypotheses in H that are not consistent with the training set D. This will result in a structure called the version space, the subset of hypotheses that are consistent with the training data. The algorithm, called the candidate elimination, utilizes the generalization and specialization operations to produce the version space with regard to H and D. It relies on a language (or restriction) bias that states that the target function is contained in H. This is an eager and supervised learning method. It is not robust to noise in data and does not have support for prior knowledge accommodation.

In decision tree learning, a target function is defined as a decision tree. Search in decision tree learning is often guided by an entropy-based information gain measure that indicates how much information a test on an attribute yields. Learning algorithms often have a bias for small trees. It is an eager, supervised, and unstable learning method, and is susceptible to noisy data, a cause for overfitting. It cannot accommodate prior knowledge during the learning process. However, it scales up well with large data in several different ways.

In neural network learning, given a fixed network structure, learning a target function amounts to finding weights for the network such that the network outputs are the same as (or within an acceptable range of) the expected outcomes as specified in the training data. A vector of weights in essence defines a target function. This makes the target function very difficult for human to read and interpret. This is an eager, supervised, and unstable learning approach and cannot accommodate prior knowledge. A popular algorithm for feed-forward networks is backpropagation, which adopts a gradient descent search and sanctions an inductive bias of smooth interpolation between data points.

Bayesian learning offers a probabilistic approach to inference, which is based on the assumption that the quantities of interest are dictated by probability distributions, and that optimal decisions or classifications can be reached by reasoning about these probabilities along with observed data. Bayesian learning methods can be divided into two groups based on the outcome of the learner: the ones that produce the most probable hypothesis given the training data, and the ones that produce the most probable classification of a new instance given the training data. A target function is thus explicitly represented in the first group, but implicitly defined in the second group. One of the main advantages is that it accommodates prior knowledge (in the form of Bayesian belief networks, prior probabilities for candidate hypotheses, or a probability distribution over observed data for a possible hypothesis). The classification of an unseen case is obtained through combined predictions of multiple hypotheses. It also scales up well with large data. It is an eager and supervised learning method and does not require search during learning process. Though it has no problem with noisy data, Bayesian learning has difficulty with small data sets. Bayesian learning adopts a bias that is based on the minimum description length principle.

Genetic algorithms and genetic programming are both biologically-inspired learning methods. A target function is represented as bit strings in genetic algorithms, or as programs in genetic programming. The search process starts with a population of initial hypotheses. Through the crossover and mutation operations, members of current population give rise to the next generation of population. During each step of the iteration, hypotheses in the current population are evaluated with regard to a given measure of fitness, with the fittest hypotheses being selected as members of the next generation. The search process terminates when some hypothesis h has a fitness value above some threshold. Thus, the learning process is essentially embodied in the generate-and-test beam search. The bias is fitness-driven. There are generational and steady-state algorithms.

Instance-based learning is a typical lazy learning approach in the sense that generalizing beyond the training data is deferred until an unseen case needs to be classified. In addition, a target function is not explicitly defined; instead, the learner returns a target function value when classifying a given unseen case. The target function value is generated based on a subset of the training data that is considered to be local to the unseen example, rather than on the entire training data. This amounts to approximating a different target function for a distinct unseen example. This is a significant departure from the eager learning methods where a single target function is obtained as a result of the learner generalizing from the entire training data. The search process is based on statistical reasoning, and consists in identifying training data that are close to the given unseen case and producing the target function value based on its neighbors. Popular algorithms include: K-nearest neighbors, case-based reasoning, and locally weighted regression.

Because a target function in inductive logic programming is defined by a set of (propositional or first-order) rules, it is highly amenable to human readability and interpretability. It lends itself to incorporation of background knowledge during learning process, and is an eager and supervised learning. The bias sanctioned by ILP includes rule accuracy, FOIL-gain, or preference of shorter clauses. There are a number of algorithms: SCA, FOIL, PROGOL, and inverted resolution.

Instead of learning a non-linear target function from data in the input space directly, support vector machines use a kernel function (defined in the form of inner product of training data) to transform the training data from the input space into a high dimensional feature space F first, and then learn the optimal linear separator (a hyperplane) in F. A decision function, defined based on the linear separator, can be used to classify unseen cases. Kernel functions play a pivotal role in support vector machines. A kernel function relies only on a subset of the training data called support vectors.

In ensemble learning, a target function is essentially the result of combining, through weighted or unweighted voting, a set of component or base-level functions called an ensemble. An ensemble can have a better predictive accuracy than its component function if (1) individual functions disagree with each other, (2) individual functions have a predictive accuracy that is slightly better than random classification (e.g., error rates below 0.5 for binary classification), and (3) individual functions' errors are at least somewhat uncorrelated. ensemble learning can be seen as a learning strategy that addresses inadequacies in training data (insufficient information in training data to help select a single best $h \in H$), in search algorithms (deployment of multiple hypotheses amounts to compensating for less than perfect search algorithms), and in the representation of H (weighted combination of individual functions makes it possible to represent a true function $f \notin H$). Ultimately, an ensemble is less likely to misclassify than just a single component function.

Two main issues exist in ensemble learning: ensemble construction and classification combination. There are bagging, cross-validation, and boosting methods for constructing ensembles, and weighted vote and unweighted vote for combining classifications. The Ada-Boost algorithm is one of the best methods for constructing ensembles of decision trees.

There are two approaches to ensemble construction. One is to combine component functions that are homogeneous (derived using the same learning algorithm and being defined in the same representation formalism, for example, an ensemble of functions derived by decision tree method) and weak (slightly better than random guessing). Another approach is to combine component functions that are heterogeneous (derived by different learning algorithms and being represented in different formalisms, for example, an ensemble of functions derived by decision trees, instance-based learning, Bayesian learning, and neural networks) and strong (each of the component functions performs relatively well in its own right).

Multiple instance learning deals with the situation in which each training example may have several variant instances. If we use a bag to indicate the set of all variant instances for a training example, then for a Boolean class the label for the bag is positive if there is at least one variant instance in the bag that has a positive label. A bag has a negative label if all variant instances in the bag have a negative label. The learning algorithm is to approximate a target function that can classify every variant instance of an unseen negative example as negative, and at least one variant instance of an unseen positive example as positive.

In unsupervised learning, a learner is to analyze a set of objects that do not have their class labels, and discern the categories to which objects belong. Given a set of objects as input, there are two groups of approaches in unsupervised learning: density estimation methods that can be used in creating statistical models to capture or explain underlying patterns or interesting structures behind the input, and feature extraction methods that can be used to glean statistical features (regularities or irregularities) directly from the input. Unlike supervised learning, there is no direct measure of success for unsupervised learning. In general, it is difficult to establish the validity of inferences from the output unsupervised learning algorithms produce. Most frequently utilized methods under unsupervised learning include: association rules, cluster analysis, self-organizing maps, and principal component analysis.

Semi-supervised learning relies on a collection of labeled and unlabeled examples. The learning starts with using the labeled examples to obtain an initial target function, which is then used to classify the unlabeled examples, thus generating additional labeled examples. The learning process will be iterated on the augmented training set. Some semi-supervised learning methods include: expectation-maximization with generative mixture models, self-training, co-training, transductive support vector machines, and graph-based methods.

When a learner has some level of control over which part of the input domain it relies on in generating a target function, this is referred to as active learning. The control the learner possesses over the input example selection is called selective sampling. Active learning can be adopted in the following setting in semi-supervised learning: the learner identifies the most informative unlabeled examples and asks the user to label them. This combination of active learning and semi-supervised learning results in what is referred to as the multi-view learning.

Analytical learning allows a target function to be generalized from a domain theory (prior knowledge about the problem domain). The learned function has a good readability and interpretability. In analytical learning, search is performed in the form of deductive reasoning. The search bias in explanation based learning, a major analytical learning method, is a domain theory and preference of a small set of Horn clauses. One important perspective of explanation based learning is that learning can be construed as recompiling or reformulating the knowledge in the domain theory so as to make it operationally more efficient when classifying unseen cases. EBL algorithms include Prolog-EBG.

Both inductive learning and analytical learning have their props and cons. The former requires plentiful data (thus vulnerable to data quality and quantity problems), while the latter relies on a domain theory (hence susceptible to domain theory quality and quantity problems). Inductive analytical learning is meant to provide a framework where benefits from both approaches can be strengthened and impact of drawbacks minimized. It usually encompasses an inductive learning component and an analytical learning component. It requires both a training set and a domain theory, and can be an eager and supervised learning. The issues of target function representation, search, and bias are largely determined by the underlying learning components involved.

Reinforcement learning is the most general form of learning. It tackles the issue of how to learn a sequence of actions called a control strategy from indirect and delayed reward information (reinforcement). It is an eager and unsupervised learning. Its search is carried out through training episodes. Two main approaches exist for reinforcement learning: model-based and model-free approaches. The best-known model-free algorithm is Q-learning. In Q-learning, actions with maximum Q value are preferred.

Machine Learning Applications in Software Engineering

In software engineering, there are three categories of entities: processes, products and resources. Processes are collections of software related activities, such as constructing specification, detailed design, or testing. Products refer to artifacts, deliverables, documents that result from a process activity, such as a specification document, a design document, or a segment of code. Resources are entities required by a process activity, such as personnel, software tools, or hardware. The aforementioned entities have internal and external attributes. Internal attributes describe an entity itself, whereas external attributes characterize the behavior of an entity (how the entity relates to its environment). Machine learning methods have been utilized to develop better software products, to be part of software products, and to make software development process more efficient and effective. The following is a partial list of software engineering areas where machine learning applications have found their way into:

- Predicting or estimating measurements for either internal or external attributes of processes, products, or resources. These include: software quality, software size, software development cost, project or software effort, maintenance task effort, software resource, correction cost, software reliability, software defect, reusability, software release timing, productivity, execution times, and testability of program modules.

- Discovering either internal or external properties of processes, products, or resources. These include: loop invariants, objects in programs, boundary of normal operations, equivalent mutants, process models, and aspects in aspect-oriented programming.

- Transforming products to accomplish some desirable or improved external attributes. These include: transforming serial programs to parallel ones, improving software modularity, and Mapping OO applications to heterogeneous distributed environments.

- Synthesizing or generating various products. These include: test data, test resource, project management rules, software agents, design repair knowledge, design schemas, data structures, programs/scripts, project management schedule, and information graphics.

- Reusing products or processes. These include: similarity computing, active browsing, cost of rework, knowledge representation, locating and adopting software to specifications, generalizing program abstractions, and clustering of components.

- Enhancing processes. These include: deriving specifications of system goals and requirements, extracting specifications from software, acquiring knowledge for specification refinement and augmentation, and acquiring and maintaining specification consistent with scenarios.

- Managing products. These include: collecting and managing software development knowledge, and maintaining software process knowledge.

Organization of the Book

This book includes sixteen chapters that are organized into five sections. The first section has three chapters (Chapters I-III) that deal with analysis, characterization, and refinement of software engineering data in terms of machine learning methods. The second section includes three chapters (Chapters IV-VI) that present applications of several machine learning approaches in helping with software systems development and deployment. The third section contains four chapters (Chapters VII-X) that describe the use of machine learning methods to establish predictive models for software quality and relevancy. Two chapters (Chapters XI-XII) in the fourth section offer some state-of-the-practice on the applications of two machine learning methods. Finally, the four chapters (Chapters XIII-XVI) in the last section of the book serve as areas of future work in this emerging research field.

Chapter I discusses the issue of how to use machine learning methods to refine a large software project database into a new database which captures and retains the essence of the original database, but contains a fewer number of attributes and instances. This new and smaller database would afford the project managers a better chance to gain insight into the database. The proposed data refinement approach is based on the decision tree learning. Authors demonstrate their approach through four datasets in the International Software Benchmarking Standard Group database.

Chapter II is concerned with analyzing software maintenance data to shed light on efforts in defect elimination. Several learning methods (decision tree learning, rule-based learning and genetic algorithm and genetic programming) are utilized to address the following two issues: the number of software components to be examined to remove a single defect, and the total time needed to remove a defect. The maintenance data from a real life software project have been used in the study.

Chapter III takes a closer look at the credibility issue in the empirical-based models. Several experiments have been conducted on five NASA defect datasets using naïve Bayesian classifier and decision tree learning. Several observations have been made: the importance of sampling on non-class attributes, and insufficiency of the ten-fold cross validation in establishing realistic models. The author introduces several credibility metrics that measure the difficulty of a dataset. It is argued that adoption of these credibility metrics will lead to better models and improve their chance of being accepted by software practitioners.

Chapter IV focuses on the applications of inductive logic programming to software engineering. An integrated framework based on inductive logic programming has been proposed for the synthesis, maintenance, reuse, testing and debugging of logic programs. In addition, inductive logic programming has been successfully utilized in genetics, automation of the scientific process, natural language processing and data mining.

Chapter V demonstrates how multiple instance learning and neural networks are integrated with Markov model mediator to address the following challenges in an advanced content-based image retrieval system: the significant discrepancy between the low-level image features and the high-level semantic concepts, and the perception subjectivity problem. Comparative studies on a large set of real-world images indicate the promising performance of this approach.

Chapter VI describes the application of genetic algorithms to reconfigurable service oriented systems. To accommodate reconfigurability in a service-oriented architecture, QoS analysis is often required to make appropriate service selections and configurations. To determine the best selections and configurations, some composition analysis techniques are needed to analyze QoS tradeoffs. The composition analysis framework proposed in this chapter employs a genetic algorithm for composition decision making. A case study is conducted on the selections and configurations of web services.

Chapter VII deals with the issue of software quality models. Authors propose an approach to define logic-driven models based on fuzzy multiplexers. The constructs in such models have a clear and modular topology whose interpretation corresponds to a collection of straightforward logic expressions. Genetic algorithms and genetic optimization underpin the design of the logic models. Experiments on some software dataset illustrate how the logic model allows the number of modifications made to software modules to be obtained from a collection of software metrics.

Chapter VIII defines a notion called relevance relation among software entities. Relevance relations map tuples of software entities to values that signify how related they are to each other. The availability of such relevance relations plays a pivotal role in software development and maintenance, making it possible to predict whether a change to one software entity (one file) results in a change in another entity (file). A process has been developed that allows relevance relations to be learned through decision tree learning. The empirical evaluation, through applying the process to a large legacy system, indicates that the predictive quality of the learned models makes them a viable choice for field deployment.

Chapter IX presents a novel software quality classification model that is based on genetic programming. The proposed model provides not only a classification but also a quality-based ranking for software modules. In evolving a genetic programming based software quality model, three performance criteria have been considered: classification accuracy, module ranking, and the size of the tree. The model has been subjected to case studies of software measurement data from two industrial software systems.

Chapter X describes a software quality prediction model that is used to predict fault prone modules. The model is based on an ensemble of trees voting on prediction decisions to improve its classification accuracy. Five NASA defect datasets have been used to assess the performance of the proposed model. Two strategies have been identified to be effective in the prediction accuracy: proper sampling technique in constructing the tree classifiers, and the threshold adjustment in determining the resulting class.

Chapter XI offers a broad view of the roles rule-based learning plays in software engineering. It provides some background information, discusses the key issues in rule induction, and examines how rule induction handles uncertainties in data. The chapter examines the rule induction applications in the following areas: software effort and cost prediction, software quality prediction, software defect prediction, software intrusion detection, and software process modeling.

Chapter XII, on the other hand, provides a state-of-the-practice overview on genetic algorithm applications to software testing. The focus of the chapter is on evolutionary testing, which is the application of genetic algorithms for test data generation. The central issue in evolutionary testing is a numeric representation of the test objective from which an appropriate fitness function can be defined to evaluate the generated test data. The chapter includes reviews of existing approaches in structural, temporal performance, and specification-based functional evolutionary testing.

Chapter XIII reviews two well-known formal methods, high-level Petri nets and temporal logic, for software system specification and analysis. It pays attention to recent advances in using these formal methods to specify, model and analyze software architectural design. The chapter opens the opportunity for machine learning methods to be utilized in learning either the property specifications or behavior models at element or composition level in a software architectural design phase. In addition, learning methods can be applied to the formal analysis for element correctness, or composition correctness, or refinement correctness.

A model-driven software engineering process advocates developing software systems by creating an executable model of the system design first and then transforming the model into a production quality implementation. The success of the approach hinges critically on the availability of code generators that can transform a model to its implementation. Chapter XIV gives a testimony to the model-driven process. It provides insights, practical considerations, and lessons learned when developing code generators for applications that must conform to the constraints imposed by real-world high-performance systems. Since the model can be construed as the domain theory, analytical learning can be used to help with the transformation process. There have been machine learning applications in program transformation tasks.

Chapter XV outlines a distributed proactive semantic software engineering environment. The proposed environment incorporates logic rules into a software development process to capture the semantics from various levels of the software life cycle. The chapter discusses several scenarios in which semantic rules are used for workflow control, design consistency checking, testing and maintenance. This environment certainly makes it possible to deploy machine learning methods in the rule generator and in the semantic constraint generator to learn constraint rules and proactive rules.

Chapter XVI depicts a role-based access control model that is augmented with the context constraints for computer security policy. There are system contexts and application contexts. Integrating the contextual information into a role-based access control model allows the model to be flexible and capable of specifying various complex access policies, and to be able to provide tight and just-in-time permission activations. Machine learning methods can be used in deriving context constraints from system or application contextual data.

This book is intended particularly for practicing software engineers, and researchers and scientists in either software engineering or machine learning field. The book can also be used either as a textbook for advanced undergraduate or graduate students in a software engineering course, a machine learning application course, or as a reference book for advanced training courses in the field.

Du Zhang
Jeffrey J.P. Tsai

Acknowledgments

We would like to take this opportunity to express our sincere appreciation to all the authors for their contributions, and to all the reviewers for their support and professionalism. We are grateful to Kristin Roth, development editor at IGI for her guidance, help, and encouragement at each step of this project.

Du Zhang
Jeffrey J.P. Tsai

Section I:

Data Analysis and Refinement

This part has three chapters that deal with analysis, characterization and refinement of software engineering data in terms of machine learning methods. There are circumstances in software engineering where data may be plentiful or scarce or anywhere in between. The questions to be asked are: What is the data quality? What do the data convey to project managers or to software engineers? Can machine learning methods help glean useful information from the data?

Chapter I discusses the issue of how to use machine learning methods to refine a large software project database into a new database which captures and retains the essence of the original database, but contains fewer number of attributes and instances. This new and smaller database would afford the project managers a better chance to gain insight into the database. Chapter II is concerned with analyzing software maintenance data to shed light on efforts in defect elimination. Several learning methods are utilized to address the following two issues: the number of software components to be examined to remove a single defect, and the total time needed to remove a defect. Chapter III takes a closer look at the credibility issue in the empirical-based models. Several experiments have been conducted on five NASA defect datasets using naïve Bayesian classifier and decision tree learning. It results in some interesting observations.

Chapter I

A Two-Stage Zone Regression Method for Global Characterization of a Project Database

J. J. Dolado, University of the Basque Country, Spain

D. Rodríguez, University of Reading, UK

J. Riquelme, University of Seville, Spain

F. Ferrer-Troyano, University of Seville, Spain

J. J. Cuadrado, University of Alcalá de Henares, Spain

Abstract

One of the problems found in generic project databases, where the data is collected from different organizations, is the large disparity of its instances. In this chapter, we characterize the database selecting both attributes and instances so that project managers can have a better global vision of the data they manage. To achieve that, we first make use of data mining algorithms to create clusters. From each cluster, instances are selected to obtain a final subset of the database. The result of the process is a smaller database which maintains the prediction capability and has a lower number of instances and attributes than the original, yet allow us to produce better predictions.

Introduction

Successful software engineering projects need to estimate and make use of past data since the inception of the project. In the last decade, several organizations have started to collect data so that companies without historical datasets can use these generic databases for estimation. In some cases, project databases are used to compare data from the organization with other industries, that is, benchmarking. Examples of such organizations collecting data include the International Software Benchmarking Standards Group (ISBSG, 2005) and the Software Technology Transfer Finland (STTF, 2004).

One problem faced by project managers when using these datasets is that the large number of attributes and instances needs to be carefully selected before estimation or benchmarking in a specific organization. For example, the latest release of the ISBSG (2005) has more than 50 attributes and 3,000 instances collected from a large variety of organizations. The project manager has the problem of interpreting and selecting the most adequate instances. In this chapter, we propose an approach to reduce (characterize) such repositories using data mining as shown in Figure 1. The number of attributes is reduced mainly using expert knowledge although the data mining algorithms can help us to identify the most relevant attributes in relation to the output parameter, that is, the attribute that wants to be estimated (e.g., *work effort*). The number of instances or samples in the dataset is reduced by selecting those that contribute to a better accuracy of the estimates after applying a version of the M5 (Quinlan, 1992) algorithm, called M5P, implemented in the Weka toolkit (Witten & Frank, 1999) to four datasets generated from the ISBSG repository. We compare the outputs before and after, characterizing the database using two algorithms provided by Weka, multivariate linear regression (MLR), and least median squares (LMS).

This chapter is organized as follows: the *Techniques Applied* section presents the data mining algorithm; *The Datasets* section describes the datasets used; and the *Evaluation of the Techniques and Characterization of Software Engineering Datasets* section discusses the approach to characterize the database followed by an evaluation of the results. Finally, the *Conclusions* section ends the chapter.

Figure 1. Characterizing dataset for producing better estimates

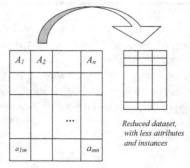

Techniques Applied

Many software engineering problems like cost estimation and forecasting can be viewed as *classification* problems. A classifier resembles a function in the sense that it attaches a value (or a range or a description), named the *class, C,* to a set of attribute values $A_1, A_2,...$ A_n, that is, a classification function will assign a class to a set of descriptions based on the characteristics of the instances for each attribute. For example, as shown in Table 1, given the attributes *size, complexity,* and so forth, a classifier can be used to predict the *effort.*

Table 1. Example of attributes and class in software engineering repository

A_1-Size	...	A_n- Complexity	C - Effort
a_{11}	...	a_{11}	c_1
...	...	...	...
a_{11}	...	a_{nm}	c_n

In this chapter, we have applied data mining, that is, computational techniques and tools designed to support the extraction, in an automatic way, of the information useful for decision support or exploration of the data source (Fayyad, Piatetsky-Shapiro, & Smyth, 1996). Since data may not be organized in a way that facilitates the extraction of useful information, typical data mining processes are composed of the following steps:

- **Data Preparation:** The data is formatted in a way that tools can manipulate it, merged from different databases, and so forth.
- **Data Mining:** It is in this step when the automated extraction of knowledge from the data is carried out. Examples of such algorithms and some usual representations include: C4.5 or M5 for decision trees, regression, and so forth.
- **Proper Interpretation of the Results:** Including the use of visualization techniques.
- **Assimilation of the Results.**

Within the available data mining algorithms, we have used M5 and linear regression classifiers implemented in the Weka toolkit, which have been used to select instances of a software engineering repository. The next sub-sections explain these techniques in more detail.

M5 and M5P

The main problem in linear regression is that the attributes must be numeric so that the model obtained will also be numeric (simple equations in a dimensions). As a solution to this problem, decision trees have been used in data mining for a long time as a supervised learning technique (models are learned from data). A decision tree divides the attribute space into clusters with two main advantages. First, each cluster is clearly defined in the sense that new instances are easily assigned to a cluster (leaf of the tree). The second benefit is that the trees are easily understandable by users in general and by project managers in particular. Each branch of the tree has a condition which reads as follows: *attribute* ≤ *value* or *attribute* > *value* that serve to make selections until a leaf is reached. Such conditions are frequently used by experts in all sciences in decision making.

Decision trees are divided into model trees in which each leaf represents the average value of the instances that are covered by the leaf and regression trees in which each leaf is a regression model. Examples of decision trees include a system called CART (Classification and Regression Trees) developed by Breiman (1984), ID3 (Quinlan, 1986) improved into C4.5 (Quinlan, 1993), and M5 (Quinlan, 1992) with the difference that in M5 the nodes represent linear regressions rather than discrete classes.

The M5 algorithm, the most commonly used classifier of this family, builds regression trees whose leaves are composed of multivariate linear models, and the nodes of the tree are chosen over the attribute that maximizes the expected error reduction as a function of the standard deviation of output parameter. In this work, we have used the M5 algorithm implemented in the Weka toolkit (Witten & Frank, 1999), called M5P. Figure 2 shows Weka's output for the M5P algorithm for one of the datasets that we used for this chapter. In this case, the M5P algorithm created 17 clusters, from LM1 to LM17. The normalized work effort (*NormWorkEff*) is the dependent variable, and a different linear model is applied depending on the number of Function Points (*FP*) and productivity (*NormPDR*). The clusters found can assign to the dependent variable either a constant or a linear equation (in the majority of the cases); in this case, each cluster or region is associated with linear equations (Figure 2, right column) In the example shown in Figure 2, the M5P algorithm created 17 leaves, and we will use *FP* and *NormPDR* to select the appropriate linear model. In this case, the tree

Figure 2. Weka's M5P output

```
FP <= 389.5 :
|   NormPDR <= 16.5 :
|   |   NormPDR <= 6.65 : LM1 (305/8.331%)
|   |   NormPDR >  6.65 : LM2 (318/5.402%)
|   NormPDR >  16.5 :
|   |   NormPDR <= 37.25 :
|   |   |   FP <= 147 : LM3 (124/5.751%)
|   |   |   FP >  147 : LM4 (107/10.878%)
|   |   NormPDR >  37.25 :
|   |   |   FP <= 161 :
|   |   |   |   NormPDR <= 56.9 : LM5 (34/8.323%)
|   |   |   |   NormPDR >  56.9 :
|   |   |   |   |   FP <= 57 : LM6 (9/17.555%)
|   |   |   |   |   FP >  57 : LM7 (34/27.858%)
|   |   |   FP >  161 : LM8 (37/58.384%)
FP >  389.5 :
|   NormPDR <= 8.05 :
|   |   FP <= 1520.5 :
|   |   |   NormPDR <= 2.65 : LM9 (62/3.559%)
|   |   |   NormPDR >  2.65 :
|   |   |   |   FP <= 610 : LM10 (50/6.205%)
|   |   |   |   FP >  610 :
|   |   |   |   |   NormPDR <= 5.7 : LM11 (38/5.155%)
|   |   |   |   |   NormPDR >  5.7 : LM12 (29/3.989%)
|   |   FP >  1520.5 : LM13 (47/23.679%)
|   NormPDR >  8.05 :
|   |   NormPDR <= 28.75 :
|   |   |   FP <= 1411.5 :
|   |   |   |   FP <= 674 : LM14 (67/11.599%)
|   |   |   |   FP >  674 : LM15 (45/26.176%)
|   |   |   FP >  1411.5 : LM16 (44/79.363%)
|   |   NormPDR >  28.75 : LM17 (40/160.629%)
```

```
Where:

LM num: 1
NormWorkEff =
0.6701 * FP
+ 5.8478 * MaxTeamSize
+ 16.1174 * DevType=New_Development, Re-development
+ 16.4605 * DevPlatf=MR
+ 7.5693 * ProjElapTime
- 9.4635 * ProjInactiveTime
+ 0.4684 * TotalDefectsDelivered
+ 12.4199 * NormPDR
+ 461.1827
LM num: 2

...

LM num: 17
NormWorkEff =
22.1179 * FP
- 15457.3164 * VAF
+ 36.5098 * MaxTeamSizy
- 634.6502 * DevType=New_Development,Re-development
+ 37.0267 * DevPlatf=MR
+ 1050.5217 * LangType=2GL,3GL,ApG
+ 328.1218 * ProjElapTime
- 90.7468 * ProjInactiveTime
+ 370.2088 * NormPDR
+ 5913.1867
```

Figure 3. Graphical view of the M5P tree

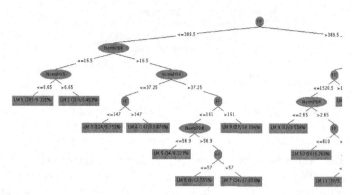

generated is composed of a large number of leaves divided by the same variables at different levels. The tree could be simplified adding a restriction about the minimum number of instances covered by each leaf; for example, saying that there should be 100 instances per leaf will generate a simpler tree but less accurate.

Figure 3 also shows the tree in a graphical way. Each leaf of the tree provides further information within brackets. For example, for LM1, there are 308 instances and an approximate error in that leaf is 8.331%.

Constructing the M5 Decision Tree

Regarding the construction of the tree, M5 needs three steps. The first step generates a regression tree using the training data. It calculates a linear model (using linear regression) for each node of the tree generated. The second step tries to simplify the regression tree generated in the previous search (first post-pruning) deleting the nodes of the linear models whose attributes do not increase the error. The aim of the third step is to reduce the size of the tree without reducing the accuracy (second post-pruning). To increase the efficiency, M5 does the last two steps at the same time so that the tree is parsed only once. This simplifies both the number of the nodes as well as simplifying the nodes themselves.

As mentioned previously, M5 first calculates a regression tree that minimizes the variation of the values in the instances that fall into the leaves of the tree. Afterwards, it generates a lineal model for each of the nodes of the tree. In the next step, it simplifies the linear models of each node by deleting those attributes that do not reduce the classification error when they are eliminated. Finally, it simplifies the regression tree by eliminating subtrees under the intermediate nodes. They are the nodes whose classification error is greater than the classification error given by the lineal model corresponding to those intermediate nodes. In this way, taking a set of learning instances E and a set of attributes A, a simplified version of the M5 algorithm will be as follows:

```
Proc_M5 (E,A)
begin
R : = create-node-tree-regression
R : = create-tree-regression (E,A,R)
R : = simplify-lineal-models (E,R)
R : = simplify-regression-tree (E,R)
Return R
End
```

The regression tree, R, is created in a divide-and-conquer method; the three functions (create-tree-regression, simplify-lineal-models and simplify-regression-tree) are called in a recursive way after creating regression tree node by (create-node-tree-regression).

Once the tree has been built, a linear model for each node is calculated and the leaves of the trees are pruned if the error decreases. The error for each node is the average of the difference between the predicted value and the actual value of each instance of the training set that reaches the node. This difference is calculated in absolute terms. This error is weighted according to the number of instances that reach that node. This process is repeated until all the examples are covered by one or more rules.

Transformation of Nominal Attributes

Before building the tree, all non-numeric attributes are transformed into binary variables so that they can be treated as numeric attributes. A variable with k values is transformed into k-1 binary variables. This transformation is based on the Breiman observation. According to this observation, the best splitting in a node for a variable with k values is one of the k-1 possible solutions once the attributes have been sorted.

Missing Values

A quite common problem with real datasets occurs when the value of a splitting attribute does not exist. Once the attribute is selected as a splitting variable to divide the dataset into subsets, the value of this attribute must be known. To solve this problem, the attribute whose value does not exist is replaced by the value of another attribute that is correlated to it. A simpler solution is to use the prediction value as the value of the attribute selected or the average value of the attribute for all the instances in the set that do not reach the node, but can be used as the value of the attribute.

Heuristics

The split criterion of the branches in the tree in M5 is given by the heuristic used to select the best attribute in each new branch. For this task, M5 uses the standard deviation as a measure of the error in each node. First, the error decrease for each attribute used as splitting point is calculated.

Smoothing

In the final stage, a regularization process is made to compensate discontinuities among adjacent linear models in the leaves of the tree. This process is started once the tree has been pruned and especially for models based on training sets containing a small number of instances. This smoothing process usually improves the prediction obtained.

Linear Regression and Least Median Squares

Linear regression (LR) is the classical linear regression model. It is assumed that there is a linear relationship between a dependant variable (e.g., effort) with a set of or independent variables, that is, attributes (e.g., *size in function points, team size, development platform,* etc.). The aim is to adjust the data to a model so that

$$y = \beta_0 + \beta_1 x_1 + \beta_2 x_2 + \dots + + \beta_k x_k + e.$$

Least median squares (LMS) is a robust regression technique that includes outlier detection (Rousseeuw & Leroy, 1987) by minimizing the median rather than the mean.

Goodness of fit of the linear models is usually measured by the correlation, co-efficient of multiple determination R^2 and by the *mean squared error*. However, in the software engineering domain, the mean magnitude of relative error (*MMRE*) and *prediction at level l—Pred (l)*—are well known techniques for evaluating the goodness of fit in the estimation methods (see the *Evaluation of the Techniques and Characterization of Software Engineering Datasets* section).

The Datasets

The International Software Benchmarking Standards Group (ISBSG), a non-profit organization, maintains a software project management repository from a variety of organizations. The ISBSG checks the validity and provides benchmarking information to companies submitting data to the repository. Furthermore, it seems that the data is collected from large and successful organizations. In general, such organizations have mature processes and well-established data collection procedures. In this work, we have used the "ISBSG release no. 8", which contains 2,028 projects and more than 55 attributes per project. The attributes can be classified as follows:

- Project context, such as type of organization, business area, and type of development;
- Product characteristics, such as application type user base;

- Development characteristics, such as development platform, languages, tools, and so forth;

- Project size data, which is different types of function points, such as IFPUG (2001), COSMIC (2004), and so forth; and

- Qualitative factors such as experience, use of methodologies, and so forth.

Before using the dataset, there are a number of issues to be taken into consideration. An important attribute is the quality rating given by the ISBSG: its range varies from A (where the submission satisfies all criteria for seemingly sound data) to D (where the data has some fundamental shortcomings). According to ISBSG, only projects classified as A or B should be used for statistical analysis. Also, many attributes in ISGSB are categorical attributes or multi-class attributes that need to be pre-processed for this work (e.g., the project scope attribute which indicates what tasks were included in the project work effort—planning, specification, design, build, and test—were grouped. Another problem of some attributes is the large number of missing instances. Therefore, in all datasets with the exception of the "reality dataset", we have had to do some pre-processing. We selected some attributes and instances manually. There are quite a large number of variables in the original dataset that we did not consider relevant or they had too many missing values to be considered in the data mining process. From the original database, we only considered the IFPUG estimation technique and those that can be considered very close variations of IFPUG such as NESMA.

We have used four datasets selecting different attributes including the one provided in the "reality tool" by ISBSG. In our study, we have selected *NormalisedWorkEffort* or *SummaryWorkEffort* as dependent variables. The normalized work effort is an estimate of the full development life cycle effort for those projects covering less than a full development life cycle while the summary work effort is the actual work effort carried out by the project. For projects covering the full development life cycle and projects where the development life cycle coverage is not known, these values are the same, that is, work effort reported. When the variable summary work effort is used, the dataset included whether each of the life cycle phases were carried out, such as, planning, specification, building and testing.

DS1: The reality dataset is composed of 709 instances and 6 attributes (*DevelopmentType, DevelopmentPlatform, LanguageType, ProjectElapsedTime, NormalisedWorkEffort, UnadjustedFunctionPoints*). The dependent variable for this dataset is the *NormalisedWorkEffort*.

DS2: The dataset DS2 is composed of 1,390 instances and 15 attributes (*FP, VAF, MaxTeamSize, DevType, DevPlatf, LangType, DBMUsed, MethodUsed, ProjElapTime, ProjInactiveTime, PackageCustomisation, RatioWEProNonPro, TotalDefectsDelivered, NormWorkEff, NormPDR*). The dependent variable for this dataset is the *NormalisedWorkEffort*.

DS3. The dataset DS3 is composed of 1,390 instances and 19 attributes (*FP, SummWorkEffort, MaxTeamSize, DevType, DevPlatf, LangType, DBMUsed, MethodUsed, ProjElapTime, ProjInactiveTime, PackageCustomisation, Planning, Specification, Build, Test, Impl, RatioWEProNonPro, TotalDefectsDelivered, ReportedPDRAdj*). In this case, we did consider the software life cycle attributes (*Planning, Specification, Build, Impl, Test*), and, therefore, we were able to use the summary work effort (*SummWorkEffort*) as the dependent variable.

DS4. The dataset DS4 is very similar to DS3 but it uses the unadjusted function points (*UnadjFP*) and the value adjustment factor (*VAF*) instead of the adjusted function points (*FP*). It is also composed of 1,390 instances. The 20 attributes are *VAF, SummWorkEffort, MaxTeamSize, DevType, DevPlatf, LangType, DBMUsed, MethodUsed, ProjElapTime, ProjInactiveTime, PackageCustomisation, Planning, Specification, Build, Test, Impl, RatioWEProNonPro, TotalDefectsDelivered, UnadjFP,* and *ReportedPDRAdj*. It also uses the summary work effort (*SummWorkEffort*) as the dependent variable.

Evaluation of the Techniques and Characterization of Software Engineering Datasets

We compare the benefits of the techniques by using linear regression and the least median square as prediction techniques before and after characterizing the database using the classical mean magnitude of relative error (MMRE) and Pred(%). In software engineering, the standard criteria for a model to be acceptable are *Pred(25) ≥ 0.75* and *MMRE ≤ 0.25*.

- *MMRE* is computed as $\frac{1}{n} \cdot \sum_{i=1}^{n} \left| \frac{e_i - \hat{e}_i}{e_i} \right|$, where in a sample of size n, $\hat{e}_i$ is the estimated value for the *i-th* element, and e_i is the actual value.

- *Pred(%)* is defined as the number of cases whose estimations are under the %, divided by the total number of cases. For example, *Pred(25)=0.75* means that 75% of cases estimates are within the inside 25% of its actual value.

Figure 4. M5P output

```
UnadjustedFunctionPoints <= 343 : LM1 (510/53.022%)
UnadjustedFunctionPoints > 343 : LM2 (199/318.225%)

where:

LM num: 1
        NormalisedWorkEffort =
                90.5723 * DevelopmentPlatform=MF,MR
                + 63.5148 * LanguageType=ApG,3GL,2GL
                + 628.9547 * LanguageType=3GL,2GL
                + 184.9949 * ProjectElapsedTime
                + 10.9211 * UnadjustedFunctionPoints
                - 545.8004

LM num: 2
        NormalisedWorkEffort =
                10189.7332 * DevelopmentPlatform=MF,MR
                - 5681.5476 * DevelopmentPlatform=MR
                + 155.8191 * LanguageType=ApG,3GL,2GL
                + 5965.379 * LanguageType=3GL,2GL
                + 551.4804 * ProjectElapsedTime
                + 4.3129 * UnadjustedFunctionPoints
                - 8118.3275
```

We will now explain how we proceeded using the reality dataset as it is the smallest of the four datasets used. Once we had our datasets ready, we applied the M5P algorithm using the Weka Toolkit. The M5P algorithm created two clusters, LM1 and LM2 (the other three datasets created a much larger number of clusters). The *NormalisedWorkEffort* is the dependent variable and a different linear model is applied depending on the *UnadjustedFunctionPoints* variable. The clusters found can assign to the dependent variable either a constant or a linear equation (in most cases). For example, for the reality dataset, M5P has produced only two branches that are interpreted as follows: if *UnadjustedFunctionPoints* is less than 343 then we apply LM1 to calculate the *NormalisedWorkEffort* (see Figure 4).

The categorical data of the linear regression function obtained by Weka is calculated substituting the value for the appropriate value wherever it occurs. For example, if we had an instance with *DevelopmentPlatform* equals to MF, *LanguageType* equals to *ApG* and *UnadjustedFunctionPoints* less than 343 then the linear equation to apply would look like this:

```
LM num: 1
    NormalisedWorkEffort =
        90.5723 * MF=MF,MR
        + 63.5148 * ApG=ApG,3GL,2GL
        + 628.9547 * ApG=3GL,2GL
        + 184.9949 * ProjectElapsedTime
        + 10.9211 * UnadjustedFunctionPoints
        - 545.8004
```

For evaluating each categorical expression, if the value of the category on the left hand side is equal to any of the categories on the right hand side of the equation, then we substitute the entire equation with value 1; otherwise with the value 0. Following the example, we obtain:

```
LM num: 1
    NormalisedWorkEffort =
        90.5723 * 1, MR
        + 63.5148 * 1
        + 628.9547 * 0
        + 184.9949 * ProjectElapsedTime
        + 10.9211 * UnadjustedFunctionPoints
        - 545.8004
```

From each cluster only those instances that were within the 25% of the actual value, that is, *Pred (25)*, are selected to be part of the characterized database.

Afterwards, we applied LR and LSM in all datasets before and after selecting instances. In the case of the reality dataset, the number of instances was reduced from 709 to 139 projects. We also created another dataset by selecting 139 instances randomly from the entire dataset (709 instances). Table 2 compares the *MMRE, Pred(25),* and *Pred(30)* results for the reality dataset where the columns named *Before* are the results obtained using the entire dataset; *After* columns are the results when applying LR and LSM with only the selected instances. Finally, *Random* columns are the result when we randomly selected a number of instances equal to the number of instances of the characterized dataset (139 in the case of the reality dataset). For the reality dataset, M5P allowed us to reduce the number of instances in the dataset from 709 to 139 (570 instances).

Table 2. DS1 dataset results (reality dataset)

	LMS			Linear Regression		
	Before (790 inst)	After (139 inst)	Random (139 inst)	Before (790 inst)	After (139 inst)	Random (139 inst)
MMRE	1.07	0.19	0.98	2.41	0.44	3.18
Pred(25)	0.18	0.73	0.24	0.14	0.34	0.10
Pred(30)	0.23	0.79	0.26	0.18	0.41	0.12

Table 3. DS2 dataset results

	LMS			Linear Regression		
	Before (1390 inst)	After (1012 inst)	Random (1012 inst)	Before (1390 inst)	After (1012 inst)	Random (1012 inst)
MMRE	0.63	0.45	0.75	2.10	1.12	2.05
Pred(25)	0.39	0.36	0.34	0.22	0.23	0.23
Pred(30)	0.47	0.42	0.41	0.27	0.27	0.27

Table 3 shows the result for the DS2 dataset. M5P allowed us to reduce the number of instances in the dataset from 1,390 to 1,012 (378 instances).

Table 4 shows the results for the DS3 dataset, and the number of instance was reduced by 375.

Table 5 shows the results for the DS4 dataset. In this case, the number of instances is reduced by 411.

Although the general estimation accuracy of LMS and LR in the datasets used is quite low using the software engineering criteria, their performance is always improved when

Table 4. DS3 dataset results

	LMS			Linear Regression		
	Before (1390 inst)	After (1015inst)	Random (1015 inst)	Before (1390 inst)	After (1015 inst)	Random (1015 inst)
MMRE	0.68	0.46	0.81	2.35	0.88	2.09
Pred(25)	0.32	0.38	0.29	0.22	0.25	0.22
Pred(30)	0.38	0.46	0.36	0.26	0.26	0.25

Table 5. DS4 dataset results

	LMS			Linear Regression		
	Before (1390 inst.)	After (979 inst)	Random (1015 inst)	Before (1390 inst)	After (979 inst)	Random (979 inst)
MMRE	0.68	0.45	0.90	2.43	0.86	2.23
Pred(25)	0.30	0.37	0.30	0.22	0.27	0.19
Pred(30)	0.36	0.43	0.36	0.26	0.32	0.24

Table 6. Differences when using LMS

	Diff instances	Diff MMRE	Diff Pred 25	Diff Pred30
DS1	570	0.88	0.55	0.53
DS2	378	0.18	0.03	0.05
DS3	375	0.22	0.06	0.08
DS3	411	0.23	0.07	0.07

selecting a fewer number of instances using M5P. Table 6 shows the differences before and after selecting the instances. It is worth noting that the best improvement is in the case where the difference in the number of instances is large. This seems to be quite logical as the larger the number of instances discarded by the data mining algorithm, the cleaner the dataset should be.

Conclusions

In this chapter, we characterized 4 datasets created from the ISBSG database selecting both attributes and instances so that project managers can have a better global vision of the data they manage. To achieve this, we first created several subsets of the ISBSG database using expert knowledge to select attributes. We then made use of Weka's M5P data mining algorithm to create clusters. From these clusters, only those instances that were within the 25% of the actual value are selected to be part of the estimation model. When we compared the goodness of using linear regression and the least median square as prediction techniques using the mean magnitude of relative error (MMRE) and Pred(%), the smaller dataset produces better or as least similar results. The result is a new database which represents the original database but with fewer number of attributes and instances so that the project manager can get a much better grasp of the information of the database, improving the performance of the rest of activities.

Further work will consist of using data mining techniques for characterizing not only the instances but also the attributes (in this work, the attributes were selected manually using expert knowledge), by using bi-clustering. More needs to be done for understanding and comparing different clusterization techniques to create segmented models and analyzing its usefulness for project managers.

Acknowledgments

This research was supported by the Spanish Research Agency (CICYT TIN2004-06689-C03).

References

Breiman, L. (1984). *Classification and regression trees*. New York: Chapman & Hall/ CRC.

COSMIC. (2004). *COSMIC-FFP measurement manual, version 2.1*. Common Software Measurement International Consortium.

Fayyad, U., Piatetsky-Shapiro, G., & Smyth, P. (1996). The KDD process for extracting useful knowledge from volumes of data. *Communications of the ACM, 39*, 27-34.

IFPUG. (2001). *Function point counting practices, release 4.1.1*. Manual. International Function Point Users Group.

ISBSG. (2005). *International Software Benchmarking Standards Group (ISBSG)*. Retrieved from http://www.isbsg.org/

Quinlan, J. R. (1986). Induction of decision trees. *Machine Learning, 1*, 81-106.

Quinlan, J. R. (1992). Learning with continuous classes. In the *Proceedings of the 5th Australian Joint Conference on Artificial Intelligence*, Hobart, Tasmania, November 16-18 (pp. 343-348). Singapore: World Scientific Press.

Quinlan, J. R. (1993). *C4.5: Programs for machine learning*. San Mateo, CA: Morgan Kaufmann.

Rousseeuw, P. J., & Leroy, A. M. (1987). *Robust regression and outlier detection*. New York: Wiley.

STTF. (2004). *Software Technology Transfer Finland (STTF)*. Retrieved from http://www. sttf.fi/eng/indexEnglish.htm

Witten, I. H., & Frank, E. (1999). *Data mining: Practical machine learning tools and techniques with Java implementations*. San Francisco, CA: Morgan Kaufmann.

Chapter II

Intelligent Analysis of Software Maintenance Data

Marek Reformat, University of Alberta, Canada

Petr Musilek, University of Alberta, Canada

Efe Igbide, University of Alberta, Canada

Abstract

Amount of software engineering data gathered by software companies amplifies importance of tools and techniques dedicated to processing and analysis of data. More and more methods are being developed to extract knowledge from data and build data models. In such cases, selection of the most suitable data processing methods and quality of extracted knowledge is of great importance. Software maintenance is one of the most time and effort-consuming tasks among all phases of a software life cycle. Maintenance managers and personnel look for methods and tools supporting analysis of software maintenance data in order to gain knowledge needed to prepare better plans and schedules of software maintenance activities. Software engineering data models should provide quantitative as well as qualitative outputs. It is desirable to build these models based on a well-delineated logic structure. Such models would enhance maintainers' understanding of factors which influence maintenance efforts. This chapter focuses on defect-related activities that are the core of corrective maintenance. Two aspects of these activities are considered: a number of software components that have to be examined during a defect removing process, and time needed to remove a single defect. Analysis of the available datasets leads to development of data models, extraction of IF-THEN rules from these models, and construction of ensemble-based prediction systems that are built based on these data models. The data models are developed using well-known tools such as See5/C5.0 and 4cRuleBuilder, and a new multi-level evolutionary-based algorithm. Single data models are put together into ensemble prediction systems that use elements of evidence theory for the purpose of inference about a degree of belief in the final prediction.

Introduction

Many organizations want to prepare reliable schedules of maintenance tasks. Such schedules would lead to on-time realization of these tasks and better management of resources. This is an important issue, especially in the case where maintenance tasks account for more than half of a typical software budget (Glass, 1989; Smith, 1999). Because of that, the software industry is exhibiting an increased interest in improving software maintenance processes. Software engineers use a number of different tools to support maintenance activities and make them more efficient. The most commonly used tools are tools for model-based software component analysis, metrics extraction, measurements presentation, and statistical analysis and evaluation. Besides that, software maintainers need tools that would help them to understand relationships between attributes of software components and maintenance tasks. Knowledge gained in this way would increase understanding of influence of software component attributes, such as size of code, complexity, functionality, and so forth, on efforts associated with realization of maintenance tasks.

There are four different categories of software maintenance: *corrective*—it involves changing software to remove defects; *adaptive*—it leads to changing software due to changes in software operating environment; *perfective*—it embraces activates that lead to improvement of maintainability, performance, or other software quality attributes; and *preventive*—it is defined as maintenance performed for the purpose of preventing problems before they happen. The corrective software maintenance is associated with activities related to elimination of software defects. This process is a key factor in ensuring timely releases of software and its updates, and high quality of software. Different tools and systems are used to support activities that are directly related to correction of defects. However, there is also a need to build systems that support decision-making tasks and lead to preparation of schedules and plans for defect removal processes. These systems should not only provide quantitative predictions but also give indications about plausibility of these predictions. Additionally, they should provide maintenance engineers with knowledge about defect removal efforts that explain obtained predictions. In summary, it is desirable to have a tool equipped with the ability to retrieve knowledge about relationships between attributes describing software and factors that directly or indirectly influence defect elimination activities.

Some of the important questions asked by managers and software maintenance engineers regarding removal of defects from software systems are:

- Does a defect removal process depend on functionality of software components?
- Does a defect removal process depend on the time when a defect entered the system?

- What are the factors that influence time needed to correct a single defect?

- What kind of relations between software component attributes and time needed to remove a defect can be found from software maintenance data?

- How confident can someone be about dependencies that have been found between a defect removal process and attributes of software components?

This chapter focuses on building software maintenance data models and their analysis. The aim is to build a prediction system that is able to provide software maintenance engineers with predictions regarding defect elimination efforts, knowledge about factors that influence these efforts, and confidence measures for obtained predictions and gained knowledge.

Fulfillment of these objectives is achieved by the application of soft computing and machine learning methods for processing software engineering data. In a nutshell, the main idea of the proposed approach is to use multiple data processing techniques to build a number of data models, and then use elements of evidence theory to "merge" the outcomes of these data models. In this context, a prediction system is built of several rule-based models. The attractiveness of these models comes from the fact that they are built of IF-THEN rules that are easy to understand by people. In this chapter, three different tools for constructing IF-THEN rules are used. One of them constructs rules directly from the data, and the other two build decision trees first and extract rules from the trees. As the result, a large set of IF-THEN rules is created. Each rule is evaluated based on its capability to perform predictions. This evaluation is quantified by degrees of belief that represent goodness of the rules. The degrees of belief assigned to the rules that are fired, for a given input data point, are used to infer an overall outcome of the prediction system. The inference engine used in the system is built based on elements of evidence theory.

This chapter can be divided into three distinctive parts. The first part embraces background information related to data models. It starts with a description of work related to the area of software engineering data models (the *Software Data Models* section). An overview of rule-based systems and ensemble prediction systems is in the *Rule-Based Models and Ensemble Systems* section. The *Evidence Theory and Ensemble-Based System* section contains a description of the proposed ensemble-based prediction system. This section also contains an overview of the concept of the proposed system, its basic components, and the inference engine. The second part of the chapter is dedicated to the description of the datasets used here and the results of their analysis. In the *Software Engineering Maintenace Data* section, a software dataset is presented. Predictions of efforts needed to remove defects are presented in the *Base-Level Data Models, Extracted Knowledge and Confidence in Results* section. This section also includes a set of IF-THEN rules which represent knowledge extracted from the software maintenance models. Descriptions of ensemble-based prediction systems and analysis of their predictions are in the *Ensemble-Based Prediction System* section. And, finally, there is the *Conclusions* section.

The third part of the chapter contains three appendices: Appendix I is a short introduction to Evolutionary Computing; Appendix II is a brief introduction to the topic of decision trees and an evolutionary-based technique used for construction of decision trees; and Appendix III describes elements of evidence theory and the transferable belief model.

Software Data Models

Software engineering data collected during development and maintenance activities are seen as a valuable source of information about relationships that exist among software attributes and different aspects of software activities. A very important aspect that becomes very often associated with software systems is software quality. Software quality can be defined two-fold: (1) as the degree to which a system, component, or process meets specified requirements; and (2) as the degree to which a system, component, or process meets customer or user needs or expectations (IEEE 610.12). In light of that definition, the most essential expectation is the absence of defects in software systems. This aspect alone touches almost every phase of a software life cycle. The coding, testing, and integration, as well as the maintenance phase are directly related to the issue of constructing high quality software. However, building and maintaining a defect-free system is not a trivial task. Many activities, embraced under the umbrella of software quality assurance, are performed in order to detect defects, localize them in a code, remove them, and finally verify that the removal process has been successful. In order to plan these activities effectively, there is a need to understand what makes a code defective, and how much time and effort is needed to isolate and eliminate defects. Development of software prediction models attempts to address those issues.

Prediction models aim at predicting outcomes on the basis of a given set of variables: they estimate what should be the outcome of a given situation with a certain condition defined by the values of the given set of variables. The steps that have to be performed during development of such models are:

- selection of the outcome attribute;
- selection of predictor (input) variables;
- data collection;
- assembly of the model;
- validation of the model; and
- updates and modifications of the model.

In the case of software engineering, prediction models that can be used to predict a number of quantities related to software quality and maintenance activities, are used for many years. These models proved to provide reasonable accuracy (Schneidewind, 1995, 1997). Many different software metrics are utilized as predictor (input) variables. The most common ones are complexity and size metrics, testing metrics, and process quality data.

The most popular software prediction models are models predicting quality-related aspects of software modules. A number of these models have been reported in the literature:

- **Tree-Based Models:** Both classification and regression trees are used to categorize software modules and functions; different regression tree algorithms—CART[1]-LS (least squares), S-PLUS, and CART-LAD (least absolute deviation)—are used to build trees to predict the number of faults in modules in Khoshgoftaar and Seliya (2002);

in another case, regression trees are constructed using a concept of fault density (Gokhale & Lyu, 1997); a study on the use of a classification tree algorithm to identify fault prone software modules based on product and process metrics is presented in Khoshgoftaar and Allen (1999); tree-based models are used to uncover relationships between defects and software metrics, and to identify high-defect modules together with their associated measurement characteristics (Takahashi, Muroaka, & Nakamura, 1997; Troster & Tian, 1995);

- **Artificial Neural Network-Based Models:** Neural networks are recognized for their ability to provide good results when dealing with data that have complex relationships between inputs and outputs; neural networks are used to classify program modules as either high or low risk based on two criteria—a number of changes to enhance modules and a number of changes to remove defects from modules (Khoshgoftaar & Allen, 1998; Khoshgoftaar & Lanning, 1995);

- **Case-Based Reasoning Models:** Case-based reasoning (CBR) relies on previous experiences and uses analogy to solve problems; CBR is applied to predict software quality of the system by discovering fault-prone modules using product and process metrics as independent variables (Berkovich, 2000);

- **Fuzzy-Based Models:** Concepts of fuzzy sets and logic are used to build data models using linguistic labels; the work related to building fuzzy-based systems for prediction purposes is presented in Reformat, Pedrycz, and Pizzi (2004), where fuzzy neural networks are constructed for defect predictions; a fuzzy clustering is used in Yuan, Khoshgoftaar, Allen, and Ganesan (2000), where a modeling technique that integrates fuzzy subtractive clustering with module-order modeling for software quality prediction is presented, a case study of a large legacy telecommunication system to predict whether each module should be considered fault-prone is conducted;

- **Bayesian Belief Network-Based Models:** Bayesian belief networks (BBN) address a complex web of interconnections between multiple factors; belief networks are used for modeling the complexities of software taking uncertainty into consideration (Neil & Fenton, 1996; Neil, Krause, & Fenton, 2003). BBN are also applied to construct prediction models that focus on the structure of the software development process explicitly representing complex relationships between metrics (Amasaki, Takagi, Mizuno, & Kikuno, 2003).

Thorough comparisons of different approaches used for building software quality prediction models can be found in Fenton and Neil (1999, 2005) and Khoshgoftaar and Seliya (2003).

Besides classification of software modules, a close attention is also given to the issues related to prediction of efforts associated with detection and correction of defects. One of the first papers dedicated to the topic of prediction of maintenance efforts is Jorgensen (1995). This paper reports on the development and use of several software maintenance effort prediction models. These models are developed applying regression analysis, neural networks, and the optimized set reduction method. The models are used to predict maintenance task efforts based on the datasets collected from a large Norwegian company. The variables included in the effort prediction models are: a cause of task, a degree of change on a code, a type of operation on a code, and confidence of maintainer. An explanation of efforts associated with software changes made to correct faults while software is undergoing development is investigated in Evanco (1999, 2001). In this case, the ordinal response models are developed to predict efforts needed to isolate and fix a defect. The predictor variables include extent of change, a type of change, an internal complexity of the software components undergoing the change, as well as fault locality and characteristics of the software components being changed. The models are developed and validated on three Ada projects. A model for estimating adaptive software maintenance efforts in person hours is described in Hayes, Patel, and Zhao (2004). A number of metrics, such as the lines of code changed and the number of operators changed, are found to be strongly correlated to maintenance efforts.

Rule-Based Models and Ensemble Systems

Data models can be categorized into two major groups: black-box models and white-box models. The black-box models provide a user with the output values without indicating a way in which those outputs are calculated. This means that knowledge about relationships existing between the inputs and the output is not discovered. Conversely, the white-box data models, also called transparent models, allow their users to gain knowledge about the data being modeled. A careful inspection of a model's structure and its analysis provides an insight into relationships existing among values of data attributes. Rule-based models are well-known examples of white-box models. A rule-based model consists of a number of IF-THEN rules. A number of different techniques for development of IF-THEN rules exist. Some of these techniques construct rules directly from the data, while others build decision tress first and then extract rules from the trees.

Rule-Based Models

Rule-based modeling is a most common form of computational model. Rules are generally well suited to study behavior of many different phenomena. These models receive information describing a situation, process that information using a set of rules, and produce a

Figure 1. Structure of a rule-based model

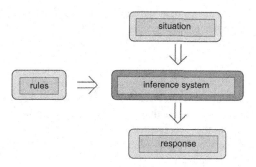

specific response as their output (Luger, 2002; Winston, 1992). Their overall structure is presented in Figure 1.

In its simplest form, a rule-based model is just a set of IF-THEN statements called rules, which encode knowledge about phenomenon being modeled. Each rule consists of an IF part called the premise or antecedent (a conjunction of conditions), and a THEN part called the consequent or conclusion (predicted category). When the IF part is true, the rule is said to fire, and the THEN part is asserted—it is considered to be a fact.

A set of IF-THEN rules is processed using Boolean logic. The expert system literature distinguishes between "forward chaining" and "backward chaining" as a method of logical reasoning. Forward chaining starts with a set of characteristics about a situation—a feature vector of independent variables—and applies these as needed until a conclusion is reached. Backward chaining, in contrast, starts with a possible conclusion—a hypothesis—and then seeks information that might validate the conclusion. Forward chaining systems are primarily data-driven, while backward chaining systems are goal-driven. A forward chaining method of reasoning is used in prediction systems.

The IF-THEN based model with forward chaining works in the following way: the system examines all the rule conditions (IF) and determines a subset, the conflict set, of the rules whose conditions are satisfied. Of this conflict set, one of those rules is triggered (fired). When the rule is fired, any actions specified in its THEN clause are carried out. Which rule is chosen to fire is a function of the conflict resolution strategy. Which strategy is chosen can be determined by the problem and is seen as one of the important aspects of the development of rule-based systems.

In any case, it is vital as it controls which of the applicable rules are fired and thus how the entire system behaves. There are several different strategies, but here are a few of the most common ones:

- **First Applicable:** Is based on the fact that the rules are put in a specified order. The first applicable rule is fired.

- **Random:** It is based on a random selection of a single rule from the conflict set. This randomly selected rule is fired.

- **Most Specific:** This category is based on the number of conditions attached to each rule. From the conflict set, the rule with the most conditions is chosen.

- **Least Recently Used:** Is based on the fact that each rule is accompanied by a time stamp indicating the last time it was used. A rule with the oldest time stamp is fired.

- **"Best" Rule:** This is based on the fact that each rule is given a "weight" which specifies how much it should be considered over other rules. The rule with the highest weight is fired.

Another important aspect of the development of rule-based models, besides the reasoning scheme, is the generation of rules. As it has been mentioned earlier, there are many different methods and techniques of doing that. IF-THEN rules can be generated on the basis of expert knowledge where they are created by a person during interaction with a domain expert, or automatically derived from available data using a variety of different approaches and tools (see Appendix II; RuleQuest; 4cData).

Ensemble Systems

A ensemble system is composed of several independently built models called base-level models. Each base-level model is developed differently by applying different construction techniques/methods using a single set of training data points, or using single technique that is applied to different data point subsets. The prediction outcome of such a system is based on processing outputs coming from all base-level models being part of the system. The process of construction of a ensemble system embraces two important phases (Todorovski & Dzeroski, 2000):

- the generation of a diverse set of base-level models; and
- the combination of outcomes generated by these models.

There are two groups of approaches for generation of base-level models. The first group can be represented by probably the most popular and simplest approach where a single learning algorithm is applied to different subsets of training data. Two best known methods are: random sampling with replacement called bagging (Breiman 1996; Todorovski et al., 2000), and re-weighting misclassified training data points called boosting (Freund & Schapire, 1996; Todorovski et al., 2000). The other group of methods is based on applying some modifications to model construction algorithms while using an identical set of training data points. A number of works is dedicated to comparison of such methods (Ali, 1995; Ali & Pazzani, 1996; Kononenko & Kovacic, 1992; Kwok & Carter, 1990).

The second important task of constructing ensemble systems is the fusion of outputs generated by base-level models. The most popular techniques applied here are distribution summation, voting, and naïve Bayesian combination (Kononenko et al., 1992). Another technique of combining models' outputs is based on the application of meta-decision trees. The role of meta-decision trees is to specify which model should be used to obtain a final classification. An extensive experimental evaluation of a new algorithm for learning meta-decision trees based on C4.5 algorithm was performed in Todorovski et al. (2000). In total, five learning algorithms of generating multi-model systems have been compared: two algorithms for learning decision trees, a rule learning algorithm, a nearest neighbor algorithm, and a naïve Bayes algorithm (Winer, Brown, & Michels, 1991). A building system based on multiple models can improve the accuracy and stability of the system significantly.

Evidence Theory and Ensemble-Based System

Application of different methods for generation of IF-THEN rules may lead to the discovery of different relationships among data attributes. The same situation occurs when a single rule-generation method is used on different subsets of the same data. The aim is to take advantage of that and build a system that combines many rule-based models and generates a single output based on the outputs of the base-level models. The fact that the rules, which constitute the models, are not equally good creates a need for taking that into consideration.

This means that a process of combining the outputs of rules has to use information about prediction capabilities of the rules, that is, information about a number of proper and false predictions made by each rule. The proposed system addresses these issues. It is based on the utilization of the following ideas:

- **Application of a number of rule-based models constructed using different methods on the same/or different subsets of data:** This provides means for thorough exploitation of different extraction techniques and increases possibilities of discovering significant facets of knowledge embedded in the data.

- **Application of the concept of basic belief masses from evidence theory (Shafer, 1976; Smets, 1988) that are used to represent goodness of the rules:** This provides assessment of quality of the rules from the point of view of their prediction capabilities.

- **Utilization of the transferable belief model (Smets, 1994):** Built on the evidence theory to reason, based on basic belief masses, about a given data point belonging to a specific category and to provide a confidence measure for the result.

Concept

The pivotal point of the proposed system is the application of elements of evidence theory. The basic concept of the theory—basic belief mass (see Appendix III for details)—is also a fundamental concept used to build the proposed prediction system. In a nutshell, the approach can be described in just a few sentences: all IF-THEN rules are treated as propositions equipped with basic belief masses (*bbm* in short); the *bbm* of all rules which are fired at a given time are used by an inference engine to derive probabilities of occurrence of different outcomes (the universe of possible outcomes is defined a priori and is related to the phenomenon under investigation).

The *bbm* represents the degree of belief that something is true. Once *bbm* is assigned to a rule it means that if the rule is satisfied by a given data point then there is the belief equal to *bbm* that this data point belongs to a category indicated by the rule. At the same time, the belief of value *1-bbm* is assign to a statement that it is not known to which category the data point belongs. In other words, every rule, which is satisfied by a given data point "generates" two numbers:

- one that indicates a belief that a given data point belongs to a category indicated by the rule (its value is equal to *bbm*); and

- one that indicates that a given data point can belong to any category (its value is *1-bbm*).

Of course, the higher the *bbm* value of the rule, the higher the belief that a given data point belongs to a category indicated by the rule, and the smaller the belief that a data point can belong to any category.

Figure 2. The structure of an ensemble-based prediction system

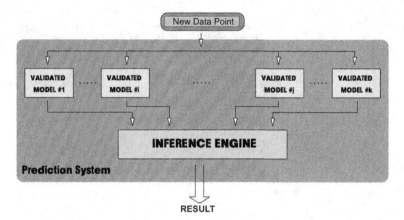

Figure 2 presents the structure of the system and the data flow during a prediction process. The system is composed of a set of validated models and an inference engine. For prediction purposes, a new data point is fed into each model. The *bbm* values of all rules fired by the data point together with categories identified by these rules constitute the input to the inference engine. Details of this engine are presented in the sub section, *Inference Engine*.

Development and Validation of IF-THEN Models

The construction stages of the proposed ensemble-based prediction system are shown in Figure 3. The first step in this process is the development of IF-THEN based models using different techniques. These models are built based on a subset of available data, which is called a training dataset.[2] This process can be performed multiple times using different training sets. This means better exploration and exploitation of the available data.

The value of *bbm* is assigned to each rule based on its coverage and prediction rate. Each rule of each model is "checked" against all training data points. This process results in generation of bbm_T (*T* stands for training) values. They are indicators of goodness of the rules. The formula (called the Laplace ratio) used for calculations of bbm_T is:

$$bbm_T = \frac{No\_Classified_T + 1}{No\_Classified_T + No\_Misclassified_T + 2} \qquad (1)$$

where $No\_Classified_T$ represents a number of training data points properly classified for a given category, and $No\_Misclassified_T$ represents a total number of training data points that has been misclassified by the rule.

Figure 3. Construction of an ensemble-based prediction system: Development and valida-tion stages

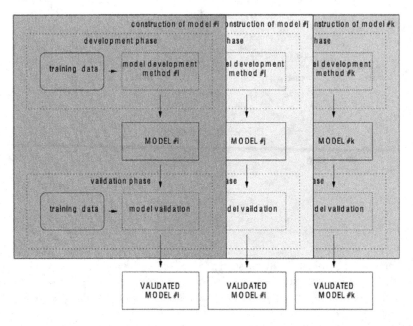

The first step in the evaluation of goodness of rules is performed based on their prediction capabilities tested against the data used for their development. To make this evaluation more reliable, the second step of the evaluation of rules' goodness is performed. This process is based on the performance of the rules when they are "tested" against data that has not been used during the development purposes. This subset of the data is called a validation dataset. Bbm_V (where V stands for validation) values are calculated:

$$bbm_V = \frac{No\_Classified_V + 1}{No\_Classified_V + No\_Misclassified_V + 2} \tag{2}$$

This time, *No_Classified$_V$* represents a number of validation data points properly classified for a given category, and *No_MisClassified$_V$* represents a total number of validation data points misclassified by the rule.

Following that, both bbm_T and bbm_V values are combined. It means that bbm_T values are *updated*. For this purpose, the Dempster's combination rule is used (Appendix III, Equation 8). The formula is:

$$bbm_{UPDATE} = (1.0 - (1.0 - bbm_T) * (1.0 - bbm_V)) \tag{3}$$

These two stages, as shown in Figure 3, constitute the construction process of the ensemble-based prediction system. For each split of data into training and validation sets, a number of different models can be constructed. Overall, the process results in a number of different base-level models, which are building blocks of the proposed prediction system.

Inference Engine

The base-level models developed using different methods and data subsets together with the inference engine constitute the ensemble-based prediction system (Figure 2). The inference engine is an implementation of the following concept. A new data point is sent to all models. It activates a number of rules that leads to generation of outputs and *bbm* (*bbm*$_{UPDATE}$ to be precise) values. The *bbm* values indicate the belief that this data point belongs either to the same or to a number of different categories. In the case where a single category is identified by all outputs, the inference engine is not engaged—it is predicted that the data point belongs to the identified category. In the case where a number of different categories are identified, the transferable belief model (TBM) (Smets & Kennes, 1994) is used to derive possibilities that the data point belongs to each of the identified categories. This process is represented in Figure 4. All models that have their rules fired provide results and *bbm* values to the inference engine. A table filled with *bbm* values is constructed. Each row of this table represents a possible combination of existing categories in the domain of interest (Ø, *A*, *B*, *A or B* in Figure 4). The TBM processes this table. The results are presented as pignistic probabilities of the data point belonging to different categories. This process is illustrated by a simple example.

Figure 4. The inference engine, its inputs and outputs (a case with two possible outcomes)

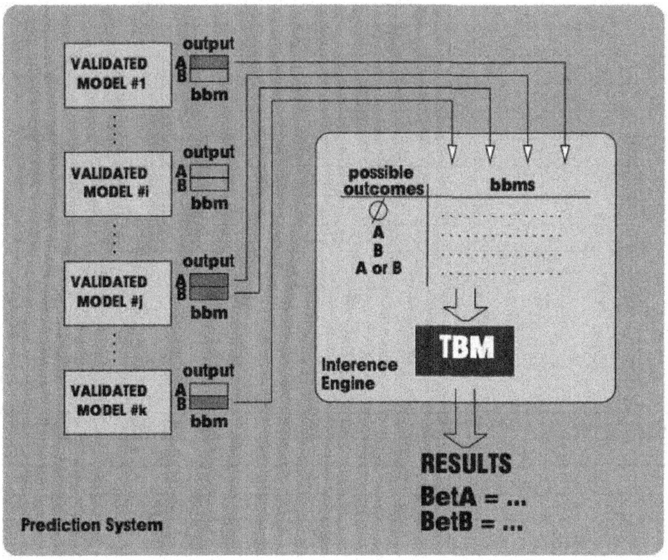

Example

Two IF-THEN based models have been built to represent relationships between an n-dimensional input and a single-dimensional output. There are two categories distinguished in the output space: *I* and *II*. Each of the models contains three IF-THEN rules for each category. Rules and their *bbm* values are shown in the Table 1.

Let's assume that a new data point has been obtained and the system is used to predict which category this point belongs to. When checked against all rules listed previously, the input data point satisfies the following set of rules: from the first model—M1-c1-R2, M1-c1-R3, and from the second—M2-c2-R1 and M2-c2-R3. *Bbm* values associated with satisfied rules are: 0.85 and 0.75 from the first model, and 0.90 and 0.85 from the second model. Table 2 is prepared based on these values. In the case of the first model, two rules are fired. The values 0.85 and 0.75 represent beliefs that the data point belongs to the category *I*, the values 0.15 and 0.25 indicate that there is still belief that this point can belong to any category—in this case, category *I* or category *II*. The same process is repeated for the rules from the second model. The values in Table 2 are the input to TBM.

Inside TBM, the *bbm* values are combined using the conjunctive combination rule (Appendix III, Equation 11). The results of this operation are presented in Table 3.

Table 1. Bbm values of model outputs

Model	Output	IF-THEN rule	bbm
first	I	M1-c1-R1	0.60
		M1-c1-R2	**0.85**
		M1-c1-R3	**0.75**
	II	M1-c2-R1	0.67
		M1-c2-R2	0.94
		M1-c2-R3	0.80
second	I	M2-c1-R1	0.80
		M2-c1-R2	0.90
		M2-c1-R3	0.67
	II	**M2-c2-R1**	**0.90**
		M2-c2-R2	0.94
		M2-c2-R3	**0.85**

Table 2. Bbms assigned to each possible category by satisfied rules

Possible outcome	M1-c1-R2	M1-c1-R3	M2-c2-R1	M2-c2-R3
0	0	0	0	0
Category I	0.85	0.75	0	0
Category II	0	0	0.90	0.85
Category I or II	0.15	0.25	0.10	0.15

Table 3. Basic belief masses assigned to each possible output

x	m(x)
0	0.9481
Category I	0.0144
Category II	0.0369
Category I or II	0.0006

Table 4. Pignistic probability (BetP) values

BetP(Category I)	0.2834
BetP(Category II)	0.7166

The next step is to calculate pignistic probabilities *BetP*. One of these probabilities represents the belief that the data point belongs to the category *I*, another that it belongs to the category *II*. These pignistic probabilities *BetP* are computed based on the *bbm* values according to the TBM using Equation 8 from Appendix III:

$$BetP(CatI) = \frac{m(CatI) + \dfrac{m(CatI\,or\,II)}{2}}{1 - m(0)} = \frac{0.0144 + \dfrac{0.0006}{2}}{1 - 0.9481} = 0.2834$$

$$BetP(CatII) = \frac{m(CatII) + \dfrac{m(CatI\,or\,II)}{2}}{1 - m(0)} = \frac{0.0369 + \dfrac{0.0006}{2}}{1 - 0.9481} = 0.7166$$

As the result of these calculations, Table 4 was created. Based on the values from this table, it can be said that in this particular case, a prediction is as follows: the new data point belongs to *Category I* with the belief of 0.2834, and to the *Category II* with the belief of 0.7166.

Software Engineering Maintenance Data

The process of development of base-level prediction models, extraction of knowledge, and construction of the ensemble-based prediction system is illustrated using the dataset from the Naval Research Laboratories (The Data and Analysis Centre for Software). The details regarding the origin of the data and their attributes are presented next. For the experimental purposes, the dataset has been divided into three sets: a training set containing data points that are used to develop base-level data models, a validation set containing data that are used to validate confidence in rules extracted from the models, and a testing set that contains data points used to evaluate prediction capabilities of the models.[3]

The data were collected at the Naval Research Laboratories (NRL) to evaluate development methodologies used on the project called The Architecture Research Facility (ARF). This project was to aid the rapid simulation of different computer architectures for research and evaluation purposes.

The original dataset consists of 117 defect reports dealing with 143 defects, which were isolated and corrected during ARF development. The dataset also includes 253 records describing each component in the project. For the purposes of the chapter, the original dataset is pre-processed. The main emphasis is put on defect elimination activates. In particular, two aspects are of interest: a number of components that have to be examined during elimination of a defect; and the effort needed to correct a defect. The modified dataset contains only data related to components with defects. There are 129 data points. Table 5 contains a few examples of these data points. The data points have been divided into three sets: a training set of 86 data points, a validation set containing 20 data points, and a testing set which has 23 data points.

The number of components that have to be examined during elimination of a defect is the first aspect of maintenance activities investigated in the chapter. The attributes of data points used in this case are represented in Table 6. There are two groups of attributes in the INPUT set. The first one represents types of defects of interest and development phases during

Table 5. Examples of data points

Type of defect	Phase of Entering	Lines of Code	No. of Comm.	Preproc. Statements	Subjective Complexity	Funct.	No. of Exam. Comp.	Elimination Time
clerical	code test	88	29	6	easy	error handling	single	<1 hour, 1day>
language	code test	83	42	2	easy	control	single	<1 hour, 1day>
clerical	code test	40	14	2	easy	control	single	< 1 hour
single design	code test	24	16	2	easy	control	single	<1 hour, 1day>
multiple	design	56	37	6	moderate	control	multiple	<1 hour, 1day>
multiple design	design	269	165	4	hard	computational	single	<1 hour, 1day>
multiple	code test	105	63	8	moderate	control	multiple	> 1 day
language	code test	188	116	3	hard	computational	multiple	<1 hour, 1day>
language	code test	168	103	5	moderate	computational	single	<1 hour

Table 6. List of attributes of the NRL data—Set I

INPUT	
type of defect	requirements_incorrect, functional_spec_incorrect, single_design_error, multiple_design_error, language_error, clerical_error, multiple_errors, other
phase when defect entered system	requirements_definition, functional_specification, design, code_testing
lines of code	<0, 635>
no. of comments	<0, 360>
no. of preprocessor statements	<0, 42>
subjective complexity	easy, moderate, hard
functionality	computational, control, data_processing, error_handling
OUTPUT	
no. of components examined	single component multiple components

Table 7. List of attributes of the NRL data—Set II

INPUT	
type of defect	requirements_incorrect, functional_spec_incorrect, single_design_error, multiple_design_error, language_error, clerical_error, multiple_errors, other
phase when defect entered system	requirements_definition, functional_specification, design, code_testing
no. of components examined	single component, multiple components
lines of code	<0, 635>
no. of comments	<0, 360>
no. of preprocessor statements	<0, 42>
subjective complexity	easy, moderate, hard
functionality	computational, control, data_processing, error_handling
OUTPUT	
time needed to eliminate a defect	less than 1 hour between 1 hour and 1 day more than 1 day

which these defects have been introduced into a system. The second set contains attributes describing software components such as line of codes, number of comments, number of preprocessor statements, as well as subjective complexity and functionality. The OUTPUT is *Number of Components Examined.*

The second point of interest is related directly to a process of elimination of defects. In this case, the attention is put on the time needed to remove a single defect. The attributes of data points used in this case are shown in Table 7. As it can be seen, the attributes chosen here are almost identical to the ones from the previous investigation. The only difference is that the attribute *Number of Examined Components* has been added to the first group of INPUT attributes. This time, the OUTPUT attribute is *Effort needed to Eliminate a Defect.*

Base-Level Data Models, Extracted Knowledge and Confidence in Results

The first step in data analysis and modeling is dedicated to the development of base-level data models that can be used for prediction purposes. The base-level models used here are rule-based models (see the *Rule-Based Models and Ensemble System* section). Three methods of building these models are selected in order to illustrate the idea of utilization of very different model development techniques. The first rule-based model is generated using See5/C5.0 (RuleQuest). The See5/C5 tool is an updated version of the well-known C4.5 algorithm (Quinlan, 1993). It has the capability of generating classifiers that are expressed as decision trees or sets of IF-THEN rules. The commercially-available tool called 4cRule-Builder (4cData) is used to build the second data model. This tool uses supervised learning techniques to generate a data model from discrete numerical or nominal data, and has built-in discretization schemes for continuous attributes. Overall, 4cRuleBuilder generates compact rules that use a small number of selectors. The third model is a set of rules extracted from a decision tree constructed using the evolutionary-based technique GAGP described in Appendix II. In general, different model development techniques can be used to build rule-based data models which become elements of the proposed prediction system.

The following step in the analysis of data focuses on the evaluation of IF-THEN rules that represent relationships between attributes of software components and different defect measures: a number of components examined to remove a defect and the time needed to eliminate a defect. At that point, the goodness of rules is estimated via monitoring and validation of prediction capabilities of the rules (see the *Development and Validation of the IF-THEN Models* sub-section).

Number of Components Examined During Elimination of Defect

First, the issue of a number of components that has to be examined in order to eliminate a defect is investigated. Three base-level prediction models have provided the prediction rates that are presented in Table 8. A visual inspection of decision trees (for See5/C5.0 and GAGP) and rules (for 4cRuleBuilder) has indicated existence of terminal nodes of trees and rules for both categories, *single component examined* and *multiple components examined*. The model generated by See5/C5.0 tool provides the highest prediction rate.[4]

Table 8. NRL data prediction models: Prediction rates for number of examined components

Model	Prediction Rate
See5/C5.0	65.22%
4cRuleBuilder	60.87%
GAGP	56.52%

Validation Process

Eleven IF-THEN rules are extracted from the decision tree generated by See5C5.0—four rules for the category *single component examined* and seven for *multiple components examined*. The application of 4cRuleBuilder tool results in six rules for *single component examined*, and five rules for *multiple components examined*. GAGP method leads to the generation of 21 rules: 14 for *single component examined* and seven for *multiple components examined*. In total, 43 rules are generated. Right now, the task is to select a relatively small set of rules that are the most significant and valuable for maintainers. Following the idea of goodness of rules (see the *Development and Validation of the IF-THEN Models* sub-section), the bbm_{UPDATE} values are used to "rank" all the rules and select the best ones.

Table 9. Original and updated bbm values

rule	bbm_T	bbm_{UPDATE}
See5/C5.0		
NC_See5_c1_1	**0.791**	**0.833**
NC_See5_c1_2	**0.770**	**0.750**
NC_See5_c2_1	**0.833**	**0.883**
NC_See5_c2_2	**0.800**	**0.889**
4cRuleBuilder		
NC_4cRB_c1_1	**0.950**	0.950
NC_4cRB_c1_2	0.929	**0.985**
NC_4cRB_c1_5	**0.941**	**0.988**
NC_4cRB_c2_1	0.818	**0.900**
NC_4cRB_c2_2	**0.898**	0.898
NC_4cRB_c2_3	**0.857**	**0.923**
GAGP		
NC_GAGP_c1_2	**0.909**	**0.952**
NC_GAGP_c1_9	**0.889**	**0.941**
NC_GAGP_c2_1	**0.800**	**0.889**
NC_GAGP_c2_3	**0.857**	0.857
NC_GAGP_c2_7	0.765	**0.907**

The *bbm* values assigned to the rules are presented in Table 9. The table contains only the rules that are best after the development stage (with the highest values of bbm_T) and the ones that are the best after the validation stage (with the highest value of bbm_{UPDATE}).

The rules generated by See5/C5.0 that are the best after the development process are also the best after the validation process (see bold entries in Table 9). For the rules NC_See5_c1_1[5] and NC_See5_c_2, their *bbm* values have increased after the validation phase. As it can be seen on the basis of other rules, none of the updated *bbm* values is smaller that the original one (there are some cases where *bbm* values do not change—this means that a rule has not been satisfied by any validation data point).

The same validation process has been performed on rules generated by 4cRuleBuilder. In the case of two rules NC_4cRB_c1_1 and NC_4cRB_c2_3, their *bbm* values have increased and the rules stay among the best ones. For the other two rules—NC_4cRB_c1_1 and NC_4cRB_c2_2—their *bbm* values have not changed. However, the *bbm* values of the other two rules NC_4cRB_c1_2 and NC_4cRB_c2_1 have increased and have become higher than the *bbm* values of NC_4cRB_c1_1 and NC_4cRB_c2_2. As the result, a set of best rules has been modified.

The validation process performed on rules generated by GAGP method has brought a single change in the category—*multiple components examined* (see Table 9). The rule NC_GAGP_c2_3 has been replaced by NC_GAGP_c2_7, which has the higher value of *bbm*. The *bbm* values of the rules from the category *single component examined* have improved.

Analysis of Best Rules

For the category *single component examined*, the range of bbm_{UPDATE} values is from 0.750 to 0.988. The rules with highest bbm_{UPDATE} values are generated by 4cRuleBuilder:

NC_4cRB_c1_2 with bbm_{UPDATE} of 0.985, and NC_4cRB_c1_5 with bbm_{UPDATE} of 0.988. The rules NC_See5_c1_1 and NC_See5_c1_2, generated by See5/C5.0, have the lowest bbm_{UPDATE} values among three sets.

An interesting observation can be made when all the rules from the category *single component examined* are compared. Rules NC_GAGP_c1_9 and NC_4cRB_c1_5 are similar (see the following rules). It looks like both of them use the attributes *defect type* and *functionality* to predict a single component examination. The set of values of the attribute *defect type* from both rules are overlapping. In the case of the attribute *functionality*, the values used by the GAGP generated rule are a subset of the values used by the rule generated by 4cRuleBuilder. Such similarity and high bbm_{UPDATE} values of these rules indicate that both of them can be used to support prediction for a single component examination. The conclusion which can be derived here is: if *defect type* is *Clerical_Error* or *Requirements_Incorrect* and *functionality* of components with these defects is *Control* or *Error_Handling* then there is a need to examine just one component to be able to understand an impact of these defects and remove them.

Rule: NC_4cRB_c1_5:

    if   DEFECT_TYPE is *Multiple_Design_Error* or *Clerical_Error* or *Functional_Spec_Incorrect* **&**
             FUNCTIONALITY is *Error_Handling* or *Control* or *Data_Accessing*
    then   SINGLE COMPONENT is examined

Rule: NC_4cRB_c1_9:

    if   DEFECT_TYPE is *Clerical_Error* or *Requirements_Incorrect* **&**
             FUNCTIONALITY is *Error_Handling* or *Control*
    then   SINGLE COMPONENT is examined

Another pair of rules that draws attention is the pair containing the rules NC_4cRB_c1_2 and NC_GAGP_c1_2 (see the following rules). The rule generated by GAGP method uses a subset of values of the attribute *defect type* that are used by the rule NC_4cRB_c1_2. Also in the case of the attribute *lines of code,* there is some substantial overlapping. Overall, the rule generated by 4cRuleBuilder seems more specific. Once again, high values of bbm_{UPDATE} make these rules good candidates for prediction activities.

Rule NC_4cRB_c1_2:

    if   DEFECT_TYPE is *Single_Design_Error* or *Multiple_Design_Error* or *Clerical_Error* or *Language_Use_Error* or *Functional_Spec._Incorrect* or *Multiple_Error* **&**
             PHASE WHEN ERROR ENTERD SYSTEM is *Requirements_Definition* or *Functional_Specification* or *Code_Testing* **&**
             LINES OF CODE is less than 85 or in the range <108, 167> or more than 207 **&**
             NUMBER OF COMMENTS is less than 29 or in the range <45, 103> or more than 128 **&**
             NUMBER OF PREPROCESSOR STATEMENTS is less than 9
    then   SINGLE COMPONENT is examined

Rule NC_GAGP_c1_2:

    if   DEFECT_TYPE is *Single_Design_Error* or *Multiple_Design_Error* or *Multiple_Error* **&**
             LINES OF CODE is less than 141 **&**
             COMPLEXITY is *Easy*
    then   SINGLE COMPONENT is examined

From rules generated by See5/C5.0, only one rule—NC_See5_c1_1—is attractive. It is a very simple rule with relatively high value of bbm_{UPDATE} and a high coverage—more than 30 data points satisfied both the antecedent and the consequential parts of this rule. It is also a very intuitive rule. Definitely it is worth considering during a prediction process.

Rule NC_See5_c1_1:

>   if   COMPLEXITY is *Easy*
>   then **SINGLE COMPONENT is examined**

In the case of the category *multiple components examined*, the rules have bbm_{UPDATE} values in the range: from 0.833 up to 0.923. Smaller maximum indicates that it is difficult to find a dominating rule describing a relationship among attributes of software components and a need for multiple components examination. The inspection of the rules points only to a single pair of rules NC_See5_c2_2 and NC_GAGP_c2_2 (see the following rules). There is a perfect much in the case of the attributes *defect type* and *complexity*. There is also some overlap existing for the attribute *lines of codes*. Based on that and high values of bbm_{UPDATE}, this pair can be treated as plausible rules describing a relationship among software attributes and a number of components which should be examined to fully understand an impact the defect *Functional_Spec._Incorrect* makes.

Rule NC_See5_c2_2:

>   if   DEFECT_TYPE is *Functional_Spec._Incorrect* &
>   LINES OF CODE Is more than 134 &
>   COMPLEXITY is *Easy*
>   then **MULTIPLE COMPONENTS are examined**

Rule NC_ GAGP_c2_2:

>   if   DEFECT_TYPE is *Functional_Spec._Incorrect* &
>   LINES OF CODE is in the range <141, 481> &
>   COMPLEXITY is *Easy* &
>   FUNCTIONALITY is *Computational*
>   then **MULTIPLE COMPONENTS are examined**

Time Needed to Eliminate a Defect

The prediction rates for the models representing effort needed to eliminate a defect are presented in Table 10. In this case, the highest prediction rate is obtained using the model generated by GAGP method.

Table 10. NRL data prediction models: Prediction rates for defect removal time

Model	Prediction Rate
See5/C5.0	56.52%
4cRuleBuilder	56.52%
GAGP	65.22%

Validation Process

Prediction models developed for the second NRL dataset leads to the extraction of 49 rules. Validation of rules generated by See5/C5.0 has brought only one change (see Table 11). The rule ET_See5_c2_2 has been replaced by the rule ET_See5_c2_4.

The bbm_{UPDATE} value of the rule ET_See5_c2_4 increased and suppressed the bbm_{UPDATE} value of the rule ET_See5_c2_2. A similar situation has occurred in the case of rules generated by 4cRuleBuilder. Only one rule has been replaced by a new rule. In this case, however, it has happened in the category *effort for elimination of a defect less than one hour*. The rule ET_4cRB_c1_1 has been replaced by ET_4cRB_c1_6. Validation of the original set of rules generated by GAGP method has also brought a single change. In the case of the category *effort for elimination of a defect more than one hour but less than one day*, the bbm_{UPDATE} value of the rule ET_GAGP_c2_4 has decreased. At the same time, the bbm_{UPDATE} value of the rule ET_GABP_c2_1 has increased from 0.666 to 0.833, and this rule has become one of the best rules.

Table 11. Original and updated bbm values

rule	bbm_T	bbm_{UPDATE}
See5/C5.0		
ET_See5_c1_1	0.938	0.974
ET_See5_c1_2	0.667	0.800
ET_See5_c2_1	0.875	0.875
ET_See5_c2_2	0.833	0.833
ET_See5_c2_4	0.727	0.842
ET_See5_c3_1	0.556	0.714
4cRuleBuilder		
ET_4cRB_c1_1	0.900	0.844
ET_4cRB_c1_2	0.944	0.966
ET_4cRB_c1_6	0.857	0.968
ET_4cRB_c2_1	0.882	0.938
ET_4cRB_c2_9	0.900	0.947
ET_4cRB_c3_1	0.500	0.500
GAGP		
ET_GAGP_c1_3	0.889	0.970
ET_GAGP_c1_7	0.889	0.889
ET_GAGP_c2_1	0.667	0.833
ET_GAGP_c2_4	0.833	0.714
ET_GAGP_c2_6	0.875	0.875

Analysis of Best Rules

As in the case of the previous experiment, let's examine the best IF-THEN rules (marked by bold fonts in Table 11). For the category *effort for elimination of a defect less than one hour* the range of bbm_{UPDATE} values is from 0.800 to 0.974. The examination of the rules from this category points to three rules ET_See5_c1_1, ET_GAGP_c1_3, and ET_GAGP_c1_7 (see the following rules). High values of bbm_{UPDATE} and similarity of the rules mean that they can be summed up with a very simple statement: if *defect type* is *Clerical_Error* then *time need to correct this defect is less than one hour*.

Rule ET_See5_c1_1:
> if   DEFECT TYPE is *Clerical_Error*
> then **DEFECT ELIMINATION TIME is less than 1 hour**

Rule ET_GAGP_c1_3:
> if   DEFECT TYPE is *Clerical_Error* &
>   FUNCTIONALITY is *Computational* or *Data_Accessing*
> then **DEFECT ELIMINATION TIME is less than 1 hour**

Rule ET_GAGP_c1_7:
> if   DEFECT TYPE is *Clerical_Error* &
>   FUNCTIONALITY is *Control*
> then **DEFECT ELIMINATION TIME is less than 1 hour**

In the category *effort for elimination of a defect more than one hour but less than one day* the rules generated by 4cRuleBuilder have the highest values of bbm_{UPDATE}. A rule ET_4cRB_c2_1 (see the following rules) seems to be a very important one. Two other rules—ET_See5_c2_4 generated by See5/C5.0 and ET_GAGP_c2_6 generated by GAGP method—are very similar. The rule ET_See5_c2_4 overlaps with ET_4cRB_c2_1 in the case of the attributes—*defect type* and *complexity*. The rule ET_GAGP_c2_6 overlaps in the case of the attributes—*defect type* and *functionality*. All this and the high bbm_{UPDATE} values indicate that these three rules can be useful in prediction of time needed to eliminate defects.

Rule ET_4cRB_c2_1:
> if   DEFECT TYPE is *Multiple_Design_Error* or
>   *Language_Use_Error* or *Functional_Spec._Incorrect* or *Other_Error* &
>   NUMBER OF COMMENTS in less than 130 or more than 181 &
>   NUMBER OF PREPROCESSOR STATEMENTS is less than 5 or more than 10 &
>   COMPLEXITY is Easy or Moderate &
>   FUNCTIONALITY is Computational or Data_Accessing or Error_Handling
> then **DEFECT ELIMINATION TIME is more than 1 hour but less than 1 day**

Rule ET_See5_c2_4:
> if   DEFECT TYPE is *Language_Use_Error* &
>   COMPLEXITY is *Easy*
> then **DEFECT ELIMINATION TIME is more than 1 hour but less than 1 day**

Rule ET_GAGP_c2_6:
> if   DEFECT_TYPE is *Single_Design_Error* or *Other_Error* &
>   FUNCTIONALITY is *Computational* or *Data_Accessing*
> then **DEFECT ELIMINATION TIME is more than 1 hour but less than 1 day**

The category *effort for elimination of a defect more than one day* is very poorly represented in the generated sets of rules. A possible reason for that is a very non-uniform distribution of data points among three categories. The category *effort for elimination of a defect more than one day* is represented by only three per cent of data points. The rule generated by See5/C5.0 is the best. Its bbm_{UPDATE} value is 0.714.

Rule ET_See5_c3_1:
   if   NUMBER_OF_COMPONENTS_EXAMINED is *Multiple* **&**
          COMPLEXITY is *Hard*
   then DEFECT ELIMINATION TIME is more than 1 day

Ensemble-Based Prediction System

The IF-THEN rules have been extracted from the base-level data models (see the *Base-Level Data Models, Extracted Knowledge and Confidence in Results* section). An important aspect of this extraction is related to the concept of rules' goodness. As the result, all rules have been evaluated and confidence measures (*bbm* values) have been assigned to them. The next step is to use this and build a system that combines different rules and takes these confidence measures into account. The results of this task are presented in the following text.

Number of Components Examined

The ensemble-based prediction system for predicting the number of components to be examined during defect removal is constructed. It is tested on all data points from the testing set. Two aspects of the results are important—a prediction rate and confidence measures for the obtained predictions.

The testing set contains 23 data points. Using only a single set of rules generated by See5/C5.0, 4cRuleBuilder, and GAGP, the prediction rates are 65.22%, 60.87%, and 56.52%, respectively (see Table 8). In the case of the ensemble-based prediction systems, the prediction rate has increased. The system that uses voting as the fusion method provides the prediction rate of 69.57%, and the system proposed here, that uses the elements of evidence theory, has the prediction rate of **73.91%** (this translates to 17 proper predictions). Among all testing data points, seven data points satisfy rules that indicate contradicting predictions. The rest of the data points are uniquely identified as belonging to a single category (most data points satisfy at least a single rule from each model, however some points satisfy only rules coming from two models). In all these cases, the pignistic probability BetP that a given data point belongs to a single category is very high at 0.99. More interesting is the case of seven data points that have led to non-unanimous prediction results. The rules that are satisfied by these seven points are presented in Table 12.

It can be easily observed that each of these points is not univocally classified to a single category. Rules generated by See5/C5.0 have problems with data points no. 1 (two rules of different categories fired), 4 (wrong rule fired), and 7 (two rules of different categories

Table 12. Rules satisfied by the seven "confusing" data points

	See5/C5.0		4cRuleBuilder		GAGP		Original Category	Predicted Category
1	cl_4	c2_4	cl_3		cl_10		I	I
2	cl_4		cl_5	c2_2	cl_4		I	I
3	cl_4					c2_3	I	II
4	cl_4			c2_1	cl_13		II	II
5	cl_1			c2_1	cl_12		I	I
6		c2_7	cl_2 cl_6	c2_1		c2_7	II	II
7	cl_4	c2_5		c2_3		c2_3	II	II

Table 13. BetP values for the seven "confusing" data points

Data points	1	2	3	4	5	6	7
BetP (cat. I: single comp. examined)	0.892	0.993	0.207	0.391	0.843	0.014	0.005
BetP (cat. II: multiple comp. examined)	0.108	0.007	0.793	0.609	0.157	0.986	0.995

fired). Rules generated by 4cRuleBuilder are misled for points no. 2 (two rules of different categories fired), 3 (no rules fired), 5 (wrong rule fired), and 6 (two rules of different
categories fired). In the case of rules generated by GAGP points no. 3 (wrong rule fired)
and 4 (wrong rule fired) are wrongly predicted. The BetP values obtained for these seven
points are shown in Table 13.

Special attention should be paid to the data point no. 4. Rules generated by See5/C5.0
(NC_See5_cl_4 with bbm_{UPDATE} of 0.545) and GAGP (NC_GAGP_cl_13 with $bbm_{UP-DATE}$ of 0.667) indicate that the point should be classified as category I. However, the rule
NC_4cRB_c2_1, which is one of the best 4cRuleBuilder rules and has bbm_{UPDATE} value of
0.900, has a strong influence on the overall result.

Time Needed to Eliminate a Defect

The ensemble-based prediction system is also built for predicting time needed to remove
a single defect. Prediction rates and the confidence measures for obtained predictions are
recorded. The testing set contains 23 data points. Using only a single set of rules generated
by See5/C5.0, 4cRuleBuilder, and GAGP, the prediction rates are 56.52%, 56.52%, and
65.22%, respectively (see Table 10). The prediction rate increases to **78.26%** (this translates
to 18 proper predictions) for the proposed ensemble-based prediction system that uses basic
belief masses. The ensemble-based system with voting has the prediction rate of 69.57%.
The analysis of the proposed prediction process indicates that 12 data points satisfy rules that
indicate contradicting predictions. The remaining 11 data points are unanimously predicted
by the rules of the system. Confidence measures for these predictions are around 0.99. The
rules fired for the 12 "confusing" points are presented in Table 14.

Table 14. Rules satisfied by the 12 "confusing" data points

	See5/C5.0	4cRuleBuilder	GAGP	Original Category	Predicted Category
1	cl_3 c2_6		cl_6	I	I
2	cl_3 c2_6	c2_3	c2_2	III	II
3	c2_6	cl_6	c2_2	III	II
4	cl_3 c2_1		c2_9	I	I
5	c2_4	c2_2 c3_1 c2_5 c2_6	c2_2	II	II
6	c3_1	cl_4 c2_2 c3_1	c2_3	III	III
7	cl_3 c2_6	cl_1 c2_4	c2_1	I	II
8	c2_8	c2_2 c3_1		II	II
9	cl_3 c2_2	c2_3 c2_7		II	II
10	cl_1 cl_3	cl_2 c2_5 cl_3	cl_3	I	I
11	cl_3 c2_4	cl_1		II	I
12	cl_1	cl_2 c2_5	cl_3	I	I

It can be easily observed that each of these points is not univocally classified to a single category. Rules generated by See5/C5.0 have problems with data points no. 1 (two rules of different categories fired), 2 (two rules of different categories fired), 3 (wrong rule fired), 4 (two rules of different categories fired), 7 (two rules of different categories fired), 9 (two rules of different categories fired), and 11 (two rules of different categories fired). Rules generated by 4cRuleBuilder are misled for points no. 1 (no rules fired), 2 (wrong rule fired), 4 (no rules fired), 5 (two rules of different categories fired), 6 (three rules of different categories fired), 7 (two rules of different categories fired), 8 (two rules of different categories fired), 10 (two rules of different categories fired), 11 (wrong rule fired), and 12 (two rules of different categories fired). In the case of the rules generated by GAGP, the points no. 2, 3, 6, 7, and 11 are wrongly predicted due to firing of the wrong rule. The values of the pignistic probabilities BetP calculated by TBM are included in Tables 15 and 16.

The most interesting are data points no. 3, 6, and 7. In the case of the point number 3, the rules generated by See5/C5.0 and GAGP indicate that this point should belong to the category I, however a higher bbm_{UPDATE} value of the 4cRuleBuilder rule (comparing to bbm_{UPDATE} of See5/C5.0 and GAGP rules) has changed the verdict of the prediction system. It can be seen that the probability that the point belongs to the category II is relatively high—0.878.

Table 15. BetP values for the 12 "confusing" data points: Points 1 to 6

Data points	1	2	3	4	5	6
BetP (cat. I: time less than 1 hour)	0.638	0.031	0.599	0.055	0.001	0.108
BetP (cat. II: time between 1 hour and 1 day)	0.308	0.962	0.381	0.932	0.996	0.434
BetP (cat. III: time more than 1 day)	0.054	0.007	0.020	0.013	0.003	0.458

Table 16. BetP values for the 12 "confusing" data points: Points 7 to 12

Data points	7	8	9	10	11	12
BetP (cat. I: time less than 1 hour)	0.119	0.014	0.002	0.999	0.673	0.999
BetP (cat. II: time between 1 hour and 1 day)	0.878	0.913	0.998	0.001	0.309	0.001
BetP (cat. III: time more than 1 day)	0.003	0.055	0.000	0.000	0.018	0.000

The point number 6, on the other hand, satisfies one rule of the category I, two rules of the category II, and two rules of the category III. The prediction system classifies this data point to a proper category. However, in the case of BetP probabilities, it can be seen that BetP(category III) is only slightly larger than BetP(category II). In the case of the point no. 7, a high bbm_{UPDATE} value of GAGP rule ET_GAGP_c2_1 (supported by bbm_{UPDATE} values of ET_See5_c2_6 and ET_4cRB_c2_4) has caused false prediction; the rules ET_See5_c1_3 and ET_4cRB_c1_1 have bbm_{UPDATE} values too small to increase the value of the probability BetP for Category I.

Conclusions

In this chapter, an intelligent method of analysis of software engineering data is illustrated. It applies evolutionary computation methods for development of models, and elements of evidence theory to combine base-level models in order to create an ensemble-based prediction system that has capabilities to determine confidence measures for the generated predictions. Application of a number of rule-based models developed with different techniques enhances prediction capabilities and allows for more comprehensive extraction of knowledge from the data. Confidence measures associated with predictions and extracted knowledge help to better understand the relationships between attributes of data and the mechanisms leading to generation of predictions.

Proposed method is applied to analysis of software corrective maintenance data. The purpose of this analysis is to find and understand relationships between attributes of software, types of defects, and efforts needed to conduct defect elimination tasks. Special attention is put on two aspects of defect elimination process: a number of software components that have to be examined to remove a single defect and a total time needed to remove a defect. The prediction systems, extracted knowledge, and results of prediction processes are described and investigated.

Acknowledgments

The author would like to acknowledge the support of the Alberta Software Engineering Research Consortium (ASERC) and the Natural Sciences and Engineering Research Council of Canada (NSERC).

References

4cData. Data mining and knowledge discovery tools and services. Retrieved September 25, 2006, from http://www.4cdata.net

Ali, K. (1995). *A comparison of methods for learning and combining evidence from multiple models*. Technical Report 95-47. Dept. of Information and Computer Science, University of California, Irvine.

Ali, K., & Pazzani, M. (1996). Error reduction through learning multiple descriptions. *Machine Learning, 24*, 173-202.

Amasaki, S., Takagi, Y., Mizuno, O., & Kikuno, T. (2003). A Bayesian belief network for assessing the likelihood of fault content. *14th International Symposium on Software Reliability Engineering,* Denver, Colorado, USA, November 17-20 (pp. 215-226). Washington, D.C.: IEEE Computer Society.

Back, T., Fogel, D. B., & Michalewicz, Z. (Eds.). (2000). *Evolutionary computations I.* Bristol, UK: Institute of Physics Publishing.

Berkovich, Y. (2000). *Software quality prediction using case-based reasoning*. PhD thesis. Boca Raton, FL: Florida Atlantic University.

Breiman, L. (1996). Bagging predictors. *Machine Learning, 24*, 123-140.

Breiman, L., Friedman, J. H., Olshen, R. A., & Stone, C. J. (1984). *Classification and regression trees*. Belmont, CA: Wadsworth International Group.

The Data and Analysis Centre for Software. Retrieved September 25, 2006, from http://www.thedacs.com

Dempster, A. P. (1968). A generalization of Bayesian inference. *Journal of Royal Statistical Society, Series B*(30), 205-247.

Evanco, W. M. (1999). Analyzing change effort in software during development. In *Proceedings of Sixth International Software Metrics Symposium (METRICS'99),* Boca Raton, FL, November 4-6 (pp. 179-188). Washington, D.C.: IEEE Computer Society.

Evanco, W. M. (2001). Prediction models for software fault correction effort. *Proceedings of the Fifth Conference on Software Maintenance and Reengineering, CSMR 2001,* Lisbon, Portugal, March 14-16 (pp. 114-120). Washington, D.C.: IEEE Computer Society.

Fenton, N. E., & Neil, M. (1999). A critique of software defect prediction models. *IEEE Transactions of Software Engineering, 25*(5), 675-689.

Fenton, N. E., & Neil, M. (2005). A critique of software defect prediction models. In D. Zhang, & J. J. P. Tsai (Eds.), *Machine learning applications in software engineering* (pp. 72-86). Singapore: World Scientific Publishing Co.

Freund, Y., & Schapire, R. E. (1996). Experiments with a new boosting algorithm. *13th International Conference on Machine Learning,* Bari, Italy, July 3-6 (pp. 148-156). San Francisco, CA: Morgan Kaufmann.

Glass, R. (1989). Software maintenance documentation. *Annual ACM Conference on Systems Documentation,* Pittsburgh, PA, November 8-10 (pp. 18-23). New York: ACM Press.

Gokhale, S. S., & Lyu., M. R. (1997). Regression tree modeling for the prediction of software quality. In the *Proceedings of the Third International Conference on Reliability and Quality of Design*, Anaheim, CA, USA, March 12-14 (pp. 31-36). New Brunswick, NJ: International Society of Science and Applied Technology.

Goldberg, D. E. (1989). *Genetic algorithms in search, optimization, and machine learning*. Reading, MA: Addison-Wesley.

Hayes, J. H., Patel, S. C., & Zhao, L. (2004). A metrics-based software maintenance effort model. In the *Proceedings of the Eighth Euromicro Working Conference on Software Maintenance and Reengineering (CSMR'04)*, Tempere, Finland, March 24-26 (pp. 254-260). Washington, D.C.: IEEE Computer Society.

Holland, J. H. (1972). *Adaptation in natural and artificial systems* (2nd ed.). Cambridge, MA: MIT Press.

IEEE 610.12. *IEEE Standard Glossary of Software Engineering Terminology.*

Jorgensen, M. (1995). Experience with the accuracy of software maintenance task effort prediction models. *IEEE Transactions of Software Engineering, 21*(8), 674-681.

Khoshgoftaar, T. M., & Allen, E. B. (1998). Neural networks for software quality prediction. In W. Pedrycz, & J. F. Peters (Eds.), *Computational intelligence in software engineering*, the Advances in Fuzzy Systems – Applications and Theory Series (pp. 33-63). Singapore: World Scientific.

Khoshgoftaar, T. M., Allen, E. B., Naik, A., Jones, W., & Hudepohl, J. (1998). Modeling software quality with classification trees. In the *Proceedings of the Fourth International Conference on Reliability and Quality of Design*, Seattle, August 12-14 (pp. 178-182). New Brunswick, NJ: International Society of Science and Applied Technology.

Khoshgoftaar, T. M., & Lanning, D. L. (1995). A neural network approach for early detection of program modules having high risk in the maintenance phase. *Journal of Systems and Software, 29*(1), 85-91.

Khoshgoftaar, T. M., & Seliya, N. (2002). Tree-based software quality models for fault prediction. In the *Proceedings of Eight International Software Metrics Symposium*, Ottawa, Canada, June 4-7 (pp. 203-214). Los Alamitos, CA: IEEE Computer Society.

Khoshgoftaar, T. M., & Seliya, N. (2003). Fault prediction modeling for software quality estimation: Comparing commonly used techniques. *Empirical Software Engineering, 8*, 255-283.

Kononenko, M., & Kovacic, M. (1992). Learning as optimization: Stochastic generation of multiple knowledge. *9th International Workshop on Machine Learning*, Aberdeen, UK, July 1-3 (pp. 257-262). San Francisco, CA: Morgan Kaufmann.

Koza, J. R. (1992). *Genetic programming: On the programming of computers by means of natural selection*. Cambridge, MA: MIT Press.

Kwok, S., & Carter, C. (1990). Multiple decision trees. *Uncertainty in Artificial Intelligence, 4*, 327-335.

Luger, G. (2002). *Artificial intelligence: Structures and strategies for complex problem-solving*. Reading, MA: Addison Wesley.

Mitchell, T. (1997). *Machine learning*. Boston, MA: McGraw Hill.

Neil, M., & Fenton, N. (1996). Predicting software quality using Bayesian belief networks. *21st Annual Software Engineering Workshop*, NASA/Goddard Space Flight Centre, Washington D.C., December 4-5 (pp. 217-230).

Neil, M., Krause, P., & Fenton, N. E. (2003). Software quality prediction using Bayesian networks. In T. M. Khoshgoftaar (Ed.), *Software engineering with computational intelligence* (Chapter 6). International Series in Engineering and Computers Science. Hingham, MA: Kluwer Academic Publishers.

Quinlan J. R. (1993). *C4.5: Programs for machine learning*. San Francisco, CA: Morgan Kaufmann Publishers.

Reformat, M., Pedrycz, W., & Pizzi, N. (2004). Building a software experience factory using granular-based models. *Fuzzy Sets and Systems, 145*(1), 111-140.

RuleQuest Research Data Mining Tools. Retrieved September 25, 2006, from http://www.rulequest.com

Savage, L. J. (1954). *Foundations of statistics*. New York: Wiley.

Schneidewind, N. F. (1995). Software metrics validation: Space shuttle flight software example. *Annals of Software Engineering, 1,* 287-309.

Schneidewind, N. F. (1997). Software metrics model for integrating quality control and prediction. In the *Proceedings of the 8th International Symposium on Software Reliability Engineering*, Albuquerque, NM, USA, November 2-5 (pp. 402-415). Washington, D.C.: IEEE Computer Society.

Shafer, G. (1976). *A mathematical theory of evidence*. Princeton, NJ: Princeton University Press.

Smets, P. (1988). Belief functions. In P. Smets, A. Mamdani, D. Dubois, & H. Prade (Eds.), *Non standard logics for automated reasoning* (pp. 253-286). London: Academic Press.

Smets, P. (1992). The concept of distinct evidence. *IPMU 92 Proceedings,* Palma de Mallorca, July 6-10, (pp. 253-286). *Lecture Notes in Computer Science, LNCS 682*. Berlin, Germany: Springer Verlag.

Smets, P., & Kennes, R. (1994). The transferable belief model. *Artificial Intelligence, 66,* 191-234.

Smith, D. (1999). *Designing maintainable software*. New York: Springer.

Takahashi, R., Muroaka, Y., & Nakamura, Y. (1997). Building software quality classification trees: Approach, experimentation, evaluation. In the *Proceedings of the Eighth International Symposium on Software Reliability Engineering*, Albuquerque, New Mexico, USA, November 2-5 (pp. 222-233). Washington, D.C.: IEEE Computer Society.

Todorovski, L. & Dzeroski, S. (2000). Combining multiple models with meta decision trees. *4th European Conference on Principles of Data Mining and Knowledge Discovery* (pp. 54-64). Berlin: Springer.

Troster, J., & Tian, J. (1995). Measurement and defect modeling for a legacy software system. *Annals of Software Engineering, 1*, 95-118.

Winer, B. J., Brown, D. R., & Michels, K. M. (1991). *Statistical principles in experimental design*. Boston, MA: McGraw-Hill.

Winston, P. H. (1992). *Artificial intelligence*. Reading, MA: Addison Wesley.

Yuan, X., Khoshgoftaar, T. M., Allen, E. B., & Ganesan, K. (2000). An application of fuzzy clustering to software quality prediction. In the *Proceedings of the Third IEEE Symposium on Application-Specific Systems and Software Engineering Technology (ASSET'00)* (pp. 85-90).

Appendix I: Evolutionary Computing

A variety of evolutionary algorithms (EAs), such as genetic algorithms (Goldberg, 1989) and genetic programming (Koza, 1992), have been successfully applied to numerous problems (Back, Fogel, & Michalewicz, 2000) both at the level of structural and parametric optimization. EAs are search methods utilizing the principles of natural selection and genetics (Holland, 1972). Concisely, EAs operate on a set of candidate solutions, called a population, to a given problem. The candidate solutions are evaluated based on their ability to solve the problem. The results of the evaluation are used in a process of forming a new set of solutions. The choice of individuals that are passed to the next population is performed in a process called selection. This process is based on "goodness" of candidate solutions. Additionally, genetic operators, that is, crossover and mutation, are employed to modify selected candidates. Such sequence of actions is repeated until some final criterion is fulfilled. The sequence of activities of EAs is presented in Figure 5.

Figure 5. Evolutionary computing algorithm

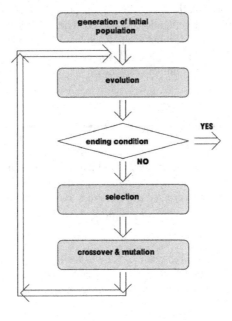

Genetic Algorithms

Genetic algorithms (GAs) (Goldberg, 1989) are one of the most popular EAs. In the case of GAs, candidate solutions to a given problem are encoded into chromosome-like data structures named genotypes. The problem to be solved is encoded into a special function called a fitness function. This function embraces all requirements imposed on the solution to the problem. The genotypes, after being decoded into phenotypes which are solutions in the problem domain, constitute inputs to the fitness function. They are evaluated based on their ability to solve the problem. The results of the evaluation are used in a selection process based on favoring individuals with higher fitness values. The selection can be performed in numerous ways. One of them is called stochastic sampling with replacement. In this method, the entire population is mapped onto a roulette wheel where each individual is represented by the area corresponding to its fitness. Individuals of the next population are chosen by repetitive spinning of the roulette wheel.

Finally, the operations of crossover and mutation are performed on the individuals. Crossover allows exchange of information among individual genotypes in the population and provides innovative capability to the GAs. Its role is to explore the search space in a process of exchanging chromosome parts. Two randomly selected chromosomes are "cut" and "merge" to "produce" a new one. Two parent chromosomes are randomly selected, and two children are created by swapping sequences of genes. In its simplest form, a single crossover point is used. The percentage of individuals that go through crossover is "controlled" by the crossover probability pc.

The role of mutation is to introduce diversity into the population and promote a probabilistic-like traversing of the search space. Mutation builds a new chromosome by making an alteration to a single gene. All genes in all chromosomes are altered with the mutation probability pm.

The evolution of candidate solutions is halted when perfect fitness is achieved or some specified maximum number of generations is passed. The candidate solution that has the best fitness, after termination, is deemed as the discovered solution. Originally, only chromosomes with binary genes have been used. However, right now there are versions of GAs that use integer or floating-point numbers as genes.

Genetic Programming

Genetic programming (GP) (Koza, 1992) can be seen as an extension of the genetic paradigm into the area of programs. It means, that objects, which constitute population, are not fixed-length strings that encode candidate solutions to the given problem, but they are programs. In general, these programs are expressed as parse trees, rather than as lines of code.

In the case of GP, each candidate solution is built using two sets:

- the function set, $F = \{f_{1(b\_1)}; f_{2(b\_2)}; \ldots; f_{n(b\_n)}\}$, of functions with arity > 0; each function from F takes a specified number of arguments, defined as $b_1; b_2; \ldots b_n$;
- the terminal set $T = \{t_1; t_2; \ldots; t_n\}$ of 0-arity functions or constants.

Figure 6. Simple programs

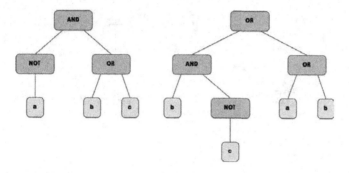

Sets F and T are defined a priori. The process of constructing candidate solutions starts by selecting a function, f_i, randomly from the set F. For each of the b_i arguments, this process is repeated where a random function or terminal may be selected to fill each argument position. If a terminal is selected, the generation process is completed for this branch of the function. If a function is selected, the generation process is recursively applied to each argument of this function. A user specifies a maximum depth of parse trees in order to limit the size of the candidates. For example, using the function set F = {AND; OR; NOT} and the terminal set T = {a; b; c; d}, two sample programs that could be created are shown in Figure 6.

Depending on the type of elements of the function and terminal sets, different structures can be built and different problems can be targeted. All stages of evolutionary algorithms—selection, crossover and mutation—are applied to all structures. Modifications of these structures are performed via manipulations on the lists (Koza, 1992).

Detailed descriptions of GP, GAs, or other evolutionary-based algorithms can be found in Back et al. (2000), Goldberg (1989), Holland (1972), and Koza (1992).

Appendix II: Decision Tress as Data Models and Their Evolutionary-Based Construction

Decision Trees

Decision trees are very attractive representations of underlying data relationships (Mitchell, 1997). They are very intuitive and relatively easy to understand by users. Their graphical representation provides a simple way of finding connections among data points and translating them into IF-THEN rules. The trees are very well suited to perform classification/prediction tasks.

Figure 7. Sample node of a decision tree

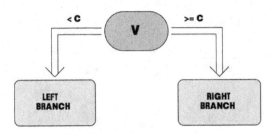

Decision trees consist of a series of nodes with a top node called the root node. Each tree is built by means of a top down growth procedure. The building process is based on training data that contain data points (vectors) with a number of attributes. One of these attributes determines the category to which the data point belongs. At each node, called the attribute node, the training data is partitioned to the children nodes using a splitting rule (see Figure 7). A splitting rule can be of the form: if $V < c$ then s belongs to L, otherwise to R, where V is a selected attribute, c is a constant, s is the data sample and L and R are the left and right branches of the node. In this case, splitting is done using one attribute and a node has two branches (two children). In general, a node can have more branches and the splitting can be done based on several attributes. The best splitting for each node is searched based on a "purity" function calculated from the data. The data is considered pure when they contain data points from only one category. Most frequently used purity functions are entropy, gini-index, and twoing-rule. The data portion that falls into each children node is partitioned again in an effort to maximize the purity function. The tree is constructed until the purity of the data points in each leaf node is at a pre-defined level. Each leaf node is then labeled with a category determined based on majority rule: node is labeled to the category to which majority of the training data points at that node belong. Such nodes are called terminal nodes.

Evolutionary-Based Construction of Decision Trees

Concept

The approach used for construction of decision trees is based on combination of genetic algorithms (GAs) and genetic programming (GP). This approach allows for targeting two problems simultaneously—searching for the best splitting in attribute domains (discretization problem) and finding the most suitable attributes for splitting rules. The approach combines GAs' strength to search through numeric spaces together with GP's strength to search symbolic spaces. Moreover, a process of construction of decision trees—defining splitting and selecting node attributes—can be "controlled" by different functions which represent different objectives essential for a given classification/prediction process. In a nutshell, the approach is to construct a decision tree via performing two-level optimization: parametric using GAs and structural using GP.

Figure 8. Genetic-based construction of decision trees

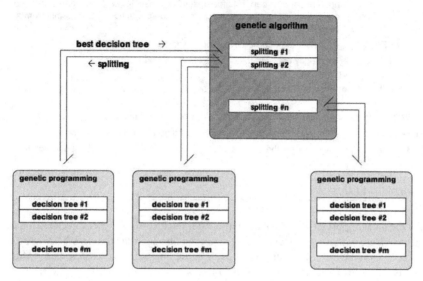

A graphical illustration of the approach is shown in Figure 8. The GA is used at the higher level and its goal is to search for the best splitting of attributes' domains. The GA operates on a population of strings, where each string—GA chromosome—is a set of possible splittings for all attributes. Each GA chromosome is evaluated via a fitness function. Evaluation of each chromosome is performed by running a GP optimization. This means that the GP searches for the best decision tree that can be constructed for the splitting represented by the GA chromosome. Consequently, the GP operates on a population of lists that are blueprints of decision trees. In other words, each individual of the GP population—a list—represents a single decision tree. The population of decision trees evolves according to the rules of selection and genetic operations of crossover and mutation. Each GP individual is evaluated by means of a certain fitness function. The GP returns the best value of the fitness function together with the best decision tree to the GA. The fitness value returned by the GP becomes the fitness value of the evaluated GA chromosome. Such approach ensures evaluation of each GA chromosome based on the best possible decision tree that can be constructed for the splitting represented by this chromosome.

To find the best solution, the GA creates and continuously modifies chromosomes—splittings and then, for each splitting, it invokes GP to generate the best decision tree. The following algorithm summarizes the steps that are used with the multi-level approach:

STEP 1: randomly generate an initial population of GA chromosomes (each chromosome contains information about a number of splittings and about splitting points for each attribute);

STEP 2: WHILE termination criterion not reached DO:

    STEP 2_1: evaluate each GA chromosome (splitting) by invoking GP

        STEP 2_1_1: randomly generate an initial population of trees for a given splitting;

        STEP 2_1_2: WHILE termination criterion not reached DO:

STEP 2_1_2_1: calculate a performance measure (fitness value) representing how well each candidate solution performs the designated task, in the case when candidate solutions are decision trees it means classification/prediction of data points from a training dataset;

STEP 2_1_2_2: select the decision trees for reproduction;

STEP 2_1_2_3: modify decision trees using crossover and mutation;

STEP 2_1_3: identify the fittest solution to the problem -- the best decision tree and return it to GA

STEP 2_2: select candidate solutions—splittings—for reproduction to the next generation;

STEP 2_3: apply genetic operators (crossover and mutation) to combine and modify splittings;

STEP 3: identify the fittest solution—the best splitting and associated with it the best decision tree.

Optimization Objective

One of the most important aspects of the approach is its flexibility to construct decision trees based on objectives that can reflect different requirements regarding the classification/prediction process and the different character of data. These objectives are represented by fitness functions. The role of the fitness function is to assess how well the decision tree classifies the training data. The simplest fitness function represents a single objective ensuring the highest classification/prediction rate without taking into consideration the classification/prediction rate for each data category. In such case, the fitness function is as follows:

$$Fit\_Fun_A = \frac{K}{N}$$

(4)

where N represents the number of data points in a training set, and K represents the number of correctly classified/predicted data points. Such fitness function gives good results when the numbers of data points in each category are comparable. In many cases, the character of processed data is such that not all categories are represented equally. In this case, a fitness function should be such that it ensures the highest possible classification/classification rate for each category. An example of such fitness functions is presented in the following:

$$Fit\_Fun_B = \prod_{i=1}^{c} \frac{k_i + 1}{n_i}$$

(5)

where c represents a number of different categories, n_i represents a number of data samples that belong to a category i, and k_i is a number of correctly classified data points of a category i.

Appendix III: Basics of Evidence Theory

Let's start with a set of worlds Ω called the *frame of discernment*. One of the worlds, denoted ω_0, corresponds to the actual world. The agent (it may be a piece of software, system) does not know which world in Ω corresponds to the actual world ω_0. Nevertheless, the agent has some idea, some opinion about which world might be the actual one. So for every subset I of Ω, called the *focal element*, the agent can express the strength of its opinion that the actual world ω_0 belongs to A. This strength is denoted *bel(A)* and called a belief function (see the following text for the formal definition). Extreme values for *bel* denote full belief (1) or no belief at all (0). The larger *bel(A)*, the stronger the agent believes that ω_0 belongs to A.

Basic Belief Assignments

One of the concepts of the theory is a basic belief assignment (*bba*). Related to belief function *bel*, one can define its so-called Moebius transform, denoted *m* and called a basic belief assignment. Let

$$m : 2^\Omega \rightarrow [0,1]$$

where *m(A)* is called the basic belief mass (*bbm*) given to $A \subseteq \Omega$. The value of *m(A)* represents belief that supports A—that is, the fact that the actual world ω_0 belongs to A without supporting any more specific subset. In the case, when ω_0 belongs to A, and nothing more is known about the value of ω_0, then some part of belief will be given to A, but no subset of A will get any positive support. In that case, $m(A) > 0$ and $m(B)=0$ for all $B \subseteq A$ and $B \neq A$.

Belief Functions

The *bbm m(A)* does not quantify belief, denoted *bel(A)*, that the actual world ω_0 belongs to A. Indeed, the *bbm m(B)* given to any subset B of A also supports that ω_0 belongs to A. Hence, the belief *bel(A)* is obtained by summing all the *bbm m(B)* for $B \subseteq A$. At the end:

$$bel(B) = \sum_{\emptyset \neq B \subseteq A} m(B) \; \forall A \subseteq \Omega, A \neq \emptyset$$

$$bel(\emptyset) = 0$$

(6)

The belief function *bel* satisfies the following inequality:

$\forall n > 1, \forall A_1, A_2, \ldots, A_n \subseteq \Omega$:

$$bel(A_1 \cup A_2 \cup \ldots \cup A_n) \geq \sum_i bel(A_i) - \sum_{i>j} bel(A_i \cap A_j) \ldots -(1)^n bel(A_1 \cap A_2 \cap \ldots \cap A_n) \tag{7}$$

As such, the meaning of these inequalities is not obvious except when $n=2$. These inequalities generalize the idea that agent's belief that the actual world belongs to $A \subseteq \Omega$ can be larger than the sum of the beliefs the agent gives to the elements of a partition of A.

Combination of Two Belief Functions

Suppose there are two "distinct" pieces of evidence Ev1 and Ev2 produced by two sources of information. Let bel_1 and bel_2 be the belief functions induced by each piece of evidence. These two belief functions, with the focal elements A_i and B_j respectively, may be combined into a new belief function using Dempster's (1968) rule of combination. The rule specifies the combined belief mass, m, assigned to each focal element C_k, where C is the set of all subsets produced by A and B. The rule is:

$$m(C_k) = \frac{\sum\limits_{A_i \cap B_j = C_k ; C_k \neq \varnothing} m(A_i)m(B_j)}{1 - \sum\limits_{A_i \cap B_j = \varnothing} m(A_i)m(B_j)} \tag{8}$$

where the focal elements of $bel_1 = A = \{A_1, A_2, \ldots, A_j\}$ and $bel_2 = B = \{B_1, B_2, \ldots, B_j\}$. The combination of two belief functions is also know as taking the orthogonal sum, $\oplus$, and is written as:

$$bel_3 = bel_1 \oplus bel_2 = (m(C_1), \ldots, m(C_k)) \tag{9}$$

The meaning of distinct for two pieces of evidence has been left undefined. It lacks rigorous definition. Intuitively, it means the absence of any relation. In this case, the belief function bel_2 induced by the second source is not influenced by the knowledge of the belief function bel_1 induced by the first source and vice versa (Smets, 1992).

Transferable Belief Model

Dempster-Shafer theory has been used to develop the transferable belief model (TBM) (Smets, 1994). The model represents quantified beliefs and is based on belief functions bel. The TBM departs from the classical Bayesian approach in that the additivity encountered in probability theory is not assumed. For instance, there is no assumption that $bel(A)=0$ implies that $bel(\neg A) = 1$. In fact $bel(A) = bel(\neg A) = 0$ is even possible. The additivity property is replaced by inequalities like:

$$bel(A \cup B) \geq bel(A) + bel(B) - bel(A \cap B) \tag{10}$$

In the TBM, one assumes that bel is a capacity monotone of order infinite. Given a belief function bel, a probability function is generated that is used to make decision by maximizing expected utilities. It requires the construction of the betting frame, that is, a list of alternatives on which the bet must be made. Let BetFrame denotes the betting frame. The granularity of BetFrame is such that if by necessity two alternatives are not distinguishable from a consequence-utility point of view, than they are pooled into the same granule.

Once the betting frame is determined, the *bbms* are transformed by the so-called pignistic transformation into the pignistic probabilities $BetP : 2^{\Omega} \rightarrow [0,1]$ with:

$$BetP(A) = \sum_{X \subseteq Bet_{Frame}, X \neq \varnothing} \frac{m(X)}{1 - m(\varnothing)} \frac{\#(A \cap X)}{\#(X)} \tag{11}$$

for all

$$A \subseteq Bet_{Frame}, A \neq \varnothing$$

$\#(X)$ is the number of granules of the betting frame BetFrame in X, and $m()$ is called the basic belief mass. By construction, the pignistic probability function $BetP$ is a probability function, but it is qualified as pignistic to avoid the error that would consist in considering this probability function as someone's beliefs. Someone's beliefs are represented by bel, and $BetP$ is just the additive measure needed to compute expected utilities when decision must be made (Savage, 1954).

Endnotes

[1]   CART stands for Classification And Regression Trees (Breiman, Friedman, Olshen, & Stone, 1984).

[2]   The proposed approach assumes the following split of data: 20% of data points are randomly selected to constitute a testing dataset, this set does not change for the time of the whole experiment, the data points from this set are used for evaluation of constructed ensemble-based prediction systems; the remaining 80% of data is randomly split into a training set (60%) and a validation set (20%).

[3]   The dataset is divided into training, validation, and testing sets to comply with the construction process of the ensemble-based prediction system (see the *Evidence Theory and Ensemble-Based System* section).

[4]   All results presented in the chapter are for testing data.

[5]   The following schema has been applied to identify generated rules: <two letters identifying dataset name>-<construction method>-<class number>-<rule number>.

Chapter III

Improving Credibility of Machine Learner Models in Software Engineering

Gary D. Boetticher, University of Houston – Clear Lake, USA

Abstract

Given a choice, software project managers frequently prefer traditional methods of making decisions rather than relying on empirical software engineering (empirical/machine learning-based models). One reason for this choice is the perceived lack of credibility associated with these models. To promote better empirical software engineering, a series of experiments are conducted on various NASA datasets to demonstrate the importance of assessing the ease/difficulty of a modeling situation. Each dataset is divided into three groups, a training set, and "nice/nasty" neighbor test sets. Using a nearest neighbor approach, "nice neighbors" align closest to same class training instances. "Nasty neighbors" align to the opposite class training instances. The "nice", "nasty" experiments average 94% and 20% accuracy, respectively. Another set of experiments show how a ten-fold cross-validation is not sufficient in characterizing a dataset. Finally, a set of metric equations is proposed for improving the credibility assessment of empirical/machine learning models.

Introduction

Software Project Management: State-of-Practice

Software project management has improved over the years. For example, the Standish Group, a consulting company, which has been studying IT management since 1994 noted in their latest release of the *Chaos Chronicles* (The Standish Group, 2003) that, "2003 Project success rates improved by more than 100 percent over the 16 percent rate from 1994." Furthermore, "Project failures in 2003 declined to 15 percent of all projects. This is a decrease of more than half of the 31 percent in 1994."

Even with these successes, there are still significant opportunities for improvement in software project management. Table 1 shows several "state-of-practice" surveys collected in 2003 from IT companies in the United States (The Standish Group, 2003); South Africa (Sonnekus & Labuschagne, 2003); and the United Kingdom (Sauer & Cuthbertson, 2003).

According to the *Chaos Chronicles* (The Standish Group, 2003), *successful projects* refers to projects that are completed on time and within budget with all features fully implemented; *project challenged* means that the projects are completed, but exceed budget, go over time, and/or are lacking some/all of the features and functions from the original specifications; and *project failures* are those projects which are abandoned and/or cancelled at some point.

Applying a weighted average to Table 1 results in 34% of the projects identified as successful, 50% are challenged, and 16% end up in failure. Thus, about one-third of the surveyed projects end up as a complete success, half the projects fail to some extent, and one sixth end up as complete failures. Considering the role of computers in various industries, such as the airlines and banking, these are alarming numbers.

From a financial perspective,[1] the lost dollar value for U.S. projects in 2002 is estimated at $38 billion with another $17 billion in cost overruns for a total project waste of $55 billion against $255 billion in project spending (The Standish Group, 2003). Dalcher and Genus (2003) estimate the cost for low success rates at $150 billion per year attributable to wastage arising from IT project failures in the Unites States, with an additional $140 billion in the European Union. Irrespective of which estimate is adopted, it is evident that software project mismanagement results in an annual waste of billions of dollars.

Table 1. State-of-practice surveys

Year	Successful	Challenged	Failure	Projects Surveyed
United States (Chaos Chronicles III)	34%	51%	15%	13,522
South Africa	43%	35%	22%	1,633
United Kingdom	16%	75%	9%	421

Empirical Software Engineering

One of the keys for improving the chances of project development success is the application of empirical-based software engineering. **Empirical-based software engineering** is the process of collecting software metrics and using these metrics as a basis for constructing a model to help in the decision-making process.

Two common types of software metrics are project and product metrics. **Project metrics** refer to the estimated time, money, or resource effort needed in completing a software project. The Standish Group (2003) perceives software cost estimating as the *most effective way to avoid cost and schedule*. Furthermore, several studies (Jones, 1998; The Standish Group, 2003) have shown that by using software cost-estimation techniques, the probability of completing a project successfully doubles. Thus, estimating the schedule, cost, and resources needed for the project is paramount for project success.

Product metrics are metrics extracted from software code and are frequently used for software defect prediction. Defect prediction is a very important area in the software development process. The reason is that a software defect dramatically escalates in cost over the software life cycle. During the coding phase, finding and correcting defects costs $977 per defect (Boehm & Basili, 2001). In the system-testing phase, the cost jumps to $7,136 per defect (Boehm et al., 2001). If a defect survives to the maintenance phase, then the cost to find and remove increases to $14,102 (Boehm et al., 2001).

From an industry perspective, Tassey (2002) estimates that the annual cost of software defects in the United States is $59.5 billion and that "feasible" improvements to testing infrastructures could reduce the annual cost of software defects in the United States by $22.2 billion. The Sustainable Computing Consortium (SCC), an academic, government, and business initiative to drive IT improvements, estimates that from a global perspective, defective computer systems cost companies $175 billion annually. Thus, there are major financial incentives for building models capable of predicting software defects.

There are primarily two methods for constructing models in empirical software engineering. The first adopts an **empirical approach** which emphasizes direct observation in the modeling process and results in one or more mathematical equations. Common examples of this approach include COCOMO I (Boehm, 1981), COCOMO II (Boehm et al., 2000), function points (Albrecht, 1979; Albrecht & Gaffney, 1983), and SLIM (Putnam, 1978) for effort estimation. The second method automates the observation process by using a **machine learning** approach to characterize relationships. Examples of machine learners include Bayesian belief networks (BBN), case-based reasoners (CBR), decision tree learners, genetic programs, and neural networks. The by-product of applying these learners include mathematical equations, decision trees, decision rules, and a set of weights as in the case of a neural network. For the purpose of this chapter, a cursory description will suffice; further details regarding the application of machine learners in software engineering may be found at Khoshgoftaar (2003), Pedrycz (2002), and Zhang and Tsai (2005).

Although the financial incentives are huge, empirical software engineering has received modest acceptance by software practitioners. A project manager may estimate a project by using a human-based approach, an empirical approach, or a machine learning approach. Even though popular models, such as COCOMO or function points, have existed for 25 or more years their application is rather low. In 2004, Jørgensen (2004) compiled a series of studies regarding the frequency of human-based estimation and found it is used 83% (Hihn & Habib-Agahi, 1991), 62% (Heemstra & Kusters, 1991), 86% (Paynter, 1996), 84% (Jørgensen, 1997), and 72% (Kitchenham, Pfleeger, McColl, & Eagan, 2002). It is evident that human-based estimation is the dominant choice relative to empirical or machine learning-based estimation. Furthermore, Jørgensen (2004) states the empirical-based estimation ranges from about 7 to 26% and machine learning-based estimation is only about 4 to 12%.

A key question is *"Why haven't empirical-based models and particularly machine learner models gained greater acceptance by software practitioners?"*

One possible answer to this question is the difficulty in assessing the credibility of these models. A model may boast accurate results, but these results may not be realistic. Thus, the lack of perceived credibility makes it difficult for software practitioners to adopt a new technology within their software development process.

It may be argued that "credibility processes" exist in the form of *n*-fold cross validation and accuracy measures. Unfortunately, none of these approaches address the issue of a dataset's difficulty (how easy or hard it is to model). An empirical model that produces spectacular results may be the consequence of a test set that closely resembles a training set rather than the capability of empirical learner. The outcome is a set of unrealistic models that is unlikely to be adopted by industry. Without a mechanism for assessing a dataset's difficulty, empirical/machine learning models lose credibility.

This chapter introduces several credibility metrics which may be incorporated into the model formulation process with the goal of giving greater credibility. Before introducing these metrics, a series of experiments are conducted to demonstrate some of the difficulties in using a dependent variable for making sampling decisions. The **dependent variable**, also known as the **class variable**, is the attribute we are trying to predict from a set of independent (non-class) variables. The initial set of experiments demonstrates the importance of sampling on non-class attributes. These experiments examine the "best case" versus "worst case" for a NASA-based defect repository dataset.

Next, a second set of experiments demonstrates that a *ten*-fold cross validation may not be sufficient in building realistic models.

After demonstrating some of the inadequacies of current validation processes, several credibility metrics are introduced. These metrics measure the *difficulty* of a dataset. Adoption of these metric equations will lead to more realistic models, greater credibility to models, and an increased likelihood that software practitioners will embrace empirical software engineering.

Related Research

This section provides a general overview of different sampling/resampling techniques, a description of the K-nearest neighbor (KNN) algorithm, and an overview of assessing models for accuracy.

Traditional sampling typically adopts a **random**, **stratified**, **systematic**, or **clustered** approach. The randomized approach, which is the simplest, randomly selects tuples to be in the test set. One way to improve estimates obtained from random sampling is by arranging the population into strata or groups. A non-class attribute (e.g., age, gender, or income) is used to stratify samples. Systematic sampling orders data by an attribute, then selects every i^{th} element on the list afterwards. Cluster sampling is a method of selecting sampling units in which the unit contains a cluster of elements (Kish, 1965). Examples of cluster samples may include all students of one major from all university students or residents from a particular state.

When extracting samples for a test set, systematic and cluster sampling focus on the class (or dependent) variable. Stratified sampling may use a non-class variable, but typically this is limited to at most one of the non-class variables and does not consider the non-class attribute in light of the class attribute. The problem is that non-class (independent) variables contain a lot of vital information which needs to be considered when partitioning tuples into training and test sets.

An **n-fold cross validation** is a resampling method for validating a model. For this technique, data is partitioned into *n*-classes, and *n* models are constructed with each of the *n*-classes rotated into the test set. *N*-fold cross validation addresses the issue of data distribution between training and test sets, but does not consider difficulty in modeling the training data.

The **K-nearest neighbor (KNN)** algorithm is a supervised learning algorithm which classifies a new instance based upon some distance formula (e.g., Euclidean). The new instance is classified to a category relative to some majority of K-nearest neighbors. Traditionally, the KNN algorithm is viewed as a machine learner, rather than a method for dividing training and test data.

Regarding approaches for measuring accuracy, Shepperd, Cartwright, and Kadoda (2000) discuss the merits of various methods for measuring accuracy including *TotalError*, *TotalAbsoluteError*, *TotalRelativeError*, *BalancedMMRE*, *MMRE*, *Pred(X)*, *Mean Squared Error*, and R^2. There is validity in using one or more of these accuracy methods. However, they do not provide any information regarding the difficulty in modeling a dataset.

A Simple Example

To illustrate why it is important to consider the relationship between non-class attributes over a training and test set, consider the dataset in Table 2. It consists of three attributes: source lines of code (SLOC); v(g), also known as cyclomatic complexity, which equals the number of decision points within a program plus one; and *defects*. For this example, defects refer to the number of software defects present in a software component. If a software component has zero defects, then it is classified as an *A*, otherwise it is classified as a *B*.

Figure 1 plots these points. The points form 4 clusters of *A*s and *B*s, respectively.

If the goal is to build a model for predicting software defects, a systematic sampling approach may be applied, which generates the training and test sets in Tables 3a and 3b.

Table 2. Simple dataset

SLOC	v(g)	Defects
81	13	A
87	13	A
182	33	A
193	32	A
53	10	B
58	10	B
140	30	B
150	27	B

Figure 1. Plot of tuples from Table 2

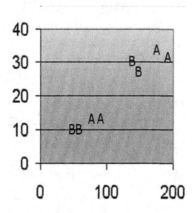

Table 3a. Training data

SLOC	v(g)	Defects
81	13	A
182	33	A
58	10	B
150	27	B

Table 3b. Test data

SLOC	v(g)	Defects
87	13	A
193	32	A
53	10	B
140	30	B

Applying a nearest neighbor approach to the non-class attributes, it is clear that the *A*s in the test set match the *A*s in the training set. This is depicted as arrows between Tables 3a and 3b. The same is true for those defects in the *B* class. It is expected that such an experiment would produce very good results irrespective of the machine learner selected. Figure 2 highlights training samples with gray boxes.

Figure 2. Plot of training and test sets (Square boxes are training samples)

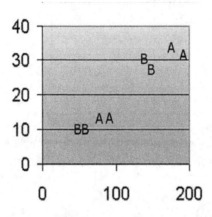

Table 4a. Training data

SLOC	v(g)	Defects
81	13	A
87	13	A
140	30	B
150	27	B

Table 4b. Test data

SLOC	v(g)	Defects
182	33	A
193	32	A
53	10	B
58	10	B

Suppose a second experiment is conducted using stratified sampling and produces the training and test sets in Tables 4a and 4b.

Applying a nearest neighbor approach to the non-class attributes, it is clear that the As in the test set match a B instance in the training set. Also, the Bs in the test set match an A instance in the training set. It is expected that such an experiment would generate very poor results irrespective of the machine learner selected. Figure 3 highlights training samples with gray boxes.

By ignoring nearest neighbors when building models, success/failure may be a function of the nearest neighbor distribution rather than the capability of the algorithm/machine-learner.

To illustrate the importance of considering nearest neighbor in training/test distribution, a series of experiments are conducted using NASA-based defect data. Although the focus is on defect data, the idea easily extends to other types of software engineering data (e.g., effort estimation data).

Figure 3. Plot of training and test sets (Square boxes are training samples)

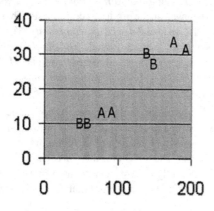

NASA Datasets

To demonstrate how non-class attributes dramatically impact the modeling process, a series of experiments are conducted against five NASA defect datasets. These experiments fall into two categories. The "nice" experiments use a test set where the non-class attributes of the test data have nearest-neighbors in the training set and are the same class value. The "nasty" experiments use a test set where the non-class attributes of the test data have nearest-neighbors in the training set with an opposite class value.

All experiments use five public domain defect datasets from the NASA Metrics Data Program (MDP) and the PROMISE repository (Shirabad & Menzies, 2005). These five datasets, referred to as CM1, JM1, KC1, KC2, and PC1, contain static code measures (e.g., Halstead, McCabe, LOC) along with defect rates. Table 5 provides a project description for each of these datasets.

Table 5. Project description for each dataset

Project	Source Code	Description
CM1	C	NASA spacecraft instrument
KC1	C++	Storage management for receiving/processing ground data
KC2	C++	Science data processing. No software overlap with KC1.
JM1	C	Real-time predictive ground system
PC1	C	Flight software for earth orbiting satellite

Each dataset contains 21 software product metrics based on the product's size, complexity, and vocabulary. The size metrics include *total lines of code, executable lines of code, lines of comments, blank lines, number of lines containing both code and comments*, and *branch count*. Another three metrics are based on the product's complexity. These include *cyclomatic complexity, essential complexity*, and *module design complexity*. The other 12 metrics are vocabulary metrics. The vocabulary metrics include *Halstead length, Halstead volume, Halstead level, Halstead difficulty, Halstead intelligent content, Halstead programming effort, Halstead error estimate, Halstead programming time, number of unique operators, number of unique operands, total operators*, and *total operands*.

The class attribute for each dataset refers to the propensity for defects. The original MDP dataset contains numeric values for the defects, while the PROMISE datasets convert the numeric values to Boolean values where *TRUE* means a component has one or more defects and *FALSE* equates to zero defects. The reason for the conversion is that the numeric distribution displayed signs of an implicitly data-starved domain (many data instances, but few of interest) where less than 1% of the data has more than five defects (Menzies, 2005a).

Data Pre-Processing

Data pre-processing removes all duplicate tuples from each dataset along with those tuples that have questionable values (e.g., LOC equal to 1.1). Table 6 shows the general demographics of each of the datasets after pre-processing.

Table 6. Data pre-processing demographics

Project	Original Size	Size w/ No Bad, No Dups	0 Defects	1+ Defects	% Defects
CM1	498	441	393	48	10.9%
JM1	10,885	8911	6904	2007	22.5%
KC1	2109	1211	896	315	26.0%
KC2	522	374	269	105	28.1%
PC1	1109	953	883	70	7.3%

Nearest Neighbor Experiments

Training and Test Set Formulation

To assess the impact of nearest-neighbor sampling upon the experimental process, 20 experiments are conducted on each of the five datasets.

For each experiment, a training set is constructed by extracting 40% of data from a given dataset. Using stratified sampling to select 40% of the data maintains the ratio between defect/non-defect data. As an example, JM1 has 8,911 records, 2,007 (22.5%) of which have one or more defects. A corresponding training set for the JM1 project contains 3,564 records, 803 (22.5%) of which are classified as having one or more defects (TRUE).

It could be argued that a greater percentage (more than 40%) of the data could be committed to the training set. There are several reasons for choosing only 40%. First, Menzies claims that only a small portion of the data is needed to build a model (Menzies, Raffo, Setamanit, DiStefano, & Chapman, 2005b). Second, since the data is essentially a two-class problem, there was no concern about whether each class would receive sufficient representation. Finally, it is necessary to insure that there is a sufficient amount of test data for assessing the results.

Once a training set is established, the remaining 60% of the data is partitioned into two test groups. Prior to splitting the test data, all of the non-class attributes are normalized by dividing each value by the *Difference* ($Maximum_k - Minimum_k$ for each column k). This guarantees that each column receives equal weighting. The next step loops through all the test records. Each test record is compared with every training record to determine the minimum *Euclidean Distance* for all of the non-class attributes. If the training and test tuples with the smallest Euclidean Distance share the same class values (TRUE/TRUE or FALSE/FALSE), then the test record is added to the "nice neighbor" test set, otherwise add it to the "nasty neighbor" test set. Figure 4 shows the corresponding algorithm.

Essentially, this is the K-nearest neighbor algorithm that determines a test tuple's closest match in the training set. Nearest neighbors from the same class are considered "nice", otherwise they are classified as "nasty."

Figure 4. Nice/nasty neighbor algorithm

```
For j=1 to test.record_count
    minimumDistance = 9999999
    For i=1 to train.record_count
    Dist = 0
        For k=1 to train.column_count - 1
        Dist = Dist + (train_ik – test_jk)²
        end k
        if (abs(Dist) < abs(minimumDistance))
            then if Train_i.defect = Test_j.defect
                then minimumDistance = Dist
                else minimumDistance = -Dist
    end i;
    if minimumDistance > 0
        then Add_To_Nice_Neighbors
    if minimumDistance < 0
        else Add_To_Nasty_Neighbors
    if minimumDistance = 0
            then if Train_i.defect = Test_j.defect
                then Add_To_Nice_Neighbors
                else Add_To_Nasty_Neighbors
end j;
```

All experiments use the training data to build a model between the non-class attributes (e.g., *size*, *complexity*, or *vocabulary*) and the class attribute *defect* (which is either *True* or *False*).

After constructing 300 datasets (one training set and two tests sets; 20 trials per software project; five software projects), attention focuses on data mining tool selection.

Data Mining Tool Selection

Since the data contains 20-plus attributes and only two class values (TRUE/FALSE), the most reasonable data mining tool in this situation is a decision tree learner. A decision tree selects an attribute which best divides the data into two homogenous groups (based on class value). The split selection recursively continues on the two or more subtrees until all children of a split are totally homogenous (or the bin dips below a prescribed threshold). Decision tree learners are described as greedy in that they do not look ahead (two or more subtree levels) due to the associated computational complexity.

One of the most popular public domain data mining tools is the Waikato environment for knowledge analysis (Weka) tool (Witten & Franks, 2000). Weka is an open-source machine learning workbench. Implemented in Java, Weka incorporates many popular machine learners and is widely used for practical work in machine learning. According to a recent KDD poll (KDD Nuggets Web site, 2005), Weka was rated number two in terms of preferred usage as compared to other commercial and public domain tools.

Within Weka, there are many learners available. The experiments specifically use the naïve Bayes and J48 learners for analysis. There are reasons for adopting these tools. First, these tools performed very well in more than 1,000 data mining experiments conducted by the author. Second, success in using these particular learners was noted by Menzies et al. (2005b) in their analysis of the NASA defect repositories.

A naïve Bayes classifier uses a probabilistic approach to assign the most likely class for a particular instance. For a given instance x, a naïve Bayes classifier computes the conditional probability

$$P\,(C = c_i \,|\, x) = P(C = c_i \,|\, A_1 = a_{i1}, \ldots A_n = a_{in}) \tag{1}$$

for all classes c_i and tries to predict the class which has the highest probability. The classifier is considered naïve (Rish, 2001) since it assumes that the frequencies of the different attributes are independent.

A second learner, J48, is based on Quinlan's C4.5 (Quinlan, 1992).

Assessment Criteria

The assessment criterion uses four metrics in all experiments to describe the results. They are:

- **PD**, which is the probability of detection. This is the probability of identifying a module with a fault divided by the total number of modules with faults.
- **PF**, which is the probability of a false alarm. This is defined as the probability of incorrectly identifying a module with a fault divided by the total number of modules with no faults.
- **NF**, which is the probability of missing an alarm. This is defined as the probability of incorrectly identifying a module where the fault was missed divided by the total number of modules with faults.
- **Acc**, which is the accuracy. This is the probability of correctly identifying faulty and non-faulty modules divided by the total number of modules under consideration.

Each of these metrics is based on simple equations constructed from Weka's **confusion matrix** as illustrate by Table 7.

PD is defined as:

$$PD = A / (A+B)$$ (2)

PF is defined as:

$$PF = C / (C + D)$$ (3)

NF is defined as:

$$NF = A / (A + B)$$ (4)

and *Acc* is defined as:

$$Acc = (A + D) / (A + B + C + D)$$ (5)

Table 7. Definition of the confusion matrix

	A Defect is Detected.	**A Defect is not Detected.**
A Defect is Present.	**A = 50** Predicted=TRUE Actual= TRUE	**B = 200** Predicted= FALSE Actual= TRUE
A Defect is not Present.	**C = 100** Predicted= TRUE Actual=FALSE	**D = 900** Predicted= FALSE Actual= FALSE

Based on the example in Table 7, the corresponding values would be:

$$PD = 50 / (50 + 200) = 20\% \tag{6}$$

$$PF = 100 / (100 + 900) = 10\% \tag{7}$$

$$NF = 200 / (200 + 50) = 80\% \tag{8}$$

$$Acc = (50 + 900) / (50 + 100 + 200 + 900) = 76\% \tag{9}$$

Results

Table 8 shows the accuracy results of the 20 experiments per project. As might be expected, the "nice" test set did very well for all five projects for both machine learners averaging about 94% accuracy. Its counterpart, the "nasty" test set, did not fare very well, averaging about 20% accuracy.

It is interesting to note that the JM1 dataset, with 7 to 20 times more tuples than any of the other projects, is above the overall average for the "nice" datasets, and below the overall average on the "nasty" datasets. Considering the large number of tuples in this dataset and how much of the solution space is covered by the JM1 dataset, it would seem that a tuple in the test set would have difficulty aligning to a specific tuple in the training set.

Regarding PD, the results as expressed in Table 9 for the "nice" test set are superior to the "nasty" test set for the learners. An overall weighted average is preferred over a regular average in order not to bias the results towards those experiments with very few defect samples.

The results in Table 9 can be misleading. Seventy-six of the 100 "nice" test sets contained zero defect tuples. Of the remaining 24 "nice" test sets, only 2 of these 24 had 20 or more samples with defects.

The "nice" test set did very well at handling false alarms as depicted in Table 10. The "nasty"

Table 8. Accuracy results from all experiments

	"Nice" Test Set		"Nasty" Test Set	
	J48	Naïve Bayes	J48	Naïve Bayes
CM1	97.4%	88.3%	6.2%	37.4%
JM1	94.6%	94.8%	16.3%	17.7%
KC1	90.9%	87.5%	22.8%	30.9%
KC2	88.3%	94.1%	42.3%	36.0%
PC1	97.8%	91.9%	19.8%	35.8%
Average	94.4%	93.6%	18.7%	21.2%

Table 9. Probability of detection results

	"Nice" Test Set		"Nasty" Test Set	
	J48	Naïve Bayes	J48	Naïve Bayes
CM1	0.0%	0.0%	5.9%	37.4%
JM1	71.9%	92.9%	14.9%	16.4%
KC1	45.8%	87.5%	22.7%	31.0%
KC2	100.0%	100.0%	42.2%	36.0%
PC1	11.7%	75.0%	10.9%	30.8%
Overall Weighted Average	45.6%	60.8%	16.8%	20.0%

Table 10. Probability of false alarms results

	"Nice" Test Set		"Nasty" Test Set	
	J48	Naïve Bayes	J48	Naïve Bayes
CM1	2.6%	11.7%	0.0%	50.0%
JM1	5.1%	5.0%	61.7%	66.1%
KC1	9.0%	12.5%	46.4%	91.7%
KC2	11.8%	5.9%	0.0%	50.0%
PC1	1.7%	7.9%	1.9%	70.6%
Overall Weighted Average	5.4%	6.3%	18.5%	37.1%

test set triggered alarms about 18 to 37% of the time depending upon learner. Overall, the sample size is small for the "nasty" test sets. Ninety percent (from the 100 experiments) of the "nasty" test sets contain zero instances of non-defective data. For the remaining 10 "nasty" datasets, only three contain 10 or more instances of non-defective modules.

To better understand these results, consider Tables 11 and 12. These tables show the weighted averages (rounded) of all confusion matrices for all 100 experiments (20 per test group). In the "nice" test data, 99.6% are defined as having no defects (FALSE). Less than 1% of the tuples actually contain defects. Although the "nice" test sets fared better than the "nasty" test sets regarding defect detection, the relatively few samples having one or more defects in the "nice" test sets discount the results.

Analyzing the "nasty" datasets in Tables 11 and 12 reveal that 97.2% (e.g., (50 + 249)/(50+249+2+7)) of the data contains one or more defects.

Referring back to the right-most column of Table 6, the percentage of defects to the total number of modules ranged from 7.3 to 28.1%. Considering that all training sets maintained their respective project ratio of defects to total components, it is quite surprising that the

Table 11. Confusion matrix, nice test set (rounded)

J48		Naïve Bayes	
2	3	3	2
58	1021	68	1011

Table 12. Confusion matrix, nasty test set (rounded)

J48		Naïve Bayes	
50	249	60	241
2	7	3	5

"nice" and "nasty" datasets would average such high proportions of non-defective and defective components, respectively.

To better understand these results, two additional experiments are conducted using the KC1 dataset. The first experiment randomly allocates 60% of the data to the training set, while the second allocates 50% of the data. Both experiments maintain a defect/non-defective ratio of 26% (see Table 6). For both experiments, the test data is divided into eight groups using a three-nearest neighbor approach. For each test vector, its three closest neighbors from the training set are determined. These neighbors are ranked based on first, second, to third closest neighbor. A "P" means that there is a positive match (same class), and an "N" means there is a negative match (opposite class). Thus, a "PPN" means that the first and second closest matches are from the same class and the third closest match is from the opposite class. Thus, the best case would be a "PPP" where the three closest training vectors are all from the same class.

Tables 13 and 14 show the results from these experiments. It is interesting to note that all eight bins contain homogenous (all TRUEs, or all FALSEs) data. There is a general trend for the bin configuration to change from all non-defective tuples (all FALSEs) to all defective tuples (TRUEs) as the neighbor status changes from all positives (PPP) to all negatives (NNN).

Table 13. KC1 data, KNN=3, 60% of training data

			Accuracy	
Neighbor Description	# of TRUEs	# of FALSEs	J48	Naïve Bayes
PPP	None	None	NA	NA
PPN	0	354	88	90
PNP	0	5	40	20
NPP	None	None	NA	NA
PNN	3	0	100	0
NPN	13	0	31	100
NNP	110	0	25	28
NNN	None	None	NA	NA

Table 14. KC1 data, KNN=3, 50% of training data

Neighbor Description	# of TRUEs	# of FALSEs	Accuracy	
			J48	Naïve Bayes
PPP	0	19	89	84
PPN	0	417	91	91
PNP	0	13	23	0
NPP	None	None	NA	NA
PNN	None	None	NA	NA
NPN	18	0	100	100
NNP	132	0	20	20
NNN	7	0	0	29

Also, the accuracy seems positively correlated to the nearest neighbor classifications.

These last two sub-experiments confirm the results achieved in Tables 11 and 12.

Ten-Fold/Duplicates Experiment

The next experiment demonstrates that a *ten*-fold cross validation does not provide a total perspective regarding the validation of a dataset.

This experiment uses the five NASA datasets described in the earlier sections. For each dataset, two types of experiments are conducted: the first uses the original dataset (less bad data) with duplicates, and a second where duplicates are removed. Note that each original dataset had only one bad data sample. Each experiment uses a *ten*-fold cross validation for each of the 20 trials. A defect prediction model is constructed based on the C4.5 learner from Weka (J48) using the default settings.

Table 15 shows the results from these experiments. For all five NASA datasets, the learner produces a better model with the inclusion of duplicates. A t-test shows that these differences are statistically significant for all five NASA datasets.

In these experiments, the duplicates are the "nice neighbors" described in the previous set

Table 15. Duplicate/no duplicate experimental results

	Accuracy Average of 29 Runs	
	With Duplicates	No Duplicates
CM1	88.07%	87.46%
JM1	79.68%	76.56%
KC1	84.29%	74.03%
KC2	81.65%	76.22%
PC1	93.43%	91.65%

of experiments. Performing a *ten*-fold cross validation insures that datasets with duplicates will have a distinct advantage over datasets without duplicates.

Discussion

In general, project managers are reluctant to embrace empirical-based models in their decision-making process. Jørgensen (2004) estimates more than 80% of all effort estimation is human-based and only about 4% is machine learning-based. If empirical software engineering is going to have any hope of gaining favor with project managers, then it is critical that the modeling process be understood very well.

The first set of experiments shows the extreme range of answers in corresponding best case/worst case scenarios. These experiments clearly indicate how significantly nearest-neighbor sampling influences the results despite the fact that no dataset had any duplicates.

The second set of experiments reflects a more realistic situation where an empirical software engineer may (or may not) include duplicates in the modeling process. The difference in results is statistically significant. For some learners, the issue of duplicates is not a problem. However, as seen with the C4.5 learner, it is a problem.

In order to avoid building artificial models, perhaps the best approach would be to not allow duplicates within datasets. Another attribute could be added to the dataset, *Number of Duplicates*, so that information regarding duplicates is not lost.

This solves the issue of duplicates within datasets, however it does not address the issue regarding the synergy between testing and training datasets ("nice" versus "nasty" test sets). The next section addresses this issue.

Better Credibility Through Nearest Neighbor-Based Sampling

As demonstrated in the first set of experiments, it is evident that nearest-neighbor test data distribution dramatically impacts experimental results. The question is *How may nearest-neighbor sampling be incorporated into the project development process in order to generate realistic models?*

There are at least two possible solutions: one of which adapts to an organization's current software engineering processes; the second solution offers an alternative process.

In the first approach, a software engineer determines the nearest neighbor for each of the tuples in the test set (based on non-class attributes), relative to the training set. If the test tuple's nearest neighbor in the training set shares the same class instance value, then add *1* to a variable called *Matches*. *Matches* will be used to define a metric called *Experimental Difficulty* (*Exp_Difficulty*) as follows:

$$Exp\_Difficulty = 1 - Matches / Total\_Test\_Instances \tag{10}$$

The *Experimental Difficulty* provides a qualitative assessment of the ease/difficulty for modeling a given dataset. Combining this metric with an accuracy metric would offer a more realistic assessment of the results. For example, a "*Exp_Difficulty * Accuracy*" would give a more complete picture regarding the goodness of a model leading to better model selection and more credible models. For an *n*-fold cross validation, the *Experimental Difficulty* could be calculated for each fold, then averaged over the *n* folds.

A second approach starts with the whole dataset prior to partitioning into training and test sets. For each tuple in the dataset, its nearest neighbor (with respect to the non-class attributes) is determined. Add 1 to the *Match* variable if a tuple's nearest neighbor is from the same class. Modifying Equation 10 results in the following equation:

$$Overall\_Difficulty = 1 - Matches / Total\_Data\_Instances \tag{11}$$

This gives an idea of the overall difficulty of the dataset. A software engineer may partition the data in order to increase (or decrease) *Experimental_Difficulty*. In the context of industrial-based benchmarks, the *Experimental_Difficulty* may be adjusted to coincide to a value adopted by another researcher. This lends greater credibility to comparing experimental results.

Considering an estimated 99% of the world's datasets are proprietary, this approach provides an additional benchmark for those models constructed on private datasets. Furthermore, these metric equations provide a means for assessing the robustness of the results.

Conclusions

Most datasets are proprietary in nature, making it impossible to replicate results in this situation. As demonstrated by the NASA experiments, not all data distributions result in similar results. This work extends previous research in defect prediction (Khoshgoftaar, 2003; Porter & Selby, 1990; Srinivasan & Fisher, 1995; Tian & Zelkowitz, 1995) by conducting nearest-neighbor analysis for gaining a deeper understanding of how datasets relate to each other, and thus the need for developing more realistic empirical/machine learning-based models. In the first set of NASA experiments, the "nice" dataset experiments (easy datasets to model) resulted in an average accuracy of 94.0% and the "nasty" dataset experiments (difficult datasets to model) produced an average accuracy of 19.5%. These results suggest that success in modeling a training dataset may be attributable to the ease/difficulty of the dataset, rather than the capability of the machine learner.

Including duplicates within a dataset reduces the difficulty of a dataset since similar tuples may appear in both the training and test sets. This research proposes removing duplicates in order to eliminate any bias.

Finally, this work proposes a set of metric equations for measuring the difficulty of a dataset. Benefits of using these metric equations include:

- **The creation of more realistic models.** These metrics will help the software engineering community better gauge the robustness of a model.

- **Greater credibility for models based on private datasets.** Since most datasets are proprietary, it is difficult to assess the quality of a model built in this context. Using the proposed metrics will make it easier to compare experiment results when the replication is impossible.

- **Greater chances of adoption by the industrial community.** As mentioned earlier, human-based estimation is still the method of choice. By providing a difficulty metric with a set of results, project managers will be able to assess the goodness of an empirical model. This will make it easier for a project manager to trust an empirical/machine learning-based model. Thus making it easier for the industrial community to more readily adopt empirical software engineering approaches.

Future Directions

This work could be extended from a two-class to an n-class problem. For example, the NASA datasets could be divided into four classes, (0, 1, 2, 3+ defects).

Another common type of software engineering dataset estimates programming effort. Thus, a likely future direction would examine these types of datasets.

Finally, it would be interesting to see whether accuracy results could be scaled by the "dataset difficulty metrics" in order to make better comparisons over datasets of varying difficulty.

References

Albrecht, A. J. (1979). Measuring application development productivity. In the *Proceedings of the Joint SHARE, GUIDE, and IBM Application Development Symposium*.

Albrecht, A. J., & Gaffney, J. E. (1983). Software function, source lines of code, and development effort prediction: A software science validation. *IEEE Transactions on Software Engineering, 9*(2).

Boehm, B. (1981). *Software engineering economics*. Englewood Cliffs, NJ : Prentice-Hall. ISBN 0-13-822122-7.

Boehm, B., Abts, C., Brown, A., Chulani, S., Clark, B., Horowitz, E., Madachy, R., Reifer, D., & Steece, B. (2000). *Software cost estimation with Cocomo II*. Pearson Publishing.

Boehm, B., & Basili, V. (2001). Software defect reduction top 10 list. *IEEE Computer, 34*(1), 135-137.

Dalcher, D., & Genus, A. (2003). Avoiding IS/IT implementation failure. *Technology Analysis and Strategic Management, 15*(4), 403-407.

Heemstra, F. J., & Kusters, R. J. (1991). Function point analysis: Evaluation of a software cost estimation model. *European Journal of Information Systems, 1*(4), 223-237.

Hihn, J., & Habib-Agahi, H. (1991). Cost estimation of software intensive projects: A survey of current practices. In *International Conference on Software Engineering* (pp. 276-287). Los Alamitos, CA: IEEE Computer Society Press.

Jones, C. (1998). *Estimating software costs.* McGraw Hill.

Jørgensen, M. (1997). An empirical evaluation of the MkII FPA estimation model. In *Norwegian Informatics Conference*, Voss, Norway, Tapir, Oslo (pp. 7-18).

Jørgensen, M. (2004) A review of studies on expert estimation of software development effort. *Journal of Systems and Software, 70*(1-2), 37-60.

KDD Nuggets Website. (2005). *Polls: Data mining tools you regularly use.* Knowledge Discovery and Data Mining Poll. Retrieved 2005, from http://www.kdnuggets.com/polls/data_mining_tools_2002_june2.htm

Khoshgoftaar, T. M. (Ed.). (2003). *Computational intelligence in software engineering, Annals of software engineering.* Kluwer Academic Publishers, ISBN 1-4020-7427-1.

Khoshgoftaar, T. M., & Allen, E. B. (2001). Model software quality with classification trees. In H. Pham (Ed.), *Recent advances in reliability and quality engineering* (pp. 247–270). World Scientific.

Kish, L. (1965). *Survey sampling.* New York: John Wiley and Sons, Inc.

Kitchenham, B., Pfleeger, S. L., McColl, B., & Eagan, S. (2002). A case study of maintenance estimation accuracy. To appear in the *Journal of Systems and Software.*

Menzies, T. (2005a). Personal conversation.

Menzies, T., Raffo, D., Setamanit, S., DiStefano, J., & Chapman, R. (2005b). Why mine repositories. Submitted to the *Transactions on Software Engineering.*

Paynter, J. (1996). Project estimation using screenflow engineering. In the *International Conference on Software Engineering: Education and Practice,* Dunedin, New Zealand (pp. 150-159). Los Alamitos, CA: IEEE Computer Society Press.

Pedrycz, W. (2002). Computational intelligence as an emerging paradigm of software engineering. In the *Proceedings of the 14th international conference on Software engineering and knowledge engineering,* Ischia, Italy (pp. 7-14). ACM.

Porter, A. A., & Selby, R. W. (1990). Empirically guided software development using metric-based classification trees. *IEEE Software,* 46-54.

Putnam, L. H. (1978). A general empirical solution to the macro software sizing and estimating problem. *IEEE Transactions on Software Engineering,* 345-361.

Quinlan, J. R. (1992). *C4.5: Programs for machine learning.* San Francisco, CA: Morgan Kaufmann.

Rish, I. (2001). *An empirical study of the naive Bayes classifier, T. J. Watson Center.* In the IJCAI-01 Workshop on Empirical Methods in Artificial Intelligence, Seattle.

Sauer, C., & Cuthbertson, C. (2003). *The state of IT project management in the UK*. Oxford: Templeton College.

Shepperd, M., Cartwright, M., & Kadoda, G. (2000). On building prediction systems for software engineers. In *Empirical Software Engineering* (pp. 175-182). Boston: Kluwer Academic Publishers.

Shirabad, J. S., & Menzies, T. J. (2005) *The PROMISE repository of software engineering databases school of information technology and engineering.* University of Ottawa, Canada. Retrieved 2005, from http://promise.site.uottawa.ca/SERepository

Sonnekus, R., & Labuschagne, L. (2003). *IT project management maturity versus project success in South Africa.* RAU Auckland Park, Johannesburg, South Africa: RAU Standard Bank Academy for Information Technology, ISBN: 0-86970-582-2.

Srinivasan, K., & Fisher, D. (1995). Machine learning approaches to estimating software development effort. *IEEE Transactions on Software Engineering*, 126-137.

The Standish Group. (2003). *The Chaos Chronicles III.*

Tassey, G. (2002). *The economic impacts of inadequate infrastructure for software testing* (Planning Report 02-3). Prepared by RTI for the National Institute of Standards and Technology (NIST). Retrieved 2005, from http://www.nist.gov/director/prog-ofc/report02-3.pdf

Tian, J., & Zelkowitz, M. V. (1995). Complexity measure evaluation and selection. *IEEE Transaction on Software Engineering*, *21*(8), 641-649.

Witten, I., & Franks, E. (2000). *Data mining: Practical machine learning tools with Java implementations.* San Francisco, CA: Morgan Kaufmann.

Zhang, D., & Tsai, J. J. P. (2005). *Machine learning applications in software engineering.* World Scientific Publishing, ISBN: 981-256-094-7.

Endnote

[1]   All monetary amounts are depicted in U.S. dollars.

Section II:

Applications to Software Development

This part includes three chapters (Chapters IV-VI) that cover machine learning applications in several areas of software systems development and deployment. Chapter IV focuses on the applications of inductive logic programming to software engineering. An integrated framework based on inductive logic programming is proposed by the author for the synthesis, maintenance, reuse, testing, and debugging of logic programs. Chapter V demonstrates how multiple instance learning and neural networks are integrated with Markov model mediator to address the challenges in an advanced content-based image retrieval system: the significant discrepancy between the low-level image features and the high-level semantic concepts, and the perception subjectivity problem. Finally, Chapter VI describes the application of genetic algorithms to a service-oriented system.

Chapter IV

ILP Applications to Software Engineering

Daniele Gunetti, Università degli Studi di Torino, Italy

Abstract

Though inductive logic programming (ILP for short) should mean the "induction of logic programs", most research and applications of this area are only loosely related to logic programming. In fact, the automatic synthesis of "true" logic programs is a difficult task, since it cannot be done without a lot of information on the sought programs, and without the ability to describe in a simple way well-restricted searching spaces. In this chapter, we argue that, if such knowledge is available, inductive logic programming can be used as a valid tool for software engineering, and we propose an integrated framework for the development, maintenance, reuse, testing, and debugging of logic programs.

Introduction to Inductive Logic Programming

Inductive logic programming is normally defined as the research area at the intersection of machine learning and logic programming. An ILP system receives as input some examples of the program's input/output behavior (plus other kinds of information about the desired program) and must produce a logic program that behaves as expected on the given examples, or at least on a high percentage of them. Typically, the obtained programs will then be used on new examples, not given to the ILP system during the learning phase. From the point of view of a computer scientist, this is just a form of program synthesis from examples, but the view presented in this chapter emphasizes the fact that examples are absolutely not the only input to practical ILP methods. Another important source of information comes from a priori knowledge about the target program, including partially-developed software components, and properties of the needed sub-procedures, such as the number and the type of the arguments and of the returned values. To stress this observation, and also the fact that practical tools will have to be embedded in more complex environments, this chapter looks at ILP as logic program development with the help of examples, and not just automatic programming from examples.

In other words, ILP may be seen as a modern approach to automatic programming, and as a software engineering tool for logic program development. The choice of Prolog as a programming language for the learned programs is a good one. This was noticed early on by Ehud Shapiro when he developed the first automatic logic programming method, called MIS, during the early 1980s (Shapiro, 1983). Prolog's simple syntax identifies procedures with clauses, which can be expanded simply by adding literals to the antecedents. Examples are just predicates applied to constant arguments, and no complicated example specification language is needed. On the other hand, one is not limited to providing input/output examples for the top-level procedure only. Examples of predicates corresponding to sub-procedures will follow the same simple syntax. For instance, for learning multiplication, one may provide:

times(2,3,6), times(1,3,3), add(3,3,6).

Thus, we may give the ILP system information for the main computation (times), and also for the sub-calls that are needed (add). Finally, nondeterminism makes the code more concise and substantially shorter than in imperative languages; as a consequence, learning a program may require fewer steps.

Examples are not the only source of information: previous knowledge about parts or properties of the target program may be used by the ILP system. In other words, we consider a scenario where a competent programmer, with a diverse set of programming tools, will also consider examples and inductive inference methods as an option. Assistance during software development is probably the most natural, but certainly not the only, software engineering application of ILP. First of all, it must be noted that the kind of software development that is achieved through ILP techniques includes a simple form of maintenance. After an initial version of a program has been coded or generated automatically, it may be used on specific cases that arise in the end application. If an error is detected, the corresponding and corrected input/output example may be added to the example base, and the program may be corrected automatically, or a new program may be learned from scratch. ILP techniques have been also used for test-case generation (Bergadano & Gunetti, 1996b) "reversing" the induction process: we go from programs to relevant, input values instead of learning a program from some of its input/output examples. If examples are seen as a specification of the learned program, this kind of test-case generation may also be viewed as a type of reverse engineering (from existing programs to specifications).

Most approaches to ILP are actually derived from previous machine learning research, and typically devoted to classification problems. The view of ILP as a source of software engineering tools is the main contribution of this chapter.

Logic Programs and Their Examples

Inductive logic programming is mainly concerned with the problem of learning logic programs from examples. In the rest of this chapter, we will assume a basic knowledge of predicate logic and logic programming. Here, we start by introducing the notion of an example of the input/output behavior of a logic program. (Throughout the chapter, we will use the standard Prolog notation for Horn clauses, with the consequent on the left side of the clause, the body on the right, and ":-" in place of the arrow symbol. Also, as it is common in ILP, we will often use a *flattened* representation of clauses, so as to avoid function symbols and arbitrary complex terms in literals. For example, the clause "member(car,[car])" can be flattened to the following set of clauses:

"member(X,Y) :- cons(X,Y,Z),car(X),null(Z)." "cons(A,B,[A|B])." "car(car)." "null([]).").

Intuitively, an example should describe the input/output behavior of a program in a specific case. For instance, an example for the *intersection* of two lists could be:

input: [4,2,6],[6,5,2,8]
output: [2,6].

For logic programs, this is easily formalized by requiring examples to be ground literals, that is, literals that do not contain variables. These examples of *intersection* would then be written as int([4,2,6],[6,5,2,8],[2,6]).

Examples need not only describe the desired behavior of a program, but can also provide negative information, that is, things that the program should not compute. In general, inductive learning systems use positive examples and negative examples. Positive examples are ground literals that are regarded as true by the user, while negative examples are ground literals that the user labels as false. For instance, the ground literal int([4,2,7],[6,5,2,8],[2,6]), could be a negative example for *intersection*. The learned program should perform computations that do not contradict the examples. If we consider a set E+ of positive examples and a set E– of negative examples, this is made precise in the following:

Definition 1: A logic program P is complete (with respect to E+) if and only if (iff), for all examples e ∈ E+, P ⊢ e.

Definition 2: A logic program P is consistent (with respect to E–) iff, for no example e ∈ E–, P ⊢ e.

For instance, if:

      E+ = int[4,2,7],[4],[4]), int([4,2,7],[],[]),
      E– = int([4,2,7],[6],[6]), and
      P = int(X,Y,Y).

then P is complete, because it derives both positive examples, but is not consistent, because it derives the negative example. Completeness and consistency are, in a sense, a minimum requirement for inductive program synthesis. At the very least, the user will want the learned program to be correct for the specific cases that are described in the given examples. Typically, one would then also use the learned program on other input values that did not occur in the examples, while still hoping that an adequate result is produced.

The ILP Problem

We can now define a basic form of an ILP problem:

Given:

      a set P of possible programs

      a set E+ of positive examples

      a set E– of negative examples

      a consistent logic program B, such that

      B ⊬ e+, for at least one $e+$ ∈ E+.

find:

      a logic program P ∈ P, such that the program B,P is complete and consistent.

A few technical comments are needed:

- The logic program B, which is given as an input of the learning system, is often referred to as *background knowledge*; it represents a part of the desired program that the user has already available or is willing to program directly.

- The program B,P is obtained by adding the clauses of P after the clauses of B. We could have written B ∪ P or B ∧ P, but when dealing with Prolog programs, the order of the clauses is also relevant.

- The set P of the programs that may be learned is called a *hypothesis space*. These words are more often used to define a set of possible clauses, but our definition (possible programs) is more general. In fact, even if some clauses may be viewed as individually possible, the user might know that no meaningful program could contain all of them at the same time.

Below, an instantiation of this basic ILP problem is given for learning the program computing the intersection of two lists:

Given:

P: all logic programs containing clauses of the type "int(X,Y,Z) :- α",

where α is a conjunction of literals chosen from among the following:

null(X), null(Y), null(Z), cons(X1,X2,X), int(X2,Y,W),

    int(X2,Y,Z), cons(X1,W,Z), member(X1,Y), notmember(X1,Y).

E+: int([4,2,6],[5,2,8],[2])

E–: int([4,2,6],[5,2,8],[2,6]), int[4,2,6],[5,2,8],[4,2,6])

B: null([]).

    cons(X,Y,[X|Y]).

    member (X,[X|Y]).

    member(X,[Z|Y]) :- member(X,Y).

    notmember(X,Q).

    notmember(X,[Z|Y]) :- X=Z, notmember(X,Y).

Find:

a program P1 for computing intersection that is complete and consistent with respect to E+ and E–.

For instance, the following program would be an acceptable solution:

P1:

int(X,Y,Z) :- null(X), null(Z).

int(X,Y,Z) :- cons(X1,X2,X), member(X1,Y), int(X2,Y,W), cons(X1,W,Z).

int(X,Y,Z) :- cons(X1,X2,X), int(X2,Y,Z).

It is easy to verify that this program is complete and consistent. However, it is not guaranteed to be correct for cases that are not given with the positive and negative examples, and in fact it is not. For instance, it derives the ground literal int([1],[1],[]), which is false. The proposed basic ILP problem statement does not require that the learned program be correct for examples that were not given.

Soundness and Completeness

When considering methods and systems for solving the basic ILP problem, the notion of an inductive inference machine (IIM) can be used. An IIM is a formalization of the concept of a learning system. If M is an IIM, then we write M(P,E+,E–,B)=P to indicate that, given a hypothesis space P, positive and negative examples E+ and E–, and a background knowledge B, the machine outputs a program P. We write M(P,E+,E–,B)=⊥ when M does not produce any output, either because it does not terminate or because it stops without having found an appropriate program. Saying that an IIM has solved the basic ILP problem will then involve two different requirements: producing only programs that are complete and consistent, and finding one such program when it exists. This is captured by the following definitions:

Definition 3: An IIM M is sound iff

if M(P,E+,E–,B)=P,

then P ∈ P and P is complete and consistent with respect to E+ and E–.

Definition 4: An IIM M is complete iff

if M(P,E+,E–,B)=⊥,

then there is no P ∈ P that is complete and consistent with respect to E+ and E–.

It is easy to notice an analogy with deductive inference. Soundness of an IIM is the property of making correct inferences. Completeness is the ability to make correct inferences whenever it is possible. However, it is important to grasp the difference between the completeness of a learned program P and the completeness of an IIM. The former means that P entails all the positive examples used during the learning task. The latter means that the IIM is able to find a complete and consistent program (with respect to the given examples) whenever it exists in P.

We conclude this section with an important consideration: where is generalization, in this understanding of learning? The answer is that the requirement of generalization, as well as the concerns of predictive accuracy, are hidden in the fact that the learned program P must belong to the hypothesis space P. For example, the hypothesis space will normally exclude a conjunction of positive examples as an acceptable inductive hypothesis. More essentially, in program synthesis applications, the hypothesis space will be small and well chosen by a programmer, and the inductive use of the examples will lead to choosing a subset of possible clauses that are already meaningful and sufficiently general.

This view may be biased toward an understanding of ILP as mainly a software engineering tool. More generally, the issue of correctness on new examples has been addressed in a number of different ways. On the experimental side of machine learning and pattern recognition, the performance on unseen data is estimated by means of cross-validation procedures. Basically, the learned program would have to be tested on separate and independent examples. Such an approach has also been followed in ILP-related research; for instance, new ILP methods are typically compared to well-established systems, such as, above all, FOIL (Quinlan, 1990), on the basis of their cross-validation accuracy as measured in some application domain. However, this perspective may be adequate for classification tasks but questionable in program synthesis applications. In this case, a more valuable evaluation of the learned program would come from sophisticated program testing techniques, while cross-validation would correspond to some kind of brute-force random testing. Important, although rare, errors may be hidden in the structure of the generated program, and accuracy is not always the only relevant parameter.

A Language for Defining
Spaces of Clauses

In this section, we describe a language for defining spaces of clauses which allows the user to specify a hypothesis space P in a formalism very close to that of the sought program. In this way, the user can easily express all the knowledge he/she has about the wanted computational rule, and can control the size of the hypothesis space and hence (at least partially) the complexity of the learning process. The description of a hypothesis space P is part of what is known as *inductive bias* of the learning process.

Clause Sets

The formalism that will be used in the rest of this chapter uses standard Prolog notation, with the addition of clause, literal, and term sets. The hypothesis space will be described by a pair <known clauses, possible clauses>. A program P belongs to the hypothesis space if P = known clauses ∪ P1, where P1 is a subset of the possible clauses. The simplest syntactic tool for specifying inductive bias within the present framework is given by clause sets: known clauses are listed as in a Prolog program, while possible clauses are surrounded by brackets denoting a set. For instance, there follows a possible description of a priori information for learning a logic program for member:

```
member(X,[X|_]).
{member(X,[Y|Z]) :- cons(X,W,Z).}
cons(X,Y,[X|Y]).
{member(X,[Y|Z]) :- X=Y, member(X,Z).
member(X,[Y|Z]) :- cons(Y,Z,W).
member(X,[Y|Z]) :- memberX,Z).}
```

This means that the learned program will have to include the first clause, which is known, possibly followed by the second clause "member(X,[Y|Z]) :- cons(X,W,Z)".; the third clause "cons(X,Y,[X|Y])" will have to follow. Finally, some or all of the remaining clauses may be appended to the program. There are 16 different logic programs satisfying these very strict requirements; among these some represent a correct implementation of member. All the user will need to do at this point is provide positive and negative examples, for example, member(a,[b,a]), member(c,[b,d,c]) and ¬member(a,[b]). The learning procedure described in the next section will select, from among the 16 possible inductive hypotheses, a program deriving the positive examples and not deriving any negative example. As the bias is so strong, the task is very easy in this case, and the learned program can only be a correct version of member.

Unfortunately, a priori information is not always so precise, and the set of possible clauses may be much larger. As a consequence, the user may find it awkward, or even impossible, to type them one after the other. To this purpose, we define literal sets. If a clause occurs in a clause set, then some conjunctions of literals of its antecedent may be surrounded by brackets, denoting a set. In this case, the clause represents an expansion given by all the clauses that may be obtained by deleting one or more literals from the set. Formally:

$$\{P :\text{-} A, \{B, C, ...\}, D\} = \{P :\text{-} A, \{C, ...\}, D\} \cup \{P :\text{-} A, B, \{C, ...\}, D\}$$

In other words, the expansion of a clause is the set of clauses obtained by replacing the literal set with a conjunction of any of its literals. With this syntactic mechanism, one can define in a concise way a large set of possible clauses. Figure 1 gives an example of inductive bias for learning intersection. The clause set contains $2^5 + 2^6 = 96$ clauses, and there are 2^{96} permitted programs. Then, even if the given bias may seem quite informative, it still allows for a very large set of different inductive hypotheses. The learning procedure will select a program that is correct with respect to given examples, for example:

int([a],[a],[a]), int([],[a],[]), int([b,a],[a],[a]),
¬int([a],[a],[]), ¬int([],[a],[a]), ¬int([b],[a],[b]),
member(a,[a]), member(a,[b,a]), ¬member(a,[]).

The possible programs that are consistent with these examples are all correct versions of *intersection* and *member*.

For defining sets of possible clauses even more concisely, the last tool is given by *term sets*: a term occurring in a literal within a literal set may be replaced by a set of terms listed within brackets. The literal is then duplicated in the set where it occurs with different arguments, as indicated by the term set. For instance:

{..., p({X,Y,Z},W), ...}

is the same as:

{..., p(X,W), p(Y,W), p(Z,W),...}.

One predicate may have more than one argument that is a term set. For example:

Figure 1. Inductive bias for intersection

```
------------------------------------------------------------------------
int([[],_,[]).
{
int([X1|X2],Y,Z) :- {member(X1,Y),notmember(X1,Y)},
                    {int(X2,Y,Z), int(X2,Y,W), cons(X1,W,Z)}.
member(X,Y) :- {cons(X,Y,Z), cons(X,Z,Y), cons(W,Y,Z),
                    cons(W,Z,Y), member(X,Z), member(W,Z)}.
}
cons(X,Y,[X|Y]).
notmember(X,[]).
notmember(X,[Y|Z]) :- X≠Y, notmember(X,Z).
------------------------------------------------------------------------
```

{..., p({X,Y},{W,Z}), ...} is the same as

{..., p({X,Y},W), p({X,Y},Z), ...} and therefore the same as

{..., p(X,W), p(Y,W), p(X,Z), p(Y,Z), ...}.

This syntactic device is useful to avoid the rewriting of a predicate with similar arguments. The a priori information shown in Figure 2 defines a larger set of $2^{10} + 2^5 + 2^9 = 1568$ possible clauses by using term sets. Inductive bias specified as described earlier is both flexible and adequate for the inductive synthesis of more complex programs. Flexibility is achieved by allowing the user to provide a priori information of different strength and to adapt it to the particular case study. Stronger and more informative prior knowledge is defined by a large set of known clauses and a limited number of possible clauses, that is, the literal sets must be small and well constrained within the structure of the rest of the program. This will lead to efficient induction, and few examples are required.

If such strong information is not available, while examples abound, then a larger set of possible clauses may be defined with more frequent literal and term sets. The approach can also be applied to complex, real-size programs, and represents a different perspective on inductive synthesis. Learning very complex programs is maybe just a dream, but this does not mean that ILP cannot be a useful tool for building large software systems. Most clauses in these programs must be hand-coded, and the basic structure of the program must be determined with traditional techniques. However, our approach would allow the programmer to leave some parts of the code underdetermined, and to fill the gaps with examples. Inductive bias could be defined in our framework and would look like a normal Prolog program, with small literal sets and optional clauses occurring here and there.

In any case, the presented framework can be applied to common ILP problems, and usual forms of bias can be formulated with clause and literal sets. In some cases, it may be cumbersome to avoid the use of large literal sets and specify the possible clauses on a one-by-

Figure 2. Inductive bias for intersection with term sets

```
-------------------------------------------------------------------------------------
{ int(X,V,Z) :- {null({X,Z}), head(X,X1), tail(X,X2),
                            assign(W,Z), cons(X1,W,Z),
                            member(X1,Y), notmember(X1,Y),
                            int(X2,Y,{Z,W})
              }.
member(X,Y) :- {head(Y,{X,KW}),tail(Y,Tail),
                            member({X,KW},Tail)}.
notmember(X,Y) :- {head({Y,Z},{X,KW}), diff(X,KW),
                            tail({Y,Z},Tail), notmember({X,KW},Tail)}.
}
notmember (X,[]).
null([]).
cons(X,Y,[X|Y]).
head(X,[X|_]).
tail(X,[_|X]).
diff(X,Y) :- X≠Y
assign(X,X).

-------------------------------------------------------------------------------------
```

one basis. To this purpose, general mechanisms for eliminating clauses from a set that is considered too large can be used:

1. **Predicate modes may be provided that indicate their desired input/output behavior.** Every argument of a predicate is labeled as either input or output. Modes need not be unique, for example, we may have both append(input, input, output) and append(output, output, input). Clause sets can be reduced according to predicate modes as follows: a clause is permitted only if any input variable of any predicate in the antecedent either occurs earlier in the antecedent or is an input variable in the head. This is called a requirement of instantiated inputs.

2. **The output variables in the head of a possible clause may be required to occur as an output of some predicate in the antecedent.** This guarantees that an instantiated output is produced when the clause is called.

3. **Once an output is produced, one may require that it is not instantiated again.** Syntactically, this means that any variable cannot occur as output in the antecedent more than once.

4. **Forcing outputs to be used:** Any output variable in the antecedent must occur either as input in some literal to the right or as output in the head.

5. **Forcing inputs to be used:** All input variables in the head must occur in the antecedent.

6. **Forbidden Clauses:** It is sometimes easier to define a large set of clauses, and list a smaller number of clauses to be removed from the set, rather to list one by one the clauses that are possible.

7. **Forbidden Conjunctions:** With the same motivations as mentioned earlier, some conjunctions of literals may be ruled out, meaning that no antecedent of a possible clause may contain them. This can be useful for two reasons: the conjunction is always true, for example, Y is $X+1 \wedge X=Y-1$, or it is contradictory, for example, head(L,A) $\wedge$ null(L).

For example, the hypothesis space of Figure 2 can be completed with the information shown in Figure 3.

As clauses become more structured into sequences of input/output computations, and as programs become more deterministic, it is likely that restrictions 1-7 do not exclude the solution while greatly reducing the space of possible clauses to be searched by the inductive method. Obviously, for efficiency reasons, clauses are not generated and then filtered. Instead, a clause is produced only if it is permitted with respect to the specified constraints. Note that in our approach, constraints 1 through 7 play the role of heuristics: the learning procedure will explore only that part of the original hypothesis space delimited by the employed constraints.

Figure 3. Completion of the hypothesis space for learning intersection

```
-----------------------------------------------------------------------------------
/* forbidden conjunctions of predicates */
! (null(A),head(A,_)).
! (null(A),tail(A,_)).
! (member (A,B),notmember(A,B)).
! (head(_,_),head(_,_)).
! (member(_,_),member(_,_),member (_,_)).
! (notmember (_,_),notmember (_,_),notmember (_,_)).
/* mode declaration */
int_inout(in,in,out).
null_inout(out).
head_inout(in,out).
tail_inout(in,out).
assign_inout(in,out).
cons_inout(in,in,out).
diff_inout(in,in).
member_inout(in,in).
notmember_inout(in,in).
-----------------------------------------------------------------------------------
```

The last point that we must discuss for clause sets is the problem of recursive clauses and termination. The learned program must of course terminate, at least on the given examples. Besides that, the inductive method presented in the next section may require that even the possible clauses form a terminating program. This requirement can either be left to the user or handled automatically.

If left to the user, the set of possible clauses must be designed so that no infinite chain of recursive calls can take place. For example, the inductive bias of Figure 1 does not have this property, because it allows for the clause:

    member(X,Y) :- cons(X,Y,Z), member(X,Z).

which produces a loop when called on any input.

If handled automatically, all the user has to do is indicate which predicates define a well-order relation. For instance, cons(X,Y,Z) determines the well-ordering Y<Z. The procedure transforming the presented formalism into a set of possible clauses will then remove all the recursive clauses that do not match the following pattern:

    P(X1, ..., Xi, ..., Xn) :- ..., rel(Y,Xi), ..., P(X1, ..., Y,..., Xn), ...

where *rel* is any well-order relation. In other words, the recursive call must have the same arguments as the head of the clause, except for one that makes it one step closer to termination. This guarantees that clauses will always terminate, not only on the available examples. Obviously, some information is required, that is, the indication of the well-order relations.

Some of the biases described in this section may seem too strong or too difficult to specify for the user. However, efficient learning requires that both the examples and the set P of possible programs be carefully selected. This is certainly not as demanding as writing the very program that we want to learn, because (1) instantiated information such as positive and negative examples is easier to define and check for correctness, and (2) a set P of possible programs is less informative than a precisely-defined computation rule: it is easier to say that intersection is linearly recursive, and requires member, than it is to provide a correct program.

An Induction Procedure

We introduce in this section a generic induction procedure that synthesizes a logic program P from a set of alternative programs P, and from a set of input/output values for its main predicate p. The main loop in the proposed procedure follows the basic scheme of many machine-learning methods, all based on the classical works of Michalski (1980) and Quinlan (1990): clauses are generated one at a time, independently of each other, and the examples that they "cover extensionally" are deleted. We stop when all examples are covered by some generated clause. This is the so-called "top-down" approach within ILP literature.

A peculiarity of the induction procedure presented here is that functionality constraints are used, so that negative examples are not necessary, and only functional relations can be employed and learned. In other words, we restrict the inductive hypotheses to logic programs that are functional, that is, such that each n-ary predicate can be associated to a total function as follows: m of its arguments are labeled as input, while the remaining n-m are labeled as output, and for every given sequence of input values, there is one and only one sequence of output values that makes the predicate true. Output values must always exist and be unique, and the whole program must correspond to a total function. The functionality restrictions are built on top of the input/output modes that are available with clause sets (recall restriction 1 introduced at the end of the previous section). Thus, functionality must be determined by the user and is assumed also for the examples that are not seen. This is necessary because some examples may be missing and will be queried later to the user. These requirements do not affect expressive power, as any computable function can be represented by a functional logic program and, on the other hand, make the learning task much easier, because many clauses that would otherwise need to be generated and checked against the examples are now disallowed a priori, and the order of the literals within a clause antecedent is somehow constrained by the need for computing an output value before it can be used as input in another literal. The queries that are asked to the user are existential queries, because they contain unbound variables that must be instantiated. However, these variables are labeled as output and, as a consequence, there is always one and only one answer to every such query.

Thus, we will assume that for every literal in P, a functional mode for its variables is provided. For example, if the *append* predicate occurs in P, it is labeled with the functional mode *append*(in,in,out). In this way, a positive example for *append* such as *append*+([a,b],[c,d],[a,b,c,d]) implicitly defines also all possible negative examples of the kind *append*–([a,b],[c,d],Z) with $Z \neq [a,b,c,d]$. On the contrary, a mode such as *append*(out,out,in) (which is perfectly legal in logic programming, since it can be used, for example, to split a list into two sub-lists) would not be allowed in the induction procedure, because it does not represent a function. A functional mode for all predicates is then used to constrain the allowed clauses as follows:

1. Suppose Q and P have mode Q(in,out) and P(in,out); the literal Q(W,Z) can occur in an intermediate clause P(X,Y) :- α, Q(W,Z), γ (where α and γ represent generic conjunctions of literals) iff either (a) W=X (i.e., the input is bound because it is passed as input in the head of the clause) or (b) W occurs in α (i.e., it is computed before Q is called);

2. A clause is in an acceptable final form only if the output variables of its head occur in the body, that is, only if the output is not left unbound.

For example, suppose we have to learn a concept c with a mode for variables c(in,in,out), using predicates a, b, d with a mode for variables a(in,out), b(in,out), d(in,in,in,out). Then the clause "c(X,Y,Z) :- a(X,W),b(Y,K),d(X,W,K,Z)" is a legal one because every input variable is defined before being used, and the output variable of c is at last instantiated. As a consequence of this functional constraint, a smaller number of allowed inductive hypotheses must be taken into consideration by the induction procedure, and its efficiency results increased. In the following, we will call the predicates that we need to learn the inductive predicates, while the others will be either built-in or defined by the user. The induction procedure follows. Since it learns functional relations, in the rest of this chapter, we will refer to it with the name of FILP (i.e., functional ILP):

The Induction Procedure FILP:

for all inductive predicates P to be learned **do**

while examples(P) $\neq \varnothing$ **do**

      Generate one clause "P(X1, ..., Xn) :- α"

      examples(P) $\leftarrow$ examples(P) – covered (α)

Generate one clause:

$\alpha \leftarrow$ true

while covered(α)$\neq \varnothing$ **do**

    if consistent(α) **then** return(P(X1, ..., Xn) :- α)

    else   1. choose a predicate Q and its arguments Args

               2. if no such Q is found, then backtrack on 1.

               3. $\alpha \leftarrow \alpha \wedge Q(\text{Args})$

where every predicate Q can be defined by the user (intensionally) by means of logical rules or (extensionally) simply by giving some examples of its input-output behavior. Clauses can be recursive and, in this case, Q = P, and its truth value can be determined only by the available examples.

Definition 5: We say that the clause P(X,Y) :- α(X,Y) *extensionally covers* P(a,b) iff α(a,Y) extensionally computes Y = b, where extensional computation is defined as follows:

- $\alpha = Q(a,Y)$ with functional mode Q(in,out). Then Q(a,Y) *extensionally computes* Y = b iff Q(a,b) is derivable from the definition of Q or is a given example of Q.

- $\alpha = \gamma(X,T), Q(T,Y)$ with functional mode γ(in,out) and Q(in,out). Then γ(a,T), Q(T,Y) *extensionally computes* Y = b iff γ(a,T) *extensionally computes* T = e and Q(e,b) is derivable from the definition of Q or is a given example of Q.

In the algorithm, an example P(a,b) belongs to covered(α) iff α(a,Y) extensionally computes Y=b, and consistent(α) is true iff, for no such example, α(a,Y) extensionally computes Y=c and c$\neq$b. The choice of the literal Q(Args) to add to α is guided by heuristic information and is a backtracking point.

Unfortunately, it can be proved that the induction procedure just presented is neither complete (Definition 4) nor sound (Definition 3), a problem that, in general, affects all ILP methods based on an extensional interpretation of recursion and of the other inductive relations (see, e.g., Bergadano & Gunetti, 1996a, for an indepth discussion of the problem). It is possible to overcome this problem by querying the user for some of the missing examples. Every possible clause in C of the type:

P(X,Y) :- A(X,W),Q(X,W,Z),α.

where Q is an inductive predicate with mode Q(in,in,out), is processed with the following:

completion procedure:
for every example P(a,b) **do**

        extensionally compute A(a,W), obtaining a value W = c

        ask the user for the value Z computed by Q(a,c,Z)

        add this example to examples(Q)

Adding one example may cause the request for others. Suppose, for instance, that an example A(a,d) is added for A. Then this procedure might add an example for Q, for example, the one matching Q(a,d,Z). As a consequence, the procedure must be repeated for every clause, again and again, until no more examples are added for the inductive predicates.

Both for making this procedure terminate and for guaranteeing the termination of learned programs, we may adopt the termination constraint defined at the end of the previous section. When functionality is in force, however, the well-order relation must be a function. To summarize, any recursive call must be of the type

P(X1, ... , Xi, ..., Xn) :- ..., Q(Xi,Y), ..., P(X1, ..., Y, ..., Xn), ...

where Q(X,Y) is a well-order function. It is possible to show that if every recursive clause in P satisfies the earlier-mentioned constraint, then the example completion procedure terminates. For instance, consider the following clause: reverse(X,Y) :- tail(X,T), reverse(T,W). It satisfies the constraint on recursive calls because when tail(X,T) is true, then T is a shorter list than X and this is a well-order relation.

If the examples passed to FILP are completed by this completion task it can be proved (Bergadano & Gunetti, 1996a) that the induction procedure is a sound and complete induction method, and is also automatically suitable for multiple predicate learning. In the rest of this chapter, when referring to the induction method presented in this section, we will always assume that the examples passed to the procedure have been completed by the described completion procedure.

Software Development, Maintenance, and Reuse

The technique described in the previous section, though so simple, can be regarded as a truly alternative method for producing software, within the declarative paradigm. Many others have been devised within the ILP community. An ILP system can be seen as putting together a given set of basic software components in different ways, in order to find a program consistent with the computation rule observed in the examples. In this and the next section, we propose ILP as an alternative approach to software engineering, especially (but not limited to) in the logic programming paradigm. In an inductive setting, development, maintenance, reuse, and the debugging phases of logic programs become different aspects of the same inductive process, and will be discussed in this section. In the next one, we will discuss the problem of program testing.

It is now commonly believed that the examples provided to an ILP system are, by themselves, insufficient for the generation of a logic program: one needs strong constraints on the clauses that could possibly be generated. In the section on clause sets, we saw a proposal for describing such constraints. The constraints must be sufficiently strong to make the induction process feasible and reliable, but are normally much less informative than the actual program that we want to learn. This can suggest a different understanding of the ILP problem: constraints and examples are seen as a real programming language, and we move from program induction to *inductive programming*. In other words, we do not want to "learn" a computation rule from the available information; we actually "program" this computation rule by means of syntactic requirements and examples of the desired input/output behavior. As a first consequence, examples should be few and well chosen, and not taken as coming from random experiments, as is usually done in machine learning. The goodness of chosen examples is a well-known problem in machine learning, but is not so important in ILP, if the goal is the synthesis of true logic programs. If one has in mind a certain computation rule that must be translated into an actual program, typical examples of that computation rule are normally also "available" in his/her mind. Often, the computation rule is precisely the one defined by the available examples. That is, the examples one has in mind define the computation rule, and not vice versa.

An *inductive program*, then, represents a set of possible object programs: the ones that are defined as possible by the constraints and are consistent with the examples. It is obviously easier to define a space of possible programs than to choose precisely which of these programs is the correct one. Inductive inference will play the role of a compilation into one of the possible object Prolog codes that will compute correct outputs for the given examples. Logic programming is a good object language for inductive programming, because the intermediate computations correspond to intermediate predicates or to recursive calls, and can be instantiated with separate examples. Moreover, it allows us to specify constraints as sets of possible clauses in a natural way.

Software development in an inductive logic programming language is a truly incremental process unifying traditionally separate phases, such as programming, debugging, maintenance, and re-engineering. Detecting a wrong output or realizing that we now want a different output often results only in the addition or in the modification of some examples, while the constraints, which require most of our programming work, can normally remain unchanged. Another form of program refinement is the process of making the constraints stronger, and is required from the programmer when the compilation is too slow. In fact, this is not exactly a compilation in the sense of a straightforward translation, but a search within a space of possible object programs. This space needs to be kept small by providing meaningful constraints, if we want the generation of the object code to be reasonably efficient. Programming time is traded off against compilation time and, in a sense, the user can choose how "inductive" a certain program should be.

It must be stressed that a number of constraints were present in classical machine learning research and in the earlier approaches to ILP that were not always known to the user. We move from program induction to inductive programming if we make these constraints explicit and "programmable". For instance, from this point of view, the source files of Figure 2 and Figure 3 which describe a hypothesis space and some constraints, together with a set of positive and negative examples for learning *intersection* actually represent an inductive program for *intersection*. Figure 2 (together with Figure 3 and some examples) is a program because it describes a computation rule: the one defined to be consistent with the examples while still lying within the space of possible clauses defined by the constraints. In this perspective, what is shown in Figure 2 and Figure 3 is the user program, while the usual logic program for *intersection*, which could be learned by an ILP system, plays the role of an object code. In inductive programming, the inductive inference of the object code corresponds to a form of compilation.

Inductive Logic Programming Languages

An inductive program is made from examples and constraints. The constraints specify the set of possible object codes and the inductive compilation procedure will select one of these object codes, so that it is consistent with the given examples. An *inductive programming language* is mainly a language for specifying constraints of this kind, that is, for specifying a set of allowed object programs. As we consider the case of logic object programs, what we are actually considering are *inductive logic programming languages*.

An inductive program represents, in fact, a set of clauses. We can also call this hypothesis space an *expansion*, since the description given in the ILP language could be expanded to build that explicit set of possible clauses. Of course, normally ILP systems do not require an expansion to be produced. Next, an object Prolog code is defined as possible if its clauses belong to the expansion of the inductive program. This represents an inductive constraint in the sense that the object program output by the compilation procedure will have to be among those possible and to be consistent with the examples (i.e., covering the positive examples and not covering the negative examples).

The notion of expansion of an inductive program is naturally associated with the possibility of having constraints of different strengths for a particular object program: the larger the expansion, the weaker the constraint, as the number of possible programs will be larger in this case. More knowledge and more programming time should result in stronger constraints, while weaker inductive programs are easier to write but require more examples and more time for compiling into an object Prolog code. An inductive logic programming language should allow the user to express easily his/her approximate intuitions of the final shape of the object program. Even if the actual compilation into a Prolog code is done, one predicate at a time, this should be transparent to the user, who will simply think in terms of possible global object programs and will work on the inductive program by refining the constraints and by adding examples, as will be illustrated in the next sub-section.

As an ILP language, the clause sets notation is well suitable, mainly because it is pretty simple: it differs from the logic programming language only in the use of brackets. In fact, the typical situation when using clause sets is when the target program is not learned from scratch and much information is available to the user, who could be, in fact, a logic programmer. Consider, for example, the case of a logic program that must be revised, since it does not cover some positive example and/or some negative example is covered. Then the program is wrong, but it is plausible to assume it is not "completely" wrong. As a consequence, it can be used as a starting point, a template to define a possible hypothesis space, by surrounding clauses and literals with brackets. The programmer, who is supposed to have some knowledge about the desired program, may know some clause that is correct and may put it in the background knowledge. Other clauses may be perceived as wrong, or at least not completely correct, and a set of mutants of each of them can be defined by using brackets. The actual number of allowed clauses defined in this way depends on the particular problem and on the programmer's knowledge, and it can be very easily controlled by means of brackets and available constraints. The resulting space of clauses turns out to be designed on the basis of the initial program as a set of possible mutations. The set of positive and negative examples not properly classified by the initial program is added, and the learning system can search for a revised version of the program.

Even if not for theory revision, similar situations are quite common in program development. Normally, a programmer has in mind a basic idea of the program, but some points can be (at least initially) unclear. These include deciding whether a clause should be recursive or doubly recursive, if a particular operation should be made on the input list or on its tail, if a test for *less* or *less_or_equal* should be made, and so forth. With clause sets, the user can easily define the basic structure of the target program and a set of alternative choices for (some) clauses of the program. Testing for the correct alternative is then left to the induction procedure, on the basis of the provided examples.

The Inductive Software Process

An inductive program does not describe a unique computation rule; it defines a *set* of such computations. Inductive inference will play the role of a compilation phase and will select an object (Prolog) program that is (1) defined as *possible* by the constraints and (2) consistent with the examples. The complexity of this compilation phase depends on the strength of the constraints, that is, on the number of possible programs, not on the size of the object programs, which may be much more complicated than the examples given in this section. There may be more than one object program satisfying conditions (1) and (2), and this is the set of computation rules that is described with the inductive program. The programmer does not need to know which actual object program will be selected from among this set of possibilities, any more than a C programmer knows how the translation and optimization phases work in the C compiler in use. As the constraints are refined and as more examples are added, the possible computation rules will reduce to a few, and may be equivalent on most inputs.

Software development is, in general, a process that is never completely finished. Inductive programming acknowledges this fact to a greater degree than traditional programming. An inductive program starts with approximate constraints that may need improving for two reasons: they may be too weak (they define too large a set of object programs) and/or they may exclude the "correct" object program. Initially, a few negative and positive examples are given: the examples the programmer feels to be representative of the computational rule s/he has in mind. This initial program is not expected to be close to the solution, but it may be compiled and executed. As mistakes are found in specific cases, they are simply added to the examples of the inductive program. When we reach the moment when the compilation fails to find an object code that covers all the positive examples, the constraints need to be relaxed in order to allow for more possible object programs. When the compilation becomes unacceptably slow, the constraints need to be made stronger in order to reduce the space of object programs to be searched. This continues until the run-time performance of the program is found to be acceptable. Programming, debugging, and maintenance merge into the same development process.

We show an example of inductive software development leading to a correct program for *intersection*. An initial version of the inductive program is given in Figure 4 by means of the clause sets language. As will be discovered later, the program is faulty because several examples are missing, and the constraints rule out the correct object program because one predicate is missing from the clause set. Some predicates, by contrast, are useless, but this only slows down the compilation process.

The compiler we use, the FILP system, translates the inductive program of Figure 4 into the following Prolog program:

```
int(X,Y,Z) :- tail(X,X2).
int(X,Y,Z) :- null(Z).
```

Figure 4. An initial version of the inductive program for intersection

```
-----------------------------------------------------------------------------------------
{
int(X,Y,Z) :- {null(X,Z), head(X,X1), tail(X,X2),
                    member(X1,Y), head(Y,Y1), member(Y1,X),
                    int(X2,Y,{Z,W}), cons(X1,W,Z)}.

}
head([X|_],X).
tail([_|X],X).
cons(X,Y,[X|Y]).
null([]).
member(X,[X|_]).
member(X,[_|Y]) :- member(X,Y).
int+([],[a],[]), int+([a],[a],[a]).
-----------------------------------------------------------------------------------------
```

Using a different inductive compiler could, in principle, lead to another object program that is consistent with the examples that were given, but this would not affect the user very much or change the basic development of this discussion. By using the earlier-mentioned program, it will not take long before bugs are found, for example:

```
? - int([a],[],[a]).
yes
```

while we would have expected to get a "no" answer. The inductive program is debugged simply by adding this case as a negative example (actually, since FILP only needs positive examples, by adding int+([a],[],[])). After recompiling, we obtain the following object program:

```
int(X,Y,Z) :- null(X), null(Z).
int(X,Y,Z) :- head(X,X1), tail(X,X2), int(X2,Y,W), cons(X1,W,Z).
```

This code, although still quite incorrect, can already be used and often produces the desired answers, not only on the given examples but also on new data:

```
? - int([],[a,b],[]).
yes
? - int([a],[a,b],[a]).
yes
? - int([],[a,b],[a]).
no
? - int([b,a],[a,b],[a]).
no
```

But when we ask for "int([b],[a],[])", we get a "no" answer, which is wrong. Again, we debug the program by adding the faulty case to the data as a new positive example. Unfortunately, the compilation now fails to find a program that is consistent with the requirements: this means that the constraints are too strong and exclude the correct object program. This is a more serious form of debugging, as it requires the addition of a predicate to the set defining intersection. The compiler signals that the positive example that cannot be covered is "int([b],[a],[])", and since "b" is not member of "[a]", it may be a good idea to add "notmember(X1,Y)" (defined as "not member(X1,Y)"). The semi-automatic generation of the predicate to be added on the basis of the uncovered example and of a given set of possible choices seems to be a problem worth investigating. Here, we may suppose that this is done by the programmer. After adding the new predicate, the following object program is obtained:

```
int(X,Y,Z) :- null(X), null(Z),
int(X,Y,Z) :- head(X,X1), null(Z), notmember(X1,Y).
int(X,Y,Z) :- head(X,X1), tail(X,X2), int(X2,Y,W), cons(X1,W,Z),
```

This program may not show its errors well for some time. It may be used together with other subprograms until new bugs are found:

```
? - int([b,a],[a],[a]).
no
? - int([b,a],[a],[]).
yes
```

If the first is added to the positive examples (so that the second turns automatically to be a negative example), we obtain a correct inductive program for intersection, leading to the usual Prolog implementation.

After some time, when the program is accepted as more or less final, it may be worthwhile to simplify it: the literals that do not occur in the object program ("head(Y,Y1)" and "member(Y1,X)") may be removed. Moreover, some examples may be removed as long as the object code does not change. This leads to a version closer to the one of Figure 2, that is easier to read and explain to others, as well as faster to compile.

For software maintenance and reusability, inductive programming is quite appropriate. If the application does not change completely, one can often revise a program for a new goal problem by modifying only the examples. This is easier to do, since one has to deal with concrete data rather than with general computation rules, and less error prone. For instance, if we wanted a set difference operation, instead of an intersection, we could reuse the constraints in the programs of Figure 2 and just change the data. If the predicate for the set difference X–Y is now called "sd(X,Y,Z)", we can keep the same predicate set and sub-programs used for *intersection*, and replace the examples with the following:

```
sd+([b],[a],[b]), sd+([],[a],[]), sd+([a,b],[a],[b]), sd+([a],[a],[])
```

Even if one knows the exact shape of the object code, it may be worthwhile to write an inductive program instead, with some predicate sets, in order to improve the reusability of that software. In fact, the program may be used and modified in the future by a less experienced programmer, who will need to change only the relevant examples.

Testing

Though it can be formally proved that no algorithm exists to generate for an arbitrary program a set of test data that allows to discover all the errors in the program, testing is necessary and widely used in software development. It is practical and (relatively) easy to apply, and can give some information about the correctness of a program. After having written a program, the first thing one usually does is run the program on some typical input, in order to check the result of the computation. In fact, this is a simple form of testing, but not always very reliable.

Testing can be seen as a way of distinguishing a program from all the possible (syntactically correct) alternatives to that program. This is very similar to ILP, where a program in the hypothesis space must be identified from among all the other possible programs on the basis of the given examples. More precisely, testing and ILP are, in some way, symmetric. The latter goes from examples to programs, whereas the former goes from programs to examples (input values). In this section, we show how this relationship and the ILP techniques presented so far can be fruitfully used for program testing. We start by giving some basic notion on testing.

Introduction to Testing

The first thing that comes out when testing a program is that both for checking the output and for generating meaningful test cases, we need some information about the "correct" program Pc.

For example, one might have available a correct version of the program or an executable specification. In this case, program testing reduces to checking whether the two programs are equivalent, at least on a chosen set of test cases, a set of input/output examples. This also will account for probabilistic equivalence of the two programs on the input values not taken into consideration. This intuitive notion of correctness allows us to define the notion of reliability for test sets (Budd & Angluin, 1982):

Definition 6: Let there be given a test set T for the program P. Let Pc be a correct program. We say that T is *reliable* with respect to Pc if and only if $[\forall x \in T\ P(x) = Pc(x)]$ implies the equivalence of P and Pc

As a consequence of this definition, if P contains errors, this will be shown by the test cases in T. However, this notion of reliability is impractical, since it requires testing for the equivalence of the programs P and Pc on some inputs, and is based on the existence of an executable specification Pc.

In fact, what most often happens in practice is that the error detection is done through a direct inspection of the outputs during the normal execution of the program. That is, the user tests the program on the only basis of the "correct program she or he has in mind". It is common in this case to assume that although the correct program is unknown, there is a known set of programs that can be seen as alternative implementations and should contain at least one correct solution. This leads to a more practical definition of meaningful test data (Budd & Angluin, 1982):

Definition 7: Let there be a given test set T for a program P and a set P of alternative programs. We say that T is *adequate* with respect to P if and only if it is reliable with
respect to every program in P

As a consequence, if P contains at least one correct program Pc, then the test set will also
be reliable for P. Many different testing techniques are based on a relation between the
program P to be tested and a set of possible alternatives Pc (e.g., DeMillo & Offutt, 1991),
and testing based on the inductive learning of logic programs also relies on Definition 7 of
adequateness of a test set.

Induction and Testing Compared

An intuitive symmetry between induction and testing can almost immediately be noticed
(Weyuker, 1983): induction is the inference from examples to programs; testing is the
inference from programs to input values. Given a test set T of input values for a program
P, the examples of P for T are defined as $E(P,T)=\{<i,o> \mid i \in T$ and $P(i)=o\}$. This notion is
formalized by Weyuker (1983) as follows:

Definition 8: A test set T is *inference adequate* for a program P intended to satisfy a specification S if and only if P_I is inductively inferred from $E(P,T)$ and $P_I \equiv P \equiv S$. If only
$P_I \equiv P$ is true, then T is said to be *program adequate*, and if only $P_I \equiv S$ is true, then T
is said to be *specification adequate*.

Here, we are interested in the case where a specification S is not given and, therefore, we
will use only the notion of a program-adequate test set. The intuitive meaning of this definition is as follows: If, given a set $E(P,T)$ of input/output examples, we inductively infer a
program $P_I \equiv P$, then T is likely to be useful for testing the program P.

Definition 8 must refer to some form of induction, and ILP systems could be fruitfully applied to Definition 8 for testing a given program P. In particular, we can rely on the learning
method FILP, which is terminating and explicitly makes use of a finite set of legal programs
P (i.e., a hypothesis space described by means of clause sets). The learned program P_I must
belong to P. This is consistent with the fact (noted earlier) that all test case generation procedures that are not specification based refer (sometimes implicitly) to a set P of alternative
programs. As a consequence, Definition 8 can then be rephrased in terms of "sound and
complete ILP" instead of "inductive inference". Moreover, test data adequacy (Definition 7)
turns out to be strongly related to finite identification: T is adequate for P if and only if P is
the only program that can be learned from $E(T,P)$ with a sound and complete ILP method.
The restriction to a finite set of alternative programs P seems to be acceptable for testing;
for instance, all approaches to fault-based testing, such as mutation analysis, are based on
this assumption.

The intuitive symmetry between induction and testing can now be made clear: induction is an inference from the pair <E(T,P), *P*> to a program P in *P*, whereas testing is an inference from <P, *P*> to the test set T. Theoretical comparisons of induction and testing can be found in Budd and Angluin (1982) and Cherniavsky and Smith (1987), while the problem of *checking* test set adequacy is faced in Weyuker (1983). In the next sub-section, we show how ILP techniques can be used in actually *generating* the adequate test cases for a logic program. In particular, the FILP system will be used in our test case generation procedure.

Inductive Test Case Generation

A sequence of inductions of programs from examples is used to generate test cases. Initially, there are no examples and, in the end, the generated set of examples will be adequate in the sense of Definition 7. Let P be the program to be tested. At any given moment, the examples generated so far are used to induce a program P'. New examples that distinguish P from P' are added, and the process is repeated until no program P' that is not equivalent to P can be generated. This procedure is described in more detail in the following.

Test case generation procedure:

Input: a program P to be tested,

a finite set *P* of alternative programs

Output: an adequate test set T

$T \leftarrow \varnothing$;

loop:

<P',T> $\leftarrow$ FILP(E(T,P),*P*)

if P' = "fail" **then return** T

if ($\exists$ i) P'(i) $\neq$ P(i)

then $T \leftarrow T \cup \{i\}$

else $P \leftarrow P - P'$

goto loop

In order for this procedure to work, the learning algorithm FILP must be complete and sound, as it is proven in Bergadano and Gunetti (1996a). In the test case generation procedure, the test set T is initially empty. The main step in the loop consists of using FILP to learn a program P' that is consistent with the examples generated so far. P' is then ruled out either by (1) adding an input value to T or by (2) removing it from *P*. As a consequence, P' will not be learned again. When FILP cannot find a program P' $\in$ *P* that is consistent with the examples, then the only programs with this property are P and those equivalent to it, that is, the test set T is adequate. This is proved by the following:

Theorem: Let equivalence be decidable for programs in P. Then this test case generation procedure outputs an adequate test set T for P.

Proof: See Bergadano and Gunetti (1996b).

The requirement of decidable equivalence is not easily verified or accepted. Program equivalence was found to be a major theoretical (Budd & Angluin, 1982) and practical (DeMillo & Offutt, 1991) issue in program testing. In the implementation of our test case generation method, we approximate it by means of its time-bounded semi-decision procedure. Except for this approximation, the system produces adequate test sets with respect to any finite class of programs P.

We conclude with two remarks. We have seen that the test case generation procedure outputs an adequate test set, in the sense that it distinguishes the program to be tested from all alternatives. It is worth noting that if P contains at least one correct implementation, then the obtained test set will also be reliable, that is, it will demonstrate any errors that may be present.

Moreover, as already noted, inductive program learning can be useful in the debugging phase of a program. Software is often verified and validated through testing and debugging. Testing is used to expose the presence of errors. Debugging is then used to locate and remove the known errors. In our setting, examples showing the errors of the tested program P are found during the execution of the test case generation procedure. These examples can then be used to learn a program correct with respect to the discovered errors. In other words, by means of program learning, P can be automatically debugged with respect to the errors located in the testing phase.

Example

We consider the problem of merging two lists. Let the following program P for merging two ordered lists, to be tested:

```
P:
1) merge(X,Y,Z) :- null(X), Y=Z.
2) merge(X,Y,Z) :- null(Y), X=Z.
3) merge(X,Y,Z) :- head(X,X1), head(Y,Y1), tail(X,X2), X1≤Y1,
                       merge(X2,Y,W), cons(X1,W,Z).
4) merge(X,Y,Z) :- head(X,X1), head(Y,Y1), tail(Y,Y2), X1>Y1,
                       merge(X,Y2,W), cons(Y1,W,Z).
```

This program is wrong: in clause 3) the comparison $X1 \leq Y1$ must be replaced by $X1 < Y1$. Another clause must be inserted for the case $X1=Y1$. As a consequence of the error, elements occurring in both input lists X and Y are repeated in the output Z. We define the set of alternatives P on the basis of P by means of clause sets as follows:

{

```
merge(X,Y,Z) :- {null(X), null(Y), X=Z, Y=Z,
                 head(X,X1), tail(X,X2), head(Y,Y1), tail(Y,Y2),
                 X<Y1, X1=Y1, X1>Y1, X1≤Y1, X1≥Y1
                 merge(X2,Y,W), merge(X,Y2,W), W=Z,
                 cons(X1,W,Z), cons(Y1,W,Z)}

}
```

The usual definitions for all the predicates in this clause set (except for merge) are given. It is easy to check that the hypothesis space HS is defined simply by putting in the literal set all the literals of P, plus some other literals for comparing some of the variables. Hence, HS can be seen as a space of mutations of (clauses of) P. HS contains 2^{18} possible clauses and, as a consequence, P contains 2^{262144} alternative programs, that is, all possible subsets of the space of clauses. Among the subsets, there are versions of the correct implementation of merge (in the following, we will use P as an input of FILP, instead of HS, to conform to the notation used in this section).

The test case generation procedure starts with an empty test set T_0 of input values, and calls FILP. As $E(T_0,P)$ contains no examples, the empty program P_0 is an acceptable output of $FILP(E(T_0,P),P)$.

Pairs of lists X and Y are then enumerated, so that

$P_0 \vdash$ merge(X,Y,Z'), $P \vdash$ merge(X,Y,Z) and $Z \neq Z'$

The first such pair that is found is $<X,Y> = <[],[]>$; for this input, P_0 produces no output and P outputs Z=[]. The new test set is then $T_1 = \{<[],[]>\}$.

$FILP(E(T_1,P),P)$ is called again, yielding P_1:

```
merge(X,Y,Z) :- X=Z.
```

This program is an acceptable output of FILP because merge([],[],[]) is derived from it, and the output is the same as that of P.

Pairs of lists X and Y are enumerated, so that

$P_1 \vdash$ merge(X, Y, Z'). $P \vdash$ merge(X, Y, Z) and $Z \neq Z'$.

The first such pair that is found is: $<X,Y>=<[],[1]>$; for this input, P_1 outputs Z=[] while P outputs Z=[1]. The new test set is then $T_2 = T_1 \cup \{<[],[1]>\}$.

$FILP(E(T_2,P),P)$ is called again, yielding P2:

```
merge(X,Y,Z) :- Y=Z.
```

This program is an acceptable output of FILP because merge([],[],[]) and merge([],[1],[1]) are derived from it.

$T_3 = T_2 \cup \{<[1],[]>\}$.
P_3:
merge(X,Y,Z) :- null(X), Y=Z.
merge(X,Y,Z) :- head(X,X1), X=Z.
merge(X,Y,Z) :- head(Y,Y1), Y=Z.

$T_4 = T_3 \cup \{<[1],[2]>\}$.
P_4:
merge(X,Y,Z) :- null(Y), X=Z.
merge(X,Y,Z) :- null(X), Y=Z.
merge(X,Y,Z) :- head(X,X1), tail(X,X2), merge(X2,Y,W), cons(X1,W,Z).

In this case, FILP queries the user for a missing example, yielding:

$T_4' = T_4 \cup \{<[],[2]>\}$.

$T_5 = T_4' \cup \{<[2],[1]>\}$.
P_5:
merge(X,Y,Z) :- null(Y), X=Z.
merge(X,Y,Z) :- null(X), Y=Z.
merge(X,Y,Z) :- head(X,X1), head(Y,Y1), tail(X,X2), X1<Y1,
                  merge(X2,Y,W), cons(X1,W,Z).
merge(X,Y,Z) :- head(X,X1), head(Y,Y1), tail(Y,Y2), X1>Y1,
                  merge(X,Y2,W), cons(Y1,W,Z).

$T_6 = T_5 \cup \{<[1],[1]>\}$.
P_6:
merge(X,Y,Z) :- null(Y), X=Z.
merge(X,Y,Z) :- null(X), Y=Z.
merge(X,Y,Z) :- head(X,X1), head(Y,Y1), tail(X,X2), X1<Y1,
                  merge(X2,Y,W), cons(X1,W,Z).
merge(X,Y,Z) :- head(X,X1), head(Y,Y1), tail(Y,Y2), X1>Y1,
                  merge(X,Y2,W), cons(Y1,W,Z).
merge(X,Y,Z) :- head(X,X1), head(Y,Y1), tail(X,X2), X1=Y1,
                  merge(X2,Y,W), cons(X1,W,Z).

As $P_6 \equiv P$, it is removed from P and no test case is generated. With FILP, removing P_6 from P can be done in practice by means of the "forbidden clauses" option in the clause sets language, as described earlier. A few more programs equivalent to P are then generated, and, finally, no other program consistent with T_6 can be found and FILP fails, ending the test generation process. T_6 is adequate, and it contains an input, namely X=[1] and Y=[1], that demonstrates the error of P, giving Z=[1,1] as output. The correct output would be Z=[1],

Only seven examples have been required to locate the error, whereas many more would have been necessary in random testing, if there are many possible element values with respect to the average list length. In general, methods presented in the literature and cited in the references would have problems with this program. The reason is that the correct program is not a simple mutation of the program P to be tested: it requires one simple modification and the addition of one entire clause. Most approaches to fault-based testing, for example, are only able to generate minor and syntactically simple modifications. More complex cases can be found in Bergadano and Gunetti (1996a).

To conclude, it is worth noting that, although the program to be tested could be used as a black box and could even be written in a language other than Prolog, its use as a white box still has some advantages. The main issue here is that the program to be tested can help the tester to determine the set P of mutations, as it was done in the example of this section. Another minor point is that if the program to be tested is written in Prolog, the method described in this chapter can also be useful for automated debugging, where a debugged program can be based on the logic program learned from the final adequate test set and the corresponding corrected outputs.

Conclusion

There are many and diverse application areas where inductive logic programming has been proven successful, and recent advances have been achieved from genetics (Bryant, Muggleton, Oliver, Kell, Reiser, & King, 2001) to the automatization of the scientific process (King et al., 2004), from natural language processing (Aitken, 2002) to data mining (Dzeroski, 2001). A very long (but still incomplete) list of applications may be found at the site of ILP Network of Excellence (www-ai.ijs.si/~ilpnet2/apps).

On the contrary, the application of ILP techniques to the development of true logic programs, like those found in textbooks such as Clocksin and Mellish (1981) and Coelho and Cotta (1988), has received less attention from the ILP and machine learning community. The reason is not difficult to understand: real logic programs are very difficult to learn, since they may require learning many clauses, often self-recursive or mutually recursive.

In this chapter, we have argued that ILP techniques and algorithms can be a valid tool for the development, maintenance, reuse, testing, and debugging of logic programs, and we have presented (relatively simple) examples of the proposed methodology. Examples involving more complex programs can be found in Bergadano and Gunetti (1996a, 1996b). *Inductive programming* is possible only if we are able exploit all the possible knowledge we may have about the target programs. But software engineering is precisely the field where such information is available, since the user of the ILP system is also supposed to be a Prolog programmer. As we already noted, learning very complex programs may still be just a dream for the available ILP systems, but it could become a reality for techniques, systems, and hardware architectures of the (hopefully near) future; this chapter represents a contribution to this aim. (Note: this chapter is an updated revision of part of the work found in Bergadano & Gunetti, 1996a, 1996b).

References

Aitken, J. (2002). Learning information extraction rules: An inductive logic programming approach. In *Proceedings of ECAI*, Lyon, France, July 21-26 (pp. 355-359). Amsterdam, The Netherlands: IOS Press.

Bergadano, F., & Gunetti, D. (1996a). *Inductive logic programming: From machine learning to software engineering*. Cambridge, MA: MIT Press.

Bergadano, F., & Gunetti, D. (1996b). Testing by means of inductive program learning. *ACM Transactions on Software Engineering and Methodology, 5*(2), 119-145.

Bryant, C., Muggleton, S., Oliver, S., Kell, D., Reiser, P., & King, R. (2001). Combining inductive logic programming, active learning, and robotics to discover the function of genes. *Electronic Transactions on Artificial Intelligence, 5*, 1-36.

Budd, T. A., & Angluin, D. (1982). Two notions of correctness and their relation to testing. *Acta Informatica, 18*, 31-45.

Cherniavsky, J. C., & Smith, C. H. (1987). A recursion theoretic approach to program testing. *IEEE Transactions on Software Engineering, 13*(7), 777-784.

Clocksin, W. F., & Mellish, C. S. (1981). *Programming in prolog*. New York, NY: Springer-Verlag.

Coelho, H., & Cotta, J. C. (1988). *Prolog by example: How to learn teach and use it*. New York, NY: Springer-Verlag.

DeMillo, R. A., & Offutt, A. J. (1991). Constraint-based automatic test data generation. *IEEE Transactions on Software Engineering, 17*(9), 900-910.

Dzeroski, S. (Ed.) (2001). *Relational data mining*. Berlin, Germany: Springer-Verlag.

King, R., Whelan, K., Jones, F., Reiser, P., Bryant, C., Muggleton, S., Kell, D., & Oliver, S. (2004). Functional genomic hypothesis generation and experimentation by a robot scientist. *Nature, 427*, 247-252.

Michalski, R. S. (1980). Pattern recognition as rule-guided inductive inference. *IEEE Transactions on PAMI, 2*, 349-361.

Quinlan, R. (1990). Learning logical definitions from relations. *Machine Learning, 5*, 239-266.

Shapiro, E. Y. (1983). *Algorithmic program debugging*. Cambridge, MA: MIT Press.

Weyuker, E. J. (1983). Assessing test data adequacy through program inference. *ACM Transactions on Programming Languages and Systems, 5*(4), 641-655.

Chapter V

MMIR:
An Advanced Content-Based Image Retrieval System Using a Hierarchical Learning Framework

Min Chen, Florida International University, USA

Shu-Ching Chen, Florida International University, USA

Abstract

This chapter introduces an advanced content-based image retrieval (CBIR) system, MMIR, where Markov model mediator (MMM) and multiple instance learning (MIL) techniques are integrated seamlessly and act coherently as a hierarchical learning engine to boost both the retrieval accuracy and efficiency. It is well-understood that the major bottleneck of CBIR systems is the large semantic gap between the low-level image features and the high-level semantic concepts. In addition, the perception subjectivity problem also challenges a CBIR system. To address these issues and challenges, the proposed MMIR system utilizes the MMM mechanism to direct the focus on the image level analysis together with the MIL technique (with the neural network technique as its core) to real-time capture and learn the object-level semantic concepts with some help of the user feedbacks. In addition, from a long-term learning perspective, the user feedback logs are explored by MMM to speed up the learning process and to increase the retrieval accuracy for a query. The comparative studies on a large set of real-world images demonstrate the promising performance of our proposed MMIR system.

Introduction

Content-based image retrieval (CBIR), which was proposed in the early 1990s, has attracted a broad range of research interests from many computer communities in the past decade. Generally speaking, in a CBIR system, each image is first mapped to a point in a certain feature space, where the features can be categorized into color (Stehling, Nascimento, & Falcao, 2000), texture (Kaplan et al., 1998), shape (Zhang & Lu, 2002), and so forth. Next, given a query in terms of image examples, the system retrieves images with regard to their features (He, Li, Zhang, Tong, & Zhang, 2004). Though extensive research efforts have been directed into this area, it still remains a big challenge and an open issue in terms of retrieving the desired images from the large image repositories effectively and efficiently. In short, some of the major obstacles can be summarized as follows.

- First, it is widely accepted that the major bottleneck of CBIR systems is the large semantic gap between the low-level image features and high-level semantic concepts, which prevents the systems from being applied to real applications (Hoi & Lyu, 2004).
- Second, the perception subjectivity problem poses additional challenges for CBIR systems. In other words, in viewing the same image (e.g., Figure 1a), different users might possess various interests in either a certain object (e.g., the house, the tree, etc.) or the entire image (e.g., a landscape during the autumn season). In this case, Figure 1b, Figure 1c, or Figure 1d, respectively, might be considered as the relevant image

Figure 1. Example images

(a)   (b)

(c)   (d)

with regard to Figure 1a. In addition, even a same user can have different perceptions toward the same image at various situations and with different purposes.

To address the earlier-mentioned challenges and issues, a certain form of adaptive (i.e., data-driven) description is required to capture the salient meaning of each image. In addition, the system should be able to expedite the navigation process through a large image database with the facilitation of users' relevance feedbacks. In other words, the search engine should be equipped with an inference engine to observe and learn from user interactions. To this extent, we believe that there are both a need and an opportunity to systematically incorporate machine learning techniques into an integrated approach for content-based image retrieval. In this chapter, we introduce an advanced content-based image retrieval system called MMIR, where Markov model mediator (MMM) and multiple instance learning (MIL) techniques are integrated seamlessly and act coherently as a hierarchical learning engine to boost both the retrieval accuracy and efficiency.

Markov model mediator (MMM) is a statistical reasoning mechanism, which adopts the mathematically sound Markov model and the concept of mediators. As presented in our earlier studies (Shyu, Chen, Chen, Zhang, & Shu, 2003; Shyu, Chen, & Rubin, 2004a), MMM possesses the extraordinary capability in exploring the semantic concepts in the image level from the long-term learning perspective. In contrast, multiple instance learning (MIL) incorporated with the neural network (NN) technique aims at learning the region of interests based on the users' relevance feedbacks on the whole image in real time. Integrating the essential functionalities from both MMM and MIL has the potential in constructing a robust CBIR system, which is the attempt of this study.

The remainder of this chapter is organized as follows. The next section, *Background and Related Work*, gives a broad background introduction as well as the literature review. The system is detailed in the *Hierarchical Learning Scheme* section and the *Experimental Results* section, followed by the discussions of the possible future trends in terms of the CBIR research in the *Future Trends* section. Finally, the chapter ends with the *Conclusions* section.

Background and Related Work

The existing work in CBIR can be roughly classified into the following four categories:

- **Feature Analysis and Similarity Measures:** Many early-year studies on CBIR focused primarily on feature analysis and similarity measures (Pass, 1997; Zhou, Rui, & Huang, 1999). However, due to the semantic gap and the perception subjectivity issues, it is extremely difficult to discriminate the images by solely relying on the similarity measure upon the low-level features in the real-world image databases (Hoi et al., 2004).

- **Relevance Feedback (RF):** A variety of RF mechanisms from heuristic techniques to sophisticated learning techniques have been proposed and actively studied in recent years to mitigate the semantic gap issue (Rui, Huang, & Mehrotra, 1997; Tong

& Chang, 2001). The principle of RF is to adjust the subsequent queries by altering the position of the query point (or called the query center) and/or the feature weights based on the information gathered from the user's feedback, which can be regarded as a form of supervised learning. From the past research studies, RF has been shown as an effective scheme to improve the retrieval performance of CBIR and has already been incorporated as a key part in designing a CBIR system. However, it typically takes quite a number of iterations to converge the learning process to obtain the high-level concepts. Moreover, in case when the relevant samples are scarce in the initial query or the relevant images are widely scatted in the feature space, the RF technique is often inadequate in learning the concepts (Jin & French, 2003). Furthermore, most of the existing RF based applications regard each image as a whole, which often fails to produce satisfactory results when the user's query interest is just the salient region(s) in the image.

- **Region-Based Approaches:** With the assumption that human discernment of certain visual contents could be potentially associated with the semantically meaningful object(s) in the image, region-based retrieval (Chen & Wang, 2004; Jing, Li, Zhang, & Zhang, 2000) and MIL (Chen, Rubin, Shyu, & Zhang, in press; Huang, Chen, Shyu, & Zhang, 2002) techniques offer an alternative solution by decomposing the images into a set of homogeneous regions for analysis. It is worth noting that, as will be discussed in a later section, to some extent, the MIL technique might be considered as a hybrid of the RF technique and the region-based approach. In fact, semantically accurate image segmentation is an ambitious long-term goal for computer vision researchers, which highly limits the performance of these approaches. Here, semantically accurate image segmentation means the capability of building a one-to-one mapping between the segmented regions and the objects in the image (Chen et al., 2004). In addition, the assumption of the existence of salient object(s) in the images does not always hold.

- **Log-Based Retrieval (or called Long-Term Learning):** Due to the complexity of image understanding, the regular learning techniques, such as RF and MIL, need quite a number of rounds of feedbacks to reach satisfactory results. Consequently, log-based retrieval was proposed recently (Hoi et al., 2004; Shyu, Chen, Chen, & Zhang, 2004b; Zhou et al., 1999), which seeks to speed up the convergence of the learning process in terms of the high-level semantic concepts in a query with the as- sistance of the historical feedback logs accumulated in the system from the long-term learning perspective. However, most of the existing log-based retrieval frameworks solely capture the general user concepts but fail to adjust or customize the high-level semantic concepts in a query with regard to a specific user. Also, similar to most of the RF techniques, they have difficulties in propagating the feedback information across the query sessions toward the region or object level.

From these discussions, we observe that by acting alone, the earlier-mentioned approaches have certain limitations in terms of retrieval accuracy and/or processing costs. However, via the intelligent integration, we aim at offering a potentially promising solution for the CBIR system with the assistance of MIL (the region-based learning approach with NN as the core) and MMM (a statistical reasoning and log-based retrieval mechanism). We will detail these two techniques in the next section. To this extent, we seek to develop a unified framework that (1) explores the high-level semantic concepts in a query from both the object-level and the image-level and (2) addresses the needs of serving the specific user's query interest as well as reducing the convergence cycles.

To our best knowledge, very few efforts have been directed to serve this purpose. In He, King, Ma, Li, and Zhang (2003), the authors suggested to incorporate the RF technique with the singular value decomposition (SVD) based long-term learning. In addition, Hoi et al. (2004) studied the log-based relevance feedback for the purpose of improving the retrieval performance and reducing the semantic gap in CBIR. In our earlier study (Shyu, Chen, Chen, Zhang, & Shu, 2006), we also proposed a unified framework which integrates the MMM mechanism with the RF technique. However, these approaches solely direct the focus on the image level. In our recent work (Chen, Zhang, Chen, & Chen, 2005), we extended our research efforts to the object level by incorporating the latent semantic indexing (LSI) based long-term learning and one-class support vector machine (SVM) based MIL technique. However, to record the query logs, the users are asked to pick the interested region in the segmented image, which imposes a heavy burden to the users.

Hierarchical Learning Scheme

As discussed earlier, integrating the essential functionalities from both MMM and MIL has the potential in constructing a robust CBIR. In the following two sub-sections, we will introduce MIL and MMM, respectively, followed by the detailed discussions of the proposed hierarchical learning framework in our proposed MMIR system.

Multiple Instance Learning

Motivated by the *drug activity prediction problem*, Dietterich, Lathrop, and Lozano-Perez (1997) introduced the multiple instance learning model. Since its introduction, it has become increasingly important in machine learning.

In a traditional supervised learning problem, the task is to learn a function

$$y = f(x_1, x_2, ..., x_n), \tag{1}$$

given a group of examples $(y_i, x_{i1}, x_{i2}, ..., x_{in})$, $i = 1, 2, ... Z$.

Here, Z represents the number of input examples and n denotes the number of features for each example object. In other words, each set of input values $(x_{i1}, x_{i2}, ... x_{in})$ is tagged with the label y_i, and the task is to learn a hypothesis (function f) that can accurately predict the labels for the unseen objects.

In MIL, however, the input vector $(x_{i1}, x_{i2}, ... x_{in})$ (called an *instance*) is not individually labeled with its corresponding y_i value. Instead, one or more instances are grouped together to form a *bag* $B_b \in \beta$ and are collectively labeled with a $Y_b \in L$. Here, β denotes the bag space and

L represents the label space with $L = \{0(\text{Negative}), 1(\text{Positive})\}$ for binary classification. Let α be the instance space and assume there are m instances in B_b, the relation between the bag label Y_b and the labels $\{y_{bj} \mid y_{bj} \in L\}$ $(j = 1,...,m)$ of all its instances $\{I_{bj} \mid I_{bj} \in \alpha\}$ is defined as follows.

$$Y_b = \begin{cases} 1 & \text{if } \exists_{j=1}^m y_{bj} = 1 \\ 0 & \text{if } \forall_{j=1}^m y_{bj} = 0 \end{cases}$$

(2)

In other words, the label of a bag (i.e., Y_b) is a disjunction of the labels of the instances in the bag (i.e., Y_b where $j = 1,...,m$). That is, the bag is labeled as positive if and only if at least one of its instances is positive; whereas it is negative when all the instances in that bag are negative. The goal of the learner is to generate a hypothesis $h : \beta \rightarrow L$ to accurately predict the label of a previously unseen bag.

In terms of image representations in the region-based retrieval, images are first segmented into regions, where each of them is roughly homogeneous in color and texture and is characterized by a feature vector. Consequently, each image is represented by a collection of feature vectors. From the perspective of learning, the labels (positive or negative) are directly associated with images instead of individual regions. It is reasonable to assume that if an image is labeled as positive, at least one of its regions is of user's interest. Intuitively, the basic idea is essentially identical to the MIL settings, where a *bag* refers to an *image*; whereas an *instance* corresponds to a *region*. With the facilitation of MIL, we can expect a reasonably good query performance by discovering and applying the query-related objects in the process and filtering out the irrelevant objects.

In this study, for the sake of accuracy, the real-valued MIL approach developed in our earlier work (Huang, Chen, & Shyu, 2003) is adopted. The idea is to transfer the discrete label space $L = \{0(\text{Negative}), 1(\text{Positive})\}$ to a continuous label space $L_R = [0, 1]$, where the value indicates the degree of positive for a bag, with label "1" being 100% positive. Therefore, the goal of the learner is to generate a hypothesis $h_R : \beta \rightarrow L_R$. Consequently, the label of the bag (i.e., the degree of the bag being positive) can be represented by the maximum of the labels of all its instances and Eq. (2) is then transformed as follows.

$$Y_b = \max_j \{y_{bj}\}.$$

(3)

Let $h_I : \alpha \rightarrow L_R$ be the hypothesis to predict the label of an instance, we have the relationship between hypotheses h_R and h_I as depicted in Equation (4).

$$Y_b = h_R(B_b) = \max_j \{y_{bj}\} = \max_j \{h_I(I_{bj})\}.$$

(4)

Then the minimum square error (MSE) criterion is used. That is, we try to learn the hypotheses $\hat{h}_R$ and $\hat{h}_I$ to minimize the following function.

$$S = \sum_b \left(Y_b - \hat{h}_R(B_b) \right)^2 = \sum_b \left(Y_b - \max_j \{ \hat{h}_I(I_{bj}) \} \right)^2. \tag{5}$$

In this study, the multilayer feed-forward neural network is adopted to represent the hypothesis $\hat{h}_I$ and the back-propagation learning method is used to train the neural network to minimize S. More detailed discussion can be found in Huang et al. (2003). In the *Experimental Results* section, we will discuss the structure and parameter settings of the neural network.

It is worth noting that to some extent, the MIL approach can be considered as a hybrid of the RF technique and the region-based retrieval. In other words, MIL intends to achieve better query results in the next round by analyzing the training bag labels (i.e., user's feedback), which resembles the RF concepts. Nevertheless, the main focus of MIL is to explore the region of users' interest, which is the reason that we classify MIL as a region-based approach.

Markov Model Mediator

Markov model mediator (MMM) is a statistical reasoning mechanism, which adopts the mathematically sound Markov model and the concept of the mediators. The Markov model is one of the most powerful tools used to analyze the complicated systems, whereas a mediator is defined as a program to collect and combine information from one or more sources to yield the resulting information (Wiederhold, 1992).

Generally speaking, an MMM is a stochastic finite state machine with a stochastic output process attached to each state to describe the probability of the occurrences of the output symbols (states) (Shyu et al., 2004b). Its structure and settings are determined by three model parameters, that is, state transition probability distribution, observation symbol probability distribution, and initial state probability distribution denoted by A, B and Π, respectively. The parameter B is determined by the states' characteristics (or attributes), whereas parameters A and Π are defined by two kinds of information extracted from the historical database query logs, namely access patterns P and access frequencies F.

Let q_k be a query in the logs that accessed a certain number of states, $f_k \in F$ represents the number of such query q_k issued and recorded, and $P_{m,k} \in P$ denotes the access pattern of state m with respective to q_k, where

$$P_{m,k} = \begin{cases} 1 & \text{if state } m \text{ is accessed by } q_k \\ 0 & \text{otherwise} \end{cases} \tag{6}$$

Let $a_{m,n} \in A$ be the transition probability between two states m and n, we have

$$a_{m,n} = \frac{\sum_k P_{m,k} \times P_{n,k} \times f_k}{\sum_n \sum_k P_{m,k} \times P_{n,k} \times f_k} \tag{7}$$

The initial state probability $\pi_m \in \Pi$ for state m is defined as follows.

$$\pi_m = \frac{\sum_k P_{m,k}}{\sum_n \sum_k P_{n,k}}$$

(8)

Then a dynamic programming based stochastic output process is carried out to produce the probability of the occurrences of the output states. A more detailed discussion can be found in Shyu et al. (2003). Owing to its strong reasoning capability, it has been widely applied to a variety of domains including database clustering (Shyu et al., 2004a), multimedia database management (Shyu et al., 2004b), and so forth.

Intuitively, in terms of the applications in image retrieval, an MMM can be readily converted to model the semantic network by regarding the images as the states and accumulating the users' feedbacks in the query logs. It is worth noting that because of the perception subjectivity issue, each user's feedback will be recorded distinctly in the logs. In other words, the access frequency $f_k \in F$ is set to 1, and Equation (6) is redefined as

$$P_{m,k} = \begin{cases} 1 & \text{if image } m \text{ is positive in the } k^{th} \text{ feedback} \\ 0 & \text{otherwise} \end{cases}$$

(9)

Then given a query image (the starting state), the stochastic output process is applied to traverse the network to yield the probability of the occurrences (or the similarity values) of the output states (the other images), where the greater the probability is, the higher the image is ranked in the retrieved image set. It is worth noting that as a statistical reasoning mechanism, MMM effectively learns the concepts adopted by the majority of users (or called general concepts), which has been fully demonstrated in Shyu et al. (2003, 2004b). However, it fails to serve the specific user's query need if it is far from the general concepts. In addition, if the query image has no access record in the query logs, the retrieval process will end up using solely the low-level image features to calculate the similarity values.

Hierarchical Learning Framework in the MMIR System

In this sub-section, we will present the basic idea and procedure of constructing the hierarchical learning framework (for short, MMM_MIL framework) by integrating these two techniques for the MMIR system, which is illustrated in Figure 2. As can be seen in this figure, the MMM_MIL framework consists of an off-line process which aims at extracting the image and object-level features to obtain the MMM parameters, and an online retrieval process. These two processes work closely with each other in the sense that the off-line process prepares the essential data for the online process to reduce the online processing time. In addition, the feedbacks provided in the online process can be accumulated in the logs for the off-line process to update the MMM parameters periodically. In this section, we will focus on the online retrieval process.

Figure 2. The hierarchical learning framework

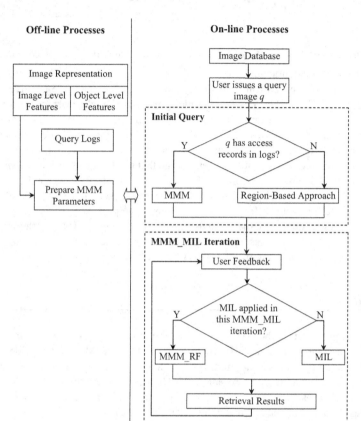

Initial Query

In most of the existing CBIR systems, given a query image, the initial query results are simply computed using a certain similarity function (e.g., Euclidean distance, Manhattan distance, etc.) upon the low-level features either in the image or the object level. For instance, in the general MIL framework, since there is no training data available for the outset of the retrieval process, a simple distance-based metric is applied to measure the similarity of two images (Huang et al., 2003). Formally, given a query image q with R_q regions (denoted as $q = \{q_i\}$, $i = 1, \dots, R_q$), its difference with respect to an image m consisting of R_m regions (denoted as $m = \{m_j\}, j = 1, \dots, R_m$) is defined as:

$$Dist(q,m) = \sum_{i} \min_{j}\{|q_i - m_j|\}$$

(10)

Here, $|q_i - m_j|$ represents the distance between two feature vectors of regions q_i and m_j.

However, due to the semantic gap issue, it is highly possible that the number of "positive" images retrieved in the initial run is relatively small (e.g., less than five positives out of the top 30 images). This lack of positive samples greatly hinders the learning performance for most of the learning algorithms, including the NN-based MIL approach we discussed earlier. In contrast, MMM possesses the capability of representing the general concepts in the query and outperforms the region-based approach defined in Equation (10) on the average. One exception, though, is that any query image that has not been accessed before will force the MMM mechanism to perform the Euclidean distance function upon the low-level image features (discussed earlier). In this case, the region-based approach will be applied as it captures more completed information. Therefore, in our proposed hierarchical learning framework, the initial query is carried out as illustrated in Figure 2. It is worth noting that the test of whether an image q has been accessed before (its access record) in the log can be formally transformed to test whether $\sum_{j} a(q, j)$ equals 0, where $a(q, j) \in A$.

MMM_MIL Iteration

With the initial query results, the users are asked to provide the feedbacks for the MMM_MIL iteration, which is defined as an MIL process followed by MMM. The basic idea is that based on the region of interest (e.g., instance I_p in image or bag B_p) MIL learned for a specific user, the semantic network represented by MMM is intelligently traversed to explore the images which are semantically related to B_p. Obviously, it can be easily carried out by treating B_p as the query image and using the algorithms described earlier. However, in case that a group of positive bags (images) are identified, which is actually the general case, the situation becomes relatively complicated in the sense that a number of paths need to be traversed and the results are then aggregated to reach the final outputs.

Therefore, an extended MMM mechanism called MMM_RF (Shyu et al., 2006) is used to solve this problem. In brief, the difference between MMM and MMM_RF is that MMM considers only the direct relationship between the query image q and the other images in the database; whereas MMM_RF adopts an additional relationship called indirectly related (RI) relationship which denotes the situation when two images are connected to a common image. With the introduction of RI, the multiple paths mentioned earlier can be effectively merged into a new path, where the same dynamic programming based stochastic output process can be applied to produce the final results (please refer to Shyu et al., 2006).

Experimental Results

Experimental Datasets

To perform rigorous evaluation of our proposed framework, we chose 9,800 real-world images from the COREL image CDs, where every 100 images represent one distinct topic of interest. Therefore, our data set contains 98 thematically diverse image categories, including antique, balloon, car, cat, firework, flower, horse, and so forth, where all the images are in JPEG format with size 384*256 or 256*384.

Experimental Setup

In order to evaluate the performance of the proposed MMIR system, the off-line process needs to be carried out first, which includes feature extraction and query log collection. In addition, the neural network structure for MIL should be defined before the online process can be conducted.

Image Representation

Each image is represented by the color and texture features extracted from both the image and object levels.

Color: Color feature is widely adopted in a CBIR system for its simplification and effectiveness. In addition, HSV color space and its variants are proven to be particularly amenable to color image analysis. Also as discussed in Goldstein (1999), though the wavelength of visible light ranges from 400 to 700 nanometers, the colors that can be named by all the cultures are generally limited to be around 11. Therefore, we quantify the color space using color categorization based on H, S, V value ranges and identify 13 representative colors. Besides *black* and *white*, 10 discernible colors (*red, red-yellow, yellow, yellow-green, green, green-blue, blue, blue-purple, purple* and *purple-red*) are extracted by dividing the Hue into five main color slices and five transition color slices. Here, each transition color slice like *red-yellow, yellow-green,* and so forth, is considered between two adjacent main color slices. In addition, we add a new category *gray* for the remaining value ranges.

Texture: Texture is an important cue for image analysis. It has been shown in a variety of studies (Smith & Chang, 1995; Tong et al., 2001) that characterizing texture features in terms of structure, orientation, and scale fits perfectly with the models of human perception. A number of texture analysis approaches have been proposed. In this study, a one-level wavelet transformation using Daubechies wavelets is used to generate the horizontal detail sub-image, the vertical detail sub-image, and the diagonal detail sub-image. The reason for selecting Daubechies wavelet transform lies in the fact that it is proven to be suitable for image analysis. For the wavelet co-efficients in each of the earlier-mentioned three sub-bands, the mean and variance values are collected respectively. Therefore, six texture features are extracted.

In terms of image-level features, the extraction process is relatively straightforward when an image is considered as a whole and a vector of 19 features (13 color features and 6 texture features) is generated as discussed earlier. As far as the region level features are considered, an image segmentation process needs to be carried out beforehand.

Image Segmentation: In this study, the *WavSeg* algorithm proposed in our earlier work (Zhang, Chen, & Shyu, 2004) is applied to partition the images. In brief, *WavSeg* adopts a wavelet analysis in concert with the SPCPE algorithm (Chen, Sista, Shyu, & Kashyap, 2000) to segment an image into a set of regions. By using Daubechies wavelets, the high-frequency components will disappear in larger scale sub-bands and the possible regions will be clearly evident. Then by grouping the salient points from each channel, an initial coarse partition is obtained and passed as the input to the SPCPE segmentation algorithm, which has been proven to outperform the random initial partition based SPCPE algorithm. In addition, this wavelet transform process can actually produce the region-level texture features together with the extraction of the region-of-interest within one entry scanning through the image data.

Once the region information becomes available, the region-level color features can be easily extracted.

Query Logs

The collection of query logs is a critical process for learning the essential parameters in this framework. Therefore, in MMIR, a group of seven users were asked to create the log information. In other words, the users are requested to perform the query-by-example (QBE) execution on the system and provide their feedbacks on the retrieved results.

In order to ensure that the logs cover a wide range of images, each time a query image is randomly seeded from the image database and the system returns the top 30 ranked images by employing the region-based approach defined earlier. The user then provides the feedbacks (positive or negative) on the images by judging whether they are relevant to the query image. Such information is named as a query log and is accumulated in the database. Currently, we have collected 896 query logs. It is worth noting that though the users may give noisy information to the logs, it will not significantly affect the learning performance as long as it only accounts for a small portion of the query logs.

Neural Network

As discussed earlier, a three-layer feed-forward neural network is used in our study to map an image region with a low-level feature vector into the user's high-level concept.

Figure 3. The three-layer feed-forward neural network

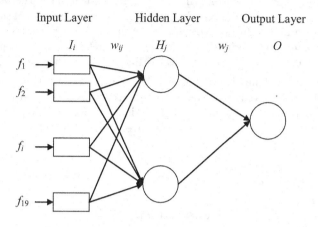

As can be seen from Figure 3, the network consists of an input layer, a hidden layer, and an output layer. Here, the input layer contains 19 input units, where each of them represents a low-level feature of an image region. Therefore, the notations $f_1, f_2, ..., f_{19}$ correspond to the 19 low-level features described previously. The hidden layer is composed of 19 hidden nodes with w_{ij} being the weight of the connection between the ith input unit I_i and the jth hidden node H_j (where $i, j = 1, ..., 19$). Note that the output layer contains only one node, which outputs the real value $y \in L_R = [0, 1]$ indicating the satisfactory level of an image region with regard to a user's concept. The weight between the output node and the jth hidden node H_j is in turn denoted as w_j. The Sigmoid function with slope parameter 1 is used as the activation function and the back-propagation (BP) learning method is applied with a learning rate of 0.1 with no momentum. The initial weights for all the connections (i.e., w_{ij} and w_j) are randomly set with relatively small values (e.g., in the range of [-0.1, 0.1]) and the termination condition of the BP algorithm is defined as follows.

$$\left| S^{(k)} - S^{(k-1)} \right| < \alpha \times S^{(k-1)} \qquad (11)$$

Here, $S^{(k)}$ denotes the value of S at the kth iteration and α is a small constant, which is set to 0.005 in our experiment.

Performance Comparison

The performance measurement metric employed in our experiments is *accuracy*, which is defined as the average ratio of the number of relevant images retrieved over the number of total returned images (or called scope). In order to evaluate the performance of the hierarchical learning framework (denoted as MMM_MIL), we compare it with the neural network-based MIL technique with relevance feedback (for short, MIL_RF) which does not support the log-based retrieval. In addition, we also compare the performance of our system with another general feature re-weighting algorithm (Rui et al., 1997) with relevance feedback using both Euclidean and Manhattan distances, denoted as RF_Euc and RF_Mah, respectively.

Fifty query images are randomly issued. For each query image, the initial query results are first retrieved and then followed by two rounds of user feedbacks with regard to MIL_RF, RF_Euc and RF_Mah algorithms. Correspondingly, besides the initial query, one MMM_MIL iteration is performed as each iteration consists of two rounds of feedbacks. In our data-

Figure 4. Experimental results

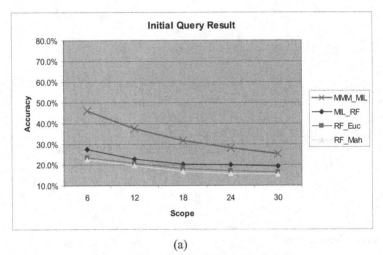

(a)

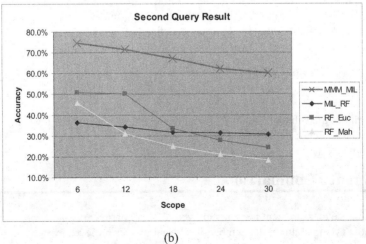

(b)

base log, totally 896 distinct queries have been recorded which are used by MMM_MIL. In addition, the region-level features used by MIL_RF are the same as the ones used by MMM_MIL. Similarly, the image-level features used by RF_Euc, RF_Mah and MMM_MIL are also identical.

The accuracy within different scopes, i.e., the percentages of positive images within the top 6, 12, 18, 24, and 30 retrieved images are calculated. The results are illustrated in Figure 4, where Figures 4a and 4b show the initial query results and the second query (or the first round of MMM_MIL) results, respectively.

As can be seen from this figure, the accuracy of MMM_MIL greatly outperforms all the other three algorithms in all the cases. More specifically, with regard to the initial query results (Figure 4a), MMM_MIL (represented by the red line) performs far better than the remaining three algorithms with more than 10% difference in accuracy on average, which demonstrates MMM's strong capability in capturing the general concepts. Furthermore, by comparing Figure 4a and Figure 4b, we observe that the MMM_MIL results improve tremendously where the increment of the accuracy rate reaches 30% on average. In contrast, the improvements of the other approaches are relatively small (with the improvement of the accuracy rate ranging from 10% to 20%), which indicates that MMM_MIL can achieve an extremely fast convergence of the concept.

Future Trends

Machine learning and other artificial intelligence (AI) approaches have attracted increasing interests in the content-based image retrieval (CBIR) area. Many research works have been conducted, which led to quite a few encouraging achievements. However, there remain a number of emerging challenges and open issues to be addressed. Correspondingly, we list some of the future trends as follows.

- **Better interaction scheme to alleviate the manual efforts**
  Generally, for an interactive CBIR system, the query performance is achieved at the cost of huge human efforts. Take the relevance feedback system as an example. Normally, the users are asked to go through 3 to 4 iterations to provide their feedbacks (positive, negative, or even the level of relativity in some approaches) for tens of images in each iteration. It can be expected that the level of manual efforts required for image retrieval will be one of the most important factors that determine the potential and popularity of the CBIR system in the real application domains. Therefore, a trend has been emerged to accumulate and analyze the historical feedbacks to improve the long-term system performance.

- **Faster converging process to speed up the retrieval task**
  The converging speed is another important issue that affects the potentials of applying AI technique to the CBIR system. Considering the explosive growth of image data and the normally high-dimensional image representations, the converging speed of the learning process becomes especially critical for the real-time image retrieval process.

The singular value decomposition (SVD) has been used for dimension reduction and noisy data removal to facilitate the converging process. More studies for this issue are certainly expected.

- **Noise-tolerate mechanism**
  In the current CBIR research, various assumptions are made in terms of the amount of noise data contained in the image database. For instance, we presume that the image quality is of reasonably good. In addition, most of the existing log-based CBIR frameworks assume that while a certain user might introduce the noise information into the query log, the rate is negligibly low (Hoi et al., 2004). As we know, many of the assumptions do not hold in the real-world applications, especially in this era of information explosion. Therefore, the construction of the noise-tolerate mechanism becomes essentially important, where the techniques like outlier detection, fuzzy logic, and so forth, might be introduced for this purpose.

Conclusions

As an emerging topic, the application of the learning techniques in the CBIR system has attracted increasing attentions nowadays. With the aim of addressing the semantic gap and the perception subjectivity issues, in this chapter, we introduced an advanced content-based image retrieval system called MMIR that is facilitated with a hierarchical learning framework called MMM_MIL. The unique characteristic of the proposed MMM_MIL learning framework is that it not only possesses the strong capabilities in real-time capturing and learning the object and image semantic concepts, but also offers an effective solution to speed up the learning process by intelligently exploring the feedback logs. The comparative experiments with the well-known learning techniques fully demonstrate the effectiveness of the proposed MMIR system.

References

Chen, S.-C., Rubin, S. H., Shyu, M.-L., & Zhang, C. (in press). A dynamic user concept pattern learning framework for content-based image retrieval. Accepted for publication, *IEEE Transactions on Systems, Man, and Cybernetics: Part C*.

Chen, S.-C., Sista, S., Shyu, M.-L., & Kashyap, R. L. (2000). An indexing and searching structure for multimedia database systems. In the *Proceedings of the IS&T/SPIE International Conference on Storage and Retrieval for Media Databases*, San Jose, CA, January 23-28 (pp. 262-270). Bellingham, WA: SPIE Press.

Chen, Y., & Wang, J. Z. (2004). Image categorization by learning and reasoning with regions. *Journal of Machine Learning Research*, 5, 913-939.

Chen, X., Zhang, C., Chen, S.-C., & Chen, M. (2005). A latent semantic indexing based method for solving multiple instance learning problem in region-based image retrieval.

In the *Proceedings of IEEE International Symposium on Multimedia,* Irvine, CA, December 12-14 (pp. 37-44). Los Alamitos, CA: IEEE Computer Society.

Dietterich, T. G., Lathrop, R. H., & Lozano-Perez, T. (1997). Solving the multiple-instance problem with axis-parallel rectangles. *Artificial Intelligence, 89,* 31-71.

Goldstein, E. B. (1999). *Sensation and perception* (5th ed.). Pacific Grove, CA: Brooks/ Cole.

He, X., King, O., Ma, W.-Y., Li, M., & Zhang, H. J. (2003). Learning a semantic space from user's relevance feedback for image retrieval. *IEEE Transactions on Circuits and Systems for Video Technology, 13*(1), 39-49.

He, J., Li, M., Zhang, H.-J., Tong, H., & Zhang, C. (2004). Mean version space: A new active learning method for content-based image retrieval. In the *Proceedings of ACM International Conference on Multimedia,* New York, NY, October 10-16 (pp. 15-22). New York: ACM Press.

Hoi, C.-H., & Lyu, M. R. (2004). A novel log-based relevance feedback technique in content-based image retrieval. In the *Proceedings of ACM International Conference on Multimedia,* New York, NY, October 10-16 (pp. 24-31). New York: ACM Press.

Huang, X., Chen, S.-C., & Shyu, M.-L. (2003). Incorporating real-valued multiple instance learning into relevance feedback for image retrieval. In the *Proceedings of the IEEE International Conference on Multimedia & Expo,* Baltimore, MD, July 6-9 (pp. 321-324). Los Alamitos, CA: IEEE Computer Society Press.

Huang, X., Chen, S.-C., Shyu, M.-L., & Zhang, C. (2002). User concept pattern discovery using relevance feedback and multiple instance learning for content-based image retrieval. In the *Proceedings of the Third International Workshop on Multimedia Data Mining,* Edmonton, Alberta, Canada, July 23 (pp. 100-108). Edmonton, Alberta, Canada: University of Alberta.

Jin, X., & French, J. C. (2003). Improving image retrieval effectiveness via multiple queries. In the *Proceedings of ACM International Workshop on Multimedia Database,* New Orleans, LA, November 7 (pp. 86-93). New York: ACM Press.

Jing, F., Li, M., Zhang, H.-J., & Zhang, B. (2000). An effective region-based image retrieval framework. In the *Proceedings of ACM International Conference on Multimedia,* Los Angeles, CA, October 30-November 3 (pp. 456-465). New York: ACM Press.

Kaplan, L. M. et al. (1998). Fast texture database retrieval using extended fractal features. In the *Proceedings of IS&T/SPIE Conference on Storage and Retrieval for Media Databases,* San Jose, CA, January 28-30 (pp. 162-173). Bellingham, WA: SPIE Press.

Pass, G. (1997). Comparing images using color coherence vectors. In the *Proceedings of ACM International Conference on Multimedia,* Seattle, WA, November 9-13 (pp. 65-73). New York: ACM Press.

Rui, Y., Huang, T. S., & Mehrotra, S. (1997). Content-based image retrieval with relevance feedback in MARS. In the *Proceedings of the International Conference on Image Processing,* Washington D.C., October 26-29 (pp. 815-818). Piscataway, NJ: IEEE Press.

Shyu, M.-L., Chen, S.-C., Chen, M., & Zhang, C. (2004b). Affinity relation discovery in image database clustering and content-based retrieval. In the *Proceedings of ACM*

International Conference on Multimedia, New York, NY, October 10-16 (pp. 372-375). New York: ACM Press.

Shyu, M.-L., Chen, S.-C., Chen, M., Zhang, C., & Shu, C.-M. (2003). MMM: A stochastic mechanism for image database queries. In the *Proceedings of the IEEE Fifth International Symposium on Multimedia Software Engineering,* Taichung, Taiwan, ROC, December 10-12 (pp. 188-195). Los Alamitos, CA: IEEE Computer Society Press.

Shyu, M.-L., Chen, S.-C., Chen, M., Zhang, C., & Shu, C.-M. (2006). Probabilistic semantic network-based image retrieval using MMM and relevance feedback. *Multimedia Tools and Applications, 30*(2), 131-147.

Shyu, M.-L., Chen, S.-C., & Rubin, S. H. (2004a). Stochastic clustering for organizing distributed information source. *IEEE Transactions on Systems, Man and Cybernetics, Part B, 34*(5), 2035-2047.

Smith, J., & Chang, S.-F. (1995, July). Automated image retrieval using color and texture. Technical report CU/CTR 408-95-14, Columbia University.

Stehling, R. O., Nascimento, M. A., & Falcao, A. X. (2000). On shapes of colors for content-based image retrieval. In the *Proceedings of ACM International Workshop on Multimedia Information Retrieval,* Los Angeles, CA, November 4 (pp. 171-174). New York: ACM Press.

Tong, S., & Chang, E. (2001). Support vector machine active learning for image retrieval. In the *Proceedings of ACM International Conference on Multimedia,* Ottawa, Ontario, Canada, September 30-October 5 (pp. 107-118). New York: ACM Press.

Wiederhold, G. (1992). Mediators in the architecture of future information systems. *IEEE Computers, 25*(3), 38-49.

Zhang, C., Chen, S.-C., & Shyu, M.-L. (2004). Multiple object retrieval for image databases using multiple instance learning and relevance feedback. In the *Proceedings of IEEE International Conference on Multimedia and Expo,* Taipei, Taiwan, ROC, June 27-30 (pp. 775-778). Los Alamitos, CA: IEEE Computer Society Press.

Zhang, D. S., & Lu, G. (2002). Generic fourier descriptors for shape-based image retrieval. In the *Proceedings of IEEE International Conference on Multimedia and Expo,* Lausanne, Switzerland, August 26-29 (pp. 425-428). Los Alamitos, CA: IEEE Computer Society Press.

Zhou, X. S., Rui, Y., & Huang, T. (1999). Water-filling: A novel way for image structural feature extraction. In the *Proceedings of IEEE International Conference on Image Processing: Vol. 2,* Kobe, Japan, October 25-28 (pp. 570-574). Piscataway, NJ: IEEE Press.

Chapter VI

A Genetic Algorithm-Based QoS Analysis Tool for Reconfigurable Service-Oriented Systems

I-Ling Yen, University of Texas at Dallas, USA

Tong Gao, University of Texas at Dallas, USA

Hui Ma, University of Texas at Dallas, USA

Abstract

Reconfigurability is an important requirement in many application systems. Many approaches have been proposed to achieve static/dynamic reconfigurability. Service-oriented architecture offers a certain degree of reconfigurability due to its support in dynamic composition. When system requirements change, new composition of services can be determined to satisfy the new requirements. However, analysis, especially QoS based analysis, is generally required to make appropriate service selections and service configurations. In this chapter, we discuss the development of QoS-based composition analysis techniques and propose a QoS specification model. The specification model facilitates QoS-based specification of the properties of the Web services and the requirements of the application systems. The composition analysis techniques can be used to analyze QoS tradeoffs and determine the best selections and configurations of the Web services. We develop a composition analysis framework and use the genetic algorithm in the framework for composition decision making. The framework currently supports SOA performance analysis. The details of the genetic algorithm for the framework and the performance analysis techniques are discussed in this chapter.

Introduction

Reconfigurability is an important feature that is required in many modern application systems (Aksit & Choukair, 2003). For example, avionics systems, intelligent vehicle control systems, and remote monitoring systems frequently require dynamic adaptability so that the system can adapt to changes due to the failure of system components, reduced power level, unexpected operating conditions, and so forth. Also, some systems are multiple-mission and mission-specific, that is, they have to handle a class of missions that have similar system requirements but they also require adaptations to satisfy mission-specific needs.

Service-oriented architecture (SOA) is an ideal vehicle for achieving reconfigurability (Tsai, Song, Paul, Cao, & Huang, 2004). Desired functionalities can be achieved in SOA by dynamically composing appropriate services. Many research works focus on Web service composition (BEA et al., 2002; Hamadi & Benatallah, 2003; Sirin, Parsia, & Hendler, 2004). Most of these investigate various language issues. Business process execution language (BPEL) is an XML-based language for specifying the business processes and interaction protocols. Web services are then composed together to meet the specified functional requirements. The concept of semantic Webs extends the current Web with well-defined meanings for each Web service to facilitate their compositions. Based on semantic Webs, Sirin et al. (2004) have proposed a service composition tool including two main modules, namely, a composer and an inference engine. A user can interact with the composer to generate the composition and filter the results. The inference engine is a Web ontology language (OWL; W3C, 2004a) reasoner. The OWL reasoner searches the related services for the generated composition. Petri net-based algebra has also been used to help the composition by modeling the control flow. These composition methods can be used for adapting a system to new functional requirements (by composing a new set of services to achieve the modified functionalities).

Service composition generally focuses on composition of Web services to achieve some desired functionality. To achieve reconfiguration, new compositions can be derived for the modified functionalities. Actually, many adaptive systems require reconfigurability in terms of quality of service (QoS) behaviors. For example, some unmanned systems allow degraded QoS when some system failures occur. Many systems tradeoff the quality of their outputs versus the execution time to cope with periods of heavy loads or contentions for resources. In SOA-based systems, QoS reconfiguration can be achieved by, for example, selecting different services among those providing the same functionalities but, perhaps, having different QoS behaviors. Thus, systems can be dynamically assembled to fit the changing functional as well as QoS requirements.

Though SOA provides a convenient framework for reconfigurability, advanced techniques are still required to achieve actual adaptation (dynamic or static). For example, when the functional requirements of a system are modified, it is necessary to decompose the new requirements and then find the matching services in order to compose the new system. Similarly, when the QoS requirements of a system are modified due to changes in the execution environment, it is necessary to reconfigure the current services or choose new services to satisfy the new QoS requirements. To determine the correct service selections and configurations, it is necessary to analyze the QoS behaviors of the composed system.

The focus of this chapter is on QoS-based system reconfiguration. The goal is to develop analysis techniques and tools to facilitate static and dynamic system QoS behavior analysis such that correct decisions regarding service selections and configurations can be made. The next section, *SOA Background*, introduces the SOA concept. The *QoS Specification Model* section presents the QoS specification model, and the *Analysis of Adaptive SOA Systems* section describes the analysis process of adaptive SOA systems. Then the composition analysis framework and genetic algorithm-based decision support are presented in the *Composition Analysis Framework* and the *Genetic-Algorithm-Based Decision Support* sections, respectively. And, the associated performance analysis method for SOA system is introduced the *Performance Analysis* section. The next section after that is *Case Study,* and finally, the *Conclusion* section summarizes this chapter.

SOA Background

The SOA concept is probably one of the most significant software engineering concepts after the currently widely adopted object-oriented technologies. The SOA term expresses the software architectural concept and essentially a collection of services. In SOA, each service encapsulates certain information and data to implement the functionality, and such service can then be consumed by clients in other applications through the exposed interfaces. These services communicate with each other to achieve the system requirements. SOA is an architecture style which is distributed, loosely coupling, highly interoperable between the services, hence, will maximize system flexibility and independent evolvability. Also, due to the potential of reuse and dynamic composition of core services, SOA offers high system reusability and reconfigurability. Legacy systems can be wrapped and reused without significant changes, while new applications can be incorporated into the architecture easily.

Web service-based SOA is a specialized realization of SOA (W3C, 2002). In this specific SOA, Web service (WS) takes the concept of the service and delivers the service over the Web using the technologies such as XML, simple object access protocol (SOAP), Web services description language (WSDL), and universal description, discovery, and integration (UDDI). SOAP provides a way to communicate between the services which are implemented in different programming languages, different technologies, and run on different operating

Figure 1. Web services system model

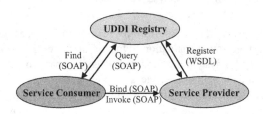

systems. WSDL provides a standard format to describe the Web services by using XML. UDDI is a repository which stores the information of the Web services and facilitates publishing and finding of the Web services.

Web service-based SOA adopts register-find-bind-invoke paradigm which is shown in Figure 1. In this paradigm, service provider registers the Web services in the public UDDI registry and publishs the Web services. Service consumer searches in the public UDDI registry and finds the desired Web services, then binds and invokes it.

Web service composition enable user to rapidly build a system or create a process by assembling individual Web services. Through specifying some details of the composition, such as when to invoke the appropriate Web services, the calling sequence of the Web services, the developer can implement the needed tasks. To facilitate the composition, several Web service composition languages are proposed, including business process execution language for Web services (BPEL4WS, also called BPEL; BEA Systems et al., 2002) and OWL-based Web Service Ontology (OWL-S; W3C, 2004b).

BPEL provides an abstract business protocol to facilitate the specification of compositions. A BPEL process specifies a set of partners and their interactions and invocation sequence. Each partner is a unit in the process and it is linked to the process via a partner link. The BPEL process coordinates with all involved clients and Web services and interacts with them, coordinates the execution sequence to achieve the desired goal. The process specification is kept at the abstract level, and it only specifies the relations and exchanged messages between partners without considering the internal details of the partner. With certain extensions, the BPEL process can be used to flexibly specify service composition and allows each partner to be associated with alternate Web services.

OWL-S provides a set of markup language constructs for describing the properties and capabilities of the Web services. It facilitates the automated Web service discovery, composition, and execution. It supports similar features as BPEL does for composition specification. OWL-S is widely used in semantic Web community while BPEL is used commonly in business sectors.

QOS Specification Model

The QoS behavior of a WS-based system can be adapted due to three factors, including: (1) resource allocation, (2) selection of different services that offer the same functionalities, and (3) tuning QoS control parameters within the services. First, for resource allocation, we consider allocating available physical platforms to involved services. Services with higher access rates in the system may be replicated on multiple platforms while multiple services with lower access rates may share a single platform. Second, different services implementing the same functionality may yield different QoS tradeoffs. Thus, appropriate selection of the services can help with achieving the QoS goals of the applications. Third, each service may be reconfigurable in terms of its QoS behavior. Some QoS control parameters within a service unit can be tuned to control the tradeoffs of the QoS behavior. For example, a search program may obtain better results when given more time and the tradeoffs between time and output quality can be controlled by certain parameters within the program. Here, all three types of adaptivity for QoS analysis and reconfiguration in SOA systems are considered.

The goal of QoS-based composition analysis for reconfigurable SOA systems is to determine the best configuration for the system based on system QoS requirements. The configuration should consider the three adaptation factors, resource allocation, Web service selection, and QoS control parameter determination. To achieve QoS-based composition analysis, it is necessary to first establish the model for QoS related specifications. For example, the QoS behavior of the application system is derived from the QoS behavior of individual Web services. Thus, QoS behavior of the Web services to be considered for composing the application systems should be known a priori to facilitate the analysis. Also, it is necessary to specify the QoS requirements of the application systems and based on which the satisfatory system configuration can be determined. In this section, we step-by-step introduce the model for QoS specification.

QoS Attribute Vector

To support all QoS-related specifications, the first step is to define the set of QoS attributes that need to be measured. Some standard QoS attributes include time and resource consumption metrics. Some application-specific QoS attributes include, for example, picture quality for image compression algorithms, precision of a relaxation based computation, and so forth. Consider a system S. Let $Q_S = (q_1, q_2, ..., q_N)$ denote the quality attribute vector of S, where Q_S includes N quality attributes. For different Web services, different quality attribute vectors may be considered. When specifying the QoS requirements of S, Q_S should be defined first. Note that the quality attribute vectors of the Web services that compose S may not have exactly the same elements, and they may be different from Q_S. When performing composition analysis, the quality attributes that are of interests are the overall system quality attributes (which is Q_S). If a Web service has additional quality attributes, they can simply be ignored. If a Web service does not contribute to a certain quality attribute in Q_S, then, a *null* value can be assigned to it.

System QoS Requirements

Let Γ_S denote the system QoS requirements for system S. Γ_S is defined on Q_S. Generally, system QoS requirements can be in the form of constraints that has to be satisfied and/or objectives that should be optimized. Let $\Gamma_S = (O, R)$, where $O = (o_1, o_2, \ldots)$ is the set of objectives, and $R = (r_1, r_2, \ldots)$ is the set of constraints. An objective o_i is an optimization function defined on one or more QoS attributes in Q_S. For example, maximize(q_1) and minimize ($aq_2 + bq_3$) are possible QoS objectives. A constraint r_i specifies a specific QoS constraint that need to be satisfied, and it is also defined on one or more QoS attributes in Q_S. For example, r_i may specify that the power consumption of the system should be within 100 walts per unit time, denoted as r_i: $q_3 \leq 100$ walts/sec, where q_3 is the power consumption quality attribute.

The goal of the system is to satisfy all the QoS constraints while obtaining optimal solutions in terms of the QoS objectives. Since there may be multiple objectives, the Pareto-optimal solutions can be considered.

Service Composition

The application system S is composed of Web services. We can use BPEL to specify the composition of services. In order to specify the functional requirements and associated candidate Web services of the partner, we extend the definition of the "partner" in BPEL by adding the tags "functional_req" and "associated_ws" respectively. Let Ω_S denote the composition specification for system S. Ω_S consists of a set of partners, $\{\omega_i \mid 1 \leq i \leq M\}$. The functionality of each partner ω_i is specified using the "functional_req" tag. From the functional specification, the actual Web services can be selected to instantiate a partner. Partner ω_i can be instantiated by m_i Web services, $ws_{i,j} \mid 1 \leq j \leq m_i$, which are included in the "associated_ws" tag of ω_i.

QoS Properties of the Individual Web Services

To facilitate QoS analysis and system configuration decision making, it is necessary to know the QoS properties of individual Web services and how to compose them to derive the QoS behavior of the composed system. The QoS property of a Web service is generally a function of the input and the operation environment parameters. For a reconfigurable Web service, the control parameters in the Web service program also impact its QoS property. Consider the candidate Web services, $ws_{i,j}$, for all i and j, for composing the system S. Let $I_{i,j}^{ws}$ denote the set of input parameters, $E_{i,j}^{ws}$ denote the set of operation environment parameters, and $X_{i,j}^{ws}$ denote the set of configurable parameters for $ws_{i,j}$. $I_{i,j}^{ws}$ is specified by the parameters in client requests. $E_{i,j}^{ws}$ can be, for example, the platform capability. For a given set of $I_{i,j}^{ws}$, $E_{i,j}^{ws}$, and $X_{i,j}^{ws}$ values, the properties of $ws_{i,j}$ in terms of quality attribute q_i can be measured. Let $^*V_{i,j}^{ws} = ({}^1V_{i,j}^{ws}, {}^2V_{i,j}^{ws}, \ldots, {}^NV_{i,j}^{ws})$ denote the QoS properties of $ws_{i,j}$, where $^kV_{i,j}^{ws}$ is the QoS property of $ws_{i,j}$ in terms quality attribute q_k. $^kV_{i,j}^{ws}$ is a function of $I_{i,j}^{ws}$, $E_{i,j}^{ws}$, and $X_{i,j}^{ws}$, i.e., $^kV_{i,j}^{ws}$ can be expressed as $^kV_{i,j}^{ws}(I_{i,j}^{ws}, E_{i,j}^{ws}, X_{i,j}^{ws})$. $^kV_{i,j}^{ws}$ is actually a set of QoS measurement data collected based on various $I_{i,j}^{ws}$, $E_{i,j}^{ws}$, and $X_{i,j}^{ws}$ or a function representing the QoS measurement data. In this chapter, we assume that the measurement data can be fitted to a function.

A configurable parameter is a parameter in a Web service that, when adjusted, can impact the measurements of one or more of the QoS attributes. Different QoS properties of a Web service and the composed system can be obtained by tuning the configurable parameters. For example, the iteration number in a relaxation algorithm can be the control parameter to balance the tradeoffs between execution time and computation precision. The set of configurable parameters $X_{i,j} = (x_{i,j}^1, x_{i,j}^2, ...)$ is the tunable parameters for Web service $ws_{i,j}$ and it includes $\chi_{i,j}$ parameters.

QoS Property Composition

As discussed earlier, how to compose QoS properties of the individual Web services to derive QoS behavior of the composed system is also a necessary entity in QoS-based composition analysis and service configuration decision making. However, the model for QoS property composition depends on the quality attributes and a specific property composition algorithm needs to be defined for each individual quality attribute. The details regarding the QoS property composition algorithms will be discussed in details in the *Genetic Algorithm-Based Decision Support* section.

Resource Specification

Resource allocation can have a significant impact on QoS behavior of the system. QoS properties of each Web service depends on the operation environment $E_{i,j}^{ws}$, which, in turn, depends on the resources allocated to the Web service. In this chapter, the resource allocation problem only considers the allocation of Web services to hardware platforms. Also, heterogeneous platforms are assumed. Multiple platforms may be allocated to a heavily loaded Web service. Let $RS = \{rs_1, rs_2, ..., rs_L\}$ denote the set of L resources (platforms) in the system. The configuration decision maker needs to allocate the L platforms to the M Web services that are selected for the M partners.

Analysis of Adaptive SOA Systems

The major goal for QoS-based composition analysis process is to determine the best composition of Web services, their configurations, and mapping of the services to hardware platforms. A general analysis process is illustrated in Figure 2.

In this QoS-based composition analysis process, the candidate configuration is first determined and then analyzed. After analysis, either some potentially better configurations are further considered or the best candidate configuration is selected. More details of each of the steps is given in the following.

Figure 2. QoS analysis process for adaptive SOA systems

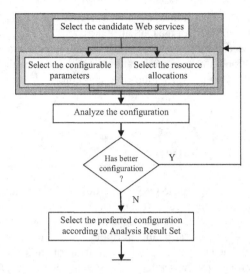

Select the Candidate Web Services

Each partner ω_i may be instantiated by multiple candidate Web services $ws_{i,j}$, $1 \leq j \leq m_i$. In this step, one of the Web services need to be selected for each partner in the system.

Select the Configurable Parameters

Some of the Web services $ws_{i,j}$ may be reconfigurable and has a set of configurable parameters $X_{i,j}^{ws} = (x_{i,j}^{1}, x_{i,j}^{2}, ...)$. Each configurable parameter has a value range. In this step, a specific value in the value range is selected for each configurable parameter.

Select the Resource Allocations

In this step, a specific resource allocation that maps the Web services to the platforms in RS is determined.

Analyze the Configuration

After selecting the specific Web services for each partner, setting each of the configurable parameters, and allocating of the platforms to Web services, the configuration of the system is fixed. Based on the configuration and the component properties of the selected Web services, a QoS property composition algorithm is applied to derive the overall system behavior. The result is then evaluated to determine whether it is satisfatory.

Select the Preferred Configurations

If the QoS behavior of the composed system is not satisfactory, then new configurations are generated and evaluated repeatedly. The process terminates either after a number of iterations or after a satisfactory solution is selected. The final solution is then used for system configuration.

The Composition Analysis Framework

The goal of the composition analysis process is to find Pareto-optimal configurations for the given SOA system specifications. A composition analysis framework has been developed to realize the QoS analysis process. The architecture of the framework is shown in Figure 3. The framework includes a specfication parser, a genetic-algorithm based decision support unit, and various composition analysis algorithms. The specification parser parses

Figure 3. The architecture of the composition analysis framework

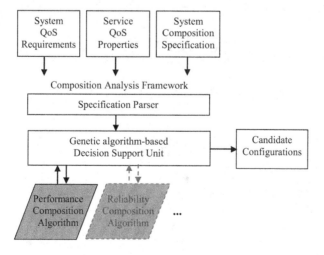

the "system composition specification", "system QoS requirements", and "service QoS properties". The parsed information is integrated and sent to the genetic-algorithm based decision support unit. The genetic-algorithm based decision support unit provides efficient composition decision making.

The genetic algorithm-based decision support unit is responsible for configuration selection, including the steps "select the candidate Web services", "select the configurable parameters", and "select the resource allocations". The selected configurations are passed to the framework. Then the framework invokes the appropriate QoS composition analysis algorithm and pass the selected configuration to it for analysis. The analysis results are then passed back to the decision support unit and the decision support unit either continues to generate new candidate configurations or selects the configuration as the final decision.

QoS composition analysis process may involve the analysis of various QoS attributes, such as performance, reliability, and so forth. Since the analysis of different QoS attributes requires different methods and the QoS analysis algorithms are highly application-dependent, the composition analysis framework provides a registry table to allow users to plug-in application-specific analysis algorithms. The user can register a QoS property composition algorithm to the framework through the publicly exposed interface. Currently, the algorithm for performance analysis of the SOA is available.

Genetic Algorithm-Based Decision Support

We use a genetic algorithm-based process for the decision support unit in the composition analysis framework. The genetic algorithm is responsible for candidate configuration genera-

Figure 4. Genetic algorithm outline

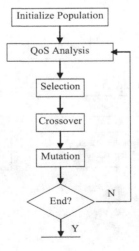

tion and optimal decision making. An outline of the genetic algorithms is shown in Figure 4. It begins with the initialization phase which randomly selects a set of individuals to form the initial population. An individual represents a solution or, for our specific problem, a configuration. A population, in turn, is a group of individuals. Each individual is composed of a sequence of genes. For our problem, the genes can represent a configurable parameter, selection of a Web service for a partner, and a specific allocation of platforms. The initial population is called the first generation. The individuals in the population are evaluated using a fitness function. For example, in the model discussed in the *QoS Specification Model* section, the performance and/or other quality attributes are measured to evaluate the fitness of the configurations. Based on the evaluation results, the generic "selection" operator is used to select the better individuals as parents. From the parents, the "crossover" and "mutation" operators are applied to generate a new generation of population. The process is repeated until a satisfactory set of solutions are obtained.

In the next sub-section, we introduce the background for multi-objective evolutionary algorithms. The mapping of the composition analysis process to the evolutionary algorithm paradigm is discussed in the *Mapping the Composition Analysis Problem to the Genetic Algorithm* sub-section. The detailed algorithms are discussed in the *Genetic Algorithm for Composition Analysis* sub-section.

Multi-Objective Evolutionary Algorithms (MOEA)

The composition analysis process has some difficulties, including the conflicting objectives, the exponential search space, and a mix of continuous and discrete configurable parameters of the Web services. The classical search algorithms, such as linear programming and gradient search, are not efficient for the multi-objective problems (Deb, 1995). Randomized algorithm can be used to deal with the problem such as local minimal trap but it is very inefficient. The genetic algorithm is a partly randomized exploratory procedure based on biological evolution. Specifically, the multi-objective evolutionary algorithms (MOEA) is a specialized genetic algorithm commonly used to find the Pareto-optimal solutions.

The main objective of the MOEAs is to quickly converge to the true Pareto-optimal front with a widely spread solution set. Initial ones, such as MOGA (Fonseca & Fleming, 1993), non-dominated sorting genetic algorithm (NSGA) (Srinivas & Deb, 1994), and niched Pareto genetic algorithm (NPGA) (Hamadi et al., 2003) realize this objective using non-dominated sorting along with a niching mechanism. These algorithms have shown some successes in finding Pareto optimal solutions. In Zitzler, Deb, and Thiele (2000), the elitism concept is introduced and has been shown to have significant impact on performance improvement. Elitism is a strategy to preserve the better solutions for new population generation. Many subsequent algorithms, for example, NSGA-II (Deb, Pratap, Agarwal, & Meyarivan, 2002), Pareto envelope-based selection (PESA) (Corne, Knowles, & Oates, 2000), and strength Pareto evolutionary algorithm 2 (SPEA2) (Zitzler, Laumanns, & Thiele, 2002) apply the elitism strategy and demonstrate substantial performance improvements.

In Deb et al. (2002), an elitism-based algorithm, NSGA-II, along with improvements in diversity preservation and constraint handling, has been proposed. It has been shown that the algorithm outperforms Pareto archived evolution strategy (PAES) and SPEA (Zitzler & Thiele, 1999) in terms of finding a diverse set of solutions and converging toward the true

Pareto-optimal set. Khare, Yao, and Deb (2003) compared the scalability of NSGA-II, PESA, and SPEA2 with respect to the number of objectives (2 to 8). PESA was shown to be the best in terms of converging to the Pareto-optimal front, but it does not have good diversity maintenance. Both SPEA2 and NSGA-II have good performance in terms of convergence and diversity maintenance, but NSGA-II runs much faster than SPEA2. Thus, NSGA-II is chosen to be the algorithm for the composition analysis process, more specifically, to generate and select promising system configurations. Some modifications are made to adapt NSGA-II to the composition analysis problem and to achieve problem-specific improvements.

Mapping the Composition Analysis Problem to the Genetic Algorithm

To map the composition analysis problem to the genetic algorithm flow, it is necessary to first determine the individuals and genes. In the *Genes and Individuals for Configuration Representation* sub-section, the design of individuals and genes for the composition analysis problem is given. To evaluate the individuals, the fitness function should be defined next. The fitness function is discussed in the *QoS Analysis Algorithms* sub-section.

Genes and Individuals for Configuration Representation

QoS-based SOA composition process supports adaptation in terms of resource allocation, Web service selection, and configurable parameter configuration within services. Thus, each individual includes three types of genes: one represents resource allocation, one represents service selection, and one represents configurable parameter setting. Figure 5 illustrates the different types of genes.

One individual includes L genes which comprise the allocation representations for the L resources in RS. Each gene represents the allocation of a resource rs_i, denoted as $A(rs_i)$. $A(rs_i)$ is an integer value from 1 to M. $A(rs_i) = k$ denotes that rs_i is allocated to the Web service instantiating partner ω_k. It is assumed that resources are independent of the Web services

Figure 5. Mapping of the system configurations

$A(rs_1)$	$A(rs_2)$	$\ldots$	$A(rs_L)$	L genes representing resource allocation
$I(\omega_1)$	$I(\omega_2)$	$\ldots$	$I(\omega_M)$	M genes representing service selection
$D(x_{1,1}{}^1)$	$D(x_{1,1}{}^2)$	$\ldots$		
$D(x_{1,2}{}^1)$	$D(x_{1,2}{}^2)$	$\ldots$		$\chi_{1,2}$ genes representing settings of c.p. in $ws_{1,2}$
$D(x_{2,1}{}^1)$	$D(x_{2,1}{}^2)$	$\ldots$		$\chi_{2,1}$ genes representing settings of c.p. in $ws_{2,1}$
$D(x_{M,1}{}^1)$	$D(x_{M,1}{}^2)$	$\ldots$		

and assumed that these resources can be allocated to any Web services, that is, Web services are not resource dependent. Also, it is assumed that each resource can only be allocated to a single Web service. Hence, the number of resource, L, is greater than or equal to the number of partners, M.

For each partner, a gene is used to represent the selection of the instantiating Web service and there are a total of M such genes. Let $I(\omega_i)$ denote the gene for service selection. Since ω_i can be instantiated by Web services $ws_{i,j}$, $1 \le j \le m_i$, $I(\omega_i)$ is the index of the Web service selected for instantiating ω_i and its value range is from 1 to m_i. In other words, if $I(\omega_i) = j$, then $ws_{i,j}$ is selected to realize ω_i.

For the configurable parameters within individual services, each gene, denoted as $D(x_{i,j}{}^k)$, represents a setting of the corresponding configurable parameter $x_{i,j}{}^k$, where $x_{i,j}{}^k$ is a tunable parameter in Web service $ws_{i,j}$. For $ws_{i,j}$, there are $\chi_{i,j}$ configurable parameters. Thus, there are a total of $\sum_{i,j} \chi_{i,j}$ genes representing configurable parameter settings. Each $D(x_{i,j}{}^k)$ has its own data type and value range. The data type and value range definitions for $x_{i,j}{}^k$ are defined in the Web service QoS property specification and can be retrieved to define $D(x_{i,j}{}^k)$.

QoS Analysis Algorithms

The individuals in a population are evaluated using the fitness functions. The fitness functions are defined and realized by QoS analysis algorithms. Essentially, each individual represents a specific configuration of the system (selection and configuration of the Web services and resource allocation for them). Based on the configuration, the overall system properties, such as performance, reliability, and so forth, are determined. In this chapter, we use performance metric as an example to illustrate the QoS Analysis. The performance analysis for the SOA systems is discussed later in the *Performance Analysis* section.

Genetic Algorithm for Composition Analysis

In this section, we discuss the detailed algorithms in the GA paradigm. The overall genetic algorithm is discussed in the *NSGAII-CAA* sub-section. The GA operations, including selection, crossover, and mutation, are discussed in *Selection Operator*, *Mutation Operator*, and *Crossover Operator* sub-sections, respectively.

NSGAII-CAA

The algorithm NSGAII-CAA (non-dominated sorting genetic algorithm II – composition analysis algorithm) is a modified version of NSGA-II. It is specifically adapted for the composition analysis process with some performance improvement features. The algorithm is shown in the following.

Algorithm NSGAII-CAA

Input: N_s: population and initial elite set size
            D: generation number
Output: Pr: result non-dominated set

1   Initialize population P_0
2   QoS analysis on P_0
3   Create empty elite set P_0'
4   $d := 0$
5   while $(d < D)$ do
6   generate a new elite set $P_{d+1}' :=$ NSGAII-crowding-pick (P_d, P_d', N_s)
7   generate the new population $P_{d+1} :=$ Mutation(Recombination(BTS(N_s, P_{d+1}')))
8   QoS analysis on P_{d+1}
9       $d := d + 1$
10 end while
11 $Pr :=$ non-dominated-set (P_d')

The algorithm follows closely the general genetic algorithm flow. In the following sub-sections, the major steps specifically designed for the composition analysis process are discussed.

Selection Operator

For selecting promising configurations in a population, a comparision standard has to be provided. NSGA-II uses the crowding pick approach (NSGAII-crowding-pick). First, each individual is assigned a priority using non-dominated sort. Then, the individuals are further sorted using the crowding distance sort. Non-dominated sort first identifies the non-dominated solutions and gives them the highest priority and, after priority assignment, moves them out of the set. Then the non-dominated solutions of the remaining individuals are identified and given the second highest priority. This process continues until priorities are assigned to all the individuals. Based on each objective, the crowding distance computation first sorts the individuals with the same priority according to their values. The distances are normalized cross objectives by equalizing the maximum distances (between the highest and lowest values) of the objectives and proportionately adjusting the distances of all pairs of adjacent individuals. For each individual, the distances for all the objectives are summed together. The individual with a larger distance value gets a higher priority.

Based on the priorities, the best individuals can be picked to form the elite set, which stores a fixed number of best individuals ever generated and serves as the mating pool for next generation. Initially, the elite set is empty. For every generation, the population and the elite set from the previous generation are merged into one set. N_s individuals with the highest priorities are picked from the set to form the new elite set, where N_s is the population size. For a J-objective problem with population size N_s, NSGA-II has a storage requirement of $O(N_s^2)$ and time complexity of $O(J N_s^2)$.

The NSGAII-CAA algorithm uses a binary tournament selection (BTS) algorithm to select N_s individuals from the elite set to generate a new set, from which the new generation can be produced by recombination and mutation. Each time two individuals are randomly picked from the elite set and one individual with the higher priority is selected. It continues till N_s individuals are selected. The complete BTS algorithm is shown as follows.

Algorithm BTS

Input: N_s: population size
                P: elite set
Output: P': result new population

```
1   i := 0
2   while (i < Ns) do
3        randomly pick up two configurations s1, s2 from P
4        if s1 has higher priority
5              put s1 in P'
6        else
7              put s2 in P'
8        i := i + 1
9   end while
```

Mutation Operator

In a mutation process, a new individual is generated from a randomly picked configuration by slightly modifying it. The probability of mutation of one individual is controlled by a mutation rate, which is normally set as $1/N_s$ where N_s is the population size. In the case study to be discussed later, the mutation rate is set as 0.01. For the individual to be mutated, the mutation point is chosen randomly and the gene of the mutation point is modified. For our specific problem, a random value in a pre-determined range of the chosen gene is used to replace the existing value. Each configurable parameter should have a fixed range so that a random value can be selected for the corresponding gene.

Crossover Operator

While mutation generates a new individual from one parent, crossover process exchanges the genes of one or more parents to reproduce new individuals. We use one-point recombination due to its effectiveness and simplicity. Similar to the mutation process, the crossover point for recombination of two individuals is generated randomly. The one-point recombination process exchanges the genes of two parents on and after the crossover point to reproduce two offsprings.

Performance Analysis

We use the Markov chain model to assess the performance for the SOA-based system (Bose, 2001). The SOA-based system consists of multiple Web services that may invoke one another (assume that there is no cyclic invocation). So the system is modeled as a multi-tier client-server system, which include multiple levels of client-server subsystems. In the following sub-sections, we first review the Markov model for performance analysis in the *Markov Model for Performance Analysis* sub-section. Then, in the *Performance Analysis for SOA Systems* sub-section, the method used for performance analysis for SOA system is introduced. Finally, in *A Performance Analysis Example* sub-section, an example is given to illustrate the performance analysis method.

Markov Model for Performance Analysis

Consider a simple client-server system. Let q denote the server queue. Assume that the server has service time t_s and request arrival rate λ. Also, let n denote the average population at the server. From the Markov model, we have (Bose, 2001):

Utilization: $\rho = \lambda \cdot t_s$,

Average response time: $t = \dfrac{t_s}{(1-\rho)}$,   (1)

Average population: $n = \dfrac{\rho}{(1-\rho)}$.

If the load on the server is very high, the server may become a bottleneck. To deal with this problem, a server may be replicated, that is, multiple resources are allocated to that server. In this case, we use the *M/M/m* queuing model to compute the system performance, which has the following performance characteristics (Bose, 2001).

Utilization: $\rho' = \dfrac{\lambda \cdot t_s}{m}$,

Average response time: $t' = t_s + \dfrac{P_Q}{(m/t_s - \lambda)}$,   (2)

where P_Q denotes the probability that all m servers are busy and $p(0)$ denotes the probability that the queue length is 0. We have

$$P_Q = \left(m \cdot \rho'\right)^m \frac{p(0)}{m!} \cdot \frac{1}{1-\rho'},$$

$$p(0) = \left[\frac{\left(m \cdot \rho'\right)^m}{m! \cdot (1-\rho')} + \left(\sum_{i=0}^{m-1} \frac{\left(m \cdot \rho'\right)^i}{i!} \right) \right]^{-1}$$

Average population: $n' = P_Q \cdot \dfrac{\rho'}{(1-\rho')}$

Performance Analysis for SOA Systems

In the *Markov Model for Performance Analysis* sub-section, it is assumed that the arrival rates for the input ports of each Web service are known. When one Web service uses services provided by other Web services, it forms the client-server relationship. A Web service $ws_{1,1}$, for some requests, may invoke another Web service $ws_{2,1}$, but for some other requests, may invoke Web service $ws_{3,1}$, and for yet some other requests, may simply serve them locally. Also, a request may be propagated through several layers of service invocation. Thus, each request has a service path. To facilitate performance analysis, it is necessary to compute the effective arrival rate for each Web service in the system, and the computation is based on the invocation paths and the arrival rates from the real clients.

The SOA composition specification specifies the service architecture, including the partners and the links. The QoS specification for the individual services includes several essential parts: (1) for each partner, the arrival rates for its input ports should be specified if it takes input from real clients; (2) for each partner, the distribution of client requests that are forwarded to each of the output ports should also be specified; and (3) for each Web service, the service rate should be specified.

We assume that the client arrival rates follows a Poisson distribution. Also, we assume that the service rate of each Web service has an exponential distribution or is constant. In addition, assume that the arrival rate λ_i for partner ω_i is less than the service rate $1/t_{i,j}$ of the Web service $ws_{i,j}$ which instantiates ω_i. Thus, the output from each partner follows a Poisson distribution with rate λ_i. We also assume that if ω_i, after processing the requests, forwards the requests to other partners, then the probability for the requests going to different partners follows a uniform random distribution. Consider the case that partner ω_i has a request arrival rate λ_i and the probability that ω_i forwards a request to ω_j is $p_{i,j}$. Then, the effective arrival rate for partner ω_j has a Possion distribution with average arrival rate $\lambda_i * p_{i,j}$. From the effective arrival rate, the response time for each Web service can be computed based on the Markov model discussed in the *Markov Model for Performance Analysis* sub-section.

To compute the response time of client requests in terms of the overall system, we need to consider the individual paths of the requests flowing through the service hierarchy. First, according to the effective arrival rate, the response time for each service can be computed. For each path, the response time of the requests can be computed by adding together the response times of the multiple tiers that a request has to go through. The average response time of the overall system is the expected value of the response times of all the paths in the service architecture. The algorithm of computing the average response time is shown in the following.

Algorithm computeTotalAverageResponseTime

Input: λ : Initial arrival rate of the system
Output: T : TotoalAverageResponseTime

1   Find the starting web service $ws_{i,j}$ of the system
2   recursivePerformanceAnalysis ($ws_{i,j}$, λ)

Algorithm recursivePerformanceAnalysis

$N_{i,j}$: The number of the partners which Web Service $ws_{i,j}$ sends request to
    The requests sent by $ws_{i,j}$ are indexed into 0 to $N_{i,j}-1$

Input: $ws_{i,j}$: Web Service to be processed
            λ_i : The effective arrival rate of $ws_{i,j}$
Output: t : The response time of $ws_{i,j}$

1   if (Web Service $ws_{i,j}$ is empty)
2   return
3   if (Web Service $ws_{i,j}$ isn't replicated)
4   Compute the response time $t_{i,j}$ of $ws_{i,j}$ using $M/M/1$ formula (1)
5   else
6   Compute the response time $t_{i,j}$ of $ws_{i,j}$ using $M/M/m$ formula (2)
7   $T += (\lambda_i / \lambda) * t$
8   $j := 0$
9   while ($j < N_{i,j}$)
10   Find the Web Service $ws_{j,k}$ which the request j goes
11   Compute the effective arrival rate λ_j of $ws_{j,k}$
12   recursivePerformanceAnalysis($ws_{j,k}$, λ_j)
13 endwhile

In the SOA based system, the link delay also affects the performance of the system. A link can be viewed as a network service unit. In the QoS property specifications of the individual services, the link delay can be specified either as a fixed latency or a specific distribution.

A Performance Analysis Example

Here, an example is given to illustrate the performance analysis algorithm.

The example system is shown in Figure 6. The performance analysis is based on a given system configuration, thus, each partner in the system has been instantiated by certain Web service which is specified in Figure 6, such as ω_1 is instantiated by $ws_{1,1}$. The specification for each Web service, partner, and link are also given in Figure 6. For example, the arrival rate λ of partner ω_1 is $0.01/ms$ and the service time $t_{1,1}$ for Web service $ws_{1,1}$ (instantiates ω_1) is 50 ms. Also, from Figure 6, we can see that the service flow is initiated at ω_1. Requests from partner ω_1 are forwarded to different partners, where 70% are forwarded to partner ω_3 and 30% to ω_2. After receiving the responses from partner ω_2 and ω_3, partner ω_1 sends the requests to partner ω_9 .The possible paths for the requests include ω_1-ω_2-ω_5-ω_9-ω_{10}-ω_{11}, ω_1-ω_2-ω_6-ω_8-ω_9-ω_{10}-ω_{11}, etc. Here, we assume that the transmission time of the requests and responses between any two partners is a constant value, namely, 20 ms.

First, we compute the response time for path ω_1-ω_3-ω_7-ω_4. From the properties of partner ω_1 and partner ω_3 in Figure 6, the effective arrival rate of partner ω_3 from partner ω_1 can be computed as $0.7*\lambda$. The requests are processed by Web service $ws_{3,4}$ (instantiates ω_3) with the service time $t_{3,4} = 80$ ms. Then requests from partner ω_3 are forwarded to partner ω_7 and gets processed by Web service $ws_{7,1}$ (instantiates ω_7). Because the requests from partner ω_3 are all forwarded to partner ω_7, the effective arrival rate is the same as partner ω_3, namely,

Figure 6. An example system for performance analysis

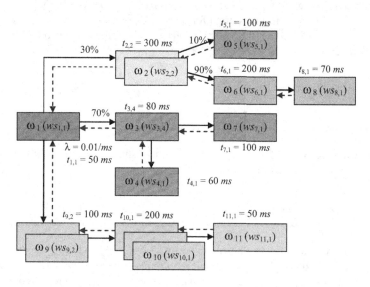

0.7*λ. After receiving the responses from partner ω_7, partner ω_3 sends the requests to partner ω_4. Similarly, the effective arrival rate of partner ω_4 is 0.7*λ. Based on the effective arrival rate, the response time of Web service $ws_{3,4}$ is computed as 182 *ms*. Similarly, the response times of Web service $ws_{7,1}$ and $ws_{4,1}$ are 333 *ms* and 103 *ms*, respectively.

Then look at path ω_1-ω_2-ω_5 and ω_1-ω_2-ω_6-ω_8. As can be seen, Web service $ws_{2,2}$ (instantiates ω_2) is replicated. It has an arrival rate 0.3*λ and the service time $t_{3,2}$ for Web service $ws_{2,2}$ is 300 *ms*. Since Web service $ws_{2,2}$ is replicated by 2, we compute the response time of Web service $ws_{2,2}$ using *M/M/m* (here *m* = 2) queuing model. Then, 10% of the requests from partner ω_2 are forwarded to partner ω_5 and 90% to partner ω_6. So the effective arrival rates of partners ω_5 and ω_6 are 0.1*0.3*λ and 0.9*0.3*λ. The requests forwarded to partner ω_6 are processed further by Web service $ws_{8,1}$ (instantiates ω_8). Thus, the response times of all Web services ($ws_{2,2}$, $ws_{5,1}$, $ws_{6,1}$, $ws_{8,1}$) are computed and they are 423 *ms*, 103 *ms*, 435 *ms*, and 86 *ms* respectively.

After receiving the responses from partner ω_2 or partner ω_3, partner ω_1 sends the requests to partner ω_9. Since partner ω_1 receives all the responses from partner ω_2 and partner ω_3 and all the responses follow Poisson distribution, the effective arrival rate of the responses for partner ω_1 is λ. The requests from partner ω_1 get processed by Web service $ws_{9,2}$ (instantiates ω_9). We compute the response time of Web service $ws_{9,2}$ using *M/M/m* (here *m* = 2) queuing model due to the replication of Web service $ws_{9,2}$ by 2. Then requests from partner ω_9 are forwarded to partner ω_{10} and gets processed by Web service $ws_{10,1}$ (instantiates ω_{10}). Web service $ws_{10,1}$ is replicated by 3, so the response time of Web service $ws_{10,1}$ is computed using *M/M/m* (here *m* = 3) queuing model. Finally the requests are forwarded to partner ω_{11} and are processed by Web service $ws_{11,1}$ (instantiates ω_{11}). Thus, the response times of all Web services ($ws_{9,2}$, $ws_{10,1}$, $ws_{11,1}$) are computed and they are 150 *ms*, 333 *ms*, 100 *ms*, respectively.

Note that the possible paths for the requests include ω_1-ω_2-ω_5-ω_9-ω_{10}-ω_{11}, ω_1-ω_2-ω_6-ω_8-ω_9-ω_{10}-ω_{11}, ω_1-ω_3-ω_7-ω_4-ω_9-ω_{10}-ω_{11}. The average response time for path ω_1-ω_2-ω_5-ω_9-ω_{10}-ω_{11} is computed as $100+423+103+150+333+100+10*20 = 1509\,ms$. Similarly, the average response time for path ω_1-ω_2-ω_6-ω_8-ω_9-ω_{10}-ω_{11} is computed as $100+423+435+86+150+333+100+12*20$ $= 1867ms$ and the average response time for path ω_1-ω_3-ω_7-ω_4-ω_9-ω_{10}-ω_{11} is computed as $100+182+333+103+150+333+100+12*20 = 1541\,ms$. Thus, the average response time of the overall system is $0.3*0.1*1509 + 0.3*0.9*1867 + 0.7*1541 = 1625\,ms$.

Case Study

We use the example system shown in Figure 6 as a case study to illustrate the composition analysis approach. Let S denote the example system.

System QoS Specification

In the example system S, the QoS attribute vector $Q_S = (q_1, q_2)$, where q_1 represents time and q_2 represents accuracy. The system QoS requirements include the objectives $O = (o_1, o_2)$ and $R = \phi$, where o_1 is "*minimize* (q_1)" and o_2 is "*maximize* (q_2)". Here, q_1 represents response time. For composition specification, we have $\Omega_S = \{\omega_i \mid 1 \le i \le 11\}$. The set of Web services for each partner is shown in Table 1. For example, Web service $ws_{1,1}$ is associated with partner ω_1, Web services $ws_{2,1}$, $ws_{2,2}$ are associated with partner ω_2, Web services $ws_{3,1}$, $ws_{3,2}$, $ws_{3,3}$, $ws_{3,4}$ are associated with partner ω_3, and so forth.

For simplicity, we do not consider the execution environment $E_{i,j}^{ws}$ for Web services $ws_{i,j}$ and the input parameter set $I_{i,j}^{ws}$, for all i,j, in the example system S. The configurable parameter set $X_{i,j}^{ws}$ of each involved Web services $ws_{i,j}$ are specified in Table 2. For example, Web service $ws_{1,1}$ has two configurable parameters $x_{1,1}^1, x_{1,1}^2$, Web service $ws_{2,1}$ has one configurable parameter $x_{2,1}^1$, Web service $ws_{3,2}$ doesn't have configurable parameters, and so forth.

The QoS property functions of the Web services are shown in Table 3. Since we have quality attributes q_1 and q_2, correspondingly, we have QoS property functions ${}^1V_{i,j}^{ws}$ and ${}^2V_{i,j}^{ws}$, where ${}^1V_{i,j}^{ws}$ represents the time property function and ${}^2V_{i,j}^{ws}$ represents the accuracy property function. Note that ${}^1V_{i,j}^{ws}$ and ${}^2V_{i,j}^{ws}$ are functions of the configurable parameters $X_{i,j}^{ws}$ (it is assumed that the impacts of $I_{i,j}^{ws}$ and $E_{i,j}^{ws}$ are not considered). Since the service time of the Web services follows the exponential distribution, we have

$$ {}^1V_{i,j}^{ws}\left(t, X_{i,j}^{ws}\right) = 1 - \frac{1}{\mu_{i,j}\left(X_{i,j}^{ws}\right)} \times e^{-\frac{1}{\mu_{i,j}\left(X_{i,j}^{ws}\right)} \times t} $$

Note that $\mu_{i,j}(X_{i,j}^{ws})$ denotes the service rate of $ws_{i,j}$,

$$ \mu_{i,j}\left(X_{i,j}^{ws}\right) = \frac{1}{t_{i,j}\left(\mu_{i,j}\left(X_{i,j}^{ws}\right)\right)}, $$

Table 1. Partners and associated Web services

Partner	Web Service	Partner	Web Service	Partner	Web Service
ω_1	$ws_{1,1}$	ω_5	$ws_{5,1}$, $ws_{5,2}$, $ws_{5,3}$	ω_9	$ws_{9,1}$, $ws_{9,2}$
ω_2	$ws_{2,1}$, $ws_{2,2}$	ω_6	$ws_{6,1}$	ω_{10}	$ws_{10,1}$, $ws_{10,2}$
ω_3	$ws_{3,1}$, $ws_{3,2}$, $ws_{3,3}$, $ws_{3,4}$	ω_7	$ws_{7,1}$, $ws_{7,2}$	ω_{11}	$ws_{11,1}$
ω_4	$ws_{4,1}$	ω_8	$ws_{8,1}$		

Table 2. The configurable parameter set of individual Web service specification

Partner	Web Service	Configurable Parameter Set	Partner	Web Service	Configurable Parameter Set
ω_1	$ws_{1,1}$	$X_{1,1}^{ws} = (x_{1,1}^1, x_{1,1}^2)$	ω_6	$ws_{6,1}$	$X_{6,1}^{ws} = \phi$
ω_2	$ws_{2,1}$	$X_{2,1}^{ws} = (x_{2,1}^1)$	ω_7	$ws_{7,1}$	$X_{7,1}^{ws} = \phi$
	$ws_{2,2}$	$X_{2,2}^{ws} = (x_{2,2}^1)$		$ws_{7,2}$	$X_{7,2}^{ws} = (x_{7,1}^1, x_{7,2}^2)$
ω_3	$ws_{3,1}$	$X_{3,1}^{ws} = (x_{3,1}^1)$	ω_8	$ws_{8,1}$	$X_{8,1}^{ws} = \phi$
	$ws_{3,2}$	$X_{3,2}^{ws} = \phi$	ω_9	$ws_{9,1}$	$X_{9,1}^{ws} = \phi$
	$ws_{3,3}$	$X_{3,3}^{ws} = \phi$		$ws_{9,2}$	$X_{9,2}^{ws} = (x_{9,2}^1)$
	$ws_{3,4}$	$X_{3,4}^{ws} = (x_{3,4}^1, x_{3,4}^2, x_{3,4}^3)$	ω_{10}	$ws_{10,1}$	$X_{10,1}^{ws} = (x_{10,1}^1, x_{10,1}^2)$
ω_4	$ws_{4,1}$	$X_{4,1}^{ws} = \phi$		$ws_{10,2}$	$X_{10,2}^{ws} = \phi$
ω_5	$ws_{5,1}$	$X_{5,1}^{ws} = (x_{5,1}^1)$			
	$ws_{5,2}$	$X_{5,2}^{ws} = \phi$	ω_{11}	$ws_{11,1}$	$X_{11,1}^{ws} = \phi$
	$ws_{5,3}$	$X_{5,3}^{ws} = (x_{5,3}^1, x_{5,3}^2)$			

and here we assume that the configurable parameters in $X_{i,j}^{ws}$ impacts the average service rate. In Table 3, $\mu_{i,j}(X_{i,j}^{ws})$ for each Web service $ws_{i,j}$ is given. Property functions $^2V_{i,j}^{ws}$ for all Web services $ws_{i,j}$ are also given in Table 3. It is also a function of the configurable parameters in $X_{i,j}^{ws}$. Here, the value range of the configurable parameters in $X_{i,j}^{ws}$ is 0 to 10.

Consider the Web services $ws_{2,1}$ as an example. The property functions of $ws_{2,1}$ are

$$^1V_{2,1}^{ws}(t) = 1 - \left(\frac{1}{\left(2*x_{2,1}^1 + 280\right)} \times e^{-\left(\frac{1}{\left(2*x_{2,1}^1 + 280\right)}\right) \times t} \right)$$

and

Table 3. QoS properties of individual Web service specification

Partner	Web Service	$\mu_{i,j}(X_{i,j}^{ws})$	$^2V_{i,j}^{ws}$
ω_1	$ws_{1,1}$	$0.5*x_{1,1}^1 + 3*x_{1,1}^2 + 10$	$0.63*(x_{1,1}^2)^{0.2}$
ω_2	$ws_{2,1}$	$2*x_{2,1}^1 + 280$	$0.31*(x_{2,1}^1)^{0.5}$
	$ws_{2,2}$	$5*x_{2,2}^1 + 250$	$0.63*(x_{2,2}^2)^{0.2}$
ω_3	$ws_{3,1}$	$3*x_{3,1}^1 + 50$	$0.31*(x_{3,1}^1)^{0.5}$
	$ws_{3,2}$	130	0.98
	$ws_{3,3}$	200	0.96
	$ws_{3,4}$	$3*x_{3,4}^1 + x_{3,4}^2 + 2*x_{3,4}^3 + 20$	$0.39*(x_{3,4}^1)^{0.4}$
ω_4	$ws_{4,1}$	60	0.92
ω_5	$ws_{5,1}$	$3*x_{5,1}^1 + 70$	$0.31*(x_{5,1}^1)^{0.5}$
	$ws_{5,2}$	90	0.99
	$ws_{5,3}$	$x_{5,3}^1 + x_{5,3}^2 + 80$	$0.63*(x_{5,3}^2)^{0.2}$
ω_6	$ws_{6,1}$	200	0.96
ω_7	$ws_{7,1}$	100	0.98
	$ws_{7,2}$	$3*x_{7,2}^1 + x_{7,2}^2 + 60$	$0.39*(x_{7,2}^1)^{0.4}$
ω_8	$ws_{8,1}$	70	0.92
ω_9	$ws_{9,1}$	120	0.94
	$ws_{9,2}$	$2*x_{9,2}^1 + 80$	$0.5*(x_{9,2}^1)^{0.3}$
ω_{10}	$ws_{10,1}$	$2*x_{10,1}^1 + x_{10,1}^2 + 160$	$0.63*(x_{10,1}^2)^{0.2}$
	$ws_{10,2}$	170	0.93
ω_{11}	$ws_{11,1}$	50	0.97

$$^2V_{2,1}^{ws}(t) = 0.31*(x_{2,1}^2)^{0.5}.$$

The resources in the example system S is $RS = \{rs_1, rs_2, ..., rs_{15}\}$, including 15 platforms. We assume that all the platforms have the same computation power.

Configuration and Gene Mapping

We map the specification for S given in the *System QoS Specification* sub-section to the genetic algorithm paradigm. An example individual for S is given in Figure 7. The genes for selection of Web services are given in the second line. For example, $I(\omega_1) = 1$ represents that $ws_{1,1}$ instantiates ω_1. The genes for resource allocation are given in the first line. We can see

Figure 7. Mapping of the system configurations

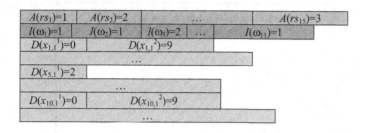

that, for example, rs_1 hosts Web service $ws_{1,1}$ since $A(rs_1) = 1$ and $I(\omega_1) = 1$. The remaining genes are for the configurable parameter settings, one line per partner (actually, the Web service that instantiates the partner). For example, $x_{1,1}^2 = 9$, it means the first configurable parameter $x_{1,1}^2$ of the Web service $ws_{1,1}$ is set to 9.

Some other parameters for the genetic algorithm are as follows. The population size N_s and elite set size P are set to 100. The number of generations D is set to 60. These settings are determined based on the convergence speed and output quality we observed.

Performance Analysis

Each system configuration is analyzed by the performance composition algorithm. For the system configuration shown in Figure 7, the service time and accuracy of each Web service, which instantiates the corresponding partner in the example system, are computed according to the configuration mapping and QoS properties of individual Web service specification shown in Table 3. For example, Web service $ws_{1,1}$ is selected to instantiate partner ω_1. The service time and accuracy of $ws_{1,1}$ are $0.5*0 + 3*9 + 10 = 37$ *ms* and $0.63*(9)^{0.2} = 0.98$, here $x_{1,1}^1 = 0$, $x_{1,1}^2 = 9$. Similarly, Web service $ws_{11,1}$ is selected to instantiate partner ω_{11}. Since Web service $ws_{11,1}$ doesn't have configurable parameters, the service time and accuracy of $ws_{11,1}$ are fixed, namely, 50 *ms* and 0.97, respectively. The average response time of this example system with the given configuration is then computed according to the algorithm "computeTotalAverageResponseTime" presented in the *Performance Analysis for SOA Systems* sub-section and the result is 1412 *ms*. To compute the accuracy of client requests in terms of the overall system, we consider the individual paths of the requests flowing through the service hierarchy. For each path, the accuracy of the requests can be computed by multiplying together the accuracy of the multiple tiers that a request has to go through. The accuracy of the overall system is the summation of the accuracy of all the paths in the service architecture. The accuracy of the example system with the given configuration is 0.12.

Figure 8. The relationship between accuracy and response time

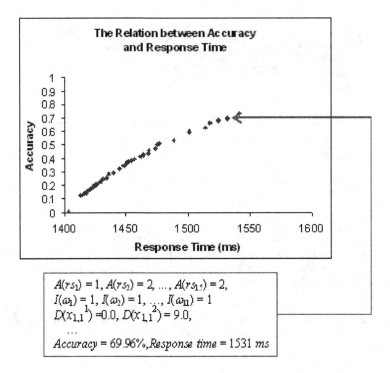

$A(rs_1) = 1, A(rs_2) = 2, ..., A(rs_{15}) = 2,$
$I(a_1) = 1, I(a_2) = 1, ..., I(a_{11}) = 1$
$D(x_{1,1}^{1}) = 0.0, D(x_{1,1}^{2}) = 9.0,$
...
Accuracy = 69.96%, Response time = 1531 ms

Analysis Results

For the example system, we consider the tradeoffs of the two QoS objectives—response time and accuracy. Figure 8 shows the Pareto front for the two objectives. There are many possible configurations to meet the functional and QoS requirements of the system S and the Pareto front are the configurations that are better than the eliminated solutions in at least one of the objectives. As we can see, in order to obtain higher accuracy, we need longer execution time. Each point in Figure 8 corresponds to a configuration. For example, the configuration corresponding to the point pointed by the arrow in Figure 8 is given in the corresponding box. In this configuration, the configurable parameters for the Web service $ws_{1,1}$ are set to: $x_{1,1}^{1} = 0.0, x_{1,2}^{2} = 9.0$, etc. The *average response time* of the system S is 1531 millisecond and *accuracy* of the system S is 69.96%.

Based on the analysis results, the system can be adapted statically and/or dynamically according to the modified QoS requirements. When the execution environment or operation condition changes, the system simply searches for the configuration(s) that satisfy the new requirements and constraints. From the case study, we can see that the framework can be used to effectively analyze QoS tradeoffs. The GA algorithm generally converges very fast and, hence, can be used for efficient adaptation decision making.

Conclusion

In this chapter, we have presented the QoS analysis process to facilitate dynamic reconfiguration in SOA-based systems. We consider the selections and configurations of Web services to compose a system. We also consider the resource allocation for Web services. The goal is to find the best configurations that satisfy the changing QoS requirements. A case study is used to validate the feasibility of our QoS-based composition analysis techniques and tools.

There are many research directions that can be explored further. The most important direction is to further develop techniques and tools for general QoS behavior analysis. For example, reliability, availability, and so forth, are also important QoS attributes. Currently, we are developing compositional analysis techniques to compute system reliability based on the reliability of individual services. Other QoS attributes will also be considered. Though some quality attributes are very difficult to assess and/or to compose, we plan to investigate these attributes and develop some common mechanisms for thorough analysis.

Dynamic reconfiguration requires the analysis process to be performed in real time so that the adaptation can be completed in a timely way. For the case study discussed in this chapter, the configuration analysis takes close to one second. For large-scale systems, the analysis process may take longer. Thus, it is necessary to investigate mechanisms for achieving real-time performance. For example, special composition analysis service sites can be offered and analysis can be done off-line and results can be provided efficiently to the clients.

We also plan to extend the toolset and develop a complete suite of tools to facilitate QoS analysis of SOA-based systems. We will consider more complicated service architectures and various composition mechanisms. Also, analysis algorithms for various QoS attributes will be incorporated.

References

Aksit, M., & Choukair, Z. (2003). Dynamic, adaptive and reconfigurable systems overview and prospective vision. In the *Proceedings of the 23rd International Conference on Distributed Computing Systems Workshop*, Providence, Rhode Island, USA, May 19-22 (pp. 84-89). Los Alamitos, CA: IEEE Computer Society.

BEA Systems, IBM, Microsoft, SAP AG, & Siebel Systems. (2002). *Business process execution language for Web services*. Retrieved May 2005, from http://www-128.ibm.com/developerworks/library/specification/ws-bpel/

Bose, S. K. (2001). *An introduction to queueing systems*. New York: Kluwer/Plenum Publishers.

Corne, D. W., Knowles, J. D., & Oates, M. J. (2000). The pareto envelop-based selection algorithm for multiobjective optimization. In M. Schoenauer et al. (Eds.), *Parallel problem solving from nature – PPSN VI* (pp. 839-848). Berlin: Springer.

Deb, K. (1995). *Optimization for engineering design: Algorithms and examples*. New Delhi: Prentice-Hall.

Deb, K., Pratap, A., Agarwal, S., & Meyarivan, T. (2002). A fast and elitist multiobjective genetic algorithm: NSGA-II. *IEEE Transactions on Evolutionary Computation, 6*(2), 182-197.

Fonseca, C. M., & Fleming, P. J. (1993). Genetic algorithms for multiobjective optimization: Formulation, discussion and generalization. In S. Forrest (Ed.), *Proceedings of the Fifth International Conference on Genetic Algorithms,* UIUC, July 17-22 (pp 416-423). San Mateo, CA: Morgan Kaufmann.

Hamadi, R., & Benatallah, B. (2003). A petri-net-based model for Web service composition. In K.-D. Schewe, & X. Zhou (Eds.), *Proceedings of the Fourteenth Australasian Database Conference on Database Technologies*, Adelaide, Australia, February 4-7 (pp. 191-200). Australia: Australian Computer Society Inc.

Khare, V., Yao, X., & Deb, K. (2003). Performance scaling of multi-objective evolutionary algorithms. In M. Carlos Fonseca, P. J. Fleming, E. Zitzler, K. Deb, & L. Thiele (Eds.), *Proceedings of the 2nd International Conference on Evolutionary Multi-Criterion Optimization (EMO '03)*, Faro, Portugal, April 8-11 (pp. 376-390). Portugal: Springer.

Sirin, E., Parsia, B., & Hendler, J. (2004). Filtering and selecting semantic Web services with interactive composition techniques. *IEEE Intelligent Systems, 19*(4), 42-49.

Srinivas, N., & Deb, K. (1994). Multiobjective optimization using nondominated sorting in genetic algorithms. *Evolutionary Computation, 2*(3), 221-248.

Tsai, W. T., Song, W., Paul, R., Cao, Z., & Huang, H. (2004). Services-oriented dynamic reconfiguration framework for dependable distributed computing. In the *Proceedings of the 28th Annual International Computer Software and Applications Conference*, Hong Kong, China, September 28-30 (pp. 554-559). Los Alamitos, CA: IEEE Computer Society.

W3C (2002). Web services. Retrieved May 2005, from http://www.w3.org/2002/ws/

W3C (2004a). OWL. Retrieved May 2005, from http://www.w3.org/TR/2004/REC-owl-features-20040210/

W3C (2004b). OWL-S. Retrieved May 2005, from http://www.w3.org/Submission/OWL-S/

Zitzler, E., Deb, K., & Thiele, L. (2000). Comparison of multiobjective evolutionary algorithms: Empirical results. *Evolutionary Computation, 8*(2), 173-195.

Zitzler, E., Laumanns, M., & Thiele, L. (2002). SPEA2: Improving the strength pareto evolutionary algorithm for multiobjective optimization. In K. C. Giannakoglou et al. (Eds.), *Proceedings of the EUROGEN2001 Conference: Evolutionary methods for design, optimization and control with application to industrial problems*, Athens, Greece, September 19-21 (pp. 95-100). Barcelona, Spain: International Center for Numerical Methos in Engineering (CIMNE).

Zitzler, E., & Thiele, L. (1999). Multiobjective evolutionary algorithms: A comparative case study and the strength pareto approach. *IEEE Transactions on Evolutionary Computation, 3*(4), 257-271.

Section III:

Predictive Models for Software Quality and Relevancy

This part contains four chapters (Chapters VII-X) that describe the use of machine learning methods to learn predictive models for software quality and relevancy. Chapter VII deals with the issue of software quality models. The authors propose an approach to define logic-driven models based on fuzzy multiplexers for software quality prediction. Genetic algorithms and genetic optimization underpin the design of the logic models. Chapter VIII introduces a concept called relevance relation among software entities and develops a process to learn the relevance relations through decision trees. The availability of relevance relations makes it possible to predict whether a change to one software entity (one file) results in a change in another entity (file). Chapter IX presents a novel software quality classification model that is based on genetic programming. The proposed model provides not only a classification but also a quality-based ranking for software modules. Finally, Chapter X describes a software quality prediction model that is used to predict fault prone modules. The model is based on an ensemble of trees voting on prediction decisions to improve its classification accuracy.

Chapter VII

Fuzzy Logic Classifiers and Models in Quantitative Software Engineering

Witold Pedrycz, University of Alberta, Canada

Giancarlo Succi, Free University of Bolzano, Italy

Abstract

The learning abilities and high transparency are the two important and highly desirable features of any model of software quality. The transparency and user-centricity of quantitative models of software engineering are of paramount relevancy as they help us gain a better and more comprehensive insight into the revealed relationships characteristic to software quality and software processes. In this study, we are concerned with logic-driven architectures of logic models based on fuzzy multiplexers (fMUXs). Those constructs exhibit a clear and modular topology whose interpretation gives rise to a collection of straightforward logic expressions. The design of the logic models is based on the genetic optimization and genetic algorithms, in particular. Through the prudent usage of this optimization framework, we address the issues of structural and parametric optimization of the logic models. Experimental studies exploit software data that relates software metrics (measures) to the number of modifications made to software modules.

Introduction: Modeling Software Products and Processes

The important objectives of quantitative software engineering revolve around building models that help express software quality in terms of some software metrics (measures) (Canfora, García, Piattini, Ruiz, & Visaggio, 2005; Cant, Jeffery, & Henderson-Sellers, 1995; Chhabra, Aggarwal, & Singh, 2004; Lanubile & Visaggio, 1997; Lee, 1993; Offutt, Harrold, & Kolte, 1993; Poels & Dedene, 2000). There have been numerous approaches to such modeling pursuits. In addition to some "standard" linear and non-linear regression models, we can witness other techniques exploiting neural networks, machine learning, neural networks and fuzzy sets (Ebert, 1994, 1996; Mantere & Alander, 2005; Pedrycz, Han, Peters, Ramanna, & Zhai, 2001; Pedrycz & Succi, 2005; Pedrycz, Succi, Musílek, & Bai, 2001; Reformat, Pedrycz, & Pizzi, 2003; Thwin & Quah, 2005).

There are several compelling reasons behind studying different approaches to modeling software processes and software products.

- Typically, the available software data are quite limited yet they may involve a significant number of variables; in this sense, their sparse character requires careful attention.

- As the models produce results to be presented to the user (designers, managers, testers, etc.), it is highly advisable to assure high transparency (user-centricity) of the overall modeling process. In particular, this feature supports an interpretation of results and reveals relationships between software metrics and software quality.

- Software processes are human-oriented and not governed by any laws of physics. This strongly suggests considering modeling practices realized at some abstract levels engaging logic constructs.

- It is highly advisable to develop models in such a way that they could accommodate heterogeneous input information not necessarily being confined to numeric data.

- The models should be endowed with a significant level of flexibility and learning mechanisms to accommodate commonly encountered non-linear relationships and potential variability of the individual projects and software products.

Being aware of these main objectives, we may conclude that ideally the modeling framework should support the development of models in such a way that they combine a high degree of plasticity and learning abilities with an evident transparency and a significant level of interpretability. Interestingly enough, we could state without any exaggeration that the fundamentals of such modeling are inherently rooted in the world of multi-valued or fuzzy logic. The underlying logic nature of the models makes them transparent, and this transparency contributes to a highly interpretative insight into experimental data. The agenda of fuzzy modeling is inherently associated with the transparency of fuzzy models. While this facet of modeling has already started to gain visibility and properly balance the otherwise accuracy-driven fuzzy models, there are still a number of fundamental issues as to the definition of interpretability itself, granularity of models vis-à-vis the characteristics of experimental data, and assessment of the readability of the structure of the model itself (Reformat et al., 2003).

Two-valued logic forms a well-known boundary case of the fuzzy logic. The design of digital systems comes with a diversity of well-established, highly efficient, and scalable architectures and related development algorithms. By acknowledging a point of view that the two-valued logic is just a special case of fuzzy logic, we are then somewhat tempted to generalize or reformulate the already existing architectures and design practices of digital systems and cast them in the framework of fuzzy logic. This point of view is the crux of this approach to the development of fuzzy logic models. We focus on a certain standard technique of implementation of combinational systems by means of multiplexers (the approach which results in an array of multiplexers implementing any Boolean function); see McCluskey (1986) and generalize this concept to the world of fuzzy logic. In essence, we are concerned with the three main phases: (1) building a generic structure of a fuzzy multiplexers; (2) developing models (networks) exploiting fuzzy multiplexers as their building components (we will be referring to them as networks of fuzzy multiplexers); and (3) designing such networks with the aid of methods of structural and parametric optimization.

As emphasized, the embedding principle (where fuzzy logic subsumes two-values logic and inherits from its fundamental constructs), makes that this starting point of view becomes especially justifiable and appealing considering that multiplexers have been commonly used in the design of digital systems and come with a well-developed design methodology (Ciletti, 1999).

The organization of the material is structured in a way that reflects the research agenda outlined earlier. First, we introduce a basic processing module of a fuzzy multiplexer (fMUX) and discuss its characteristics (the *Fuzzy Multiplexer as a Generic Processing Unit* section). This naturally leads us to the networks formed by fuzzy multiplexers, *A Realization of the Network of fMUXs* section, relates their structure to the expansion theorem by Shannon, and emphasizes the nature of the function decomposition completed in this manner. *The General Development Environment of the Network-Interfaces Issues* section is concerned with the general development of fMUX networks and serves as a pre-requisite to the comprehensive discussion on the design of the networks. *The Development of the fMUX Networks* section concentrates on the genetic optimization of the networks using which we address an issue of their structural optimization (concerned with a selection of an optimal subset of input variables) and parametric learning. The discussion covers architectural considerations of GAs as well as presents the underlying genetic operators pertinent to the optimization realized here. Experimental results dealing with synthetic and software data are included in the *Experimental Studies* section.

The terminology used here adheres to the standards encountered in two-valued logic, digital systems, and fuzzy logic. The logic operators are modeled via t- and t-conorms. If not stated otherwise, we use two standard realizations of t- and t-conorms coming in the form of a product and probabilistic sum. An overbar denotes a complement treated in a usual way encountered in logic (that is $\bar{x} = 1\text{-}x$).

Fuzzy Multiplexer as a Generic Processing Unit

We are concerned with the development of logic-based models of data in the unit hypercube. More precisely, such models realize logic transformations that map the unit hypercubes (say $[0,1]^n$) into $[0,1]$ and come with some well-defined semantics. We require that such mapping is made modular meaning that it is formed on a basis of a collection of some generic processing units (nodes). The basic processing node, referred to as a fuzzy multiplexer (fMUX), realizes a mapping from $[0,1]^2$ into $[0,1]$ that comes in the following form

$$y = c_0 * \overline{x} + c_1 * x \tag{1}$$

where the logic operations (* and +) are implemented using some t- and t-conorms. For the sake of completeness of the presentation, let us recall that by a t-norm we mean a two argument function t: $[0,1]^2 \to [01,]$ such that it is monotonic, associative, distributive, and satisfies two boundary conditions of the form $0tx = 0$ and $1tx = x$ for all x in $[0,1]$. For any t-conorm all these conditions hold true while the boundary condition reads as $0sx = x$ and $1sx = 1$. Given these t- and t-conorm realizations, (1) is governed by the expression

$$y = (c_0 t \overline{x}) \, s \, (c_1 tx) \tag{2}$$

The structure of (1) can be schematically illustrated as visualized in Figure 1. The variable (x) standing in the earlier-mentioned expression plays a role of a *switching* (selection or select) variable that allows two fixed *information* inputs (c_0 or c_1) to affect the output. The degree to which the produced result depends on these fixed information values is controlled by the select variable. To emphasize the role played by all these signals, we use a concise notation $y = fMUX(x, \mathbf{c})$ where $\mathbf{c}$ ($=[c_0 \ c_1]$) denotes a vector of the information inputs. In

Figure 1. A schematic view of the fuzzy multiplexer with one select input (x) and two fixed information inputs (c_0 and c_1)

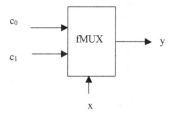

the two boundary conditions the select variable may assume, we produce a binary switch (as being used in digital systems). It means that if $x = 1$ then $y = c_1$. Likewise the value of x set up to 0 leads to the output being equal to c_0 meaning that the value of c_0 is transferred to the output of the device.

Figure 2 includes a series of plots of the characteristics of the fuzzy multiplexer being treated as a function of x; noticeable is a fact that different configurations of the values of the information inputs (c_0 and c_1) give rise to different non-linear input-output relationships of the device. By choosing a certain value of the select input, we logically "blend" the two constant logic values present at the information inputs. The detailed non-linear form of the relationship depends on the use of the t-norms and t-conorms. In the specific example illustrated in Figure 2, the t-norm is realized as a product operator that is $atb = ab$ while the t-conorm is treated as the probabilistic sum, $asb = a + b - ab$, $a,b \in [0,1]$.

Figure 2. Input-output characteristics of the fuzzy multiplexer for selected values of c_0 and c_1, $y = fMUX(x,c_1,c_0)$:

$a - c_0 = 0.9 \ c_1 = 0.8$
$b - c_0 = 0.2, \ c_1 = 0.8$
$c - c_0 = 1.0, \ c_1 = 0.0$
$d - c_0 = 0.6, \ c_1 = 0.3$

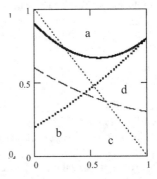

Figure 3. A two-layer network of fuzzy multiplexers

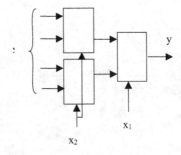

Using fuzzy multiplexers, we can easily form cascade structures (networks) as commonly encountered in the two-valued logic constructs (digital systems). An example of a two-layer structure, a network of fMUXs is displayed in Figure 3. The input-output characteristics of the network that are regarded as a function of the select signals x_1 and x_2 are shown in Figure 4. Depending upon the numeric values in the vector of the information inputs (**c**), we encounter various types of non-linearities. Figure 5 includes the corresponding character-istics for the minimum and maximum operations; it becomes apparent that the piece-wise

Figure 4. 3D plots of the input-output characteristics of the fMUX for selected combinations of the parameters and t- and t-conorms:

$$\mathbf{c} = [0.7 \ \ 0.8 \ \ 0.9 \ \ 0.5] \qquad (a)$$
$$\mathbf{c} = [0.1 \ \ 0.8 \ \ 0.9 \ \ 0.5] \qquad (b)$$
$$\mathbf{c} = [0.7 \ \ 0.8 \ \ 1 \ \ 0] \qquad (c)$$
$$\mathbf{c} = [1 \ 1 \ 1 \ 1] \qquad (d)$$

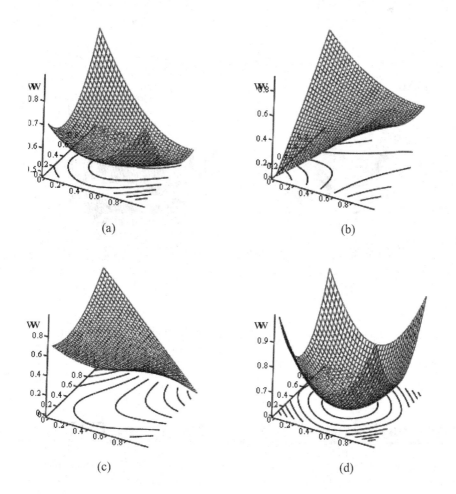

(a)

(b)

(c)

(d)

Figure 5. 3D plots of the characteristics of the fMUX for selected combinations of the parameters; here t- and t-conorms are realized as a minimum and maximum:

$$c = [0.7\ \ 0.8\ \ 0.9\ \ 0.5]\qquad (a)$$
$$c = [0.1\ \ 0.8\ \ 0.9\ \ 0.5]\qquad (b)$$
$$c = [0.7\ \ 0.8\ \ 1\ \ 0]\qquad\quad (c)$$
$$c = [1\ 1\ 1\ 1]\qquad\qquad\quad (d)$$

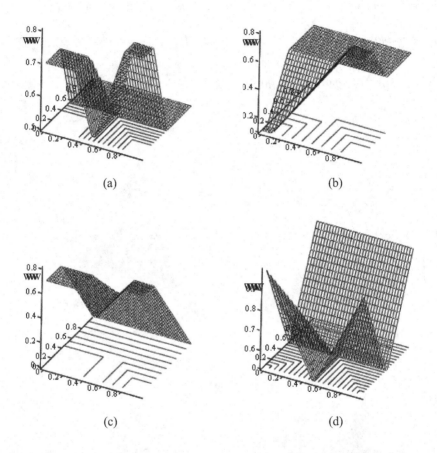

(a)   (b)

(c)   (d)

character of the relationships becomes predominant. Regarding the notation, Figure 3, the switching variables as listed from left to right visualize their location across the network with the last variables being the one realizing the final switching.

A Realization of the Network of fMUXs

The functional module of the fuzzy multiplexer introduced earlier is a generic building block that can be efficiently used to construct larger structures. Its functionality is minimal (in the sense we have here only a single switching variable, that is x). If we are dealing with more variables $(x_1, x_2, \ldots, x_n)$, the resulting structure is formed as a regular multi-level architecture composed of the basic fMUXs as visualized in Figure 6. Noticeably at each level of the network, we assign a single selection variable. Moreover at each level of the network, the number of multiplexers doubles; the output layer comprises one multiplexer, the layer next to it two multiplexers, the next one four units, and so forth. With the substantial number of select variables, we can envision some scalability problems (and these have to be addressed at the design phase).

The fMUX network comes with an interesting motivation and exhibits a clear interpretation. As functionality is concerned, it is instructive to go back to the two-valued logic which clearly reveals a rationale behind the use of such networks of multiplexers (Kohavi, 1970). Consider a two-variable Boolean function $f(x_1, x_2)$. According to the classic Shannon expansion theorem, the function can be written down as a sum of products, that is

$$
\begin{aligned}
y = f(x_1, x_2) &= \overline{x}_2 f(x_1, 0) + x_2 f(x_1, 1) \\
&= \overline{x}_2 [\overline{x}_1 f(0,0) + x_1 f(1,0)] + x_2 [\overline{x}_1 f(0,1) + x_1 f(1,1)]
\end{aligned}
\tag{3}
$$

In essence $\mathbf{c} = [f(0,0)\ f(1,0)\ f(0,1)\ f(1,1)]$ becomes a vector of constant information inputs here; these numeric values uniquely define the given Boolean function.

This successive expansion of the Boolean function maps directly on the two-level structure of the multiplexers; the information inputs to the multiplexer are the functions of one variable, namely $f(x_1, 0)$ and $f(x_1, 1)$, which are realized by the two multiplexers in the first layer of the network. Here, $f(0,0)$, $f(1,0)$, and so forth, are the information inputs to these multiplexers. The network of the fuzzy multiplexers is just a generalization of this fundamental result to fuzzy functions defined in the unit interval.

Figure 6. Network architecture built with the use of the basic functional modules of fuzzy multiplexers; for illustrative purposes, shown are only three layers of the network

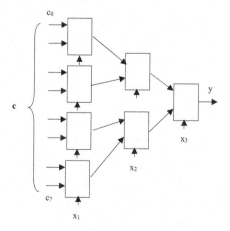

When it comes to the interpretation, the network exhibits several interesting properties. We start with the input layer. The outputs of these fMUXs are just logic expressions of a single input (select) variable (being more specific, the variable and its complement). In the sense of involving only one variable, they are general. There are also a lot of them (especially if we are dealing with the multi-player network). In this sense, what becomes realized at the first layer is just a list of partial realizations of the function, and the outputs there can be treated as generalized variables. In the subsequent layers, these are specialized (by involving another variable), and their number becomes reduced.

The General Development Environment of the Network-Interfaces Issues

The fuzzy multiplexer completes a logic-based processing of input variables and realizes a certain logic-driven mapping between input and output spaces. As they interact with a physical world whose manifestation does not arise at the level of logic (multi-valued) signals, it becomes apparent that there is a need for some interface of the model. Such interfaces are well known in fuzzy modeling. They commonly arise under a name of fuzzifiers (granular coders) and defuzzifiers (granular decoders). The role of the coder is to convert a numeric input coming from the external environment into the internal format of logic membership grades associated with each input variable. This can be shown in the form outlined in Figure 7.

The choice of the fuzzy sets coming as the components of the interfaces is essential to the performance of the fuzzy models. In particular, this concerns: (1) the number of fuzzy sets and (2) their membership functions. The number of fuzzy sets implies a certain level of granularity of the model while the form of the membership function could help in further parametric optimization of the model.

Figure 7. A general-layered structure of fuzzy modeling; the granular decoder is used in case of several networks of fuzzy multiplexers

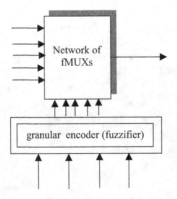

In this study, we consider one of the simplest scenarios. While being quite straightforward, this design alternative exhibits interesting properties, supports computational simplicity and implies a significant level of the interpretability of the model.

For an input variable that assumes values in the range of [a, b], let us consider two fuzzy sets with triangular membership functions defined as

$$A_1(x) = (x-a)/(b-a) \tag{4}$$

and

$$A_2(x) = 1 - (x-a)/(b-a) \tag{5}$$

Evidently, the family $\{A_1, A_2\}$ forms a fuzzy partition of the space as $A_1(x) + A_2(x) = 1$. These two fuzzy sets overlap at the level of 0.5. The linear model of membership is quite common and simple to interpret. It is also highly legitimate in all those cases where we do not have any additional knowledge about the problem at hand. We can look at these membership functions from a different standpoint. The linear normalization of the input variable from the interval of [a, b] to the unit interval [0,1] is just expressed by (4) so in essence A_1 is a result of such normalization. A_2 complements A_1. A_1 is monotonically (linearly) increasing while A_2 is monotonically (linearly) decreasing.

The Development of the fMUX Networks

In this section, we discuss some general design scenarios and envision their suitability in the development of the fMUX networks.

Selecting Among General Design Scenarios

The development of the fMUX networks entails two fundamental design scenarios:

1. If we consider all input variables $(x_1, x_2, \ldots, x_n)$ to be used in the development of the system then the values of the entries of the vector $\mathbf{c} = [c_0\ c_1\ c_2\ c_k \ldots]$ have to be estimated

2. If the number of the input variables is high (and this implies a high dimensionality of $\mathbf{c}$ along with all drawbacks of learning we envision under such circumstances), the design of the network has to involve a selection of an optimal subset of the variables and a simultaneous estimation of the pertinent vector of constants ($\mathbf{c}$).

In the first scenario, we can use a standard gradient-based learning. It is straightforward; for a given structure (that is the variables being specified in advance along with their arrangement within the network), a detailed form of a performance index to be minimized (Q), specific models of t- and t-conorms, the gradient of Q taken with respect to **c** navigates the optimization process realized throughout the search space,

$$\mathbf{c}(\text{iter} + 1) = \mathbf{c}(\text{iter}) - \beta \nabla_c Q \qquad (6)$$

where **c**(iter) denotes the values of the input constants at a certain iteration step (iter); $\beta > 0$ is a learning factor implying an intensity of adjustments of the values of **c**. The gradient of Q can be easily determined. In spite of that, there could be some potential shortcomings of this learning scheme. The most profound one comes with a high dimensionality of the network. If there are a significant number of the variables in the problem, the computed gradient assumes low values. As a result, the learning becomes very inefficient. Note also that the dimensionality of the input vector is equal to 2^n and this expression gives rise to a prohibitively high dimensionality quite quickly even for relatively small values of "n". In light of these, it is very likely that the gradient-based methods will come with a limited applicability and we have to proceed with caution when dealing with the increased problem dimensionality.

The second design scenario involves an optimization of the structure (selection of variables) that helps handle the dimensionality problem in an efficient manner. The parametric optimization concerning the vector of the co-efficients in some reduced format becomes then more efficient. We may also envision frequent situations in which not all variables become essential to the design of the logic mapping (the same holds in pattern recognition where a stage of feature selection becomes a necessity). With the structural and parametric optimization at hand, we have to confine ourselves to some techniques of global and structural optimization. An appealing way to follow is to consider genetic algorithms (GAs).

Genetic Development of the fMUX Networks

Having recognized the primary design objectives, we now concentrate on the details of the underlying genetic optimization. GAs (Goldberg, 1989; Michalewicz, 1996) are well-documented in the literature including a long list of their numerous applications to neuro-fuzzy systems. Bearing this in mind, we elaborate on the fundamental architecture of the GA, its parameters, and discuss some implementation details.

Genotype Representation

The proposed genotype is a direct reflection of the structure of the fMUX network. We consider a floating point coding as this results in compact chromosomes. Let us assume that the number of input variables to be used in the network is given in advance and equal to n' where n' < n. The chromosome consists of two sub-strings of real numbers. The first

Figure 8. The structure of the fMUX network and its genetic representation (a) and details of the coding of the subset of the input variables (b) through ranking and using the first n' entries of the sub-string

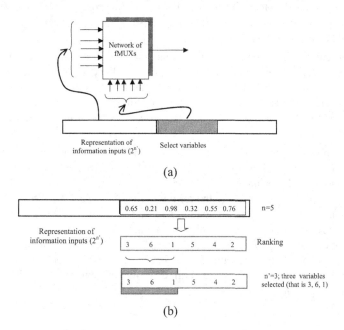

block (sub-string) contains $2^{n'}$ values of the information inputs, vector. The second block (with n inputs) deals with the subset of the variables to be used in the design. The details are schematically visualized in Figure 8.

As far as the structure of network is concerned, it is instructive to discuss a way in which the select variables are coded in the second block of the chromosome. The second portion of the chromosome corresponds to the subset of the original inputs that are chosen as select variables and requires some processing before being used to identify the structure of the network. As the entries of the chromosome are real-coded, the likelihood of encountering two identical entries is zero (to be on the safe side, we can always break a tie randomly). With the pre-defined number of the inputs (n'), we then use only the first n' entries of the chromosome, and this produces the sequence of the input variables. The entries are ranked (in the increasing order), and the first n' entries of the sub-string are used to choose among all variables. This ordering is directly mapped onto the network where the first variable is the one switching the first layer of the network.

N.B. One could easily optimize the number of the subset of the input variables (n') instead of supplying it externally yet this does not to seem to be very attractive. It is perhaps more justifiable to do a systematic search by sweeping n' from 1 to n. In essence, this systematic search helps us assess approximation and generalization abilities of the networks and get a better sense as to the plausible subset of the variables.

When it comes to the *selection process*, we use an elitist ranking selection (Michalewicz, 1996). This selection mechanism means that individuals to be selected for the next generation are based on their relative rank in the population, as determined by the fitness function. The best individual from each generation is always carried over to the next generation (elitist mechanism) meaning that the solution found so far during the genetic optimization is guaranteed to never disappear.

The *mutation* operator is a standard construct encountered in a number of genetic algorithms, cf. . 0. Given an individual string $\mathbf{a} = [a_1, a_2, ..., a_{2n}]$, we generate a new string $\mathbf{a}' = [a_1', a_2', ..., a_{2n}']$ where a_i', i=1, 2,...,2n, is a random number confined in the range of [0,1] and subject to the following replacement (mutation) rule: a_i is mutated that is replaced by a_i' with some probability of mutation (p_m) otherwise the entry of the chromosome is left intact, that is $a_i' = a_i$.

The *crossover* operation is realized as the BLX-0.5 crossover operator (Baker, 1985; Eshelman & Schaffer, 1993; Goldberg, 1991; Herrera, Lozano, & Verdegay, 1998) which is carried out as follows. Given are two individuals $\mathbf{a} = [a_1, a_2, ..., a_{2n}]$ and $\mathbf{b} = [b_1, b_2, ..., b_{2n}]$. The resulting offsprings are formed in the form $\mathbf{a}' = [a_1', a_2', ..., a_{2n}']$ and $\mathbf{b}' = [b_1', b_2', ..., b_{2n}']$, where a_i', b_i', i=1,2,...,2n, are random numbers located in the range [max(0, min_i-0.5I), min(1, max_i+0.5I)]. Here, $min_i = \min(a_i, b_i)$, $max_i = \max(a_i, b_i)$, and $I = max_i - min_i$. This particular crossover operation provides a good balance between using the information of the parents and avoiding premature convergence. The crossover operator ensures that all values of the generated offspring are confined to the unit interval [0, 1]. The operator is employed with probability of crossover, p_c, otherwise the individuals are left unchanged $\mathbf{a}' = \mathbf{a}$ and $\mathbf{b}' = \mathbf{b}$.

Fitness Function

The fitness function quantifies how the network approximates the data and is taken as

$$1 - \frac{Q}{Q+1}$$

with Q being a sum of squared errors between the target values (experimental output data) and the corresponding outputs of the network. The other option is the standard root mean squared error (RMSE). A small positive constant ε standing in the denominator of the earlier expression assures that the fitness function remains meaningful even for Q = 0 (which in practice never occurs).

Experimental Studies

In the experimental part of the study, we start with some illustrative material dealing with Boolean expressions and then move on to the software data.

Realization of Boolean Functions

In this experiment, we are concerned with Boolean data; this helps us compare the result produced by the fuzzy multiplexer with the solutions obtained using standard techniques used to design digital systems. The data set comprises of 12 input-output pairs of binary data with 5 inputs and a single output,

$(\mathbf{x}(k)\text{-}y(k))$: ([1 0 0 0 0] 0), ([1 0 0 0 1] 1), ([1 0 0 1 0] 1), ([1 0 0 1 1] 1), ([1 1 1 0 0] 1), ([1 1 1 0 1] 0), ([1 1 1 1 0] 1), ([1 1 1 1 1] 1), ([1 1 0 0 0] 0), ([1 1 0 0 1] 1), ([1 1 0 1 0] 0), ([1 1 0 1 1] 0)

The development of the network is completed for a varying number of inputs starting from one variable and ending up with all the variables. The results are summarized in Table 1.

From this table (based on the values of the classification error), it becomes obvious that four variables are optimal for the problem. The resulting inputs are shown in Figure 9. With the

Table 1. Structure of the multiplexer network and associated errors; by the classification error, we mean the number of mismatches between the binary (that is subjected to some threshold) output of the network and the data

Number of variables	1	2	3	4	5
Order of variables	x_3	x_5, x_3	x_3, x_5, x_2	x_4, x_3, x_2, x_5	x_4, x_1, x_2, x_5, x_3
MSE	0.478	0.408	0.354	$1.29*10^{-4}$	$2.09*10^{-5}$
Classification error	3	2	4	0	0

Figure 9. Values of the information inputs; observe that their distribution is highly bimodal with the values of information inputs being close to 1 or 0 with a very few exceptions

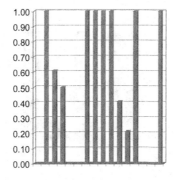

threshold value of 0.5, we are left with eight significant inputs. Noticeably, all those very close to 1 identify the min terms existing in the data. The one extra here with the value equal to 0.61 (and still deemed relevant) corresponds to the combination of the inputs equal to 0100 (that is $\overline{x}_4 x_3 \overline{x}_2 \overline{x}_5$), and it is subsumed by the remaining sum of the minterms. Alluding to the problem variables being identified by the genetic algorithm, it is interesting to note that x1 has been eliminated. It is not surprising at all noting that it fixed at 1 and thus becomes redundant in the problem. For this optimal number of the inputs, Figure 10 shows how GA performs in terms of the optimization; evidently most learning occurs at the beginning of the process, and this becomes evident for the best individual as well as the average fitness in the population.

The second example is shown here to visualize the effectiveness of the genetic optimization. The binary data describe a three-dimensional XOR problem. With the population of 50 chromosomes, 50 generations, the mutation rate of 0.05, and crossover rate equal to 0.8, the ideal result is obtained after a few initial generations. As expected, the information inputs are either close to 1 or become practically equal to zero (Figure 11).

Figure 10. Fitness function (average and best individual) in successive generations

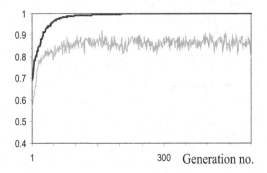

Figure 11. Information inputs of the network of fuzzy multiplexers

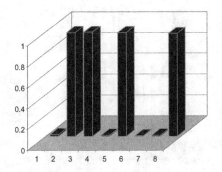

Experiments with Software Data

In the ensuing comprehensive suite of experiments, we consider a well-documented MIS data set (Munson & Khoshgoftaar, 1996) which has already been used in other experimentation with models of quantitative software engineering. The dataset includes software modules described by a collection of typical software metrics and associated number of changes made to the corresponding module. For the purpose of this experimentation, we focused only on the selected software measures leaving some others out (such as, e.g., number of characters, number of code characters, number of comments); refer to Table 2.

For further experimentation, we eliminated one data point for which the number of changes was overly high (98) in comparison to the rest of the data and which could easily skew up the entire picture. Note that the average number of changes was 7.25. In the learning process, we use 60% of randomly selected data. The rest (40%) is left for testing purposes. The t- and t-conorm are implemented as the product and probabilistic sum.

As discussed in *The General Development Environment of the Network-Interfaces Issues* section, the software measures were linearly normalized to the unit interval. The evolutionary optimization was realized with the following parameters of the GA whose values are quite typical and quite similar to those found in the literature, namely

> size of population –300,
>
> number of generations – 500,
>
> mutation rate – 0.05,
>
> crossover rate – 0.8

As a matter of fact, it is worth noting that those parameters could be fine-tuned, however the process might be quite tedious and geared only towards a specific dataset.

Table 2. A collection of software metrics (measures) used in the experiments

	Software metrics	notes
x_1	Number of lines of code, including comments	
x_2	Program length	$N = N1 + N2$; N1- the total number of operators, N2-total number of operands
x_3	Estimated program length	$n_1 \log_2 n_1 + n_2 \log_2 n_2$ n_1-the number of unique operators, n_2 – the number of unique operators
x_4	Jensen's estimator of program length	$(\log_2 n_1)! + (\log_2 n_2)!$
x_5	McCabe cyclomatic complexity number	number of decision nodes +1
x_6	Belady's bandwidth metric	average level of nesting

Table 3. Results of genetic optimization of the logic model of the network of fuzzy multiplexers (the switching variables are listed starting from the first layer of the fuzzy multiplexers in the overall architecture)

Number of input variables	1	2	3	4	5	6
				x_1	x_3	x_4
		x_1	x_1	x_4	x_1	x_1
		x_3	x_5	x_3	x_4	x_3
Software metrics and their arrangement	x_1		x_3	x_5	x_6	x_5
					x_5	x_6
						x_2
Performance index (training data)	5.42	**5.37**	5.37	5.41	5.53	5.76

In the series of experiments, we modified the number of allowed input variables starting from a single software metrics and moving on to the entire set. The results are reported in terms of the performance index (RMSE) for the training and testing set as well as the corresponding subsets of the variables (see Table 3).

We observe that the performance index on the training set achieves the minimum for two and three variables. With the increase of the dimensionality, there is some increase in the values of the performance index. Given this, we may regard the two software metrics, that is, the number of lines of code, and the estimated program length to form a suitable subset of software metrics. By adding the third metrics, that is, McCabe cyclomatic complexity, we are not witnessing any improvement (the performance index stays the same). As a matter of act, the performance index on the testing set reaches 8.09 for two metrics and 5.37 for the suite of the three metrics. The topologies of the networks with a single input and two inputs along with their characteristics are visualized in Figure 12.

The findings are intuitively appealing as far as the specific software metrics are concerned and their occurrence in the overall expression. In the case of the single input, the number of lines of code is a fairly compelling indicator of possible changes. The logic expression identifies a direct relationship between the increase in the values of this metrics and the resulting increase in the number of changes made to the software module. This observation is drawn from the logic expression; see Figure 12, $y = 0.92 \, t \, x_1 = 0.92 \, x_1$ (as the t-norm has been implemented as the product operator). This relationship is linear as illustrated in Figure 12. Given the underlying logic of the fuzzy multiplexer, one could infer that the increase of the number of lines of code leads to the increase of the number of changes in the code. With the two inputs, we observe that the x1 is the first switching variable and the results produced at the first layer are combined by the fuzzy multiplexer guided by x_3 (estimated program length). The logic expression governing the relationships is intuitively appealing: roughly speaking, the increase in the number of changes occurs when both the number of lines and the estimated program length are increasing or at least one of them with the more significant impact caused by the high number of lines. This slightly asymmetric behavior is also reflected in Figure 12.

Figure 12. The detailed architecture of the network with the values of the inputs to the fuzzy multiplexers; shown are also the input-output characteristics of the networks for the two software metrics

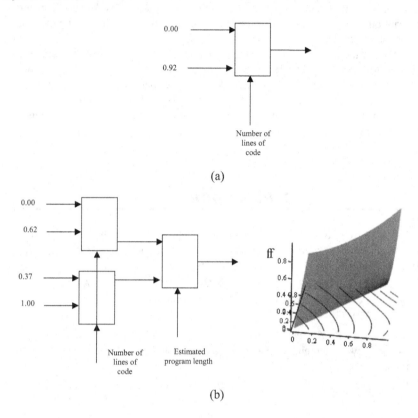

(a)

(b)

Conclusions

We have introduced a logic-driven architecture of fuzzy models based on a concept of fuzzy multiplexers (fMUXs). fMUXs are direct generalizations of fundamental building blocks encountered in two-valued (digital) logic and being used in a design process therein. The design of the fMUX networks has been carried in the framework of genetic optimization. The GA is effectively used at the level of structural and parametric optimization. It is worth stressing that the structural optimization becomes indispensable in case of multi-variable problems. The selected (optimized) subset of input variables leads to an efficient dimensionality reduction of the problem and helps concentrate on the most significant variables. With this regard, the resulting transparency of the model is also worth emphasizing. Given the topology of the network itself and the processing therein, its structure becomes highly interpretable. Any fMUXs construct is translated into a coherent logical description of the experimental data being used in its development. Taking full advantage of this aspect, we were able to reveal and quantify immediate links between some software metrics and the quality of the software product (in our case, it related to the number of changes that were made to the software modules). We emphasize that the network of fMUXs translates into a logic description of experimental software data we used in their development. Given the form of the input interface that linked the data with the logic processing realized through two linear membership functions, we came up with an interesting and highly readable semantics of the relationships conveyed by the logic model. In essence, the logic model endowed with this type of interface expresses "gradual" dependencies between the inputs (software metrics) and some ensuing effects (the number of changes) and quantifies the strength of these relationships (which is done with the use of the numeric values of the data inputs of the fMUXs positioned at the input layer of the network).

References

Baker, J. E. (1985). Adaptive selection methods for genetic algorithms. In J. J. Grefenstette (Ed.), *Proceedings of the First International Conference on Genetic Algorithms* (pp. 101-111). Mahwah, NJ: L. Erlbaum Associates.

Canfora, G., García, F., Piattini, M., Ruiz, F., & Visaggio, C. A. (2005). A family of experiments to validate metrics for software process models. *Journal of Systems and Software, 77*(2), 113-129.

Cant, S. N., Jeffery, D. R., & Henderson-Sellers, B. (1995). A conceptual model of cognitive complexity of elements of the programming process. *Information and Software Technology, 37*(7), 351-362.

Chhabra, J. K. , Aggarwal, K. K., & Singh, Y. (2004). Measurement of object-oriented software spatial complexity. *Information and Software Technology, 46*(10), 689-699.

Ciletti, M. D. (1999). *Modeling, synthesis and rapid prototyping with the Verilog HDL.* Upper Saddle River, NJ: Prentice Hall.

Ebert, C. (1994). Rule-based fuzzy classification for software quality control. *Fuzzy Sets and Systems, 63*(3), 349-358.

Ebert, C. (1996). Fuzzy classification for software criticality analysis. *Expert Systems with Applications, 11*(3), 323-342.

Eshelman, L. J., & Schaffer, J. D. (1993). Real-coded genetic algorithms and interval schemata. In D. Whitley (Ed.), *Foundations of genetic algorithms 2* (pp. 187-202). San Mateo, CA: Morgan Kaufmann Publishers.

Goldberg, D. E. (1989). *Genetic algorithms in search, optimization, and machine learning.* Boston, MA: Addison-Wesley.

Goldberg, D. E. (1991). Real-coded genetic algorithms, virtual alphabets, and blocking. *Complex Systems, 5,* 139-167.

Herrera, F., Lozano, M., & Verdegay J. L. (1998). Tackling real-coded genetic algorithms: Operators and tools for behavioral analysis. *Artificial Intelligence Review, 12*, 265-319.

Kohavi, Z. (1970). *Switching and finite automata theory*. New York: McGraw-Hill.

Lanubile, F., & Visaggio, G. (1997). Evaluating predictive quality models derived from software measures: Lessons learned. *Journal of Systems and Software, 38*, 225-234.

Lee, H. (1993). A structured methodology for software development effort prediction using the analytic hierarchy process. *Journal of Systems and Software, 21*(2), 179-186.

Mantere, T., & Alander, J. T. (2005). Evolutionary software engineering: A review. *Applied Soft Computing, 5*(3), 315-331.

McCluskey, E. J. (1986). *Logic design principles*. Englewood Cliffs, NJ: Prentice Hall.

Michalewicz, Z. (1996). *Genetic algorithms + data structures = evolution programs* (3rd ed.). Heidelberg: Springer-Verlag.

Munson, J., & Khoshgoftaar, T. M. (1996). Software metrics for reliability assessment. In M. R. Lyu (Ed.), *Handbook of software reliability engineering* (pp. 493-530). New York: McGraw Hill.

Offutt, A. J., Harrold, M. J., & Kolte, P. (1993). A software metric system for module coupling. *Journal of Systems and Software, 20*(3), 295-308.

Pedrycz, W., Succi, G., Musílek, P., & Bai, X. (2001). Using self-organizing maps to analyze object-oriented software measures. *Journal of Systems and Software, 59*(1), 65-82.

Pedrycz, W., Han, L. , Peters, J. F., Ramanna, S., & Zhai, R. (2001). Calibration of software quality: Fuzzy neural and rough neural computing approaches. *Neurocomputing, 36*(1-4), 149-170.

Pedrycz, W., & Succi, G. (2005). Genetic granular classifiers in modeling software quality. *Journal of Systems and Software, 76*(3), 277-285.

Poels, G., & Dedene, G. (2000). Distance-based software measurement: Necessary and sufficient properties for software measures. *Information and Software Technology, 42*(1), 35-46.

Reformat, M., Pedrycz, W., & Pizzi, N. J. (2003). Software quality analysis with the use of computational intelligence. *Information and Software Technology, 45*(7), 405-417.

Thwin, M. M. T., & Quah, T.-S. (2005). Application of neural networks for software quality prediction using object-oriented metrics. *Journal of Systems and Software, 76*(2), 147-156.

Chapter VIII

Modeling Relevance Relations Using Machine Learning Techniques

Jelber Sayyad Shirabad, University of Ottawa, Canada

Timothy C. Lethbridge, University of Ottawa, Canada

Stan Matwin, University of Ottawa, Canada

Abstract

This chapter presents the notion of relevance relations, an abstraction to represent relationships between software entities. Relevance relations map tuples of software entities to values that reflect how related they are to each other. Although there are no clear definitions for these relationships, software engineers can typically identify instances of these complex relationships. We show how a classifier can model a relevance relation. We also present the process of creating such models by using data mining and machine learning techniques. In a case study, we applied this process to a large legacy system; our system learned models of a relevance relation that predict whether a change in one file may require a change in another file. Our empirical evaluation shows that the predictive quality of such models makes them a viable choice for field deployment. We also show how by assigning different misclassification costs such models can be tuned to meet the needs of the user in terms of their precision and recall.

Introduction

Software maintenance is widely recognized to be the most expensive and time-consuming aspect of the software process. To maintain a system properly one needs to have at least a partial understanding of the system; this, in turn, requires knowing about the relationships among elements of the system. As the software ages and grows in size, one would expect to see that an increasing proportion of the relationships become undocumented. In particular, latent relationships among system components are created, and some existing relationships become deprecated, that is, remain present for historical purposes only. In a large, "legacy" system there is no single person who completely understands the system and its network of relationships, yet such systems control many aspects of modern society. It is important to note that while there is no crisp definition for most complex relationships in software systems, in many cases one can identify instances of such relations among some components of the system.

The complexity of a software system is clearly related to the complexity of the network of relationships in the system. A key tenet of our research is that a software engineer who needs to investigate software problems and maintain a software system will benefit from knowing what elements of the system are related to each other. In this chapter, we introduce an abstraction called the *relevance relation* that is used to represent relationships that would be useful for a maintainer to know. A relevance relation maps a tuple of system elements to a value indicating how related they are. Each tuple in a relevance relation therefore contains a set of related elements.

Well-managed software projects maintain repositories that keep track of software revisions and use mechanisms to record software problem reports as well as the changes applied to the software to address these problems. These software change repositories reflect a history of the system, which includes actions that result in the creation of new relationships and the strengthening of the existing relationships in the software. This history also reflects the collective experience and knowledge of software engineers who have maintained the system.

Conceptually, machine learning systems learn models from past experience that can be applied in future unseen situations or scenarios. Therefore, the main thrust of this chapter is to show how one can use machine learning and data mining algorithms and techniques to discover relevance relations hidden in the historic data available in software.

To better demonstrate these ideas, we will present a case study where we learn a specific relevance relation among source files in a software system. We will derive this relation from maintenance history: files that have been changed together when making previous changes are considered to be relevant to each other for the purposes of future changes. However, in principle, relevance relations can hold among any type of element or component in a software system.

Background

Despite their established track record and widespread use in other domains, machine learning techniques are applied relatively infrequently in software engineering and to an even lesser degree in software maintenance. There are a few examples of application of machine learning, however; among them, Cohen and Devanbu (1997, 1999) discuss the application of inductive logic programming (ILP) to predict faulty classes. Merlo reports on the usage of neural nets in design recovery. They incorporate expert input, including providing a taxonomy of concepts recognizable from the comments in the source code (Melro & De Mori, 1994; Merlo, McAdam, & De Mori, 1993). Porter (1994) used decision tree-based techniques to isolate high risk software modules while Briand, Thomas, and Hetmanski (1993) use logistic regression and optimized set reduction methods in the task of identifying high risk components in Ada designs. In Briand, Melo, and Wüst (2002), the authors use a regression-based method called MARS (multi-variate adaptive regression splines) to build a fault-proneness prediction model from a set of OO measures collected from a mid-sized Java project. They also evaluated the accuracy of this model when it is applied to another Java system developed by the same team. Almeida and Matwin (1999) have applied machine learning to the task of software quality prediction. In Fouqué and Matwin (1993), the authors applied ILP to help and enhance the reuse process. More recently, Graves, Karr, Marron, and Siy (2000) evaluated statistical models developed from modules' change history to investigate which characteristics of this history would be better indicators of introduction of additional faults in modules as they continued to be developed. Khoshgoftaar and Seliya (2003) have performed a comparative evaluation of fault prediction models using CART-LS and CART-LAD decision tree learners, S-PLUS multiple regression, neural networks, and case-based reasoning. Finally, Zimmermann, Weißgerber, Diehl, and Zeller (2004) applied association rule mining to version histories of the Eclipse programming environment to suggest program entities that would change together. Software change history has been analyzed by other researchers such as Gall, Krajewski, and Jazayeri (2003) to find architectural weaknesses in a system. Their techniques were based on locating classes that had changed together in the past. However, this and similar research does not involve learning generalized models as is the case when machine learning techniques are used, therefore we have limited their mention in this chapter.

Generally, the two most prevalent applications of machine learning in software engineering are building models that can predict fault proneness of software modules or the cost associated with a software project. In both these cases, and most applications mentioned earlier, the models built make predictions regarding a single entity such as a class, a module, or a software project. In contrast, relevance relations capture relationships among multiple entities, and therefore the models representing them make predictions regarding multiple entities in a software system.

Relevance Among Software Entities

In this section, we provide the definitions of relevance relation and other concepts closely related to it. We will also describe a specific application that aims to extract a useful relevance relation in the context of software maintenance.

Relevance Relations

Definition: A *software entity* is any semantically or syntactically valid construct in a software system that can be seen as a unit with a well-defined purpose.[1] Examples of software entities include documents, source files, routines, modules, variables, and even the entire software system.

Definition: A *predictor* is a relation that maps tuples of *one* or more software entities to values that show a prediction made about the elements of the tuples.

Definition: A *relevance relation* is a predictor that maps tuples of *two* or more software entities to a value r quantifying how *relevant*, that is, connected or related, the entities are to each other. In other words, r shows the strength of *relevance* among the entities. Therefore, "relevant" here is embedded in, and dependent on, the definition of the relation.

A *continuous relevance relation* maps the tuples of entities into a real number between 0 and 1. In this setting, 0 stands for the lack of relevance, and 1 shows 100% relevance. Instead of a real number, the strength can be one of k discrete values, in which case we call R a *discrete relevance relation*. For instance, if k is two, we could have a Boolean relevance relation R that maps the tuple of entities $e_1, ..., e_n$ ($n \geq 2$) to *true* or *false* depending on whether, based on the definition of R, the entities $e_1, ..., e_n$ are *relevant* or *not relevant* to each other, respectively.

The definition of the relevance relation can capture simple or very complex interactions among the entities mapped by the relation. The definition can be based on a combination of the existing relations among the mapped entities themselves, or between the mapped entities and other entities in the system. For instance, a relevance relation between files can be defined in terms of a combination of the file inclusion relation among files, and a variable reference relation among files and variables to which they refer.

Definition: A *system relevance graph* for a relevance relation R or SRG_R is a weighted hypergraph G(V, E, R) where the set of vertices V is a subset of the set of software entities in the system. Each hyperedge in E connects vertices that, according to relevance relation R, are relevant to each other.[2] The relevance value of the vertices on a hyperedge is the weight of that hyperedge. If each tuple of entities mapped by R is ordered then SRG_R is a directed graph, otherwise it is undirected. A *system relevance subgraph* $SRG_{R,r}$ is a subgraph of SRG_R where software entities on each hyperedge are mapped to a relevance value r by relevance relation R.

Figure 1. A system relevance graph and its two system relevance subgraphs

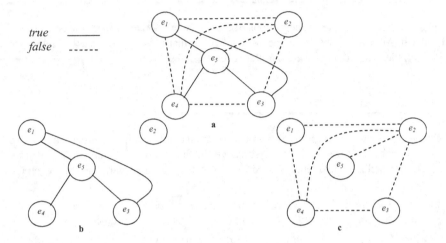

Figure 1a shows a system relevance graph for a system with five entities e_1,..., e_5 and a Boolean relevance relation R that maps every two entities to *true* (solid lines) if these entities belong to the same sub-system and *false* (broken lines) otherwise.

Figures 1b shows $SRG_{R, true}$ where based on the definition of R the entities in the following tuples are in the same sub-system

$$(e_1,e_3), (e_1,e_5), (e_3,e_5), (e_4,e_5)$$

According to $SRG_{R, false}$, shown in Figure 1c, entities in the following tuples are in different sub-systems:

$$(e_1,e_2), (e_1,e_4), (e_2,e_3), (e_2,e_4), ,(e_2,e_5), (e_3,e_4)$$

Definition: A *system static relevance graph* ($SSRG_R$) is an SRG in which R is defined in terms of static relations[3] in the source code. For instance, if relation R in Figure 1 would map a tuple to true if both entities called the same function, and false otherwise, then this figure would show an SSRG.

A software system can be depicted by different SRGs. The topology of an SRG for a given release of the system only depends on the definition of the relevance relation. Two SRGs of the same system may share one or more connected sub-graphs suggesting the possibility of the existence of a *meta-relation* between two relevance relations. For instance, an SRG based on the *Is-In-Subsystem* relevance relation and an SRG based on the *documents-entity* relevance relation may share a common sub-graph suggesting that there is documentation for a sub-system.

An SRG can be used both for redocumentation and design recovery during a reverse engineering effort. Most organizations that produce software have access to tools that allow programmers to browse or query low level static source code relations. *TkSee* (Lethbridge, 2000; Lethbridge & Anquetil, 1997), a tool in use at Mitel Networks[4] is an example of such a system which allows one to explore a software systems and issue queries such as "what are the routines called" or "what are the variables referred to" in a file. Such tools can be used to better understand or reverse engineer software systems, and associate design decisions with the source code; however some SRGs can speed up this process considerably. TkSee uses a database that stores variety of information generated by parsing the source files in the system. For instance, for each routine r in the software system, this database keeps a list of routines called by r[5]. Using this information one can create an $SRG_{calls(ri,rj) \to Boolean}$ in which *calls* is a relevance relation that maps two routine entities r_i and r_j to *true* if r_i calls r_j in the source code, and *false* otherwise. Note that $SRG_{calls(ri,rj) \to Boolean}$ is an example of an SRG that can be used in redocumenting a system.

A Real-World Relevance Relation

The level of abstraction represented by an SRG depends upon the definition of the relevance relation it is based on. The most basic SRGs are based on relevance relations defined in terms of a single static source code relation such as calls(r_i,r_j). Although these SRGs can be extremely useful for a developer in the maintenance task, they fail to capture non-trivial relationships among entities in a software system. In this chapter, we investigate the existence of other relevance relations that may assist a maintenance programmer in his or her job. Therefore, *within the context of maintenance activity,* we are trying to seek the answer to the following question:

- Using a combination of static source code relations and/or other sources of information, *can we find other useful and non-trivial relevance relation(s) in a software system?*

Static source code relations are widely used by both software developers and researchers in various areas of software engineering such as reverse engineering, software visualization, and mining software repositories. This leads us to ask:

- *What are the important static relations that a maintenance programmer should be aware of?[6]*

We believe finding a *maintenance relevance relation* (MRR) could provide an answer to these questions. Such a relation should incorporate information about the changes applied to the system as part of the maintenance process. Consequently, it has the potential to reflect the interconnections among the entities of a system, which are influenced by the changes applied to the system. Such interconnections may or may not conform to the original or perceived design of the system. Instead, they could show the existence and interplay of the actual interconnections among the entities, which cause changes in one entity to influence another one. Lack of documentation and/or awareness of these is believed by many to be a major source of complexity and cost in maintaining software.

This chapter is primarily focused on answering the first question. However, we note that after finding a definition for a useful MRR, one could further study and analyze this definition to find an importance ranking among its constituting elements, including the ones based on static relations.

The definition of software entity given earlier is very broad in nature. In the context of software maintenance, there is a much smaller set of software entities that seem to be interesting. Examples of such software entities are files, routines, variables, modules, subsystems, and documents.

When a maintenance programmer is looking at a piece of code, such as a file or a routine, one of the important questions that he needs to answer is:

- *"Which other files should I know about, that is, which other files might be relevant to this piece of code?"*

The ability to answer this question is essential in understanding and maintaining any software system regardless of the type of maintenance activity. Therefore, in this chapter, we will focus on SRGs in which the nodes are files We would like to learn a special class of maintenance relevance relations called the *Co-update* relation:

$$\text{Co-update}(f_i, f_j) \rightarrow \{\text{Relevant, Not-Relevant}\} \text{ where,}$$
$$i \neq j \text{ and } f_i \text{ and } f_j \text{ are any two files in the system.}$$

Co-update$(f_i, f_j) \rightarrow$ ***Relevant*** means that a change in f_i may result in a change in f_j, and vice versa.[7]

A relevance relation such as Co-update could be used to assist a maintenance programmer in answering the previous question about files.

The reason to limit the number of files in the tuples to two is based on the following observations:

- A relation with two-entity tuples provides the most basic kind of relevance relation in terms of number of entities. Consequently, it can potentially capture more general interconnections among entities. Tuples with three or more entities result in a more restricted relation than the basic two-entity case.
- Usually, most changes involve a very few entities, and there are fewer examples of changes involving larger numbers of entities. This is also true for the system we used in our case study.

We chose a discrete relevance relation as opposed to a continuous one partly due to the learning method that we experimented with, namely decision tree learning, and partly due to the fact that in a large software system, an SRG can be very complex. It is not clear to us whether providing a software engineer with a large set of objects with different relevance rankings will be more beneficial than providing him or her with a smaller set that is believed to contain the relevant objects. A real-valued variable can be easily discretized to a Boolean variable, however this will introduce the issue of finding the proper threshold value.[8]

To learn the Co-update MRR, we propose the application of inductive learning methods to the data extracted from a real-world legacy system[9] using the following sources:

- Static source code analysis
- Historical maintenance records

In other words, we *mine*[10] these sources of data to extract the Co-update relation. The motivation here is that such a relation learned from the examples of the past maintenance experience could be used to assist the software engineers, especially the newcomers to the team, in future similar maintenance activities.

From Relevance Relations to Classification

The problem of learning a relevance relation can be directly mapped to a classification learning problem where the *concept* we are trying to learn is the relevance relation of interest. Here, the classifier represents the *learned* relevance relation. In most practical settings, the *definition* of the concept is not known but some *instances* of the concept are known. For example, by looking at a software change repository, we can find past instances of the Co-update relation without knowing the definition of the relation itself. If we knew the definition, we could use it to predict whether for any pair of files in the system a change in one may require a change in another, even if we do not have a record of them being changed together in the past.

We start from the instances of an undefined relevance relation and try to find a definition for it by learning a *classifier* or *model*. This classifier is learned from *training examples* that describe the entities mapped by each known instance of the relevance relation. In the supervised learning paradigm, each example has a *label*, which in our case is the relevance value of entities described by the example. To describe an instance, we use a pre-defined set of *features*.

The mapping between a relevance relation and a classifier modeling this relevance relation is shown in Figure 2. As this figure suggests, once a model is learned a previously unseen tuple of entities $(e_i, e_j, \ldots, e_z)$ can be translated to a *case* with feature or attribute values $(a_1, a_2, \ldots, , a_N)$, and input to the learned model. The output of the model r' is an approximation of the actual relevance value r. If a model is always correct in predicting cases, it accurately represents the corresponding relevance relation. In a real world setting, for all but simple

Figure 2. The mapping between a relevance relation and a classifier

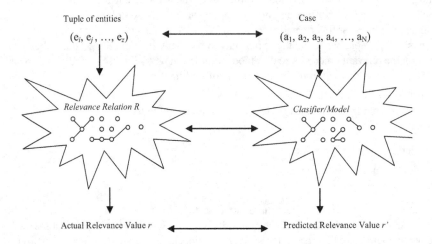

relevance relations, one would expect that the model would make wrong predictions for some of the cases.

Here we emphasize that any relevance relation can be modeled by a classifier learned from the instances of that relation. For the special case of suggesting software entities that tend to change together, one could also employ other techniques such as association rule learning as discussed in Zimmermann et al. (2004). However, compared to classification learning, association rule learning is much more specific in its applications and consequently more limited as a general learning technique.

Figure 3 shows the process of learning a relevance relation in the context of software maintenance. With the exception of the data and knowledge sources which are geared towards the ones available in a software development and maintenance, this process is general enough to be used in other applications of machine learning, and it is closely related to the ones suggested by other researchers such as Saitta and Neri (1998) and Piatetsky-Shapiro, Brachman, Khabaza, Kloesgen, and Simoudis (1996). Obviously, the assumption is that the maintenance problem we are trying to address is already defined. In the discussion that follows, we will mostly focus on source-code-level software maintenance. We show the feasibility of learning a useful maintenance relevance relation and report the difficulties and challenges involved in the process.

The process can be divided into three stages: pre-learning, learning, and post learning. As seen in Figure 3, there are backward arrows, indicating that at many of the steps in the process one may need to revisit an earlier step. The following sections provide more details about each of these stages.

Figure 3. *The process of learning a maintenance relevance relation*

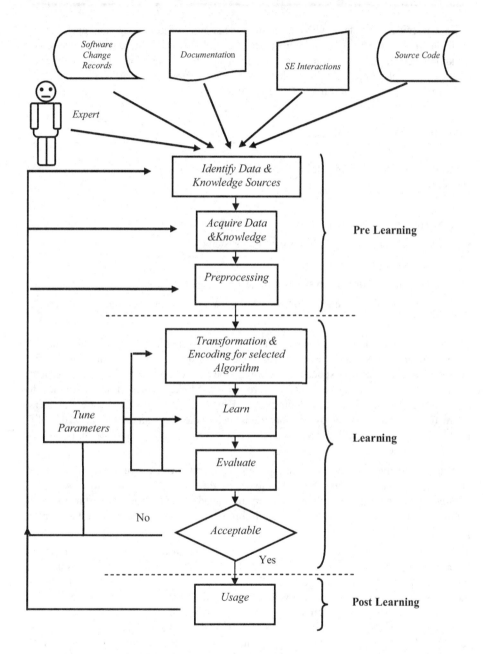

Pre-Learning Stage

The pre-learning stage starts with determining the sources of knowledge and data that are available to solve the problem of interest. This step is followed by the actual acquisition of the knowledge and data, and transforming the raw information to a format that can be used in the learning phase. It is estimated that these steps contribute to 50-80% of all the effort in the real-life data mining projects (Pyle, 1999).

Identifying Sources of Data and Knowledge

Some of the sources of knowledge and data available in software development/maintenance environments are:

- Source code
- Bug tracking and software configuration systems
- Documentation
- Experts in the software system of interest
- Software engineers' interaction with the source code while maintaining software

We have used these first three resources fairly extensively in our research. Due to the lack of software engineers' time, we had to minimize the burden on them by using some of the available documents at the expense of our time. To be able to use the fifth knowledge source, one needs to instrument the tools used by programmers to keep track of their activities. In a real-world setting, effective recording of, and subsequent usage of software engineers' interactions may be hindered by considerations such as the wide range of tools used by different people, lack of availability of the source code to instrument the tools, and usability and privacy concerns.

Although most medium-to-large size software development companies keep a record of changes made to their software, almost universally the information is not stored with data mining or machine learning in mind. Also, one may need to pull together data from disparate sources and further process them to create information and data to be used in the learning phase.

To be able to learn the Co-update relation, we need to find instances of files being changed together during the maintenance process. At Mitel Networks, the target of our case study, the process of applying changes to the source files starts with posting a problem report in SMS, the software management system developed and used in the company. SMS provides the functionality of source management and bug tracking systems. By using SMS, developers can keep track of the problems reported about a system, along with a history of responses to the problem. Problem reports typically include a textual description of the problem with possible additional information such as the hardware's status at the time the problem was observed, and so forth.

The changes made to the system in response to a problem report are recorded in the form of an *update*. As noted in Bryson and Kielstra (1992), *"An update is the basic unit of identifying actual (as opposed to planned) updates to the software."*

Once the changes are tested, verified, and deemed to be acceptable, the update is assigned a "closed" status, which means it is frozen and cannot be reopened or altered. An update records the problem reports that it intends to address, and the name of the files changed as the result of applying the update. A similar process is followed in many other companies, although the terminology and some of the finer details may vary from one company to the other.

Acquire Data and Knowledge

SMS provides queries that show files changed by an update. However, to be able to create a relatively reliable list of files changed as a result of an update, results generated by more than one query needed to be programmatically combined and filtered.

To classify the relevance between m software entities, for example, files, one needs to define k classes, or categories, of relevance. In the case of Co-update relation, both m (number of files) and k (number of classes) are equal to two[11]. The two classes of relevance used in this chapter are:

- Relevant (a change in one will likely result in a change in the other)
- Not-Relevant (a change in one file will likely not have an effect on the other)

Ideally, an expert should provide the best examples of these two classes of relevance between pairs of files. They could also dismiss some of the examples extracted by other means as not important, or non-representative. However, due to the industrial setting of our project, the size of the software system under study, and the shortage of software engineers' time, we cannot rely on them to classify each pair of software objects. Consequently, we have used heuristics that solely rely on the stored maintenance data to label our examples. One would only expect to generate better results than what is reported here, should there be a well-established expert support structure in the target organization.

The reader might ask, *"why should we learn if there are already heuristics that can label examples?"* Arguably, the most important feature of a learning system is its ability to *generalize* or extrapolate *beyond* the examples used to learn a concept. Models generated by these systems can make predictions about cases that were not seen during the training phase; a system that merely memorizes examples of a concept is not capable of classifying unseen cases. The heuristics that label examples are based on the information extracted for a certain period of time. They will generate a set of file pairs with the corresponding class labels. These heuristics cannot predict the class label for a new file pair that is not in this set.

Another benefit of learning is that if the learning method generates an *explainable* model, for example, a decision tree, we may be able to document nontrivial relations among files and use this information as part of a reverse engineering effort.

Our heuristic to classify a training example as Relevant relies on information stored in SMS.

Co-Update Heuristic: Files which have been changed together in the same update are *relevant* to each other.[12]

Motivation: Updates are capable of capturing design decisions at the level of implementation. They can indirectly show parts of the SRG that have been traversed in the process of system maintenance over a certain period of time. In other words, they can provide clues to the kind of relations that exist among software entities that have been subject to the maintenance process.

Not-Relevant Heuristic: Two files that have never[13] been changed together are *not relevant* to each other.

If $T=[T_1,T_2]$ is the period of time to which the Co-update heuristic was applied, $T'=[T_3,T_2]$ the period of time to which the Not-Relevant heuristic is applied includes T that is, $T_3 \leq T_1$.[14]

Motivation: If two files have not been changed together in response to problems occurring in a software system over a period of certain number of years, this could be considered as a good evidence of independence among these files, or perhaps the existence of a relation that is not effected by typical maintenance activities applied to these files.

Figure 4 shows the relation between T and T'.

An update can change zero or more files. We are interested in updates that affect more than one file. These are files that we consider to be relevant to each other. If an update changes N files, we generate $\binom{N}{2}$ pairs of Relevant files.[15] This is because we are not pairing a file with itself, and the co-update relation is symmetric in nature. However, some updates change a large number of files. We refer to the number of files changed by an update its *group size*. A group size of n is written as G_n, and if there is no group size limit, it is indicated as NGSL.[16] It seems logical to assume that the smaller the size of a group, the closer the relationship between its member files is. Other way of interpreting this is that perhaps for small n the problem addressed by the update was very specific, affecting a small number of files, which are closely related to each other.

Corresponding to a set S_R of Relevant file pairs, there is a set S_{NR} of Not-Relevant file pairs, where $S_R \cap S_{NR} = \emptyset$. Effectively, each file f is paired with j files in the set f_R of files relevant to f, and with k files in set f_{NR} of files not relevant to f, where $|f_R|=$j, $|f_{NR}|=$k, and $f_R \cap f_{NR} = \emptyset$.

We denote the training set of file pairs as TRS, and the testing set of file pairs as TSS. The

Figure 4. The relation between time periods the Co-update and Not-Relevant heuristics are applied

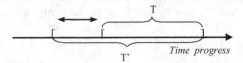

Relevant and Not-Relevant subsets in these sets are denoted as TRS_R, TRS_{NR}, TSS_R, and TSS_{NR}.

In general, we assume the world is *closed*. To create the set S_{NR} of Not-Relevant file pairs, we generate a *set of potential file pairs* in the target software system, and then remove all the pairs that we know are relevant to each other, including the set S_R. For instance, we may have access to additional sources of knowledge indicating that some of the pairs in the potential Not-Relevant set are indeed Relevant. The general relation between Relevant and Not-Relevant pairs is shown in Figure 5.

A Relevant file pair (f_i, f_j) is generated based on existing facts; that is, f_i and f_j are changed by the same update in time period T. However, a Not-Relevant pair (f_i, f_k) is generated because within the time period T' considered there was no update changing f_i and f_k together, or in other words due to the lack of a fact to the contrary. In general, the Not-Relevant heuristic can introduce some labeling or classification noise due to lack of knowledge. Short of expert feedback, or other sources of information, the only way to reduce the number of mislabeled Not-Relevant file pairs is to consider a longer period of time T' in the change history of the system. This is because the evidence to the contrary, that is, that they are updated together, does not exist in a larger time period. Assuming such a history exists, since software systems evolve over time, the larger the size of this history window, the higher the possibility that the extracted information is no longer valid for the current version of the system. Additionally, the number of Relevant file pairs grows slowly with the increase of the size of the time window, which means the reduction in the number of Not-Relevant file pairs also grows slowly.

To reduce the size of S_{NR}, instead of choosing all possible file pairs, or even a subset of these files such as the high level programming language file pairs, we can pair files in S_R with other files in the system. Due to the smaller size of S_R, the number of files used to generate the pairs will be smaller, which means the number of generated pairs will be smaller. The number of Not-Relevant pairs can be further reduced if we only focus on files f_i that appear as the *first* file in some pair (f_i, f_j) in S_R. We refer to this approach the *relevant-based* method of creating the set of potential Not-Relevant file pairs. Conceptually by applying the relevant-based method, we are pairing each file f_i with files that are relevant to it and files that are not relevant to it.

Figure 5. Relation between Relevant and Not-Relevant pairs

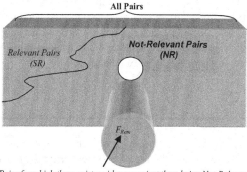

Pairs for which there exists evidence against them being Not-Relevant

Figure 6. File pairs, features, and examples

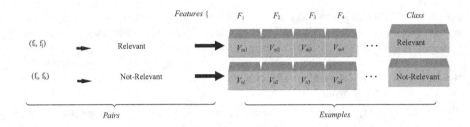

In the remainder of this chapter we use the notation $S_{c, n, y}$ to denote a set S of file pairs of class c, a group size restriction of n, and for time period indicated by y, where $c \in \{R, NR\}$ (R = Relevant, NR = Not-Relevant), n is a positive integer or NGSL, and y is a valid year or year range $y1$-$y2$ where $y1 < y2$.

When repeated file pairs are allowed, that is, S is a bag of file pairs instead of a set, we use $S_{c*, n, y}$ notation.

Definition: first_of_pairs(S) = $\{x_i | (x_i, y_j) \in S, S$ is a set of file pairs$\}$

Definition: dnrp[17] (S_R, F_2, F_{Rem}) = $\{(x, y) | (x, y) \in$ first_of_pairs$(S_R) \otimes F_2 - F_{Rem} \}$

where S_R is a set of Relevant file pairs, F_2 is a set of files[18] which can be the second element of a file pair, and F_{Rem} is a set of file pairs that should not be included in the resulting set.

Once the set of Relevant and Not-Relevant file pairs are created, one can generate the examples by calculating the value for the pre-defined features. A class label must be assigned to an example if the learning algorithm is one of supervised learning methods. This is shown in Figure 6.

Pre-Processing

The pre-processing stage deals with cleaning the data, removing noise, and making decisions, such as what subset of data to use, what features are relevant, and what to do with features with unknown values. The selection of a subset of data is an issue particularly when there is imbalance among the distribution of the classes. Many learning algorithms tend to be influenced by extreme skew in the distribution of data among the classes.

Learning Stage

The datasets generated in the previous steps need to be transformed to the format required by the learning system. In the next step, the learning system will take this dataset and create a classifier (or model). The classifier should be empirically evaluated to make sure it provides the desired level of performance according to appropriate measure or measures. If this evaluation succeeds, the process moves to the post-learning stage. Otherwise, one can either move to a previous step in the process, or change the value of a parameter of the learning algorithm and generate a new classifier.

Transformation and Encoding

Different learning systems have different number of input files, and use different formats and encoding conventions to represent the data processed by the system. The type of the data accepted by a learning algorithm varies from one algorithm to the other. For instance, some algorithms only accept numeric data, while others may accept categorical data as well. More modern learning systems allow data types such as strings or dates. Depending on the algorithm used there may be a need to transform the data generated in the pre-learning stage to an algorithm and implementation specific format. The output of the transformation step is the training dataset to be used by the learning system.

Learning

In the learning or modeling step, the learning system reads the training examples in the training set and generates a classifier (or model). This is depicted in Figure 7.

In this figure, an induction algorithm reads N pre-classified *training examples* $E_1, ..., E_N$ of the relevance relation we are interested in. Each example E_i is described by n *attributes* or *features* a_{ij}, $j=1, ..., n$, and is assigned a class c_i which is one of k pre-defined possible classes or a number between 0 and 1 if the relevance relation is continuous. The induction algorithm generates a classifier that can be used to classify an unseen (or unclassified) case X.

Machine learning research has generated a rich set of learning algorithms and new methods are still being introduced. However, not every method has been proven robust or scalable when it comes to dealing with real-world datasets. Other factors that influence the choice of the learning method include:

Figure 7. Classification learning

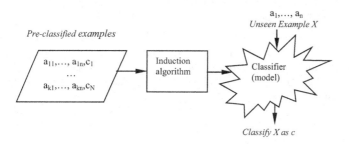

- implementation reliability and free versus commercial availability;
- the type of acceptable input by the algorithm, and whether a meaningful or even worthwhile transformation exists to convert the data to the desired input types;
- explainable versus black box models;
- the familiarity of the machine learning experts with other existing methods and even their motivation. In a more research-oriented setting, it will not be surprising to see the machine learning experts use their own algorithms as a means to validate their effectiveness.

Evaluating the Usefulness of the Learned Concept

We have used the term *usefulness* earlier in a very broad sense. For the purpose of empirical evaluation of the learned *relevance* concept, there is a need to present a more tangible measure. The evaluation process requires the learned classifier to be tested on a test set that is independent from the training set used to generate the classifier. In the section titled *Experiments: The Learning Stage*, we introduce some of the performance measures we have employed in our research. The details of the test sets used in evaluating the classifiers are presented in the following section.

Parameter Tuning

Most algorithms employed by learning systems use a variety of tunable parameters. Instead of changing the training set, one can change the value of these parameters to generate alternative models with improved predictive performance.

Post-Learning Stage

The post-learning phase mostly deals with putting the learned classifier into use. This is a compulsory step in deployed research (Saitta & Neri, 1998). As a result of feedback received from the user, one may revise some of the decisions made in the pre-learning and learning stages, such as data representation, sampling techniques, learning algorithms, and so forth. Such changes will require repetition of some of the earlier steps of the process, as shown by the backward arrows from this stage to the previous ones in Figure 3.

However such an endeavor demands a different set of resources and research priorities than those available in an academic setting such as ours.

In the next two sections, we present a case study where we learn the Co-update relation by mining various sources of data and knowledge about a real-world software system. *A Real-World Case Study: The Pre-Learning Stage* section covers the pre-learning stage while the *Experiments: The Learning Stage* section discusses the learning stage of the process discussed previously.

A Real World Case Study:
The Pre-Learning Stage

We would like to predict, given two files, whether when one file changes, the other may need to be changed as well. We can formulate this as a classification problem where we use k distinct classes to indicate how likely it is that two files change together. The learned classifier, embedded in an application with a proper user interface, could be used at least in one of the following scenarios:

- An expert software engineer who suspects changing file f_i may require a change in file f_j can receive a measure of their relevance for file pair (f_i, f_j).

- A software engineer who wants to know what other files may be affected by a change in a file f_i submits the file name f_i to the application and receives a list $f_j, ..., f_z$ of such files in return. If the classifier suggests too many files, a ranking between the returned results may further assist the software engineer in the maintenance task. However, a good classifier typically would not generate too many unrelated answers.

Furthermore, the classifier can also be used in other applications such as sub-system clustering that can benefit from the knowledge of existing relations between files.

Creating Training and Testing Repositories

We used a large legacy telephone switch system, that is, a PBX, developed by Mitel Networks as a case study. This system is written in a high level programming language (HLL) and assembler. The version of the PBX software which we used in our experiments had close to 1.9 million lines of code distributed among more than 4,700 files, out of which about 75% were HLL source files.

Before creating the training examples, we need to create the set of Relevant and Not-Relevant file pairs. For this, we processed the updates for the 1995-1999 time period. We found 1,401 closed updates in response to 1,213 problem reports. An update can change one or more files. Out of all closed updates in the earlier-noted time period, 43% changed two or more files. However, some updates change a large number of files. For instance, we encountered updates that changed more than 280 files. As discussed earlier, it makes sense to assume that updates that change a smaller number of files capture relationships that exist between files that are more closely related. We found that updates with a group size of 2 to 20 constitute 93% of updates with a group size larger than 1. Our experiments with no limit on update group size showed that better results can be obtained by limiting the group size. We have used a group size limit of 20 for the experiments reported in this chapter.

Our version of the Co-update relation will only focus on the HLL (high level programming language) files. Due to the less-structured nature of the assembler code, the information created by the parsers available to us was not as accurate as we had wished. The number of Relevant HLL file pairs changed by updates with a group size limit of up to 20 in the 1995-1999 time period was 4,547. This number includes repeated file pairs if two files were changed together

Table 1. Training repository and the testing set class distribution

	Relevant	Not-Relevant	#Relevant/#Not-Relevant
All	4547	1226827	0.00371
Training	3031	817884	0.00371
Testing	1516	408943	0.00371

in more than one update, that is, $|S_R|=|S_{R*,20,1995-1999}|=4,547$. In experiments not reported here, we observed that for files that are changed together more than once repeating Relevant file pairs generate better results than creating only one Relevant file pair.

For N source files, we can create $\binom{N}{2}$ pairs of files as a set of potential file pairs. The set of Not-Relevant file pairs is created by removing the set of Relevant file pairs from this set. The number of potential file pairs when all the source files in the system are used is close to 11 million pairs. The very skewed distribution of classes is a major difficulty with learning the Co-update relation. The number of files changed together in a year, that is, the relevant files, is much smaller than all the possible combinations of file pairs. Using only HLL files (in excess of 3,500 files), generates more than six million file pairs. This is still a very large number of pairs that, besides imposing severe computational limitations, introduces extreme imbalance between the Relevant and Not-Relevant pairs.

The relevant-based method of creating the Not-Relevant pairs further reduces the size of this set. Following the notation introduced in the section on acquiring data and knowledge, this dataset corresponds to

$$S_{NR} = \text{dnrp} (S_{R,20,1995-1999}, \text{HLL}, S_{R,NGSL,1995-1999})$$

$S_{R,NGSL,1995-1999}$ is the set of all the file pairs that were changed together by updates in the 1995-1999 time period, and includes $S_{R,20,1995-1999}$. HLL is a set that contains the names of source files written in a high level programming language.

For the purpose of evaluating our classifiers, we used the *hold out* method which involves randomly splitting the set of file pairs into three parts. Two parts form a training repository, and one part is used for testing. The test set is independent of the training repository and maintains the original distribution of classes.

Table 1 shows the distribution of file pairs in the training repository and the testing set.

As can be seen in Table 1, despite great reduction in the number of Not-Relevant file pairs, the set of file pairs is nevertheless very imbalanced. Such imbalanced data frequently appears in real-world applications and poses difficulties to the learning task (AAAI, 2000). We discuss how we learn from less-skewed training sets when we present our experimental setup.

Attributes Used in the Experiments

The attributes or features used to describe the examples of the Co-update relation can be based on a property of one of the files in the pair but more often are a function of both of these files. The attributes we have used to learn the Co-update relation can be divided into two groups:

- Syntactic attributes
- Text-based attributes

In this section, we present and discuss each of these attribute sets.

Syntactic Attributes

Syntactic attributes are based on syntactic constructs in the source code such as function calls, or data flow information such as variable or type definitions. These attributes are extracted by static analysis of the source code. They also include attributes based on names given to files. In Table 2, we have shown a set of such attributes used in our experiments.

Table 2. Syntactic attributes

Attribute Name	Attribute Type
Same File Name	Boolean
ISU File Extension	Text
OSU File Extension	Text
Same Extension	Boolean
Common Prefix Length	Integer
Number of Shared Directly Referred Types	Integer
Number of Shared Directly Referred non Type Data Items	Integer
Number of Routines Directly Referred in ISU and Defined in OSU	Integer
Number of Routines Directly and Indirectly Referred in ISU and Defined in OSU	Integer
Number of Routines Defined in ISU and Directly Referred in OSU	Integer
Number of Routines Defined in ISU and Directly and Indirectly Referred by OSU	Integer
Number of Shared Routines Directly Referred	Integer
Number of Shared Routines Among All Routines Referred in the Units	Integer
Number of Shared Direct and Indirectly Referred Routines	Integer
Number of Shared Files Included	Integer
Directly Include You	Boolean
Directly Include Me	Boolean

Computing the value of some of these attributes involves steps similar to the ones taken to measure well known static software product metrics such as fan-in, fan-out, and cyclomatic complexity (McCabe, 1976). Many of the entries in this table are self-explanatory. However, the term "interesting software unit" (ISU) denotes the first file in a pair and "other software unit" (OSU) denotes the second file. We say a sub-routine is directly referred to if it appears in the main executable portion of a source file, for example, main function in a C program. Sub-routines that are referred to outside the main executable part of a source file are said to be *indirectly* referred to.

Text-Based Attributes

In addition to extracting syntactic features of the file pair, we also analyze some of the English text related to the files. This includes problem reports affecting a file, and the comments embedded in the file.

Problem reports contain the description of the problem or potential bug in English and may also include other information deemed to be helpful to the person who will fix the problem. This additional information may include program traces, memory dumps, hardware status information, and so forth. They are stored and maintained in SMS, independently from source files themselves.

Most source files include comments that describe what the program is intended to do.

Both problem reports and source file comments provide additional sources of knowledge that can be used to extract attributes. The idea here is to associate a set of words with each source file. Therefore, instead of looking at a source file as a sequence of syntactic constructs, we can view them as documents.

To learn the Co-update relation, we have adapted the *vector* or *bag of words representation* (Mladenic, 1999) by associating a vector of Boolean features with each *pair of files*. The bag of words representation is frequently used in information retrieval and text classification. Each document in a set of documents is represented by a bag of words appearing in all the documents in the set. In the Boolean version of this representation, the vector corresponding to a document consists of Boolean features. A feature is set to *true* if the word corresponding to that feature appears in the document, otherwise it is set to *false*. Therefore, for each source file, we first create a *file feature vector* from the set of words associated with the source files.

However, the Co-update relation involves a *pair* of files. To create a *file pair feature vector* for a pair of source files (f_i, f_j), we find the intersection of the file feature vectors associated with f_i and f_j. The idea here is to find similarities between the two files. In the intersection vector, a feature is set to *true* if the word corresponding to the feature is in both documents that are associated with the files in the pair.

An important issue in using a bag of words approach in text classification is the selection of the words or features. We created a set of *acceptable words* by first using an acronym definition file which existed at Mitel Networks. These acronyms belong to the application domain; therefore they include some of the most important and commonly used words. From this set, we removed an expanded version of the set of stop words, that is, words not to be included, proposed in Lewis (1992). We further refined this initial set of acceptable words through a few semi-automatic iterations where we filtered a set of problem reports against the set of acceptable words, and then manually updated the set of acceptable words by analyzing the word frequencies of rejected words as well as our knowledge of application-domain vocabulary.

Although this acceptable word list was created by a non-expert and as a proof of concept, we were motivated by an earlier promising work in creating a lightweight knowledge base about the same application domain that used a similar manual selection technique for the initial set of concepts (Sayyad Shirabad, Lethbridge, & Lyon, 1997). The word extractor program detects words in uppercase in an otherwise mostly lowercase text. In many cases, such words are good candidates for technical abbreviations or acronyms and domain specific terms. To reduce the noise in the extracted words, the program detects memory dumps or distinguishes a word followed by a period at the end of a sentence from a file name or an assembler instruction that includes a period. We believe the results presented in this chapter would be further improved if we could benefit from the domain experts' knowledge in creating these word lists.

As part of the process of creating the set of acceptable words, we also manually created two other lists that we called the *transformation list* and the *collocation list*. The word extractor program uses the transformation list to perform actions such as lemmatization or conversion of plurals to singulars. The collocation list is used to preserve sequences of interesting words that appear together even though the participating words may not be deemed acceptable on their own.

While the process of creating these three lists can be further automated, the best lists are application dependent and finding them could be a separate research topic on its own. One of the active research areas in machine learning is feature selection; this deals with closely related issues. One could also use techniques from the field of natural language processing such as parsing and stemming in this process.

In the following two sub-sections, we discuss how we can use the source comments and problem report words as features.

Source File Comment Attributes

Finding comments in a source file is a relatively trivial task. We used the three lists mentioned previously to filter the comments in each source file and associate each file with a set of comment words. We then used the bag of words representation discussed earlier to create the file pair feature vectors.

Problem Report Attributes

An update can be in response to one or more problem reports and can change one or more files. We can therefore associate each file with one or more problem reports. Since description of a problem can be viewed as a document, a bag of words can be associated with each problem report. Lets assume that a file f_i is changed to address problem reports $p_1, p_2, ...,$ p_n. Furthermore assume that these problem reports are represented by bags of words called $W_{p_1}, W_{p_2}, ..., W_{p_n}$. We create a bag of words for a file f_i by finding the union of problem report bags of words $\bigcup_{k=1}^{n} W_{p_k}$ for problem reports that resulted in a change in f_i. This bag contains

Figure 8. Creating source file-bag of words using problem reports

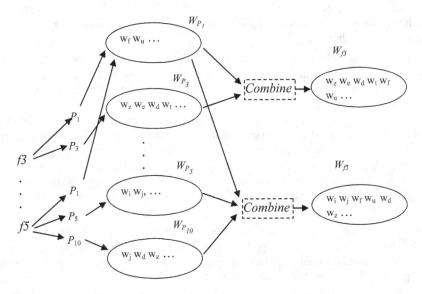

all the words that appear in some problem report that caused the file to change. The use of a union allows us to account for different reasons resulting in a file being changed.

Figure 8 shows how problem reports can be used to associate a bag of words with a source file. Since there is a 1-to-N relation between problem report words and source files, this process will not generate attributes that uniquely identify examples. The new bag of words is filtered using the three lists discussed earlier.

Once a file is associated with a bag of problem report words, it can be represented as a feature vector, and a file pair feature vector can be created using these individual file feature vectors.

Experiments: The Learning Stage

To generate the models discussed in this chapter, we used C5.0 (RuleQuest Research, 1999)[19] for the following reasons:

- Decision tree learning algorithms have been widely studied and successfully used by machine learning and other researchers.
- Decision trees are explainable models and can be analyzed by an expert to identify the reason for a prediction. The study of the tree could also result in finding relationships that were not known before. This is in contrast to black box methods such as neural networks or support vector machines.

- During the course of our research we have tried alternative methods, but none were able to generate significantly better results than decision trees.[20] Many times decision trees generated better results.

In a decision tree, each non-leaf node is a test of the value of one of the pre-defined feature used to describe the example. A leaf node stores the classification for the cases that satisfies the conditions on the path from the root of the tree to that particular leaf. A case is classified by starting at the top of the tree, and following the branches of the tree based on the outcome of each test, until the case reaches a leaf.

To compare and evaluate the effects of using different feature sets, we first need to choose a performance measure or method of comparison that is appropriate for the particular task at hand. Table 1 shows the large imbalance between the Relevant and the Not-Relevant classes. In settings such as this, *accuracy*, which is the number of cases correctly classified over the total number of cases classified, is not the best performance measure. A simple classifier that always chooses the majority class will have a very high accuracy, however such a classifier has no practical value.

To learn the Co-update relation, we created less-skewed datasets from the training repository and tested the generated classifiers using the complete and independent testing set. Each training set included all the Relevant examples and K times as many Not-Relevant examples from the training repository. We used the following 18 values for K:

$$1, 2, 3, 4, 5, 6, 7, 8, 9, 10, 15, 20, 25, 30, 35, 40, 45, 50$$

In the experiments using the syntactic attributes, the Not-Relevant examples were formed by selecting a stratified sample of the Not-Relevant examples in the training repository. In other words in the training sets we tried to maintain, as much as possible, the same proportion of Not-Relevant examples with a certain attribute value pattern as was present in the skewed training repository.

Precision and recall are standard metrics from information retrieval, and are also used in machine learning. *Precision* tells one the proportion of returned results that are in fact valid (that is, assigned the correct class). *Recall* is a complementary metric that tells one the proportion of valid results that are in fact found.

While precision and recall of the Relevant class are appropriate measures for this application, they are not always convenient to use to compare classifiers' performance. We frequently found that, when comparing classifiers generated by different methods of creating training sets, while the precision plot for one method was more dominant, the recall plot for the other method tend to be more dominant.

ROC plots (Egan, 1975) allow us to depict measures which are equally important as precision and recall but on one single plot. In an ROC plot, the horizontal axis represents the *false positive rate* and the vertical axis represent the *true positive rate*. For our application, the Relevant class is the same as the positive class. Using the *confusion matrix* in Figure 9, the true and false positive rates and precision and recall of the Relevant class are defined as

Figure 9. A confusion matrix for a two class classification problem

		Classified as	
		Relevant	Not-Relevant
True class	Not-Relevant	a	b
	Relevant	c	d

$$TP_R = Recall_R = \frac{\text{Relevant cases correctly classified}}{\text{Number of Relevant cases}} = \frac{c}{c+d} \qquad (1)$$

$$FP_R = \frac{\text{Not-Relevant cases incorrectly classified}}{\text{Number of Not-Relevant cases}} = \frac{a}{a+b} \qquad (2)$$

$$Precision_R = \frac{\text{Relevant cases correctly classified}}{\text{Number of cases classified as Relevant}} = \frac{c}{a+c} \qquad (3)$$

Figure 10 shows the ROC plots for two classifiers A and B. In an ROC curve, the following holds:

- Point (0,1) corresponds to *perfect classification*, where every case is classified correctly.
- Point (1,0) is a classifier that misclassifies every case.
- Point (1,1) is a classifier that classifies every case as positive.
- Point (0,0) is a classifier that classifies every case as negative.

Figure 10. Two example ROC curves

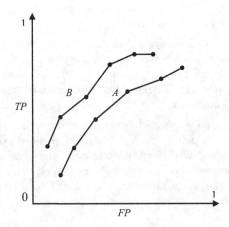

Better classifiers have (FP, TP) values closer to point (0, 1). A classifier *dominates* another classifier if it is more "north west" of the inferior classifier. In Figure 10, classifier B clearly dominates classifier A.

In our application domain, a high true positive rate means that the classifier correctly classifies most of the Relevant examples in the testing set. A low false positive rate indicates that the classifier does not classify many Not-Relevant examples as Relevant. After using the ROC plot to determine the superiority of one classifier over another classifier, one can further investigate the quality of the better classifier by other means such as precision and recall plots.

Syntactic Versus Text-Based Attributes

Figure 11 shows the ROC plots generated for the 18 ratios of skewness between Not-Relevant and Relevant examples using syntactic and text-based features.

The same set of file pairs were used for experiments with the same skewness ratio. In each plot, the classifier with imbalance ratio 1 corresponds to the rightmost point on the plot, while the lower leftmost point corresponds to an imbalance ratio 50 classifier. The true and false positive ratios decrease as the ratio of Not-Relevant to Relevant examples in the training set increases. Generally, an increase in the training set skewness causes the true positive rate to decrease, however the amount of change in the case of problem report based classifiers is much less than the classifiers using other feature sets.

Figure 11. Comparison of syntactic and text-based feature sets

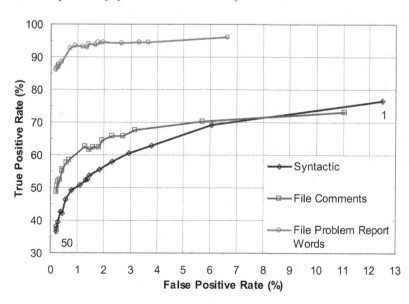

Figure 12. Comparison of the precision of classifiers generated from syntactic and text-based feature sets

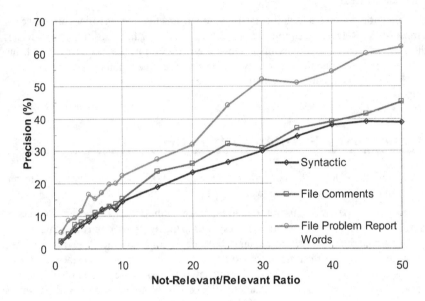

Figure 13. Comparison of the recall of classifiers generated from syntactic and text-based feature sets

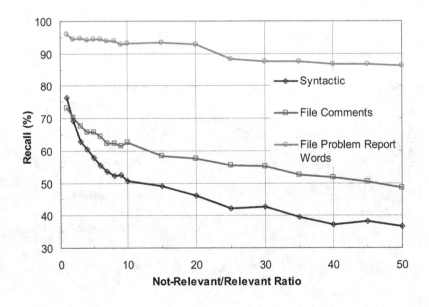

While the classifiers learned from syntactic attributes generate interesting true and false positive rates, their performance is not sufficient to use them in the field. The figure shows that the classifiers generated from the problem report feature set clearly dominate the classifiers generated from source file comment and syntactic feature sets. Although the comment feature set does not perform as well as the problem report feature set, the classifiers generated from this feature set still dominate the classifiers generated form syntactic features.

Figures 12 and 13 show the precision and recall plots for the 18 skewness ratios discussed earlier. The increase in skewness ratio results in an increase in the precision and a decrease in the recall of the Relevant class However for problem report based classifiers, the degradation of recall values occurs at a much slower rate. For the imbalance ratio of 50, the problem report based classifier achieves 62% precision and 86% recall. In other words, for 62 out of every 100 file pairs the classifier correctly predicts that they change together. The classifier correctly identifies 86 out of every 100 file pairs that actually change together. The importance of such performance values becomes more apparent when we take into account that a maintenance programmer may be faced with thousands of potential source files in the system. These empirical results suggest that we can answer yes to the question we posed regarding the possibility of finding a non-trivial and useful relevance relation.

Combining Feature Sets

Feature sets can be combined by simply concatenating features in each set. This is the obvious choice when combining syntactic and text-based features because they are different in their nature. In the case of text-based features, such as problem report word features and the source file comment word features, we have at least two other alternatives. We can create a combined feature set by either finding the intersection or the union of the two feature sets. In the first case, the new feature set consists of words appearing both in the comments and problem report words associated with a source file. In the second case, a word need only appear in the comments of a source file or in a problem report associated with a source file.

We have performed extensive experiments using the concatenation and the union method of combining problem report word and source file comment feature sets. The union representation did not improve the results in most cases, including the more interesting results such as the ones obtained for ratio-50 problem report word features classifier discussed in the previous section. Due to space limitation, we will not discuss these experiments here.

Figure 14 shows the ROC plots for classifiers generated from examples using the concatenation of syntactic and source file comment features. We only used a subset of features that appeared in the decision trees generated in the comment word feature set experiments presented in the previous section. This in effect is performing a limited feature selection on source file comment feature set. The idea behind feature selection is to choose a subset of available features to describe the example without the loss of quality of the results obtained. A smaller feature set reduces the number of calculations or observations required to create an example. Sometimes, a smaller feature subset improves the quality of the obtained results.

This figure shows that the concatenation of these two feature sets generated classifiers that considerably dominate both syntactic and source file comment feature sets.

Figure 14. Combining syntactic and source file comment features

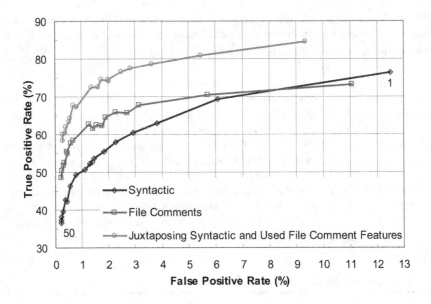

Figure 15. Combining syntactic and problem report word features

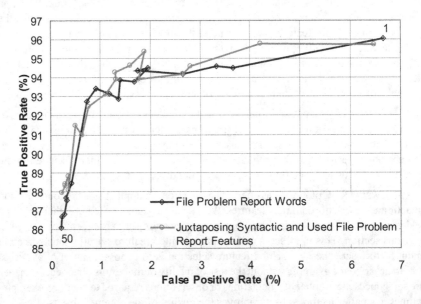

We also combined syntactic features with a subset of features that appeared in the decision trees generated in the problem report feature set experiments discussed in the previous sub-section. As shown in Figure 15, again the combination of syntactic and text-based features improved the existing results for most of the ratios including the more interesting classifiers generated from more skewed training sets. It should not be surprising to see the improvements are less than the ones seen in the case of combining file comment and syntactic features, as problem report word features on their own generate high quality results.

Summary of Experiments

In the previous two sections, we discussed experiments that learned classifiers approximating the Co-update maintenance relevance relations using syntactic, as well as text-based features extracted from source file comments and problem reports. These experiments show that the classifiers learned from the text-based features, especially the problem report features, considerably outperform syntactic feature classifiers. Generally, independently of the feature set, increasing the Not-Relevant/Relevant ratio in the training set improves the precision and degrades the recall of the Relevant class. The problem report feature set classifiers not only have higher recall values, they are also less sensitive to the increase in the skewness of the training set. The performance values obtained from the ratio 50 problem report feature set classifier indicates that one can learn models that are reasonably good candidates for field deployment.

Figures 14 and 15 show the results obtained from some of the possible combinations of syntactic and text-based features. Generally, classifiers learned from combined feature sets improved the results of classifiers learned from the individual feature sets. The improvements for comment-based classifiers were more significant than the ones for problem report based classifiers.

Incorporating Costs in the Learned Models

While it is ideal to have a classifier that is always correct, hardly if ever is this the case for real-world classifiers. In a two-class classification setting, we could misclassify Relevant cases as Not-Relevant or misclassify Not-Relevant cases as Relevant. In Figure 9, these would be the entries indicated as d and a respectively. If we think of the Relevant class as positive and the Not-Relevant class as negative, these correspond to *false negative* and *false positive* errors.

The results discussed so far were based on the assumption that a false positive and false negative errors have equal weight. Many learning algorithms including C5.0 can create models that assign different weights or importance to different misclassification errors. We will explore the effects of learning under different misclassification costs in the following sub-sections.

The behavior of a classifier can be further analyzed based on the confusion matrix generated from testing cases. This is done by assigning different cost factors to each kind of error and calculating the total error cost. An example of such analysis can be found in Sayyad Shirabad et al. (2004).

Learning when Misclassifying Relevant Cases Costs More

We ran experiments using the problem report based training sets where misclassifying a Relevant example as Not-Relevant costs 2, 5, 10, 15, and 20 times more than misclassifying a Not-Relevant example as Relevant. We generated classifiers for training sets with Not-Relevant/Relevant ratios 30, 35, 40, 45, and 50.[21] In each case, a classifier was trained and tested on the same testing repository as we discussed earlier.

Figure 16 shows the ROC comparison of these classifiers. As the figure shows, increasing the misclassification cost of Relevant (positive) examples generates classifiers with better true-positive rates. In other words, these classifiers manage to classify more of the Relevant test cases correctly. However, the increase in true positive rate is accompanied by increase in the false positive rate In other words, these classifiers tend to classify more cases as Relevant and as a result end up misclassifying more Not-Relevant examples as Relevant. Figure 16 also shows that cost values 10, 15, and 20 generate worse classifiers than the ones generated for the cost value 5. Figures 17 and 18 show the precision and the recall of the classifiers generated for the misclassification costs mentioned earlier.

These figures show that by changing the cost of misclassifying Relevant examples we can improve the recall of the Relevant class at the expense of its precision. Such classifiers could be preferable in scenarios where the user cares to find as many relevant files as possible and can afford sifting through extra not relevant files.

Figure 16. ROC comparison for varying Relevant misclassification costs

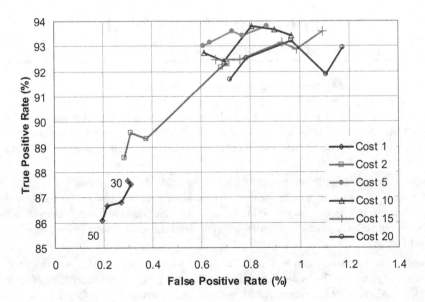

Figure 17. Precision comparison for varying Relevant misclassification costs

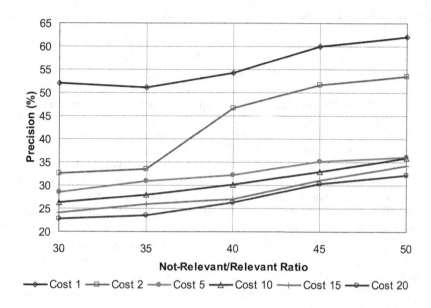

Figure 18. Recall comparison for varying Relevant misclassification costs

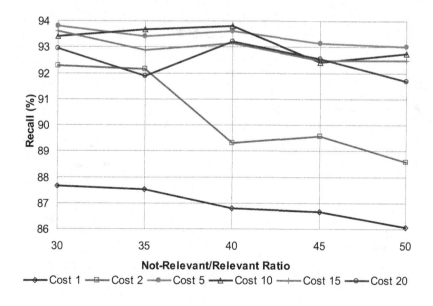

Learning when Misclassifying Not-Relevant Cases Costs More

We also performed experiments using the problem report word feature set where misclassifying a Not-Relevant example as Relevant was 2, 5, 10, 15, and 20 costlier than misclassifying a Relevant example as Not-Relevant. As shown in Figure 19, increasing the misclassification cost of Not-Relevant examples generates classifiers that classify more of the Not-Relevant test cases correctly and therefore have better false positive rates. However, the decrease in false positive rate is accompanied by a decrease in true positive rate. These models classify more cases as Not-Relevant and subsequently misclassify more Relevant examples as Not-Relevant. Furthermore, for cost values 10, 15, and 20 the true positive rate decreases more rapidly compared to cost values 2 and 5. The reason for the true positive value of zero for cost value 20 and skewness ratio 50 is that the generated classifier was a single node decision tree that classified every test case as Not-Relevant. Consequently, this classifier would misclassify all the Relevant cases. Figures 20 and 21 show the precision and recall plots under the earlier-mentioned misclassification cost settings.

These figures show that by changing the cost of misclassifying Not-Relevant examples, we can improve the precision of the Relevant class, however this is achieved at the expense of the reduced recall of this class. Such classifiers could be preferable in scenarios where the user wants the suggested files to be actually relevant even though there maybe many such files that are missed by the classifiers.

Figure 19. ROC comparison for varying Not-Relevant misclassification costs

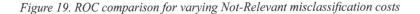

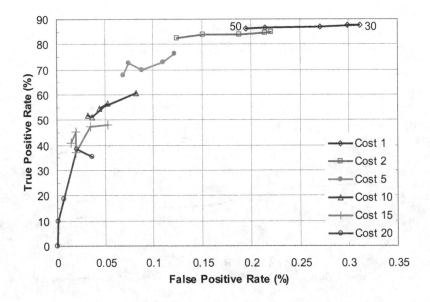

Figure 20. Precision comparison for varying Not-Relevant misclassification costs

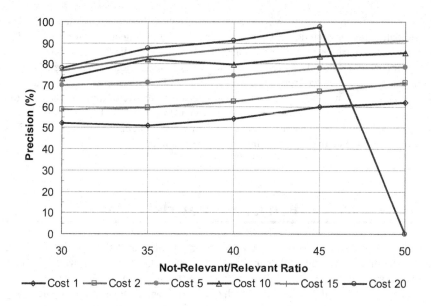

Figure 21. Recall comparison for varying Not-Relevant misclassification costs

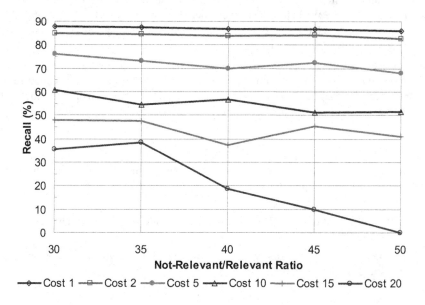

Summary of Experimental Results

In the previous two sub-sections, we presented the effects of learning classifiers modeling the Co-update relevance relation when the costs of misclassifying cases are not equal. We performed these experiments using the problem report feature set. We showed that by assigning a higher cost to misclassifying Relevant cases, one can learn models that generate better recall than the ones generated from equal cost classifiers. This is achieved at the expense of reduced precision. Assigning higher costs to misclassified Not-Relevant examples has the reverse effect where one can obtain better precision at the expense of lost recall. In both cases, the experiments showed that cost ratios 10 and higher generally resulted in classifiers with lower performance than the ones trained for cost ratio 5.

Future Trends

The notion of the relevance relation is very general and flexible, so that it can capture a wide range of relationships among entities in a software system. In this chapter, we discussed a specific relevance relation called Co-update, however the modeling of a relevance relation by a classifier as well as the process by which one learns such a model is applicable to any relevance relation. We, therefore, envision that these ideas will be replicated to learn other relationships in software systems.

As we use supervised learning to model a relevance relation, first we need to find instances of the relation of interest and then describe them in the form of examples using properly designed set of features. Therefore, the main obstacle in the wider applications of the ideas discussed in this chapter is availability of data. By availability we mean both collection of data and access to it. We believe that open source system will be the major target for discovery of relevance relations in the future, since many of these systems collect historic project related data that are freely accessible.

However, we recognize that discovery of relevance relations and building high-quality models that represent them are time consuming and require a lot of effort as well as expertise in data mining techniques. Therefore, we expect that research in this area will grow slowly at the beginning. Some of the potential future research directions for us include:

- Using alternative features sets, that is, file name based attributes;
- Improving the attribute creation process for text based attributes by refining the word filtering lists and employing more sophisticated natural language processing and information retrieval techniques;
- Experimenting with feature selection methods to create classifiers with better predictive quality;
- Using learning methodologies, such as co-training (Blum & Mitchell, 1998) as alternatives to example labeling heuristics;

- Investigating alternative methods to reduce the size of the majority class and other techniques to learn from imbalanced datasets (AAAI, 2000; ICML, 2003);

- Learning from one class (Relevant), for example, training an autoassociator (Japkowicz, 2001);

- Using methods that generate a probability estimation of the relevance, for example, probability estimation trees (Provost & Domingos, 2000). Such methods can be used to rank files classified as Relevant;

- Field testing the generated models and evaluate their use in a real world setting;

- Using the learned Co-update relation in other applications such as clustering to find the sub-systems in the legacy system;

- Discovering other interesting relevance relations. For instance, models that can classify a new problem report as one or more of a set of pre-defined problem types; and

- Using open source software as an alternative to proprietary legacy software.

Conclusions

This chapter presents the notion of relevance relations, which maps tuples of two or more software entities to a value quantifying how relevant, that is, connected or related, the entities are to each other. Such an abstraction allows one to capture most, if not all, of existing and important interactions among entities in a software system. We showed how the problem of learning a relevance relation can be mapped to a classification learning problem. We also discussed the process of learning a relevance relation in the context of software maintenance.

We presented an example of a real-world relevance relation called Co-update which maps tuples of file pairs to a relevance value of Relevant or Not-Relevant indicating whether or not a change in one file may result in a change in the other file. We then provided detailed discussions of the steps involved in the process when learning the Co-update relevance relation in the case of a real-world legacy telephony system.

We experimented with both syntactic and textual feature sets to model the Co-update relation. Our experiments showed that text-based feature sets outperform syntactic feature sets. Among text-based feature sets, problem-report feature sets resulted in superior models. We also showed that combining syntactic- and text-based feature sets in most cases improves the results obtained from using each feature set individually.

We further experimented with learning models of Co-update relevance relation at in the presence of different misclassification costs during learning. The results show that by assigning a higher misclassification cost to misclassifying Relevant examples one can learn classifiers that can find a larger portion of all the existing Relevant file pairs, however these models also tend to suggest a larger number of Not-Relevant pairs as being Relevant. On the other hand by assigning a higher cost to misclassifying Not-Relevant examples, one can learn classifiers that are more often correct when suggesting two files as being "relevant", however these models tend to find a *smaller* portion of all the existing Relevant file pairs.

In other words the software engineer has a choice between the accuracy of suggested relevant pairs and the comprehensiveness of these suggestions, and in principle one can learn a classifier that best suits the needs of the user.

Acknowledgments

This research was sponsored by CSER and supported by Mitel Networks and NSERC. The authors would like to thank the members of SX 2000 team for their support and help with our project.

References

AAAI (2000). *AAAI 2000 Workshop on Learning from Imbalanced Data Set*, Austin, Texas, July 31, 2001. American Association for Artificial Intelligence.

Almeida, M. A., & Matwin, S. (1999). Machine learning method for software quality model building. In the *Proceedings of 11th International Symposium on Methodologies for Intelligent Systems (ISMIS)*, Warsaw, Poland, June 8-11 (pp. 565-573). *Lecture Notes in Computer Science, 1609*. Springer.

Blum, A., & Mitchell, T. (1998). Combining labeled and unlabeled data with co-training. In the *Proceedings of the 11th Conference on Computational Learning Theory*, Madison, WI, July 24-26 (pp. 92-100). Morgan Kaufmann Publishers.

Briand, L. C., Melo, W. L., & Wüst, J. (2002). Assessing the applicability of fault-proneness models across object-oriented software projects. *IEEE Transactions on Software Engineering, 28*(7), 706-720.

Briand, L. C., Thomas, W. M., & Hetmanski, C. J. (1993). Modeling and managing risk early in software developments. In the *Proceedings of 15th International Conference on Software Engineering*, Baltimore, MD (pp. 55-65). IEEE.

Bryson, C., & Kielstra, J. (1992). *SMS—Library system user's reference manual*. DT.49, Version A18. Mitel Corporation.

Cohen, W., & Devanbu, P. (1997). A comparative study of inductive logic programming methods for software fault prediction. In the *Proceedings of Fourteenth International Conference on Machine Learning*, Vanderbilt University, Nashville, TN, USA, July 8-12 (pp. 66-74). Morgan Kaufmann.

Cohen, W., & Devanbu, P. (1999). Automatically exploring hypotheses about fault prediction: A comparative study of inductive logic programming methods. *International Journal of Software Engineering and Knowledge Engineering, 9*(5), 519-546.

Egan, J. (1975). *Signal detection theory and ROC analysis*. New York: Academic Press.

Fouqué, G., & Matwin, S. (1993). Composition software reuse with case-based reasoning. In the *Proceedings of the 9th IEEE Conference on AI for Applications*, Orlando, FL, March 1-5 (pp. 128-134). IEEE.

Gall, H., Krajewski, J., & Jazayeri, M. (2003). CVS release history data for detecting logical couplings. In the *Proceedings of the International Workshop on Principles of Software Evolution (IWPSE)*, Helsinki, Finland, September 1-2 (pp. 13-23). IEEE CS Press.

Graves, T. L., Karr, A. F., Marron, J. S., & Siy, H. (2000). Predicting fault incidence using software change history. *IEEE Transactions on Software Engineering, 26*(7), 653-661.

Holte, R. C. (1993). Very simple classification rules perform well on most commonly used datasets. *Machine Learning, 3*, 63-91.

ICML. (2003). *Workshop on Learning from Imbalanced Data Sets II*, Washington, D.C., August 21. International Conference on Machine Learning.

Japkowicz, N. (2001). Supervised versus unsupervised binary-learning by feedforward neural networks. *Machine Learning, 42*(1/2), 97-122.

Khoshgoftaar, T. M., & Seliya, N. (2003). Fault prediction modeling for software quality estimation: Comparing commonly used techniques. *Empirical Software Engineering, 8*, 255-283.

Lethbridge, T. C. (2000). Integrated personal work management in the TkSee software exploration tool. In the *Second International Symposium on Constructing Software Engineering Tools CoSET*, Limerick, Ireland, June 5 (pp. 31-38). IEEE.

Lethbridge, T. C., & Anquetil, N. (1997). *Architecture of a source code exploration tool: A software engineering case study*. Technical Report TR-97-07, Department of Computer Science, University of Ottawa.

Lewis, D. D. (1992). *Representation and learning in information retrieval*. Doctoral dissertation, University of Massachusetts.

Marchand, M., & Shawe-Taylor, J. (2002). The set covering machine, *Machine Learning, 3*, 723-746.

McCabe, T. J. (1976). A complexity measure. *IEEE Transactions on Software Engineering, 2*(4), 308-320.

Merlo, E., & De Mori, R. (1994). Artificial neural networks for source code information analysis. In the *Proceedings of International Conference on Artificial Neural Networks, 2*(3), Sorrento, Italy, May 26-29 (pp. 895-900).

Merlo, E., McAdam, I., & De Mori, R. (1993). Source code informal information analysis using connectionist models. In the *Proceedings of the 13th International Joint Conference on Artificial Intelligence (IJCAI)*, Chambery, France, August 28-September 3 (pp. 1339-1345). Morgan Kaufmann.

Mladenic, D. (1999). Text-learning and related intelligent agents: A survey. *IEEE Intelligent Systems, 14*(4), 44-54.

Piatetsky-Shapiro, G., Brachman, R., Khabaza, T., Kloesgen, W., & Simoudis, E. (1996) An overview of issues in developing industrial data mining and knowledge discovery. In E. Simoudis, J. Han, & U. Fayyad (Eds.), *Proceedings of the Second International*

Conference on Knowledge Discovery and Data Mining, Portland, Oregon, USA, August 2-4 (pp. 89-95). AAAI Press.

Porter, A. (1994). Using measurement-driven modeling to provide empirical feedback to software developers. *Journal of Systems and Software, 20*(3), 237-254.

Provost, F., & Domingos, P. (2000). *Well-trained PETs: Improving probability estimation trees.* CeDER Working Paper # , Stern School of Business, New York University, NY.

Pyle, D. (1999). *Data preparation for data mining.* San Francisco, CA: Morgan Kaufmann.

Quinlan, J. R. (1993). *C4.5: Programs for machine learning* (P. Langley, Series Ed.). San Mateo, CA: Morgan Kaufmann Publishers.

RuleQuest Research. (1999). Data mining tools See5 and C5.0. Retrieved from http://www.rulequest.com/see5-info.html

Saitta, L., & Neri, F. (1998). Learning in the "real world". *Machine Learning, 30*(2-3), 133-163.

Sayyad Shirabad, J., Lethbridge, T. C., & Lyon, S. (1997). A little knowledge can go a long way towards program understanding. In the *Proceedings of the 5th International Workshop on Program Comprehension*, Dearborn, MI, May 28-30 (pp. 111-117). IEEE Computer Society.

Sayyad Shirabad, J., Lethbridge, T. C., & Matwin, S. (2004). Mining software change repository of a legacy telephony system. In the *Proceedings of MSR 2004 – The International Workshop on Mining Software Repositories* (An ICSE 2004 workshop), Edinburgh, Scotland, May (pp. 53-57).

Zimmermann, T., Weißgerber, P., Diehl, S., & Zeller, A. (2004). Mining version histories to guide software changes. In the *Proceedings of 26th International Conference on Software Engineering,* Edinburgh, Scotland, May 23-28 (pp. 563-572). IEEE.

Endnotes

[1]   Unless otherwise stated, in this chapter an entity means a software entity.

[2]   Depending on the entities chosen and the definition of R, there could be a large number of *SRGs* for a system.

[3]   A static relation can be contrasted with a run-time or dynamic relation. For instance, while the source code of a routine r_1 may refer to another routine r_2 (a static relation), during execution time, it may never call that routine (it would be absent from the corresponding dynamic relation). On the other hand, the use of function pointers results in tuples that exist in a dynamic relation but not in a static one.

[4]   Mitel Networks has been our industrial partner in this research.

[5]   This is a static source code call reference.

[6]   Note that by "important" here we mean that the static relation has more influence in making entities relevant to each other.

[7]   This definition is the same as Co-update(f_i, f_j) → Boolean, where *Relevant* is the same as *true*, and *Not-Relevant* is the same as *false*.

[8] It is also possible to assign a confidence value to a discrete relevance value should there be a need for such a finer ranking.

[9] Real-world systems introduce challenges that are not present when working with artificial or "toy" systems. Unfortunately, in many cases, past research has not dealt with large systems and consequently the methods proposed in such a research usually do not scale up.

[10] *Data mining* can be defined as a set of methods and practices for extracting interesting, actionable, relationships from large datasets.

[11] Although there are two categories of relevance, one can assign a real valued confidence factor to each classification.

[12] A stronger statement would be: Files which have always changed together due to updates applied to a software system are relevant to each other. To be more precise, always here means always within the period of time in which updates were studied. We have chosen to use a more relaxed heuristic, in the hope of finding a wider scope relevance relation.

[13] Never here means, within the period of time under study.

[14] In the experiments discussed in this chapter we have used a time period T'=T or in other words $T_3 = T_1$.

[15] In other words, for each two potential permutations of two paired files, only one file pair is generated.

[16] No Group Size Limit.

[17] Default Not Relevant Pairs.

[18] A set of file names, to be precise.

[19] This is a successor of C4.5 decision tree learner (Quinlan, 1993). We also experimented with a simple learning algorithm called 1R (Holte, 1993). As expected, 1R did not produce satisfactory results due to the complexity of the data.

[20] The learners we used included Ripper (a rule learner), Timbl (a memory-based learner) and svm-light a popular implementation of support vector machines and set covering machines (SCM) (Marchand & Shawe-Taylor, 2002). We have not reported these results mostly because the experimental setups were different from the ones presented in this chapter. Also, the earlier statement should not be interpreted as universal. With proper parameter tuning, some of these learners can generate models that outperform C5.0 models. However one may also be able generate better results by better tuning parameters of C5.0. Our limited experiments with these alternative methods did not provide us with enough reason to consider using them as the main learning method instead of C5.0, especially considering the other benefits of C5.0 discussed earlier.

[21] These are the ratios that generated some of the better results using problem report based features.

Chapter IX

A Practical Software Quality Classification Model Using Genetic Programming

Yi Liu, Georgia College & State University, USA

Taghi M. Khoshgoftaar, Florida Atlantic University, USA

Abstract

A software quality estimation model is an important tool for a given software quality assurance initiative. Software quality classification models can be used to indicate which program modules are fault-prone (FP) and not fault-prone (NFP). Such models assume that enough resources are available for quality improvement of all the modules predicted as FP. In conjunction with a software quality classification model, a quality-based ranking of program modules has practical benefits since priority can be given to modules that are more FP. However, such a ranking cannot be achieved by traditional classification techniques. We present a novel software quality classification model based on multi-objective optimization with genetic programming (GP). More specifically, the GP-based model provides both a classification (FP or NFP) and a quality-based ranking for the program modules. The quality factor used to rank the modules is typically the number of faults or defects associated with a module. Genetic programming is ideally suited for optimizing multiple criteria simultaneously. In our study, three performance criteria are used to evolve a GP-based software quality model: classification performance, module ranking, and size of the GP tree. The third criterion addresses a commonly observed phenomena in GP, that is, bloating. The proposed model is investigated with case studies of software measurement data obtained from two industrial software systems.

Introduction

Software quality assurance is a vital component of any given software development process and consists of various techniques and methods used toward software quality improvement. A software quality model aims to find the underlying relationship between software measurements and software quality. The problem of predicting, during the software development process, which program modules are likely to be problematic is of practical importance in software engineering practice (Khoshgoftaar & Seliya, 2004).

Any given software development project usually has a finite amount of resources it can expend. In addition, the amount of resources allocated for software quality improvement is typically a fraction of the total budget. Therefore, it is of practical importance that the software development team seeks effective ways to achieve the best possible software quality within the allocated budget. One of the commonly-adopted methods for improving software quality is to classify program modules into two risk-based groups, such as fault-prone (FP) and not fault-prone (NFP) (Briand, Melo, & Wust, 2002; Ping, Systa, & Muller, 2002; Runeson, Ohlsson, & Wohlin, 2001). Subsequent to the calibration of a software quality classification model, all the modules predicted as FP are subjected to software quality improvement activities. A software quality model can also be built to predict the number of defects in program modules (Ganesan, Khoshgoftaar, & Allen, 2000; Khoshgoftaar & Seliya, 2002b, 2003).

In related literature, various techniques have been explored for calibrating metrics-based software quality classification models (Schneidewind, 2002). Some commonly used techniques include logistic regression (Khoshgoftaar & Allen, 1999), classification trees (Khoshgoftaar & Allen, 2001; Khoshgoftaar & Seliya, 2002a), case-based reasoning (Khoshgoftaar, Cukic, & Seliya, 2002), and computational intelligence-based methods (Pizzi, Summers, & Pedrycz, 2002; Reformat, Pedrycz, & Pizzi, 2002; Suarez & Lutsko, 1999). The definition of what constitutes a FP program module is dependent on the project management team and the software quality objectives of the system under consideration. Usually, the number of software faults or defects associated with a program module determines whether it is to be considered as high-risk (FP) or low-risk (NFP). In cases where defect data is not available, the amount of code churn (changes to source code to fix a problem) for a given module may determine whether it is FP or NFP.

The underlying assumption behind a FP-NFP software quality classification model is that all program modules predicted as FP will be subjected to inspections. Since each development organization has a pre-defined procedure for conducting software quality improvements, all the FP modules will be subjected to the same inspection process. This implies that the software project should have enough resources to inspect all the FP modules. Though preferable, such a scenario may not always occur in software engineering practice, raising the issue of which (or what number) of the modules predicted as FP should be subjected to software quality improvements.

In software engineering practice, the problems of limited time and limited budget are arguably the two most critical aspects of a software development project. In the case when the allocated resources are not sufficient to inspect all the predicted FP modules, the development team is likely to randomly pick and inspect only a portion of the FP modules. On the other hand if all the FP modules are to be inspected by the allocated resources, then the modules will be given below-normal (often not feasible according to organizational procedures) inspections and reviews. A traditional software quality classification model does not provide any guidance regarding the relative quality among the FP modules. We believe that this shortcoming of classification models affects their effectiveness as software quality improvement tools.

A logical solution to the previously-described shortcoming of software quality classification models is to provide a quality-based ranking of the program modules in addition to classifying modules as FP or NFP. For example, all the program modules can be ranked in an ascending order according to the predicted number of faults for each module (Khoshgoftaar & Allen, 1999). Subsequently, if the allocated software quality improvement resources are not enough to inspect all the FP modules, then the development team can select (after ranking the modules) a cut-off percentile covering the number of modules that can be inspected with the allocated resources.

Incorporating the module-ranking feature into a software quality classification model requires the optimization of both the classification accuracy and the predicted ranking performance as compared to the actual ranking. However, traditional classification techniques such as logistic regression and classification trees are not suitable for achieving such a simultaneous optimization.

We present an improved software quality classification model based on the multi-objective optimization feature of genetic programming (GP) (Eschenauer, Koski, & Osyczka, 1971). Since none of the existing software quality classification models facilitate such a multi-objective optimization, a comparison of the proposed technique to other classification techniques is not appropriate. The proposed model is based on our previous work related to calibrating software quality classification models using GP (Khoshgoftaar, Liu, & Seliya, 2003; Liu & Khoshgoftaar, 2001). Moreover, this is one of the first studies to introduce the concept of module ranking (module-order modeling; Adipat, 2001; Khoshgoftaar & Allen, 1999) into a GP-based software quality classification model.

In comparison to the various existing classification models, the proposed technique provides an additional flexibility to project managers who face limited quality improvement resources. Instead of randomly picking the predicted FP modules for quality improvement, the development team can begin by inspecting the most faulty ones and continue doing so according to the predicted ranking of the program modules. GP is an appropriate choice for a multi-objective optimization problem since it is based on the process of natural evolution which involves the simultaneous optimization of several factors (Koza, 1992). GP performs a global stochastic search across the space of computable functions to discover the form and the parameters of the prediction model.

The proposed GP-based software quality classification model strives to simultaneously optimize three objectives: (1) minimize the average weighted cost of misclassification; (2) for a given module, its predicted rank is the same as its actual rank; and (3) the size of the GP tree. The improved classification model is demonstrated through empirical case studies of software measurement data obtained from two industrial software systems. For each case study, a software quality classification model is calibrated based on the program modules of the training dataset. The modules in the training dataset are described by a set of software metrics and a known class-membership. Subsequently, the predictive performance of the calibrated model is evaluated by applying it to the test dataset.

Since the cost of misclassifying a FP module is invariably greater (see the next section) than the cost of misclassifying a NFP module (Khoshgoftaar & Allen, 2000), the first objective is the most important criterion for software quality classification models. The second objective addresses the issue of improving the usefulness of software quality classification models by optimizing the quality-based relative ranking of program modules. The third objective is the least significant criterion and is introduced in our modeling process in order to address the "bloat" problem which is inherent to modeling with GP. The bloat problem creates modeling difficulties such as increasing the search process time and creating very large trees which lends to the incomprehensibility of the GP model. Moreover, the bloat problem is often associated with the overfitting of the training data (Iba, Garis, & Sato, 1996; Jong, Watson, & Pollack, 2001; Langdon, 1996; Liu & Khoshgoftaar, 2004).

The chapter continues with a brief discussion on software quality classification models and module-order models. Next, we provide a brief overview of GP, discussing specific issues related to GP-based modeling. The following section presents the multi-objective optimization solution for the improved GP model. The remaining sections present and discuss the empirical case studies, followed by a summary of this chapter.

Software Quality Classification Model

Software complexity metrics have been shown to be indicative of software quality, and have been used extensively to model software quality estimation models (Briand, Melo, & Wust, 2002; Ping, Systa, & Muller, 2002; Schneidewind, 2002). A two-group software quality classification (SQC) model is usually calibrated to identify FP and NFP modules based on software metrics and quality data from similar software projects or previously developed system releases (Khoshgoftaar, Yuan, & Allen, 2000; Reformat, Pedrycz, & Pizzi, 2002). Subsequently, the software quality assurance team can target the predicted FP modules for inspections. The definition of a FP and NFP program module is specific to the development team's software quality objectives, and is often based on a pre-selected threshold value of the quality factor, such as number of faults.

Typically, a training dataset (with known software metrics and quality data) is used to fit a SQC model. Its predictive performance is then measured by estimating the class-membership of the modules of a test dataset. Depending on when such a model is to be applied, the appropriate software metrics are used to train the classification model. For example, design-level metrics are used to estimate the software quality during the implementation phase, providing a guidance for placing experienced programmers to implement the likely problematic modules.

A SQC model is usually not perfect, that is, it will have some misclassifications. In the context of the SQC models in our study, a Type I error occurs when a NFP module is misclassified as FP, whereas a Type II error occurs when a FP module is misclassified as NFP. From a software engineering point of view, the cost of a Type II error is more severe since it entails a missed opportunity for improving a poor quality module, leading to corrective efforts during system operations. In contrast, the cost of a Type I error is relatively lower since it entails unproductive inspections (prior to deployment) of a module that is already of good quality. Therefore, it is important to incorporate the disparity between the two costs of misclassifications during the classification modeling process.

In our previous studies with SQC models, we have observed an inverse relationship between the Type I and Type II error rates for a given classification technique and its modeling parameters. More specifically, as the Type II error rate decreases the Type I error rate increases, and vice versa. This relationship is important in obtaining the preferred balance (between the error rates), which may be dictated by the software application domain and the quality improvement goals of the project. The usefulness of a SQC model is affected by the attained balance between the two error rates. For example, a medical or safety-critical software system may prefer a model with a very low Type II error rate, regardless of its Type I error rate. On the other hand, a high-assurance software system with limited quality improvement resources may prefer approximately equal misclassification error rates (Khoshgoftaar, Yuan, & Allen, 2000).

Module-Order Model

A module-order model predicts the relative quality-based ranking of each program module (Khoshgoftaar & Allen, 1999). More specifically, the program modules are ranked (predicted order) based on a quality factor such as number of faults. The basic advantage of such a software quality model over a software quality classification model is that it enables project managers to enhance modules in their predicted quality-based order, beginning with the most FP. Usually, a module-order model will be built based on the following steps:

- Build an underlying quantitative software quality prediction model, such as a software fault prediction model.
- Rank the program modules according to a quality measure predicted by the underlying model.
- Evaluate the accuracy of a model's predicted ranking.

Initially, a quantitative software quality prediction model is calibrated to predict the dependent variable. In our studies, the dependent variable is the number of faults associated with a program module. For a given quantitative model, the number of faults, F_i, in module i is a function $F_i = f(x_i)$ of its software measurements, the vector x_i. Let $\hat{F}(x_i)$ be the estimate of F_i by a fitted model, $\hat{f}(x_i)$. In module-order modeling, the predicted values of the dependent variable obtained by $\hat{F}(x_i)$ are only used to obtain the (predicted) relative order of each program module. We now discuss the details of module-order modeling.

Let R_i be the percentile rank of observation i in a perfect ranking of modules according to F_i. Let $\hat{R}(x_i)$ be the percentile rank of observation i in the predicted ranking according to $\hat{F}(x_i)$. In module-order modeling, the emphasis is on whether a module falls within a certain cut-off percentile that indicates the proportion of modules that are to be inspected. All the modules within the cut-off percentage will be inspected, and hence their relative order is not important. Similarly, the relative order among the modules that do not belong to the cut-off percentage is not important either. According to the allocated software quality improvement resources, the project management team will select a certain cut-off percentile and apply the quality enhancement processes to the whole cut-off group.

The following illustrates the evaluation procedure for a module-order model. Given a model and a validation dataset indexed by i:

- Management will choose to enhance modules in priority order, beginning with the most faulty. However, the rank of the last module enhanced is uncertain at the time of modeling. Determine a range of percentiles that covers management's options for the last module, based on the schedule and resources allocated for a software quality improvement. Choose a set of representative cut-off percentiles, c, from that range.

- For each value of c, determine the number of faults accounted for by modules above the percentile c. This is done for both the perfect and predicted ranking of the modules: $G(c)$ is the number of faults accounted for by the modules that are ranked (perfect ranking) above the percentile c, and $\hat{G}(c)$ is the number of faults accounted for by the modules that are predicted as falling above the percentile c.

$$G(c) = \sum_{i:R_i \geq c} F_i$$

$$\hat{G}(c) = \sum_{i:\hat{R}_i \geq c} F_i$$

- Calculate the percentage of faults accounted for by each ranking, namely, $G(c)/G_{tot}$ and $\hat{G}(c)/G_{tot}$, where G_{tot} is the total number of actual faults of the program modules in the given dataset.

- Calculate the performance of the module-order model, $\phi(c)$, which indicates how closely the faults accounted for by the model ranking match those of the perfect module ranking.

$$\phi(c) = \frac{\hat{G}(c)}{G(c)}$$

If the resources for quality enhancements are limited, it is unlikely to cover more than 50% of the modules. In our empirical studies, we choose c from the 50 to 95 percentiles with an increment of 5%. However, the cut-off percent of interest depends on the software project under consideration. We plot "Alberg diagrams" (Ohlsson & Alberg, 1996) to give an informal depiction of a model's performance accuracy. Usually, an "Alberg diagram" consists of two curves, $G(c)/G_{tot}$ and $\hat{G}(c)/G_{tot}$ as functions of the percentage c. The closer the two curves are, the more accurate is the module-order model.

Genetic Programming

As a part of evolutionary computation systems, genetic programming (GP) was initially proposed by John Koza (1992), and has been applied to a large number of fields, including data mining (Ghosh & Freitas, 2003) and bioinformatics (Handley, 1995).The primary advantage of using GP-based models is that a solution to the given problem is automatically evolved based on certain objectives. More specifically, the analyst does not have to assume a mathematical form or structure for the problem solution.

The evolution process of GP is based on imitating the Darwinian principle of survival and reproduction of the fittest individuals. Each individual in GP can be an S-expression tree in the Lisp language, and its fitness value indicates the individual's quality with respect to the objective (fitness) function. An individual in GP is composed of functions and terminals provided by a given problem. This fitness value of individual also defines a probability of who can be selected for mating and reproduction.

Characteristics of GP

The basic units in GP are the function set and the terminal set. The function set is composed of the statements, operators, and functions available to the GP system (Banzhaf, Nordin, & Keller, 1998). The terminal set contains the inputs to the GP program, the constants to the GP program, and the zero-argument functions with side-effect executed by the GP system (Banzhaf et al., 1998). The function and terminal sets are required to have the "closure" and "sufficiency" properties. Each individual can be a tree-based structure that may have different size, shape, and structure than other individuals.

GP mimics the randomness of natural evolution by using pseudo-random generators to choose and control operators for the entire evolution process. The first population is generated by a random search in the search space, which contains all individuals that could be assembled by the function set and the terminal set. Subsequently, each individual is evaluated and assigned a fitness value to indicate how "fit" it is. The reproduction, crossover, and mutation operations contribute to the stochastic nature of GP. In our study, we used all three genetic operators.

The three genetic operators—reproduction, crossover, and mutation—are used to perform the genetic evolution of the population. Individuals are chosen based on fitness-based selection. The fitness of each individual is assigned by some well-defined explicit evalua-tive procedure. Each individual is usually evaluated over a set of fitness cases, which are a sample of the entire domain space. In this research, the set of fitness cases is the fit dataset, in which each fitness case is a software module. The individuals that have higher fitness values will have higher probabilities of being selected, thus having higher probabilities to survive and produce offspring.

Process of Evolution

The process of a GP run is made of the following steps: initialization, evaluation, selection, and breeding.

- **Initialization:** The first step of GP algorithm is initialization, in which GP randomly generates the first population using a random search in the problem domain. There-fore, the individuals in the first population have extremely poor fitness except when the problem is so simple that it can be solved by a random search. Three methods of randomly generating the first population—full, grow, and half-and-half—can be used to obtain individuals of different sizes and shapes (Koza, 1992).

- **Evaluation:** After the first population has been generated, each individual is evaluated against a set of fitness cases, and assigned a fitness value by a fitness function. There are several measures of fitness that are widely used: raw fitness, standardized fitness, adjusted fitness, and normalized fitness (Koza, 1992).

- **Selection:** After the performance of each individual is known, a selection algorithm is carried out to select individuals. Two commonly applied selection algorithms are: fitness-proportional selection and tournament-based fitness. With fitness-proportional selection, the probability of an individual that is selected depends on its ability com-pared to others in the population. It is given by

$$p_i = \frac{f_a(i)}{\sum_{k=1}^{n} f_a(k)}$$

where n is the number of individuals and $f_a(i)$ is the adjusted fitness of an individu-al—the higher the adjusted fitness of an individual, the greater the probability of it being selected. The formula also shows that every individual has some opportunity to be selected.

In tournament-based fitness, some individuals are selected (to compete) at random and the fittest of them is selected: for example, a binary tournament selection will select two individuals and the fitter one will be chosen. When the tournament is over (that is, only one individual is left), the relative fitness of each member of the population is awarded according to the level of the tournament it has reached. This method al-lows for adjusting the selection pressure by choosing different tournament sizes. The benefits of this method include accelerating the evolution process and parallelizing the competition.

- **Breeding:** After GP randomly selects an operator, the breeding process starts. It first selects a GP operator, then chooses one or two individuals based on the operator—reproduction, crossover, and mutation. All offspring(s) obtained from the operations are sent to the next generation.

  After breeding, the new population replaces the old one. Then GP will measure the fitness of the individuals in the new generation, select the fitter ones, and repeat the breeding process. The entire process continues until the terminating conditions are satisfied. The terminating conditions could be either that an individual is found to solve the problem, or that the number of maximum generations is reached. As the process goes on, the average fitness of the population is expected to increase. The best individual of the run is the solution found by GP. The entire process of GP is shown in Figure 1, where M is the maximum number of individuals in the population and i is the number of offspring currently present in the generation.

Figure 1. Flowchart of GP procedure

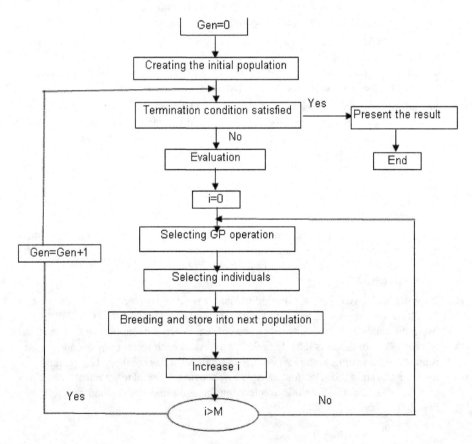

Bloat Problem in GP

In the context of GP-based modeling, the bloat or code growth problem is very likely to occur. The problem indicates the accelerated growth of the tree size as the GP process continues. This problem occurs because the search space contains larger solutions than smaller ones (Cowan & Reynolds, 1999; Langdon & Poli, 1997). Another reason is that larger trees are more likely to produce offspring because of intron which provides some protection against crossover (Nordin, Francone, & Banzhaf, 1996). Nordin and Banzhaf (1995) indicated that the length of the effective code of individuals decreases over time since a large number of intron appear, resulting in the rapidly increasing size of the individuals. From a practical point of view, the bloat problem slows down the search process by increasing the computation time of each individual and creating large solutions. Furthermore, growth in solution size may indicate "overfitting" of the model (Tackett, 1993).

There are two popular methods that are used to control bloat. The most widely used method provides an upper bound either on tree depth or program length (Koza, 1992). However, some research works have illustrated unexpected problems with this approach (Gathercole & Ross, 1996; Langdon & Poli, 1997). The other commonly used method incorporates program size into the fitness measure (Iba, Garis, & Sato, 1996; Koza, 1992). Some studies presented an analysis of the effect of parsimony pressure (Nordin & Banzhaf, 1995; Rosca & Ballard, 1996). The key aspect of this method is how to choose the weight for the size in the fitness measure. Soule, Foster, and Dickinson (1996) found that a single value of such a weight is difficult to obtain. In order to avoid such a problem, multi-objective fitness measures have been used where one objective was to obtain compact or fast programs (Jong, Watson, & Pollack, 2001; Langdon, 1996). Though other methods have been proposed (Rosca & Ballard, 1996; Soule, Foster, & Dickinson, 1996), they are rarely used due to their implementation difficulty and algorithm complexity. In our empirical studies with the improved GP model, we select the tree size as an optimization objective. We reward the smaller trees whose number of nodes are greater than 10.

Random Subset Selection

The success of building a GP-based prediction model is largely dependent on the selected fitness cases, that is, the cases in the fit or training dataset. Generally speaking, a large dataset will result in a better GP model. It is important that the selected fitness cases are the proper representatives of the problem under consideration. This allows GP to learn and extract the underlying solution to the problem, instead of simply memorizing the fitness cases. However, the number and availability of the fit data cases is dependent on the problem domain. In the context of software quality estimation modeling, a model is initially calibrated based on the fit dataset and subsequently, the predictive performance of the model is evaluated by a test dataset.

In the context of metrics-based software quality estimation models, the number of cases in the fit dataset is usually fixed after the data collection process is completed. Moreover, during the software development life cycle, the phase at which the software quality models are to be calibrated also determines which cases are to used as fitness cases. Once the data collection process is completed, the number of fitness cases that will be used by a GP-based software quality estimation model is fixed. Therefore, it is important to utilize the fitness cases in the best possible way.

A commonly used approach is to use the entire fit dataset as the training data and evaluate the fitness of the individuals with respect to all the cases in the fit dataset. However, such an approach has a disadvantage of increasing the risk of overfitting, a problem that is often seen in estimation tasks (Khoshgoftaar, Allen, & Deng, 2001). Overfitting occurs when a calibrated model performs well for the fit dataset, but has a relatively poor performance for the test dataset. Because a higher fitness may indicate overfitting, selecting the model with the highest fitness may not be a good method.

Another commonly used approach is to use an additional dataset as a validation dataset during the training process. The usual procedure to achieve this is to randomly split the available fit dataset into two subsets: one is used for training while the other is used to validate the trained model. The predictive capability of the model is validated by the test dataset. The approach of using a validation dataset to avoid overfitting has been investigated by Thomas and Sycara (1999), they concluded that "the validation issues raised by these experiments are puzzling. It seems that neither allowing the validation window to move with the test set, nor trying to use information from the validation set to select better rules provides much gain."

In our study with GP-based software quality classification models, we use the random subset selection method during the training process. In this method, a model is not evaluated by the entire fit dataset, and moreover, a fixed subset of the fit dataset is not used to evaluate the trained model. In the random subset selection method, a subset from the fit dataset is randomly selected for each generation. The fitness of each individual in a generation is evaluated with respect to this subset, and not the entire fit dataset. Hence, the individuals in each generation are assessed by different data cases during evaluation. The individuals can only survive if they do well with many different subsets. The memorization of one or more subsets will not ensure survival. Since the surviving individuals are always confronted with different datasets in each generation, they are more likely to represent the underlying rules behind the data.

An additional advantage of the random subset selection method is that computation time for the fitness evaluation is reduced when we have a large dataset. This is because we randomly pick a subset with a smaller number of fitness cases than the entire fit dataset for each generation. The smaller the size of the subset, the shorter is the evaluation time. In the two case studies presented in this chapter, we randomly pick two-thirds of the NFP modules and two-thirds of the FP modules from the fit dataset to use as the fitness subset for a given generation.

Multi-Objective Optimization

In a real-world system, several performance criteria have to be usually addressed simultaneously. Consequently, a multi-objective optimization is desired by analyzing the conflicting tradeoff (if any) between the different criteria. A multi-objective optimization gives a clear and sound basis for the decision-maker to solve an overall decision-making problem in a systematic way. A multi-objective optimization solution always strives for a set of Pareto-optima, which represents feasible solutions such that no criterion can be improved without deteriorating some other criterion. Therefore, the critical analysis component is obtaining the best solution among the set Pareto-optima.

A Pareto-optimal set is defined as a mathematical expression such that (Eschenauer, Koski, & Osyczka, 1971; Stadler, 1975): Let x be a vector of the independent variables, $f(x)$ be an objective function. A vector x^* is Pareto-optimal if and only if there is no vector x that exists with the characteristics:

$$f_j(x) \leq f_j(x^*), \text{ for all } j \in \{1,\ldots,m\} \text{ and}$$

$$f_j(x) < f_j(x^*), \text{ for at least one } j \in \{1,\ldots,m\}$$

where m is the number of objective functions.

The most frequently used methods for generating Pareto-optima are based on the idea of replacing the multi-objective optimal problem by a parameterized scalar problem. Typically, by varying the value of each parameter for each objective, it is possible to generate all or parts of the Pareto-optimal set. The method used in this chapter is based on the constraint-oriented transformation (Eschenauer, Koski, & Osyczka, 1971), in which an objective is initially chosen to be minimized and the other objectives are transformed into constraints.

For example, $\min(f_1(x))$, with $f_j(x) \leq \bar{y}_j$, where $j = 2,\ldots,m$. $f_1(x)$ is the primary objective, generally the most important one for the given system; $f_2,\ldots,f_m$ are the secondary objectives, and $\bar{y}_j$ is the jth constraint defined for the system. Therefore, given a set of selected/allowable values, different solutions are obtained. By varying the limits of the allowable values, a Pareto-optima set will be generated.

In this chapter, instead of transforming $f_2,\ldots,f_m$ into constraints, we minimize the objectives one at time according to their importance as defined by the analyst. More specifically, we first minimize the most important objective, then minimize the second one, then the third one, and so on. That is for $x \in X$: $\min(f_1(x))$, $\min(f_2(x))$, $\ldots$, $\min(f_m(x))$. In our study, the most important objective is to correctly classify the software modules into the FP and the NFP groups. Subsequently, the secondary objective is to optimize the predicted quality-based module ranking with respect to the actual ranking. Finally, the third optimization objective is the size of the GP model, that is, among the trees which have at least 10 nodes the smaller trees are rewarded.

Calibrating the GP-Based Model

Genetic programming allows an analyst to define customized fitness functions based on the problem requirements. Our goal is to achieve a software quality model that can, in addition to correctly classifying program modules as FP and NFP, provide a correct quality-based

Table 1. Parameter list for GP

pop_size	1000
max_generations	100
output.bestn	5
init.method	half_and_half
init.depth	2 to 10
max_depth	20
breed_phases	2
breed[1].operator	crossover, select =fitness
breed[1].rate	0.6
breed[2].operator	reproduction, select =fitness
breed[2].rate	0.1
breed[3].operator	mutation, select =fitness
breed[3].rate	0.3
function set	GT, VGT +, -, *, / sin, cos, log,exp
terminal set	independent variables and constants
termination-criterion	exceeding the maximum generation

ranking of the program modules. Moreover, the size of the GP tree is optimized to control the bloat problem. The tool we selected is "lilgp 1.01", developed by Zongker and Punch of Michigan State University. Implemented using the C programming language, the tool is based on the LISP works of John Koza. When applying lilgp for a genetic programming application, each individual is organized as a tree in which each node is a C function pointer.

The GP parameters used during our modeling process for the case studies are summarized in Table 1, which includes the function and terminal sets. While most of the parameters are self explanatory, we explain a few of them. The parameter, output.bestn, represents the number of best individuals selected after each run. The function, GT, in the function set is defined to return a 0.0 if its first parameter is larger than the second parameter, and a 1.0 otherwise. The function, VGT, is defined to return the maximum of the its two parameters. The selection of individuals is based on fitness-proportional selection. The optimization of these parameters is out of scope of this study, however, will be considered as part of our future research.

Fitness Function for Classification

In the context of software quality modeling, the cost of misclassifying a FP module is invariably greater than that of a NFP module. During the process of SQC modeling, the disparate misclassification costs should be incorporated. However, since the actual costs of misclassifications are unknown at the time of modeling, we use a weighted approach for determining the costs of a Type I and Type II error (Khoshgoftaar & Allen, 2000). Therefore, a SQC model that achieves the lowest average weighted cost of misclassification will be selected for the first objective, as shown later in this section.

We define C_I as the (modeling) cost for a Type I error and C_{II} as the modeling cost for a Type II error. Since $C_{II} > C_I$, we express C_{II} in terms of C_I, that is, the misclassification costs are normalized with respect to C_I. For convenience, we denote the normalized C_{II} as ξ, which can also be viewed as the cost ratio, $\frac{C_{II}}{C_I}$. For a given individual, if a NFP module is misclassified as FP, a penalty of C_I is added to the fitness of the individual; and if a FP module is misclassified as NFP, a penalty of C_{II} is added to the fitness of the model. Moreover, if the absolute value of the predicted number of faults (or lines of code churn) is extremely large, then a penalty of C_{III} is added to the fitness. The addition of the third cost penalty is done to address the practical problem observed during the GP modeling process, that is, sometimes the predicted value of the dependent variable is extremely large.

The measurement of fitness includes the raw fitness and the number of hits, which is defined as the number of correct classifications. The raw fitness for the first fitness function is given by,

$$fitness = C_I * N_I + C_{II} * N_{II} + C_{III} * N_{III}$$

where N_I and N_{II} are respectively the numbers of the Type I and Type II errors, and N_{III} is the number of modules which have an extremely large predicted value of the quality factor. Theoretically speaking, only the first two terms of the fitness function constitute the average weighted cost of misclassification for a given model. The third term is added to the fitness function to address a practical problem observed (discussed previously) in the GP modeling process. In our studies, C_{III} is empirically set to the value of C_{II}.

Fitness Function for Module Rank

The program modules in the fit dataset are ranked according to their number of faults. The modules are then grouped with respect to the cut-off percentile, c. Recall (see the *Module-Order Model* section) that R_i is the percentile rank of observation i in a perfect ranking of modules according to F_i. In addition, $\hat{R}_i(x_i)$ is the percentile rank of observation i in the predicted ranking according to $\hat{F}_i(x_i)$ (Khoshgoftaar & Allen, 1999). The basic idea of the second fitness function is to apply a penalty if the actual ranking and the predicted ranking of a module are different. The larger the differences are in the respective ranking, the higher are the penalties applied to the individual. The fitness function for module ranking is given by:

$$fitness = \sum_{i=1}^{n} | R_i - \hat{R}(x_i) |$$

where n is the number of observations in the fit dataset.

Fitness Function for Tree Size

Obtaining a comprehensible model is a desirable feature for a software quality estimation model. We define the third fitness function as the number of tree nodes, in order to avoid the bloat problem. Among the individuals that have at least 10 nodes, the smaller trees are rewarded while the larger trees are penalized.

The GP Modeling Process

In the process of GP, a lower value of the raw fitness indicates a better individual and a greater probability of survival. The individual selection process during a GP run is summarized in the following:

- Group the individuals (models) according to the first fitness function. Thus, each group will have the same value for the first fitness function.
- Select one group based on the first fitness function.
- Check whether only one member is in this group. If yes, go to *End*, otherwise continue.
- Select the individuals in this group using the value for the second fitness function. If there are two or more individuals with the same value, then continue. Otherwise go to *End*.
- Select one individual (among those with the same value for the second fitness function) according to the third fitness function.
- *End:* The selection process ends. One individual is selected to crossover, mutate or reproduce.

Model Selection Procedure

In the context of two-group software quality classification models calibrated for both case studies, model selection among competing classification models was based on two factors: (1) a preferred balance of equality (approximately) between the Type I and Type II error rates, with the Type II error rate being as low as possible; and (2) the module-order model performances. The first model selection factor was considered to yield classification models that are useful for the software quality improvement of the two high-assurance systems being modeled. Another software system may consider a different preferred balance between the error rates as more appropriate. The second model selection factor, which improves the usefulness of classification models, provided a way to select the best model among those with similar performances for the first factor.

The GP training process is a stochastic and emergent phenomenon, and hence, each run generates different models. Some GP runs may produce good models, while others may produce inferior models. Moreover, the problem of overfitting and sampling errors makes model selection a difficult problem. The ideal classification model is one that has a very low value for both the Type I and Type II error rates. In the context of software quality classification models, it has been shown that for a given modeling technique the Type I and Type II error rates have an inverse relationship (Khoshgoftaar & Allen, 1999; Khoshgoftaar, Yuan, & Allen, 2000). More specifically, if one is lowered, the other one increases. That is, it is not possible to simultaneously lower both error rates.

During the GP modeling process, if several models have the same values for the first fitness function, we select one as our preferred model with better performance in the second fitness function. Different classification models were calibrated by varying the value of the cost ratio, ξ. For a given ξ, the top five individuals are selected for each run of GP. We performed 20 runs for every value of ξ. Subsequently, 100 classification models were obtained for the given case study. The final preferred classification model is then selected among these 100 models. The following model selection process illustrates how we select a preferred model:

- For a given ξ, recalculate the fitness of the 100 individuals based on the entire fit dataset. The entire dataset is used for validation purposes based on the random-subset selection process discussed previously. Although most of the 100 individuals have similar fitness when a run finishes, they have different fitness values when we measure them on the entire fit dataset. This step ensures that we always pick the preferred one based on the entire fit dataset.

- Select the preferred model of each ξ from the 100 individuals. In this step, only the first model selection factor is used (i.e., the two error rates are approximately equal with the Type II error rate being as low as possible) to obtain the preferred model for a given ξ.

- Among the preferred models for the various ξ values, choose a final preferred classification model for the system being modeled. In this step, both (preferred balance between error rates and module-order model performances) model selection factors are used to obtain the final preferred model. In order to verify the accuracy of the results, the experiment was repeated 10 times and a t-test was performed to obtain a 90% confidence interval.

A Command Control Communication System

System Description

This case study consists of software metrics and fault data collected from a military command, control, and communications system written in the Ada programming language. Abbreviated as "CCCS", this full-scale industrial software system was developed in a large organiza-

Table 2. Software product metrics for CCCS

Symbol	Description
U_1	Number of unique operators(Halstead,1977)
N_1	Total number of operators(Halstead,1977)
U_2	Number of unique operands(Halstead,1977)
N_2	Total number of operands(Halstead,1977)
V(G)	McCabe's cyclomatic complexity
N_L	Number of logical operators
LOC	Lines of code
ELOC	Executable lines of code

tion by professionals using the procedural programming paradigm. A program module was identified as an Ada package, comprising of one or more procedures.

The number and selection of software metrics used were determined by available data collection tools. The software product measures used for our study are presented in Table 2. However, a different project might collect another set of measures (Fenton & Pfleeger, 1997; Ohlsson & Runeson, 2002). The number of faults was attributed to each module during the system integration and test phase, and during the first year of deployment. Fifty-two percent of the modules have no faults, while 25% of them have greater than two faults. The top 20% of modules contained 82.2% of the faults, whereas the top 5% of modules accounted for 40.2% of the faults.

The original dataset consisted of 282 program modules measured by the software developers. Using an impartial data splitting technique, we defined the *fit* (188 modules) and *test* (94 modules) datasets for our case study. A CCCS module was considered FP if it had at least four faults, and NFP otherwise. Another software system may determine a different threshold value as more appropriate. The fit dataset was used to train the models while the test dataset was used to evaluate their predictive performances.

Empirical Results

According to the model calibration process described earlier and the three fitness functions, GP-based software quality classification models are built based on the CCCS software metrics. Several different values of the modeling parameter, ξ, are considered for the first fitness function. The ξ values that yielded models of interest include 1, 2, 3, 4, and 5. For each value of ξ, 20 runs were performed for a total of 100 runs of the GP process. In order to gain confidence in our proposed model, we performed 10 experiments, each consisting of the 100 runs. We performed 20 runs for each value of ξ, and during each run the five best individuals were recorded. Hence, for each value of ξ, we obtained 100 candidate models. This procedure was repeated for all five values of ξ, and among all the candidate models, we selected the preferred model (from all values of ξ) according to the first model selection factor that was discussed earlier.

The preferred classification models for each of the 10 experiments are shown in Table 3. The error values shown in the table are for the entire fit dataset. The average error rates for the 10 experiments indicate a Type I error rate of 12.75%, a Type II error rate of 5.71%, and an overall error rate of 11.44%. According to our two model selection factors, the best model occurs in the eighth experiment which yielded (for fit data) a Type I error rate of 11.76% and a Type II error rate of 5.71%. In addition to having the best preferred balance between the two error rates, this classification model also had the best module-order model performance. This implies that for the fit dataset the predicted rankings of the best model had the closest match to the actual rankings.

Table 3. CCCS: Best models for fit dataset

Experiment	Type I	Type II	Overall
1	12.42%	5.71%	11.17%
2	13.07%	5.71%	11.70%
3	13.07%	5.71%	11.70%
4	13.07%	5.71%	11.70%
5	12.42%	5.71%	11.17%
6	13.07%	5.71%	11.70%
7	12.42%	5.71%	11.17%
8	11.76%	5.71%	10.64%
9	13.07%	5.71%	11.70%
10	13.07%	5.71%	11.70%
Average	12.75%	5.71%	11.44%

Table 4. CCCS: Best models for test dataset

Experiment	Type I	Type II	Overall
1	16.00%	10.53%	14.89%
2	14.67%	10.53%	13.83%
3	14.67%	10.53%	13.83%
4	14.67%	10.53%	13.83%
5	14.67%	10.53%	13.83%
6	14.67%	10.53%	13.83%
7	17.33%	10.53%	15.96%
8	16.00%	5.26%	13.83%
9	14.67%	10.53%	13.83%
10	14.67%	10.53%	13.83%
Average	15.20%	10.00%	14.15%

The usefulness of a classification model should be gauged according to its predictive performance for the program modules of the test dataset. The predictive performances of the classification models for the test dataset are shown in Table 4. We observe that the preferred model (Experiment 8) performs the best also for the test dataset: a Type I error rate of 16.00% and a Type II error rate of 5.26%. We performed a t-test to obtain the 90% confidence interval for the Type I and Type II misclassification error rates, yielding the values of (14.66%, 15.74%) and (9.04%, 10.96%), respectively. The 90% confidence interval of the overall error rate is (13.75%, 14.54%). The average size of the tree across the 10 experiments was only 22 nodes.

The average (for 10 experiments) module-order model performances for the test dataset are shown in Table 5. The first column is the cut-off percentile, c; the second and the third columns indicate $\hat{G}(c)/G_{tot}$ and $G(c)/G_{tot}$, respectively. The last column indicates the performance of the model as a module-order model, indicating the usefulness of the software quality classification model with respect to limited resource availability scenarios. The minimum c value considered is 0.5, implying that we assume at most only half of the program

Table 5. Average performance of MOM on CCCS test dataset

c	$\hat{G}(c)/G_{tot}$	$G(c)/G_{tot}$	$\phi(c)$
0.95	0.335	0.419	0.8
0.9	0.578	0.631	0.917
0.85	0.702	0.751	0.935
0.8	0.754	0.822	0.917
0.75	0.83	0.884	0.939
0.7	0.855	0.925	0.924
0.65	0.864	0.942	0.917
0.6	0.881	0.963	0.915
0.55	0.909	0.983	0.924
0.5	0.917	1	0.917

Table 6. Performance of MOM in the best model on CCCS test dataset

c	$\hat{G}(c)/G_{tot}$	$G(c)/G_{tot}$	$\phi(c)$
0.95	0.311	0.419	0.743
0.9	0.598	0.631	0.947
0.85	0.672	0.751	0.895
0.8	0.784	0.822	0.954
0.75	0.822	0.884	0.929
0.7	0.867	0.925	0.938
0.65	0.88	0.942	0.934
0.6	0.896	0.963	0.931
0.55	0.905	0.983	0.92
0.5	0.917	1	0.917

Figure 2. CCCS: Module-order model results

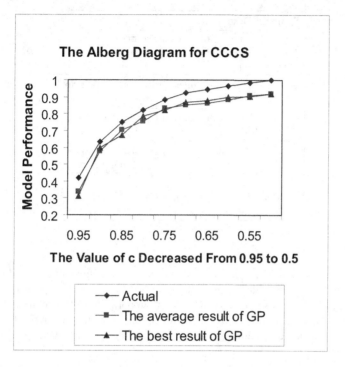

modules will be inspected for quality improvement. Table 6 lists the module-order model performance of the preferred model for the test dataset.

In the case of a high assurance system such as CCCS, the module-order model performance for the top 25%, that is, $c=0.75$, modules is the most important. In the case of the best model, we note that for $c=0.75$, a performance of almost 93% is obtained. A graphical representation of the module-order model performances of the preferred classification model, and the average of 10 experiments is shown in Figure 2. The graphical representation of the performances indicates that the predicted ordering of the modules is very close to the perfect ordering of the modules.

Wireless Configurations Systems

System Description

The case study (denoted as WLTS) involved data collection efforts from initial releases of two large Windows-based embedded system applications used primarily for customizing the configuration of wireless telecommunications products. The two embedded applications,

Table 7. WLTS software metrics

Symbol	Description
NUMI	Number of times the source file was inspected prior to the system test release.
LOCB	Number of lines for the source file prior coding phase.
LOCT	Number of lines of code for the source file prior to system test release.
LOCA	Number of lines of commented code for the source file prior to coding phase.
LOCS	Number of lines of commented code for the source file prior to system test release.

each with over 27 million lines of C++ code provide similar functionality and contained common source code. The systems are analyzed simultaneously, and the primary difference between them is the type of wireless product they support. The software metrics obtained reflected aspects of source files. Hence, a module in this case study comprised of a source file. The available data collection tools determined the number and the types of software metrics collected.

Software measurement and quality data was collected for 1,211 modules. The software metrics used to calibrate the models included four product metrics one process (inspection) metric, as shown in Table 7. The module quality factor was the number of faults discovered during system test. A random and impartial data splitting of the 1,211 modules was performed such that the *fit* dataset consisted of 807 modules while the *test* dataset consisted of 404 modules. A threshold value of two faults was selected based on our discussions with the software development team. Accordingly, the fit dataset consisted of 632 NFP modules and 175 FP modules, while the test dataset consisted of 317 NFP modules and 87 FP modules.

Empirical Results

A modeling procedure similar to the CCCS case study is adopted for the WLTS case study. For this case study, the considered values of ξ include: 1, 1.5, 2, 2.5, ..., 5, that is, a total of nine values. It was observed that other values of ξ yielded models that were not of interest with respect to our model selection strategy. For each of the 10 experiments, 180 runs were performed which consisted of 20 runs for each ξ value.

The performances (for fit dataset) of the preferred classification model for each of the 10 experiments are shown in Table 8. According to our model selection strategy discussed earlier, the best model appeared in the first experiment. This model had a Type I error rate of 28.64% and a Type II error rate of 21.14%. As compared to this model, the classifica-

Table 8. WLTS: Best models for fit dataset

Experiment	Type I	Type II	Overall
1	28.64%	21.14%	27.01%
2	28.00%	29.00%	28.38%
3	28.96%	18.86%	26.77%
4	31.49%	24.00%	29.86%
5	26.58%	26.29%	26.52%
6	28.16%	25.14%	27.51%
7	27.06%	29.14%	27.51%
8	25.32%	28.57%	26.02%
9	28.80%	24.00%	27.76%
10	30.70%	23.43%	29.12%
Average	28.37%	24.96%	27.65%

Table 9. WLTS: Performance (fit dataset) of MOM for Experiment 1

c	$\hat{G}(c)/G_{tot}$	$G(c)/G_{tot}$	$\phi(c)$
0.95	0.5	0.58	0.86
0.9	0.59	0.72	0.82
0.85	0.65	0.83	0.78
0.8	0.71	0.9	0.78
0.75	0.76	0.95	0.8
0.7	0.8	0.98	0.82
0.65	0.83	1	0.83
0.6	0.87	1	0.87
0.55	0.88	1	0.88
0.5	0.89	1	0.89

Table 10. WLTS: Performance (fit dataset) of MOM for Experiment 3

c	$\hat{G}(c)/G_{tot}$	$G(c)/G_{tot}$	$\phi(c)$
0.95	0.38	0.58	0.66
0.9	0.49	0.72	0.68
0.85	0.53	0.83	0.64
0.8	0.58	0.9	0.65
0.75	0.62	0.95	0.65
0.7	0.77	0.98	0.79
0.65	0.85	1	0.85
0.6	0.88	1	0.88
0.55	0.91	1	0.91
0.5	0.91	1	0.91

tion model obtained in Experiment 3 has a similar Type I error rate but has a lower (only 2.28%) Type II error rate. This implied that according to our first model selection factor (i.e., approximately equal error rates with the Type II error rate being as low as possible) the model obtained in Experiment 3 is a better choice. However, we did not select this model as the best model because it did not yield better module-order modeling performances as compared to the model obtained in Experiment 1. Moreover, the obtained balance between the error rates for the two models can be considered quite similar.

The module-order modeling performance of the classification models obtained in Experiments 1 and 3 are presented in Table 9 and Table 10, respectively. We observe that for all values of $c \geq 0.65$, the model obtained in Experiment 1 yielded a better performance than the model obtained in Experiment 3. This implies that if 35% of the modules were to be inspected, then the model obtained in Experiment 1 would catch more faults as compared to the model obtained in Experiment 3. Therefore, we selected the model obtained in Experiment 1 as the final preferred classification model for this case study.

Table 11. WLTS: Best models for test dataset

Experiment	Type I	Type ||	Overall
1	25.24%	17.24%	23.51%
2	25.00%	28.00%	25.50%
3	29.65%	16.09%	26.73%
4	29.02%	21.84%	27.48%
5	26.18%	22.99%	25.50%
6	26.50%	24.14%	25.99%
7	23.97%	27.59%	24.75%
8	26.18%	22.99%	25.50%
9	28.39%	24.14%	27.48%
10	29.02%	21.84%	27.48%
Average	26.92%	22.69%	25.99%

Table 12. WLTS: Average MOM performances for test data

c	$G(c)/G_{tot}$	$G(c)/G_{tot}$	$\phi(c)$
0.95	0.426	0.569	0.749
0.9	0.566	0.716	0.79
0.85	0.641	0.827	0.775
0.8	0.698	0.901	0.775
0.75	0.74	0.946	0.783
0.7	0.777	0.979	0.794
0.65	0.807	1	0.807
0.6	0.846	1	0.846
0.55	0.863	1	0.863
0.5	0.876	1	0.876

The performances of the 10 classification models when applied to the test dataset are shown in Table 11. The average Type I, Type II, and overall misclassification error rates of the test dataset are 26.92%, 22.69%, and 25.99%, respectively. The test dataset performances of the selected model (Experiment 1) indicated a Type I error rate of 25.24% and a Type II error rate of 17.24%. The standard deviations of the Type I and Type II error rates are 1.97% and 3.82%, respectively. A t-test was performed to obtain a 90% confidence interval for the

Table 13. WLTS: MOM performances (test data) of preferred model

c	$\hat{G}(c)/G_{tot}$	$G(c)/G_{tot}$	$\phi(c)$
0.95	0.463	0.569	0.813
0.9	0.613	0.716	0.856
0.85	0.667	0.827	0.807
0.8	0.722	0.901	0.801
0.75	0.773	0.946	0.817
0.7	0.832	0.979	0.85
0.65	0.863	1	0.863
0.6	0.885	1	0.885
0.55	0.896	1	0.896
0.5	0.908	1	0.908

Figure 3. WLTS: Module-order modeling results

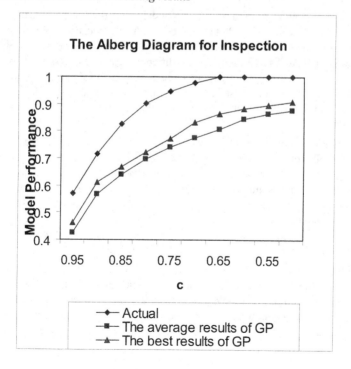

average Type I and Type II misclassification rates, yielding the values of (25.77%, 28.06%) and (20.47%, 24.90%). The mean, standard deviation, and 90% confidence interval for the overall rate are 25.99%, 1.32% and (25.22%, 26.75%), respectively.

The average (across 10 experiments) module-order model performances for the test dataset are shown in Table 12. We observe that for $c = 0.75$, the average performance of the GP modeling procedure is about 78%. The module-order model performances (for test dataset) of the preferred classification model are shown in Table 13. We observe that for $c = 0.75$, a performance of about 82% is obtained. A graphical representation of the module-order model performance for the test dataset is shown in Figure 3. We observe that the predicted ranking of the program module is very close to the perfect ranking, indicating a good performance with respect to the second fitness function.

Conclusion

Software quality classification models that classify program modules as either fault-prone or not fault-prone are effective for software quality improvement endeavors. With the aid of such models, the software quality assurance team can target the FP or high-risk modules in order to achieve the best quality improvement results with the allocated resources. We have noted that software quality classification models are based on the assumption that the available software quality improvement resources are such that all the program modules predicted as FP will be inspected for quality improvement.

This underlying assumption limits the usefulness of such models when the allocated resources are not sufficient to target all the predicted FP modules. This is because classification models do not indicate the relative fault-proneness of the modules predicted as FP. If a quality-based ranking of program modules was available in addition to the FP-NFP classifications, then the development team can have a better guidance regarding which FP modules are more risky than others. However, commonly used classification techniques such as logistic regression, decision trees, and so forth, are not suitable for predicting the quality-based ranking of the program modules.

We propose an improved GP-based software quality classification model that, in addition to providing FP-NFP classifications, provides the needed quality-based ranking of program modules. From a practical software engineering point of view, such a model is very attractive to a software development team. More specifically, when the inspection of all the predicted FP modules is beyond the scope of the allocated resources, project managers can allocate the resources toward the predicted FP modules based on their estimated quality-based rank. Moreover, in order to control the bloat and overfitting problems of GP-based models, the proposed modeling procedure rewards smaller trees through a fitness function.

A multi-objective optimization is the foundation for building such a classification model. Three objectives, that is, classification, module ranking, and tree size, were indicated for the multi-objective optimization problem. The constraint transformation method, which was changed based on our requirement, was the basic methodology behind our classification model. We ranked the three objectives based on their importance. Subsequently, we changed the GP selection process in order to implement the model. Two full-scale industrial case studies demonstrate the effectiveness of the improved classification model.

To our knowledge, this is a new approach for calibrating software quality classification models using a multi-objective optimization solution based on genetic programming. Future research will focus on the effectiveness of our model by adding diversity to the GP process. Moreover, the performance of the GP-based model will be compared with other classification and module-order modeling techniques.

References

Adipat, B. (2001) *An empirical study of moduleorder models*. Master's thesis, Florida Atlantic University, Boca Raton, FL.

Angeline, P. J., & Pollack, J. P. (1993). Competitive environments evolve better solutions for complex tasks. In S. Forrest, (Ed.), *Proceedings of the 5th International Conference on Genetic Algorithms* (pp. 264-270).

Banzhaf, W., Nordin, P., & Keller, R. E. (1998). *Genetic programming: An introduction on the automatic evolution of computer programs and its application*. New York: PWS Publishing Company.

Briand, L. C., Melo, W. L., & Wust, J. (2002). Assessing the applicability of faultproneness models across objectoriented software projects. *IEEE Transactions on Software Engineering, 28*(7), 706-720.

Cowan, G. S., & Reynolds, R. G. (1999). Learning to assess the quality of genetic programs using cultural algorithms. In the *Proceedings of the 1999 Congress on Evolutionary Computation, 3* (pp. 1679-1686).

Eschenauer, H., Koski, J. , & Osyczka, A. (1971). *Multicriteria design optimization*. Heidelberg, Germany: SpringerVerlag.

Fenton, N. E., & Pfleeger, S. L. (1997). *Software metrics: A rigorous and practical approach* (2nd ed.). ITP, Boston, MA: PWS Publishing Company.

Ganesan, K., Khoshgoftaar, T. M., & Allen, E. B. (2000). Casebased software quality prediction. *International Journal of Software Engineering and Knowledge Engineering, 10*(2), 139-152.

Gathercole, C., & Ross, P. (1996). An adverse interaction between crossover and restricted tree depth in genetic programming. In the *Proceedings of the First Annual Conference* (pp. 291-296).

Ghosh, A., & Freitas, A. A. (2003). Guest editorial: Data mining and knowledge discovery with evolutionary algorithms. *IEEE Trans. on Evolutionary Computation, 7*(6), 517-518.

Halstead, M. H.(1977). *Elements of software science*. New York: Elsevier NorthHolland.

Handley, S. (1995). Predicting whether or not a nucleic acid sequence is an e. coli promoter region using genetic programming. In the *Proceedings of the 1st International Sym-*

posium on Intelligence in Neural and Biological Systems (pp 122-127). Washington, DC: IEEE Press.

Iba, H., Garis, H., & Sato, T. (1996). Genetic programming using a minimum description length principle. *Advances in genetic programming* (pp. 265-284).

Jong, R. A., Watson, D. & Pollack, J. B. (2001). Reducing bloat and promoting diversity using multiobjective methods. In the *Proceedings of the Genetic and Evolutionary Computation Conference* (pp. 11-18).

Khoshgoftaar, T. M., & Allen, E. B. (1999). A comparative study of ordering and classification of faultprone software modules. *Empirical Software Engineering: An International Journal*, 4, 159-186.

Khoshgoftaar, T. M., & Allen, E. B. (1999). Logistic regression modeling of software quality. *International Journal of Reliability, Quality and Safety Engineering*, 6(4), 303-317.

Khoshgoftaar, T. M., & Allen, E. B. (2000). A practical classification rule for software quality models. *IEEE Transactions on Reliability*, 49(2), 209-216.

Khoshgoftaar, T. M., & Allen, E. B. (2001). Modeling software quality with classification trees. In H. Pham (Ed.), *Recent advances in reliability and quality engineering* (pp. 247-270). World Scientific Publishing.

Khoshgoftaar, T. M., Allen, E. B., & Deng, J. (2001). Controlling overfitting in software quality models: Experiments with regression trees and classification. In the *Proceedings of 7th International Software Metrics Symposium* (pp. 190-198). London, UK: IEEE Computer Society.

Khoshgoftaar, T. M., Cukic, B., & Seliya, N. (2002). Predicting faultprone modules in embedded systems using analogybased classification models. *International Journal of Software Engineering and knowledge Engineering*, 12(2), 201-221.

Khoshgoftaar, T. M., Liu, Y., & Seliya, N. (2003). Genetic programmingbased decision trees for software quality classification. In the *Proceedings of 15th International Conference on Tools with Artificial intelligence* (pp. 374-383). Sacramento, CA, USA: IEEE Computer Society.

Khoshgoftaar, T. M., & Seliya, N. (2002a).Software quality classification modeling using the SPRINT decision tree algorithm. In the *Proceedings of 14th International Conference on Tools with Artificial intelligence* (pp. 365-374). Washington, DC, USA: IEEE Computer Society.

Khoshgoftaar, T. M., & Seliya, N. (2002b). Tree-based software quality models for fault prediction. In the *Proceedings of 8th International Conference Metrics Symposium* (pp. 203-214). Ottawa, Ontario, Canada: IEEE Computer Society

Khoshgoftaar, T. M., & Seliya, N. (2003). Fault prediction modeling for software quality estimation: Comparing commonly used techniques. *Empirical Software Engineering Journal*, 8(3), 255-283

Khoshgoftaar, T. M., & Seliya, N. (2004). Comparative assessment of software quality classification techniques: An empirical case study. *Empirical Software Engineering Journal*, 9(3), 229-257.

Khoshgoftaar, T. M., Yuan, X., & Allen, E. B. (2000). Balancing misclassification rates in classification tree models of software quality. *Empirical Software Engineering Journal, 5,* 313-330.

Koza, J. R. (1992). *Genetic programming, volume I.* New York: MIT Press.

Langdon, W. B. (1996). *Data structures and genetic programming, Advances in Genetic Programming 2.* Cambridge: MIT Press.

Langdon, W. B., & Poli, R. (1997). A analysis of the max problem in genetic programming. *Genetic Programming 1997: Proceedings of the Second Annual Conference* (pp. 231-245).

Langdon, W. B., & Poli, R. (1998). Fitness causes boat: Mutation. In the *Proceedings of the First European Workshop on Genetic Programing* (pp. 37-48).

Liu, Y., & Khoshgoftaar, T. M. (2001). Genetic programming model for software quality prediction. In the *Proceedings of 6th International High Assurance Systems Engineering Symposium* (pp. 127-136).

Liu, Y., & Khoshgoftaar, T. M. (2004). Reducing overfitting in genetic programming models for software quality classification. In the *Proceedings of the IEEE International Symposium on High Assurance Systems Engineering* (pp. 56-65).

Nordin, P., & Banzhaf, W. (1995). Complexity compression and evolution. In the *Proceedings of the 6th International Conference on Genetic Algorithms* (pp. 310-317).

Nordin, P., Francone, F., & Banzhaf, W. (1996). Explicitly defined introns and destructive crossover in genetic programming. *Advances in genetic programming 2, volume 2.* MIT Press.

Ohlsson, M. C., & Runeson, P. (2002). Experience from replicating empirical studies on prediction models. In the *Proceedings: 8th International Software Metrics Symposium* (pp. 217-226). Ontario, Canada: IEEE Computer Society.

Ohlsson, N., & Alberg, H. (1996). Predicting faultprone software modules in telephone switches. *IEEE Transactions on software Engineering, 22*(12), 886-894.

Ping, Y., Systa, T., & Muller, H. (2002). Predicting faultproneness using OO metrics: An industrial case study. In T. Gyimothy, & F. B. Abreu (Eds.), *Proceedings of 6th European Conference on Software Maintenance and Reengineering* (pp. 99-107), Budapest, Hungary.

Pizzi, N. J., Summers, R., & Pedrycz, W. (2002). Software quality prediction using median adjusted class labels. In the *Proceedings: International Joint Conference on Neural Networks, volume 3* (pp. 2405-2409). Honolulu, HI: IEEE Computer Society.

Reformat, M., Pedrycz, W., & Pizzi, N. J. (2002). Software quality analysis with the use of computational intelligence. In the *Proceedings: IEEE International Conference on Fuzzy Systems, volume 2,* Honolulu, HI, USA (pp. 1156-1161).

Rosca, J. P., & Ballard, D. H. (1996). *Complexity drift in evolutionary computation with tree representations.* Technical Report NRL5, University of Rochester, Computer Science Department.

Runeson, P., Ohlsson, M. C., & Wohlin, C. (2001). A classification scheme for studies on faultprone components. *Lecture Notes in Computer Science, 2188,* 341-355. Springer Link.

Schneidewind, N. F. (2002). Body of knowledge for software quality measurement. *IEEE Computer, 35*(2), 77-83.

Soule, T., & Foster, J. A. (1999). Effects of code growth and parsimony presure on populations in genetic programming. *Evolutionary Computation*, 293-309.

Soule, T., Foster, J. A., & Dickinson, J. (1996). Code growth in genetic programming. In the *Proceedings of the First Annual Conference* (pp. 215-223).

Stadler, W. (1975). *Preference optimality and application of Pareto optimality*. New York.

Suarez, A., & Lutsko, J. F. (1999). Globally optimal fuzzy decision trees for classification and regression. *Pattern Analysis and Machine Intelligence, 21*(12), 1297-1311.

Tackett, W. A. (1993). Genetic programming for feature discovery and image discrimination. In the *Proceedings of the 5th International Conference on Genetic Algorithms* (pp. 303-309).

Thomas, J., & Sycara, K. (1999). The importance of simplicity and validation in genetic programming for data mining in financial data. In the *Proceedings of the Joint AAAI1999 and GECCO1999 Workshop on Data Mining with Evolutionary Algorithms*.

Chapter X

A Statistical Framework for the Prediction of Fault-Proneness

Yan Ma, West Virginia University, USA

Lan Guo, West Virginia University, USA

Bojan Cukic, West Virginia University, USA

Abstract

Accurate prediction of fault-prone modules in software development process enables effective discovery and identification of the defects. Such prediction models are especially valuable for the large-scale systems, where verification experts need to focus their attention and resources to problem areas in the system under development. This chapter presents a methodology for predicting fault-prone modules using a modified random forests algorithm. Random forests improve classification accuracy by growing an ensemble of trees and letting them vote on the classification decision. We applied the methodology to five NASA public domain defect datasets. These datasets vary in size, but all typically contain a small number of defect samples. If overall accuracy maximization is the goal, then learning from such data usually results in a biased classifier. To obtain better prediction of fault-proneness, two strategies are investigated: proper sampling technique in constructing the tree classifiers, and threshold adjustment in determining the "winning" class. Both are found to be effective in accurate prediction of fault-prone modules. In addition, the chapter presents a thorough and statistically sound comparison of these methods against many other classifiers frequently used in the literature.

Introduction

Early detection of **fault-prone** software components enables verification experts to concentrate their time and resources on the problem areas of the software system under development. The ability of **software quality models** to accurately identify critical faulty components allows for the application of focused verification activities ranging from manual inspection to automated formal analysis methods. Software quality models, thus, help ensure the reliability of the delivered products. It has become imperative to develop and apply good software quality models early in the software development life cycle, especially for large-scale development efforts.

The basic hypothesis of software quality prediction is that a module currently under development is fault prone if a module with the similar product or process metrics in an earlier project (or release) developed in the same environment was fault prone (Khoshgoftaar, Allen, Ross, Munikoti, Goel, & Nandi, 1997). Therefore, the information available early within the current project or from the previous project can be used in making predictions. This methodology is very useful for the large-scale projects or projects with multiple releases.

Accurate prediction of fault-prone modules enables the verification and validation activities focused on the critical software components. Therefore, software developers have a keen interest in software quality models. To meet the needs of developers, fault-prone prediction models must be efficient and accurate.

Many modeling techniques have been developed and applied for software quality prediction. These include: logistic regression (Basili, Briand, & Melo, 1996); discriminant analysis (Khoshgoftaar, Allen, Kalaichelvan, & Goel, 1996; Munson & Khoshgoftaar, 1992); the discriminative power techniques (Schneidewind, 1992); optimized set reduction (Briand, Basili, & Hetmanski, 1993); artificial neural network (Khoshgoftaar & Lanning, 1995); fuzzy classification (Ebert, 1996); genetic algorithms (Azar, Precup, Bouktif, Kegl, & Sahraoui, 2002); and classification trees (Gokhale & Lyu, 1997; Khoshgoftaar & Seliya, 2002; Selby & Porter, 1988; Troster & Tian, 1995). Following more than a decade of research, Fenton and Neil (1999) critically evaluated software quality models. They proposed the Bayesian belief networks (BBNs) as the most promising method for further consideration. In the Bayesian networks, nodes (variables) are interrelated by links representing causal relationships. The BBNs predict an event (here an occurrence of a fault-prone module) based on an uncertainty measure computed by the Bayesian inference methods. The ability of the BBNs in modeling complex inter-relationship among the variables cannot be achieved by the conventional methods such as multi-variate analysis. The introduction of the BBNs to software quality prediction was certainly a positive step forward. However, the drawbacks of the BBNs have also been recognized by the researchers. First, the BBNs connect variables based on causal relationship. However, not all variables are causally related. Software quality predictors are generally software metrics, such as McCabe metrics, Halstead metrics, or process metrics. It is not reasonable, for instance, to model the causal relationship between the *lines of code* and *unique arithmetic operators* (a basic Halstead metric). Second, BBNs require a (subjective) prior to perform the inferences. However, such a prior may not always be available or reasonable. To overcome the limitations of the BBN model, the Dempster-Shafer belief networks (DSBNs) were recently developed and applied to software quality prediction (Guo, Cukic, & Singh, 2003). The DSBNs model the relationship of the variables using prediction logic, which integrates formal logic and statistics. In addition, the DSBNs do not require any prior probabilities, and the inference process can start with zero knowledge. The DSBN methodology holds promise for future software quality and reliability modeling. However, it is not widely deployed in real-life statistical tools, which is the reason for its sparse utilization in software engineering research.

In all software quality models, there is a tradeoff between the defect detection rate and the overall prediction accuracy. Thus, if performance comparison between various models is based on only one criterion (either the defect detection rate or the overall accuracy) the results of comparison will be only partially relevant. A software quality model can be considered superior over its counterparts if it has both a higher defect detection rate, and a higher overall accuracy. About *65-75%* of critical modules and non-fault-prone modules were correctly predicted in Hudepohl, Aud, Khoshgoftaar, Allen, and Mayrand (1996), Khoshgoftaar et al. (1996), and Khoshgoftaar & Seliya (2002) using the overall accuracy criterion. Decision trees (Selby & Porter, 1988) correctly predicted *79.3%* of high development effort fault-prone modules (detection rate), while the trees generated from the best parameter combinations correctly identified *88.4%* of those modules on the average. The discriminative power techniques correctly classified *75* of *81* fault free modules, and *21* of *31* faulty modules (Schneidewind, 1992). In one case study, among five common classification techniques: Pareto classification, classification trees, factor-based discriminant analysis, fuzzy classification, and neural network, fuzzy classification appears to yield better results with a defect detection rate of 86% (Ebert & Baisch, 1998). Since most of these studies have been performed using different datasets, reflecting different software development environments and processes, the final judgment on "the best" fault-prone module prediction method is difficult to make.

In this chapter, we present a novel software quality prediction methodology based on balanced random forests. We compare the proposed methodology with many existing approaches using the same datasets. Our approach to predicting fault-prone modules runs efficiently on large datasets and it is more robust to outliers and noise compared to other classifiers. Hence, it is especially valuable for the large systems. The prediction accuracy of the proposed methodology is higher as compared to the algorithms available in three statistical and/or data mining software packages, *Weka*, *See5* and *SAS*, for the same datasets obtained from **NASA**. The difference in the performance of the proposed methodology over other methods is statistically significant. As performance comparison between different classification algorithms for detecting fault-prone software modules has been one of the weakest points in software engineering literature, we believe the procedure we outline here, if followed, has a potential to enhance the statistical validity of future experiments.

The remainder of this chapter is organized as follows. The next section describes *Random Forest* classification algorithm. The *Balanced Random Forests* section introduces the balanced Random Forests algorithm. The datasets used in this study are presented in the *Experimental Data* section. The *Performance Measurement Indices* section defines performance measurement parameters used in the experiments. The *Experiments* section presents the experiments, including the methodology, a short description of the classifiers used, and a detailed comparison between the proposed methodology over related work, that is, logistic regression, discriminant analysis, and classifiers available in three machine learning software packages, *See5, SAS* and *Weka* (Witten & Frank, 2005). The *Discussion* section includes a brief discussion of experimental results. The *Conclusion* section summarizes the chapter and provides final remarks.

Random Forests

A classification tree (Breiman, Friedman, Olshen, & Stone, 1984) is a top-down tree-structured classifier. It is built through a process known as recursive partitioning whereby the measurement space is successively split into subsets, each of which is equivalent to a terminal node in the tree.

Starting from the top node of the tree that contains the entire sample, all the candidate splits are evaluated independently, the most appropriate one is selected. The "appropriateness" of a split can be evaluated by different measures. The most popular one is based on impurity functions. Impurity measures are the quantification of how well the classes are being separated. In general, the value of an impurity measure is the largest when data are split evenly among all the classes and zero when all the data points belonging to a single class. There are various impurity measures used in the literature. The most commonly used are: *entropy-based measure* (Quinlan, 1993) and *Gini index* (Breiman et al., 1984). Purity (or homogeneity) of class labels is measured before and after the split. The split that produces the most discrimination between classes is the most appropriate one. The classification tree is grown to a point where the number of instances in the terminal node is small or the class membership of instances in the node is pure enough. The label of the class that dominates the instances in the terminal node is assigned to this node. The fully-grown tree may overfit the data and need to be cut back by using criteria which balance the classification performance and the tree's complexity.

In a tree model, an edge from a parent node to one of its children nodes indicates a rule. This child node is reachable only when the rule is satisfied. A path from the root node to a terminal node of the tree, which consists of at least one edge, specifies a classification rule. Such classification rule is the combination of the functions associated with all of the edges on the path. The decision associated with each classification rule is stated by the label attached to the terminal node. For a new data instance characterized by the input vector x, we would expose it to the root node of the tree and then follow along the path in which x satisfies all the rules. Obtained class label at the terminal node represents the classification decision.

Trees represent an efficient paradigm in generating understandable knowledge structures. But, experience shows that the lack of accuracy is the reason that prevents classification trees from being the ideal tool for predictive learning (Hastie, Tibshirani, & Friedman, 2001). One way to improve accuracy of classification trees is to utilize ensemble learning. Ensemble methods learn a large number of models instead of a single model and combine the predictions of all the models with a learning algorithm.

Bagging (Breiman, 1996) and **random forests** (Breiman, 2001) are ensemble methods. They construct a collection of base models and simply average their predictions. Bagging generally works for different unstable classifiers, including trees or neural networks, while random forests use only trees as base models. Random forests algorithm stems from bagging and can be considered as a special case of bagging (Speed, 2003).

The idea behind bagging is to take a bootstrap replicate (a sample collected with replacement) from the original training set and build a classifier. By bootstrapping, different versions of the learning set can be generated and a collection of classifiers is obtained. For overall classification, the predicated class is determined by plurality voting among the classes C, that is, the class label most frequently predicted by the models is selected.

Like bagging, a random forest consists of a collection of K tree classifiers $h_1(x)$, $h_2(x)$, ..., $h_K(x)$. Each classifier is built upon a bootstrap replica of the training set and votes for one of the classes in C. A test instance is classified by the label of the wining class. With bootstrap sampling, approximately 36.8% of the training instances are *not* used in growing each tree (due to sampling with replacement). These data instances are called out-of-bag (OOB) cases. Random forest algorithm uses OOB cases to estimate the classification error and evaluate the performance of the forest.

Besides bagging, another source of randomness is introduced in constructing the forest ensemble. At each node of the tree, the learning algorithm randomly selects and evaluates a subset of m features. The "best" feature in the subset is chosen as the basis for the decision which splits the node. The value of m is kept fixed at all nodes. In the random forests algorithm implemented in R toolset (http://www.r-project.org), the default value of m is selected to be the integer nearest to $\sqrt{M}$, where M is the total number of features in the dataset (Breiman & Cutler, 2004).

Let us denote the aggregated classifier as *h(x)*. The classification margin function indicates the extent to which the percentage vote for the correct class y exceeds the maximum proportion of vote obtained by a class in C other than y. It is defined as:

$$m\arg in(x, y) = P(h(x) = y) - \max_{i=1, i \neq y}^{c} P(h(x) = i)$$

The classification margin is estimated from all the tree classifiers in the forest. In the binary classification problem, the margin of an observation is the difference between the proportion of votes for the true class and the proportion of votes for the other class. The calculated margin lies between -1 and 1 (inclusive). A positive margin indicates a correct classification decision. The larger the margin, the more confidence we may have in the conclusion. If the margin of an observation is negative, then an erroneous decision is made.

The classification error of a forest depends on the strength of individual tree classifiers in the forest and the correlation between them (Breiman, 2001, 2004; Breiman & Cutler, 2004).

- **Correlation between tree classifiers in the forest**. No improvement could be obtained by generating identical trees. Two sources of randomness described earlier—bagging and random feature selection—make the trees look different and therefore lower the correlation between trees. Low correlation lowers the classification error rate.

- **Strength of individual tree in the forest.** Strength of the forest, measured by the average margin over the learning set, relies on the strength of individual tree models. A tree with a low error rate is a strong classifier. Having more diverse strong classifiers in the forest lowers the overall error.

Every tree in a forest expresses specific classification rules. Given a new instance with feature vector $x = \{x_1, x_2, ..., x_p\}$, the classification starts with *tree #1* in the forest. The traversal begins from the root, and the splitting rule determines the child node to descend to. This process is repeated until the terminal node is reached. The class label attached to the terminal node is assigned to the case. Thus, *tree #1* has made its decision. The classification continues with *tree #2* and follows the same procedure in finding the class label for the same data instance. Upon classifying the instance by every single tree in the forest, the algorithm has K votes, each indicating the likely class to which the data instance belongs to. The class with the majority of votes wins. Figure 1 shows the construction of a random forest from Bootstrap Samples (denoted by BS_i).

Random forest algorithm overcomes the disadvantages of a single classification tree. Trees are built from different bootstrap samples of the original dataset. Random feature sets used for determining optimal splits at each node stabilize the classifier. Finally, making the classification decision by voting improves the performance over a single tree. The advantages of random forest outlined in the literature include (Breiman, 2001, 2004; Breiman & Cutler):

- Easy to use and simplicity;
- Low classification error;
- Robustness with respect to noise;
- Easy handling of large feature spaces;
- Relatively fast tree growing algorithm and absence of the need for tree pruning;
- Built-in cross validation by using OOB cases to estimate classification error rates;
- High level of predictive accuracy without overfitting.

From a single run of a random forest, we can obtain a wealth of information such as classification error rate, variable importance ranking, proximity measures and so forth. Detailed description can be found in Breiman and Cutler (2004). Next, we describe a few that are important for the application of random forests to the software engineering data.

- **Classification Error Rate Estimation:** In a random forest, there is no need for cross-validation, that is, the use of a separate test set to get an unbiased estimate of the classification error (Breiman & Cutler, 2004). As mentioned earlier, the OOB cases are used for validation. This feature simplifies the design of software engineering experiments, especially in cases when datasets are rather small and the division into a training set and a test set diminishes the statistical representativeness of each of them. OOB testing is performed as follows. OOB cases of the kth tree in the forest

Figure 1. Construction of random forests

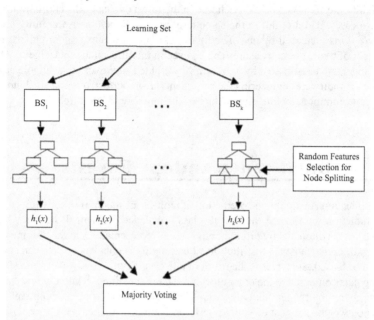

are used to test that tree as well as all the other trees in the forest, followed by voting. Comparing the overall classification with the known class affiliation from the dataset provides an unbiased estimate of the OOB set error rate.

- **Feature Importance Evaluation:** In a random forests algorithm, the importance of a variable is defined in terms of its contribution of predictive accuracy. The implementation of the random forest algorithm in R offers users two importance measures. The first importance measure, "Mean Decrease in Accuracy" is defined through OOB testing. Randomly permuting the values of the ith variable in the OOB set of each tree results in a permuted OOB set. Random forest is run on such a permuted OOB set. The decrease in the margin resulting from random permutation of the values of ith variable averaged across all the cases in the OOB set produces the importance measure. The second measure, "Mean Decrease in Gini", is based on the *Gini* index. If a split of a node is made on the ith variable, as cases in the children nodes become more pure, the *Gini* impurity criterion for the children nodes should be lower than that measured in the parent node. The sum of all decreases in impurity in the forest due to this variable, normalized by the number of trees, forms a variable importance measure. When software engineering metrics are used to predict quality attributes, ranking the importance of measurements is very important because it helps explain the dependencies in the development life cycle. Having importance measures incorporated in the classification toolset further simplifies the experimental design.

- **Proximity Measurements:** The proximity measurements provide intrinsic measures of similarities between cases. Each tree in the forest evaluates the entire training set. If two cases, *a* and *b*, fall in the same terminal node, then their proximity measure *prox(a, b)* is increased by one. The final proximity measures are normalized by the number of trees. These measures can be used in missing value replacement, where a missing value is estimated by a proximity-weighted sum over the available attribute values. As software engineering measurements are imperfect, missing attribute values are quite common, making this feature of random forests appealing.

Balanced Random Forests

In many applications including the prediction of fault-prone modules in software engineering, the prediction models are faced with class imbalance problem. It occurs when the classes in *C* have a dramatically different numbers of representatives in the training dataset and/or very different statistical distributions. Learning from imbalanced data can cause the classifier to be biased. Such bias is the result of one class being heavily over-represented in the training data compared to the other classes. Classes containing relatively few cases can be largely ignored by the learning algorithms because the cost of performing well on the large class outweighs the cost of doing poorly on the much smaller classes, provided that the algorithm aims at maximizing overall accuracy (Chawla, Bowyer, Hall, & Kegelmeyer, 2002). For instance, a binary classification problem such as the identification of fault-prone modules may be represented by *1,000* cases, *950* of which are negative cases (majority class, not fault-prone modules), and *50* are positive cases (minority class, fault-prone modules). Even if the model classified all the cases as negative and misclassified all the positive cases, the overall accuracy could reach *95%*, a great result for any machine learning classification algorithm. In many situations, the minority class is the subject of our major interest. In practice, we want to achieve a lower minority classification error even at the cost of a higher majority class error rate. For example, if the goal of identifying fault-prone modules early in software development is exposing them to a more rigorous set of verification and validation activities, the imperative is to identify as many potentially faulty modules as possible. If we happen to misclassify non-faulty modules as faulty, the verification process will increase its cost as some modules are unnecessarily analyzed. But, the consequence of misclassifying faulty software module as non-faulty may be a system failure, a highly undesirable outcome.

In the random forest algorithm described in the *Random Forests* section, every single tree is built upon a bootstrapped sample from the original learning set. In cases where classes represented in the original learning set are unbalanced, the bootstrapped sample is also unbalanced.

Consequently, learning from such data would result in a biased classifier. To make use of all available information in the training data and avoid producing a biased classifier, a proper sampling technique needs to be introduced into the random forests algorithm.

One way is to randomly partition the majority class S_{maj} into subsets $S_{maj1}, S_{maj2}, ..., S_{majk}$ of (approximately) equal size. The number of subsets k depends on the size of the minority class S_{min}, since the number of cases in each partition of S_{maj} should be comparable with the number of cases in S_{min}. For instance, software project JM1 (see Table 1) consists of *10,885* modules and around *19%* are faulty modules. We could randomly partition the non-effective instances into five subsets. Combining each subset of S_{maj} with S_{min} results in k (relatively) balanced samples. Let's call them "communities". We could then run random forests algorithm on each community. The final classification decision would be made by plurality voting among k communities.

The other modification of the conventional random forest algorithm could be to build each tree in the forest on a balanced sample. Instead of taking a bootstrapped sample from the entire learning dataset, each single tree is build upon a set which mixes the two classes samples of approximately the same size: one is a bootstrapped sample from S_{min} and the other sample is taken randomly with replacement from S_{maj} (Chen, Liaw, & Breiman, 2004). The size of the balanced set from which a tree is grown is dependent on the size of minority class. Take the project CM1, for example. Each tree would be built on a balanced sample with 49 fault-prone modules and a subset of non-defective modules of approximately the same size. As the number of the trees in the forest becomes large, all the instances in the original learning set tend to be selected to build the forest. Trees can be grown to maximum size without pruning. As in the conventional random forest, only a random subset of features is selected to make the splitting. This "balanced tree" feature has already implemented in the random forests package in R. This feature has been used in the conduct our experiments, in addition to traditional random forests algorithm.

Experimental Data

The defect datasets used in our case studies have been collected from mission critical projects at NASA, as a part of the Software Metrics Data Program (MDP). Table 1 provides the simple description of the characteristics of software projects which served as the origin of the metrics datasets. Basic datasets properties such as sample size, proportion of defects, and data pre-processing methods are described in Table 2. Only the dataset describing project JM1 contains some missing values. These were removed prior to the statistical analysis. Each dataset contains 21 **software metrics**, which describe product's size, complexity, and

Table 1. Projects description

Projects	Source Code	Description
KC1	C++	Storage management for receiving/ processing ground data
KC2	C++	Science data processing
JM1	C	Real-time predictive ground system
PC1	C	Flight software for earth orbiting satellite
CM1	C	A NASA spacecraft instrument

some structural characteristics (Boetticher, 2005) (see Table 3). Each module is measured in terms of the same software product metrics. A class label is associated with each module, indicating if the module is defect-free or fault-prone. Defects were detected during the development or in the deployment. From Table 2, we can see that the fault-prone modules constitute only a small portion of the datasets. Therefore, the class distribution in the learning set does not reflect their importance in the problem.

Table 2. Datasets characteristics

Projects	# of Instances	Pre-processing	% Defects
KC1	2,109	-	15%
KC2	523	-	21%
JM1	10,885	missing values removed	19%
PC1	1,109	-	7%
CM1	498	-	10%

Table 3. Metric descriptions of five datasets

Metric Type	Metric	Definition
McCabe	v(G) ev(G) iv(G) LOC	Cyclomatic Complexity Essential Complexity Design Complexity Lines of Code
Derived Halstead	N V L D I E B T	Length Volume Level Difficulty Intelligent Count Effort Effort Estimate Programming Time
Line Count	LOCode LOComment LOBlank LOCodeAndComment	Lines of Code Lines of Comment Lines of Blank Lines of Code and Comment
Basic Halstead	UniqOp UniqOpnd TotalOp TotalOpnd	Unique Operators Unique Operands Total Operators Total Operands
Branch	BranchCount	Total Branch Count

Performance Measurement Indices

Figure 2 shows the confusion matrix of defect prediction. Several standard terms have been defined for this two-class matrix. In our study, we call the software modules with defects "positive" cases, while the modules without defects are termed "negative" cases. In order to be able to evaluate how well classification algorithm performs, we define several performance metrics below.

The *PD, the Probability of Detection (or recall)* is the percentage of fault-prone modules that are correctly predicted by the classification algorithm. It is defined as:

$$PD = \frac{TP}{TP + FN}$$

The *PF (Probability of False Alarm)* is the proportion of defect-free modules that were erroneously classified as fault-prone, calculated as:

$$PF = \frac{FP}{FP + TN}$$

The *ACC (Accuracy)* measures the chance that the total number of modules was predicted correctly. It is calculated as follows:

$$ACC = \frac{TP + TN}{TN + FP + FN + TP}$$

The *True Negative Rate (TNR)* is the proportion of correctly identified defect-free modules. It is calculated as:

$$TNR = \frac{TN}{TN + FP} = 1 - PF$$

Figure 2. Confusion matrix of defect prediction

		Defect Predicted?	
		No	Yes
Module with defect?	No	True Negative (TN)	False Positive (FN)
	Yes	False Negative (FN)	True Positive (TP)

The *precision* is percentage of correctly predicted fault-prone modules, calculated as:

$$Precision = \frac{TP}{TP+FP}$$

In our case studies, the number of fault-prone modules is much smaller than the number of non-defective modules. Therefore, the accuracy might not be a good measure of classification performance (Kubat, Holte, & Matwin, 1998). Figure 3 shows the margin plot (please review the *Random Forests* section for the definition of *"margin"*) for projects PC1 and KC2 using the random forest algorithm (majority voting). Since maximizing overall accuracy is the goal, a good overall accuracy measures were obtained. However, a large proportion of fault-prone modules (cases belonging to minority class) were misclassified. The performance measures that take the "imbalance of data" into account when assessing classification success include *geometric mean (G-mean)* (Kubat et al., 1998) and *F-measure* (Lewis & Gale, 1994), defined as follows:

$$G-mean_1 = \sqrt{PD \times Precision}$$

$$G-mean_2 = \sqrt{PD \times TNR}$$

$$F-measure = \frac{(\beta^2+1) \times Precision \times PD}{\beta^2 \times Precision + PD}$$

Figure 3. Margin plot: A graphical representation of the confusion matrix. The horizontal axis is case index. Cases from majority class and minority class are represented by "o" and "x", respectively. A positive margin associated with a case indicates a correct decision while a negative margin means an erroneous decision.

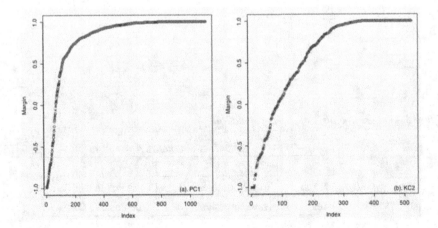

Parameter β in the *F-measure* calculation takes any non-negative value and is used to manipulate the weight assigned to *PD* and *precision*. In our study, equal weights are given to *PD* and *precision* by setting the value of β to *1.0*. Of course, different projects are likely to assign different weights for *PD* and *precision*. For example, risk adverse projects may increase the weight of PD, thus stressing the importance of detecting all faulty modules even if that implies checking many modules which are not faulty. To the contrary, projects with very limited verification and validation budgets may want to put emphasis on precision, thus limiting the number of non-faulty modules exposed to costly reviews. The calculation of *F-measure* should be adjusted accordingly. If all the fault-prone modules are predicted incorrectly, both *G-mean's* and *F-measure* result in a score of *0*.

Receiver operating characteristic (ROC) curves can also be used to evaluate the performance of classifiers. An ROC curve provides a visual tool for examining the tradeoff between the ability of a classifier to correctly identify positive cases (*PD*) and the number of negative cases that are incorrectly classified (*PF*). The higher the *PD* at low *PF* values, the better the model. A numerical measure of the accuracy of the model can be obtained from the area under the curve (AUC), where an area of *0.5* is equivalent to random guessing and an AUC of *1.0* suggests perfect accuracy (Hanley & McNeil, 1983).

Experiments

In this study, we first compare the classification performance of the random forest algorithm with a set of diverse but well-known classifiers. We report various performance measures. Then, the performance of the balanced random forest classifier is investigated with respect to the conventional random forests algorithm.

Methodology

Having grown a forest of decision trees using the random forests algorithm, given a new instance of a software module, each tree in the forest casts a vote and makes its own classification decision. Consequently, a proportion of the trees vote the module as "fault-prone" and the rest classify it as "not-fault-prone". In binary classification problems using majority voting rule, if at least *50%* of the trees reach an agreement such agreement is considered the final decision. Random forests, aiming at the minimization of the overall error rate, keep the error rate low in the majority class and possibly high in the minority class. This obviously causes a problem for software quality prediction since many possibly flawed modules will be misclassified as fault-free and released into the later phase of the software life cycle without proper verification and validation checks.

Imbalance makes classification error lean towards the minority class. Random forests can adjust for imbalance by altering the voting thresholds. User-specified voting cut-offs make the random forest algorithm flexible. If user-defined voting thresholds are used, the "winning" class is the one with the maximum ratio of proportion of votes to cut-off. The default cut-off is $1/c$ where c is the number of classes (i.e., majority vote wins). The fault proneness problem in software engineering has binary predictive outcomes ("fault-prone" and "not-fault-prone"), so the cut-off is a vector of length two $\{c_{fp}, c_{nfp}\}$, with the condition that c_{fp} + c_{nfp} = 100%. With a module to be classified, suppose p_{fp} is the proportion of the trees in the forest that vote for "fault-prone" and $p_{nfp} = 1 - p_{fp}$ in favor of "not-fault-prone", then the module is predicted to be fault-prone if $\frac{p_{fp}}{c_{fp}} > \frac{p_{nfp}}{c_{nfp}}$. Under the constrains that both c_{fp}, c_{nfp} and p_{fp}, p_{nfp} sum up to 1, as long as $p_{fp} > c_{fp}$, the module is identified as fault-prone.

In the experiment with the regular random forests algorithm, we use a sequence of user-defined thresholds between 0 to 1 (exclusive), with the increment of 0.02, as c_{fp}. Consequently, c_{nfp} takes the value of $1 - c_{fp}$. Software quality engineers who conduct this type of studies can decide to choose a threshold value that produces the best classification results for their specific projects. By changing the threshold of voting, different combination of PD and PF can be obtained. The ROC curves can thus be constructed. This is one way of addressing the imbalance problem in software engineering datasets.

The alternative solution of the problem caused by data imbalance is to use the balanced random forests approach, discussed in the *Balanced Random Forests* section. To remind readers, this approach calls for the base classifiers (trees) in the ensemble to be built from a balanced sample. A simple majority voting thresholds are then used by the balanced random forests classifier and the corresponding ROC curve represents its performance characteristics. In our experiments with balanced random forests, the area under the ROC curve is calculated using the trapezoidal rule (Hanley & McNeil, 1982).

It has been shown using the large number theory that random forests are not overfitting the dataset from which they learn the theory (Breiman, 2001). The classification error rate fluctuates at first and then converges as more trees are added to the forests. In our experiments, we constructed forests of 800 trees.

Comparing Classification Results

The performance of the regular random forest algorithm using various user-defined thresholds is first compared with statistical methods such as logistic regression, discriminant function analysis, a single classification tree, boosting, and so forth. Some of these methods are implemented in *See5*, some of them in *Weka*, an open source software issued under the GNU public license (Witten & Frank, 1999) and some in *SAS*. We used 10-fold cross-validation to evaluate the prediction accuracy of the algorithms whose classification performance were compared with random forests. The 10-fold cross-validation was run for at least 10 times in each experiment on the original datasets. The result with the least variance was chosen as the final result. Next, we briefly describe the classifiers included in our study.

Logistic Regression

Binary logistic regression is a form of regression which is used when the dependent is a dichotomy and the variables are of any type. Logistic regression applies maximum likelihood estimation after transforming the dependent into a logit variable. In this way, logistic regression estimates the probability of defect occurrence in a software module. The LOGISTIC procedure in *SAS* was used in our experiments.

Discriminant Analysis

Discriminant analysis is a very useful statistical tool. It takes into account the different variables of an instance and works out which class the instance most likely belongs to. Linear discrimination is the classification algorithm most widely used in practice. It optimally separates two groups, using the Mahalanobis metric or generalized distance. It also gives the same linear separation decision surface as Bayesian maximum likelihood discrimination in the case of equal class covariance matrices. In our experiments, the DISCRIM procedure from *SAS* was used on the datasets describing five NASA projects.

Classification Tree

This is one of the classifiers included in the commercial tool *See5*. It builds a tree-structured model for classification.

Boosting

Like random forests, boosting is also an ensemble methodology. Base models are constructed sequentially on modified versions of the data with the modification being that the weights of the cases are re-evaluated in order to emphasize misclassified cases. The predictions of the models are integrated through a weighted voting (Dettling, 2004). We used the boosting algorithm's implementation from *Weka*.

Ruleset

Rulesets are classifiers generated by *See5*. Rulesets contain an unordered collection of if-then rules. Each rule consists of one or more conditions that must all be satisfied if the rule is to be applicable. There is also a class label associated with each rule.

J48

This non-parametric machine learning algorithm is implemented in *Weka*. J48 is based on Quinlan's C4.5 algorithm (Quinlan, 1993) for generating trees.

IBk

IBk is a *Weka* classifier which implements the k-nearest neighbor (KNN) algorithm. To classify a new instance, the KNN rule chooses the class that is the most common among this new case's k neighbors "closest in distance" in the learning set. IB1 is KNN with $k=1$.

VF1

VF1 is a *Weka* classifier implementing the voting feature interval classifier. For numeric attributes, upper and lower boundaries (intervals) are constructed around each class. Discrete attributes have point intervals. Class counts are recorded for each interval on each attribute. Classification is made by voting.

Naïve Bayes

Naïve Bayes learner is a classifier implemented in *Weka*. It is based on probability models that incorporate strong independence assumptions. Naïve Bayes classifiers can handle an arbitrary number of independent variables. Given a set of variables, $\mathbf{X} = \{X_1, X_2,..., X_p\}$, Naïve Bayes constructs the posterior probability for the class c_j among a set of possible classes in C,

$$P(c_j \mid X) = P(c_j)\prod_{i=1}^{p}P(X_i \mid c_j)$$

Naïve Bayes classifier calculates the previously-mentioned conditional probability for each class in C and the predicted class is the one with the highest probability.

Kernel Density

This simple kernel density classifier is implemented in *Weka*. A detailed description of kernel-based learning can be found in Shawe-Taylor and Cristianini (2004).

Voted Perceptron

This *Weka* classifier implements the voted perceptron algorithm by Freund and Schapire (1999). A list of all prediction vectors is generated after each and every classification error during training. For each such vector, the algorithm counts the number of iterations it "survives" until the next classification error is made. This count is treated as the "weight" of the prediction vector. To make a prediction, voted perceptron algorithm computes the binary prediction of each prediction vector and combines all the predictions using a weighted majority vote. The weights used are the survival times described earlier. This makes sense since good predictions vectors tend to survive for a long period of time and, thus, have higher weight in the majority vote.

Hyper Pipes

It is a *Weka* classifier. For each class, a Hyper Pipe is constructed to contain all points of that class. The algorithm records the attribute bounds observed for each class. Test instances are classified according to the class that mostly contains the attributes of the new instance.

Decision Stump

Decision Stump builds simple binary decision "stumps" for classification problems. "Stumps" are tree models that limit growth to just two terminal nodes. This method copes well with missing values by treating "missing" as a separate attribute value. Decision Stump is mainly used in conjunction with the logitboost method and it is implemented in *Weka*.

KStar

KStar (Cleary & Trigg, 1995) is an instance-based classifier. The class of a test instance is based upon the class of those instances in the training set similar to it, as determined by some similarity measurement. The underlying assumption of this type of classifiers is that similar cases belong to the same class.

ROCKY

ROCKY is a defect detector toolset used in experimental selection of modules for software inspection at NASA IV&V facility in Fairmont, West Virginia (Menzies et al., 2003). ROCKY detectors are built by exhaustively exploring all singleton rules of the form: *attribute* $\geq$ *threshold*, where *attribute* is every numeric attribute present in the dataset, and *threshold* is a certain percentile value of the corresponding attribute. ROCKY has been applied to predicting fault-prone modules in projects KC2 and JM1. Predictions based on individual metrics were presented in Menzies et al. (2003).

These classifiers have been chosen for our case study either because they have been applied in the past, in one of the related software engineering experiments or because machine learning literature recommends them as robust tools for two-class classification problems.

Experimental Results: Traditional Random Forests Algorithm

In this section, we report the comparison of classification performance among the tools and techniques mentioned earlier on the five NASA software engineering datasets. We discuss the performance measures such as *PD, ACC, Precision, G-mean$_1$, G-mean$_2$* and *F-measure*. The comparison results are summarized in Tables 4-8. Since both *G-mean* and *F-measure* are more appropriate for assessing the performance on the imbalanced datasets, in the tables we highlight the highest three values of *G-mean* and *F-measure* across all the classifiers under study. Due to space constraints, not all the results from the random forest algorithm are shown here. Only the classification outcomes associated with three cut-offs: (0.9, 0.1), (0.8, 0.2) and (0.7, 0.3) are listed in the tables. By adjusting the thresholds in random forests, the algorithm tends to focus more on the accuracy of the minority class while trading off accuracy in the majority class. The performance of balanced random forests algorithm is reported in the next sub-section.

As the classification results vary across different NASA datasets, we present them for each dataset first and then generalize the observations later in the discussion. For project JM1, presented first, we compare the performance results of random forests to more than a dozen different classifiers. For projects that follow JM1, fewer classifiers are included for comparison. In all cases, our tables include the best classifiers and leave out those that do not perform well.

Table 4. Performance comparison on project JM1

Methods	PD(Recall)	ACC	Precision	G-mean$_1$	G-mean$_2$	F-measure
Logistic	0.654	0.658	0.315	0.454	**0.656**	0.425
Discriminant	0.509	0.736	0.368	0.433	0.634	**0.427**
Tree	0.131	0.811	0.546	0.268	0.357	0.211
RuleSet	0.115	0.810	0.540	0.249	0.335	0.190
Boosting	0.118	0.808	0.515	0.246	0.339	0.192
KernelDensity	0.194	0.810	0.523	0.319	0.431	0.283
NaiveBayes	0.197	0.803	0.477	0.306	0.432	0.279
J48	0.247	0.802	0.476	0.343	0.481	0.325
IBk	0.369	0.761	0.379	0.374	0.562	0.374
IB1	0.376	0.756	0.371	0.373	0.564	0.373
VotedPerceptron	0.604	0.560	0.243	0.383	0.576	0.347
VF1	0.868	0.418	0.232	0.448	0.519	0.366
HyperPipes	1.000	0.195	0.194	0.440	0.046	0.324
ROCKY	0.338	0.752	0.352	0.345	0.536	0.345
RF (0.9,0.1)	0.827	0.557	0.281	**0.482**	0.638	0.419
RF (0.8,0.2)	0.645	0.696	0.346	**0.472**	**0.676**	**0.450**
RF (0.7,0.3)	0.483	0.784	0.445	**0.463**	**0.643**	**0.463**

JM1 Project

JM1 is the largest dataset in our study. It contains software metrics and fault-proneness information on *10,885* modules. Table 4 shows that random forests outperform almost all the other classification techniques. Random forests at cut-offs *(0.8, 0.2)* and *(0.7, 0.3)* achieve the highest values in both *G-mean* and *F-measure*. Logistic regression produces an acceptable value in *G-mean₂*, but a low result in *F-measure*, while discriminant function analysis has the third highest *F-measure*, but a relatively low *G-mean* scores. Several classifiers used on this project achieve accuracy of up to *81%* but are associated with very low probability of detection. Hyper Pipes, on the other hand, beats all the other methods in probability of detection, but the overall accuracy is abysmal. JM1 dataset is known to suffer from noisy software engineering measurements and it is not surprising that random forests outperform other classifiers on a large and noisy data.

PC1 Project

PC1 is a fairly large dataset with 1,109 modules. The random forests algorithm shows clear advantage over the other methods (see Table 5). Although classifier VF1 obtains a superior result on *PD*, the other performance measures prevent it from being a candidate model for software quality prediction. The instance-based classifier IB1 achieves an acceptable *F-measure* compared with other methods except for random forest, but its *G-mean* values are low. Some of the prediction models, such as ruleset, boosting and VF1, either have a high value in *PD* or accuracy, but not both, therefore can not be used in software quality prediction.

Table 5. Performance comparison on project PC1

Methods	PD(Recall)	ACC	Precision	G-mean$_1$	G-mean$_2$	F-measure
Logistic	0.234	0.885	0.208	0.221	0.467	0.220
Discriminant	0.429	0.849	0.211	0.301	0.615	0.283
Tree	0.221	0.929	0.476	0.324	0.466	0.302
RuleSet	0.177	0.932	0.531	0.307	0.418	0.265
Boosting	0.130	0.940	1.000	0.361	0.361	0.230
J48	0.247	0.934	0.556	0.370	0.493	0.342
IB1	0.416	0.914	0.389	0.402	0.629	**0.402**
KStar	0.273	0.921	0.399	0.330	0.514	0.324
NaiveBayes	0.299	0.887	0.244	0.270	0.528	0.269
VF1	0.883	0.193	0.071	0.251	0.353	0.132
RF (0.9,0.1)	0.740	0.823	0.245	**0.426**	**0.784**	0.368
RF (0.8,0.2)	0.506	0.908	0.379	**0.438**	**0.689**	**0.433**
RF (0.7,0.3)	0.442	0.934	0.531	**0.484**	**0.655**	**0.482**

Table 6. Performance comparison on project KC1

Methods	PD(Recall)	ACC	Precision	G-mean$_1$	G-mean$_2$	F-measure
Logistic	0.752	0.711	0.317	0.488	**0.727**	0.446
Discriminant	0.638	0.790	0.390	0.499	0.722	0.484
Tree	0.193	0.848	0.523	0.318	0.432	0.282
RuleSet	0.187	0.852	0.564	0.325	0.427	0.281
Boosting	0.169	0.862	0.732	0.352	0.409	0.275
KStar	0.509	0.855	0.532	**0.521**	0.684	**0.520**
VF1	0.957	0.195	0.156	0.387	0.231	0.269
RF (0.9,0.1)	0.844	0.711	0.330	**0.528**	**0.761**	0.475
RF (0.8,0.2)	0.700	0.782	0.387	**0.520**	**0.747**	**0.498**
RF (0.7,0.3)	0.561	0.825	0.447	0.501	0.700	**0.498**

KC1 Project

KC1 project reports the measurements on *2,109* software modules. Generally speaking, random forests surpass almost all the compared methods (see Table 6) in terms of *G-mean* and *F-measure*. KStar produces comparable results in *G-mean$_1$* and *F-measure*, but worse in *G-mean$_2$*. Logistic regression has a relatively high *G-mean$_2$*, but achieves low value in *F-measure*. Classifiers such as single classification tree, ruleset and boosting achieve accuracy up to around *85%*, but the *PD* is not acceptable. VF1, on the other hand, has an impressive *PD*, but the accuracy and precision measures are not satisfactory.

KC2 Project

KC2 contains software measurements of *523* modules. Table 7 compares the performance of random forests with 10 other classification models on the project KC2. Clearly, random

Table 7. Performance comparison on project KC2

Methods	PD(Recall)	ACC	Precision	G-mean$_1$	G-mean$_2$	F-measure
Logistic	0.849	0.685	0.382	0.569	0.738	0.527
Discriminant	0.632	0.821	0.559	**0.594**	**0.742**	**0.593**
Tree	0.547	0.819	0.564	0.555	0.698	0.555
RuleSet	0.500	0.836	0.630	0.561	0.680	0.557
Boosting	0.434	0.835	0.651	0.531	0.638	0.521
IBk	0.509	0.812	0.548	0.528	0.673	0.528
DecisionStump	0.642	0.808	0.529	0.583	0.739	**0.580**
VotedPerceptron	0.849	0.376	0.228	0.440	0.463	0.360
VF1	0.887	0.586	0.319	0.532	0.671	0.469
ROCKY	0.722	0.727	0.409	0.543	0.725	0.522
RF (0.9,0.1)	0.880	0.723	0.419	**0.607**	**0.774**	0.567
RF (0.8,0.2)	0.806	0.769	0.465	**0.612**	**0.782**	**0.590**
RF (0.7,0.3)	0.620	0.784	0.482	0.547	0.716	0.543

Table 8. Performance comparison on project CM1

Methods	PD(Recall)	ACC	Precision	G-mean$_1$	G-mean$_2$	F-measure
Logistic	0.776	0.657	0.192	**0.386**	**0.707**	**0.308**
Discriminant	0.694	0.841	0.346	**0.490**	**0.771**	**0.462**
Tree	0.204	0.906	0.561	0.338	0.448	0.299
RuleSet	0.102	0.882	0.253	0.161	0.314	0.145
Boosting	0.020	0.892	0.145	0.054	0.141	0.035
KStar	0.204	0.859	0.243	0.222	0.436	0.222
NaiveBayes	0.306	0.849	0.267	0.286	0.527	0.285
VF1	0.898	0.339	0.120	0.328	0.450	0.211
RF (0.9,0.1)	0.714	0.651	0.179	**0.358**	**0.678**	0.287
RF (0.8,0.2)	0.490	0.805	0.250	0.350	0.641	**0.331**
RF (0.7,0.3)	0.224	0.855	0.244	0.234	0.456	0.234

forest at cut-off *(0.8, 0.2)* produces the best result based on *G-mean* and *F-measure*. Discriminant function analysis also provides decent performance measures. It seems that except for voted perceptron, most other classifiers achieve comparable results.

CM1 Project

CM1 is the smallest dataset in our study. It contains only *498* modules. From the results in Table 8, we conclude that there is no significant advantage of random forests over the compared methods. Logistic regression and discriminant function analysis appear to perform well on project CM1 based on *G-mean* and *F-measure*. NASA quality engineers noted that this is probably the most straightforward dataset for predicting fault-prone modules. It appears that the strengths of random forests algorithm are not reflected in better performance on CM1.

Comparison Between Traditional and Balanced Random Forests

The next step in our study is to compare the performance of balanced random forests (BRF) with the regular random forests (RF) algorithm. An appropriate way to compare the performance of these two variants of the same classification algorithm is by using ROC curves to describe the results of their application to the same datasets. The results of our first experiment suggest that the traditional RF algorithm is the most suitable choice for the classification tool for most NASA datasets. Our goal here is to examine whether the application of BRF can bring additional tangible benefits to the prediction of fault-prone modules in these datasets.

The ROC curves in Figure 4 indicate that the performance differences between RF and BRF are minimal on all the NASA projects. BRF seems to be slightly better than RF in most of the

Figure 4. AUC of RF and BRF. The solid line is the ROC produced by RF and dashed line is generated by BRF. The datasets correspond to ROC curves as follows: (a) PC1, (b) KC1, (c) JM1, (d) CM1, (e) KC2

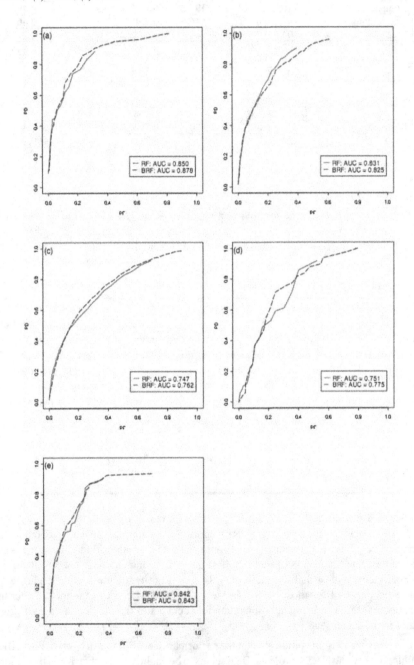

Table 9. Comparing RF and BRF by use of AUC

Projects	AUC (RF)	AUC (BRF)
JM1	0.7471	0.7616
PC1	0.8504	0.8781
KC1	0.8309	0.8245
KC2	0.8424	0.8432
CM1	0.7514	0.7750

cases. We wanted to further quantify this difference by measuring the area under the ROC curve (AUC). The AUC can take on any value between *0* and *1*, since both the *x* and *y*-axes have values ranging from *0* to *1*. The area under the curve is calculated using the trapezoid rule. Table 9 summarizes AUC information. Balanced random forests provide a better classification of fault-prone modules over the conventional random forests algorithm on projects JM1, PC1 and CM1. Of the remaining two projects, in KC1 there is a slight decrease in the value of AUC, while KC2 shows a slight improvement. However, performance differences between RF and BRF on these two datasets are not statistically significant.

Discussion

This chapter compares many statistical methods and machine learning algorithms in the context of predicting fault-prone modules in software development. Our experiments demonstrate that some of the evaluated classification algorithms (for example, ruleset, boosting, single tree classifiers) are not likely to perform well in the context of software quality prediction, even though they may have been considered a few times in the literature over the past decade. Many classifiers used in our performance comparison exhibit either a low defect detection rate *PD* or a low overall accuracy, or both. Other classifiers (Logistic, Discriminant, for example) should be included in the software quality engineer's toolbox, that is, these algorithms are the candidates for building good models for software quality prediction.

Compared with all the classifiers we got to analyze, random forests (and balanced random forests) always achieve better prediction performance, or at least achieve the performance that matches that of the best performing classification algorithms. Random forests work especially well on large and diverse datasets, such as JM1 and PC1. As mentioned in the *Random Forests* section, the prediction performance of random forests depends on the (low) correlation between trees in the forest. Each tree is built upon a bootstrapped sample from the original software metrics dataset. When the sample size is not large, there is a good chance that the same instance from the training set is used in almost all the bootstrapped samples. This causes an increase in the correlation between tree classifiers in the forest and, consequently, limits the performance of the forest.

Regarding the overall performance of random forests, two important observations emerge from our experiments. One is that the random forest algorithm is always one of the best classifiers if the user-specific voting thresholds approximate the proportion of fault-prone modules in the project's training set. The second observation relates the classification performance of two variants of the random forest algorithm. Balanced random forests provide a moderate performance increase over the traditional random forest algorithm. Since the improvement is moderate, software quality engineers have to decide whether it is worth additional effort in the design of experiments.

Conclusion

This chapter offers several insights into the field of software quality prediction. The first and foremost observation we want the readers to remember is that the performance of predictive models for the detection of fault-prone modules in software projects needs to be evaluated from multiple points of view. Overall prediction accuracy may be a misleading criterion as faulty modules are likely to represent a minority of the modules in the database. These training sets favor the classification of software modules in the majority class, that is, not-fault-prone. The probability of detection index measures how likely a fault-prone module is to be correctly classified. Further, precision index measures the proportion of correctly predicted fault-prone modules. In case the precision index is low, many fault-free modules will be unnecessarily exposed to rigorous software verification and validation thus increasing the cost of the process and the time needed for the project completion. Due to these observations, we propose to use a different set of performance indicators when comparing the performance of classification algorithms.

We also present a novel methodology for software quality prediction. This methodology is based on the two variants of the random forests algorithm. It is valuable for real-world applications in software quality predictions. First, it is more robust with respect to noise in the software metrics measurements than other methods. Therefore, it works especially well for the prediction of fault-proneness in large-scale software systems. Second, the methodology based on random forests runs efficiently on large datasets and provides high level of predictive power without overfitting. Therefore, based on our results, random forests are probably the most promising "best guess" when selecting a classification algorithm to apply to a dataset that describes the static characteristics (software metrics) of fault-prone modules in software engineering.

Another important characteristic of this study is that it has compared results from many different classification and machine learning algorithms on five different but highly relevant software engineering datasets. The results of our experiments provide a "proving grounds" for new methods that will be developed in the future. All our experiments can be repeated, as the tools and datasets can be easily obtained by fellow researchers. Thus, new methods for predicting fault-prone modules in software development projects can be and probably should be compared with our results in a clear and consistent way.

References

Azar, D., Precup, D., Bouktif, S., Kegl, B., & Sahraoui, H. (2002). Combining and adapting software quality predictive models by genetic algorithms. *ASE2002, the 17th IEEE International Conference on Automated Software Engineering,* Edinburgh, UK, September 23-27 (pp. 285-288). Los Alamitos, CA: IEEE Computer Society.

Basili, V. R., Briand, L. C., & Melo, W. L. (1996). A validation of object-oriented design metrics as quality indicators. *IEEE Transactions on Software Engineering, 22*(10), 751-761.

Boetticher, G. D. (2005). Nearest neighbor sampling for better defect prediction. *ACM SIGSOFT Software Engineering Notes, 30*(4), 1-6.

Breiman, L. (1996). Bagging predictors. *Machine Learning, 24,* 123-140.

Breiman, L. (2001). Random forests. *Machine Learning, 45,* 5-32.

Breiman, L. (2004). *Wald Lecture II, Looking inside the black box.* Retrieved May 2004, from http://www.stat.berkeley.edu/users/breiman.

Breiman, L., & Cutler, A. (2004). *Random forests: Classification/clustering.* Retrieved May 2004, from http://www.stat.berkeley.edu/users/breiman/RandomForests

Breiman, L., Friedman, J. H., Olshen, R. A., & Stone, C. J. (1984). *Classification and regression trees.* Belmont, CA: Wadsworth International Group.

Briand, L. C., Basili, V. R., & Hetmanski, C. J. (1993). Developing interpretable models with optimized set reduction for identifying high-risk software components. *IEEE Transactions on Software Engineering, 19*(11), 1028-1044.

Chawla, N. V., Bowyer, K. W., Hall, L. O., & Kegelmeyer, W. P. (2002). Smote: Synthetic minority over-sampling technique. *Journal of Artificial Intelligence Research, 16,* 321-357.

Chen, C., Liaw, A., & Breiman, L. (2004). *Using random forest to learn imbalanced data.* Technical Report No. 666. Berkeley, CA: University of Berkeley, Department of Statistics.

Cleary, J. G., & Trigg, L. E. (1995). K*: An instance-based learner using an entropic distance measure. In the *Proceedings of the 12th International Conference on Machine Learning,* Tahoe City, CA, July 9-12 (pp. 108-114). San Francisco, CA: Morgan Kaufmann.

Dettling, M. (2004). BagBoosting for tumor classification with gene expression data. *Bioinformatics, 20*(18), 3583-3593.

Ebert, C., & Baisch, E. (1998). Industrial application of criticality prediction in software development. *ISSRE, the Ninth International Symposium on Software Reliability Engineering,* Paderborn, Germany, November (pp. 80-89). Washington, D.C.: IEEE Computer Society.

Ebert, C. (1996). Classification techniques for metric-based software development. *Software Quality Journal, 5*(4), 255-272.

Fenton, N., & Neil, M. (1999, September/October). A critique of software defect prediction models. *IEEE Transactions on Software Engineering, 25*(5), 675-689.

Freund, Y., & Schapire, R. E. (1999). Large margin classification using the perceptron algorithm. *Machine Learning, 37*(3), 277-296.

Gokhale, S. S., & Lyu, M. R. (1997). Regression tree modeling for the prediction of software quality. In H. Pham (Ed.), *The Third ISSAT International Conference on Reliability and Quality in Design*, Anaheim, CA, March 12-14 (pp.31-36). New Brunswick, NJ: ISSAT.

Guo, L., Cukic, B., & Singh, H. (2003). Predicting fault prone modules by the dempster-shafer belief networks. *ASE2003, the 18th IEEE International Conference on Automated Software Engineering,* Montreal Canada, October (pp. 249-252). Los Alamitos, CA: IEEE Computer Society.

Hanley, J. A., & McNeil, B. J. (1983). A method of comparing the areas under receiver operating characteristic curves derived from the same cases. *Radiology, 148*, 839-843.

Hanley, J. A., & McNeil, B. J. (1982). The meaning and use of the area under a receiver operating characteristic (ROC) curve. *Radiology, 143*, 29-36.

Hastie, T., Tibshirani, R., & Friedman, J. H. (2001). *The elements of statistical learning.* New York: Springer-Verlag.

Hudepohl, J. P., Aud, S. J., Khoshgoftaar, T. M., Allen, E. B., & Mayrand, J. (1996). Emerald: Software metrics and models on the desktop. *IEEE Software, 13*(5), 56-60.

Khoshgoftaar, T. M., & Lanning, D. L. (1995). A neural network approach for early detection of program modules having high risk in the maintenance phase. *Journal of Systems and Software, 29*(1), 85-91.

Khoshgoftaar, T. M., Allen, E. B., Kalaichelvan, K. S., & Goel, N. (1996). Early quality prediction: A case study in telecommunications. *IEEE Software, 13*(1), 65-71.

Khoshgoftaar, T. M., Allen, E. B., Ross, F. D., Munikoti, R., Goel, N., & Nandi, A. (1997). Predicting fault-prone modules with case-based reasoning. *ISSRE 1997, the Eighth International Symposium on Software Engineering,* Albuquerque, New Mexico, November (pp. 27-35). Los Alamitos, CA: IEEE Computer Society.

Khoshgoftaar, T. M., & Seliya, N. (2002). Tree-based software quality estimation models for fault prediction. *METRICS 2002, the Eighth IIIE Symposium on Software Metrics,* Ottawa, Canada, June 4-7 (pp. 203-214). Los Alamitos, CA: IEEE Computer Society.

Kubat, M., Holte, R. C., & Matwin, S. (1998). Machine learning for the detection of oil spills in satellite radar images. *Machine Learning, 30*(2-3), 195-215.

Lewis, D., & Gale, W. (1994). A sequential algorithm for training text classifiers. In the *Proceedings of the 17th Annual International ACM-SIGIR Conference on Research and Development in Information Retrieval,* Dublin, Ireland, July 3-6 (pp. 3-12) (special issue of the SIGIR Forum). New York, NY: ACM/Springer-Verlag.

Menzies, T., Stefano, J. D., Ammar, K., McGill, K., Callis, P., Chapman, R. M., & Davis, J. (2003). When can we test less? In the *9th IEEE International Software Metrics Symposium (METRICS2003),* Sydney, Australia, September 3-5 (pp. 98). Los Alamitos, CA: IEEE Computer Society. Retrieved 2004, from http://menzies.us/pdf/03metrics.pdf

Munson, J. C., & Khoshgoftaar, T. M. (1992). The detection of fault-prone programs. *IEEE Transactions on Software Engineering, 18*(5), 423-433.

Quinlan, J. R. (1993). *C4.5 programs for machine learning*. San Francisco, CA: Morgan Kaufmann.

Remlinger, K. S. (2003). *Introduction and application of random forest on high throughput screening data from drug discovery*. Retrieved October 2003, from http://www4.ncsu.edu/~ksremlin

Schneidewind, N. F. (1992). Methodology for validating software metrics. *IEEE Transactions on Software Engineering, 18*(5), 410-422.

See5. (2005). Software package. Retrieved 2004, from http://www.rulequest.com/see5-info.html

Selby, R. W., & Porter, A. A. (1988). Learning from examples: generation and evaluation of decision trees for software resource analysis. *IEEE Transactions on Software Engineering, 14*(12), 1743-1757.

Shawe-Taylor, J., & Cristianini, N. (2004). *Kernel methods for pattern analysis*. Cambridge, UK: Cambridge University Press.

Speed, T. (Ed.). (2003). *Statistical analysis of gene expression microarray data*. Boca Raton, FL: Chapman & Hall/CRC Press.

Troster, J., & Tian, J. (1995). Measurement and defect modeling for a legacy software system. *Annals of Software Engineering, 1*, 95-118.

Witten, I. H., & Frank, E. (2005). *Data mining: Practical machine learning tools and techniques with java implementations*. San Francisco, CA: Morgan Kaufmann.

Section IV:

State-of-the-Practice

This part comprises two chapters (Chapters XI-XII) that offer some state-of-the-practice review on the applications of two machine learning methods. Chapter XI focuses on the roles rule-based learning plays in software engineering. It provides some background information, discusses the key issues in rule induction, and examines how rule induction handles uncertainties in data. The chapter examines the rule induction applications in the following areas: software effort and cost prediction, software quality prediction, software defect prediction, software intrusion detection, and software process modeling. Chapter XII, on the other hand, centers on genetic algorithm applications to software testing. The highlight of the chapter is on evolutionary testing, and the application of genetic algorithms for test data generation. The chapter includes reviews of existing approaches in structural, temporal performance, and specification-based functional evolutionary testing.

Chapter XI

Applying Rule Induction in Software Prediction

Bhekisipho Twala, Brunel University, UK

Michelle Cartwright, Brunel University, UK

Martin Shepperd, Brunel University, UK

Abstract

Recently, the use of machine learning (ML) algorithms has proven to be of great practical value in solving a variety of software engineering problems including software prediction, for example, cost and defect processes. An important advantage of machine learning over statistical analysis as a modelling technique lies in the fact that the interpretation of production rules is more straightforward and intelligible to human beings than, say, principal components and patterns with numbers that represent their meaning. The main focus of this chapter is upon rule induction (RI): providing some background and key issues on RI and further examining how RI has been utilised to handle uncertainties in data. Application of RI in prediction and other software engineering tasks is considered. The chapter concludes by identifying future research work when applying rule induction in software prediction. Such future research work might also help solve new problems related to rule induction and prediction.

Introduction

Machine learning (ML), which has been making great progress in many directions, is a hallmark of machine intelligence just as human learning is the hallmark of human intelligence. The ability to learn and reason from observations and experience seems to be crucial for any intelligent being (Forsyth & Rada, 1986; Holland, 1975; Winston, 1992).

One major problem for applying ML algorithms in software engineering is the unavailability and scarcity of software data, that is, data for training the model. Surveys for collecting software engineering data are usually small but difficult and expensive to conduct. This is due to the lack of expertise with required knowledge to carry out and maintain high quality information and the nature of software development which cannot be collected in an environmental setting. Also, the lack of data could arise from the need for confidentiality—industrial companies are often reluctant to allow access to data on software failures because of the possibility that people might think less highly of their products. Another problem as far as ML application is concerned is the form that the dataset takes, that is, the dataset characteristics. Most learning techniques assume that the data are presented in a simple attribute-value format. Another important feature of a problem domain is the quality of the data available. Most real data is imperfect: incomplete; irrelevant; redundant; noisy; and erroneous. The aim of a learning system is to discover a set of decision rules that is complete, in that it describes all of the data and predicts the data accurately.

In this chapter, we explore what RI can do in the software engineering domain to increase the awareness of learning methods when building software prediction models. However, our main focus is on the application of rule induction to software prediction.

The topic is significant because:

1. RI is an emerging technology that can aid in the discovery of rules and patterns in sets of data.

2. RI has an advantage over statistical analysis as a modelling technique due to the fact that the interpretation of production rules is more straightforward and intelligible to human beings than, say, principal component and patterns with numbers that represent their meaning.

3. Due to the lack of adequate tools to evaluate and estimate software project estimation, RL strategies have been used to tackle such problems, including software prediction.

Rule induction is one of the most established and effective data mining technology in use today that has been applied successfully in several disciplines and to real-world domains. These include: preventing breakdowns in electric transformers (Riese, 1984); increasing yield in chemical process control (Leech, 1986); improving separation of gas from oil (Guilfoyle, 1986); making credit card decisions (Michie, 1989); diagnosis of mechanical devices (Giordana, Neri, & Saitta, 1996); monitoring quality of rolling emulsions (Karba & Drole, 1990); coronary heart disease diagnosis and risk group delivery (Gamberger, Lavrac, & Krstacic, 2002); categorising text documents (Johnson, Oles, Zhang, & Goetz, 2002); and among other areas.

The remainder of this chapter is organised as follows. The *Supervised Learning Methods* section briefly describes the problem of supervised and unsupervised learning. In the *Applying Rule Induction in Prediction* section, we give an overview of the principles of rule induction. In particular, we describe how rule induction has been applied to handle some machine learning problems. The *Applying Rule Induction in Software Engineering Tasks* is the following section. Afterwards is the *Discussion* section, and finally, the *Concluding Remarks* section draws conclusions and some directions for future research.

Supervised Learning Methods

Supervised learning is a ML technique for creating a function from training data. The training data consist of pairs of input objects and desired output.

Classification and regression are critical types of prediction problems. RI can be used for predicting numerical and continuous dependent variables (regression) and discrete-valued or categorical predictor variables (classification). Regression-type problems are generally those where one attempts to predict values of a continuous variable from one or more continuous and/or categorical variables. For example, one may be interested in predicting software effort (a continuous dependent variable). Classification-type problems predict values of a categorical dependent variable from one or more continuous or categorical variables. For example, one may be interested in predicting which one of different software languages (for example, visual basic) a project manager decides to purchase.

There are many ways of looking for particular patterns in data. One way is extracting classification rules—rules that enable one to predict the particular classification (of some sort) about the data that the learner has not been presented with before. This is also known as the task of supervised classification (Duda, Hart, & Stork, 2000; Hastie, Tibshirani, & Friedman, 2001), which is discussed in the next section.

Classification can be thought as the base of ability to knowledge acquisition (Pawlak, 1991). There are therefore two types of classification problems: supervised classification and unsupervised classification.

For supervised classification, we have a model whereby the class structure and the training data are known *a priori* (pre-specified by a *teacher* or *supervisor*). The main goal is to formulate "good" rules that will allow one to allocate new objects to their appropriate classes. Decision trees (DTs) fall into this category of supervised learning, and have been used for classification tasks by both the ML and statistics communities. DTs are induced from a training set of labelled attribute vectors in order to classify unlabelled data.

In contrast, the aim of unsupervised learning (clustering) is to formulate a class structure, that is, to decide how many classes there are as well as assigning instances to their appropriate classes. For unsupervised classification, there is no model and the number of classes (clusters, categories, groups, species, types, and so on) and the specifications of the classes are not defined or given.

In supervised learning, for multi-variate data, a classification function $y = f(x)$ from training instances of the form $\{(x_1, y_1),\ldots, (x_m, y_m)\}$, predicts one (or more) output attribute(s) or dependent variable(s) given the values of the input attributes of the form $(x, f(x))$. The x_i values are vectors of the form $\{x_{i1},...,x_{in}\}$ whose components can be numerically ordered, nominal or categorical, or ordinal. The y values are drawn from a discrete set of classes $\{1,..., K\}$ in the case of *classification*. Depending on the usage, the prediction can be "definite" or probabilistic over possible values. Given a set of training instances and any given prior probabilities and misclassification costs, a learning algorithm outputs a *classifier* or *predictive model*. The classifier is an hypothesis about the true classification function that is learned from, or fitted to, *training data*. The classifier is then tested on *test data*.

It is also important to note that numerical attribute values cannot be used in rules induced by some data mining systems since there is a very small chance that these values may match values of unseen, testing cases. In other words, such data mining systems require a discrete feature space. The normal approach to processing data with numerical attributes is to convert numerical attributes into intervals through the process called discretisation (Dougherty, Kohavi, & Sahami, 1995; Grzymala-Busse, 2002; Quinlan, 1993). The features can be discretised in advance or during rule induction. In rule induction methods such as C4.5 rules, continuous values are discretised during the learning process.

A wide range of machine learning paradigms have been developed for this task of supervised learning. These include instance-based or memory-based learning—which also consists of variations on the nearest neighbour techniques (Cover & Hart, 1967; Dasrathy, 1991; Hand, 1997); decision trees (Breiman, Friedman, Olshen, & Stone, 1984; Quinlan, 1993); neural networks (Patterson, 1996; Ripley, 1996); genetic learning (Grefenstette, 1991; Koza, 1992); association rules (Agrawal, Imielinski, & Swami, 1993; Pearl, 1988); rule induction (Clark & Boswell, 1991; Cohen, 1995); analytic learning (Mitchell, 1997); naïve Bayes classifier (Kononenko, 1991; Langley & Sage, 1994; Zheng & Webb, 1997); and so on. However, as mentioned earlier, our focus is on supervised learning using rule induction within the context of software engineering.

Applying Rule Induction in Prediction

Rule induction is a machine learning technique that induces decision rules from data. These rules are simple, logic rules that are often highly predictive.

There are various ways of deriving rule sets. One of them is using a decision tree, that is, converting a tree into an equivalent set of rules. This is the approach we follow in this chapter, which can also be called decision tree rule induction. The starting point is laid out in detail by Quinlan (1993), in the discussion of how C4.5 creates rule sets from trees. Although rules and decision trees may seem similar at first, they are in fact different both in terms information they discover from datasets and in terms of their behaviour on new data items. In fact, decision tree algorithms are very similar to rule induction algorithms which produce rule sets without a decision tree. In addition, the RI methods covered in this chapter are attribute-based, and they have drawbacks which have been handled by another approach in ML called inductive logic programming (Bratko & Muggleton, 1995; Lavrac & Dzeroski, 1994; Muggleton, 1991, 1992; Muggleton & Feng, 1990; Quinlan, 1990; Srinivasan, Muggleton, King, & Sternberg, 1994). However, inductive logic programming is not within the scope of this chapter.

Figure 1. A decision tree framework

When we have some data, and some conclusions which we would like to evaluate in light of these data, it is necessary to lay out the reasoning process which connects data to conclusions. This is sometimes called inductive learning or affinity grouping and it involves classification.

Most ML algorithms use a training set of examples as the basis for learning. The general framework for a tree classifier, Figure 1, is a variation of the decision tree framework.

The first step is to select the types of data that will be used by the classifier or mining algorithm (decision tree). The *search procedure* is part of the system that carries out the task. It explores the search space defined by a set of possible representations and derives a rule or set of rules for associating input descriptions with output decisions (Forsyth, Clarke, & Wright, 1994).

Associated with each search strategy is the evaluation component or function that can be used to estimate the distance from the current state to the goal state. If we compute these estimates at each choice point, then the estimates can be used as a basis for choice. It is worth mentioning that such a type of framework could apply within different research communities. For an example, statisticians would allow models to be used for estimation purposes (as a search procedure), like, utilising the maximum likelihood (ML) for estimating missing values. Recently, Hand, Mannila, and Smyth (2001) have shown how such a framework could apply for data mining.

Rules: A Formalism for Thought Processes

The computer requires defining ones thinking in some formal way. Various formalisms have been tried. The one which has shown the greatest flexibility and similarity to human thought processes is the rule, although other formalisms have been used, mostly in very special cases. The formalism used by expert production systems learn a set of condition-action rules from data (such as: "IF item *A* is part of an event, THEN x percent of the time, item B is part of products, training and support"). The left hand side of the rule, or the IF part, is known technically as the antecedent, or the LHS; the right hand side, or the THEN part is called the consequent, or RHS. The antecedent consists of tests to be made on existing data; the consequent holds actions to be taken if the data pass in the antecedent.

Disjunction normal form is a logical formula consisting of a disjunction of conjunctions where no conjunction contains a disjunction. For example, the disjunction normal formula of (A or B) and C is (A and C) or (B and C). This is the most common representation used for rules induced by such algorithms.

Examples of rule learning systems are AQ15 (Michalski, Mozetic, Hong, & Lavrac, 1986), CN2 (Clark & Niblett, 1989), GREEDY3 (Pagallo & Haussler, 1990), PVM (Weiss, Galen, & Tadepelli, 1990), RIPPER (Cohen, 1995), and many more. All of these techniques, and almost all related algorithms, are strictly classifiers, and all use some form of restricted rule structure (tree, decision list) allowing the search algorithm to use a divide-and-conquer strategy in searching the data. These algorithms induce rules for each class and instances directly whereby each rule covers a subset of the positive instances, and few or no negative ones, then "separating out" the newly covered examples and starting again on the remainder. The rule is composed of a consequent (predicted class) and an antecedent (a condition involving a single attribute). The only vaguely similar approaches to the problem of generalised rule induction of which we are aware is a Bayesian approach presented by Cheeseman (1984) and the ENTAIL algorithm of Gaines and Shaw (1986), which is based on fuzzy logic measures rather than probability theory. In addition, in this volume, Piatetsky-Shapiro (1991) describes an approach which looks at generalised rule induction for strong rules, where "strong" is defined in the sense of having rule transition probabilities near 1.

Many rule-induction algorithms which use a statistical basis fall into the tree-based classifier category, for example the well known ID3 algorithm (Quinlan, 1986) and its variants. These algorithms derive classification rules in the form of a tree structure. The restriction to a tree structure makes the search problem much easier than the problem of looking for general rules. Quinlan (1987, 1993) has more recently proposed the C4.5 algorithm, which prunes back an original ID3-like tree structure to a set of modular rules called *rule sets*. These *rule sets* make accurate predictions on future data.

The decision tree example displayed in Figure 2 can be converted to the following rules:

R_1:   **IF** (Execution Time Constraint > 1.415) and (Programmer Experience with underlying hardware and operating system > 1.0)

   THEN Likely to require high effort

R_2:   **IF** (Execution Time Constraint > 1.415) and (Programmer Experience with underlying hardware and operating system <= 1.0)

   THEN Not likely to require high effort

and so on.

In this fictitious example, the goal is to classify an unknown instance in terms of high development effort based on attributes related to software development.

Learning algorithms in the rule-induction framework usually select the "best" rule by a greedy search through a space of rule sets and utilising the evaluation function to select attributes for incorporating in the knowledge structure. The choice of the evaluation function is of great importance to that algorithm's performance. The AQ algorithm (Michalski et al., 1986) uses the accuracy of the rule on the training set given in a formula as:

$$E(i_+, i_-) = \frac{i_+}{i_+ + i_-}$$

(1)

Figure 2. Example of a binary axis-parallel decision tree for a three-dimensional feature space and two classes for predicting software development effort. Ovals represent internal nodes; rectangles represent leaf nodes or terminal nodes

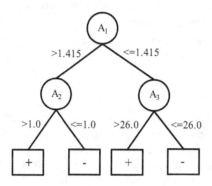

where i_+ is the number of positive instances that satisfy the rule and i_- is the number of negative instances that satisfy the rule. Given the rule, E should increase with i_+ and decrease with i_-. The CN2 system originally used the entropy rule (Quinlan, 1986). Both measures tend to favour overly specific rules and to overcome this problem a Laplace correction is used (Niblett, 1987):

$$E(i_+, i_-) = \frac{i_+ + 1}{i_+ + i_- + c}$$

(2)

where c is the number of classes.

Induced decision rules are the basis for classifying new or testing instances. Classification prediction of a new instance is performed by matching each rule with that particular instance, and selecting those it satisfies. If there is only one such rule, its class is assigned to the instance. If there are none a "default rule" is used, that is, assigning the instance to the class that occurs most frequently in the entire training set, or among those instances not covered by any rule. Finally, if more than one rule covers the example one strategy is to order rules into a "decision list", and select only the first rule that fires (Rumelhart, Hinton, & Williams, 1986). The other strategy is to let different rules vote, and select the class with most votes (Clark & Boswell, 1991).

The main difference between rule learners and decision trees is that even though they both partition a space, rule learners do not do it recursively in the manner of trees. In fact, once a decision tree has been constructed, it is then translated into an equivalent set of rules. However, techniques that directly generate rules from data are also available, which overcome some of the drawbacks of decision tree modelling.

We shall now look at how rule induction has been applied to handle some common machine learning problems.

Handling Uncertainties in Data

One problem is that large amounts of data are needed for inductive learning. In many real problems, there is a degree of uncertainty or error (imperfection) present in the data. These could lead to errors in the classification process.

The four sources of uncertainty in data are discussed in the following sub-sections:

Inconsistent Data

Occasionally, two or more independent sources of information (e.g., databases) may contain values that purport to represent the same real-world value. If these values are different, the representations are said to be inconsistent. Two instances are inconsistent if they have identical attribute values for the condition attributes, but are labelled as belonging to different concepts. Data inconsistency could lead to errors in the classification process and thus result in solutions that are inconclusive. Inconsistencies in software data may not only confuse a learning algorithm and result in failure in deriving decision rules but produce negative effects in prediction as well. Therefore, in order to guarantee correctness and efficiency in software prediction, it is necessary to be able to handle inconsistencies in data.

Given that inconsistency is often viewed as a logical concept, thus, it is appropriate that inconsistency handling should be based on logic. Pawlak (1991) proposed a procedure for dealing with the problem of inconsistency called rough set theory. A method of rule induction, based on rough set theory, in which each missing attribute value was replaced by all possible values was introduced by Grzymala-Busse (1991) and further developed by Kryszkiewicz (1998). Stefanowski and Tsoukias (1999) show how a second rough set approach could be used when extracting classification rules from incomplete data. Their proposed procedure is based on two groups. The first group is focused on inducing the complete set of all rules in the given syntax, which can be generated from the instances, while the other group is focused on minimal set of rules.

Noise and Overfitting

Another source of uncertainty is that of random errors or "noise" which is inevitable. There are many kinds of "noise" that could occur in the examples. These include errors, spurious correlations (i.e., correlations that are due mostly to the influences of one or more "other" variables), attributes that are not recorded, two examples having the same attribute/value pairs but different classifications, some values of attributes being incorrect because of errors in the data acquisition process or the processing phase, values of attributes being missing, and the classification or class label being wrong (for example, 1 instead of 2) because of some error. Monago and Kodratoff (1987) present a more detailed analysis of the sources of noise in data.

The next problem is also related to unnecessary attributes (which can be caused by noise) which, besides making no contribution to the predictive performance of the learning system, will simultaneously impose an extra computational burden. This situation is generally referred to as overfitting (Cohen & Jensen, 1997; Forsyth et al., 1994; Schaffer, 1993), that is, overfitting the training example data. For example, if the hypothesis space has many dimensions because of a large number of attributes, meaningless regularity may be found in the data that is irrelevant to the true, important, distinguishing features. Overfitting is harmful for several reasons. First, overfitted models are incorrect; they indicate that some variables are related when they are not. Second, overfitted models are difficult to understand due to the unnecessary component that complicates attempts to integrate induced models with existing knowledge derived from other sources, and overfitting avoidance has some-times been justified solely on the grounds of producing comprehensible models. Finally, overfitted models can have lower accuracy on new data than models that are not overfitted as demonstrated with a variety of domains and systems by Quinlan (1987).

In the area of decision tree rule induction, overfitting is avoided or fixed, to a certain extent, by: (1) stop growing the tree when further splitting the data does not yield a statistically significant improvement; or by (2) growing a full tree, then pruning the tree by eliminating nodes. In practice, the latter approach has been more successful.

Incomplete Data

Another problem that is related to noise is that of incomplete data or missing values. The presence of missing values is commonplace in large real-world databases. This has become one of the most important problems in academic research since most learning systems and statistical analysis were in the early stages not designed to handle missing data (incomplete vectors). There are several reasons why there are missing values in data. An item could be missing because it was unavailable or arises by "default" in data recording activities. Missing values could also occur because of confusing questions in the data gathering or because of sensor malfunction. In some situations, the missingness could be caused by the relationships between the attribute variables themselves. That is, the information that is missing on a given attribute variable could be as a result of its relation to values of other attribute variables in the dataset. An extreme case is that the missing value could be as result of its relation to an unobserved (missing value) in the dataset.

Both large and small amounts of missing and/or faulty details in data might mislead the learning process and have an influence in various statistical measures, yet not a lot of work has been done in the research field.

Outliers

The presence of outliers in the training data can affect the performance of software quality classification models. Khoshgoftaar, Bullard, and Gao (2003) proposed a rule-based model-ling (RBM) procedure for detecting and removing outliers in the training data in an effort to improve the data quality and thus improve the accuracy of a case-based reasoning (CBR) classification model. Their results showed that applying the RBM rule-based significantly improved the accuracy of CBR software quality classification models.

Applying Rule Induction in Software Engineering Tasks

How to estimate the cost of a project is a very important issue in software project management. Many software organisations frequently do not allocate enough resources for software quality. As a result, building and evaluating prediction systems is an important activity for software engineering researchers with implications for practitioners if poor models are used (Shepperd, Cartwright, and Kadoda, 2000). Lack of adequate tools to evaluate and estimate software quality is one of the main challenges in software engineering. There is a small, but growing body of work in which ML is applied in software quality prediction. Most of the existing work is based on algorithmic models of effort (Boehm, 1981; Shepperd & Schofield, 1997). One of the practical problems in applying ML is that it is hard to acquire a variety of learning tools and experiment with them in a uniform way. Researchers also seek to build accurate and reliable predictors based upon legacy data. As prediction success depends on the relationship between training and test data, this is a very difficult task when one considers the scarcity of software quality data. This makes it difficult to use ML algorithms and formulate theories from data in order to construct decision support tools early in the software cycle. A variety of ML techniques that have been applied for prediction tasks include: artificial neural networks (Boetticher, 2001; Jørgensen, 1995; Srinivasan & Fisher, 1995); Bayesian belief networks (Fenton, Krause, & Neil, 2001; Fenton & Neil, 1999); clustering techniques (Krohn & Boldyreff, 1999; Podgurski, Masri, McCleese, & Wolff, 1999); decision trees (Srinivasan & Fisher, 1995); genetic algorithm (Cordero, Costramagna, & Paschetta, 1997); genetic programming (Dolado, 2001; Kaminsky & Boetticher, 2004); instance-based learning (Mitchell, 1997; Zhang & Tsai, 2003). However, none has proven consistently accurate.

Many techniques have been developed for learning rules and relationships automatically from diverse datasets, to simplify the often tedious and error-prone process of acquiring knowledge from empirical data. While these techniques are plausible, theoretically well-founded, and perform well on more or less artificial datasets, they depend on their ability to make sense on real-world datasets. However, there is little data available for the application of ML despite the fact that application of ML is not only concerned with the form that the dataset takes but on the quality of the data as well. In this section, we show how rule induction has been used in tackling software engineering problems. Related research consisting of the utilisation of various ML algorithms for predicting software is also looked at.

Software Effort (Cost) Prediction

Tree-based modelling has been investigated by Selby and Porter (1988) to identify software modules that have high or low development effort based on attributes of the module and its system. Their work involves discretisation of continuous features, especially for the predictor variable. Decision tree learning is also used to help predict software development by Srinivasan and Fisher (1995). Their results compared favourably with conventional methods such as COCOMO (Boehm, 1981) and function points (Symons, 1988).

Software cost estimates are critical inputs for managers' decision making in the early planning stages of constructing projects. Madachy (1995) developed a model to assess the applicability of rule-based reasoning to the difficult problem of early software project cost estimation. Madachy argues that at present it appears impossible to identify features early in the life cycle that reliably define the size of the project. Madachy proposed that the best alternative was to pursue a solution that produced estimate of potential risk for a specific project based on previous experiences. The proposed approach uses cost factors to estimate risk rather than effort. The results help users determine and rank associated sources of project risk.

Chatzoglou and Macaulay (1998) developed a technique based on a combination of rule-based models. The proposed approach is to planning which enables project managers to learn from the experience of others. Their technique, which is in three parts, adopts the idea that different stages of the development cycle must have different planning models, which in turn must use different measures or factors. The first part deals with the problem of planning each iteration of the requirements capture and analysis (RCA) process; the second deals with the problem of planning the whole RCA process; and the third with planning the whole project development process. The technique gives predictions of the resources (time, effort, cost, people) needed for the completion of an outcome of the requirements capture and analysis (RCA) process. Based on the predictions about the RCA process, the procedure then attempts to predict the resources and outcomes of the whole development process. The strength of technique is that it incorporates both qualitative and quantitative factors that can be easily identified and measured in the beginning of the development process. Despite its strengths, the technique struggles with small datasets and datasets with missing values, which are both common in software engineering research. When applied to an industrial dataset with 107 instances, each of the three rule-based models achieved high predictive accuracy rates.

However, not all experiences of using RI for prediction tasks have been positive, as shown by Mair and Shepperd (1999) who carried out a preliminary investigation on the use of RI methods to accurately predict software effort. Their results showed how RI methods can be unstable and predict less accurately as do other methods that are not considered as good predictors.

Software Quality (Fault) Prediction

The problem of finding fault-prone elements in software systems (Basili, Briand, & Melo, 1996; Briand, Devanbu, & Melo, 1997; Chidamber & Kemmerer, 1994) has received much attention. Cohen and Devanbu (1999) investigated the utility of ILP programs for the task of classifying programs. The idea was to explore the use of ILP methods, FLIPPER (Cohen, 1995) and FOIL (Quinlan, 1990) for the task of predicting software fault density in C++ classes. FLIPPER and FOIL were compared using natural and artificial datasets, and the results showed FLIPPER outperforming FOIL in terms of computational speed and predictive accuracy, especially for the natural dataset. Reasons for the differences in performance were analyzed and, based on the analysis, extensions on FLIPPER were proposed. One such extension was the introduction of a user-directed bias towards easy to evaluate clauses (a special case of the number of restrictions frequently used in description logics) that enabled an improved performance by FLIPPER but at some cost in accuracy. Also, the use of counting clauses greatly improved the performance of FLIPPER.

Selby and Porter (1988) use Quinlan's ID3 system to build classification trees to identify classes of objects (software modules) with high development effort or high number of faults. The data collected from NASA production environment included 4,700 software modules with 74 measured attributes (or metrics). A total of 9,600 decision trees were automatically generated and evaluated. The decision trees correctly identified 79.3% of the software modules that had high development effort of faults, on the average across all 9,600 trees. As a follow up to their previous paper, Porter and Selby (1990a) summarises the software metric-based classification tree generation approach and outlines a multi-phase methodology for applying classification tree techniques to large scale, evolving systems. Their approach is validated using NASA and Hughes project data, with promising results. A comparison of five variations on their original classification tree algorithm is presented by Porter and Selby (1990b). The techniques are quartiles, octiles, and three methods based on least weight sub-sequence analysis. Accuracy and complexity of the generated trees resulting from different techniques for partitioning the attribute data values during the tree generation process is considered. The results show distribution-sensitive partition techniques that use only relatively few partitions resulting to increases in accuracy but decreases in complexity when using classification trees.

Basili, Condon, El Emam, Hendrink, and Melo (1997) conducted a study to model and understand the cost of rework for a library of reusable software components. A predictive model of the impact of error source on rework effort was built using C4.5 rules and metrics extracted by the AMADEUS tool. The model was also used to develop proscriptive coding rules that can be used by programmers as guidelines to reduce the cost of work in the future. The model demonstrates good prediction accuracy and is recommended for managers to allocate resources for corrective maintenance activities.

Almeida, Lounis, and Melo (1998) have continued the work by Basili et al. (1997) by comparing the models built with C4.5 with models built with NewID, CN2 and FOIL with regard to their capabilities to generate accurate and easily interpretable correctability models. The metrics are extracted with the ASAP tool from a set of ADA faulty components from the NASA SEL. Their results show FOIL achieving a superior performance compared to the other algorithms. The application of FOIL rules also shows some promise. Their results further show C4.5 rules working better than C4.5 trees as it was the case with results achieved by Basili and his colleagues.

Khoshgoftaar and Seliya (2002) present an empirical comprehensive evaluation of tree-based methods to identify fault-prone software modules based on product and process metrics. The algorithms are compared based on accuracy, structure, and complexity. The data is drawn from large telecommunications software systems at Nortel consisting of almost 13 million lines of code. The results not only show poor predictive accuracy rates by the SPLUS trees but large and complex trees. However, CART trees achieve good accuracy rates and the trees are simple and easy to interpret.

Genetic programs against several industrial-level repositories in predicting software faults are applied by Evett and Khoshgoftaar (1998). The authors' assess their GP models by ranking datasets according to defect counts and comparing the top n percent of actual and predicted models where n ranges from 75 to 90%.

So, Cha, and Kwon (2002) have shown how applying flexible inference rules and a fuzzy logic approach could be used for software quality prediction. Their proposed approach shows how potentially error-prone software components could be identified from software inspection data due to the ability of fuzzy logic to naturally handle both numerical and nominal attributes for such datasets. Hence, obtaining insights on how software processes could be improved.

Predicting the quality of object-oriented software is a complex task. One of the major problems for building reliable predictive models is the lack of representative samples which makes it hard to generalise and validate existing models. An ideal predictive model can be seen as the mixture of two types of knowledge: common knowledge of the domain and context specific knowledge for a company. In existing models, one of the two types is often missing. To solve this problem, Bouktif, Azar, Sahaoui, and Kégl (2003) proposed two evolutionary (genetic)-algorithm-based approaches for combining and adapting existing object-oriented software quality predictive models to the context of a specific company. Their approaches are based on studying the prediction of the stability at the class level in object-oriented software systems using rule-based learning. One evolutionary (genetic) algorithm is used to *combine* rules into one classifier while the other is used for *adapting* a rule set, that is, one rule set is evolved into another by adapting it to a training set (context). Their results show that combining experts can yield significantly better results then using individual models. The adaptation approach gave a slight improvement over the initial model generated by C4.5 (Quinlan, 1993) even though their results were not conclusive.

Software Defect Prediction

Software defect prediction is a very useful and important tool to gauge the likely delivered quality and maintenance effort before software systems are deployed (Fenton et al., 1999). Despite the efforts of various researchers there seems to be little consensus regarding what to measure when formulating defect prediction models.

Fenton et al. (1999) develops a Bayesian belief network tool called AID (Assess, Improve, Decide) to predict software defects by testing the model on 28 software projects. The results of this study show some potential. However, it is later shown that such models require a great deal of data to train (Fenton et al., 2001).

The application of neural networks to predict software has received a great deal of attention. Hochmann, Hudepohl, Allen, and Khoshgoftaar (1997) extends the use of neural networks to predict software defects by building 30 classification models with an equal distribution of fault-prone and non-fault prone software. They then compare evolutionary neural networks (ENNs) to discriminant analysis (DA). Their experimental results show ENNs outperforming DA.

Kaminsky and Boetticher (2004) propose a technique called genetically engineerable evolvable program (GEEP) for predicting software defects. In this approach, explicit breadth-based knowledge is incorporated within the genetic programming modeling process. Their experimental findings show GEEP producing statistically superior results than models without access to any explicit knowledge.

Software Intrusion Detection

There has been a steadily growing interest in the research and development of intrusion detection systems due to the risks and chances of malicious intrusions to system resources and data. A new rule-based approach for detecting computer intrusion is proposed by Il-gun, Kemmerer, and Porras (1995). Their state transition analysis (STA) approach models penetrations as a series of state changes that lead from an initial secure state to a target compromised state. State transition diagrams are written to correspond to the states of an actual computer system, and these diagrams form the basis of a rule-based expert system for detecting penetrations. Their approach manages to address the weaknesses of current penetration identification tools and uses rules to identify site-specific policy violations that might have gone unnoticed.

Lee and Stolfo (2000) describe a framework that uses data mining algorithms to compute activity patterns from system audit data and extracts predictive features from the patterns. Machine learning algorithms are then applied to the audit records that are processed according to the feature definitions to generate intrusion detection rules. Their work provides another layer of defence against malicious (or otherwise unauthorised) uses of computer systems by sensing a misuse or attack once it has taken place. Future work in this area would be to develop algorithms for learning anomaly detection models (i.e., models that can detect "innovative" intrusions).

Software Process Modelling

Software process modelling is a direction within software engineering that aims at provid-ing support for capturing software development processes. A programming language based on a rule learning approach is applied as a software process modelling procedure for the effectiveness and efficiency of both development and use of software engineering standards by Verlage and Münch (1997). Their work show how software process modelling can be a useful tool for initiating and sustaining software process improvement, hence, the product quality and business value. They also show how software process modelling can overcome the shortcomings of informal representation of software engineering knowledge.

One other application of rule induction has been in rule based-systems (Giarratano & Riley, 1998; Hayes-Roth, 1985; Ignizio, 1991; Jacob & Froscher, 1990), which have been used in very few cases of effort prediction. However, rule-based systems are not within the scope of this chapter.

Discussion

It can be argued that ML has done an immense amount for software engineering. This chapter has attempted to provide the reader with the key issues of rule induction techniques and how such techniques have been used for software engineering tasks, especially prediction. To achieve our goal, we investigated the utility of the machine learning algorithm known as rule induction for software engineering tasks, especially software prediction. We have shown how rule-based learning approaches can be used in tackling software engineering problems, especially for predicting software development effort. One major advantage of using machine learning techniques such as rule induction is that they are adaptable and nonparametric: they do not make any assumptions on the distributional form of the data. Also, they do not require a structured specification of the model, therefore making them less sensitive to model misspecification or to the presence of outliers. In addition, one major value of rule learning is that a human user can understand and modify a rule set much more easily than he or she can understand and modify, say, a decision tree. We have also noted the important practical advantages of using rule learning methods. One scenario involves a user's desire to update an existing system in order to improve performance that may have degraded due to changing environment without fully recreating the system from scratch. Other strengths of the rule-based approaches include their use of domain knowledge and low storage requirement. Rule-based learners use a tree structure to split the instance space into sub-spaces defined by the path of the tree, which is a powerful way to represent hypotheses. In other words, these rules essentially correspond to decision regions that overlap each other in the data space. Due to the flexibility of allowing different classifiers for different sub-instances in data space, rule induction systems have sometimes achieved better accuracy than decision tree—from which the rule set was formed (Zheng, 1998). Also rule-based systems often succeed in identifying small sets of highly predictive features and make effective use of statistical measures to combat problems such as noise (as already discussed in previous sections). Despite their strengths, rule induction approaches are less appropriate for estimation tasks where the goal is to predict the value of a continuous variable such as software effort. Rule induction approaches are also error-prone when the number of training instances per class gets small. This can happen rather quickly in a tree with many levels and/or many branches per node. The process of growing a decision tree, hence classification rules, is computationally expensive. At each node, each candidate splitting field must be sorted before its best split can be found. In some algorithms, combinations of fields are used and a search must be made for optimal combining weights. Pruning algorithms can also be expensive since many candidate sub-trees must be formed and compared. Finally, most decision-tree algorithms only examine a single field at a time. This leads to rectangular classification boxes that may not correspond well with the actual distribution of instances in the decision space.

Apart from RI, current researchers have focussed on how to integrate both RI and case-based reasoning (CBR) approaches to solve problems more efficiently and effectively (Babka, 1998; Cercone, An, & Chan, 1999; Golding & Rosenbloom, 1993; Prentzas & Hatzilygeroudis, 2002). RI represents general knowledge of the domain while CBR represents specific knowledge. The motivation for integrating two reasoning approaches is to achieve a synergy which produces results that could not be obtained if each approach were operating individually. This is due to the fact that each reasoning approach has its own strengths and weaknesses. Therefore, the integration of the two approaches turns out to be natural and useful. This trend is very likely to carry on the following years.

Finally, an open issue that continues to be explored is characterisation of datasets, using either simple measures, statistical measures, or information theoretic measures that will allow an educated mapping of the most appropriate prediction technique to a dataset for maximising the accuracy of resulting solution. However, the chapter demonstrates that rule induction has a potential to be used as an alternative machine learning tool for software prediction.

Concluding Remarks

Software is nowadays a critical component of our lives and everyday-work working activities. However, as the technological infrastructure of the modern world evolves a great challenge arises for developing high quality software systems with increasing size and complexity. Software engineers and researchers are striving to meet this challenge by developing and implementing software engineering methodologies able to deliver software products of high quality, within budget and time constraints. The field of machine learning in software engineering has recently emerged to provide means for addressing, studying, analysing, and understanding critical software development issues and at the same time to offer mature machine learning technologies such as artificial neural network, Bayesian networks, decision trees, fuzzy logic, genetic algorithms, and rule induction. We have shown that using rule induction in estimation or prediction produces rules that are easily interpreted. Moreover, rule set pruning techniques may be applied to the induced rule sets to simplify them. In addition, pruning often improves accuracy with little loss in coverage. We have also shown how rules could be used for handling inconsistent data. Not only do individual rules provide "nuggets" of useful information, but rule sets may be used as classifiers which have many uses, such as predicting software faults, effort, or defect. As future work, expanding rule induction methods to recognise wider range of software engineering tasks would be an interesting research topic. Future research might include learning of rule parameters, identification of software project elements and rules through training, and handling of uncertainties in the segmentation stage. The goal is to realise the flexibility of this framework for more general software prediction tasks. Application of machine learning early in the software life cycle against empirical data might be useful for future research. Finally, future work might include not just learning a single predictive model but learn a set of predictive models and then combine the predictions of multiple models. This kind of work is also known as ensemble of predictive models.

References

Agrawal, R., Imielinski, T., & Swami, A. (1993). Mining association rules between sets of items in large databases. In P. Buneman, & S. Jajodia (Eds.), *SIGMOD93*, Washington, D.C. (pp. 207-216).

de Almeida, M., Lounis, H., & Melo, W. (1998). An investigation on the use of machine learned models for estimating correction costs. In the *International Conference on Software Engineering* (pp. 473-476).

Babka, O. (1998). Decision support system learning from history cases. In the *Proceedings of the IASTED International Conference Intelligent Systems and Control (ISC '98)*, Halifax, Nova Scotia, Canada, June 1-3.

Basili, V. R., Briand, L. C., & Melo, W. L. (1996). A validation of object-oriented design metrics as quality indicators. *IEEE Transactions on Software Engineering, 22*(10), 751-761.

Basili, V. R., Condon, S. E., El Emam, K., Hendrink, R. B., & Melo, W. (1997). Character-izing and modelling the cost of rework in a library of reusable software components. In the *Proceedings of 19th International Conference on Software Engineering,* Boston, MA, May 17-23 (pp. 282-291).

Boehm, B. W. (1981). *Software engineering economics.* Englewood Cliffs, NJ: Prentice Hall.

Boetticher, G. (2001). Using machine learning to predict project effort: Empirical case studies in data-starved domains. *Model Based Requirements Workshop, 16th IEEE International Conference,* San Diego, November 26-29 (pp. 17-24).

Bouktif, S., Azar, D., Sahaoui, H., & Kégl, B. (2003). Improving rule set-based software quality prediction: A genetic algorithm-based approach. *Journal of Object Technology, 3*(4), 227-241.

Bratko, I., & Muggleton, S. (1995). Applications of inductive logic programming. *Communications of the ACM, 38*(11), 65-70.

Breiman, L., Friedman, J. H., Olshen, R. A., & Stone, C. J. (1984). *Classification and regression trees.* New York: Chapman & Hall (Wadsworth, Inc.).

Briand, L., Devanbu, P., & Melo, W. (1997). Defining and validating measures for object-based high level design. *IEEE Transactions on Software Engineering, 25*(5), 722-743.

Cercone, N., An, A., & Chan, C. (1999). Rule induction and case-based reasoning: Hybrid architectures appear advantageous. *IEEE Transactions on Knowledge and Data Engineering, 11*(1), 166-174.

Chatzoglou, P. D. & Macaulay, L. A. (1998). A rule-based approach to developing software development prediction models. *Automated Software Engineering, 5*(2), 211-243.

Cheeseman, P. (1984). *Learning of expert systems from data.* First IEEE Conference on Applications of Artificial Intelligence. Los Alamitos, CA: IEEE Computer Society.

Chidamber, S. R., & Kemmerer, C. F. (1994). A metrics suite for object-oriented design. *IEEE Transactions on Software Engineering, 20*(6), 476-493.

Clark, P., & Boswell, R. (1991). Rule induction with CN2: Some recent improvements. In Y. Kodratoff (Ed.), *Machine Learning – EWSL-91,* Berlin, Germany (pp. 151-163). Springer Verlag.

Clark, P., & Niblett, T. (1989). The CN2 induction algorithm. *Machine Learning, 3,* 261-283.

Cohen, P. R., & Jensen, D. (1997). Overfitting explained. In the *Preliminary Papers of the Sixth International Workshop on Artificial Intelligence and Statistics,* Fort Lauderdale, FL, January (pp. 115-122).

Cohen, W. W. (1995). Fast effective rule induction. In the *Proceedings of the Twelfth International Conference on Machine Learning* (pp. 115-123). San Francisco, CA: M. Kaufmann.

Cohen, W. W., & Devanbu, P. (1999). Automatically exploring hypotheses about fault prediction: A comparative study of inductive logic programming methods. *International Journal of Software Engineering and Knowledge Engineering, 9*(5), 519-546.

Cordero, R., Costramagna, M., & Paschetta, E. (1997). A genetic algorithm approach for the calibration of COCOMO-like models. *12th COCOMO Forum,* USC Campus, Los Angeles, CA, October 9-10.

Cover, T. M., & Hart, P. E. (1967). Nearest neighbour pattern classification. *IEEE Transactions on Information Theory, 13*(1), 21-27.

Dasrathy, B. V. (1991). *Nearest neighbour (NN) norms: NN pattern classification techniques.* Los Alamitos, CA: IEEE Computer Society Press.

Dolado, J. J. (2001). On the problem of the software const function. *Information and Software Technology, 43,* 61-72.

Dougherty, J., Kohavi, R., & Sahami, M. (1995). Supervised and unsupervised discretization of continuous features. In the *Proceedings of the 12th International Conference on Machine Learning (ICML-95)* (pp. 194-202). San Francisco, CA: Morgan Kaufmann Publishers.

Duda, R. O., Hart, P. E., & Stork, D. G. (2000). *Pattern classification* (2nd ed.). New York: John Wiley and Sons, Inc.

Evett, M., & Khoshgoftar, T. (1998). GP-based software quality prediction. In the *Genetic Programming 1998: Proceedings for the 3rd Annual Conference,* Madison, Wisconsin, July 22-25 (pp. 60-65). San Francisco: Morgan Kaufmann.

Fenton, N., Krause, P., & Neil, M. (2001). Probabilistic modeling for software quality control. *Lecture Notes in Computer Science, 2143,* 444-453. Berlin, Heidelberg: Springer Verlag.

Fenton, N., & Neil, M. (1999). A critique of software defect prediction models. *IEEE Transactions and Software Engineering, 25*(5), 675-689.

Forsyth, R., & Rada, R. (1986). *Machine learning: Applications in expert systems and information retrieval.* Chichester: Ellis Horwood Limited.

Forsyth, R. S., Clarke, D. D., & Wright, R. L. (1994). Overfitting revisited: An information-theoretic approach to simplifying discrimination trees. *Journal of Experimental and Theoretical Artificial Intelligence, 6*(3), 289-302.

Gaines, B. R. & Shaw, M. L. G. (1986). Induction of inference rules for expert systems. *Fuzzy Sets and Systems, 18*(3), 315-328.

Gamberger, D., Lavrac, N., & Krstacic, G. (2002). Confirmation rule induction and its applications to coronary heart disease diagnosis and risk group discovery. *Journal of Intelligent Fuzzy Systems, 12*(1), 35-48.

Giarratano, J., & Riley, G. (1998). *Expert systems: Principles and programming* (3rd ed.). Boston, MA: PWS Publishing Company.

Giordana, A., Neri, F., & Saitta, L. (1996). Automated learning: An application to industrial diagnosis. In P. Langley, & Y. Kodratoff (Eds.), *Machine learning applications.* San Francisco, CA: Morgan Kauffman, San Francisco.

Golding, A. R., & Rosenbloom, P. S. (1993). Improving rule-based systems through case-based reasoning. In B. G. Buchanan, & D. C. Wilkins (Eds.), *Readings in knowledge acquisition and learning: Automating the construction and improvement of expert systems* (pp. 759-764). San Mateo, CA: Morgan Kaufmann Publishers, Inc. ISBN 1-55860-163-5.

Grefenstette, J. J. (1991). Strategy acquisition with genetic algorithms. In L. D. Davis (Ed.), *Handbook of genetic algorithms*. Boston: Van Nostrand Reinhold.

Grzymala-Busse, J. W. (1991). On the unknown attribute values in learning from examples. In the *Proceedings of the ISMIS-91, 6th International Symposium on methodologies for Intelligent Systems*, Charlotte, North Carolina, October 16-19 (pp. 368-377). *Lecture Notes in Artificial Intelligence, 542*. Berlin, Heidelberg, New York: Springer Verlag.

Grzymala-Busse, J. W. (2002). Discretization of numerical attributes. In W. Klösgen, & J. Zytkow (Eds.), *Handbook of data mining and knowledge discovery* (pp. 218-225). Oxford: Oxford University Press.

Guilfoyle, C. (1986). Ten minutes to lay the foundations. *Expert Systems User, 8*, 16-19.

Hand, D. J. (1997). *Construction and assessment of classification rules*. Chichester: John Wiley and Sons.

Hand, D. J., Mannila, H., & Smyth, P. (2001). *Principles of data mining*. MIT Press.

Hastie, T., Tibshirani, R., Friedman, J. (2001). *The elements of statistical learning: Data mining, inference, and prediction*. New York: Springer Verlag.

Hayes-Roth, F. (1985). Rule-based systems. *Communications of the ACM, 28*(9), 921-932.

Hochmann, J. P., Hudepohl, E. B., Allen, T. M., & Khoshgoftaar, R. (1997). Evolutionary neural networks: A robust approach to software reliability. *8th International Symposium on Software Reliability Engineering (ISSRE '97)* (pp. 13-26).

Holland, J. H. (1975). *Adaptation in natural and artificial systems*. Ann Arbor, MI: University of Michigan Press.

Ignizio, J. P. (1991). *Introduction to expert systems: The development and implementation of rule-base expert systems*. McGraw-Hill, Inc.

Ilgun, K., Kemmerer, R. A., & Porras, P. A. (1995). State transition analysis: A rule-based intrusion detection approach. *IEEE Transactions on Software Engineering, 21*(3), 181-199.

Jacob, R. J. K., & Froscher, J. N. (1990). A software engineering methodology for rule-based systems. *IEEE Transactions on Knowledge and Data Engineering, 2*(2), 173-189.

Johnson, D. E., Oles, F. J., Zhang, T., & Goetz, T. (2002). A decision-tree based symbolic rule induction system for text categorization. *IBM Systems Journal, 41*, 428-437.

Jørgensen, M. (1995). Experience with the accuracy of software maintenance task effort prediction models. *IEEE Transactions on Software Engineering, 21*(8), 674-681.

Kaminsky, K., & Boetticher, G. (2004). *Building a genetically engineerable evolvable program (GEEP) using breadth-based explicit knowledge for predicting software defects*. North American Fuzzy Information Processing Society (NAFIPS), Banff, Canada, June 27-30.

Karba, N., & Drole, R. (1990). Expert system for the cold rolling mill of Steel Works Jesenice. In the *Proceedings of the 13th Symposium on Information Technologies*, Sarajevo.

Khoshgoftaar, T. M., Bullard, L. A., & Gao, K. (2003). Detecting outliers using rule-based modelling for improving cbr-based software quality classification models. In K. D. Ashley, & D. G. Bridge (Eds.), *Proceedings of the 5th International Conference on Case-Based Reasoning. LNAI, 1689*, 216-230. Springer Verlag.

Khoshgoftaar, T. M. & Seliya, N. (2002). Tree-based software quality estimation models for fault prediction. In the *Proceedings of the 8th IEEE International Symposium on Software Metrics*.

Kononenko, I. (1991). Semi-naïve Bayesian classifier. In the *Proceedings of European Conference on Artificial Intelligence* (pp. 206-219).

Koza, J. R. (1992). *Advances in genetic programming*. Cambridge, MA: MIT Press.

Krohn, U., & Boldyreff, C. (1999). Application of cluster algorithms for batching of proposed software changes. *Journal of Software Maintenance: Research Practices, 11*, 151-165.

Kryszkiewicz, M. (1998). Rough set approach to incomplete information systems. *Information Sciences, 112*, 39-49.

Langley, P., & Sage, S. (1994). Induction of selective Bayesian classifiers. In the *Proc. Conf. on Uncertainty in AI*. Morgan Kauffmann.

Lavrac, N., & Dzeroski, S. (1994). *Inductive programming techniques and applications*. Chichester, UK: Ellis Horwood.

Lee, W., & Stolfo, S. J. (2000). A framework for constructing features and models for intrusion detection systems. *ACM Transactions on Information and System Security, 3*(4), 227-261.

Leech, W. J. (1986). A rule-based process control method with feedback. *Advances in Instrumentation, 41*, 169-175.

Madachy, R. (1995). Knowledge-based risk assessment and cost estimation. In W. L. Johnson, & A. Finkelstein (Eds.), *Automated software engineering* (pp. 219-230). Hingham, MA: Kluwer Academic Publishers.

Mair, C., & Shepperd, M. J. (1999). *An investigation of rule induction based prediction systems*. Presented at IEEE ICSE Workshop, Empirical Studies of Software Development and Evolution, Los Angeles.

Michalski, R. S., Mozetic, I., Hong, J., & Lavrac, N. (1986). The multi-purpose incremental learning system AQ15 and its testing application to three medical domains. In the *Proceedings of the 5th National Conference on Artificial Intelligence* (pp. 1041-1045). Philadelphia, PA: AAAI Press.

Michie, D. (1989). Problems of computer aided concept formation. In J. R. Quinlan (Ed.), *Applications of expert systems, 2*. Wokingham, UK: Addison-Wesley.

Mitchell, T. M. (1997). *Machine learning*. McGraw Hill.

Monago, M. M., & Kodratoff, Y. (1987). Noise and knowledge acquisition. In J. McDermott (Ed.), *IJCAI-87* (pp. 348-354). CA: Kaufmann.

Muggleton, S. (1991). Inductive logic programming. *New Generation Computing, 8*(4), 295-318.

Muggleton, S. (1992). *Inductive logic programming*. London: Academic Press.

Muggleton, S., & Feng, C. (1990). Efficient induction of logic programs. In S. Arikawa, S. Goto, S. Ohsuga, & T. Yokomori (Eds.), *Proceedings of the 1ˢᵗ Conference on Algorithmic Learning Theory* (pp. 368-381). Tokyo: Japanese Society for Artificial Intelligence.

Niblett, T. (1987). Constructing decision trees in noisy domains. In the *Proceedings of the Second European Working Session on Learning* (pp. 67-78). Bled, Yugoslavia: Sigma.

Pagallo, G., & Haussler, D. (1990). Boolean feature discovery in empirical learning. *Machine Learning, 5*, 71-100.

Patterson, D. W. (1996). *Artificial neural network: Theory and practices.* Singapore: Prentice-Hall.

Pawlak, Z. (1991). *Rough sets.* Dordrecht: Kluwer Academic.

Pearl, J. (1988). *Probabilistic reasoning in intelligent systems: Networks of plausible inference.* San Mateo, CA: Morgan Kauffman.

Piatetsky-Shapiro, G. (1991). Discovery, analysis, and presentation of strong rules. In G. Piatetsky-Shapiro, & W. J. Frawley (Eds.), *Knowledge discovery in databases* (pp. 229-248). Cambridge, MA: MIT Press.

Podgurski, A., Masri, W., McCleese, Y., & Wolff, F. G. (1999). Estimation of software reliability by stratified sampling. *ACM Transactions on Software Engineering and Methodology, 8*(3), 263-283.

Porter, A. A., & Selby, R. W. (1990a). Empirically guided software development using metric-based classification trees. *IEEE Software, 7*(2), 46-54.

Porter, A. A., & Selby, R. W. (1990b). Evaluating techniques for generating metric-based classification trees. *Journal of Systems Software, 12*, 209-218.

Prentzas, J., & Hatzilygeroudis, I. (2002). Integrating hybrid rule-based with case-based reasoning. In S. Craw, & A. Preece (Eds.), *Advances in case-based reasoning. Proceedings of the 2002 European Conference on Case-Based Reasoning, LNAI 2416* (pp. 336-349). Springer Verlag.

Quinlan, J. R. (1986). Induction of decision trees. *Machine Learning, 1*, 81-106.

Quinlan, J. R. (1987). Generating production rules from decision trees. In the *Proceedings of the 10ᵗʰ International Joint Conference on Artificial Intelligence* (pp. 304-307).

Quinlan, J. R. (1990). Learning logical definitions from relations. *Machine Learning, 5*, 239-266.

Quinlan, J. R. (1993). *C4.5: Programs for machine learning.* Philadelphia, PA: Morgan Kaufmann.

Riese, C. (1984). *Transformer fault detection and diagnosis using Rule-Master by Radian.* Technical Report, Radian Corp., Austin, TX.

Ripley, B. D. (1996). *Pattern recognition and neural networks.* Cambridge: Cambridge University Press.

Rumelhart, D. E., Hinton, G. E., & Williams, R. J. (1986). Learning international representation by error propagation. In D. E. Rumelhart, & J. L. McClelland (Eds.), *Parallel distributed processing: Explorations in the microstructure of cognition, Volume 1: Foundations.* Cambridge, MA: MIT Press.

Schaffer, C. (1993). Overfitting avoidance as bias. *Machine Learning, 10,* 153-178.

Selby, R. W., & Porter, A. A. (1988). Learning from examples: Generation and evaluation of decision trees for software resource analysis. *IEEE Transactions on Software Engineering, 14*(12), 17431757.

Shepperd, M., Cartwright, M., & Kadoda, G. (2000). On building prediction systems for software engineers. *Empirical Software Engineering, 5*(3), 175-182.

Shepperd, M., & Schofield, C. (1997). Estimating software project effort using analogies. *IEEE Transactions and Software Engineering, 23*(12), 736-743.

So, S. S., Cha, S. D., & Kwon, Y. R. (2002). Empirical evaluation of a fuzzy logic-based software quality prediction model. *Fuzzy Sets and Systems, 127*(2), 198-208.

Srinivasan, A., Muggleton, S. H., King, R. D., Sternberg, M. J. E. (1994). Mutagenesis: ILP experiments in non-determinate biological domain. In the *Proceedings of the 4th International Workshop on Inductive Logic Programming ILP – 94,* Bad Honeef/Bonn.

Srinivasan, K., & Fisher, D. (1995). Machine learning approaches to estimating software development effort. *IEEE Transactions on Software Engineering, 21*(2), 126-137.

Stefanowski, J., & Tsoukias, A. (1999). On the extension of rough sets under incomplete information. In the *Proceedings of the 7th International Workshop on New Directions in Rough Sets, Data Mining and Granular-Soft Computing,* Yamaguchi, Japan (pp. 73-81).

Symons, C. R. (1988). Function point analysis: Difficulties and improvements. *IEEE Transactions on Software Engineering, 14*(1), 2-11.

Verlage, M., & Münch, J. (1997). Software engineering standards and forum, 1997. Emerging international standards. *ISESS, Third IEEE International* (pp. 196-206).

Weiss, S., Galen, R., & Tadepelli, P. (1990). Maximizing the predictive rule of production rules. *Artificial Intelligence, 45,* 47-71.

Winston, P. (1992). *Artificial intelligence. Part II: Learning and regularity recognition* (3rd ed.). Addison-Wesley.

Zhang, D., & Tsai, J. (2003). Machine learning and software engineering. *Software Quality Journal, 11*(2), 87-119.

Zheng, Z. (1998). Scaling up the rule generation of C4.5. In the *Proceedings of PAKDDC '98* (pp. 348-359). Berlin: Springer Verlag.

Zheng, Z., & Webb, G. I. (1997). *Lazy Bayesian trees.* Technical Report (TR C97/07), Deakin University, Australia.

Chapter XII

Application of Genetic Algorithms in Software Testing*

Baowen Xu, Southeast University & Jiangsu Institute of
Software Quality, China

Xiaoyuan Xie, Southeast University & Jiangsu Institute of
Software Quality, China

Liang Shi, Southeast University & Jiangsu Institute of
Software Quality, China

Changhai Nie, Southeast University & Jiangsu Institute of
Software Quality, China

Abstract

Genetic algorithms are a kind of global meta-heuristic search technique that searches intelligently for optimal solutions to a problem. Evolutionary testing is a promise testing technique, which utilises genetic algorithms to generate test data for various testing objectives. It has been researched and applied in many testing areas, including structural testing, temporal performance testing, safety testing, specification-based testing, and so forth. Experimental studies have shown that compared with the traditional techniques, evolutionary testing can greatly improve the testing efficiency.

Background of Evolutionary Testing

Motivation of Software Testing

Software engineering is always a complicated domain characterised by a large number of competing and inter-related constraints. With the rapid development of software scale and complexity, more and more software engineering problems, such as initial planning, requirements analysis, cost estimation, system integration, software testing, system maintenance, and so on, become vague and hard to solve, which makes it more difficult to balance these problems in the limited budget and schedule. Since traditional methods may not meet the continuous increasing complexity, promising techniques based on artificial intelligence have been proposed and researched. Nowadays, many software engineering problems have been considered from a new perspective as search problems, which meta-heuristic search techniques can be applied to.

Software testing is one of the significant components of software engineering with many complex and inter-related constraints. Efficient testing requires systematic and automatic test data generation to satisfy pre-defined standards. However because of the increasing complexity of software systems, usual testing techniques have demonstrated their limitation in certain areas.

- In functional testing and structural testing, test data are often generated manually according to some testing standards. Yet, it is hard to automate the generation task, which makes it too resource intensive.

- In safety testing and performance testing, it is always required to generate test data to examine software behaviours in some critical or dynamic situations. Since there are many implicit factors that influence the system's behaviours unpredictably, it may be a hard task for test data generation. In many cases, the manual work can hardly increase the confidence in software correctness.

- Random testing can be completely automated. However, since it is not performed systematically, it may generate excessive test data that have low possibility to satisfy the testing requirements and low efficiency to detect errors in software.

Test data generation can be transformed into a search problem in which meta-heuristic techniques are applied. Meta-heuristic search techniques refer to a set of generic algorithms that search intelligently for optimal or near optimal solutions to a problem within various search space. Since the search space of software testing is usually large, non-linear, and discontinuous, local search-based methods, such as hill climbing, are inefficient to find good solutions. However, genetic algorithms are a kind of global search-based strategy, which has been proved suitable for software testing (Clark et al., 2003; Wegener, 2001).

Evolutionary testing is a promise testing technique, which utilises genetic algorithms to generate test data for various testing objectives. Experimental studies have shown that evolutionary testing can be very efficient in various testing areas, including structural testing, temporal performance testing, safety testing, specification-based testing, and so forth. This new testing technique has been regarded as complementary and supplementary to existing approaches.

Process and Techniques of Genetic Algorithms

Evolutionary testing utilises a meta-heuristic search technique, genetic algorithms, for test data generation. Genetic algorithms represent a kind of adaptive search techniques based on the processes of natural genetics and Darwin's theory of biological evolution. The fundamental concept behind genetic algorithms is to evolve successive generations of increasingly better combinations of those parameters that significantly affect the overall performance of a design. It is characterised by an iterative procedure and work parallel on a number of potential solutions for a population of individuals, whose typical process is shown in Figure 1 and Figure 2 (Wegener, Baresel, & Sthamer, 2001).

At the very beginning of genetic algorithms, a population is randomly or heuristically initialised by some solutions. Each individual in the population is encoded into certain *code representation* (chromosome or genotype), which maps the original solution space into a gene-type search space. Since genetic algorithms search in the gene space instead of operating on solutions directly, the choice of coding method can affect the performance and efficiency of genetic algorithms significantly. The commonly used methods include *binary code, Gray code, decimal code, dynamic code, real code,* and so forth. Choice of coding scheme depends on the nature of the optimisation problem and influences the selection of genetic operations.

After initialisation, each individual should be evaluated by a pre-defined *fitness function,* which is a kind of measurement of the solution's quality. Solutions that are closer to an optimum are judged with higher value than others by the fitness function. This usually results in a spectrum of solutions ranging in fitness from poor to good like natural world. The design

Figure 1. Genetic algorithm

```
Set generation number, m=0;
Initialize the population P(0);
Evaluate the fitness function for
   each individual of P(0);
WHILE (optimization criterion is not met
OR end condition is not satisfied)
{
   Define a population P_parent=P(m)
   Selection:       P(m)=S(P(m));
   Crossover:       P(m)=C(P(m));
   Mutation:        P(m)=M(P(m));
   Evaluation:  F(P(m));
   Survival:        P(m+1)=Sur(P(m), P_parent);
   m=m+1;
}
```

Figure 2. Flow graph of genetic algorithm

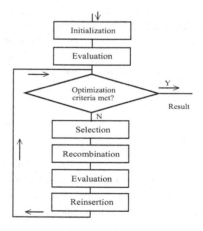

of fitness function always depends on the object of optimisation, which should reflect the nature of the optimum and guide the search. Actually the genetic algorithms are blind; they know nothing of the problem except the fitness information. Fitness function varied in different problem areas, which will be introduced in detail in next sections.

Afterward, a series of *genetic operations* that mimic natural evolution are proceeded orderly and iteratively, whose typical sequence is *selection, crossover (recombination), mutation, evaluation* by fitness function, and *survival (reinsertion).* Genetic algorithms renew a population iteratively with the genetic operations continuously, until optimum is achieved, or another stopping condition is fulfilled.

Selection

In the iterative process, pairs of individuals are selected from the population according to the pre-defined selection strategy. Many selection schemes are based on the fitness values of individuals, such as *roulette wheel* and *N-tournament.* In the *roulette wheel,* the population's cumulative fitness is normalised to give a set of selection probabilities for each individual. In the *N-tournament,* N individuals are selected at random from a population and the fittest ones are chosen. They both provide higher selection probability to individuals with higher fitness values. The reason for the bias is that a good solution is assumed to be composed of good genes. Selecting such solutions as parents increases the chances that their offspring will inherit these genes and will be at least as fit. Although the selection is biased toward the better solutions, the worst members of the population still have a chance of being selected as parents—even a poor solution may have a few good genes that may benefit the population. However in some cases this kind of schemes may not turn out to be better than random selection, which selects pairs of individuals randomly without considering their fitness values. Thus, the choice of selection scheme may be difficult, which should be made according to the optimal problem.

Crossover

With the selected parents, crossover operation exchanges the information between them. It provides a mechanism for mixing genetic material within the population. Crossover is varies from different code representation. To binary code the common used crossover operators include *single-point crossover, uniform crossover,* and so forth. And to decimal code, the usual crossover methods include *discrete crossover, arithmetical crossover,* and so forth.

Mutation

This operator provides a probability of independent random change in some bits of the gene of an individual. It is a vital scheme to introduce new genetic material to population thereby preventing the search from stagnating. Similar with crossover, mutation is also related with coding scheme. In binary code, mutation is just to change 0 to 1 (or 1 to 0) of one bit in an individual. And in decimal code, some commonly used methods include normal *distributed mutation, self-adaptation mutation, non-consistency mutation,* and so forth. And in decimal code, different mutation operators can be utilised together, which may bring better performance.

Survival

Newborn individuals through crossover and mutation form the offspring population. They need to be evaluated for their fitness and shifted into the next generation. The next population of solution is chosen from the parent and offspring generations in accordance with a survival strategy that normally favors fit individuals but nevertheless does not exclude the survival of the worse solutions. The most common one is *roulette wheel,* whose mechanism is that the population's cumulative fitness is normalised to give a set of survival probabilities for each individual.

There is an example which shows one generation of the evolution. We choose binary code as code representation and choose random selection, single crossover, bit mutation, and random survival as genetic operations. First, as shown in Figure 3a, select two individuals from the parent population randomly. With the operation of crossover and mutation, whose processes are shown in Figure 3b and Figure 3c, we can get two newborn individuals in offspring population. After several times of the genetic operation, we can acquire an offspring population in the same size with the parent population. At last, the random survival strategy procedures the next generation by parent and offspring populations, which is shown in Figure 3d.

Figure 3. Illustration of some genetic operation

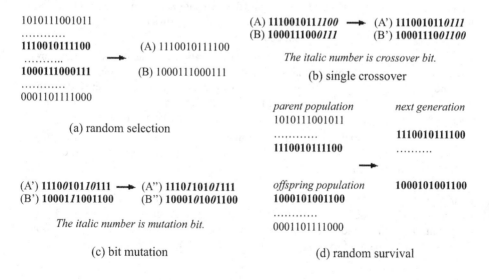

The power of genetic algorithms is in the technique of applying crossover and mutation operators to individuals. Despite their randomised nature, genetic algorithms are not simple random search. It takes advantage of the old knowledge held in a parent population to generate new solutions with improved performance. Thereby, the population is improved at each generation. Relatively good solutions reproduce; relatively bad ones die out and are replaced by fitter offspring.

The adaptation of the genetic algorithms is achieved by using selection and survival procedures based on fitness. The selection strategy controls which individuals are selected for reproduction, and the survival strategy determines how many, and which, individuals are taken from the parent and offspring populations to form the next generation. The fitness value is a numerical value that expresses the performance of an individual with regard to the current optimum, so that different individuals can be compared. The notion of fitness is fundamental to the application of genetic algorithms, and the fitness is required to change neither too rapidly nor too slowly with the design parameters. The fitness function must guarantee that individuals can be differentiated according to their suitability for solving the optimisation problem (Sthamer, 1996).

Under the guide of the fitness function, genetic algorithms perform those genetic operations iteratively. And after several generations of iteration, the population could gradually evolve toward optimal solutions. However, genetic algorithms cannot guarantee to obtain an optimal solution, since there are too many unpredictable factors in the search. For example, the stopping condition is one of the critical factors, which decides the stop time of iteration. Without a properly defined stopping condition, the search of genetic algorithms may terminate too early to find optimal solution or step too further without any improvement of population which leads to unnecessary computation cost (Back, 1996; Srinivas & Patnaik, 1994).

Introduction of Evolutionary Testing

Evolutionary testing is the application of genetic algorithms for test data generation, which has been used for systematising and automating the conventional test methods, such as structural testing, functional testing, and the non-functional properties testing, such as temporal testing (Wegener, Sthamer, & Baresel, 2001).

In evolutionary testing, the test object under consideration is transformed into a search problem. For the problem of generating test data for software, the input domain of the system under test is mapping onto the search space of genetic algorithms, and the individuals are the test data which should be encoded into gene representations to perform the genetic operations, such as crossover and mutation, according to genetic algorithms.

The central issue of evolutionary testing is a numeric representation of the test objective, from which a suitable fitness function for the evaluation of generated test data can be derived. Different testing activities consider different testing objects and these objects should be incorporated into the design of fitness functions. For example, when the temporal behaviour of an application is tested, the fitness evaluation of the test data is based on the measured execution time. For safety testing, fitness values are derived from pre-conditions and post-conditions of modules, and for the automation of structural test data design the control-flow executed by a test datum forms the starting point for the fitness evaluation.

The whole process of evolutionary testing has the same skeleton as genetic algorithms. An initial set of test data is generated usually at random; the system under test is then executed with these test data; and the execution for each test datum is monitored. A fitness value is calculated for the corresponding test datum to assess its suitability for the test aim based on the monitoring results. Next, selection, crossover, and mutation operations are performed in order to generate the offspring test data. The test data generated are also evaluated by executing the system under test. Finally, the next generation set of test data is formed by surviving from parent and offspring test data. The evolution process continues until the test objective is fulfilled or another given stopping condition is reached (Wegener, Baresel, & Sthamer, 2002).

Up to now, genetic algorithms have been proved to be applied successfully in many areas of software testing. There are two possible reasons.

Firstly, genetic algorithms are appropriate for test data generation. Due to the non-linearity of software (if-statement, loops, etc.) the conversion of test data generation problems to optimisation tasks mostly results in complex, discontinuous, and non-linear search spaces. Since local search methods like hill climbing are not suitable in such cases, there is a need for strategies which is global, efficient, and robust over a broad spectrum of problems. Fortunately, genetic algorithms, which are global search strategies, can perform very effectively when searching spaces are not smooth or continuous. Starting with a selection of good individuals genetic algorithms try to achieve the optimum solution by means of the random exchange of information between increasingly fit individuals (recombination), and the introduction of a probability of independent random change (mutation). They offer a kind of robust non-linear search techniques that are particularly suited to problems involving large numbers of variables.

Secondly, it dose not take much cost to apply genetic algorithms in many fields of test data generation. Clark et al. (2003) proved that some objects of software testing can be transformed into a search problem and the construction of a suitable fitness function is relative easy, which makes it feasible for the usage of genetic algorithms. The only pre-requisites for those fields are an executable test object and its interface specification. In addition, for the automation of structural testing, the source code of the test object must be available to enable its instrumentation (Wegener, Sthamer, & Baresel, 2001). Besides, some previous experiments have shown that the execution time of test data generation using genetic algorithms in those fields is reasonable, and most fitness functions do not take much cost for evaluation. Consequently, it is practical to apply genetic algorithm in test data generation (Wegener, 2001).

Structural Evolutionary Testing

In structural testing, genetic algorithms can be applied to generate test data that can cover specific structural constructs. Because of its high automaticity, it can improve the efficiency of structural testing greatly. In comparison with random testing that produces large quantity of test data inefficiently, evolutionary testing can generate a small test suite according to the testing objectives in a short time.

Introduction of Structural Testing

In structural testing, the task is to consider certain structural constructs in source code and generate test data that can execute these constructs as many as possible.

Suppose a C function that determines the type of a triangle is under test. Figure 4a shows the source code of the function, which has three input variables, a, b, and c, and Figure 4b depicts the corresponding *control-flow graph*. Structural testing tries to design proper test data to execute certain paths, nodes, conditions, and so forth, in the control-flow graph according to a pre-defined testing criterion. In testing practice, the usual structural testing criteria include statement coverage, branch coverage, path coverage, and so forth.

- *Statement coverage criterion* requires that all reachable program statements or predicates (nodes of the control-flow graph) should be executed during testing. For example in Figure 4b, there are seven nodes of statements or predicates: #1, #3, #4, #5, #6, #8, #11. To achieve statement coverage criterion, a test suite is required to execute all the seven nodes.

- *Branch coverage criterion* requires that all feasible program braches (edges of the control-flow graph) should be covered during testing. In Figure 4b, there are six branches: (#1, #11), (#1, #3), (#3, #4), (#3, #5), (#5, #6), (#5, #8). To achieve branch coverage criterion, a test suite is required to execute all the six branches.

- *Path coverage criterion* requires that all the feasible paths through the control-flow graph should be covered during testing. In Figure 4b, the feasible paths include (#1, #11), (#1, #3, #4), (#1, #3, #5, #6) and (#1, #3, #5, #8). To achieve path coverage criterion, a test suite is required to execute all the four paths.

In structural testing, traditional test approaches have their insufficiency in some cases. For example, random testing is a commonly used automatic testing technique. Although test data

Figure 4. Sample code of a C function

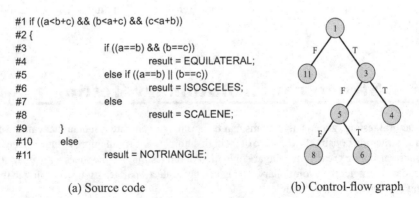

```
#1 if ((a<b+c) && (b<a+c) && (c<a+b))
#2 {
#3              if ((a==b) && (b==c))
#4                      result = EQUILATERAL;
#5              else if ((a==b) || (b==c))
#6                      result = ISOSCELES;
#7              else
#8                      result = SCALENE;
#9      }
#10     else
#11             result = NOTRIANGLE;
```

(a) Source code   (b) Control-flow graph may be produced easily, cheaply, and rapidly by random testing, the method is inefficient and ineffective. Since the information about the testing requirement and the program under test is not incorporated into the generation process, the process of generation will be under no guidance. Therefore, the test data generator may create too many test data or even fail to find test data to satisfy the requirement (Pargas, Harrold, & Peck, 1999). Conversely, manual design may generate error-sensitive test data exactly according to the testing requirement. However, the manpower is also very expensive which may increase the cost of the software testing.

Fortunately, some researches have proved that genetic algorithms can generate test data automatically and systemically for structural testing. The produced test data can execute certain required structural constructs in a program, which makes structural testing more effective.

Structural Evolutionary Testing

Structural evolutionary testing utilises genetic algorithms for test data generation to satisfy certain coverage criteria. In the process of evolution, an individual is a single test input and the fitness function is determined by a particular structural construct. Evolutionary testing performs evolutionary search to select out a test input that can cover the structural construct. In this way, a set of test input can automatically be produced to achieve the structural testing criterion. Because of its complete automation, evolutionary testing can contribute to the reduction of testing cost.

The central issue of structural evolutionary testing is the construction of fitness function according to test objects for pre-defined testing criteria. Depending on the construction of the fitness function, previous work on structural evolutionary testing can be divided into three categories: the coverage-oriented approach, the distance-oriented approach, and the hybrid approach (Wegener, Baresel, & Sthamer, 2001).

Coverage-Oriented Approach

In the coverage-oriented approach, the fitness function is determined by the coverage of the corresponding test data. The test data cover more designated program constructs are assigned with higher fitness values on the basis of *control-flow graph* (Roper, 1997; Watkins, 1995; Weichselbaum, 1998) or *control-dependence graph* (Pargas et al., 1999). Roper, Weichselbaum, and Pargas et al. concentrate on statement and branch coverage criteria. Weichselbaum addresses condition coverage criterion in addition.

The coverage-oriented approach usually evaluates the fitness values according to the dynamic execution information of corresponding test data. The fitness function for a specified testing objective may be constructed like:

$$Fitness\ (test,\ objective) = \frac{the\ number\ of\ executed\ construts\ of\ the\ objective}{the\ number\ of\ all\ the\ constructs\ of\ the\ objective} \qquad (1)$$

Figure 5. Two execution paths

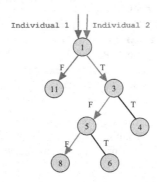

This fitness value calculated by formula (1) is expected to be maximised during the optimisation. When an individual obtains the maximum fitness value, the specified objective is satisfied by the test datum.

For example, in the program control-flow graph shown in Figure 4b, each node represents a statement or a predicate in the source code. In the coverage-oriented approach, the fitness value is computed according to the number of covered nodes for each corresponding individual. One of the possible fitness functions for a specified path may be:

$$Fitness\ (test,\ path) = node_{exe}\ /\ node_{all} \tag{2}$$

In formula (2), $node_{exe}$ means the number of nodes that the test data has executed in the specified path, and $node_{all}$ stands for the number of all the nodes in the path. Figure 5 traces two individuals' execution paths. If the target path to be covered is (#1, #3, #5, #6), the fitness value of *Individual 1* is 1/4 and the fitness value of *Individual 2* is 3/4.

Some empirical results have shown that this method has much better performance than random testing. Pargas et al. (1999) investigate six programs in their experiments, which are described in Table 1. With the same times of experiments, they compare the average performance of evolutionary testing and random testing when the two methods achieve full statements coverage. Table 2 lists the average, max, and min iteration times of both random and evolutionary testing for *Bisect.c, Fourballs.c* and *Tritype.c*.

It is obvious that in this three programs evolutionary testing consumes less average, max, and min iteration time when it achieves 100% coverage. For example in *Bisect.c,* evolutionary testing achieved 100% statement coverage after iterating an average of 29 times, while random testing achieved 100% statement coverage after iterating an average of 40 times. And in *Tritype.c* the difference is more significant; the average iteration time is 145 in evolutionary testing but is 1,259 in random testing.

Other empirical results show that evolutionary testing has its limitation in some cases. For example in other three programs *Bub.c, Find.c* and *Mid.c*, evolutionary testing dose not show its advantage over random testing, which may be due to that the programs do not involve

Table 1. Object programs under testing

Programs	Line of code	Cyclomatic complexity	Description of the program
Bub.c	32	4	Given an array of integers, bubble sorts the array.
Find.c	66	5	Given array A [ ], and index F, places all elements less than or equal to A [F] to the left of A [F], and all elements that are greater than or equal to A [F] to the right of A [F].
Mid.c	21	4	Given three integers, determines the middle value.
Bisect.c	36	3	Given an epsilon and X, computes $sqrt(X)$ to within epsilon using bisection method.
Fourball.c	82	7	Given four integers representing the weights of balls, determines the weights of the balls relative to each other.
Tritype.c	61	7	Given three integers, representing possible lengths of a triangle's sides, determines the type of triangle (if any).

Table 2. Comparison between evolutionary testing and random testing[*]

Programs	Times of experiments	Mean number of iteration		Min number of iteration		Max number of iteration	
		Evo.test	Ran.test	Evo.test	Ran.test	Evo.test	Ran.test
Bisect.c	32	29	40	13	23	70	62
Fourballs.c	32	95	159	52	110	168	229
Tritype.c	32	145	1259	21	24	392	3707

[*] *Evo.test means evolutionary testing; Ran.test means random testing.*

nested conditionals. Since the simple predicates are easy to be satisfied by random input, the meta-heuristic search seems to be too complex and expensive in this condition.

Therefore, it can be concluded that with the proper coverage-oriented fitness function, evolutionary testing can be applied in some cases successfully, which generates test data more effectively than random testing.

However there are also some criticisms about the demerits of the coverage-oriented approach. One criticism mentions its exclusive use of coverage as fitness criteria. Therefore, the search will mainly be directed by the execution of a few long program paths, thereby making it more difficult to attain complete coverage. Actually some researchers suggest that the coverage-oriented approach is the most suitable for path coverage criterion, while for condition coverage, they prefer another approach of fitness function construction, the distance-oriented approach.

Distance-Oriented Approach

In structural testing, another method of fitness function construction is the distance-oriented approach. In this approach, certain structure constructs as testing objects are partitioned into separate sub-goals. The task is to generate test data that lead to an execution of all the desired sub-goals, such as branches or conditions.

Up to now the emphasis of these works has lied in the automation of statement and branch coverage (Jones, Sthamer, & Eyres, 1996; McGraw, Michael, & Schatz, 1998; Sthamer, 1996; Tracey, Clark, Mander, & McDermid, 1998). In addition, some researchers have also worked upon the condition coverage (McGraw et al., 1998).

In this approach, a specialised fitness function is formulated for each sub-goal. Different from measuring the coverage of test data, the fitness function computes a distance for each test datum that indicates how far it is away from satisfying the predicate of the desired sub-goal. And a set of fitness functions should be utilised in turn as needed in order to guide the generation of test data to cover the sub-goals one by one. Therefore, the test suite determined through the evolution for each sub-goal would then serve as the test data for the coverage of the structural test criterion.

Table 3 shows some examples of fitness function that are derived from the predicates of the sub-goals. These fitness values are expected to be minimised during optimisation. Only if a test datum obtains the minimum fitness value 0, the predicate turns true. Meanwhile the desired sub-goal is achieved by the test datum and the evolutionary testing will proceed to aim at the next sub-goal (Wegener, Baresel, & Sthamer, 2001).

Take the program shown in Figure 4a as an example, and consider the statement coverage (Jones, Sthamer, & Eyres, 1996). If #4 is a sub-goal, which requires to satisfy the predicate (a==b && b==c). It means that when the test datum has arrived at #3, which is the initial node of the branches, it needs going on to execute the *true* branch. The fitness value depends upon how close the state variables are to the correct branch. The fitness function can be

*Table 3. Construction of fitness functions for basic condition expressions**

expr.	Fitness value (when expr. is false)	Fitness value (when expr. is true)
a=b	$f(expr.)=|a-b|$	$f(expr.)=0$
a≠b	$f(expr.)=k$	$f(expr.)=0$
a<b	$f(expr.)=(a-b)+k$	$F(expr.)=0$
a≤b	$f(expr.)=(a-b)$	$f(expr.)=0$
a>b	$f(expr.)=(b-a)+k$	$f(expr.)=0$
a≥b	$f(expr.)=(b-a)$	$f(expr.)=0$
a‖b	$f(expr.)=min(f(a), f(b))$	$f(expr.)=0$
a&&b	$f(expr.)=f(a)+f(b)$	$f(expr.)=0$

In the table, expr. is short for expression, and k is a small step size.

Table 4. Number of test data generated by evolutionary testing and random testing in quadratic solver and triangle classifier for full branch coverage

Range of input	Quadratic Solver		Triangle Classifier	
	Evolutionary testing	Random testing	Evolutionary testing	Random testing
±100	1373	7354	17789	160752
±200	1975	25536	48490	571983
±400	2642	92348	126943	1967674

Table 5. Number of test data generated by evolutionary testing and random testing in linear search and remainder for full branch coverage

Range of input	Linear Search		Remainder	
	Evolutionary testing	Random testing	Evolutionary testing	Random testing
±20000	762	76733	680	63260
±40000	788	146637	1002	119597
±80000	813	298058	2131	238080
±100000	829	375661	2476	317773

designed as |a-b|+|b-c| according to Table 3. Only if the test data reaching #3 goes down the *true* branch, the value of fitness function is 0.

Some experiments have shown that this approach also has better performance than random testing (Jones et al., 1996; Sthamer, 1996). Sthamer (1996) investigates several programs, including *quadratic solver, triangle classifier, linear search,* and *remainder*.

Table 4 compares the average number of test data generated by evolutionary testing and random testing with full branch coverage in *quadratic solver* and *triangle classifier*, which have no loops in programs. It can be discovered that with the same input range random testing needs to generate much more test data than evolutionary testing to achieve a full coverage. Poor performance of random testing on such a simple program arises because it is always very difficult to satisfy the desired condition and execute the desired branch. Take *quadratic solver* as an example, within the input range ±100 of three parameters, there are over 8 million possible test inputs, but only 1,104 (0.014%) will satisfy the desired condition. Thus, random testing with no guidance on the search will give a poor performance, while evolutionary testing with proper configuration can provide a definite direction of search which can improve the efficiency of test data generation.

In *linear search* and *remainder* that have loops, experiments are conducted for branch coverage. The average number of test data generated by evolutionary testing and random testing for full branch coverage are compared in Table 5. It can be discovered that with the same input range, random testing still needs to generate much more test data than evolutionary testing. For example, when testing is carried out in *linear search*, the number of tests generated by random testing is 76,733, while the number of tests in evolutionary testing is 762.

Compared with the coverage-oriented approach, the distance-oriented approach fitness function enables more purposeful search for program structures. Therefore, it is assumed that this approach will yield better results for more complex test objects. However in programs with long paths to be covered or with complex condition expressions, the fitness function in the distance-oriented approach may betoo difficult to design, whereas the fitness function in the coverage-oriented approach is always easy to be constructed.

Combination of Coverage-Oriented and Distance-Oriented Approaches

As previously mentioned, the fitness function, which represents the test aim accurately and provides the guidance of the search, can be defined according to the execution trace of each test datum, which is described in the coverage-oriented approach. Also it can be constructed based on the predicate conditions, which is described in the distance-oriented approach. However both two approaches have their limitations. Wegener, Baresel, and Sthamer (2001) combined the ideas of the two approaches, and introduced the conceptions of *approximation_level* and *distance.*

The *approximation_level* is defined according to the execution trace of a test datum, which indicates how many structural constructs still require to be covered for the pre-defined partial aim. In this sense, *approximation_level* corresponds to "distance from target". Apart from the information of testing coverage, *distance* is measured in the predicate statement with undesired branching, which is the same with the condition-oriented fitness function. Therefore the fitness function can be defined like:

*Table 6. Object programs under testing**

programs	LOC	No.bran/loop	Cycl.comp	Max.nest	Myer.interv
Atof	64	57/4	16	2	27
Is_line_covered_by_rectangle	71	24/1	8	4	6
Is_point_located_in_rectangle	5	5/0	2	1	3
Search_field	108	37/4	13	2	10
Netflow	154	153/0	34	7	40
Complex_flow	42	41/2	13	2	10
Classify_triangle	35	38/0	14	2	7

In the table, LOC means lines of codes; No.bran/loop means number of branches or loops; Cycl. comp means the cyclomatic complexity of the object program; Max.nest means the maximum nesting level for each testing object of structural construction, which could indicate the difficulty in reaching a partial aim with respect to the control flow graph; Myer.interv means the complexity of certain branching conditions.

Figure 6. Coverage comparison between evolutionary testing () and random testing (RT)

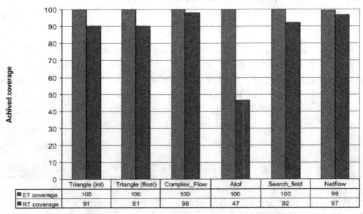

	Triangle (int)	Triangle (float)	Complex_Flow	Atof	Search_field	Netflow
ET coverage	100	100	100	100	100	99
RT coverage	91	91	98	47	92	97

Fig. 9. Mean coverage achieved by evolutionary and random testing in the experiments.

Figure 7. Number of test data comparison between evolutionary testing (ET) and random testing (RT)

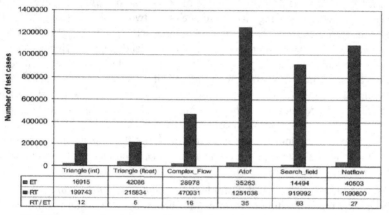

Fig. 10. Mean number of test data generated for the evolutionary and the random test in the experiments.

$$Fitness(test,\ objective) =$$

$$approximation\_level(test,\ objective)+ distance(test,\ objective) \quad (3)$$

Consider the target path (#1, #3, #5, #6) in Figure 5. Test individual 1 is (3, 3, 6), whose execution path is (#1, #11); test individual 2 is (3, 4, 5), whose execution path is (#1, #3, #5, #8). Thus, for individual 1, its *approximation_level* should be *4-1=3*, and according to Table 3, its *distance* should be $min(|3-3|,|3-6|)=0$. For individual 2, is *approximation_level* should be *4-3=1*, and its *distance* should be $min(|3-4|,|4-5|)=1$. Therefore, the fitness value of individual 1 is *3+0=3*, and the fitness value of individual 2 is *1+1=2*.

Some experiments have shown that under the same input ranges and the same maximum of iteration, this approach also has better performance than random testing (Wegener, Baresel, & Sthamer, 2001). Wegener et al. tested seven programs which are shown in Table 6, and the average empirical results are shown in Figure 6 and Figure 7. It can be discovered from Figure 6 that evolutionary testing can achieve full branch coverage for all test objects, while random testing only achieves between 46% and 98% on average. And, Figure 7 indicates that evolutionary testing generates much less test data compared to random testing.

Flag Variable Problem

Many empirical studies have shown that genetic algorithms can be properly applied in structural testing, and can improve the efficiency of test data generation greatly in comparison with random testing. However some problems in structural evolutionary testing may affect the performance of genetic algorithms. Flag variable problem is one of the critical problems that severely diminish the performance of evolutionary testing (Baresel, Binkley, Harman,

& Korel, 2004; Harman et al., 2002a; Harman, Hu, Hierons, Baresel, & Sthamer, 2002b; Harman et al., 2004).

A *flag variable* is one variable with the value of either *true* or *false*. It reduces the input state space, with few values being mapped to one of the two possible outcomes and all the other being mapped to the other one. This kind of input space can greatly reduce the effectiveness of the search. That is, it creates a coarse fitness landscape, which consists of two plateaus, corresponding to the two possible flag values. One of these plateaus will be super fit and the other super unfit. For example in Figure 8, it can be discovered that flag is a flag variable with only two value, *true* and *false*. And only with the input value "10" the fitness value can reach the maximum, while the other inputs lead to the fitness value "0" (Harman et al., 2004). This kind of fitness landscape could provide almost no guidance to direct the evolutionary search from unfit regions to fit regions, since the fit plateau is too narrow in comparison with the unfit wide plateau. This results in evolutionary testing yielding even poorer performance than random testing.

One of the solutions of the flag variable problem is *testability transformation* (Harman et al., 2004). Testability transformation is a source-to-source program transformation technique that removes any structural impediment in testing to improve the performance of automatic test data generation. Practically, it can be applied in flag variable removal in evolutionary testing.

Harman et al. summarise the transformation problem into five levels according to the difficulty of *flag* removal, which are shown in Table 7. The aim of testability transformation is to transform a flag-using program (level 1, 2, 3, and 4) into a flag-free program (level 0).

Figure 8. Fitness landscape of a predicate with a flag variable

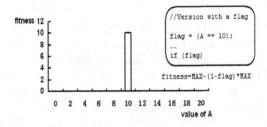

Figure 9. Fitness landscape of a predicate with no flag variable

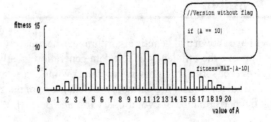

*Table 7. Five four levels of transformation problem**

Level	Description
$Level_0$	There is no *flag* in the program
$Level_1$	There is only a single Assign(*flag*) and no intervening assignments of other variables in Assign(*flag*) before Pred(*flag*) in the program.
$Level_2$	There is only a single Assign(*flag*) but several intervening assignments of other variables in Assign(*flag*) before Pred(*flag*) in the program.
$Level_3$	There is a sequence of Assign(*flag*) interleaved with several intervening assignments of other variables in Assign(*flag*) before Pred(*flag*).
$Level_4$	There is a sequence containing conditional statements, which consist of several Assign(*flag*) and assignments of other variables in Assign(*flag*) before Pred(*flag*).

In the table, flag means a flag variable, Assign(flag) means the assignments of flag, and Pred(flag) means the predicate first using flag.

*Table 8. Different methods for four levels**

Level	Description
$Level_1$	Replace the *flag* in Pred(*flag*) with the Assign(*flag*).
$Level_2$	Record the original value of the other variables in Assign(*flag*) with temp variables at the beginning of the program, redefine *flag* with the temporal variables as Assign'(*flag*), and replace *flag* in Pred(*flag*) with the Assign'(*flag*).
$Level_3$	Utilise the technique of amorphous slicing to redefine *flag* with the temporal variables as Assign'(*flag*), and replace *flag* in Pred(*flag*) with the Assign'(*flag*).
$Level_4$	Utilise the bushing and blossoming techniques to redefine *flag* with the temporal variables as Assign'(*flag*), and replace *flag* in Pred(*flag*) with the Assign'(*flag*).

In the table, flag means a flag variable, Assign(flag) means the assignments of flag, and Pred(flag) means the predicate first using flag.

The essential idea is to "collect" the disparate assignments together and merge them into a single assignment statement to substitute the *flag* in the predicate. Testability transformation provides different methods for different levels which are shown in Table 8.

The effect of the transformation is depicted by Figure 8 and Figure 9. Figure 8 shows the fitness landscape of the original program, and Figure 9 shows the situation after the transformation. It can be discovered that the flag variable problem has been resolved by the transformation, and the fitness landscape provides more guidance to direct the search.

It can be proved that testability transformation is original meaning preserving since the overall effect upon the program is only the substitution for the use of *flag*. Besides it is also the branch coverage adequacy criterion preserving, since substitution for an expression has no effect upon the edges of the control flow graph. Some empirical studies have shown that with the help of testability transformation evolutionary testing can generate test data in much less iterations and acquire higher coverage, especially in the system with many flag variables, such as some embedded systems (Harman et al., 2004).

Prematurity Problem

Besides the flag variable problem, there is another problem, the prematurity problem, which influences the performance of structural evolutionary testing greatly. During the process of evolutionary search, the population sometimes may prematurely converge on one local optimal solution, which badly delays the progress of evolution. And there is a lack of self-adaptation methods to avoid the stagnation.

We have presented one kind of dynamic optimisation strategies for evolutionary structural testing, which is denoted as **DOMP** (**D**ynamic **O**ptimisation of **M**utation **P**ossibility) (Xie, Xu, Shi, Nie, & He, 2005). The basic idea of DOMP is that the mutation possibility P_m should be adjusted dynamically according to the population. When the phenomena of population prematurity are observed, P_m should be increased sharply to bring more various genes into the population. It helps to eliminate the mono-structural genes in the population, and break the stagnant status of the evolution. When the population diversity is recovered, P_m should be dropped to the ordinary value. Otherwise, the evolutionary search will degenerate to random search.

The empirical results show that DOMP can greatly improve the performance of the evolutionary testing in many cases. Three functions, shown in Table 9, were tested in the experiments for statement coverage. Figure 10 compares the average performance between evolutionary testing with DOMP and without DOMP. In the figure, P_h means the hit percent of evolutionary testing. $P_h = T_h/T_0$, where T_h is the number of experiments that generate desired test data and T_0 is the total number of experiments. The higher P_h is, the more effective evolutionary testing is.

It is obvious that P_h is increased by DOMP in *Triangle* and *Quadratic*. In our experiments, P_h is elevated by 35.5% at most in *Triangle* and by 48.2% at most in *Quadratic*. However, it is also can be observed that DOMP has little influence upon *LineCover*. One possible reason may be that the testing objective of *LineCover* is so complex that it is difficult for evolutionary search to find optimal solutions. It can be concluded from Table 9 that the target condition of *Triangle* is

Table 9. Different functions in experiments

Function	Input	Condition to satisfy	Corresponding result	Description of the function
Triangle	a, b, c	$(a=b)$ && $(b=c)$	The triangle is an equilateral one.	a, b and c are the edges of a triangle. The program uses them to classify the triangle.
Quadratic	a, b, c	$b^2-4*a*c=0$	The equation has two equal real solutions.	a, b and c are the coefficients of a quadratic equation. The discriminator $b^2-4*a*c$ is used to investigate the distribution of the solutions.
LineCover	l1x, l2x, l1y, l2y, rx, ry, w, h	$(rx = \min(l1x, l2x))$ && $(ry = \min(l1y, l2y))$ && $(rx+w=\max(l1x, l2x))$ && $(ry+h=\max(l1y, l2y))$	The line segment is the diagonal of the rectangle.	(l1x, l1y) and (l2x, l2y) are two end points of a line segment. (rx, ry) is the bottom left point of a rectangle. (w, h) are the width and height of the rectangle. The program checks the position relationship between the line segment and the rectangle.

*Figure 10. P_h comparison between DOMP and Un-DOMP**

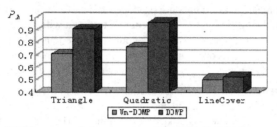

DOMP means evolutionary testing with DOMP; Un-DOMP means evolutionary testing without DOMP.

an algebraic equations, and the target condition of *Quadratic* is a combination of several simple Boolean expressions. However the target condition of *LineCover* is a combination of four Boolean expressions, and each of them is an equation whose requirement is harder to satisfy than the other two programs. Thus, due to the complex condition, the population may hardly converge prematurely, and DOMP has no chance to optimise the evolution process in *LineCover*.

In conclusion, for programs with simple conditions to satisfy, such as *Triangle* and *Quadratic*, it is helpful to use DOMP in structural evolutionary testing for statement coverage or branch coverage, since DOMP may improve P_h significantly for these programs. Besides, some empirical results also advise that is should be careful to utilise genetic operations with high selection pressure, such as roulette wheel selection, N-tournament selection, roulette wheel survival, and so forth, in these programs. The combinations of those operations may bring high selection pressure, which could make the population very prone to be premature and lead to poor performances of evolutionary testing.

For programs with complex conditions to satisfy, such as *LineCover*, DOMP may not be very effective, since there is rarely prematurity in the evolution process. However, DOMP is also suggested to use, since it provides more protection for evolutionary testing from losing the population diversity. For this kind of programs, genetic operations with high selection pressure are preferred. Since in these programs, increasing the selection pressure may help to speed up the process of convergence and finally help to elevate P_h.

Temporal Performance Evolutionary Testing

Introduction of Temporal Performance Testing

Nowadays more and more industrial applications are real-time systems. Different from testing the conventional software systems, testing real-time systems is more complex, since it is critical to add a new dimension to the testing of such systems—not only the logical behaviors, but also the temporal behaviors of the systems require thorough testing.

The aim of temporal performance testing is to find the inputs to produce temporal errors. Temporal behavior errors usually result from a violation of specified timing constraints. In general, a violation means that outputs are produced too early or their computation takes too long. Therefore, the task of testers is to generate test data with the longest or shortest execution time in order to check whether they could produce temporal errors. Practically in most cases testers only focus on inputs that result in the maximum execution time. If the execution time exceeds the specified constraint, an error has been detected.

Unfortunately the examination of the temporal requirements like timeliness, simultaneity, and predictability makes the test complex and costly, since in real-time systems testing is usually complicated by technical characteristics like the development in host-target environments, the strong connection with the system environment, the frequent use of parallelism, distribution, and fault-tolerance mechanisms as well as the utilisation of simulators (Wegener, Grimm, Grochtmann, Sthamer, & Jones, 1996). Therefore, it is a difficult task for manual testing even if the tester is quite familiar with the function, since there are many latent factors that influence the temporal behaviors. Random testing, however, provides little confidence in searching for the maximum execution time of the temporal behavior.

Therefore it is important to investigate a specialised approach to check temporal correctness. Some researchers find that it is very effective to use genetic algorithms in searching for test data which are executed at worst-case scenarios, which can enhance the confidence in the temporal correctness.

Evolutionary Testing Applied in Temporal Performance Testing

The task of temporal performance testing is to find inputs with the longest (shortest) execution time to check whether they produce temporal errors. In evolutionary testing, the search for such inputs is interpreted as a discontinuous, non-linear optimisation problem, with the input domain of the test object as search space, and execution time as objective value. In order to solve this optimisation problem, genetic algorithms are used to approximate the longest execution time of a test object (Wegener, Pitschinetz, & Sthamer, 2000).

Similar to other applications of evolutionary testing, each individual of the population represents a test datum with which the system under testing is executed. The difference is that for each test datum the execution time is measured and is used to determine the fitness of the respective individual. Naturally we can just set the value of execution time as the fitness function to search for the longest execution time (Wegener, Grochtmann, & Jones, 1997):

$$Fitness\ (test) = execution\_time \qquad (4)$$

Then test data with longer execution time will obtain higher fitness values. If the shortest execution time is searched for, we can just set the reciprocal of execution time as the fitness function (Wegener, Grochtmann, & Jones, 1997):

Fitness (test) = 1 / *execution_time*   (5)

Then test data with shorter execution time will obtain higher fitness values.

The evolutionary process continues until a given stopping condition is reached or a temporal error is detected. If all the execution meets the specified timing constraints of the system, confidence in the temporal correctness of the system is substantiated.

Wegener, Grochtmann, and Jones have conducted a series of experiments to compare the performance between evolutionary testing and random testing in temporal behavior testing. They picked up six time-critical tasks from an engine control system in their previous work as the target programs. In the experiments, fitness function is determined by either the duration of execution for the longest path or the reciprocal for the shortest path. They used processor cycles as the measurement for duration of executions, in order to rule out the dependence on the hardware and software platform.

The average results of the experiments are shown in Table 10. It can be discovered from the table that for each program evolutionary testing runs less test data and obtains better results than random testing, regardless of whether the shortest or the longest execution times were searched for. In the search for test data with shortest execution time, only for the *Computer Graphics I* and *Auto Electronics* random testing gives the same results as evolutionary testing, while for other programs random testing generates test data with longer execution time than evolutionary testing does. Similarly in the search for test data with longest execution time, random testing generates test data with shorter execution time than evolutionary testing dose except for *Computer Graphics* ☐ and *Auto Electronics I*.

Figure 11 (Wegener, Grochtmann, & Jones, 1997) shows the comparison of *Auto Electronics* ☐ in searching for the longest execution time on average. It can be seen that random testing reaches its maximum execution time after only about 30 generations, whereas for genetic optimisation a continuous improvement up to the 100th generation can be observed. And after only eleven generations, the execution time found by genetic optimisation is above that of random testing.

Figure 12 (Wegener, Grochtmann, & Jones, 1997) shows the comparison of *Railroad Technology* in searching for the longest execution time on average. It becomes clear that after

Table 10. Comparison between random testing and evolutionary testing in temporal performance testing

Applications	Random Testing			Evolutionary Testing		
	No. of test runs	Shortest time	Longest time	No. of test runs	Shortest time	Longest time
Computer Graphics I	9200	99	384	1200	99	392
Computer Graphics ☐	4600	359	1839	800	355	1839
Auto Electronics I	2700	66	104	1350	45	104
Auto Electronics ☐	5000	366	10774	4850	366	12185
Railroad Technology	10000	1050	11529	9500	399	14175
Defense Electronics	56000	27258	110842	30000	27154	114160

Figure 11. Comparison of execution time variation between random testing and evolution-ary testing in Auto Electronics ☐

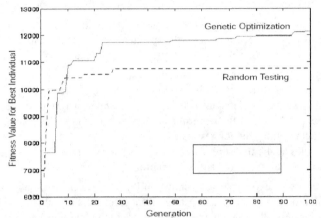

Figure 5: Comparison of Genetic Optimization and Random Testing Searching
for the Longest Execution Time for the Airbag Controller

Figure 12. Comparison of execution time variation between random testing and evolution-ary testing in Railroad Technology

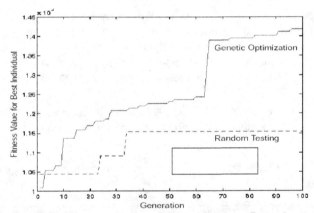

Figure 7: Comparison of Genetic Optimization and Random Testing Searching   for the Longest Execution Time for the Railroad System

the fourth generation genetic optimisation is superior to random testing. While random testing stagnates after 35 generations, genetic optimisation, however, manages once again to improve the execution times continuously. And, a significant leap of more than 1,500 cycles can be noted in the 70th generation.

Therefore, these curve traces suggest that the evolutionary testing would find longer execution time if the number of generation was increased. However the execution time found by random testing would be stagnant from a low generation level and could not become higher even with the increasing of generations.

Besides random testing, evolutionary testing have also been proved superior to manual work even though it treats the software as black boxes, whereas in manual work developers are familiar with the function and structure of the software. An explanation might be that the developers can hardly figure out the performance factors affected by hardware structure, system calls, linkage, and compiler optimisation (Wegener et al., 2000).

From the earlier discussion, it could be concluded that evolutionary temporal performance testing exceeds random testing and manual work in many cases. However, the sole use of genetic algorithms is not sufficient for a thorough and comprehensive examination of real-time systems. A combination of systematic testing and genetic optimisation is promising and necessary to develop an effective test strategy for embedded systems.

Functional Evolutionary Testing Based on Specification

Apart from the structural testing and the temporal performance testing in real-time systems, another testing activity in practice is functional testing, which examines the correctness of the system behaviors according to the specification. Practically genetic algorithms can be applied in a variety of functional testing. Two of the most common applications are specification-based testing and safety testing.

Specification-Based Evolutionary Testing

In specification-based testing, the aim is to find out whether the input-output behavior of the program does agree with its functional specification. In this testing, the test data can be derived early in the development cycle.

Tracey et al. consider the testing task based on a formal specification consisting of a set of (disjoint) pre/post conditions (Clark et al., 2003; Tracey, Clark, & Mander, 1998; Tracey, Clark, McDermid, & Mander, 1999). For such a system, test data leads to a failure if the execution satisfies the precondition P but fails the post condition Q. A predicate $E(P, Q)=Q \Box \neg P$ is defined for each pre/post condition pair (P, Q). Thus the aim of testing is to generate test data that make $E(P, Q)$ to be false. Usually the predicate $E(P, Q)$ should be rewritten into disjunctive normal form E'. Thus, when the predicate $E(P, Q)$ is false, it means each conjunct in this normal form is false and at least one term in each conjunct is false.

Therefore in order to satisfy the testing aim, the fitness function is designed according to how close the execution is to making $E(P, Q)$ false, which equals to how close the execu-

Table 11. Some examples of fitness function construction of $f(N)$*

Expression N	Value of $f(N)$ when N is false	Value of $f(N)$ when N is true
$e_1=e_2$	0	$|e_1-e_2|$
$e_1>e_2$	0	e_1-e_2+k
$e_1<e_2$	0	e_2-e_1+k
$e_1 \neq e_2$	0	k

In the table, k is a small step size.

tion is to making each conjunct in $E(P, Q)$ false. The fitness value could be expected to be minimised during the search. The smaller the fitness value is, the closer the test datum is away from the target. When $E(P, Q)$ becomes false, the value of fitness function could be the minimum 0.

Consequently, the fitness function should be constructed based on the following rules:

- For the normal form E', the fitness value could be the summary of the fitness value of each conjunct.
- For each conjunct in E', the fitness value should be the multiply of all the terms of this conjunct.
- And for each term N in the conjuncts, the fitness value could be computed according to Table 11.

For example, if $E(P, Q) = (A \square B) \square (C \square D)$, the fitness function can be defined like:

$$Fitness\ (test) = f(A)*f(B) + f(C)*f(D) \tag{6}$$

In formula (6), $f(A), f(B), f(C), f(D)$ can be defined by Table 11 according to the sub-expressions. It is obvious that when at least one term of A and B, and one term of C and D are false, *Fitness (test)* will be 0. On the contrary, if both A and B are true, the value of $f(A)*f(B)$ cannot be 0, and *Fitness (test)* is above 0. And the higher the fitness value is, the farther the test datum is away from the target.

Safety Evolutionary Testing

For safety critical systems, it is not sufficient to only focus on demonstrating consistency between the implementation and the functional specification. Safety constraints and safety properties of the system should also be tested. If there are test data which result in a violation of a safety constraint, the system under testing may have errors.

Safety constraint is normally defined in terms of hazardous conditions which may lead (or contribute) to an accident. It is important to note that not all errors cause hazards and conversely not all software, which correctly implements its specification, is safe. The objective of safety testing is to provide confidence for the system that each of the identified hazardous conditions cannot occur (or that the probability of failure is acceptably low) (Tracey, Clark, McDermid, & Mander, 1999; Tracey, Clark, Mander, & McDermid, 2000).

In safety testing, the target is to generate test data which violate some specified safety constraints. For example, in a car engine control system, the input parameters may be the speeds of wheels and motors, and the safety constraint may be specified as *speed_of_car <150 km/h*. Therefore some techniques are needed to transform the specified safety constraint into a condition, denoted as *safety condition*, about the input parameters, which will be applied in the design of the fitness function (Tracey, Clark, McDermid, & Mander, 1999; Wegener, 2001).

One of the transformation techniques is *software fault tree analysis* (Tracey, Clark, McDermid, & Mander, 1999). With the safety constraints specification, it is assumed that the system has failed in some manner. The process basically analyses paths backwards through the software statement-by-statement to eventually determine the set of possible safety conditions that may cause the identified failure or potential hazardous outputs.

The fitness function can be defined as the distance from violating a safety condition. Suppose there are two input parameters a and b in the expression P, the fitness function for safety testing can be designed according to Table 12. If P is in a conjunct or a disjunctive form, the design of fitness function is similar to the method for the specification-based testing in the *Specification-Based Evolutionary Testing* sub-section. If there are two terms A and B in the expression P, the fitness function for safety testing can be designed according to Table 13, in which $f(A)$ and $f(B)$ are calculated in the same way as $f(P)$.

Traditionally safety testing can be conducted with static analysis techniques, such as model checking, formula verification, and so forth. Static analysis techniques do not require execution of the software; instead they examine a representation of the software. Usually static analysis could be used to verify the safety properties of the system, however, these methods are very complex and costly, which may greatly increases the cost of software development.

Table 12. Some examples of fitness function construction of f (P) *

Expression P	Value of $f(P)$ when P is true	Value of $f(P)$ when P is false
$a = b$	0	$|a\text{-}b|$
$a \neq b$	0	k
$a < b$	0	$a\text{-}b + k$
$a \leq b$	0	$a\text{-}b$
$a > b$	0	$b\text{-}a + k$
$a \geq b$	0	$b\text{-}a$

In the table, k is a small step size.

Table 13. Some examples of fitness function construction of f (P) *

Expression P	Value of $f(P)$
$\neg A$	$F(A)$
$A \vee B$	$Min\ (f(A), f(B))$
$A \wedge B$	$f(A) + f(B)$

In the table, k is a small step size.

Evolutionary testing can help to reduce the cost of safety testing. Prior to attempting static analysis, evolutionary testing can be applied first. For a possible safety constraint, test data are generated to show situations in which the safety constraint is violated. If no such test data are found, the software needs to be verified by static analysis further. Even though we still need static analysis, the time of static analysis can be decreased sharply. Empirical studies show that with the help of evolutionary safety testing, 89% of the static analysis could be discharged automatically. There are only 11% left which requires manual proof effort (Tracey, Clark, McDermid, & Mander, 1999).

Conclusions

Evolutionary testing uses a kind of meta-heuristic search techniques, genetic algorithms, to convert the task of test data generation into an optimal problem and search for relevant test data in the input domain of the system under test.

Genetic algorithms are applicable when the good solutions are easy to recognise but hard to generate. Due to the situation of software testing, where competing constraints have to be balanced against one another, it can be concluded that testing is an attractive and ripe area for the application of genetic algorithms.

Actually empirical studies have proved that evolutionary testing can be applied very successfully in testing data generation to various testing objectives, such as structural testing, temporal performance testing, and specification-based testing, whenever the test aim can be expressed numerically.

With the help of genetic algorithms, evolutionary testing has many advantages over the traditional testing techniques, which makes it a promising testing technique. First it enables the complete automation of test data design, which allows the system to be tested with a large number of different input situations. In most cases, more than several thousand test data are generated and executed within a few minutes, which is a great saving of manpower. Second it generates test data systematically. Unlike other automatic testing techniques such as random testing, evolutionary testing can generate test data which are more sensitive to software defects. These two features of evolutionary testing may contribute to the quality improvement as well as to the reduction of development costs.

Though evolutionary testing has performed well in many testing areas, there are still several open problems that need further research (Wegener, 2001).

Process Control of Evolutionary Testing

Evolutionary testing is based on the genetic algorithms, and the process of evolution may greatly affect the performance of test data generation. Therefore the process control of evolution is very important.

Different configuration strategies select different genetic operators to carry out evolutionary testing, which may lead to different performances. Commonly in practice, evolutionary testing has to face various testing tasks with different test objectives, different program structures, and different input domains, which lead to different searching spaces. Thus the diversity of testing environment may have influences on the difficulty of searching for optimal solutions. Empirical studies show that sometimes a configuration strategy that is optimal for one kind of programs may sharply decrease the performance of evolutionary testing for another kind of programs (Sthamer, 1996; Wegener & Bühler, 2002). Apparently, the genetic algorithms need to be configured properly according to the features of the search space to achieve the best performance.

Up to now many researchers have concentrated on searching for some generic indications on configuration for different testing environments to optimise the performance of evolutionary process (Baresel, Sthamer, & Schmidt, 2002; Harman, Hu, Hierons, Baresel, & Sthamer, 2002; Harman et al., 2004; Sthamer, Wegener, & Baresel, 2002; Wegener, Baresel, & Sthamer, 2001; Wegener & Bühler, 2002). Apart from the static configuration, proper dynamic controlling methods are also necessary, such as DOMP, which is introduced in the sub-section *Prematurity Problem* (Xie et al., 2005).

Stopping Criteria

In genetic algorithms, it is always critical to define a proper stopping criterion for the evolution. Evolutionary testing generates test data continuously, until the optimum is achieved, or another stopping condition is fulfilled. If the process ends because of the desired test data being found, the testing turns out to be a successful one. However if the evolution ends due to certain stopping criterion being satisfied, the evolutionary process has failed to find the optimal test data.

Practically it is difficult to define a proper stopping criterion. This criterion has to decide when to stop a so far unsuccessful testing, since errors have not yet been found but may be detected if the evolution is continued for a while. For example, in structural testing some sub-goals of the program that have not been covered could be just some unreachable constructs or some feasible constructs that have not yet been found by evolutionary testing. In the first case the evolution should be ended timely to save testing resources, while in the second case the evolution may be expected to continue for a while. However it may be too complicated to decide whether a test generation is definitely a failed one or a promising one during the evolution process. Additionally even if the test generation is a promising one, the cost may be so great that it is unworthy to continue the optimisation.

Therefore the definition of a proper stopping criterion should balance the successful rate and the cost of the testing. The desired evolutionary testing should be both an efficient and economic one. Up to now, some usual stopping criteria in evolutionary testing include:

* Assign a constant value to the maximum of generation according to the experience value and the empirical studies. Once the number of generation exceeds the maximum, the evolution ends.

* Define a lowest increasing rate of the sum (or maximum) of fitness values in a population. After several generation of evolution, if the increasing rate is lower than the pre-defined lowest value, the process of evolution is terminated.

However these criteria are not suitable for every situation, since they do not take the test progress into account, such as the number of generations, the number of target function calls or the computation time (Wegener, 2001).

Invalid Test Data

A program usually has pre-conditions that are part of its abstract model and contract. If the input doses not satisfy the pre-conditions, the system may throw an exception or exit immediately. During the evolution, genetic algorithms sometimes generate test data that are not in the valid input domains, which violate the pre-conditions. Some of those individuals may even have quite high fitness values, which disturbs the normal optimisation process. Therefore there must be some measures to avoid the invalid test data. Some common methods include generating new individuals randomly to replace the invalid ones, mapping invalid data to valid data, and so on (Wegener, 2001).

Some Other Questions

To utilise genetic algorithms in various testing activities, some other questions need to be considered besides these open problems.

Is the system suitable for evolutionary testing? First of all, the testing target should be able to be converted into an optimal problem, which means it is possible to design a proper fitness function for the task. Second the fitness function should be easy to calculate without costing many resources.

Are the results from evolutionary testing reliable? We can consider the following situations like: can we say a module is safe if no violation of safety properties has been found during evolutionary testing? Are those statements, branches, or paths that have not executed during evolutionary testing infeasible?

At last analysis, evolutionary testing is a promising technique, and the future work in field should be focused on two areas. First, it is promising to extend further application fields of genetic algorithms in software testing, such as regression testing, mutation testing, integration testing, system testing, and so on. Second, it will be helpful to combine genetic algorithms with other analysis and testing techniques, such as model checking, regression testing, object-oriented testing, and so forth.

References

Back, T. (1996). *Evolutionary algorithms in theory and practice*. Oxford: Oxford University Press.

Baresel, A., Binkley, D., Harman, M., & Korel, B. (2004). Evolutionary testing in the presence of loop-assigned flags: A testability transformation approach. *International Symposium on Software Testing and Analysis*, Boston, Massachusetts (pp.108-118).

Baresel, A., Sthamer, H., & Schmidt, M. (2002). Fitness function design to improve evolutionary structural testing. *Genetic and Evolutionary Computation Conference*, New York, USA (pp.1329-1336).

Clark, J., Dolado, J., Harman, M., Hierons, R., Jones, B., Lumkin, M., Mitchell, B., Mancoridis, S., Rees, K., Roper, M., & Shepperd, M. (2003). Reformulating software engineering as a search problem. *IEE Proceedings - Software, 150*(3), 161-175.

Harman, M., Hu, L., Hierons, R., Baresel, A., & Sthamer, H. (2002b). Improving evolutionary testing by flag removal. In the *Genetic and Evolutionary Computation Conference*, New York, USA, July (pp.1359-1366).

Harman, M., Hu, L., Hierons, R., Fox, C., Danicic, S., Wegener, J., Sthamer, H., & Baresel, A. (2002a). Evolutionary testing supported by slicing and transformation. In the *International Conference on Software Maintenance*, Montreal, Canada, 18th.

Harman, M., Hu, L., Hierons, R., Wegener, J., Sthamer, H., Baresel, A., & Roper, M. (2004, January). Testability transformation. *IEEE Transactions on Software Engineering, 30*(1).

Jones, B., Eyres, D., & Sthamer, H. (1998). A strategy for using genetic algorithms to automate branch and fault-based testing. *Computer Journal, 41*(2), 98-107.

Jones, B., Sthamer, H., & Eyres, D. (1996). Automatic structural testing using genetic algorithm. *Software Engineering Journal, 11*(5), 299-306.

Jones, B., Sthamer, H., Yang, X., & Eyres, D. (1995). The automatic generation of software test data sets using adaptive search techniques. In the *3rd International Conference on Software Quality Management*, Sevilla, Spain (pp. 435-444).

McGraw, G., Michael, C., & Schatz, M. (1998). *Generating software test data by evolution*. Technical Report RSTR-018-97-01, RST Corporation, Sterling, Virginia, USA.

Pargas, R., Harrold, M., & Peck, R. (1999). Test-data generation using genetic algorithm. *Software Testing, Verification & Reliability, 9*(4), 263-282.

Roper, M. (1997). Computer-aided software testing using genetic algorithms. In the *10th International Software Quality Week (QW'97)*, San Francisco, USA.

Srinivas, M., & Patnaik, L. (1994, June). Genetic algorithms: A survey. *IEEE Computer, 27*(6), 17-26.

Sthamer, H. (1996, April). *The automatic generation of software test data using genetic algorithms*. PhD Thesis, University of Glamorgan, Pontyprid, Great Britain.

Sthamer, H., Wegener, J., & Baresel, A. (2002). Using evolutionary testing to improve efficiency and quality in software testing. In the *2nd Asia-Pacific Conference on Software Testing Analysis & Review*, Melbourne, Australia, July 22-24.

Tracey, N., Clark, J., & Mander, K. (1998). The way forward for unifying dynamic test case generation: The optimisation-based approach. In the *IFIP International Workshop on Dependable Computing and Its Applications*, Johannesbourg, South Africa (pp. 169-180).

Tracey, N., Clark, J., Mander, K., & McDermid, J. (1998). An automated framework for structural test-data generation. In the *13th IEEE Conference on Automated Software Engineering*, Hawaii, USA.

Tracey, N., Clark, J., Mander, K., & McDermid, J. (2000, January). Automated test-data generation for exception conditions. *Software Practice and Experience, 30*(1), 61-79.

Tracey, N., Clark, J., McDermid, J., & Mander, K. (1999). Integrating safety analysis with automatic test-data generation for software safety verification. In the *17th International System Safety Conference* (pp. 128-137).

Tracey, N., Clark, J., McDermid, J., & Mander, K. (2000, January). A search based automated test-data generation framework for high-integrity systems. *Journal of Software Practice and Experience*.

Watkins, A. (1995). A tools for the automatic generation of test data using genetic algorithms. In the *Proceedings of the Software Quality Conference'95*, Dundee, Great Britain (pp. 300-309).

Wegener, J. (2001). Overview of evolutionary testing. *IEEE Seminal Workshop*, Toronto, Canada, May 14.

Wegener, J., Baresel, A., & Sthamer, H. (2001). Evolutionary test environment for automatic structural testing. *Information and Software Technology Special Issue on Software Eng. Using Metaheuristic Innovative Algorithms, 43*(14), 841-854.

Wegener, J., Baresel, A., & Sthamer, H. (2002). Suitability of evolutionary algorithms for evolutionary testing. In the *26th Annual International Computer Software and Applications Conference*, Oxford, Great Britain (pp. 287-289).

Wegener, J., & Bühler, O. (2002). Evaluation of different fitness functions for the evolutionary testing of an automatic parking system. In the *Genetic and Evolutionary Computation Conference*, Seattle, Washington (pp. 1400-1412).

Wegener, J., Grimm, K., Grochtmann, M., Sthamer, H., & Jones, B. (1996). Systematic testing of real-time systems. In the *4th European Conference on Software Testing, Analysis & Review*, Amsterdam, Netherlands.

Wegener, J., & Grochtmann, M. (1998). Verifying timing constraints of real-time systems by means of evolutionary testing. *Real-Time Systems, 15*(3), 275-298.

Wegener, J., Grochtmann, M., & Jones, B. (1997). Testing temporal correctness of real-time systems by means of genetic algorithms. In the *10th International Software Quality Week (QW '97)*, San Francisco, USA, May.

Wegener, J., Pitschinetz, R., & Sthamer, H. (2000). Automated testing of real-time tasks. In the *Proceedings of the 1st International Workshop on Automated Program Analysis, Testing and Verification*, Limerick, Ireland, June.

Wegener, J., Pohlheim, H., & Sthamer, H. (1999). Testing the temporal behaviour of real-time tasks using extended evolutionary algorithms. In the *7th European Conference on Software Testing, Analysis and Review*, Barcelona, Spain.

Wegener, J., Sthamer, H., & Baresel, A. (2001). Application fields for evolutionary testing. *European Software Testing Analysis & Review,* Stockholm, Sweden, November.

Wegener, J., Sthamer, H., Jones, B., & Eyres, D. (1997). Testing real-time systems using genetic algorithms. *Software Quality Journal, 6*(2), 127-135.

Weichselbaum, R. (1998). Software test automation by means of genetic algorithms. In the *6th International Conference on Software Testing, Analysis and Review (EuroSTAR '98),* Munich, Germany.

Xanthakis, S., Ellis, C., Skourlas, C., LeGall, A., & Katsikas, S. (1992). Application of genetic algorithms to software testing. In the *5th International Conference on Software Engineering,* Toulouse, France.

Xie, X., Xu, B., Shi, L., Nie, C., & He, Y. (2005). A dynamic optimization strategy for evolutionary testing. In the *12th ASIA-PACIFIC Software Engineering Conference,* Taipei, Taiwan.

Some Web Resources

Evolutionary Testing:

- University of York (Nigel Tracey, John Clark, etc.)
  http://www.cs.york.ac.uk/testsig/publications
- Reliable Software Technologies/Cigital (Christoph Michael, Gary McGraw, etc.)
  http://www.cigital.com/papers
- DaimlerChrysler (Harmen Sthamer, Andre Baresel, Joachim Wegener, etc.)
  http://www.systematic-testing.com
- Aristotle Research Group (Pargas, R., Harrold, M., and Peck, R)
  http://www.cc.gatech.edu/~harrold/

Introduction to Evolutionary Algorithms by Hartmut Pohlheim

  http://www.geatbx.com/docu/algindex.html

Endnote

*   This work was supported in part by the National Natural Science Foundation of China (60425206, 60373066, 60403016), National Grand Fundamental Research 973 Program of China (2002CB312000), and National Research Foundation for the Doctoral Program of Higher Education of China (20020286004).

Section V:

Areas of Future Work

The last part is composed of four chapters (Chapters XIII-XVI). Though they each focus on a different and challenging software engineering endeavor, they serve as areas of what can be pursued in this emerging research field. Chapter XIII reviews two well-known formal methods, high-level Petri nets and temporal logic, for software system specification and analysis. The chapter opens the opportunity for machine learning methods to be utilised in learning either the property specifications or behavior models at element or composition level in a software architectural design phase. In addition, learning methods can be applied to the formal analysis for element correctness, or composition correctness, or refinement correctness. Chapter XIV pertains to an important step, that is, code generators in a model-driven software engineering process that advocates developing software systems by creating an executable model of the system design first and then transforming the model into a production quality implementation. Since the model can be construed as the domain theory, analytical learning can be used to help with the transformation process. Chapter XV outlines a distributed proactive semantic software engineering environment. The proposed environment incorporates logic rules into a software development process to capture the semantics from various levels of the software life cycle. This environment certainly makes it possible to deploy machine learning methods in the rule generator and in the semantic constraint generator to learn constraint rules and proactive rules. Finally, Chapter XVI depicts a role-based access control model that is augmented with the context constraints for computer security policy. Machine learning methods can be used in deriving context constraints from system or application contextual data.

Chapter XIII

Formal Methods for Specifying and Analyzing Complex Software Systems

Xudong He, Florida International University, USA

Huiqun Yu, East China University of Science and Technology, China

Yi Deng, Florida International University, USA

Abstract

Software has been a major enabling technology for advancing modern society, and is now an indispensable part of daily life. Because of the increased complexity of these software systems, and their critical societal role, more effective software development and analysis technologies are needed. How to develop and ensure the dependability of these complex software systems is a grand challenge. It is well known that a highly dependable complex software system cannot be developed without a rigorous development process and a precise specification and design documentation. Formal methods are one of the most promising technologies for precisely specifying, modeling, and analyzing complex software systems. Although past research experience and practice in computer science have convincingly shown that it is not possible to formally verify program behavior and properties at the program source code level due to its extreme huge size and complexity, recently advances in applying formal methods during software specification and design, especially at software architecture level, have demonstrated significant benefits of using formal methods. In this chapter, we will review several well-known formal methods for software system specification and analysis. We will present recent advances of using these formal methods for specifying, modeling, and analyzing software architectural design.

Introduction

It is wildly agreed that the main obstacle to "help computers help us more" and relegate to these helpful partners even more complex and sensitive tasks is not inadequate speed and unsatisfactory raw computing power in the existing machines, but our limited ability to design and implement complex systems with sufficiently high degree of confidence in their correctness under all circumstances (Clarke, Grumberg, & Peled, 1999). This problem of design validation—ensuring the correctness of the design at the earliest stage possible—is the major challenge in any responsible system development process, and the activities intended for its solution occupy an ever increasing portion of the development cycle cost and time budgets.

Two major approaches to analyze the system quality are *testing* and *verification*. Traditional and widely used quality assurance techniques based on software testing are inadequate to ensure the reliability of complex systems. In addition to the inherent limitation of testing from being able to guarantee system properties, many of today's software systems are designed to adapt in a wide range of environments and evolve over time. Because of this, the range of possible testing scenarios at code level becomes extremely large and potentially uncontrollable.

Formal methods (Harel, 1987; Hoare, 1985; Manna & Pnueli, 1992; Milner, 1989; Murata, 1989) for software specification and *verification* have been viewed as a promising way to address the problems associated with testing. These methods are precise and rigorous and can prevent and detect system defects introduced at the early stages of development, which are often more costly to fix and have more severe consequences. Despite tremendous advances (Clarke & Wing, 1996), however, widely spread application of *formal methods* in practical system development still remains to be seen (Craigen, Gerhart, & Ralston, 1995). A major cause for the problem is that results on *formal methods* are to large extent fragmented. Formal techniques are viewed as difficult and expensive to use because their application is ad hoc, and they are too fine grained to deal with the complexity in practical-sized development. Thus it is necessary to precisely define, measure, and analyze software dependability at a level higher than source code. Recent research (Knight, 2002) has shown that it is especially important to explore technologies how to handle dependability attributes at the *software architecture* level for the following reasons:

- A *software architecture* description presents the highest-level design abstraction of a system (Shaw & Garlan, 1996). As a result, it is relative simple compared to a detailed system design. Thus it is more likely to develop an effective methodology to study dependability attributes.

- As the highest-level design abstraction, a *software architecture* description precedes and logically and structurally influences other system development products. Thus an error in a *software architecture* has a much larger impact than an error introduced at a later development stage. Prevention and detection of errors at software architectural level are thus extremely important. Hence, it is necessary to study and measure dependability attributes before the actual software systems are developed and deployed.

Many studies, especially those done at the Software Engineering Institute at Carnegie Mellon University (Kazman, Klein, & Clements, 2000), have shown that a *software architecture* reveals, influences, or even dictates many system dependability features such as reliability, performance, security, and faulty-tolerance. Therefore, the dependability attributes measured at *software architecture* level can serve as the basis to predict and validate the dependability attributes of the developed and deployed systems.

In this chapter, we will review several well-known *formal methods* for complex software system specification and analysis. We will illustrate these methods and their applications in the *software architecture model* (*SAM*) (He & Deng, 2002; Wang, He, & Deng, 1999), which is a general *software architecture* model for developing and analyzing *software architecture* specifications.

Background

Visualizing the Structures of Software Architectures

Specification is the process of describing a system and its desired properties. Formal specification uses a language that is usually composed of three primary components: (1) a *syntax* that defines the specific notation with which the specification is represented; (2) a *semantics* that helps to define a "universe of objects" (Wing, 1990) that will be used to describe the system; and (3) a set of *relations* that define the rules that indicate which objects properly satisfy the specification.

In *SAM*, a *software architecture* is visualized by a hierarchical set of boxes with ports connected by directed arcs. These boxes are called *compositions*. Each composition may contain other compositions. The bottom-level compositions are either *components* or *connectors*. Various constraints can be specified. This hierarchical model supports compositionality in both *software architecture* design and analysis, and thus facilitates scalability. Figure 1 shows a graphical view of an *SAM software architecture*, in which *connectors* are not emphasized and are only represented by thick arrows. Each *component* or *connector* is defined using a *Petri net*. Thus the internal logical structure of a *component* or *connector* is also visualized through the *Petri net* structure.

Textually, an *SAM software architecture* is defined by a set of compositions $C = \{C_1, C_2, ...,C_k\}$ (each composition corresponds to a design level or the concept of sub-architecture) and a hierarchical mapping h relating compositions. Each composition $C_i = \{Cm_i, Cn_i, Cs_i\}$ consists of a set Cm_i of *components*, a set Cn_i of *connectors*, and a set Cs_i of composition

Figure 1. An SAM architecture model

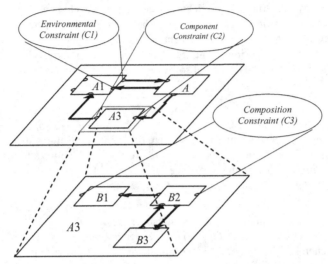

constraints. An element $C_{ij} = (S_{ij}, B_{ij})$, (either a *component* or a *connector*) in a composition C_i has a *property specification* S_{ij} (a *temporal logic* formula) and a *behavior model* B_{ij} (a *Petri net*). Each composition constraint in Cs_i is also defined by a *temporal logic* formula. The interface of a *behavior model* B_{ij} consists of a set of places (called ports) that is the intersection among relevant *components* and *connectors*. Each *property specification* S_{ij} only uses the ports as its atomic propositions/predicates that are true in a given marking if they contain appropriate tokens. A composition constraint is defined as a *property specification*; however it often contains ports belonging to multiple *components* and / or *connectors*. A *component* C_{ij} can be refined into a lower-level composition C_l, which is defined by $h(C_{ij}) = C_l$.

Modeling the Behaviors of Software Architectures

In *SAM*, the behavior of a *component* or a *connector* is explicitly defined using a *Petri net*. The behavior of an overall *software architecture* is implicitly derived by composing all the bottom-level *behavior models* of *components* and *connectors*. *SAM* provides both the modeling power and flexibility through the choice of different *Petri net* models. We have used several *Petri net* models including time *Petri nets* (Wang, He, & Deng, 1999), condition event nets, and predicate transition nets (He & Deng, 2000, 2002) in our previous work. The selection of a particular *Petri net* model is based on the application under consideration. A simple *Petri net* model such as condition event nets is adequate when we only need to deal with simple control flows and data-independent constraints; while a more powerful *Petri net* model such as predicate transition nets is needed to handle both control and data. To study performance related constraints, a more specialized *Petri net* model such as stochastic *Petri nets* is more appropriate and convenient. In the following sections, we give a brief definition of predicate transition nets (*PrT* nets) using the conventions in He (1996). Readers not interested in the technical details may skip this section, and just look at the examples.

The Syntax and Static Semantics of PrT Nets

A *PrT* net is a tuple (*N*, *Spec*, *ins*) where

1. $N = (P, T, F)$ is the net structure, in which

    i.   *P* and *T* are non-empty finite sets satisfying $P \cap T = \varnothing$ (*P* and *T* are the sets of places and transitions of *N* respectively),

    ii. $F \subseteq (P \times T) \cup (T \times P)$ is a flow relation (the arcs of *N*);

2.   *Spec* = (*S*, *OP*, *Eq*) is the underlying specification, and consists of a signature **S** = (*S*, *OP*) and a set *Eq* of **S**-equations. Signature **S** = (*S*, *OP*) includes a set of sorts *S* and a family $OP = (OP_{s_1,...,s_n, s})$ of sorted operations for $s_1, ..., s_n, s \in S$. For each $s \in S$, we use CON_S to denote OP_s (the 0-ary operation of sort *s*), that is, the set of constant symbols of sort *s*. The **S**-equations in *Eq* define the meanings and properties of operations in *OP*. We often simply use familiar operations and their properties without explicitly listing the relevant equations. *Spec* is a meta-language to define the tokens, labels, and constraints of a *PrT* net. Tokens of a *PrT* net are ground terms of the signature S, written $MCON_S$. The set of labels is denoted using $Label_s(X)$ (*X* is the set of sorted variables disjoint with *OP*). Each label can be a multiple set expression of the form $\{k_1 x_1, ..., k_n x_n\}$. Constraints of a *PrT* net are a subset of first order logic formulas (where the domains of quantifiers are finite and any free variable in a constraint appears in the label of some connecting arc of the transition), and thus are essentially propositional logic formulas. The subset of first order logical formulas contains the S-terms of sort *bool* over *X*, denoted as $Term_{OP,bool}(X)$.

3.   *ins* = (φ, *L*, *R*, M_0) is a net inscription that associates a net element in *N* with its denotation in *Spec* :

    i. $\varphi: P \rightarrow \wp(S)$ is the data definition of *N* and associates each place *p* in *P* with a subset of sorts in *S*.

    ii. $L: F \rightarrow Label_s(X)$ is a sort-respecting labeling of *PrT* net. We use the following abbreviation in the following definitions:

$$\overline{L}(x,y) = \begin{cases} L(x,y) & \text{iff } (x,y) \in F \\ \varnothing & \text{otherwise} \end{cases}$$

    iii. $R: T \rightarrow Term_{OP,bool}(X)$ is a well-defined constraining mapping, which associates each transition *t* in *T* with a first order logic formula defined in the underlying algebraic specification. Furthermore, the constraint of a transition defines the meaning of the transition.

    vi. $M_0: P \rightarrow MCON_S$ is a sort-respecting initial marking. The initial marking assigns a multi-set of tokens to each place *p* in *P*.

Dynamic Semantics of PrT Nets

1.   Markings of a *PrT* net *N* are mappings $M: P \rightarrow MCON_S$;

2.   An occurrence mode of N is a substitution $\alpha = \{x_1 \leftarrow c_1, ..., x_n \leftarrow c_n\}$, which instantiates typed label variables. We use $e:\alpha$ to denote the result of instantiating an expression e with α, in which e can be either a label expression or a constraint;

3.   Given a marking M, a transition $t \in T$, and an occurrence mode α, t is α_enabled at M iff the following predicate is true: $\forall p: p \in P.(\overline{L}(p,t):\alpha) \subseteq M(p)) \wedge R(t):\alpha$;

4.   If t is α_enabled at M, t may fire in occurrence mode α. The firing of t with α returns the marking M' defined by $M'(p) = M(p) - \overline{L}(p,t):\alpha \cup (t,p):\alpha$ for $p \in P$. We use $M[t/\alpha>M'$ to denote the firing of t with occurrence α under marking M. As in traditional *Petri nets*, two enabled transitions may fire at the same time as long as they are not in conflict;

5.   For a marking M, the set $[M>$ of markings reachable from M is the smallest set of markings such that $M \in [M>$ and if $M' \in [M>$ and $M'[t/\alpha>M''$ then $M'' \in [M>$, for some $t \in T$ and occurrence mode α (note: concurrent transition firings do not produce additional new reachable markings);

6.   An execution sequence $M_0 T_0 M_1 T_1 ...$ of N is either finite when the last marking is terminal (no more enabled transition in the last marking) or infinite, in which each T_i is an execution step consisting of a set of non-conflict firing transitions;

7.   The behavior of N, denoted by *Comp(N)*, is the set of all execution sequences starting from the initial marking.

The Dining Philosophers problem is a classic multi-process synchronization problem introduced by Dijkstra. The problem consists of k philosophers sitting at a round table who do nothing but think and eat. Between each philosopher, there is a single chopstick. In order to eat, a philosopher must have both chopsticks. A problem can arise if each philosopher grabs the chopstick on the right, then waits for the stick on the left. In this case, a deadlock has occurred. The challenge in the Dining Philosophers problem is to design a protocol so that the philosophers do not deadlock (i.e., the entire set of philosophers does not stop and wait indefinitely), and so that no philosopher starves (i.e., every philosopher eventually gets his/her hands on a pair of chopsticks). The following is an example of the *PrT* net model of the Dining Philosophers problem.

Figure 2. A PrT Net model of the Dining Philosophers problem

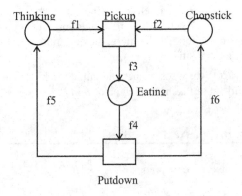

Putdown

There are three places (*Thinking, Chopstick* and *Eating*) and two transitions (*Pickup* and *Putdown*) in the *PrT* net. In the underlying specification *Spec* = (*S, OP, Eq*), *S* includes elementary sorts such as Integer and Boolean, and also sorts PHIL and CHOP derived from Integer. *S* also includes structured sorts such as set and tuple obtained from the Cartesian product of the elementary sorts; *OP* includes standard arithmetic and relational operations on Integer, logical connectives on Boolean, set operations, and selection operation on tuples; and *Eq* includes known properties of these operators.

The net inscription (φ, L, R, M_0) is as follows:

- Sorts of predicates:

  $\varphi(Thinking) = \wp(\text{PHIL})$, $\varphi(Eating) = \wp(\text{PHIL} \times \text{CHOP} \times \text{CHOP})$,

  $\varphi(Chopstick) = \wp(\text{CHOP})$,

  where $\wp$ denotes power set.

- Arc definitions:

  $L(f1) = \{ph\}$, $L(f2) = \{ch1, ch2\}$, $L(f3) = \{<ph, ch1, ch2>\}$,

  $L(f4) = \{<ph, ch1, ch2>\}$, $L(f5) = \{ph\}$, $L(f6) = \{ch1, ch2\}$.

- Constraints of transitions:

  $R(Pickup) = (ph = ch1) \wedge (ch2 = ph \oplus 1)$, $R(Putdown) = $ true.

- The initial marking m_0 is defined as follows:

  $M_0(Thinking) = \{1, 2, ..., k\}$, $M_0(Eating) = \{\ \}$, $M_0(Chopstick) = \{1, 2, ..., k\}$.

Table 1. A possible run of five Dining Philosophers problem

Markings m_i			Transitions n_i	
Thinking	Eating	Chopstick	Fired Transition	Token(s) consumed
{1,2,3,4,5}	{ }	{1,2,3,4,5}	Pickup	ph=1, ch1=1, ch2=2
{2,3,4,5}	{<1,1,2>}	{3,4,5}	Putdown	<ph,ch1,ch2>=<1,1,2>
{1,2,3,4,5}	{ }	{1,2,3,4,5}	Pickup	ph=2, ch1=2, ch2=3
{1,3,4,5}	{<2,2,3>}	{1,4,5}	Pickup	ph=4, ch1=4, ch2=5
{1, 3, 5}	{<2,2,3>, <4,4,5>}	{1}	Putdown	<ph,ch1,ch2>=<2,2,3>
{1, 2, 3, 5}	{<4,4,5>}	{1,2,3}	Putdown	<ph,ch1,ch2>=<4,4,5>
{1,2,3,4,5}	{ }	{1,2,3,4,5}	Pickup	ph=5, ch1=5, ch2=1
{1,2,3,4}	{<5,5,1>}	{2,3,4}	Pickup	ph=3, ch1=3, ch2=4
{1,2,4}	{<5,5,1>, <3,3,4>}	{2}	Putdown	<ph,ch1,ch2>=<3,3,4>
{1,2,3,4}	{<5,5,1>}	{2,3,4}	Putdown	<ph,ch1,ch2>=<5,5,1>
{1,2,3,4,5}	{ }	{1,2,3,4,5}	...	...

This specification allows concurrent executions such as multiple non-conflicting (non-neighboring) philosophers picking up chopsticks simultaneously, and some philosophers picking up chopsticks while others putting down chopsticks. The constraints associated with transitions Pickup and Putdown also ensure that a philosopher can only use two designated chopsticks defined by the implicit adjacent relationships. Table 1 gives the details of a possible run of five dining philosophers PrT net.

Specifying SAM Architecture Properties

In SAM, *software architecture* properties are specified using a *temporal logic*. Depending on the given Petri net models, different *temporal logics* are used. In this section, we provide the essential concepts of a generic first order linear time *temporal logic* to specify the properties of *components* and *connectors*. We follow the approach in Lamport (1994) to define vocabulary and models of our *temporal logic* in terms of PrT nets without giving a specific *temporal logic*.

Values, State Variables, and States

The set of values is the multi-set of tokens $MCON_S$ defined by the *Spec* of a given PrT net N. Multi-sets can be viewed as partial functions. For example, multi-set $\{3a, 2b\}$ can be represented as $\{a \mapsto 3, b \mapsto 2\}$.

The set of state variables is the set P of places of N, which change their meanings during the executions of N. The arity of a place p is determined by its sort $\varphi\ (p)$ in the net inscription.

The set of states **St** is the set of all reachable markings $[M_0>$ of N. A marking is a mapping from the set of state variables into the set of values. We use $M[|x|]$ to denote the value of x under state (marking) M.

Since state variables take partial functions as values, they are flexible function symbols. We can access a particular component value of a state variable. However there is a problem associated with partial functions, that is, many values are undefined. This problem can easily be solved by extending state variables into total functions in the following way: for any n-ary state variable p, any tuple $c \in MCON_S{}^n$ and any state M, if $p(c)$ is undefined under M, then let $M[|\, p(c)\, |] = 0$. This extension is consistent with the semantics of PrT nets, that is, there is no token c in place p under marking M. Furthermore, we can consider the meaning $[|p(c)|]$ of the function application $p(c)$ as a mapping from states to **Nat** using a postfix notation for function application $M[|p(c)\, |]$.

Rigid Variables, Rigid Function, and Predicate Symbols

Rigid variables are individual variables that do not change their meanings during the executions of N. All rigid variables occurring in our *temporal logic* formulas are bound (quantified), and they are the only variables that can be quantified. Rigid variables are variables appearing in the label expressions and constraints of N. Rigid function and predicate symbols do not change their meanings during the executions of N. The set of rigid function and predicate symbols is defined in the *Spec* of N.

State Functions, Predicates, and Transitions

A *state function* is an expression built from values, state variables, rigid function, and predicate symbols. For example $[|p(c) + 1|]$ is a state function where c and 1 are values, p is a state variable, $+$ is a rigid function symbol. Since the meanings of rigid symbols are not affected by any state, thus for any given state M, $M[|p(c) + 1|] = M[|p(c)|] + 1$.

A *predicate* is a boolean-valued state function. A predicate p is said to be satisfied by a state M iff $M[|p|]$ is true.

A *transition* is a particular kind of predicates that contain primed state variables, for example, $[|p'(c) = p(c) + 1|]$. A transition relates two states (an old state and a new state), where the unprimed state variables refer to the old state and the primed state variables refer to the new state. Therefore, the meaning of a transition is a relation between states. The term transition used here is a *temporal logic* entity. Although it reflects the nature of a transition in a PrT net N, it is not a transition in N. For example, given a pair of states M and M': $M[|p'(c) = p(c) + 1|]M'$ is defined by $M'[|p'(c)|] = M[|p(c)|] + 1$. Given a transition t, a pair of states M and M' is called a "transition step" iff $M[|t|]M'$ equals true. We can easily generalize any predicate p without primed state variables into a relation between states by replacing all unprimed state variables with their primed versions such that $M[|p'|]M'$ equals $M'[|p|]$ for any states M and M'.

Temporal Formulas

Temporal formulas are built from elementary formulas (predicates and transitions) using logical connectives $\neg$ and $\wedge$ (and derived logical connectives $\vee$, $\Rightarrow$, and $\Leftrightarrow$), universal quantifier $\forall$ and derived existential quantifier $\exists$, and temporal operators always $\Box$, sometimes $\Diamond$, and until U.

The semantics of *temporal logic* is defined on behaviors (infinite sequences of states). The behaviors are obtained from the execution sequences of PrT nets where the last marking of a finite execution sequence is repeated infinitely many times at the end of the execution sequence. For example, for an execution sequence $M_0,...,M_n$, the following behavior $\sigma = <<M_0,...,M_n,M_n,... >>$ is obtained. We denote the set of all possible behaviors obtained from a given PrT net as $\mathbf{St}^\infty$.

Let u and v be two arbitrary temporal formulas, p be an n-ary predicate, t be a transition, $x, x_1,...,x_n$ be rigid variables, $\sigma = <<M_0, M_1, ... >>$ be a behavior, and $\sigma^k = <<M_k, M_{k+1}, ... >>$ be a k step shifted behavior sequence; we define the semantics of temporal formulas recursively as follows:

1. $\sigma [|p(x_1,...,x_n)|]$ $\equiv$ $M_0[| p(x_1,...,x_n)|]$

2. $\sigma [|t|]$ $\equiv$ $M_0[| t|]M_1$

3. $\sigma[|\neg u|]$ $\equiv$ $\neg\,\sigma[|u|]$

4. $\sigma[|u \wedge v|]$ $\equiv$ $\sigma[|u|] \wedge \sigma[|v|]$

5. $\sigma[|\forall x.\, u|]$ $\equiv$ $\forall x. \sigma[|u|]$

6. $\sigma[|\Box\, u|]$ $\equiv$ $\forall n \in \mathbf{Nat}.\ \sigma^n[|u|]$

7. $\sigma[|uUv|]$ $\equiv$ $\exists\, k.\sigma^k[|v|] \wedge \forall\, 0 \le n \le k.\sigma^n[|u|]$

A temporal formula u is said to be *satisfiable*, denoted as $\sigma \models u$, iff there is an execution σ such that $\sigma[|u|]$ is true, i.e. $\sigma \models u \Leftrightarrow \exists\, \sigma \in \mathbf{St}^\infty.\ \sigma[|u|]$. u is *valid* with regard to N, denoted as $N \models u$, iff it is satisfied by all possible behaviors $\mathbf{St}^\infty$ from N: $N \models u \Leftrightarrow \forall \sigma \in \mathbf{St}^\infty.\ \sigma[|u|]$.

Defining System Properties in Temporal Logic

Specifying architecture properties in *SAM* becomes defining *PrT* net properties using *temporal logic*. Canonical forms for a variety of system properties such as safety, guarantee, obligation, response, persistence, and reactivity are given in Manna and Pnueli (1992). For example, the following *temporal logic* formulas specify a safety property and a liveness property of the *PrT* net in Figure 2, respectively:

*   Mutual exclusion:

    $\forall ph \in \{1, ..., k\}\Box\neg(< ph, \_, \_ >\in Eating \wedge\, < ph \oplus 1, \_, \_ >\in Eating)$,

    which defines that no adjacent philosophers can eat at the same time.

*   Starvation freedom: $\forall ph \in \{1, ..., k\}\Diamond(< ph, \_, \_ >\in Eating)$,

    which states that every philosopher will eventually get a chance to eat.

Formal Methods for Designing Software Architectures

There are two distinct levels of *software architecture* specification development in *SAM*: element level and composition level. The element level specification deals with the specification of a single *component* or *connector*, and the composition level specification concerns how to combine (horizontal) specifications at the same abstraction level together and how to relate (vertical) specifications at different abstraction levels.

Developing Element Level Specifications

In *SAM*, each element (either a *component* or a *connector*) is specified by a tuple $<S, B>$. S is a *property specification*, written in *temporal logic*, that specifies the required properties of the element, and B is a *behavior model*, defined by a *PrT* net, that defines the behavior of the element. S and B can be viewed as the specification and the implementation respectively as in many other *software architecture* models such as Wright (Allen & Garlan, 1997). Therefore to develop the specification of an element is essentially to write S and B.

Although many existing techniques for writing *temporal logic* specifications (Lamport, 1994; Manna & Pnueli, 1992) and for developing *Petri nets* (He & Yang, 1992; Jensen, 1992; Reisig, 1992) may be directly used here. There are several unique features about <S, B>. First, S and B are related and constrain each other. Thus we have to develop either S or B with respect to a possibly existing B or S. Depending on our understanding of a given system; we can either develop S or B first. Second, the predicate symbols used in S are exterior (either input or out) ports of B. Third, S should in general be weaker than B, that is, B may satisfy more properties than S. Thus the view of implementation as implication is valid here. With these unique features in mind, we offer the following heuristics for developing S and B:

Heuristic 1: How to Write S

To define an element constraint, we can either directly formulate the given user requirements or carry out a cause effect analysis by viewing input ports as causes and output ports as effects. Canonical forms (Manna & Pnueli, 1992) for a variety of properties such as Safety, Guarantee, Obligation, Response, Persistence, and Reactivity are used as guidelines to define property specifications.

A simple example of applying Heuristic 1 is as follows. Let us consider a simple automated library system that supports typical transaction types such as checkout and return a book. A transaction is initiated with a user request that contains user identification, a book title, and a transaction type (checkout/return). The transaction is processed by updating the user record and the book record, and is finished by sending the user a message—either successful or a failure reason. One desirable property of an automated library system is that each request must be proposed. This property is a type of response property (Manna & Pnueli, 1992), and thus can be defined as $\forall(req).(\Box(\text{Request}(req) \Rightarrow \Diamond \text{Response}(msg)))$, where *req* and *msg* stand for a request and message (Success or Failure) respectively, and Request and Response are predicate symbols, and must correspond to an input port and an output port respectively.

Heuristic 2: How to Develop B

We follow the general procedure proposed in He and Yang (1992) to develop B.

Step 1: Use all the input and output ports as places of B.

Step 2: Identify a list of events directly from the given user requirements or through Use Case analysis (Booch, Rumbaugh, & Jacobson, 1999).

Step 3: Represent each event with a simple PrT net.

Step 4: Merge all the PrT nets together through shared places to obtain B.

Figure 3. (a) A PrT model of checkout; (b) A PrT model of return; (c) A connected PrT model; (d) A PrT model of checkout

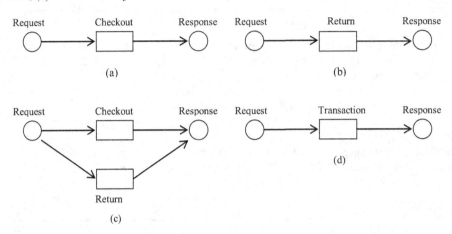

Step 5: Apply the transformation techniques (He & Lee, 1991) to make B more structured and / or meaningful.

Again, we use this simple library system as an example. We only provide a partial *behavior model* without the complete net inscription to illustrate the application of Heuristic 2. A more complete example of a *PrT* net specification of a library system can be found in He and Yang (1992). Since we developed a *property specification* first in this case and we identified an input port Request and an output port Response, we use them as places in the *behavior model B* according to Step 1. We can easily identify two distinct types of events: checkout and return. According to Step 3, we come up with the following two *PrT* nets Figures 3a and b, each of which models an event type. Figure 3c is obtained by merging shared places according Step 4, and Figure 3d is obtained by restructuring Figure 3c through combining Checkout and Return into a generic transaction type.

Developing Composition Level Specifications

SAM supports both top-down and bottom-up system development approaches. The top-down approach is used to develop a *software architecture* specification by decomposing a system specification into specifications of *components* and *connectors* and by refining a higher level *component* into a set of related sub-*components* and *connectors* at a lower level. The bottom-up approach is used to develop a *software architecture* specification by composing existing specifications of *components* and *connectors* and by abstracting a set of related *components* and *connectors* into a higher level *component*. Thus the top-down approach can be viewed as the inverse process of the bottom-up approach. Often both the top-down approach and the bottom-up approach have to be used together to develop a *software architecture* specification.

Heuristic 3: How to Refine an Element Specification <S, B>

Step 1: Refining B:

> *A behavior model B may be refined in several ways, for example, structure driven refinement, in which several sub-components and their connectors are identified, or functionality driven refinement, in which several functional units can be identified. Although, we do not exactly know what refinement approaches are effective in general. One thing is for sure, that is, the input and output ports of the element must be maintained at a lower level. Petri net specific heuristics (He & Lee, 1991; He & Yang, 1992) may be used to maintain the validity of resulting lower level B'. If only behavior-preserving transformations are used to obtain B' from B, we can assure the correctness of <S, B'> based on the correctness of <S, B>; otherwise new analysis is needed to ensure the satisfiability of S (He, 1998).*

Step 2: Refining S:

> *Refining S into S' in general indicates the change of requirements (a special case is when S is logically equivalent to S'), and thus results in the change of B. Once S' is known, the new B' can be developed using the approach for developing element level specification. Not any S' can be taken as a refinement of S. We require that S' maintain S, which can be elegantly expressed as S' ⇒ S (Abadi & Lamport, 1991). Simple heuristics such as strengthening S always result in a valid refinement S'.*

As an example, Figure 4 shows a possible refinement of transaction into two possible scenarios in the dotted box, one is for valid request and the other for invalid request. A corresponding refinement of the *property specification* is

$$\forall(req).(\Box(\text{Request}(req) \wedge req \in \text{Valid} \Rightarrow \Diamond \text{Response}(\boldsymbol{S}))) \wedge$$
$$\forall(req).(\Box(\text{Request}(req) \wedge req \notin \text{Valid} \Rightarrow \Diamond \text{Response}(\boldsymbol{F})))$$

Figure 4. A refined PrT model of transactions

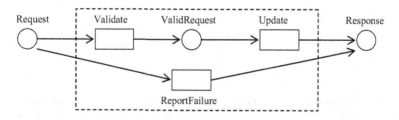

where S and F stand for success and failure respectively. This refinement implies the original *property specification* and is thus a correct refinement according to Heuristic 3.

Heuristic 4: How to Compose Two Element Specifications $<S_1, B_1>$ and $<S_2, B_2>$

In SAM, only a pair of related component and connector can be composed meaningfully.
Step 1: Compose B_1 and B_2 by merging identical ports.
Step 2: Compose S_1 and S_2 by conjoining $S_1 \wedge S_2$.

The soundness of viewing specification composition as logical conjunction has been shown by several researchers (Abadi & Lamport, 1993; Zave & Jackson, 1993).

If we view the two transaction types, Checkout and Return, in the preceding library example as two separate *components*, then Figure 3c illustrates the application of Heuristic 4.

Specify Element Instances

An element specification $<S, B>$ obtained earlier is generic when the initial marking in B is ignored. In *PrT* net, instances sharing the same net structure are distinguished through token identifications. Thus to obtain concrete elements, we only need to provide specific initial marking and generalize transition constraints to differentiate tokens with unique identifications. In general, there is no need to change the *property specification S*. For example, let B_1, B_2, and B_3 be three *PrT* nets with the same net structure and net inscription except the initial markings; then $<S, B_1>$, $<S, B_2>$, and $<S, B_3>$ are three element specifications. The above view shows the expressive power of *PrT* nets and first order *temporal logic* over that of low-level *Petri nets* and propositional *temporal logic*.

Formal Software Architecture Analysis

Formal Analysis Techniques

A *SAM* architecture description is well-defined if the ports of a *component* are preserved (contained) in the set of exterior ports of its refinement and the proposition symbols used in a *property specification* are ports of the relevant *behavior model*(s). The correctness of a *SAM* architecture description is defined by the following criteria:

1. **Element (*Component/Connector*) Correctness:** The *property specification* S_{ij} holds in the corresponding *behavior model* B_{ij}, that is, $B_{ij} \models S_{ij}$. Note we use B_{ij} here to denote the set of behaviors or execution sequences defined by B_{ij}.

2. **Composition Correctness:** The conjunction of all constraints in Cs_i of C_i is implied by the conjunction of all the *property specifications* S_{ij} of C_{ij}, i.e. $\wedge\, S_{ij} \vdash \wedge\, Cs_i$. An alternative weaker but acceptable criterion is that the conjunction of all constraints in Cs_i holds in the integrated *behavior model* B_i of composition C_i; i.e. $B_i \models \wedge\, Cs_i$.

3. **Refinement Correctness:** The *property specification* S_{ij} of a *component* C_{ij} must be implied by the composition constraints Cs_l of its refinement C_l with $C_l = h(C_{ij})$, that is, $\wedge\, Cs_l \vdash S_{ij}$. An alternative weaker but acceptable criterion is that S_{ij} holds in the integrated lower level *behavior model* B_l of C_l, that is, $B_l \models S_{ij}$.

The refinement correctness is equivalent to the composition correctness when the *property specification* S_{ij} is inherited without change as the composition constraint Cs_l of its refinement $C_l = h(C_{ij})$. This correctness criteria are the *verification* requirements of a *SAM* architecture description.

To ensure the correctness of a *software architecture* specification in *SAM*, we have to show that all the constraints are satisfied by the corresponding *behavior models*. The *verification* of all three correctness criteria given can be done by demonstrating that a *property specification* S holds in a *behavior model* B and, that is, $B \models S$. The structure of *SAM* architecture specifications and the underlying *formal methods* of *SAM* nicely support an incremental formal analysis methodology such that the *verification* of above correctness criteria can be done hierarchically (vertically) and compositionally (horizontally).

Two well-established approaches to *verification* are *model checking* and theorem proving.

- *Model checking* is a technique that relies on building a finite model of a system and checking that a desired property holds in that model. Roughly speaking, the check is performed as an exhaustive state space search that is guaranteed to terminate since the model is finite. The technical challenge in *model checking* is in devising algorithms and data structures that allow us to handle large search spaces. *Model checking* has been used primarily in hardware and protocol *verification* (Clarke & Kurshan, 1996); the current trend is to apply this technique to analyzing specifications of software systems.

- *Theorem proving* is a technique by which both the system and its desired properties are expressed as formulas in some mathematical logic. This logic is given by a *formal system*, which defines a set of axioms and a set of inference rules. Theorem proving is the process of finding a proof of a property from the axioms of the system. Steps in the proof appeal to the axioms and rules, and possibly derived definitions and intermediate lemmas. Although proofs can be constructed by hand, here we focus only on machine-assisted theorem proving. Theorem provers are increasingly being used today in the mechanical *verification* of safety-critical properties of hardware and software designs.

Element Level Analysis

For each $<S_{ij}, B_{ij}>$ in composition C_i, we need to show that B_{ij} satisfies S_{ij}, that is, $B_{ij} \models S_{ij}$. Both *model checking* and theorem proving techniques are applicable to element level analysis.

In the following, we briefly introduce *model checking* technique by *reachability tree* (Murata, 1989), and theorem proving technique by *temporal logic* (He, 1995, 2001).

Model Checking

A *reachability tree* is an unfolding of a *PrT* net, which explicitly enumerates all possible markings or states that the *behavior model* B_{ij} generates. The nodes of a *reachability tree* are reachable markings and directed edges represent feasible transitions (Murata, 1989). The main advantage of *reachability tree* technique is that the tree can be automatically generated. Once the tree is generated, different system properties can be analyzed. The main problem is space explosion when a *PrT* net has too many reachable states or even infinite reachable states. One possible way to deal with this problem is to truncate the tree whenever a marking is covered by a new marking and this results in a variant of *reachability tree*s called coverability trees. In this case, information loss is unavoidable. Thus this technique may not work in some cases. The following heuristic provides some guidelines to use the *reachability tree* analysis technique.

The basic idea of *model checking* technique for element level analysis is: (1) generating a *reachability tree* from B_{ij}; and (2) evaluating S_{ij} using the generated reachability or coverability tree. It should be noted that when a formula contains an always operator □, the formula needs to be evaluated in all nodes of the tree before a conclusion can be made.

As an example, we use the simple library system given in Figure 4 with the assumption of one valid token *req1* and one invalid token *req2* in place Request. When transition Update receives a valid request, it updates the user and book records, and generates a response **S** denoting success. When transition ReportFailure receives an invalid request, it produces a failure message **F**. The resulting *reachability tree* of Step (1) is shown in Figure 5.

Based on Step (2), it is easy to see that the following *property specification*

$$\forall (req).(\square(\text{Request}(req) \wedge req \in \text{Valid} \Rightarrow \Diamond \text{Response}(S)))$$

Figure 5. The reachability tree of Figure 4

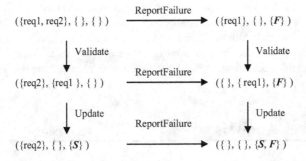

is satisfied in the *reachability tree* by all three possible paths: Validate—Update, Report-Failure—Validate—Update, and Validate—ReportFailure—Update. Similarly, we can evaluate the following *property specification*: $\forall(req).(\Box(\text{Request}(req) \wedge req \notin \text{Valid} \Rightarrow \Diamond\text{Response}(F)))$.

Theorem Proving

The basic idea is to axiomatize B_{ij} (He & Ding, 1992; He & Lee, 1990) and then use the obtained axiom system to prove S_{ij}, that is, Axiom(B_{ij}) $\vdash S_{ij}$. The axiom system consists of general system independent axioms and inference rules and system dependent axioms and inference rules (Manna & Pnueli, 1983). Each transition in B_{ij} generates a system dependent *temporal logic* rule that captures the causal relationships between the input places and output places of the transition. The canonical form of system dependent inference rules has the form: *fired*(t/M) $\Rightarrow$ *enabled*(t/M), where t is a transition, M is a given marking. *Fired* and *Enabled* are two predicates representing the post-condition and precondition of t under M respectively. The advantage of this technique is that a syntactic approach rather than a semantic approach is used in *verification*. Since no explicit representation of states is needed, there is no space explosion problem as in the *reachability tree* technique. The main problems are that the technique is often difficult to automate and its application requires substantial knowledge of first order *temporal logic* and general knowledge of theorem proof.

To demonstrate the application of this heuristic, we axiomatize the net structure in Figure 4, and the resulting system dependent inference rules after Step 1 are:

1. $\neg\ M[|\text{ValidRequest}(x)|]\ \wedge\ M'[|\text{ValidRequest}(x)|]\ \Rightarrow\ M[|\text{Request}(x)|]\ \wedge$
    $M[|R(\text{Validate})|]$

2. $\neg M[|\text{Response}(S)|] \wedge M'[|\text{Response}(S)|] \Rightarrow M[|\text{ValidRequest}(x)|] \wedge M[|R(\text{Update})|]$

3. $\neg\ M[|\text{Response}(F)|]\ \wedge\ M'[|\text{Response}(F)|]\ \Rightarrow\ M[|\text{Request}(x)|]\ \wedge$
    $M[|R(\text{ReportFailure})|]$

In these inference rules, M and M' stand for a given marking and its successor marking, respectively. $R(t)$ is the constraint associated with transition t. To prove *property specification*

$$\forall(req).(\Box(\text{Request}(req) \wedge req \in \text{Valid} \Rightarrow \Diamond\text{Response}(S)))$$

We instantiate $\Diamond$ to a marking M' and apply rule (2) to obtain $M[|\text{ValidRequest}(x)|]$, and we apply rule (1) to obtain $M[|\text{Request}(x)|]$. With some simple logical manipulations, we can easily deduce the required property.

Composition Analysis

We need to show that the connected *behavior model* B_i (again a *PrT* net) of composition C_i obtained from all the individual *behavior models* B_{ij} ($j = 1,...,k$) of *components* and *connectors* satisfies all the constraints $\bigwedge_{c \in Cs_i} c$ in Cs_i, that is, $B_i \models \bigwedge_{c \in Cs_i} c$. Due to the *SAM* framework, the analysis techniques at element level can be directly applied here. This global approach works in general, but may not be efficient.

An ideal approach is to carry out the composition level analysis compositionally. In this approach, we first analyze *components* and *connectors* individually, that is, $B_{ij} \models S_{ij}$ for all *components* and *connectors* in a composition C_i, and then synthesize the properties, that is, $\wedge S_{ij} \vdash \bigwedge_{c \in Cs_i} c$. Despite some existing results on compositional *verification* techniques in *temporal logic* (Abadi & Lamport, 1993) and *Petri nets* (Juan, Tsai, & Murata, 1998), their general use and application to *SAM* are not ready yet.

The following is a modest yet effective incremental analysis approach.

Step 1: Identify partial order relationships among the *components* and *connectors* based on their causal relationships.

Step 2: Compose and analyze the *components* and *connectors* in a partial order incrementally, starting from the least element (most independent).

Step 3: Compose and analyze mutually dependent *components* and *connectors* together.

Step 4: Once we have shown that the initial condition or marking used to prove every individual element can be ensured by the composed *behavior model*, then we can conclude that all the *property specifications* hold simultaneously.

To illustrate the ideas of this approach, let us view the refined *PrT* model of transactions in Figure 4 as a composition, which consists of three trivial *components* Request, ValidRequest, and Response, and three trivial *connectors* Validate, Update, and ReportFailure. Based on the *PrT* net structure, we can identify the following incremental analysis order:

1.   (Request, Validate, ValidateRequest);
2.   (ValidateRequest, Update, Response);
3.   (Request, Validate, ValidateRequest, Update, Response);
4.   (Request, ReportFailure, Response).

where #4 is independent of the first three analyses.

To further improve the effectiveness of this approach, we are working on some Petri net reduction techniques such that the *behavior models* used in incremental analysis are simplified versions of the original *behavior models*.

Refinement Analysis

For each *component* $C_{ij} = <S_{ij}, B_{ij}>$ with $h(C_{ij}) = C_l$, we need to show that either the connected *behavior model* B_l of composition C_l satisfies S_{ij}, that is, $B_l \models S_{ij}$ or alternatively $\wedge$ $Cs_l \vdash S_{ij}$. Three techniques discussed in element analysis can be used to show $B_l \models S_{ij}$. Formal temporal deduction technique (He & Ding, 1992, He, 1995) can be used to prove $\wedge Cs_l \vdash S_{ij}$.

As an example, if we view Figure 4 as a refinement of Figure 3d. We can easily prove the following to assure the correctness of the refinement:

$$\forall(req).(\square(\text{Request}(req) \wedge req \in \text{Valid} \Rightarrow \Diamond\text{Response}(S))) \wedge \forall(req).(\square(\text{Request}(req) \wedge req$$
$$\notin \text{Valid} \Rightarrow \Diamond\text{Response}(F))) \vdash \forall(req).(\square(\text{Request}(req) \Rightarrow \Diamond\text{Response}(msg))).$$

Studying Dependability Attributes Using SAM

We have studied a variety of functional properties and several non-functional dependability attributes at *software architecture* level using *SAM* (He & Deng, 2002; Wang, He, & Deng, 1999). We have applied *SAM* to specify and analyze schedulability (Xu, He, & Deng, 2002), performance including end-to-end latency (Shi & He, 2003a; Wang & Deng, 1999; Yu, He, Gao, & Deng, 2002), security (Deng, Wang, Beznosov, & Tsai, 2003; He & Deng, 2002), fault-tolerance (Shi & He, 2002), reliability (Shi & He, 2003a, 2003b), and many other functional behavior properties such as deadlock and response (He & Deng, 2002; He, Ding, & Deng, 2002; He, Yu, Shi, Ding, & Deng, 2004; Shi & He, 2002).

Since several Petri net models and *temporal logics* as well as a variety of formal analysis techniques were used to specify and verify these system architectures and dependability attributes. Here we just briefly mentioned our approach without providing technical details.

- End-to-End Latency

  In Wang et al. (1999), time *Petri nets* (Berthomieu & Diaz, 1991) and real-time computational tree logic (*CTL*) (Emerson, Mok, Sistla, & Srinivasian, 1992) were used to specify the *software architecture* of a control and command system. End-to-end latency was then verified by generating a *reachability tree* from the time Petri net model and evaluating timing properties specified in real-time *CTL* formulas. We also used stochastic *Petri nets* to study latency (Shi & He, 2003a).

- Schedulability

  In Yu et al (2002), predicate transition nets (*PrT* nets) (Murata, 1989) and first-order linear-time *temporal logic* (*FOLTTL*) (Manna & Pnueli, 1992) were used to specify the *software architecture* of a simplified multi-media system. Timing requirements were dealt with by adding a time stamp attribute in tokens and by adding lower and upper bounds in transition constraints in predicate transition nets. Timing properties were specified in first-order *temporal logic* formulas by an additional clock variable. *Verification* of schedulability was again done using the theorem prover *STeP*.

- Security

  In He and Deng (2002), *PrT* nets and *FOLTTL* were used to specify the *software architecture* of an access authorization subsystem. Several system *components* were explicitly modeled to handle security check process. Security policies were defined as part of transition constraints within these security-checking *components*. Security related properties were specified using *FOLTTL*. *Verification* of security properties was done using *reachability tree* technique at the *component* level and using theorem proving at the composition level.

- Fault-Tolerance

  In Shi and He (2002), *PrT* nets and *FOLTTL* were used to specify the *software architecture* a communication protocol. To handle possible communication faults such as loss of information, additional system timer *components* were introduced to detect such losses. Fault-related properties were specified using *FOLTTL* and were verified using the symbolic model checker *SMV* (McMillan, 1993).

- Reliability

  In Shi and He (2003a, 2003b), *PrT* nets were used to model a *software architecture*. *PrT* nets were then unfolded into stochastic reward nets (SRNs). Probabilistic real-time Computation Tree Logic (*PCTL*) (Hansson & Johnson, 1994) was used to specify system reliability. The probability of system failure was then calculated using tool SPNP (Trivedi, 1999) in Shi and He (2003a) and tool SMART (Ciardo, Jones, Marmorstein, Miner, & Siminiceanu, 2002) in Shi and He (2003b).

Related Work

Many *formal methods* have been developed and applied to specifying and verifying complex software systems. For example, Z (Spivey, 1992) was used to specify *software architecture* (Abowd, Allen, & Garlan, 1995), CSP (Hoare, 1985) was used as the foundation of Wright (Allen & Garlan, 1997), and CHAM (Inverardi, & Wolf, 1995) (an operational formalism) was proposed to specify *software architecture*s. Rapide (Luckham, Kenney, Augustin et al., 1995) used a multiple language approach in specifying *software architecture*s, while some language has a well-defined formal foundation (for example the specification language uses a combination of algebraic and pattern constraints), others offer constructs similar to those in a typical high-level programming language.

Two complementary *formal methods*, *Petri nets* and *temporal logic*, are used in *SAM* to define *behavior model*s and *property specification*s respectively. The selection of these *formal methods* is based on the following reasons. Well-known model-oriented *formal methods* include *Petri nets* and finite state machines. Finite state machines are simple, but have difficulty to deal with concurrent systems especially distributed systems. *Petri nets* are well suited for modeling concurrent and distributed systems, which characterize the majority of embedded systems being used by NASA and other government agencies. However, *Petri nets* are often misunderstood and even prejudiced in the U.S. Many researchers' knowledge of *Petri nets* is limited to the 1st generation low-level *Petri nets* used primarily for modeling control flows. *Petri nets* have evolved tremendously in the past 20 years, from the 2nd generation high-level *Petri nets* in 1980s (Jensen & Rozenberg, 1991) and the 3rd generation hierarchical and modular *Petri nets* in early 1990s (He, 1996; He & Lee, 1991; Jensen, 1992) to the 4th generation object-oriented *Petri nets* in late 1990s (Agha, De Cindio, & Rozenberg, 2001). More importantly, *Petri nets* have been extended in many different ways to study system performance, reliability, and schedulability (Haas, 2002; Marsan, Balbo, Conte, Donatelli, & Franceschinis, 1994; Wang, 1998), which are the central attributes of complex dependable systems. There are vast existing research results on *Petri nets* (over 10,000 publications). Despite many different types of *temporal logic*, for example, propositional vs. first-order, linear time vs. branch time, timed vs. un-timed, probabilistic vs. non-probabilistic, it is widely accepted that *temporal logic* in general is an excellent property-oriented formal method for specifying behavioral properties of concurrent systems. We are familiar with and have extensive experience in using Manna and Pnueli's (1992, 1995) linear-time first order *temporal logic*; Lamport's (1994) linear-time first order *temporal logic* (*Temporal Logic* of Actions); and Clarke and Emerson's (1981) branch time propositional logic *CTL,* and its extension *CTL** (Clarke, Emerson, & Sistla, 1986); and various timed versions of the above *temporal logic*s (Abadi & Lamport, 1994; Alur & Henzinger, 1992; Emerson et al., 1992). One major problem of using a dual-formalism is how to integrate two *formal methods* in a consistent and meaningful way, our own research results (He, 1992; He & Ding, 1992; He & Lee, 1990) and other's work (Mandrioli, Morzenti, Pezze, Pietro, & Silva, 1996) have provided a satisfactory solution to integrate *Petri nets* and *temporal logic* in *SAM.*

Almost all ADLs support the specification and analysis of major system functional properties such as safety and liveness properties (Medvidovic & Taylor, 2000). Several ADLs also provide capabilities to represent some dependability attributes. MetaH (Binns, Engelhart, Jackson, & Vestal, 1996) supported the description of non-functional properties such as real-time schedulability, reliability, and security in *components* but not in *connectors*. Unicon (Shaw, Deline, Klein et al., 1995) supported the definition of real-time schedulability in both *components* and *connectors*. Rapide (Luckham et al., 1995) supported the modeling of time constraints in architectural configurations. The analysis of non-functional properties in these ADLs was not performed at the architecture specification level instead of during the simulation and implementation. As pointed out in Stavridou and Riemenschneider (1998), "ADLs need to be extended with appropriate linguistic support for expressing dependability constraints. They also need to be furnished with an appropriate semantics, to enable formal *verification* of architectural properties."

Discussion and Conclusion

Commercial pressure to produce higher quality software is always increasing. *Formal methods* have already demonstrated success in specifying commercial and safety-critical software, and in verifying protocol standards and hardware designs. In this chapter, we have provided a well-defined integration of two well-known *formal methods* predicate transition nets and first order linear-time *temporal logic* as the foundation for writing *software architecture* specifications in *SAM*. This dual *formal methods* approach supports both behavioral modeling and property analysis of *software architectures*. Unlike many other architecture description language research efforts that primarily focus on the representation issues of *software architecture*s, we have further presented a unified framework with a set of heuristics to develop and analyze *software architecture* specifications in *SAM*. The heuristics are supported by well-developed existing techniques and methods with potential software tool assistance. We have demonstrated the applications of several of the heuristics with regard to the development and analysis in a non-trivial example. Our contributions are not limited to *software architecture* research, but also shed some light on how mature *formal methods* can be effectively used in real-world software development. While it is true that every formal method has its limits and weaknesses, it is important to rely on its strengths while avoiding and minimizing its weaknesses in practical applications. This philosophy has been used both in designing our dual *formal methods* foundation of *SAM* as well as our framework consisting of a variety of development and analysis techniques.

From our own experience in teaching and using formal methods, students can learn system modeling using high-level *Petri nets* and specification using first order *temporal logic* in a one semester course. The first author has taught these materials in several software engineering related courses in the past 15 years, and has found that the majority students can master the methods without major problems. Therefore, we are quite convinced that the *SAM* approach is practical and effective. Furthermore, we have applied *SAM* to model and analyze the *software architecture*s of several systems, including a control and command system (Wang et al., 1999), a flexible manufacturing system (Wang & Deng, 1999), popular architectural *connector*s (He & Deng, 2000), the alternating bit communication protocol, and a resource access decision system (He & Deng, 2002). More recently, we are using *SAM* to model and analyze a middleware architecture for delivering a variety of multimedia applications based on various internet communication protocols. We have developed methods to translate Petri net models into state transition systems based on several popular model checkers including *SMV* (McMillan, 1993), *STeP* (Bjorner et al., 1995), and *SPIN* (Holzmann, 2003) for property analysis. These translation algorithms are linear to the size of given Petri net models and translations can be automated. The complexity of analysis is largely dependent on given properties. In our own experience, architecture level properties are relative simple and can be effectively checked using these model checkers.

We are carrying out more case studies to explore the effectiveness of combining different development and analysis techniques and to determine the practical limitations of each individual technique. To support this whole *SAM* framework, we are adding software *component*s to our existing *SAM* environment, which consists of a graphical editor for building behavioral models, a textual editor for defining *property specification*s, a simulator to execute behavioral models, and a translator to covert a *behavior model* in *Petri nets* into a Promela program in model checker *SPIN* for property analysis.

Acknowledgements

This research was supported in part by the National Science Foundation of the USA under grant HRD-0317692, and by the National Aeronautics and Space Administration of the USA under grant NAG2-1440. Huiqun Yu's work was also partially supported by the NSF of China under grant No. 60473055.

References

Abadi, M., & Lamport, L. (1991). The existence of refinement mappings. *Theoretical Computer Science, 82*, 253-284.

Abadi, M., & Lamport, L. (1993). Composing specification. *ACM Trans. on Programming Languages and Systems, 15*, 73-130.

Abadi, M., & Lamport, L. (1994). An old-fashioned recipe for real time. *ACM Transactions on Programming Languages and Systems, 16*(5), 1543-1571.

Abowd, G., Allen, R., & Garlan, D. (1995). Formalizing style to understand descriptions of software architecture. *ACM Transaction on Software Engineering and Methodology, 4*(4), 319-364.

Agha, G., De Cindio, F., & Rozenberg, G. (Eds.) (2001).Concurrent object-oriented programming and Petri nets – Advances in Petri nets. *Lecture Notes in Computer Science, 2001.* Berlin: Springer Verlag.

Allen, R., & Garlan, D. (1997). A formal basis for architectural connection. *ACM Transaction on Software Engineering and Methodology, 6*(3), 213-249.

Alur, R., & Henzinger, T. (1992). Logics and models of real time: a survey. *Lecture Notes in Computer Science, 600*, 74-106.

Berthomieu, B., & Diaz, M. (1991). Modeling and verification of time dependent systems using time Petri nets. *IEEE Trans. Software Engineering, 17*(3), 259-273.

Binns, P., Engelhart, M., Jackson, M., & Vestal, S. (1996). Domain-specific software architectures for guidance, navigation, and control. *International Journal of Software Engineering and Knowledge Engineering, 6*(2), 201-228.

Bjorner, N. et al. (1995, November). *Step: The Stanford temporal prover – User's manual.* Technical Report STAN-CS-TR-95-1562, Department of Computer Science, Stanford University.

Booch, G., Rumbaugh, J., & Jacobson, I. (1999). *The unified modeling language – User guide.* Reading, MA: Addison Wesley.

Ciardo, G., Jones, R., Marmorstein, R., Miner, A., & Siminiceanu, R. (2002). SMART: stochastics model-checking analyzer for reliability and timing. In the *Proc. of Int'l Conf. on Dependable Systems and Networks,* Bethesda, MD, June. Los Alamitos, CA: IEEE Computer Society Press.

Clarke, E., & Emerson, E. (1981). Characterizing properties of parallel programs as fixpoints. *Lecture Notes in Computer Science, 85.*

Clarke, E., Emerson, E., & Sistla, A. (1986). Automatic verification of finite-state concurrent systems using temporal logic specifications. *ACM Trans. on Programming Languages and Systems, 8*(2), 244-263.

Clarke, E., Grumberg, O., & Peled, D. (1999). *Model checking.* Cambridge, MA: MIT Press.

Clarke, E., & Kurshan, R. (1996). Computer-aided verification. *IEEE Spectrum, 33*(6), 61-67.

Clarke, E., & Wing, J. (1996). Formal methods: state of the art and future. *ACM Computing Surveys, 28*(4), 626-643.

Craigen, D., Gerhart, S., & Ralston, T. (1995). Formal methods reality check: Industrial usage. *IEEE Trans. On Software Engineering, 21*(2), 90-98.

Deng, Y., Wang, J., Beznosov, K., & Tsai, J. P. (2003). An approach for modeling and analysis of security system architectures. *IEEE Transactions on Knowledge and Data Engineering, 15*(5), 1099-119.

Emerson, E., Mok, A., Sistla, A., & Srinivasian, J. (1992). Quantitative temporal reasoning. *Real-Time Systems, 4,* 331-352.

Haas, P. (2002). *Stochastic Petri nets: Modeling, stability, simulation.* Berlin, Germany: Springer-Verlag.

Hansson, H., & Johnson, B. (1994). A logic for reasoning about time and reliability. *Formal Aspects of Computing, 6*(4), 512-535.

Harel, D. (1987). Statecharts: A visual formalism for complex systems. *Science of Computer Programming, 8,* 231-274.

He, X. (1992). Temporal predicate transition nets – A new formalism for specifying and verifying concurrent systems. *International Journal of Computer Mathematics, 45*(1/2), 171-184.

He, X. (1995). A method for analyzing properties of hierarchical predicate transition nets. In the *Proc. of the 19th Annual International Computer Software and Applications Conference,* Dallas, Texas, August (pp. 50-55). Los Alamitos, CA: IEEE Computer Society Press.

He, X. (1996). A formal definition of hierarchical predicate transition nets. *Lecture Notes in Computer Science, 1091,* 212-229.

He, X. (1998). Transformations on hierarchical predicate transition nets: Abstractions and refinements. In the *Proc. of the 22nd International Computer Software and Application Conference,* Vienna, Austria, August (pp.164-169). Los Alamitos, CA: IEEE Computer Society Press.

He, X. (2001). PZ nets – A formal method integrating Petri nets with Z. *Information and Software Technology, 43,* 1-18.

He, X., & Deng, Y. (2000). Specifying software architectural connectors in SAM. *International Journal of Software Engineering and Knowledge Engineering, 10,* 411-432.

He, X., & Deng, Y. (2002). A framework for developing and analyzing software architecture specifications in SAM. *The Computer Journal, 45*(1), 111-128.

He, X., & Ding, Y. (1992). A temporal logic approach for analyzing safety properties of predicate transition nets. In V. Leewun (Ed.), *Information processing '92* (pp.127-133). Amsterdam: North Holland.

He, X., Ding, J., & Deng, Y. (2002). Analyzing SAM architectural specifications using model checking. In the *Proc. of SEKE2002,* Italy, June (pp.271-274). Skokie, IL: Knowledge Systems Institute.

He, X., & Lee, J. A. N. (1990). Integrating predicate transition nets and first order temporal logic in the specification of concurrent systems. *Formal Aspects of Computing, 2*(3), 226-246.

He, X., & Lee, J. A. N. (1991). A methodology for constructing predicate transition net specifications. *Software – Practice & Experience, 21*, 845-875.

He, X., & Yang, C. (1992). Structured analysis using hierarchical predicate transition nets. In the *Proc. of the 16th Int'l Computer Software and Applications Conf.,* Chicago, IL, September (pp.212-217). Los Alamitos, CA: IEEE Computer Society Press.

He, X., Yu, H., Shi, T., Ding, J., & Deng, Y. (2004). Formally analyzing software architectural specifications using SAM. *Journal of Systems and Software, 71*(1-2), 11-29.

Hoare, C. A. R. (1985). *Communicating sequential processes.* London, UK: Prentice-Hall.

Holzmann, G. (2003). *The SPIN model checker: Primer and reference manual.* Boston, MA: Addison Wesley.

Inverardi, P., & Wolf, A. (1995). Formal specification and analysis of software architectures using the chemical abstract machine model. *IEEE Transaction on Software Engineering, 21*(4), 373-386.

Jensen, K. (1992). *Coloured Petri nets.* Berlin: Springer-Verlag.

Jensen, K., & Rozenberg, G. (Eds.) (1991). *High-level Petri nets – Theory and applications.* Berlin, Germany: Springer Verlag.

Juan, E., Tsai, J. P., & Murata, T. (1998). Compositional verification of concurrent systems using Petri-net-based condensation rules. *ACM Transactions on Programming Languages and Systems, 20*(5), 917-979

Kazman, R., Klein, M., & Clements, P. (2000). *ATAM: A method for architectural evaluation.* Software Engineering Institute Technical Report CMU/SEI-2000-TR-004, Carnegie-Mellon University.

Knight, J. (2002). Dependability of embedded systems. In the *Proc. of ICSE '02,* Orlando, FL, May (pp.685-686). New York: ACM Press.

Lamport, L. (1994). The temporal logic of actions. *ACM Transactions on Programming Languages and Systems, 16*(3), 872-923.

Luckham, D., Kenney, J., & Augustin, L. et al. (1995). Specification and analysis of system architecture using Rapide. *IEEE Transaction on Software Engineering, 21*(4), 336-355.

Mandrioli, D., Morzenti, A., Pezze, M., Pietro, P. S., & Silva, S. (1996). A Petri net and logic approach to the specification and verification of real time systems. In *Formal methods for real time computing.* Hoboken, NJ: John Wiley & Sons.

Manna, Z., & Pnueli, A. (1983). How to cook a temporal proof system for your pet language. In the *Proc. Of the 10th ACM Symp. On Principle of Programming Languages,* Austin, TX, January (pp.141-154). New York: ACM Press.

Manna, Z., & Pnueli, A. (1992). *The temporal logic of reactive and concurrent systems – Specification.* Berlin: Springer-Verlag.

Manna, Z., & Pnueli, A. (1995). *The temporal verification of reactive systems – Safety.* Berlin: Springer-Verlag.

Marsan, M., Balbo, G., Conte, G., Donatelli, S., & Franceschinis, G. (1994). *Modeling with generalized stochastic Petri nets.* Hoboken, NJ: John Wiley and Sons.

McMillan, K. (1993). *Symbolic model checking.* Boston: Kluwer Academic Publishers.

Medvidovic, N., & Taylor, R. (2000). A classification and comparison framework for software architecture description languages. *IEEE Transaction on Software Engineering, 26*(1), 70-93.

Milner, R. (1989). *Communication and concurrency.* London, UK: Prentice-Hall.

Murata, T. (1989). Petri nets, properties, analysis and applications. *Proc. of IEEE, 77*(4), 541-580.

Reisig, W. (1992). *A primer in Petri net design.* Berlin: Springer-Verlag.

Shaw, M., Deline, R., & Klein, D. et al. (1995). Abstractions for software architecture and tools to support them. *IEEE Trans. on Software Eng., 21*(4), 314-335.

Shaw, M., & Garlan, D. (1996). *Software architecture.* Upper Saddle River, NJ: Prentice-Hall.

Shi, T., & He, X. (2002). Modeling and analyzing the software architecture of a communication protocol using SAM. In J. Bosch et al. (Eds.), *Proc. of the 3rd Working IEEE/IFIP Conference on Software Architecture,* Montreal, Canada, August (pp. 63-78). Boston, MA: Kluwer Academic Publishers.

Shi, T., & He, X. (2003a). Dependability analysis using SAM. In the *Proc. of the ICSE Workshop on Software Architectures for Dependable Systems,* Portland, Oregon, May (pp. 37-42).

Shi, T., & He, X. (2003b). A methodology for dependability and performability analysis in SAM. In the *Proc. of the International Conference on Dependable Systems and Networks,* San Francisco, CA, June (pp. 679-688). Los Alamitos, CA: IEEE Computer Society Press.

Spivey, J. (1992). *Z reference manual.* London, UK: Prentice-Hall.

Stavridou, V., & Riemenschneider, R. (1998). Provably dependable software architectures. In the *Proc. of 3rd International Software Architecture Workshop,* Orlando, FL, November (pp. 133-136).

Trivedi, K. (1999). *SPNP User's Manual, version 6.0.* Department of ECE, Duke University.

Wang, J. (1998). *Timed Petri nets, theory and application.* Boston, MA: Kluwer Academic Publisher.

Wang, J., & Deng, Y. (1999). Incremental modeling and verification of flexible manufacturing systems. *Journal of Intelligent Manufacturing, 10*(6), 485-502.

Wang, J., He, X., & Deng, Y. (1999). Introducing software architecture specification and analysis in SAM through an example. *Information and Software Technology, 41,* 451-467.

Wing, J. (1990). A specifier's introduction to formal methods. *IEEE Computer, 23*(9), 8-24.

Xu, D., He, X., & Deng, Y. (2002). Compositional schedulability analysis of real-time systems using time Petri nets. *IEEE Trans. On Software Engineering, 28*(10), 984-996.

Yu, H., He, X., Gao, S., & Deng, Y. (2002). Modeling and analyzing SMIL documents in SAM. In the *Proc. of Fourth IEEE International Symposium on Multimedia Software Engineering,* Newport Beach, CA, December (pp. 132-139). Los Alamitos, CA: IEEE Computer Society Publishing.

Zave, P., & Jackson, M. (1993). Conjunction as composition. *ACM Transaction on Software Engineering and Methodology, 2*(4), 379-411.

Chapter XIV

Practical Considerations in Automatic Code Generation

Paul Dietz, Motorola, USA

Aswin van den Berg, Motorola, USA

Kevin Marth, Motorola, USA

Thomas Weigert, Motorola, USA

Frank Weil, Motorola, USA

Abstract

Model-driven engineering proposes to develop software systems by first creating an executable model of the system design and then transforming this model into an implementation. This chapter discusses how to automatically transform such design models into product implementations for industrial-strength systems. It provides insights, practical considerations, and lessons learned when developing code generators for applications that must conform to the constraints imposed by real-world, high-performance systems. This deeper understanding of the relevant issues will enable developers of automatic code generation systems to build transformation tools that can be deployed in industrial applications with stringent performance requirements.

Background

Commercial software development still largely follows processes based on the software development life-cycle paradigms that were introduced in the late sixties as software engineering faced the *software crisis*: the methods and skills employed for designing software did not match the emerging hardware capabilities. While many variations to the original *Waterfall* paradigm have been put into practice, the poor performance of software engineering processes continues to undo the advances in processing capabilities due to Moore's law. The primary criticisms that have been lobbied against the software life-cycle model still hold today: software development begins with an attempt to recognize and understand the user requirements and then proceeds to implement a software system that satisfies those requirements. The requirements specification is formulated in a dialogue between users and system analysts. Typically, the requirements definition reflects the developers' interpretation of the users' needs. Where the communication of these needs has been distorted, either by preconceptions or by general unfamiliarity on either side, it is unlikely that misunderstandings become apparent until the user tests (examines) the near-ready product. Thus, maintenance is performed at the implementation level. At this point, the programmers have applied considerable skill and knowledge to optimize the code. However, optimization spreads information: it takes advantage of what is known elsewhere in the system and substitutes complex but efficient realizations for the simple abstractions of the specification. The result is a system more difficult to understand due to increased dependencies among its components and scattering of information. Correcting errors deriving from the requirements phase during software maintenance becomes exceedingly expensive.

As soon as these problems became apparent, new methodologies were proposed; see Agresti (1986) for a collection of seminal papers criticizing the waterfall model and presenting alternative approaches. An *operational specification* is a system model than can be evaluated or executed to exhibit the behavior of a software system at an early development stage. *Transformational implementation* is an approach to software development that uses automated support to apply a series of transformations that change a specification into an implementation. Together these techniques promise to overcome the limitations of the Waterfall model: an operational design specification avoids errors in the requirements phase by demonstrating to the users the system behavior during an early stage of the software development process. Transformational implementation enables the rapid realization of the specification and the maintenance of the product at the level of the specification. Together these techniques have become known as *model-driven engineering*. Weigert and Weil (2006) discuss the benefits achievable when applying model-driven engineering to the development of real-time embedded systems and give data from industrial experience.

Requirements and design verification through operational specifications became feasible by the advent of standardized executable specification languages such as SDL, or more recently, UML. These languages have been given operational interpretations and are widely supported by tools that allow users not only to develop the model of the software system, but also to exercise it against test cases, and observe and analyze the resultant behavior of the software system. Tools are able to transform the high-level specifications into implementations in popular target languages: see Czarnecki and Eisenecker (2000) or Tsai and Weigert (1993) for an overview of approaches to system implementation through program transformation. Nevertheless, commercial software development has not been able to capitalize on these advances. The obstacles proved to be the code generators–that is, the tools translating specifications into implementations. While impressive results were demonstrated in non-constrained domains or with toy examples, code generation has proven elusive in many application areas, in particular, for real-time, embedded system development. Where automated translation of specification to code is not available, engineers are reluctant to invest the effort to develop executable specifications because this effort will have to be repeated, possibly several times, when translating the specification into target code. As a consequence, development falls back onto the familiar life-cycle models.

In this chapter, we shall illustrate our experience in developing commercial-strength code generators that have proven effective in highly-constrained domains, in particular the development of telecommunications applications, both for network elements and subscriber devices (Weigert, 1999). We shall examine capabilities an automated code generation system must possess for it to effectively support these domains.

We begin by summarizing constraints on program transformation systems that are induced by the constraints under which industrial software products have to be developed. Many of the difficulties in realizing a high-performance code generation system are due to these constraints. In order to support the deployment of model-driven engineering at Motorola, we have implemented the Mousetrap program transformation system. This system accepts high-level specifications in domain-specific notations geared at the development of real-time embedded systems in the telecommunications domains: UML, SDL, and proprietary PDU definition languages. It generates high-performance product code from design specifications. A significant portion of application code on Motorola telecommunication network elements is being generated by Mousetrap.

In the *Automatic Code Generation for Industrial-Strength Systems* section, we give an overview of the Mousetrap program transformation system, summarize the language it provides to express transformation rules, and describe the architecture of the transformation process realizing high-level specifications in C target code. The *Types of Code Generation Rules* section compares the different types of transformation rules one will find in a real-life system. Finally, in the *Transformation of an Example Model* section, we illustrate the transformation process by examining the generation of an implementation for a simple yet representative system. We will pick out a number of interesting transformations and describe them in detail, showing "before/after" examples of the impact that these rules have on the program in progress. A representative part of the program is listed in the Appendix as it appears at significant stages during the transformation process.

While this chapter attempts to give a broad view of the program transformation process using the Mousetrap system as an example, and thus necessarily cannot discuss system aspects in depth, we have included sidebars illustrating important aspects of program transformation in more detail: expression lifting puts a program in a canonical form that ensures that semantic assumptions about the evaluation order of function arguments that hold for the specifications will not be violated by the C implementation. Liveness analysis determines, for each point in the program, the set of variables whose value may be used at that point. This analysis contributes essentially to many optimizations. Both expression lifting and liveness analysis, together with many other optimizations, rely on effects analysis; effects analysis computes the side effect behavior for each statement and expression in the program. These sidebars can be read independently of the rest of the chapter, and they may be ignored if only a high-level overview of program transformation is desired.

Issues with Generating Code for Industrial-Strength Systems

Current automatic code generation techniques generally either do not scale to the size needed for real applications or generate code that does not meet the constraints of the environment in which application is embedded.

Constraints on Industrial-Strength Systems

What differentiates the theory of program transformation from its practical application is the set of constraints under which a real system must be developed. While correctness of the generated code is obviously a major concern, it is also taken as a given. That is, a development method or tool that produces incorrect results will simply not be used. The distinction between approaches, then, is how well they handle these constraints.

System Size

A typical network device or network element in a telecommunications system will be composed of several million lines of code in a high-level language such as C. Each individual application that is part of the device or element will be composed of several hundred thousand lines of code. While it is sometimes the case that the applications could be broken down into even smaller independent sub-applications, this decomposition typically comes with the penalty of decreased performance of the overall component due to increased context switching and interprocess communication.

Performance Requirements

It is rarely the case that a system has no performance requirements related to execution speed, memory use, throughput capacity, latency of responses, and so forth. How well a system meets these requirements often separates the successful systems from the failed ones.

While there are no entirely typical sets of performance requirements, there is a continuum roughly following the scale from small embedded devices through large stand-alone network elements. For example, a handheld device such as a cell phone or PDA will have limited amounts of memory available, will be running on a relatively low-end processor, and will need to maximize battery life. In contrast, a network element such as a cellular base station will have relatively large amounts of memory, will be utilizing one or even several high-end processors, and will not have any requirements related to power consumption.

Even with the increasing power of processors and the lowering cost of memory, these requirements are not being relaxed significantly. The amount of work that the applications are required to do is increasing at a similar pace, often faster than the capabilities of the underlying processing hardware.

Target Platform Interaction

Real systems are being tasked with increasing sophistication related to interaction with other applications and the underlying target platform. Systems must also be "well behaved" on the target platform. This equates to being able to answer health probes in a timely manner, honoring and properly handling OS-level signals, using the dictated inter-process communication mechanisms and middleware layers, linking with supplied library files, and so forth.

Quality

It must be assumed that applications operate in a hostile environment where malevolent users try to gain control of a system for their own purposes. Attempts at exploiting system weaknesses such as buffer overruns are common in virtually every domain. In addition, there are often severe penalties for system failure, and field debugging must be facilitated.

In some domains, it may be acceptable to take relatively drastic action on system failure. For example, it is typically not considered catastrophic if a single cell phone drops a call. In contrast, an infrastructure component often cannot fail without far-reaching consequences. For an application such as a communication protocol handler that executes on both the handheld and infrastructure component, this means that the same model must often be transformed in very different ways.

System Life

Typically, systems are long-lived, are part of product families, and are incrementally enhanced for successive releases. It is rarely the case that systems are developed in isolation and then never used again.

Derived Constraints on Transformation Systems

From the earlier-mentioned characteristics, the following constraints can be derived both on the code that is generated and on the code generation system itself.

- Transformation algorithms must scale well.
- Memory used during transformation must be wisely managed.
- Overall transformation time must be kept to a reasonable level.
- Traditional correctness-proof and testing techniques either will not be tractable or will be incomplete. Therefore, the code generation system must be robust in the presence of model problems.
- For the same reason as previously mentioned, the code generation system must be able to provide appropriate and useful feedback to the modeler.

- It is very important to generate highly-optimized code. Note that generated code typically looks nothing like hand-written code, so it is likely that compilers will not be able to optimize the code well.

- For both speed and memory usage reasons, application memory must be well managed, with dynamic allocation kept at a minimum.

- Run-time interpretation must be kept at a minimum.

- Selection of concrete implementations of abstract data types is very important.

- With certain simplifying assumptions, additional optimizations can be made, but it requires the user to abide by the simplifying assumptions.

- The generated code must use applicable middle-ware layers for timers, memory allocation, signal handling, thread creation, inter-process communication, liveness monitoring, and so forth.

- System interfaces must be accommodated, including callback functions, asynchronous events, high-priority events, library APIs, and so forth.

- The generated code must be traceable back to the model.

- Security aspects outside of the scope of the model itself must be accommodated (e.g., prevention of buffer overflows, validation of input data, etc.).

- Robustness aspects outside of the scope of the model itself must be accommodated (e.g., recovery from memory allocation failures).

- Implementation-specific robustness aspects must be automatically inserted (e.g., how to detect and handle run-time problems such as accessing an array out of bounds).

- Models must be as free as possible from platform details since it is almost guaranteed that they will change as the application evolves over its life.

- Models must be maintained over many product releases.

These derived constraints set the framework for *why* industrial-strength automated code generation systems are structured the way they are and *why* they perform the transformation steps that they do.

Automatic Code Generation for Industrial-Strength Systems

The Mousetrap program transformation system (Boyle, Harmer, Weigert, & Weil, 1998) accepts SDL and UML as its main modeling languages for input and generates C code as its main output language. However, the system is generic, and the discussions in this chapter are largely independent of the modeling language used and the target language selected.

Generating code for a high-performance system such as a telecommunications infrastructure component, a telematics controller, and so forth, requires more information than is, or even should be, included in a functional model. This information derives from two general and somewhat conflicting issues: no software component exists in total isolation, and model integrity should be maintained.

The environment in which the generated component will operate imposes constraints on the model. Practical aspects of a real component such as inter-process communication, external functionality, cross-compilers, and so forth, must be taken into account. Since these issues typically dictate how the component interacts with its environment, they often have deep impacts on the details of the models.

In contrast, a model should be as free from platform considerations as possible. One would ideally like to target a given model to widely disparate platforms with no changes to the model itself. This tenet implies that considerations such as communication protocol implementations, error handling, timer and memory interfaces, and platform-generated events (such as interrupt signals) should be outside of the model itself. These considerations are, however, critical to the generation of correct and optimized code.

Figure 1 provides an overview of the full code generation process, highlighting the additional information needed to generate the code. The cylinders in the figure represent manually created inputs to be transformed into code and information to be used during the transformation. The document symbols represent generated outputs from the transformation process. The solid thick arrows represent transformation processes, and the open thin arrows represent items that are used as is.

As can be seen from Figure 1, the actual model is only one of several inputs necessary for code generation. The other inputs play an equally important role and are described here.

Figure 1. Code generation overview

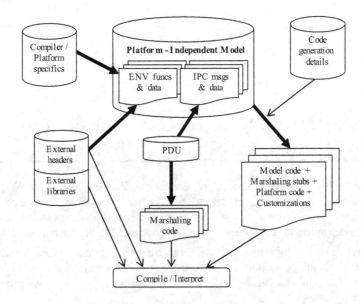

Compiler and Platform Specifics

Some aspects of target language standards are left unspecified. For example, the C standard does not define the size of int, short int, or long int. The most effective strategy is to automatically generate types that can be used in the model, but there are often other implications. For example, C compilers do not handle a literal of the most negative integer intuitively (e.g., on an 8-bit system, where signed integers can range from −128 to 127, the constant −128 is parsed as −(128), which is a problem since 128 cannot be stored directly). If this literal is in the model, how it is translated to code will depend on the word size on the target platform and how the compiler handles it.

External Headers

If functions or constants from outside of the model are used within the model, then the proper external declarations should be automatically generated from the relevant header files. This includes not only the declarations themselves, but also the closure of all the data types used by those declarations.

External Libraries

While these libraries themselves are not used in the models or code generation, they will be used by the compiler or interpreter. It is critical that the declarations used in the models be consistent so that the calls in the generated code exactly match the library functions.

Protocol Data Unit (PDU) Specifications

These specifications describe the messages that are sent to and from the component as well as the data they carry. The encoding scheme may be part of the PDU specification itself or may be separate (as is the case with ASN.1). The encoding and decoding functionality—collectively called *marshaling*—should be separate from the model itself. However, these PDU specifications should be used to automatically generate both the messages and data types used in the model and the corresponding marshaling code for the target platform (Dietz & Weigert, 2003).

Code Generation Details

The code generation details describe the special instructions needed to generate efficient code that does not violate any platform constraints. Typical information declared here includes: (1) the middleware API that must be used for timers, memory access, and so forth; (2) details of the inter-process communication mechanism; (3) details of error handling; and (4) logging and debugging information that should be added to the resultant code.

Program Transformation

The Mousetrap program transformation system manipulates a source program by the application of transformation rules to that program. A transformation rule describes a semantic relation between two programs (or fragments thereof). The most widely used semantic relations are weakened versions of equivalence. For example, a transformation rule may state that two programs produce identical output given the same input, ignoring erroneous inputs, undefined situations due to non-termination, or the like.

Typically, transformation rules do not relate actual programs, but program templates. A program template represents classes of programs. A program can be obtained from a program template by instantiating variables in the template.

Applying a transformation rule means replacing a program (or program fragment) by an "equivalent" program (or program fragment). The resultant program will be just as correct as the original program (the transformation rule promises to preserve correctness) and it is, in some sense, "better" than the original program by some criterion of interest (typically the criteria outlined in the *Transformation Rules* sub-section).

The Mousetrap program transformation system develops a program by successive application of transformation rules. Usually this means that one starts with a specification of the program and obtains the program implementing the specifications as a result of this process. However, program transformation may also result in a transition from a less efficient program to a more efficient program or from a sequential version of a program to a parallel version.

The Mousetrap system itself consists of several components:

- The bottom layer is an engine providing order-sorted, conditional term rewriting. Rewrite rules may be formulated by relying on matching modulo equational theories, such as associativity, commutativity, idempotence, and a special list theory. Identities for terms are automatically provided by the rewrite engine. Evaluation strategies are completely flexible.

- Input programs are translated into terms of an appropriate equational theory. A facility is provided which produces parsers, term compilers, unparsers, and definitions of the equational theory of the input language grammar from an extended Backus-Naur notation. Any programming language construct may be given equational properties or identities. The input grammars are restricted to be LALR-1.

- A rule compiler translates transformation rules operating over program templates into rewrite rules operating over terms in its equational theory.

Transformation Rules

The language used to write transformation rules consists of a means of defining grammars and abstract syntax trees, as well as forms for constructing, inspecting, matching, and traversing the trees. The Mousetrap system then applies these rules to an input program or program fragment and yields the representation of the resultant program. In this section, we will be mainly concerned with the mechanisms provided by the Mousetrap program transformation system to write transformation rules. Mousetrap transformation rules are expressed in an extension of Common Lisp, the implementation language of the transformation system. Via its macro facility, Common Lisp makes it easy to intermingle rule-based and procedural forms to express program transformations. In this section, we give an overview of expressive power of the language used to write Mousetrap transformation rules, without going into the syntactical detail of the notation. In subsequent examples, we will illustrate such rules in example form, showing same sample code fragment before and after the application of a rule. A detailed description of the Mousetrap rule language can be found in Boyle et al. (1998).

Simple Transformation Rules

A transformation rule is a correctness-preserving rewrite rule over parse trees. Each rule has an optional variable declaration section, a pattern part, an arrow indicating the rewriting relationship, and a replacement part. Comments may be freely interspersed. Both pattern and replacement are descriptions of a class of parse trees (we will refer to these as *terms*). In their simplest form, terms are written as source text in either the source or target grammars. A term is constructed by parsing this source text as deriving from the specified grammatical class in the respective grammar. Source and target grammars are not necessarily the same.

A term may simply be a literal description of a parse tree, or it may be the description of a parse tree with some sub-trees left unspecified but restricted to a given grammatical class (in which case there may be many instances matching the pattern). Sub-trees are left unspecified through the use of variables standing for sub-trees of a particular grammatical class. Variables must be declared before the pattern of the transformation rule. A term may also simply be a variable, matching any term deriving from the dominating symbol that the variable was declared to represent. A constructed terms may be bound to a variable to be used later in the transformation rule.

If the pattern matches a term of the input program (i.e., a term deriving from the parse tree to which this transformation rule is applied), the variables in the pattern are bound to the respective terms matched. Then a replacement term is constructed from the replacement part of the rule and the bindings for the variables previously created. Then the resultant replacement term is inserted in the input program in place of the matched term. Pattern and replacement must both derive from the same grammatical class, for this replacement to be meaningful.

Terms are matched against patterns modulo equational theories that hold for the language in which the source text is parsed. Equational matching, in particular leveraging the theory of lists, is often useful, but care must be taken in writing patterns to avoid non-scalable rules in which, for example, the time to find a match in a list increases as some higher power of the length of the list.

Of course, simply matching two terms and performing a replacement using variable substitutions alone will be sufficient only in the most trivial cases. Mousetrap provides powerful high-level abstractions to allow for convenient representation of transformation rules.

Qualifiers

A match of a pattern in an input parse tree may be seen as a condition that has to be satisfied in order for a replacement to take place. Arbitrarily many qualifiers may be inserted between the pattern and the arrow symbol. The replacement will only take place in case the additional conditions described by the qualifiers are satisfied.

Various predicates are provided to express additional conditions: one can test for equality or containment between ground terms given the variable bindings currently in place. One can test whether some term matches another term or whether an instance of a given term is contained in another term. The comparisons or matches are performed modulo any equational theory that may hold for the dominating symbols of the terms in question. Any bindings of variables created in a match performed in a qualifier can be relied upon in subsequent qualifiers and in the replacement. (Additional predicates can be constructed using the procedural mechanisms of Common Lisp.) No bindings to variables are created through negated qualifiers.

Subtransformation

Often it proves useful to be able to perform transformations on a matched term in the context of existing bindings for variables. This can be accomplished through the use of subtransformations (i.e., transformations of sub-terms of a matched term within a transformation). Subtransformations are another means of constructing a term; rather than simply describing a term by its dominating symbol and the source text to be parsed, a subtransformation takes a term and constructs a new term by applying a transformation to it. The original term as well as the transformation rule applied to it are subject to the bindings of terms to variables that have been made earlier. No bindings made during a subtransformation will persist beyond the scope of the subtransformation with the exception that information can be passed back from the subtransformation using more globally scoped variables.

Transformation Sets

Transformations may be grouped into sets that will be applied together to the same term. There is no particular order implied as to which transformation in a set takes precedence should two transformations be applicable to the same sub-term. In other words, at each sub-term of a matched term, we attempt to apply all transformations in a rule set in no stated order (albeit it is possible to impose an ordering on the sequence in which transformation rules are applied). Variable declarations hold for all rules in a set. Sets of transformation rules can also be used in subtransformations.

Traversal Order

Further, the mode of traversal may be varied. Ordinarily, we want a term to be rewritten as completely as possible. Therefore, once a match is located, we should try to rewrite the replacement term again using the same transformation set before it is inserted into the original term. This procedure guarantees that all applicable rules have actually been applied to the resultant term. In that case, the resultant term is said to be in canonical form. Sometimes, we know that no modification can happen to the replacement, or, more seriously, sometimes a rewrite sequence might not terminate if performed in the previously-noted manner. A mode of rewriting is possible in which the replacement term will not be traversed again (i.e., it is assumed to be already in canonical form). The different modes of rule application and term traversal are indicated by prefixing the pattern with an optional traversal indicator keyword: if no keyword is present, the system continues attempting to apply a set of transformation rules until a fix-point is reached. Another option is to perform a replacement at most once; the set of transformation rules is not reapplied even if the pattern were to match the replacement term. Further, there are traversal modes that either do not descend into a term, but apply the given rule to the current subterm in the matched term only, apply the given rule to the children of the current subterm only, apply rules in preorder, or apply them in postorder (the default).

Multiple Grammars

One of the strengths of Mousetrap is its ability to express transformation rules in terms of source and target language grammars. Often program transformation also facilitates the transition between different languages (say, a translation from Lisp to C). Traditional approaches require that transformation rules are intra-grammatical, that is, that pattern and replacement belong to the same grammar. This requirement has as a consequence that one must construct a grammar encompassing both source and target languages in order to allow for translation between two different languages. The development of such combined grammars is no trivial undertaking.

Mousetrap allows terms constructed from different grammars to co-exist. In particular, it is possible to operate on terms in which sub-terms have derived from source text parsed according to different grammars. After such a rule is successfully applied, the term, although constructed according to an original grammar, will contain subterms that belong a different grammar, specified in the replacement. The user is responsible that the term ultimately belongs to a single grammar. The grammars according to which the terms are constructed have to overlap at some points for a transition to be possible. Only sub-terms of the same grammatical class can be substituted for each other.

Attributes

Transformational programming often proceeds by analyzing a program fragment for certain properties and in some later step uses the result of this analysis to manipulate that fragment. It is convenient to have a mechanism that remembers the results of such analysis, or in general, marks sub-terms in the input program. For example, transformations may depend on the type of expressions in the matched term.

Mousetrap allows one to attach attributes (affixes) to sub-terms in the input program. The values of attributes can be either terms or arbitrary values, generated in standard Lisp syntax. Attributes can be tested for equality (in qualifiers), and their value can be retrieved or updated.

Attributes may be either stored directly with the term, or the attribute information may be stored elsewhere in a table indexed by terms (under term equality). The former can cause equivalent terms to be allocated separate copies, increasing the memory used to represent the program, and attributes may be lost during rewrites, requiring recomputation of the values. The latter requires that the same attribute value always be obtained for equivalent terms.

Layered Approach

The translation from the input language to the target language is performed in several major stages (see Figure 2).

This layered approach has two significant benefits: it allows the modular addition of input and output languages, and it maximizes the reuse of the rule base by allowing the majority of the transformation work to be done on one common language.

Each stage of transformation has one or more languages associated with it. For example, the Core stage operates on terms corresponding to the Core language. The translations between these languages are relatively simple syntactic changes and are independent of the main transformations within the stage.

The first transformation stage (Pre) is a pre-processing stage that converts an input model into a simpler and more uniform representation. For example, the SDL textual grammar cannot be used directly in standard parsing tools—it contains a multitude of shift-reduce and reduce-reduce errors and requires much context information to parse properly.

This first stage also simplifies the input language by using single forms to represent some constructs and by requiring or eliminating optional elements as appropriate. For example, the same grammatical form is used to represent SDL decision-statements and if-statements, and a default clause is ensured to be in all decision-statements.

The second transformation stage has two related parts: one that deals with the main functionality of a model (named CFSM for the concept of communicating finite-state machines) and one that deals with protocols (named PDU for protocol data units). This stage is responsible for understanding the semantics of the input models. The main purpose of these rules is

Figure 2. Transformation process overview

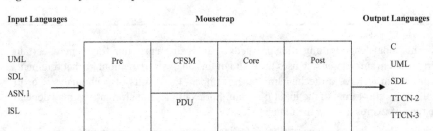

to transform the constructs that are specific to a given modeling language or protocol into the set of common, or "core" programming features. It is at this stage where the domain-specific constructs of the specification language are eliminated and realized in terms of the more generic "core" constructs. In the domain of real-time embedded telecommunication systems, the domain-specific features are primarily:

- an extended state machine concept providing means for controlling the firing of transitions, saving inputs across the firing of other transitions, returning to a variety of "previous" states after firing of a transition, executing synchronized products of several state machines, and encapsulating state machines to be reusable within larger state machines similar to procedure calls; and

- a bit-string the encoding and decoding of which is dictated by rules that map a logical representation of data onto the bit-string.

In practice, CFSM is a family of languages that share a common grammar. Transformation rules successively remove parts of the syntax while maintaining the same semantics. For example, the rules replace communication constructs such as channels, signal routes, gates, connectors, and so forth, with simple direct addressing; replace state machines with loops and decision-statements; replace import/export with global variables, and so on. Going from Core to C, the rules perform primarily syntactical transformations, such as replacing various loop forms with do, while, or for-statements, or replacing decision-statements with case-statements or if-statements.

Since the first two stages are most similar to the input model, most semantic checking is done in those stages. It is important *not* to assume that the input model will be defect free. Transformations must be structured to be able to handle syntactically correct inputs that contain violations of both the static and dynamic semantics. In addition, users of the system should be informed when constructs are encountered that are probably wrong because they cause transformations that would not likely be intended.

For example, consider the code fragments in Figure 3, which declare a variable to be in the range of 0 to 10 and then check the value of the variable.

Transformation rules can easily detect that it will never be valid for the variable var to be greater than 10, and that, therefore, the then-clause and the if-statement itself can be eliminated from the code because it can never be executed. It is unlikely, however, that the modeler deliberately put in dead code, so an appropriate message should be generated. If this is not

Figure 3. Variable range example

```
syntype small_range = Integer
 constants 0 : 10
endsyntype;
...
dcl var small_range;
...
if (var > 10) then {...} else {...}
```

done, it may be very difficult to determine in the generated code why the expected code is not present, especially if the code has been restructured as part of the transformation process or if there is a snowball effect where successively larger parts of the code are removed because the dead code causes subsequent parts of the code to become unreachable.

Care must also be taken to ensure that messages presented to the user actually represent model issues and are not artifacts of the transformation process. For example, when putting the code in canonical form, it may be the case that all decision-statements are given a default branch. If a later optimization step removes empty decision branches, it would be detrimental to present information to the user that the system removed a branch that the user has no knowledge of and no way of understanding if there is any practical effect.

The Core stage uses a domain-independent internal form as a common target language for the multiple front ends. Several classes of transformations are performed on Core. Canonicalization transformations put the program into a special form (e.g., no side effecting operations except at the statement level, unique names, and substitution of named constants). Analysis transformations walk the term, collecting information and possibly annotating it (e.g., type inference, side effect inference, and alias analysis). Optimization transformations make the term simpler, faster, or in some other way better, and often make use of the information provided by the analysis transformations. Examples here include forward propagation of values, simplification of expressions using algebraic identities, removal of unnecessary copies of large data structures, compile-time garbage collection (merging of allocation/free-statements), simplification of control flow, removal of dead code, and inlining of functions.

After optimizations are performed, a separate phase implements processes via functions operating on structures containing the part of the process state that may persist across the points where the process execution may block. This may sufficiently obfuscate the control flow of the process to the point that optimizations that could have been delayed from the previous stage would no longer be possible. This is one reason that those optimizations are not left to the C compiler. Another reason is that code generated through program transformation may not look much like code written by hand, so compilers may do a very poor job of optimizing it.

The final stage of transformation performs post-processing in what is essentially the target language. These are relatively simple translations such as applying rules related to specific compilers and changing while loops into for loops. As a final step, the resulting term is unparsed, or "pretty-printed", in the form of the target language itself.

Platform-Specific Interface

Following the model-driven engineering approach, application engineers ideally will focus their efforts on the application of their respective business domain expertise within the design model, constructing a model at a level of abstraction that is completely independent of the target platform where the application will ultimately be deployed. As applications grow more sophisticated and business domains grow more specialized, the value of engineers to a business is maximized when these engineers are fully engaged in their own areas of expertise. This expertise may well be distinct from the expertise required to effectively and efficiently realize a design model on a target platform. For example, expertise in concurrent programming is required to correctly deploy a multi-threaded application. The application engineer can reasonably be expected to provide a specification expressing the system behavior as the result of the collaboration of a set of concurrently executing processes. However, the application engineer may not possess the expertise required to resolve the lower-level issues of threading, mutual exclusion, and synchronization that are implicit in the declarative specification of concurrency. Further, it is precisely the specific choices of platform constructs that will be used to achieve the desired concurrency that transform a platform-independent model to a targeted implementation. From a practical standpoint, then, the twin goals of an ideally portable platform-independent model and an optimally applied engineering staff effectively delegate to the code generator the responsibility for transforming the model into an implementation. The transformation rules that drive the code generator are able to embody sufficient knowledge of the target platform so that the application engineers are required to specify only simple and concise choices that will parameterize the code generated for a specific platform.

Several services must be provided by the platform interface for a design model. The following basic platform services are required to implement the constructs and features used within a design model, either explicitly or implicitly.

Task/Thread/Process Management

Various operating systems treat tasks, threads, and processes disparately, and the code generator must tailor the generated platform interface to the capabilities of the target platform. When the target is a general-purpose operating system such as Linux, an application is typically mapped to a process with multiple cooperating threads of execution. Other real-time operating systems may provide only cooperating tasks without the benefits of process-based memory protection or may provide a process abstraction without an additional fine-grained thread abstraction. The knowledge of target platform capabilities embodied in the code generator enables an application to effectively utilize the abstraction(s) provided by the target platform without explicit concern for that target platform within the design model. Application engineers may parameterize the generated code by specifying stack sizes and scheduling parameters for tasks, threads, and/or processes. These parameters are not reflected in the design model but are handled by the code generator.

Memory Management

The explicit management of memory by application engineers is both error-prone and labor-intensive. The delegation of responsibility for memory management to the code generator contributes to the enhanced software quality associated with model-driven engineering. The memory management implemented by the code generator ultimately relies upon the platform memory service(s). A platform typically supports memory management via the POSIX memory API (malloc/realloc/free), but efficient memory management may require that memory is allocated and partitioned into pools with specified numbers of fixed-size blocks at application startup. When appropriately configured using capacity requirements, memory pools ensure that an application will obtain the memory it requires as it executes regardless of the behavior of other applications on the same processor. Application engineers select and configure memory pools by specifying the block size associated with each memory pool as well as the number of blocks in each memory pool.

Timer Management

The management of timers is a prime example of the separation of concerns involving a design model and its platform interface. Applications may require thousands of simultaneous timers, and application engineers should be free to specify the design model without undue concern for whether the underlying platform can actually directly support the required number of simultaneous timers. Experience with timer management has suggested the compromise of employing a single platform timer to dispatch from an internal queue that manages the timers utilized within the design model. Thus, the number of timers that can be supported in the design model is constrained only by the size of the internal timer queue (if statically allocated) or the available memory (if the timer queue is dynamically allocated and resized) and is not subject to potential limitations within the platform timer service itself that might be encountered if a one-to-one mapping of platform timers and design model timers is assumed.

The units of time and duration are left unspecified in modeling languages but must be configured when generating code from a design model. Two configuration parameters have been found to enable the flexible specification of the units of time and duration. One parameter specifies the number of duration units per second and must be specified by application engineers when manipulating timers within the design model. Application engineers are free to choose a convenient value for this parameter based on domain requirements. A second parameter specifies the number of platform clock ticks per second and must be considered when setting the single platform timer in the generated timer management code. However, this second parameter is not visible within the design model, ensuring encapsulation of platform-specific details of timer management.

Interprocess Communication

Platform middleware and operating systems support a formidable number of abstractions and mechanisms for interprocess communication (IPC), including (but not limited to) TCP and UDP sockets, message queues, mailboxes, ports, remote procedure calls, signals, and callback-based message services involving registration and subscription. The plethora of IPC abstractions and mechanisms burdens an application engineer with platform-specific detail and negatively impacts the portability of the design model if choices involving IPC are manifest within the design model. For example, a maximally portable design model simply sends and receives signals to and from its environment without any knowledge of the underlying IPC mechanisms.

In practice, it is sometimes desirable to allow platform-specific details to escape into the design model if the IPC abstraction is also a first-class abstraction within the design model or if IPC must be dynamically configured based on domain-specific logic. An example of the former might involve a design model in which IP addresses and port numbers have inherent significance within the domain and there is an advantage to exposing the associated socket and its identifier because they are useful in the design model and would ultimately be derived within the design model anyway. An example of the latter might involve a design model in which an environment signal must be sent using a message subscription service where the parameters to select a family of subscribers are dynamic and depend upon data maintained within the model.

The platform interface must strive to enable maximally portable design models while accommodating design models in which IPC is exposed when necessary. Application engineers may configure the code generator to statically associate specific IPC mechanisms and message service parameters with design model constructs such as environment channels. When more dynamic behavior is required within a design model, environment signals may be augmented with an additional field dedicated to platform-specific detail, and the generated platform interface code will utilize the dedicated field appropriately. In this case, it is obviously desirable to structure the design model with appropriate abstraction so that platform-specific IPC detail is encapsulated and not needlessly distributed throughout the design model. With this compromise, experience has shown that it is possible for an application engineer to achieve acceptable platform independence while exercising considerable control over platform-specific IPC without resorting to lower-level code outside of the design model.

Types of Code Generation Rules

The overall types of transformation rules that are necessary can be categorized as follows.

Transformational

Transformational rules are correctness-preserving rewrite rules whose primary purpose is to transform constructs in one form or language into the equivalent construct in another form or language. Examples of these rules are "flattening" of inheritance features, inlining of packages, translation of state machines into nested catch/throw constructs, and so forth.

Canonicalization

Canonicalization rules render all uses of a construct into a single form. The purpose of these steps is to minimize the number of rules that need to be written in other phases by minimizing the number of forms that must be matched against. While these rules are in a sense transformational, they are different in that they do not help the progress of the overall transformation, but instead merely mitigate how difficult it is to write the rules themselves. For example, case-statements that are (essentially) if-statements are converted to normal form in which the else-branch is empty.

In addition, Core has some syntactic forms that can be expressed in multiple ways, and canonicalization eliminates this syntactic sugar. For example, let-statements are converted to blocks; similarly, let-expressions are converted to block-expressions.

A more substantial canonicalization transformation is expression lifting (see Sidebar "Expression Lifting" beginning on p. 365). After this transformation, the program has the property that all expressions that have side effects are either the top-level expression of expression-statements or the right-hand side of assignment-statements. All more deeply-nested expressions are side-effect free. Because this transformation introduces temporary variables, it also needs the types of lifted subexpressions. Core has left-to-right evaluation order, so not only must sub-expressions with side effects be lifted out, but so must any sub-expression to their left whose value may be changed by the lifted expressions. This is achieved by annotating each expression with information on the set of "abstract locations" that it may access and the set that it may modify. With this information, it can be conservatively determined if one expression can commute with another (that is, if they yield the same results if evaluated in either order).

Yet another canonicalization transform is unique renaming. Many transformations depend on distinct entities having unique names. The unique renaming transformation maintains a table mapping names that have been used to their replacements; when a duplicate is found, the second usage is replaced with a similar, but otherwise unused, name. This symbol table should have constant access time, allow a push/pop operation for entry into/exit from scopes of local names, and have constant-time range queries. This algorithm runs in time linear in the size of the term. A naïve, purely rule-based algorithm would otherwise take time quadratic in the size of the term, in the worst case. A name is left unchanged if it does not need to be renamed; any "exported" name (that is, a name that is visible outside the module being translated) remains unchanged since it is part of the external interface of the module.

Informational

Informational rules build up information used by other rules, but do not in themselves transform the code. These rules exist for the reasons already discussed. Examples of these types of rules are addition of scopes to state machine transitions, determination of the lexical scope of all identifiers, analyzing alias usage and expression side effects, and propagation of type information and variable range bounds.

Semantic Analysis

Semantic analysis rules perform both static and dynamic analysis on the model or look for potential defects as previously discussed. Examples of static semantic errors to be caught include decision-statements in which there is not an answer part for all possible values of the question (and there is no else part) and decision-statements in which there are overlapping answer parts. Examples of dynamic semantic errors are out-of-bounds indexes in indexed types, dereferencing a Null reference, and assigning a value that is out of range to a variable. Examples of potential defects are assuming infinite-precision arithmetic, having unreachable or unused parts of the model, and sending a signal to a process that does not exist.

Sidebar: Expression Lifting

In C, the evaluation order of sub-expressions is undefined, while in the specification languages SDL and UML, the evaluation order is fixed from left to right. Code generation must, therefore, ensure that the resultant code does not rely on the order of sub-expression evaluation. Enforcing this constraint while preserving the semantics of any program requires that all sub-expressions be "lifted" if the sub-expression has side effects. Expression lifting, as is shown in the following text, replaces the sub-expression with a temporary variable, where that variable is assigned the sub-expression in a preceding statement.

```
foo(1,bar(),2);
===>
dcl tmp1 t;
tmp1 := bar();
foo(1,tmp1,2);
```

In this example, t is the type of the expression bar(). This transformation is not sufficient, however. Suppose the function call bar(), as a side effect, may modify the variable x. Then such transformation, applied as in the code snippet next, would be unsafe since the original has left-to-right evaluation order and evaluates x before bar().

```
foo(x,bar(),2);
==>
dcl tmp1 t;
tmp1 := bar();
foo(x,tmp1,2);
```

One could safely canonicalize expressions by lifting any argument to the left of a side-effecting sub-expression if that argument is not constant. However, this would introduce too many temporary variables. Instead, one can perform a global flow-insensitive analysis of the possible side effects of each expression. The transformation that performs expression lifting leveraging side-effects analysis is implemented by a series of subtransformations:

1. The attribute TYPE is computed for each sub-term deriving from an expression. This attribute contains the type of that expression.

2. The attribute SFX is computed for each expression and statement term. This attribute contains information describing the side effect behavior of a term (See the Sidebar "Effects Analysis"). Side effect analysis proceeds by abstracting the potentially very large number of memory locations in the actual program into a smaller number of *abstract locations*. Information stored in the SFX attribute includes the set of abstract locations that may be referenced when the term is executed and the set of abstract locations that may be modified when the term is executed. The information in the SFX attribute enables us to conservatively determine if the evaluation of a term t can

Sidebar: Expression Lifting continued on next page

commute with the evaluation of a term t′. This is the case if evaluating t before t′ yields the same result as evaluating t′ before t. More precisely: we say that t and t′ commute if no abstract location modified in one term is referenced or modified in the other, and if the execution of neither term may terminate abnormally.

3.   The SFX attribute is used to compute a Boolean attribute LIFT on each expression or L-value term. This attribute is defined as follows:

   a.   If the expression is a function call and if the function call has a side effect and is neither the top-level expression in an expression-statement nor the right-hand side of an assignment-statement, then the attribute is true.

   b.   If the expression is in a list of actual parameters and does not commute with some expression following it, then the attribute is true.

   c.   If an L-value occurs on the left-hand side of an assignment-statement and does not commute with the right-hand side, then the attribute is true.

   d.   Otherwise, the LIFT attribute is false.

4.   The term is traversed from left to right. Transformation rules are applied in both pre- and post-order. In pre-order:

   a.   When a statement S is first visited, a list of lifted statements is created. When S is last visited, this list is examined, and, if non-empty, the statement is re-placed by a block-statement in which S is preceded by this list of statements in reverse order.

   b.   When an expression e is visited, if its LIFT attribute is true, a temporary vari-able v is created whose type is the value of the TYPE attribute of e. Two state-ments—the declaration of v, and the assignment of e to v—are placed on the head of the list of lifted statements, and the expression is replaced by a simple variable expression containing only v.

Similarly, if an L-value lv is visited and its LIFT attribute is true, where its TYPE attribute is some type t, then a variable is created with type ref t (a pointer to t), and a declaration of the variable and its assignment of &lv are placed on the list of lifted statements. The L-value is replaced by a dereference of the variable.

When a block expression comprised of a statement-list sl and an expression e is first visited, the statement list sl is traversed. Then, the statements in sl are pushed onto the front of the lifted statement list. Finally, the expression e is traversed.

There can be more than one lifted statement list in existence at any time, because the traversal can be inside several statements at once. At any time only the most recently created active statement list is being modified.

This algorithm does not necessarily minimize the cost of lifting (in the sense of the cost of the introduced assignment-statements). For example, if expression e precedes expression e′ in an expression list and e does not commute with e′, it may be cheaper to lift a sub-expres-sion of e instead of the entire expression.

Optimization

Optimization rules create semantically equivalent code that performs better in some aspect such as execution speed or memory utilization. Once the term has been canonicalized, Mousetrap performs a series of optimizations. Generally, these are performed in a stereotyped order until either the term stops changing or a fixed number of iterations of the optimizer have occurred. The order of transformations and the number of iterations of optimizations were worked out by experience to both maximize the efficiency of the generated code and minimize the space and time used by the transformations.

Examples of optimizations include those that are standard in compiler technology such as constant folding, function inlining, and common sub-expression elimination. Other examples are more specific to higher-level model transformation such as state machine simplification, compile-time garbage collection, and variable bounds reduction.

An extensive group of optimizations involves simplification of expressions according to various algebraic laws. At this stage, canonicalization has ensured that no proper sub-expression can have side effects. This fact enables a wide variety of algebraic laws to be used without regard for the order of occurrence of sub-expressions. Expressions may also be eliminated entirely if this is algebraically allowed. The entire list of transformations (more than 400) is too large to list

A set of optimizations that are particularly important involve the elimination of unnecessary copying of values of complex aggregate types. In a modeling language with value seman-tics, such as SDL, large aggregate objects (records, arrays, sequences, etc.) are implicitly copied at each assignment, function call, or built-in operation. These copies can be very expensive, even changing the complexity of the algorithm being expressed if not removed. Transformations must recognize common idioms. For example, accessing elements of a list sequentially in a loop can be transformed into accesses using an auxiliary pointer that is moved down the list in step with the index variable. As another example, when a variable of aggregate type that is passed to a function or built-in constructor is dead immediately afterwards, one can avoid inserting the implicit copy for that variable by instead reusing its contents. Introduction of call-by-reference in place of call-by-value can also be performed if alias analysis reveals that this would not change the meaning of the program.

Transformation of an Example Model

As a unifying example of the practical application of code generation, we shall consider a simple echo server such as might be provided as a standard service by most implementations of TCP/IP. The standard echo server accepts a connection from a client and echoes any data sent by the client back to the client. The echo server inputs client requests consisting of a list of character strings and echoes back to the client a single character string constructed by concatenating the individual character strings in the input list. In addition, the echo server maintains a sequence number for each client connection that numbers the echo server responses within the context of that client connection. For example, if a client sends the

Figure 4. Echo system

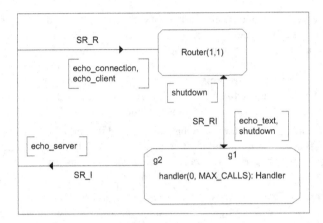

input data ('Hello', 'World') to the echo server, the echo server will reply with the pair 1, 'Hello World', assuming that this is the client's first message to the echo server. The system view of the echo server is shown in Figure 4.

The echo server handles multiple client connections concurrently, and it is therefore required that each client connection be serviced in the echo server by an active entity with its own thread of control (at least conceptually). In UML, each connection would be serviced by an instance of a specified active class.

The Router active class is the gateway into the echo server, and the single instance of the Router oversees the creation, deletion, and servicing of clients. When a client establishes a new connection to the echo server, the Router instance receives from the environment the echo_connection signal containing the client number that uniquely identifies the connection. The Router creates an instance of the Handler class dedicated to the connection. When an established connection is shut down, the Router instance also receives from the environment the echo_connection signal, but a signal parameter indicates that the connection is to be terminated. The Router then terminates the instance of the Handlerclass dedicated to the connection. When a service request from a client is received from the environment in the echo_client signal, the Router instance delegates the service request to the Handler instance dedicated to that client by sending the echo_text signal.

The specification of the state machine to handle client connections is illustrated in Figure 5. Each instance of the Handler class is parameterized by the client number, an identifier created by the platform-interface code to indicate the client connection serviced by the instance. Upon receipt of the echo_text signal containing a list of character strings, the text_list_to_text procedure is invoked, where the list of character strings will be concatenated to construct a single character string. The echo_server signal containing a sequence number, and the constructed character string will then be sent to the environment and ultimately to the client. The procedure text_list_to_text is shown in Figure 6.

Figure 5. Handler state machine

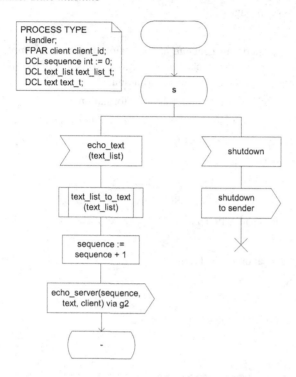

Figure 6. text_list_to_text procedure

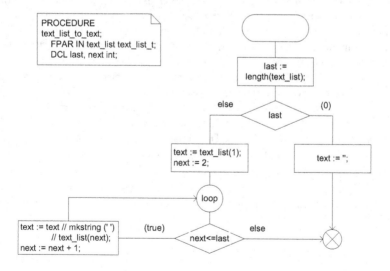

When translating an input model from the specification language through to C, the transformations occur in several stages:

- Traverse the input model to generate an equivalent model in a simpler and more uniform syntax, simultaneously checking the model for some of the simpler-to-find semantic defects and filling in derived information.
- Annotate the term with full type and scoping information.
- Analyze the annotated term to look for and report on model pathologies.
- Put the resulting model in canonical form.
- Optimize and transform the state machines.
- Choose concrete representations of abstract data types (lists, duration, time, etc.).
- Translate the resulting term from CFSM representation to Core.
- Perform initial canonicalization and preliminary optimization.
- Implement data types.
- Optimize the fully canonicalized terms.
- Implement processes.
- Translate from Core to C.
- Perform final polishing of the resultant C code.

Initial Model Translation

Graphical modeling languages such as SDL and UML have advantages to the users over purely textual languages, but they present challenges for processing tools. The equivalent textual representations of these languages, if they even exist in a standard form, are often verbose and difficult to parse with conventional techniques. The first step in translating these models, then, is to transform them into a term that can be manipulated by the rule engine. Since graphical modeling languages are effectively tied to their associated modeling tools, the initial translation process needs to be customized to each tool. Once the basic mechanism is in place to traverse the input model, the initial translation can be made. In this transformation stage, as in every stage, the system must ensure that the transformed code conforms to the proper surface syntax even if that form is rarely if ever used directly. While the correctness-preserving aspects of the rules ensure that this is true of the general syntax, it must be possible to lexically analyze the code, too. This constraint implies that the rule system must respect the keywords, punctuation, and lexical structure of the target language.

For example, if the input language has a variable named for, but that is a keyword in the target language, it must be renamed. Another example would be a variable such as a b, where the space character is a valid identifier character in the input language but not in the target language.

Annotations

Once the model has been transformed into a term representation, the term can be annotated with additional information that will aid in the further analysis and transformation of the model. Two of the most useful annotations are the type of every expression and the scope path of every identifier.

The scope annotations can be easily derived in a top-down traversal of the term by keeping a stack of the scoping units that are encountered during traversal. When an identifier is encountered, the associated name-table entry is annotated with the full stack of scope units.

The type annotations are more complicated to derive. The basic algorithm is to traverse the term, annotating expressions that are initially known such as the types of unique literals and constants. From these known points, the surrounding sub-terms can be annotated with their types and the process repeated until there is nothing else to annotate. Figure 7 shows an example of the sequence of steps used for type propagation. The top of the figure shows the initial synonym declarations. In each successive step, the derived type annotations are shown as subscripts. In the first step, MIN and MAX have known types since that is how they are declared. In the next step, the assignments indicate that the right-hand sides are also of type Integer. This gives 127 the type Integer, the type of MIN is propagated, and the + operation can be annotated with Integer assuming the Integer + operator is the only one which has the proper signature. In the third step, the 1 is given type Integer since that is what it must be from the signature of the + operator. Similarly for the * operator, only the Integer * fits the required signature. In the final step, the constant 2 is given type Integer because of the signature of the Integer * operator.

Another term annotation that is added is the indication of which process variables escape the "scope" of the transition in which they are used. By the basic semantics of SDL and UML, a state machine transition does not in itself create a scope. However, that makes it difficult to know when a variable must retain its value and when the associated memory can be freed. Analysis of the definitions and uses of the process variables, as well as any possible side effects that may be associated with them such as sending the value to another process, al-

Figure 7. Type propagation example

```
synonym MIN Integer := 127;
synonym MAX Integer := 2 * MIN + 1;
==>
synonym MIN_Integer Integer := 127;
synonym MAX_Integer Integer := 2 * MIN + 1;
==>
synonym MIN_Integer Integer := 127_Integer;
synonym MAX_Integer Integer := 2 * MIN_Integer +_Integer 1;
==>
synonym MIN_Integer Integer := 127_Integer;
synonym MAX_Integer Integer := 2 *_Integer MIN_Integer +_Integer 1_Integer;
==>
synonym MIN_Integer Integer := 127_Integer;
synonym MAX_Integer Integer := 2_Integer *_Integer MIN_Integer +_Integer 1_Integer;
```

Figure 8. Semantic check example

```
DCL var Integer;
DCL n Natural;

...

TASK n := var;
```

lows transformation rules to create virtual scopes for the transitions and to associate process variables with those scopes. (The introduction of "process-local" scopes relies on liveness analysis, see Sidebar "Liveness Analysis" beginning on p. 373.)

As an example of a semantic check that can be made once type propagation is completed, consider the code fragment shown in Figure 8. While it may be the case that operational constraints will ensure the condition that var will always be greater than or equal to zero, it may be impossible to prove that that will be the case, and an appropriate warning should be generated.

It is also possible at this point to insert runtime checks into the code for many of the potential semantic problems. Later optimization stages can remove those checks that can be statically determined to be unnecessary. However, experience has shown that not only does this significantly increase the code size since a large portion of the checks cannot be removed, but there is also no single answer on what should be done when the check fails at runtime. It is typically more effective to report such problems back to the modeler so that the underlying cause can be fixed.

Model-Level Optimizations

For performance reasons, it is important to minimize the amount of runtime processing that must occur. For size reasons, it is important to minimize the amount of non-functional infrastructure that must be kept around. An example that combines both of these involves the interprocess communication mechanism in SDL and UML. The dynamic semantics of a signal send involves the determination of the receiver of the signal by following the path that the signal takes to its destination process at runtime. Not only does this resolution take extra time during execution, but also the entire resolution mechanism as well as the signal path mechanism must be represented in the code.

It is far better to statically determine the receiver at transformation time by traversing the communication structure of the model. For example, in the process instances of the handler process type, the message send shown at the top of Figure 9 can be statically translated to the one at the bottom, indicating that the message is sent outside of the model through the channel SR_I to the environment.

If it is not possible to statically determine the receiver, either the signal is being sent directly to a process using the unique Pid of the process (in which case the receiver is a simple lookup in the process table at runtime) or the send is nondeterministic. If it is nondeterministic, the code generation system should inform the modeler since nondeterminism does not equate

Sidebar: Liveness Analysis

The goal of liveness analysis is to determine the set of live variables at specified points of interest within a program. A variable v is said to be *live* at point p in a program if the value of v may be used along some control flow path in the program that begins at p; otherwise, the variable v is said to be *dead* at point p.

In a traditional compiler, liveness analysis is typically performed on an intermediate representation of a program such as a flow graph. A flow graph is a directed graph in which the nodes are basic blocks, each composed of a sequence of low-level instructions. The edges connecting nodes within a flow graph represent control flow between basic blocks. Control flow within a basic block is entirely sequential with the exception of the last instruction in the basic block, where a branch may be taken.

In contrast, the Mousetrap code generator uses the Core language to express the intermediate representation of a design model before the ultimate translation to C. The majority of analysis and optimization steps within the code generator, including liveness analysis, are therefore performed while the design model is expressed in the Core language. The semantic distance between Core and C is not profound, as the Core language contains constructs to express both structured and unstructured flow of control. Consequently, liveness analysis in the Core language must consider control flow more varied and sophisticated than the control flow expressed in a flow graph.

The implementation of liveness analysis in the Core language is based on the same two liveness equations that are applied to basic blocks within a flow graph.

live-in[block] = use[block] ∪ (live-out[block] - def[block])
live-out[block] = ∪ live-in[block-successor]

The first equation defines the variables that are live at entry to a block as the union of

* the variables used in the block, and
* the variables not defined in the block that are live at block exit.

The second equation defines the variables that are live at block exit to be the union of the variables that are live at entry to successor blocks. A successor to a block is any block to which control can flow at exit of the block.

Information flows backward during liveness analysis since equation one consumes the liveness computed via equation two, and equation two consumes the liveness of the successors to the block of interest.

Adapting these liveness equations to the Core language requires the substitution of statement for block in the equations, as liveness must be considered in the context of individual Core procedure bodies, each containing a list of Core statements.

Sidebar: Liveness Analysis continued on next page

live-in[stmt] = use[stmt] $\cup$ (live-out[stmt] - def[stmt])
live-out[stmt] = live-in[successor of stmt]

Since a statement in a statement list has at most one successor statement, the second equation is simplified by eliminating the union operation. The second equation then equates the variables that are live after the execution of a statement to the variables that are live prior to the execution of its successor statement. Thus, the input to liveness analysis for any Core statement is the liveness computed prior to the execution of the successor to the statement. Computing the variables that are live prior to the execution of an arbitrary statement can be accomplished by applying the first equation to each specific type of Core statement. The liveness information flows backward through a statement list.

Core liveness analysis requires the def-use information computed by Core effects analysis, which is discussed in detail in the Sidebar: "Effects Analysis". It is sufficient for the purposes of this discussion to understand that each Core expression and statement term will be annotated with def-use information as a precondition for liveness analysis. The def-use information is conservative and includes all variables that *might* be defined and/or used by the term. The distinction between *might* and *must* is relevant in the following discussion, where liveness analysis for several Core statement types is considered. These Core statements have the concrete syntax shown below:

```
(ident ?n) (expr ?e) (expr-list ?el) (stmt ?s ?sc) (stmt-list ?sl)
(branch ?b) (branch-list ?bl) (node ?nd) (node-list ?ndl) (lvalue ?lv)
case-stmt              ::= CASE ?e { ?bl ELSE : { ?sl } }
branch                 ::= ?el : { ?sl }
catch-stmt             ::= CATCH ?n { ?sl }
flow-stmt              ::= FLOW { ?ndl }
node                   ::= ?n { ?sl }
loop-stmt              ::= LOOP { ?sl }
assignment-stmt        ::= ?lv := ?e ;
throw-stmt             ::= THROW ?n;
```

Case-Statement

This statement subsumes the if and case-statements found in procedural languages. The live variables prior to the execution of a case-statement include the variables that are used in the tested expression ?e as well as the live variables at entry to each of the branches, including the default else-branch. The live variables at entry to a branch are the live variables at entry to the statement list within the branch, since the expression-list ?el guarding a branch must include only ground expression, which are compile-time constants. The live variables at entry to the statement list within a branch are computed via recursive invocations of liveness analysis.

The following equations summarize liveness analysis for a Core case-statement ?s with successor statement ?sc.

live-in[?s] = use[?e] $\cup$ live-in[each ?b in ?bl] $\cup$ live-in[?sl]
live-out[?s] = live-out[each ?b in ?bl] = live-out[?sl] = live-in[?sc]

Sidebar: Liveness Analysis continued on next page

The second equation is used to compute the input to the recursive invocations of liveness analysis for each branch of the case-statement.

Catch-Statement

This statement provides the context for the transfer of control to its successor statement. Within the ?sl component of the catch-statement, execution of the statement throw ?n will transfer control to the successor statement of the catch-statement.

The following equations summarize liveness analysis for a Core catch-statement ?s with successor statement ?sc.

live-in[?s] = live-in[?sl]
live-out[?s] = live-out[?sl] = live-in[?sc]

In addition, live-out[?s] is associated with ?n for use when analyzing the statement throw ?n.

Flow-Statement

This statement indicates an irreducible control flow and enables the convenient expression of the state machines encountered in SDL and UML. A node is a named statement list. Within the context of a flow-statement, control may be transferred to the node identified by ?n by executing the statement throw ?n. If execution of the statement-list of a node does not terminate with a throw-statement, the flow of control transfers to the successor statement of the encompassing flow-statement. Execution of a flow-statement begins with the first node in ?ndl.

Liveness analysis for a flow-statement generally requires several iterations over the nodes in the ?ndl component. Since the transfer of control associated with throw-statements is central to the liveness analysis of a flow-statement, the set live-in[throw ?n] is introduced to denote the live variables upon transferring control to the node identified by ?n.

Initially, the value of live-in[throw ?n] is the empty set for each node identifier ?n, and this initialization is considered an update of each live-in[throw ?n] set. Then, while updates to any of the live-in[throw ?n] sets occur, liveness analysis is invoked recursively upon the ?sl within each node, where the live-in[throw ?n] sets will influence the analysis whenever a throw ?n statement is encountered. When liveness analysis for the ?sl within a node completes during a given iteration, the live-in[throw ?n] set is updated, if necessary, for the ?n that identifies the node. The following equations summarize liveness analysis for each node ?nd in a flow-statement ?s with successor statement ?sc.

live-in[?nd] = live-in[throw ?n] = live-in[?sl]
live-out[?sl] = live-out[?s] = live-in[?sc]

Sidebar: Liveness Analysis continued on next page

Liveness analysis for a flow-statement ?s completes when an iteration over the nodes in the ?ndl component of ?s completes without updating any live-in[throw ?n] set. At that point, the following equation summarizes liveness analysis for ?s.

```
live-in[?s] = live-out[?s], if ?ndl is empty
live-in[?s] = live-in[first(?ndl)], otherwise
```

Loop-Statement

This statement enables the expression of both definite and indefinite (perhaps infinite) iteration. The logic associated with the update and test of any loop control variables will be specified within the ?sl component of the loop-statement and will typically involve a throw-statement that exits the loop-statement via an enclosing catch-statement. The use of a single construct to express iteration simplifies analysis and optimization within the Core language since transformation rules need not consider the variety of iteration constructs commonly encountered in procedural languages. However, common idioms such as for, while, and repeat-loops are recognized during the translation of Core loop-statements to C.

Liveness analysis for a loop-statement generally requires several iterations over the ?sl component. Since the flow of control does not exit the loop-statement in the absence of a throw-statement in the ?sl component, the initial live-out set for the ?sl component is initialized to the empty set. Liveness analysis is recursively invoked on the ?sl component to compute the live-in set for ?sl, and the live-out set for ?sl is then equated to the live-in set for ?sl. The liveness analysis for a loop-statement ?s completes when a recursive invocation on the ?sl component of ?s computes a live-in set for ?sl that is equal to the live-out set for ?sl. At that point, the following equation summarizes liveness analysis for ?s.

```
live-out[?sl] = live-in[?sl] = live-in[?s]
```

Assignment-Statement

The Core assignment statement is the only Core statement type in which variables are directly defined. Alias and effects analysis are used to determine whether the ?lv component ultimately specifies a single variable (the ?lv component may include pointer dereferences). In those cases where alias analysis determines that the ?lv component *might* specify more than one variable, liveness analysis must be conservative and not consider any variable to be defined by the assignment statement. For example, consider the following Core statement list, where & is the Core reference operator and ^ is the Core dereference operator.

```
CASE x < 10 { true : { p := &w; } else : { p := &z; } }
^p := 10;
x := y;
```

Sidebar: Liveness Analysis continued on next page

The assignment statement with the L-value ^p *might* assign the value 10 to either w or z. Liveness analysis cannot conclude that the variable w *must* be defined by the assignment-statement. Similarly, liveness analysis cannot conclude that the variable z *must* be defined by the assignment-statement. On the other hand, the assignment-statement with the L-value x *must* define the variable x, since there is no aliasing involved in the assignment-statement.

Liveness analysis for an assignment-statement ?s with successor statement ?sc is directly summarized by the two liveness equations derived previously, subject to the conservative treatment of defined variables:

live-in[?s] = use[?s] ∪ (live-out[?s] - def[?s])
live-out[?s] = live-in[?sc]

Applications

Liveness analysis contributes essentially to Core optimization. For example, liveness analysis is the principal and immediate enabling input in the following transformations.

Minimization of Process Context: The variables that must be preserved in the context of a process instance are precisely those variables that are live at the point at which the process instance may block when waiting for signal input. During the course of Core process implementation, calls to the abstract API process-block are introduced at the blocking points in each process type. Liveness analysis is then invoked upon the statement list in the body of each process type. Expression statements invoking process-block will be annotated with liveness sets during the course of liveness analysis. The process context for a process type is then simply the union of all live variables across all calls to process-block within the body of the process type.

Elimination of Dead Assignment Statements: An assignment-statement is said to be *dead* if the value of the L-value defined by the statement is not used at a subsequent point in the program. At a minimum, the actual assignment to the L-value can be eliminated, since it has no useful effect. If the dead assignment statement does not involve a procedure call with non-local effects, the entire assignment statement can be eliminated. For example, consider the following Core statement list:

```
x := y;
w := f();
z := g();
```

If x, w, and z are known to be dead at the points of their respective assignments, and if it is known that f has non-local effects while g does not have non-local effects, the following optimized Core statement list can be substituted:

```
f();
```

In terms of liveness analysis, a dead assignment-statement ?s is simply an assignment statement whose ?lv component is not represented in live-out[?s].

Figure 9. Receiver transformation example

```
echo_server(sequence,
    text, client) via g2
```

```
==>
```

```
echo_server(sequence,
text, client) via ENV SR_I
```

to fairness, and *any* of the possible receivers can be statically chosen to the exclusion of all the others (which is typically not what the modeler intended).

Other model-level optimizations are performed on state machines. Simple state machines can be implemented efficiently using a case-statement within a loop. However, the state machines as defined by SDL and UML allow much more complicated structures. Any implementation must take into account the possibility of guard conditions that have side effects, signals that are discarded or saved without a state transition, priority inputs, hierarchical states with their own entry and exit points and deep history, transitions that can split and merge, and so forth.

While there is no single best method for how to translate the state machines, putting the state machine in a canonical form helps the process. The basic canonical form of the state machine is one in which the state and signal structure is fully expanded. That is, for every state and every input signal, the resulting action is present even if that action is simply to discard the signal. From this form, the states and input can be refactored so that the state and input signal combinations that occur most frequently appear near the top of the resulting decision structure. As a general rule, grouping common transitions together based on the number of signals involved at least will minimize the number of cases that need to be searched.

In this form, it is also simple to detect the cases that can be further optimized. For example, if a state machine consists of only one state but that state has several inputs, then the state itself does not need to be explicitly represented. Alternately, if there are multiple states but only one input signal, then the infrastructure that matches on the signal type can be removed. Another case that can be optimized is a state machine with multiple states and multiple signals, but each state only handles one signal and no signal is handled in more than one state. In that case, it is only the sequencing of the signals that is relevant and the states themselves do not need to be transformed.

Abstract Data Types

The concrete implementations of abstract data types must be selected. As with the implementation of state machines, there is no single best strategy for choosing the most efficient implementation of the data types and their operations. General trade-offs can be made between minimizing the space required and minimizing the execution time, and the final implementation must often be made by supplying additional information resulting from profiling of the executing code to the transformation rules.

A viable scheme to handle the selection of the concrete implementations is to have several implementations available for each abstract data type. The specific implementation can be chosen based on heuristic rules related to the expected performance of the implementation.

To help choose among candidate implementations, the transformation system can determine which operations on the data type are used (or not used) in the model. For example, suppose that the transformation rules determine that the tuples of a map are never accessed directly through the domain values except for a single delete call, but instead the data type is frequently iterated over. This would indicate that a concrete implementation that favors iteration, such as a linked list, would be preferable over one that requires extra steps to determine the next value.

The implementation of list or string data types involves three subtasks: (1) efficient implementation of their primitive operations; (2) strength reduction to improve the asymptotic efficiency of loops that traverse or construct them (typical idioms of linear traversal or construction by concatenation are implemented in constant time per operation); and (3) elimination of unnecessary copying that would naïvely be required by value semantics. In practice, the third sub-task is very important. Mousetrap devotes effort to analyzing situations where the source of a complex data structure becomes dead and therefore can be reused instead of copied, and to where copies can be replaced by references.

For example, models typically require the use of a data type that allows map or hash-table-like functionality. That is, one wants to be able to access some data value through the use of a domain value similar to the function of a C array, but allowing more than simple consecutive integers to be the domain values. Modeling languages may provide a suitable data type, such as Array in SDL. However, there are two main problems with using these provided types to produce high-performance code:

- Size bounds are needed in order to efficiently implement the functionality in the generated code. Most often, the maximum number of mappings to be stored is significantly smaller than the size implied by the domain type.

- An indication is needed of how dense the mapping is. That is, what is the maximum number of elements that can be in the mapping versus how many there are typically. From this information, it can be determined how to implement the map (e.g., as a sparse array, a hash table, a regular array, etc.).

Only knowing the domain and range types, the transformation system would be forced to choose a concrete data type that would allow a potentially very large number of tuples, such as a hash table created through dynamic memory allocation. However, with the additional information about the maximum and typical numbers of elements, implementations that are more efficient can be chosen, such as a static hash table or even a simple linked list.

Translation to Core

As the final stage in the process of translating from the PDU/CFSM stage to Core, the term is transformed in a single pass that changes the types of the nodes in the term into their direct equivalents in Core.

An important aspect of Core is that it assumes integers can be arbitrarily large, although all declarations of integer types have finite range. The types of expressions are typically different from the types of the associated subterms. For example, if the variables x and y have types int[0,10] and int[-100,200] (indicating Integer subranges), then the expression x + y has the type int[-100,210]. Unlike C, arithmetic operations have the normal mathematical meaning in Core–semantics dependent on word size, such as rounding and overflow, do not exist in Core. As a result, it is easier to write correctness-preserving transformations as well as reason about the types of expressions in a target-independent way.

Canonicalization

Core is a simplified procedural language for which ease of transformation was a more important goal than ease of programming. This led to a preference for uniform syntax over more convenient (for the programmer) syntactic sugar. For example, instead of using an if-statement, conditional execution is expressed using a case-statement. The equivalent of the if-statement is a Boolean case-statement.

Placing additional constraints on Core terms simplifies many of the transformations. Terms that satisfy these constraints are called "canonical". Some examples of these constraints:

- All expressions are well-typed.
- All names not externally visible in the program are distinct.
- Control flow through any procedure ends in a return-statement, even for procedures without return values.
- Defined constants do not appear in expressions.
- The only expressions that have side effects are either expression-statements (that is, top-level procedure calls) or the top-level expression in the right-hand side of an assignment-statement.

The last constraint is important for at least two reasons. First, the C language does not define a standard evaluation order for subexpressions in most cases. If one is translating a language such as SDL that does have an order defined, it must be enforced by the introduction of temporary variables.

Second, many subsequent optimizations may be more easily expressed if most expressions are guaranteed to be without side effects. Many expression optimizations in Mousetrap either cause expressions to be moved with respect to one another or cause the number of occurrences of the expression to change.

Enforcing this constraint while preserving the semantics of any program requires that all subexpressions be "lifted" (replaced with a temporary variable, where that variable is assigned in a preceding statement) if the subexpression has side effects. See the detailed discussion in Sidebar "Expression Lifting" beginning on page 365.

Optimizations

Expression simplification applies rules that represent algebraic equalities of expressions. Mousetrap has approximately 400 rules of this kind. Many can only be applied to canonicalized terms, however, a function that applies the subset that is safe on arbitrary terms is also available. The same rules may be applied in either context.

One of the most complicated (and expensive) optimizations is *forward analysis*. In this optimization, assertions about the values of variables and other expressions are propagated forward along paths of possible control flow. The optimization makes use of side effect information (attached as attributes to statements) to remove assertions as they potentially become invalidated.

Information that is propagated includes:

- that a variable or expression has a specified constant value (constant propagation);
- that a variable or expression is equal to another variable or expression, and this was the result of assignment of the second to the first (copy propagation);
- that a pointer is not null;
- that an object with nontrivial constructors is in an initialized ("nullified") state; and
- that the value of an integer expression is in a proper subrange of the range specified by its type.

Finally, some destructors ("invalidate" expressions) are partially inlined in order to expose more opportunities for optimization.

A data structure is constructed that represents information about the values of variables and other simple expressions such that if an expression e is mapped to an expression e' in this data structure, then when e is encountered the optimization can rewrite it to e'. Whether this happens depends on parameters controlling the complexity of e' vs. e (in order to avoid replacing inexpensive variable references with more expensive expressions). This data structure is propagated forward along control flow, with merging and fix-point computations occurring at conditionals and other transfers of control and at loops. Substitution of these values is performed when appropriate. In a sense, this transformation is the opposite of common sub-expression elimination. Mousetrap performs a pass of limited common sub-expression elimination after the last pass through forward analysis in order to repair performance problems that may have been introduced by replicating code unnecessarily.

Several examples of this optimization step can be observed on the echo_system.

The constant 2, assigned to the variable next, is forward propagated into the condition of a case-statement, which is subsequently simplified to its then-clause, as shown in Figure 10.

In Figure 11, the expression text_list0!length is propagated as the value of the variable last. This is an example of copy propagation. Note that the value is propagated into a loop, as the transformation recognizes that last is not modified in the loop. Figure 12 shows a further

Figure 10. Constant propagation and simplification

```
fundcl text_list_to_text (text_list0 SDL_string_impl) void {
dcl next int[1,2147483647];
...
next := 2;
dcl iter_text_list0 ref SDL_string_item;
iter_text_list0 := text_list0!first;
case next >= 2 {
  true : {
  iter_text_list0 :=    iterator_advance_SDL_string_impl
      (iter_text_list0, int_between[1, 268435456] (next) - 1);
  }
  else: { }
}
...
==>
fundcl text_list_to_text (text_list0 SDL_string_impl) void {
dcl next int[1,2147483647];
...
next := 2;
dcl iter_text_list0 ref SDL_string_item;
iter_text_list0 := text_list0!first;
iter_text_list0 := iterator_advance_SDL_string_impl
  (iter_text_list0!first, 1);
...
```

Figure 11. Copy propagation (a)

```
fundcl text_list_to_text (text_list0 SDL_string_impl) void {
...
dcl last int[1,2147483647];
last := text_list0!length;
...
catch tag32 {
loop {
...
case next > last {
    true : { return; }
    else: { }
}
...
==>
fundcl text_list_to_text (text_list0 SDL_string_impl) void {
...
dcl last int[1,2147483647];
...
catch tag32 {
loop {
...
case next > text_list0!length {
    true : { return; }
    else: { }
}
...
```

Figure 12. Copy propagation (b)

```
fundcl text_list_to_text (text_list0 SDL_string_impl) void {
...
dcl cs_conc_arg1 char_string_impl;
cs_conc_arg1 := struct (. char_string_impl : 1,
            sub_array (imprecise (& cs_data), 1), true .);
...
cs_conc_ptr1 :=    new_array [type ref array [char]]
    (cs_conc_arg1!length + cs_conc_arg1!length + cs_conc_arg2!length + 1);
...
==>
fundcl text_list_to_text (text_list0 SDL_string_impl) void {
...
cs_conc_arg1 :=
        struct (. char_string_impl : 0, imprecise (& cs_data), true .);
...
cs_conc_ptr1 := new_array [type ref array [char]]
    (text!length + 1 + cs_conc_arg2!length + 1);
...
```

example of copy propagation, where the propagated value is inferred from the constructor for the aggregate data structure.

When the pointer iter_text_list0 is dereferenced, the assertion that this pointer is not null is established. This assertion is propagated forward to a case-statement where the tested variable is compared against null; this comparison and the case statement are then simplified away, as shown in Figure 13.

Calling a destructor on a null object has no effect. Therefore, the invalidate operation (the Core destructor) on text_list immediately after its initialization (the nullify operation puts the object into a clean state) is a noop, and is removed (see Figure 14).

Figure 13. Assertion propagation (a)

```
fundcl text_list_to_text (text_list0 SDL_string_impl) void {
...
cs_conc_arg3 := (^iter_text_list0)!item;
...
case iter_text_list0 != null [type ref SDL_string_item__char_string] () {
true : { iter_text_list0 := (^iter_text_list0)!next; }
    else: { }
}
...
==>
fundcl text_list_to_text (text_list0 SDL_string_impl) void {
...
cs_conc_arg3 := (^iter_text_list0)!item;
...
iter_text_list0 := (^iter_text_list0)!next;
...
```

Figure 14. Assertion propagation (b)

```
...
nullify [fun SDL_string_impl] (& text_list);
...
invalidate [fun SDL_string_impl] (& text_list);
...
==>
...
nullify [fun SDL_string_impl] (& text_list);
...
```

Figure 15. Partial inlining of destructor

```
...
echo_text_msg := process_pop_current [type echo_text_signal] ();
...
invalidate [fun O_echo_text_signal] (& echo_text_msg);
echo_text_msg := null [type ref echo_text_signal] ();
...
==>
...
echo_text_msg := process_pop_current [type echo_text_signal] ();
...
invalidate [fun echo_text_signal] (echo_text_msg);
free (echo_text_msg);
echo_text_msg := null [type ref echo_text_signal] ();
...
```

The partial inlining of destructors is shown in Figure 15. At this point, it is known that echo_text_msg is non-null. In these situations, destructors will be transformed as follows: the object is invalidated first and then its memory is freed. The main reason for performing this change is to expose the opportunity to later combine sequences of creation and destruction of memory to avoid unnecessary allocation of new memory.

Mousetrap also performs several kinds of interprocedural optimizations. Most important is function inlining. If a function is called in sufficiently few places, and is not "too big" (more precisely, if the term will not grow by more than a given factor), the inlining transformation replaces each call with an expression that contains a copy of the body of the function. The formal parameters become temporary variables that are assigned the actual parameters. After the inlining transformation has been performed, the term may no longer be in canonical form, so unique renaming and a limited form of expression lifting are again performed.

One very important class of optimizations involves the elimination of copying of large data structures. In some modeling languages such as SDL, aggregate data types such as arrays or sequences have value semantics: assignment or parameter passing involves implicit copies of the data structure. These copies can be very expensive, so effort is devoted to their elimination.

In one class of transformations, certain common idioms are recognized and replaced with forms that are more efficient. For example, Figure 16 shows an example of a string idiom optimization performed in text_list_to_text. The optimization recognizes that an SDL string (a sequence data structure), is being traversed sequentially in a loop. It performs strength reduction, introducing an iterator variable. Because Mousetrap implemented these SDL strings as linked lists, this optimization turns a quadratic time algorithm into a linear time algorithm.

At this point, the string and iterator types are still abstract. They will be made concrete by later transformations; other transformations will simplify some of the intermediate code. The case statement introduced here is later eliminated by the forward analysis transformation (see Figure 10). In this example, the transformation identifies the index variable next and the string variable text_list0. A new variable, iter_text_list0, an iterator for the string type, is introduced. Three statements are rewritten:

- When the variable next is initialized, code is added to initialize the iterator.
- When next is incremented, code is added to advance the iterator.
- When next is used to index into text_list0, the call is transformed into a call using the iterator variable. (The iterator points to the next-1 location in the string.)

Another very important optimization transforms function calls in which some arguments have expensive copy operations into calls where the arguments have only shallow copies. This can be done by introducing pointers or by changing the types of arguments to "demoted" types (for which copy operation do not follow certain internal pointers, but instead continue to refer to the data structure being copied).

Figure 16. Iterator optimization example

```
fundcl text_list_to_text (text_list0 SDL_string_impl) void {
    ...
    text := char_string_Concat (text,
            ^_SDL_string_Extract_ref (& text_list0, next - 1));
    next := next + 1;
    ...
==>
fundcl text_list_to_text (text_list0 SDL_string_impl) void {
    ...
    text := char_string_Concat (text,
                ^ iterator_extract_ref (& text_list0, iter_text_list0));
    case iter_text_list0 != iterator_after_end (text_list0) {
      true : {
        iter_text_list0 := iterator_advance (text_list0, iter_text_list0, 1);
      }
      else: { }
    }
    next := next + 1;
    ...
```

This optimization is safe only if the source data structure and the copied data structure are not modified during the function call, and if no references to the copied data structure or its components can escape. The alias analyzer is used to conservatively verify the first of these preconditions, and patterns on the body of the function are matched. Escape is ruled out by determining that the formal parameter is never used in a referenced L-value in the body of the function.

In the echo system example, the function text_list_to_text is passed an argument of a linked-list type. The transformation determines that this type can be replaced by a demoted list type, which is equivalent to passing just the head structure of the linked list, rather than copying the entire linked list and its contents (see Figure 17). A similar transformation shown in Figure 18 converts call-by-value on "expensive" types—that is, large structure, union, or array types—into call-by-reference to these types. Side effect information is used to confirm that this transformation is safe. Linked-list types could be passed by reference as well, but for "small" types (the header structure of the Mousetrap list implementation is not a large structure) passing by demotion proves to provide better performance. The reason is that variables that have had their addresses taken (by the & operator) are less amenable to other optimizations; they also confuse the alias analyzer. Structure parameters can exploit a scalarization transformation in which the fields of the structure are passed individually,

Figure 17. Call-by-value to call-by-demotion optimization

```
fundcl text_list_to_text ( text_list0 SDL_string
        [type char_string [], 0, 4294967295]) void { ... }
...
text_list_to_text (text_list);
...
==>
fundcl text_list_to_text ( text_list0 demote
        [SDL_string [type char_string [], 0, 4294967295]]) void { ... }
...
text_list_to_text (@ text_list);
...
```

Figure 18. Call-by-value to call-by-reference optimization

```
fundcl text_list_to_text ( text_list0 SDL_string
        [type char_string [], 0, 4294967295]) void { ... }
...
text_list_to_text (text_list);
...
==>
fundcl text_list_to_text ( text_list0 ref
        SDL_string [type char_string [], 0, 4294967295]) void { ... }
...
text_list_to_text (& text_list);
...
```

and eliminated if they are always passed constant or globally accessible values, or if they are not used in the called function.

One can also reduce the cost of passing data structures through "structure explosion". In this optimization, variables and actual parameters that are structures and that are not aliased (by having their address taken with the & operator) are converted to a set of variables, one for each field of the structure. Assignments to the variable are changed to assignments to its fields; assignments from the variable are changed to structure constructor expressions, and formal parameters are replaced by a set of formal parameters for their fields.

In Figure 19, the parameter to text_list_to_text is separated into four parameters, one for each field of the SDL_string_impl structure type. Two of these parameters (for the finger and

Figure 19. Structure explosion optimization

```
fundcl text_list_to_text ( text_list0 SDL_string_impl ) void {
    ...
    iter_text_list0 := text_list0!first;
    ...
    case next > text_list0!length {
    true : { throw tag32; } else: { }
    }
    ...
==>
fundcl text_list_to_text (text_list0_length int[0,268435455],
                          text_list0_first ref SDL_string_item
                          text_list0_finger ref _SDL_string_item,
                          text_list0_fingidx int[0,268435455] ) void {
    ...
    iter_text_list0 := text_list0_first;
    ...
    case next > text_list0_length {
    true : { throw tag32; } else: { }
    }
    ...
```

Figure 20. Array size reduction example

```
const lookup_table array [array [array [int[0,255], 5], 1] :=
    array (. array [array [int[0,255], 5], 1] :
        array (. array [array [int[0,255], 5] : 255, 3, 2, 1, 0 .) .);
    ...
    transition_number := lookup_table [[0]] [[(message_lookup_table
            [[(_enum_to_int (current_message_kind))]]) ]];
==>
    const lookup_table array [int[0,255], 5] :=
        array (. array [int[0,255], 5] : 255, 3, 2, 1, 0 .) .);
    ...
    transition_number := lookup_table [[(message_lookup_table
            [[(_enum_to_int (current_message_kind))]]) ]];
```

fingidx fields) are not used in the function body, so a later optimization will eliminate them entirely.

Another means of reducing the cost of manipulating large data structures is to reduce these data structures in size. For example, a transformation looks for array variables that are indexed by values that are in a proper sub-range of the declared range of indices of the array. These arrays are replaced by either smaller arrays of the same dimensionality or arrays of reduced dimensionality (if one or more indices are always constant). In the echo_system example, this happens to the state-transition lookup table since the process has only one state (this degenerate case of an array is often introduced by state machines having only single state, see Figure 20).

Implementation of Core Processes

Instances of a UML active class or an SDL process map directly to instances of an associated Core process type. The efficient and practical implementation of Core process types requires knowledge of the target platform, including the relative costs of threading and synchronization. If a platform provides extremely lightweight threading and synchronization, it may be appropriate to assign each instance of a Core process type to a dedicated thread. In this case, scheduling of process instances reduces to the platform scheduling of threads, and the state of a process instance can be treated as thread-specific data. However, experience with several popular operating systems and design models with thousands of process instances has shown that the cost of task/thread synchronization eliminates the one-to-one mapping of threads and process instances from consideration. In fact, significant success has been achieved using the simple approach of executing all instances of all Core process types within a single thread.

The implementation of Core processes via a single-threaded approach is accomplished by transforming each Core process type into a procedure that accepts a specified instance of the process type as a parameter. This parameter uniquely identifies the process instance and aggregates the state and signal management for the process instance. Since multiple process instances are sharing the same thread of execution, it is essential that a process instance waiting for signal input not block within the process procedure. Rather than blocking, the process implementation must save the relevant state of the process instance currently executing and arrange for a return from the process procedure. When signal input arrives for a blocked process instance, the procedure will again be invoked with the process instance as a parameter, and execution will effectively resume within the process procedure at the point where the process instance previously would have blocked.

The identification of the relevant state that must be preserved across the points at which a process instance may block is of great practical significance. The naïve approach would simply save the values of all process variables that are in-scope at the points at which a process instance might block. With realistic design models, however, the memory required to implement this strategy can easily exceed hundreds of kilobytes for each process type and overwhelm the capacity of the underlying platform when these storage requirements are multiplied by the thousands of processes that may be active simultaneously. It is therefore essential to minimize the preserved state and retain the values of only those process variables that are actually "live" at the point(s) at which a process instance might block. Here, "live" means variables whose values may be consumed when a process instance resumes execution after potentially blocking.

The relevant process state is identified through liveness analysis (see Sidebar "Liveness Analysis" beginning on p. 373). It utilizes the alias and effects analysis based on sets of abstract locations (see Sidebar "Effects Analysis" beginning on p. 390). That is, the abstract locations that are live prior to the execution of a statement are either the abstract locations used by the statement or the abstract locations used by a successor statement that are not defined (assigned-to) by the statement. As with forward analysis, merging and fixed-point computation must be executed when considering liveness across conditional and loop-statements.

As a concrete example, consider the minimization of the context to be preserved for instances of the Handler active class in the echo server example. Instances of this active class will block when waiting on an echo_text or shutdown signal. The process variables sequence, text_list, and text are all in-scope at these points. However, analysis of the body of this active class reveals that only the sequence variable need be preserved for an instance of this active class. The values of both the text_list and text variables are not required once the echo_server signal is sent to the environment, so these variables are not live across any point at which an instance of this active class might block. Since both of these variables have complex types that will consume several words of storage, their elimination from the process context significantly reduces the required context size when compared to the naïve approach.

Translation to C

Once optimizations are completed, Mousetrap begins the process of transforming the internal representation to C. Mousetrap supports "mixed" terms, in which operators from different grammars can co-exist, so this process is gradual, transforming only part of the grammar at each step.

One of the products of this transformation stage is a set of header files containing declarations of the type, functions, and global variables of the transformed code. One file contains only the externally visible entities; this file is included by anything that needs to invoke functions visible in the external interface. Declarations are topologically sorted (and stub definitions added) so the rules of C regarding use-before-definition are satisfied.

Since the arithmetic operators of the intermediate language have cleaner semantics than those of C, care needs to be taken in their translation. Mousetrap assumes that the target C environment has types for 8, 16, 32, and (optionally) 64-bit integers, both signed and un-signed. Integer sub-range types are translated to the lowest enclosing C type in the integer type hierarchy of C. This means, for example, that the type int[0,100000] is translated to a signed 32-bit integer type, since signed types upgrade to unsigned types in C. Appropriate upward casts are added when implementing arithmetic operators. Arbitrary fixed precision integer arithmetic is provided as well, but is much more costly.

At times, it is known that certain branches in the code are unlikely to occur. For example, code can be generated that tests each heap allocation to determine if the request succeeds, and jumps to an error handling routine if it failed. This presumably will not occur often. In this situation, C macros are introduced that inform the C compiler that the relevant if-statements

Sidebar: Effects Analysis

The purpose of effects analysis is to compute the side effect behavior for each statement and expression. This information is then used to determine the validity of program transformations and to perform various analyses for the purpose of program transformation. Examples of such analysis and transformations are expression lifting (see Sidebar "Expression Lifting"), code motion (changing the order of statements in a statement list), forward analysis, and liveness analysis (see Sidebar "Liveness Analysis").

The end result of effects analysis is the SFX attribute that is computed for each statement and expression and contains, among others, the following two parts: a *use* effects set and a *def* effects set. A use set is an abstraction of the memory locations that are potentially *accessed* during the execution of the statement or expression. A def set is an abstraction of the memory locations that are potentially *modified* during the execution of the statement or expression. Another field of the SFX attribute, which is not discussed here, contains information on whether the term may terminate abnormally (by a return or goto-statement) rather than falling through.

Let def(s) denote the def set of statement s and use(s) denote the use set of s. Let def(e) denote the def set of expression e and use(e) denote the use set of expression e. An example of the use of these effects sets is that any statement s with empty def(s) can be deleted. As another example consider the sequence of two statements s1 s2. The order of these statements can be reversed only if def(s1) does not intersect use(s2) and use(s1) does not intersect def(s2).

Effects Sets and Abstract Locations

We represent effects sets (the def and use sets of a statement or expression) by sets of abstract locations. Abstract locations represent the set of memory locations for program variables and allocations and their components. For example, if v is a variable of structure type with a field x, then the set represented by the abstract location for v, denoted by [v], contains the set represented by the abstract location for v!x, denoted by [v!x].

The effects set constructors are union, singleton and difference. Predicates on effects sets are is-empty, is-singleton, and intersects. Since abstract locations represent sets of runtime memory locations, the set denoted by an effects set is defined as the union of all the memory locations denoted by its abstract locations. For example, the effects set {[v]} intersects with {[v!x]} because the set of possible runtime locations for [v] intersects with the set of possible runtime locations for [v!x]. In other words, changing v!x changes v.

Since, obviously, we do not know the set of runtime memory locations associated with an abstract location at transformation time, we need to use a static abstraction of runtime memory. We do this by associating numbers with sets of runtime locations. For example, for each variable v we assign a single integer i to represent all the possible starting locations of that variable v and we assign another integer i+size(v)-1 with the ending locations. We represent abstract locations by intervals of these numbers and effects sets by the union of these intervals. For example, if v is a variable of structure type with two integer fields x

Sidebar: Effects Analysis continued on next page

and y, then we represent the abstract locations for v, v!x, and v!y by the intervals [1,2], [1,1] and [2,2] and it follows that the interval set for {[v]} intersects with the interval set for {[v!x]}. Therefore, given a program p we create a virtual static memory space with locations 0 to the size of p. Abstract locations are pairs of the start and end location in this memory space. We also associate other information with abstract locations like their types and whether they are aliased.

Effects analysis comprises the following steps:

- Perform alias analysis; this creates the points-to-graph.
- Annotate the points-to-graph with effects sets.
- Compute the SFX attributes in the bottom-up order given by the call graph.

Alias Analysis

The goal of alias analysis is to create a points-to-graph. A points-to-graph is a graph where the nodes represent abstract locations and where the nodes for all pointers that can potentially point to the same memory location point to the same node. For example, if two variables of pointer type, p and q, are aliased (for example by an assignment p := q), then the nodes for p and q point to the same node. The algorithm used for doing alias analysis is inspired by Steensgaard's (1996) algorithm, which is context and flow insensitive and has near linear time and space complexity. We cannot utilize super linear methods, which might produce more refined points-to-graphs, because of scalability concerns.

There are four node types: simple, pointer, structure, and array. We define corresponding predicates for testing the type of a node. For a pointer node, we can access the referenced node with the operation pointee. For a structure node, we can access its fields with fields. For an array node, we can access its element node with elem. For each expression e and lvalue lv we have a way to access their node by node. A simple node can turn into a pointer, structure or array node with the operations expand-to-pointer, expand-to-structure, and expand-to-array. The node kinds simple, pointer, array, and structure are sufficient to handle all the data types of typical languages. Union types are modeled using structure nodes.

Our algorithm is based on union-find with path compression: Each node represents an equivalence class. When two nodes, n1 and n2, are *joined*, then one node is made equal to the other (for example, by setting a table is(n1) to n2) and the structures of n1 and n2 are joined recursively. Given a node n, one can find the node representing its equivalence class by traversing the path of these is links; this traversal is performed by ecr(n). The function join(n1,n2) is defined as follows:

```
case
  simple (n1): is(n1) := n2;
  simple (n2): is(n2) := n1;
  pointer(n1): let np1 = pointee (n1) and np2 = pointee (n2)
                 is(n1) := n2;
                 join (ecr (np1), ecr (np2));
                 pointee (ecr(n2)) := ecr(np1);
```

Sidebar: Effects Analysis continued on next page

```
   array  (n1): let elem1 = elem (n1) and elem2 = elem (n2)
                    is(n1) := n2;
                    join (elem1, elem2);
                    elem (ecr(n2)) := ecr(elem1);
structure (n1): let flds1 = fields (n1) and flds2 = fields (n2)
                    is(n1) := n2;
                    join-fields (flds1, flds2);
                  fields(ecr(n2)) := flds2;
```

The post condition of the alias analysis algorithm is that for each assignment lv := e, node(lv) is equal to node(e). We make a distinction between node identity and node equality. Node identity means that the two nodes are the same. Two nodes are equal if and only if they have the same structure and all the referenced nodes are identical.

The basic idea of the join algorithm is as follows:

1.   Assign distinct simple nodes to each variable.

2.   For each assignment lv := e (handling function parameter passing and return value passing as assignments) unify the node structures for lv and e so that all referenced nodes are joined by applying assign_nodes. For example if two pointers p and q are assigned, then the node structures that are referenced by the nodes for p and q are joined into one node using join. The function assign-nodes unifies the node structures for lv and e such that node(lv) will be equal to node(e) afterwards. It is important that all the node structures for lv and e are expanded down to all pointer nodes so that they can be joined. For example, for assignment p := q where p and q have pointer type, we need to expand node(p) and node(q) to be pointer nodes and these nodes need to both point to the same pointee node. If we do not expand the nodes for p and q, the aliasing effect of the assignment is not taken into account.

In practice, the naïve implementation of this algorithm is not feasible because structures and unions may have many fields. For example, for assignment u1 := u2 where the type is a union of many pointer tags we would need to expand both u1 and u2 with all these tags and join the corresponding referenced nodes. This leads to the creation of too many nodes. Such data types are common in communication systems.

To circumvent this problem, we introduce the notion of a node *recipe* and the following invariant: If node n has a recipe, denoted by has-recipe(n), then that recipe, recipe(n), is more defined than n. That is, if n is a pointer node, then recipe(n) is a pointer node and pointee(n) is identical to pointee(recipe(n)). If n is a structure node, recipe(n) is a structure node with at least the fields that n has and all the field nodes that the recipe has in common with n are more defined than the corresponding field nodes of n. The intuition behind a recipe is that the node structure of n is *prescribed* by its recipe but the structure is only created when it is necessary. Node equality is extended so that a node is also equal to its recipe.

We redefine assign-nodes(n1, n2) as follows:

Sidebar: Effects Analysis continued on next page

```
case
   has-recipe(n1): assign-recipe (n2, recipe(n1));
   has-recipe(n2): assign-recipe (n1, recipe(n2));
   else: let recipe = make-simple-node()
          in { assign-recipe(n1,recipe);

                  assign-recipe(n2,recipe); },
```

where assign-recipe(n, recipe) is defined as

```
case
   has-recipe(n): join(recipe(n), recipe);
   simple(n): recipe(n) := recipe;
   pointer(n):
     expand recipe to be a pointer node and then
                          join(pointee(n),pointee(recipe))
   array(n):
     expand recipe to be an array node and then call
                        assign-recipe(elem(n),elem(recipe))
   structure(n):
     expand recipe to be a structure node that contains the fields of recipe
          and then call assign-recipe with all those fields.
```

Returning to the example u1 := u2, and for the case that node(u1) and node(u2) are simple, we create a simple recipe node and assign it to both recipe(node(u1)) and recipe(node(u2)).

Annotate the Points-to-Graph with Effects Sets

Since the nodes in the points-to-graph denote sets of memory locations we can associate an effects set with each node that represents those locations, denoted by loc(n). We do this by initially assigning the empty effects set to each node and then traversing the program in the following steps:

- for each variable v, we add is abstract location [v] to loc(node(v));

- for each field access lv!x we add the following constraint: if l is an abstract location in the effects set for node(lv) then the abstract location for the x field of l is in loc(node(lv!s));

- for each array element access lv[[i]] we add the following constraint: if l is an abstract location in the effects set for node(lv) then the abstract location for its element is in loc(node(lv[[i]])).

To see why the constraints are needed, consider the lvalue (^p)!x. Here the effects set for node((^p)!x) is dependent on the effects set of node(^p) which might not be computed yet. However, if we associate all the constraints with each node, then after the traversal we can compute the effects set for each node by evaluating its constraints.

Sidebar: Effects Analysis continued on next page

Compute the SFX Attributes

The end result of effects analysis is the SFX attribute for each statement and expression. The attribute is set in the following steps:

1. Create the call-graph.

2. Associate an SFX attribute with each procedure.

3. Starting with all procedures that do not call any other procedures (the leaves of the call graph) and then traversing bottom-up in the call graph, for each procedure

    a. Traverse its body bottom-up and

        i.   for each lvalue lv, expression e and statement s, set def(lv), def(e), def(s) and use(lv), use(e), use(s) to be the union of the def and use set of their operands;

        ii. for a dereference ^p, add the effects set for the pointer loc(node(p)) to the use set;

        iii. for a procedure call, add the use and def sets of the call to the use and def sets;

        iv. for an assignment lv := e, add loc(node(lv)) to the def set and add loc(node(e)) to the use set.

    b. Add the union of all def and use sets in the body to the def and use sets of the procedure and then remove the effects pertaining to all the local variables of the procedure (using effect set difference).

This analysis is conservative in the sense that each physical location is in the set of at least one abstract location, and if a term may modify a physical location, then the analysis determines that it modifies the abstract location containing that physical location. Because this abstraction may map two or more distinct memory locations to a single abstract location, the analysis is imprecise. Transformations that use the information are designed to work with conservative approximations of the actual program behavior.

We have implemented several optimizations to the method described. For example:

*   In many cases, we can determine the effects set of an expression or lvalue without accessing its node. For example, the effects set for v!x is {|v!x|} which is more accurate than loc(node(v!x)).

*   We only compute the effects loc(n) for those nodes for which it is necessary. These nodes turn out to be exactly those nodes that are referenced by a pointer.

*   Given the previous optimization, we can optimize assign-recipe to create a smaller number of nodes by not attaching recipes to nodes that are not referenced.

We improved the precision of effects analysis by handling some procedures in a context sensitive way. That is, the effects of a procedure call are dependent on its context. Here we rely on caching the nodes of the actual parameters.

usually branch in the common direction (this macro is defined separately and is compiler-specific; for compilers not supporting such hints the macro is trivial). Branch prediction is important for generating efficient code on some modern processor architectures.

One peculiarity of C is the ambiguity of certain if-statements. Mousetrap manipulates abstract syntax trees, which by their very nature are unambiguous, but distinct terms have the same printed representation. Such terms are recognized by a set of cleanup transformations and rewritten to forms that print unambiguously in C.

A final transformation pass is performed on the C code to clean up or reduce the size of the generated code. These rules are mostly cosmetic; the semantics of C is such that deep optimizations are more difficult to perform than on the Core internal representation. Examples of final cleanup transformations include conversion of goto-statements into break-statements or continue-statements, elimination of unneeded casts, recognition of idioms such as increment and decrement operators, and recognition of for-loops.

Conclusion

In this chapter, we have given an overview of a technique to develop programs by deriving them through the sequential application of correctness-preserving transformations from high-level specifications. This technique has been successfully leveraged in the Mousetrap program transformation system to develop application code for Motorola network elements. In contrast to compilers or code translators, a program transformation system performs the transformation from specification to implementation in a number of discrete steps that can be adjusted to the application domain and expert user experience. Consequentially, program transformation systems, like Mousetrap, have been able to consistently beat hand-written code in terms of code quality and performance even in application domains where other code generation approaches have failed.

References

Agresti, W. (Ed.) (1986). *New paradigms for software development*. Washington: IEEE Computer Society Press.

Boyle, J., Harmer, T., Weigert, T., & Weil, F. (1998). The derivation of efficient programs from high-level specifications. In N. Bourbakis (Ed.), *Artificial intelligence in automation*. Singapore: World Scientific Publishers.

Czarnecki, K., & Eisenecker, U. (2000). *Generative programming: Methods, tools, and applications*. Indianapolis: Addison-Wesley.

Dietz, P., & Weigert, T. (2003). Automated generation of marshalling code from high-level specifications. In R. Reed, & J. Reed (Eds.), *Lecture Notes in Computer Science: Number 2708. SDL 2003: System Design* (pp. 374-386). Berlin: Springer Verlag.

Steensgaard, B. (1996). Points-to-analysis in almost linear time. In the *Proceedings of the 23rd ACM SIGPLAN-SIGACT Symposium on Principles of Programming Languages*, St. Petersburg Beach, FL, January 21-24 (pp. 34-41). New York: ACM Press.

Tsai, J.-P., & Weigert, T. (1993). *Knowledge-based software development for real-time distributed systems.* Singapore: World Scientific Publishers.

Weigert, T. (1999). Lessons learned from deploying code generation in industrial projects. In M. Sant'Anna, J. Leite, I. Baxter, D. Wile, T. Biggerstaff, D. Batory, P. Devanbu, & L. Burd (Eds.), *Proceedings International Workshop on Software Transformation Systems*, Los Angeles, CA, May 16-22. Los Angeles: IEEE Computer Society Press.

Weigert, T., & Weil, F. (2006). Practical experiences in using model-driven engineering to develop trustworthy computing systems. In the *Proceedings 2006 IEEE International Conference on Sensor Networks, Ubiquitous, and Trustworthy Computing*, Taichung, Taiwan, June 5-7 (pp. 208-217). Taichung: IEEE Computer Society Press.

Appendix: Handler Process

This appendix shows the Handler process as it progresses through the various transformation stages from the original SDL input to the final resultant C code. The following code excerpts show the Handler process (and the local text_list_to_text function) as they appear at the entry to each stage. While we do not give the semantics of the constructs of the intermediate representation, by examining the results of performing the sequence of transformation phases discussed earlier the reader should gain intuition as to the impact of these transformation steps.

SDL

```
PROCESS TYPE Handler;
 FPAR client client_id;
 GATE g1
   OUT WITH shutdown;
   IN WITH shutdown, echo_text;
 GATE g2
   OUT WITH echo_server;
 DCL sequence int := 0;
 DCL text_list text_list_t;
 DCL text text_t;
 PROCEDURE text_list_to_text;
   FPAR IN text_list text_list_t;
   DCL last, next int;
   START;
   TASK last := length(text_list);
   DECISION last;
   (0):
    TASK text := '';
    RETURN;
   ELSE:
```

```
      TASK text := text_list(1),
      next := 2;
      JOIN loop;
    ENDDECISION;
    loop:
    DECISION next <= last;
    (true):
      TASK text := text // mkstring(' ') // text_list(next);
      TASK next := next + 1;
      JOIN loop;
    ELSE:
      RETURN;
    ENDDECISION;
  ENDPROCEDURE text_list_to_text;
  START;
  NEXTSTATE S;
  STATE S;
    INPUT echo_text( text_list);
      CALL text_list_to_text( text_list);
      TASK sequence := sequence + 1;
      OUTPUT echo_server( sequence, text, client) VIA g2;
      NEXTSTATE -;
    INPUT shutdown
      OUTPUT shutdown TO SENDER;
      STOP;
  ENDSTATE;
ENDPROCESS TYPE Handler;
```

Pre

```
proc handler Handler[0, MAX_CALLS](client :: client_id) {
  sigset echo_text, shutdown;
  dcl sequence :: int := 0;
  dcl text_list :: text_list_t;
  dcl text :: text_t;
  start next S;
  state S {
    input echo_text (text_list);
    join 1aea78;
    input shutdown();
    join 1ae498;
  }
  lbl 1ae498 {
    output shutdown() to sender;
    stop;
  }
  lbl 1aea78 {
    text_list_to_text(text_list);
    task sequence := sequence + 1;
    output echo_server(sequence, text, client) to Env SR_I;
    next - ;
  }
  procedures func text_list_to_text (in text_list :: text_list_t) void {
    dcl last :: int;
    dcl next :: int;
    start {
      task last := op  length(text_list );
```

```
    case (last ) {
      [ == 0] : {
        task text := "";
        return ;
      }
      else  {
        {
          task text := text_list [1];
          task next := 2;
        }

        join loop ;
      }
    }
    lbl loop case (next <= last) {
      [ == true] :  {
        task text := text // op  mkstring(' ');
        task text := text // text_list [next];
        task next := next + 1;
        join loop;
      }
      else return;
    }
   }
  }
 }
}
```

CFSM

```
proc handler [(0), MAX_CALLS] (client :: client_id) {
  sigset MT_SHUTDOWN_PROCESS, echo_text, shutdown;
  dcl self_1 :: pid := process_self ();
  dcl sender :: pid;
  dcl sequence :: int;
  dcl text_list :: text_list_t;
  dcl text :: text_t;
  func text_list_to_text (in text_list0 :: text_list_t) void {
    dcl last :: int;
    dcl next :: int;
    {
      task last := SDL_string_Length ( << text_list_t (text_list0) >> );
      case (last) {
        [== (0)] : {
          task text := char_string_Literal ((""") );
          return;
        } else {
          task text := << text_list_t (text_list0) >> [(1)];
          task next := (2);
        }
        join loop;
      }
    } /* last */
    lbl loop case (next <= last) {
      [== (true)] : {
        task text := char_string_Concat (
            char_string_Concat (text, char_string_MkString ((' ') ) ),
            << text_list_t (text_list0) >> [next] );
```

```
      task next := next + (1);
      join loop;
    }
    else return;
  } /* next <= last */
}
} /* text_list_to_text */
dcl current_state :: one_byte;
dcl unsave :: boolean := (false);
dcl conditional_input_unsave :: boolean := (false);
dcl transition_number :: one_byte;
dcl current_message_kind :: process_message_data_kind;
start {
  lbl start_node {
    task sequence := (0);
    lbl grst3
    task << text_list_t text_list >> :=
        << text_list_t (null_text_list) >>;
    process_nextstate ((1) + (0) );
    if (unsave) {
      process_unsave_all ();
      task unsave := (false);
      task conditional_input_unsave := (false);
    } /* unsave */
    task current_state := (0);
    task transition_number := lookup_transition ((0));
    join fsm_node;
  }
  lbl fsm_node case (transition_number) {
    [== (1)] : { process_consume_current (); { process_stop (); }}
    [== (2)] : {
      let_stmt (
        echo_text_msg, process_pop_current (
          type (echo_text_signal ) )
        );
      assume (echo_text_msg != << own_echo_text_signal (null) >> );
      task << text_list_t text_list >> := extract_contents (
            addr (ref_own (echo_text_msg ) ! (Element1) ) );
      task echo_text_msg := null (type (own_echo_text_signal ) );
      { join 1aea78; }
    }
    [== (3)] : { process_consume_current (); { join 1ae498; }}
    [== (255)] : {
      process_discard_current ();
      task transition_number := lookup_transition (current_state );
      join fsm_node;
    }
    else assume ((false) );
  } /* transition_number */
  lbl 1ae498 {
    dcl message_2 :: own_shutdown_signal := void ();
    dcl receiver_2 :: pid := sender;
    process_send (
      type (shutdown_signal ), receiver_2, enum (
            tag (process_message_data ), shutdown ), message_2);
    process_stop ();
  }
  lbl 1aea78 {
```

```
    text_list_to_text (<< text_list_t (text_list) >> );
    task sequence := sequence + (1);
    { dcl se_tmp :: echo_server_signal :=
        << echo_server_signal
        ((. demote (sequence ), demote (text ), demote ( client ) .)) >>;
      process_send_external (
          type (echo_server_signal ), fun ( env_output ), enum (env, SR_I ),
          enum (tag (process_message_data ), echo_server ),
          addr (se_tmp )
          );
    }
    join grst3;
    }
  }
}
```

Core

```
process handler (client client_id) message []
  dcl self_1 pid [];
  dcl sender pid [];
  dcl sequence int;
  dcl text_list text_list_t;
  dcl text text_t;
  fundcl text_list_to_text (text_list0 text_list_t) void {
    dcl last int;
    dcl next int;
    flow {
      Label_Start_4 {
      last := SDL_string_Length (text_list0);
      case last {
        0 : {
        text := char_string_Literal ("");
        return;
        } else: {
        text := ^SDL_string_Extract_ref (& text_list0, 1 - 1);
        next := 2;
        throw loop;
        }
      }
      throw loop;
      }
      loop {
        case next <= last {
        true : {
        text := char_string_Concat
          (char_string_Concat (text, char_string_MkString (' ')),
          ^SDL_string_Extract_ref (& text_list0, next - 1));
        next := next + 1;
        throw loop;
        }
        else: {
        return;
        }
        }
      }
    }
```

```
  }
  dcl current_state one_byte;
  dcl unsave bool;
  dcl conditional_input_unsave bool;
  dcl transition_number one_byte;
  dcl current_message_kind message_kind;
body {
  self_1 := process_self ();
  unsave := false;
  conditional_input_unsave := false;
  flow {
    Label_Start_5 { throw start_node; }
    1aea78 {
      text_list_to_text (text_list);
      sequence := sequence + 1;
      dcl se_tmp demote [type echo_server_signal];
      se_tmp := struct (.
        demote [type echo_server_signal] : @ sequence, @ text, @ client .);
      process_send_external [type echo_server_signal, fun env_output]
                      (enum (. env : SR_I .),
                       enum (. message_kind : echo_server .),
                       & se_tmp);
      throw grst3;
    }
    1ae498 {
      dcl message_2 own_shutdown_signal;
      message_2 := void ();
      dcl receiver_2 pid [];
      receiver_2 := sender;
      process_send [type shutdown_signal]
        (receiver_2, enum (. message_kind : shutdown .), message_2);
      process_stop ();
      throw 1aea78;
    }
    fsm_node {
      case transition_number {
        1 : { process_consume_current (); process_stop (); }
        2 : {
          let echo_text_msg := process_pop_current [type echo_text_signal] ()
            in {
            assume (echo_text_msg != null [type own_echo_text_signal] ());
            text_list :=
              extract_contents (& (^(@ echo_text_msg) ) !Element1);
            echo_text_msg := null [type own_echo_text_signal] ();
            throw 1aea78;
          }
        }
        3 : { process_consume_current (); throw 1ae498; }
        255 : { process_discard_current (); throw signals_node; }
        else : { assume (false); }
      }
      throw 1ae498;
    }
    grst3 {
      text_list := SDL_string_Empty [type text_list_t] ();
      process_nextstate (1 + 0);
      current_state := 0;
      throw next_state;
```

```
    }
    start_node { sequence := 0; throw grst3; }
    signals_node {
      case process_has_current () {
        true : {
          current_message_kind := process_get_current_kind ();
          sender := process_get_current_sender ();
          transition_number := lookup_table [[current_state]]
            [[(message_lookup_table
                [[(enum_to_int (current_message_kind))]]) ]];
          throw fsm_node;
        }
        else: { process_block (); throw signals_node; }
      }
    }
    next_state {
      case unsave {
        true : {
          process_unsave_all ();
          unsave := false;
          conditional_input_unsave := false;
        }
        else: { }
      }
      throw signals_node;
    }
  }
}
```

Post

```
fundcl text_list_to_text (text_list0_length int[0,268435455],
                text_list0_first ref SDL_string_item) void {
  dcl process_2 ref process;
  process_2 := coerce ref process process_context (process_self ());
  dcl next int[1,2147483647];
  dcl cs_conc_arg char_string_impl;
  dcl temp133_length int[0,268435455];
  dcl temp133_contents ref array [char];
  dcl temp133_is_const bool;
  dcl cs_conc_arg2 char_string_impl;
  dcl cs_conc_off int[0,268435455];
  dcl cs_conc_ptr ref array [char];
  case text_list0_length == 0 {
    true : {
      invalidate_char_string_impl (& (^process_2) !text);
      (^process_2) !text!contents := imprecise (& cs_data);
      (^process_2) !text!length := 0;
      (^process_2) !text!is_const := true;
      return;
    }
    else: { }
  }
  cs_conc_arg := (^text_list0_first)!item;
  dcl stmp7_length int[0,268435455];
  dcl stmp7_contents ref array [char];
  dcl stmp7_is_const bool;
```

```
case cs_conc_arg!is_const {
  true : {
    temp133_length := cs_conc_arg!length;
    temp133_contents := cs_conc_arg!contents;
    temp133_is_const := true;
  }
  else: {
    dcl temp5 ref array [char];
    temp5 := new_array [type ref array [char]] (cs_conc_arg!length + 1);
    case temp5 == null [type ref array [char]] () {
      true : {
        cs_conc_arg2 := zero [type char_string_impl] ();
      }
      else: {
        array_copy (temp5, cs_conc_arg!contents, cs_conc_arg!length);
        (^temp5) [[(cs_conc_arg!length)]] := '\0';
        stmp7_length := cs_conc_arg!length;
        stmp7_contents := temp5;
        stmp7_is_const := false;
        cs_conc_arg2!length := stmp7_length;
        cs_conc_arg2!contents := stmp7_contents;
        cs_conc_arg2!is_const := stmp7_is_const;
      }
    }
    temp133_length := cs_conc_arg2!length;
    temp133_contents := cs_conc_arg2!contents;
    temp133_is_const := cs_conc_arg2!is_const;
  }
}
invalidate_char_string_impl (& (^process_2) !text);
(^process_2) !text!length := temp133_length;
(^process_2) !text!contents := temp133_contents;
(^process_2) !text!is_const := temp133_is_const;
dcl iter_text_list0 ref SDL_string_item;
dcl iter2 ref SDL_string_item;
iter2 := text_list0_first;
cs_conc_off := 1;
catch return_catch9 {
  loop {
    case cs_conc_off == 0 || iter2 == null [type ref SDL_string_item] () {
      true : { throw return_catch9; }
      else: { }
    }
    iter2 := (^iter2)!next;
    cs_conc_off := int_between [1, 268435455] (cs_conc_off) - 1;
  }
} /* return_catch9 */
iter_text_list0 := iter2;
next := 2;
loop {
  case next > text_list0_length {
    true : { return; }
    else: { }
  }
  cs_conc_arg2 := (^iter_text_list0)!item;
  cs_conc_ptr :=
    new_array [type ref array [char]] ((^process_2)!text!length +
                          cs_conc_arg2!length + 2);
```

```
    case cs_conc_ptr != null [type ref array [char]] () {
     true : {
       array_copy (cs_conc_ptr, (^process_2)!text!contents,
               (^process_2)!text!length);
       (^cs_conc_ptr) [[((^process_2)!text!length)]] := cs_data [[1]] ;
       array_copy (sub_array (cs_conc_ptr,
           int_between [0, 268435454] ((^process_2)!text!length) + 1),
             cs_conc_arg2!contents, cs_conc_arg2!length);
       cs_conc_off :=
           int_between [0, 268435454] (cs_conc_arg2!length +
             int_between [0, 268435454] ((^process_2)!text!length)) + 1;
       (^cs_conc_ptr) [[cs_conc_off]] := '\0';
      }
      else: { cs_conc_off := 0; }
     }
     invalidate_char_string_impl (& (^process_2) !text);
     stmp7_length := cs_conc_off;
     stmp7_contents := cs_conc_ptr;
     stmp7_is_const := false;
     (^process_2) !text!length := stmp7_length;
     (^process_2) !text!contents := stmp7_contents;
     (^process_2) !text!is_const := stmp7_is_const;
     iter_text_list0 := (^iter_text_list0)!next;
     next := int_between [1, 2147483646] (next) + 1;
   }
 }
fundcl handler () void {
 dcl process_3 ref process;
 process_3 := coerce ref process process_context (process_self ());
 catch merge_tag2 {
   flow {
     node_0_2 {
       case (^process_3)!node {
         enum (. process_flow : node_6 .) : {
           throw node_3_2;
         }
         else: { }
       }
       (^process_3) !text := zero [type char_string_impl] ();
       (^process_3) !sequence := 0;
       throw node_2_2;
     }
     node_2_2 {
       process_nextstate (1);
       (^process_3) !text_list := zero [type SDL_string_impl] ();
       throw node_3_2;
     }
     node_3_2 {
       loop {
         case process_has_current () {
           true : {
             dcl current_message_kind message_kind;
             dcl sender pid [];
             dcl transition_number int[0,255];
             current_message_kind := process_get_current_kind ();
             sender := process_get_current_sender ();
             transition_number := lookup_table
               [[(message_lookup_table
```

```
        [[(enum_to_int (current_message_kind))]]) ]];
      catch tag9 {
       case transition_number {
        2 : {
         dcl echo_text_msg ref echo_text_signal;
         echo_text_msg :=
           process_pop_current [type echo_text_signal] ();
         invalidate_char_string_item
                   ((^process_3)!text_list!first);
         (^process_3) !text_list := (^echo_text_msg)!Element1;
         free (echo_text_msg);
         text_list_to_text ((^process_3)!text_list!length,
                     (^process_3)!text_list!first);
         dcl se_tmp echo_server_signal;
         dcl sequence_1 int[1,2147483647];
         sequence_1 := int_between [0, 2147483646]
                     ((^process_3)!sequence) + 1;
         dcl stmp8_Element1 int[-2147483648,2147483647];
         dcl stmp8_Element2 char_string_impl;
         dcl stmp8_Element3 int[-2147483648,2147483647];
         stmp8_Element1 := sequence_1;
         stmp8_Element2 := (^process_3)!text;
         stmp8_Element3 := (^process_3)!client_2;
         se_tmp!Element1 := stmp8_Element1;
         se_tmp!Element2 := stmp8_Element2;
         se_tmp!Element3 := stmp8_Element3;
         process_send_external
           [type echo_server_signal, fun env_output]
           (enum (. env : SR_I .),
            enum (. message_kind : echo_server .),
            & se_tmp);
         (^process_3) !sequence := sequence_1;
         invalidate_char_string_item
                   ((^process_3)!text_list!first);
         throw node_2_2;
        }
        3 : { process_consume_current (); }
        255 : { process_discard_current (); throw tag9; }
        else: { process_consume_current (); throw merge_tag2; }
       }
       process_send [type shutdown_signal]
        (sender, enum (. message_kind : shutdown .));
       throw merge_tag2;
      } /* tag9 */
     }
    else: {
     case process_block () {
      true : {
       (^process_3) !node := enum (. process_flow : node_6 .);
       return;
      }
      else: { }
     }
    }
   }
  }
 }
}
```

```
} /* merge_tag2 */
invalidate_char_string_impl (& (^process_3) !text);
invalidate_char_string_item ((^process_3)!text_list!first);
process_report_stop ();
return;
}
```

C

```
MT_STATIC_FUNC void text_list_to_text (mt_sint32 text_list0_length,
                          SDL_string_item *text_list0_first) {
  process *process_2;
  mt_sint32 next;
  char_string_impl cs_conc_arg;
  mt_sint32 temp133_length;
  char *temp133_contents;
  bool temp133_is_const;
  char_string_impl cs_conc_arg2;
  mt_sint32 cs_conc_off;
  char *cs_conc_ptr;
  mt_sint32 stmp7_length;
  char *stmp7_contents;
  bool stmp7_is_const;
  SDL_string_item *iter_text_list0;
  SDL_string_item *iter2;
  process_2 = (process *) mt_process_context (mt_process_self ());
  if (text_list0_length == 0) {
    invalidate_char_string_impl (& process_2 -> text);
    process_2 -> text.contents = (char *) & cs_data;
    process_2 -> text.length = 0;
    process_2 -> text.is_const = TRUE;
    return;
  }
  cs_conc_arg = text_list0_first -> item;
  if (cs_conc_arg.is_const) {
    temp133_length = cs_conc_arg.length;
    temp133_contents = cs_conc_arg.contents;
    temp133_is_const = TRUE;
  } else {
    char *temp5 = (char *)
      MT_MALLOC ((mt_sint32) (cs_conc_arg.length + 1) * sizeof (char));
    if (temp5 == NULL)
      (void) memset ((void *) & cs_conc_arg2, 0, sizeof (char_string_impl));
    else {
      (void)  memmove ((void *) temp5, (void *) cs_conc_arg.contents,
                 sizeof (char) * cs_conc_arg.length);
      temp5 [(cs_conc_arg.length)] = '\0';
      stmp7_length = cs_conc_arg.length;
      stmp7_contents = temp5;
      stmp7_is_const = FALSE;
      cs_conc_arg2.length = stmp7_length;
      cs_conc_arg2.contents = stmp7_contents;
      cs_conc_arg2.is_const = stmp7_is_const;
    }
    temp133_length = cs_conc_arg2.length;
    temp133_contents = cs_conc_arg2.contents;
    temp133_is_const = cs_conc_arg2.is_const;
```

```
}
invalidate_char_string_impl (& process_2 -> text);
process_2 -> text.length = temp133_length;
process_2 -> text.contents = temp133_contents;
process_2 -> text.is_const = temp133_is_const;
iter2 = text_list0_first;
for (cs_conc_off = 1; cs_conc_off != 0&& iter2 != NULL; -- cs_conc_off)
  iter2 = iter2 -> next;
iter_text_list0 = iter2;
for (next = 2; next <= text_list0_length; ++ next) {
 cs_conc_arg2 = iter_text_list0 -> item;
 cs_conc_ptr = (char *) MT_MALLOC ((mt_sint32) ((mt_sint32)
   (process_2 -> text.length + cs_conc_arg2.length) + 2) * sizeof (char));
 if (cs_conc_ptr != NULL) {
  (void) memmove ((void *) cs_conc_ptr, (void *)
          process_2 -> text.contents,
          sizeof (char) * process_2 -> text.length);
  cs_conc_ptr [(process_2 -> text.length)] = cs_data [1];
  (void) memmove ((void *) (cs_conc_ptr + (mt_sint32)
          (process_2 -> text.length + 1)),
          (void *) cs_conc_arg2.contents,
          sizeof (char) * cs_conc_arg2.length);
  cs_conc_off =
    (mt_sint32) (cs_conc_arg2.length + process_2 -> text.length) + 1;
  cs_conc_ptr [cs_conc_off] = '\0';
 }
 else cs_conc_off = 0;
 invalidate_char_string_impl (& process_2 -> text);
 stmp7_length = cs_conc_off;
 stmp7_contents = cs_conc_ptr;
 stmp7_is_const = FALSE;
 process_2 -> text.length = stmp7_length;
 process_2 -> text.contents = stmp7_contents;
 process_2 -> text.is_const = stmp7_is_const;
 iter_text_list0 = iter_text_list0 -> next;
}
}
MT_STATIC_FUNC void handler (void) {
 process *process_3;
 process_3 = (process *) mt_process_context (mt_process_self ());
 if (process_3 -> node == process_flow_node_6) MT_GOTO (node_3_2);
 (void) memset ((void *) & process_3 -> text, 0, sizeof (char_string_impl));
 process_3 -> sequence = 0;
 node_2_2 :
 mt_process_nextstate (1);
 (void) memset ((void *) & process_3 -> text_list, 0,
         sizeof (SDL_string_impl));
 node_3_2 :
 for (;;) {
  if (mt_process_has_current ()) {
   message_kind current_message_kind;
   mt_pid_t sender;
   mt_uint8 transition_number;
   current_message_kind = mt_process_get_current_kind ();
   sender = mt_process_get_current_sender ();
   transition_number = lookup_table [((mt_uint16)
     message_lookup_table [((mt_uint16)
              ((int) current_message_kind))])];
```

```
switch (transition_number) {
  case 2: {
    echo_text_signal *echo_text_msg;
    echo_server_signal se_tmp;
    mt_sint32 sequence_1;
    mt_sint32 stmp8_Element1;
    char_string_impl stmp8_Element2;
    mt_sint32 stmp8_Element3;
    echo_text_msg = mt_process_pop_current ();
    invalidate_char_string_item (process_3 -> text_list.first);
    process_3 -> text_list = echo_text_msg -> Element1;
    MT_FREE_FIXED (echo_text_msg, sizeof (echo_text_signal));
    text_list_to_text (process_3 -> text_list.length,
                process_3 -> text_list.first);
    sequence_1 = process_3 -> sequence + 1;
    stmp8_Element1 = sequence_1;
    stmp8_Element2 = process_3 -> text;
    stmp8_Element3 = process_3 -> client_2;
    se_tmp.Element1 = stmp8_Element1;
    se_tmp.Element2 = stmp8_Element2;
    se_tmp.Element3 = stmp8_Element3;
    mt_process_send_external ((opaque) & env_output,
                    env_SR_I,
                    message_kind_echo_server,
                    & se_tmp);
    process_3 -> sequence = sequence_1;
    invalidate_char_string_item (process_3 -> text_list.first);
    MT_GOTO (node_2_2);
  }
  case 3: mt_process_consume_current ();
  break;
  case 255: mt_process_discard_current ();
  continue;
  default : mt_process_consume_current ();
  MT_GOTO (merge_tag2);
  }
  mt_process_send (sender, message_kind_shutdown, NULL);
  break;
}
if (mt_process_block ()) {
  process_3 -> node = process_flow_node_6; return;
  }
}
merge_tag2 : invalidate_char_string_impl (& process_3 -> text);
invalidate_char_string_item (process_3 -> text_list.first);
mt_process_report_stop();
}
```

Chapter XV

DPSSEE:
A Distributed Proactive
Semantic Software
Engineering Environment[1]

Donghua Deng, University of California, Irvine, USA

Phillip C.-Y. Sheu, University of California, Irvine, USA

Abstract

This chapter presents a distributed proactive semantic software engineering environment (DPSSEE) that incorporates logic rules into a software development process to capture the semantics from all levels of the software life cycle. It introduces the syntax and semantics of the Semantic Description Language (SDL). It also introduces model-based testing and maintenance. Several working scenarios are discussed to illustrate the use of semantic rules for workflow control, design consistency checking, testing, and maintenance.

Introduction

Huge amounts of information can be derived in a software development process. Such information includes programming objects (e.g., projects, modules, functions, classes, variables, statements, etc.), their relationships and the experience knowledge that can be derived. Appropriate management and utilization of this information can guide the developers, speed up a software development process, and allow the developers to incorporate personalized logic rules to control the environment.

In this chapter, we describe a distributed proactive semantic software engineering environment (DPSSEE) that incorporates a set of advanced knowledge representation schemes and knowledge-based function modules that can capture and utilize the semantics of a software development process.

Compared with other disciplines, the nature of information for software development is much less observational. In DPSSEE, we aim to investigate such nature in a rational and empirical way. We formulate an appropriate model for a software development environment by extracting objects from a set of function modules (e.g., design tools, version control tools, project management tools, etc.), so that the model can then be used to support more systematic, complete, and efficient project management and software analysis, implementation, testing, and maintenance.

In addition, a user can assert more semantics based on experiences, observations, and so forth. Such additional semantics is expressed in terms of constraint rules and proactive rules. They can be used to strengthen the functionality of each function module, and make a software development environment more efficient and intelligent.

The organization of this chapter is as follows. The *Background* section reviews the work related to knowledge-based software engineering at different levels. The *System Architecture* section illustrates the overall architecture of DPSSEE. The *Semantic of Software Engineering* section introduces the syntax and semantics of the Semantics Description Language (SDL). The *Semantic Software Development Model (SSDM)* section illustrates the structure, annotation, and construction of the SSDM. The *Semantic Project Management Model (SPMM)* section describes the construction of the SPMM. The *Model-Based Testing and Maintenance* section presents an approach to model-based testing and maintenance based on the semantics provided by SSDM. The *Rule Generation and Applications* section discusses the syntax and applications of proactive and constraint rules. Finally, the chapter ends with the *Conclusions* section.

Background

Software tools have been developed to support different aspects of the software life cycle. For example, Microsoft Project supports project planning and progress tracking for virtual software development teams. For software design, CASE tools, such as Rational Rose, Jcomposer (Grundy, Mugridge, & Hosking, 1998), Argo/UML (Robbins, Hilbert, & Redmiles, 1998), PARSE-DAT (Liu, 1998), and Clockworks (Graham, Morton, & Urnes, 1996), are available to model, analyze, and refine a software design. Version control tools, such as Visual SourceSafe, source code control system (SCCS), and revision control system (RCS) provide a repository for file sharing during a software development process. In addition, the field of knowledge-based software engineering (KBSE) has studied the formal representations of knowledge at all levels during the software life cycle, and the utilization of such knowledge to support the design, programming, testing and maintenance of software. The following is a partial list of some existing KBSE systems.

MILOS (minimally invasive long term organizational support) (Maurer & Bowen, 2002) provides process support and experience management for software development in a distributed environment. It supports project coordination, information routing, team communication, pair programming, and experience management based on collaboration and coordination technologies.

LASSIE is a knowledge-based software information system (Devanbu et al., 1991) that addresses the invisibility and complexity problem through a knowledge representation scheme and a set of reasoning mechanisms to support relational code analysis, reuse librarians, and project management. It represents a large software system with a knowledge base, and then provides an interactive interface to give developers access to the software using some semantic views.

In the software design stage, some knowledge-based modeling and design tools are available. For example:

SoftArch (Grundy, 2000) is an environment that provides flexible software architecture modeling, analysis, design generation, and tool integration using the concept of successive refinement. It provides extensible analysis tools enabling developers to reason about their architecture models, allowing code generation from architecture-level abstractions, and supporting reuse of previously developed models and patterns. A collection of extensible "analysis agents" constrain, guide and advise architects as they build and refine their architecture models.

ADORA (analysis and description of requirements and architecture) (Glinz, Berner, Joos, Ryser, Schett, & Xia, 2001) presents an approach to object-oriented modeling of software. All information related to a system is integrated into one coherent model instead of UML, which allows consistency constraints among the views to be defined.

Knowledge-based applications can also aid the developer in programming efficiently and correctly. For example:

KIDS (Kestrel interactive development system) (Smith, 1990) is a knowledge-based programming environment that provides an automated support for the development of efficient and correct programs from formal specifications. It supports algorithm design, deductive inference, program simplification, partial evaluation, finite differencing optimization, data type refinement and compilation, and so forth.

WREN (Lüer & Rosenblum, 2001) is an environment for component-based software development (CBDE) that provides a method to name the interfaces in a globally unique way, to find potentially interesting components from component distribution sites, to evaluate the identified components for suitability to an application, to incorporate selected components into application design models, and to integrate selected components into an application.

COMET (commitment-based software development) (Mark, Tyler, McGuire, & Schossberg, 1992) facilitates a software design and development process with explicit representation and reasoning based on commitments. It aids the developer with module reuse by examining the commitments must be met, and explores the modifications of the commitments as the modules are changed.

Knowledge-based testing and maintenance has been provided in many software development systems. For example:

Rhapsody (Gery, Harel, & Palatshy, 2002) integrated a set of technologies to develop software systems in a highly reusable and platform-independent way based on the idea of executable models (Harel & Gery, 1997), where model-based testing and maintenance is able to specify and run tests, and to detect defects from the test results by visualizing the failure points within the model. It also provides a model-based testing component to facilitate consistency checking between the requirements and the system constructed.

KITSS (Kelly, 1993) is a knowledge-based translation system for test scenarios that guide the software developer with test cases for white or black testing. It provides intelligent assistance in converting test cases into an executable testing language. It prevents the lengthy, tedious, error prone work of writing test scripts by hand, and guarantees the quality of the resulting scripts.

SCENT-Method (Ryser, 2002) is a method for scenario-based validation and testing of software. It is an approach that aims to validate and verify requirements with a formalization of natural language scenarios, and provides support for the generation of test scenarios. It derives the test scenarios from state charts, and uses dependency charts for scenarios to enhance the developed test suits. It saves the time for creating scenario tests for software applications, leaves more time for running the tests and developing the system.

TACCLE (Chen, Tse, & Chen, 2001) is a unified methodology for testing object-oriented software at the class and cluster levels. In class-level testing, it determines whether the objects produced from the execution of implemented systems would retain the properties defined by the specification, for example, behavioral equivalence and non-equivalence. In cluster-level testing, it tests the behavioral dependencies and interactions among cooperating objects of different classes in a given cluster based on a formal specification language.

Korat (Boyapati, Khurshid, & Marinov, 2002) is a novel framework that generates the test
cases for a Java program automatically. Based on a formal specification for a method,
it uses the pre-condition of a method to automatically produce all test cases limited
by a given size. It then executes the method on each test case, uses the post-condition
of the method to ensure the correctness of each output.

Model-based test case generation techniques have been well developed. These techniques
are suitable for state-based systems that are modeled by a formal or semi-formal description
language, like extended finite state machine (EFSM), Specification Description Language,
and so forth. A set of tools (Alur & Yannakakis, 1998; Carver & Tai, 1998; Tahat, Vaysburg,
Korel, & Bader, 2001; Rayadurgam, 2001) has been developed based on these techniques
to generate system-level test suites from system models.

Instead of using models, some other methodologies such as genetic algorithms (GAs) have
also been proposed for test case generation. For example, in the paper about path testing,
Lin and Yeh (2000) used a set of GAs to generate the test cases to test a selected path. They
developed a new fitness function (SIMILARITY) to determine the distance between the
exercised path and the target path for a given target path. In a paper about real-time system
testing (Wegener, Sthamer, Jones, & Eyres, 1997), the authors declared an appropriate fitness function to measure the execution time of a real-time system. Through establishing the
longest and shortest execution times, GAs can be used to validate the temporal correctness.
In a paper about branch testing (Jones, Eyres, & Sthamer, 1998), the authors used GAs to
search program domains for appropriate test cases in order to satisfy the all-branch testing
criterion. The fitness functions can be derived automatically for each branch predicate.

Test selection is important for software maintenance to improve the efficiency of regression
testing. Many related techniques have been introduced, for example, TestTube, scenario-
based functional regression testing, and so forth.

TestTube (Chen, Rosenblum, & Vo, 1994) first identifies the coverage dependencies between
a test suit and a program: which functions, types, variables, and macros are covered
by each test unit in a test suit. It identifies the changed entities once the system under
testing is modified. Based on the coverage and modification information, TestTube
selects all the test suits that cover the changed entities when testing a new version of
the system.

Tsai, Bai, and Yu (2001) proposed a scenario-based functional regression testing based on
end-to-end integration test scenarios. They first represented test scenarios in a template
model that combines both test dependency and traceability information. Test dependency
information provides the ability to achieve a test-slicing algorithm to detect the scenarios
that are affected by modifications. Traceability information provides the ability to find affected components and their associated test scenarios. All these detected test scenarios are
candidates for regression testing.

MANTEMA (Polo, Piattini, Ruiz, & Calero, 1999) is a software maintenance methodology based on the ISO/IEC 12207 standard. It separates software maintenance into different types of activities and tasks, including urgent corrective, non-urgent corrective, perfective, preventive, and adaptive. This separation allows the user to apply it flexibly based on a specific application case.

In summary, different KBSE systems allow certain knowledge to be specified in an appropriate language to guide the developer in various stages of the software life cycle. Some important differences between DPSSEE and other KBSE systems include:

1. Unlike most existing KBSE tools which focus on a specific aspect of software development, it addresses all phases of the software life cycle.

2. Unlike most KBSE tools which intend to automate a specific task, it is focused on the representation and enforcement of additional knowledge that can be asserted on top of a software project and of any information that can be derived from the existing CASE tools where such knowledge is hard to be derived by such tools.

3. It addresses the representation and enforcement of additional knowledge that can be asserted on top of multiple CASE tools that allow such tools to work together seamlessly.

System Architecture

The overall system architecture of DPSSEE is shown in Figure 1. It consists of two data models: the semantic software development model (SSDM) and semantic project management model (SPMM). A set of tools (e.g., ArgoUML, Visual Version Control, etc.) is used to generate the contents for the two data models. The semantic generator allows the user to provide additional and critical information required by the two data models that cannot be captured by the existing tools. On top of SSDM and SPMM, the model-based testing and maintenance module develops different strategies of model-based test case generation and regression test selection in terms of the information and relationships provided by SSDM. Rules including proactive and constraint rules are asserted to provide further supports for software development and project management. These include, for example, rules that control the software development workflow, rules for checking the consistency of a software design, rules for testing and maintenance, and so forth. To consider authorization, DPSSEE implements role-based access control as the filter between different users and the data models.

Figure 1. System architecture of DPSSEE

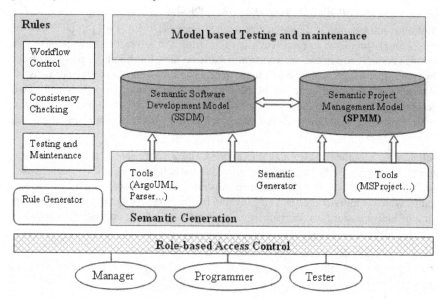

Semantic of Software Engineering

In DPSSEE, "semantics of software engineering" includes any derived knowledge and user generated logic that may be used to make a software development and project management process more intelligent.

The derivation of semantics takes place in two separate stages. The first stage is perception, where the programming objects information from the function modules becomes directly accessible to the programming database. In this stage, the information is more primitive and complete. The second stage involves the extraction of specific information by a proactive agent from these programming objects. This stage is cognition.

In addition to the empirical semantics derived from the programming objects, in DPSSEE user can also benefit from the personalized logic (semantics) that may be enforced to customize a software development process.

Semantic Description Language (SDL)

The DPSSEE applies Semantics Description Language (SDL), which includes a programming object model that allows different pieces of a software project to be encoded. Different entities of a software project are individuated as "objects", which will be referred to as *individuals*, denoted as *a, b, c*, and so on. Each object has a set of properties. In this way, the information about software development is taken to be an itemized, conceptual form, and each item of information pertains to a certain object.

Accordingly, information is digitalized as a set of infons (Devlin, 1991) in DPSSEE. We employ a single predicate to represent a specific infon. An infon that corresponds to the way things actually are in the environment is called a *fact*. Furthermore, real life "facts" always pertain to a certain interval of time. In order to deal with these kinds of facts, we need to introduce temporal locations in addition to the spatial data. Temporal locations will be denoted by t, t_1, t_2,... and they may be either the points in time or regions of time. For example, *eq(a, b, t_s, t_e, period)* means a equals to b from t_s (start time) to t_e (end time) with a period value *period*.

A software development environment is divided into a collection of situations, such as situations encountered, situations referred to, and so forth. It supports two types of situation according to Devlin (1991): real situation and abstract situation. A real situation is one kind of reality, which is individuated as a single entity by the proactive agent according to some scheme of individuation. An abstract situation is a set of infons, consisting of relations, individuals, and temporal locations.

The different situations composed of a set of infons can be linked by '→' to express specific logic rules. In this way, the semantics of software engineering can be represented as logic rules in the form of $l_1 \wedge l_2 \wedge \ldots \wedge l_n \rightarrow r_1 \wedge r_2 \wedge \ldots \wedge r_m$. Each l_i, $1 \leq i \leq n$, and r_j, $1 \leq j \leq m$, is a literal that is a predicate or a negated predicate, which represents a specific infon, and all the literals in the right hand side $r_1, r_2, \ldots r_m$ should be true if all the literals in the left hand side $l_1, l_2, \ldots l_n$ are evaluated true at the same time. The predicates in the left side are condition predicates, while in the right side are either condition predicates or action predicates.

Some condition predicates in logic rules can be described as the following:

> eq(a, b, t_s, t_e, period) -- equal, t_s: start time, t_e: end time
>
> neq(a, b, t_s, t_e, period) -- not equal
>
> le(a, b, t_s, t_e, period) -- less than or equal
>
> lt(a, b, t_s, t_e, period) -- less than
>
> ge(a, b, t_s, t_e, period) -- greater than or equal
>
> gt(a, b, t_s, t_e, period) -- greater than

where *a, b* are constants or variables representing the programming objects of the form: tuple_var.attribute (e.g., T.age). The time variable t_s, t_e and *period* are time variables or constants. The possible relationships between two time intervals are: *Before, After, Equal, During, Meet, Overlap, FinishBy, BeginWith*. For example, the predicate "The deadline of a project (*p.Deadline*) is before that of a module (*m.Deadline*)." can be represented as *Before(m.Deadline, p.Deadline)*.

For the action predicates, the user can define functions with arguments consisting of objects, properties and time locations:

> user-defined-function (arguments, t_s, t_e, period)

Constraint and Proactive Rules

In DPSSEE, the semantics knowledge base supports two types of rules: constraint rules and proactive rules.

1. **Constraint Rules**

   If the literals in both the left hand and the right hand side of a rule are condition predicates, then we classify this rule as a constraint rule. Constraint rules link various situations that are composed of a set of infons (facts). Once the situation in the left hand is evaluated to be true, the right hand side situation also should be true. Otherwise the rule is violated. For example,

   [Rule1] The programmer of a module cannot be the test engineer of the same module.

   Assignment(a, t_1, t_2) $\wedge$ TestTask(k, t_1, t_2) $\wedge$eq(a.ModuleID, k.ModuleID) $\rightarrow$ neq(a.Programmer, k.Tester)

2. **Proactive Rules**

   Different from a constraint rule, a proactive rule utilizes action predicates as its right hand side literals. Once the condition predicates in the left side are evaluated to be true, all the actions in the right hand will be performed. For example,

   [Rule 2] If a programmer can finish all his assignments one month before the deadline of the module, then increase his/her salary by 10%.

   Module(m, t_1, t_2) $\wedge$ Assignment (a, t_1, t_2) $\wedge$ Employee (e, t_1, t_2) $\wedge$ eq(a.ModuleID, m.ModuleID) $\wedge$ eq(e.EmployeeID, a.Programmer) $\wedge$ lt (a.CompletedDate, m.Deadline, '00:01:00:00:00:00') $\rightarrow$ Increase(e.Salary, '10%', t_3)

Semantic Software Development Model (SSDM)

The semantic software development model (SSDM) is the kernel of DPSSEE via which the information generated from the software requirements, design, implementation, testing, and maintenance phases is well organized.

SSDM Structure

We introduce the semantic software development model (SSDM) for object-oriented software development. It covers all phases of a software development process: requirements, design, implementation, testing and maintenance, as shown in Figure 2.

Figure 2. The SSDM structure

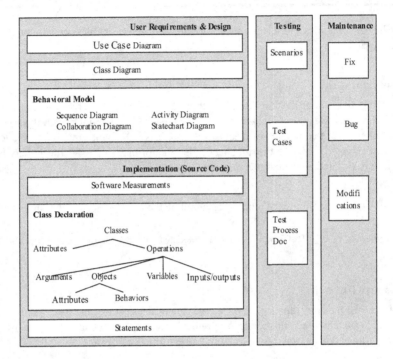

The SSDM incorporates Unified Modeling Language (UML) which is a visual object-oriented modeling language that offers a standard way to model a complex software system in all phases of software development including static modeling of structural elements such as classes, objects, and system components as well as dynamic aspects such as behaviors and interactions. All UML diagrams facilitate the design of a software system as a whole, and each one of them further refines the design and implementation details necessary to complete the software system.

In UML, the requirements of a software system in general can be described by a set of use case diagrams; the static data structure can be depicted by a set of class diagrams; the state transitions of objects can be described by a set of statechart diagrams; the interactions among objects can be described by a set of sequence/collaboration diagrams; and the control flow can be described by a set of activity diagrams.

For software implementation, we model the source codes and their measurements with a set of objects. The software measurements model computes the software metrics for each source code file, where a source code file corresponds to a class object, and a class file declares the attributes and operations of this class. The details of an operation include its arguments, the objects and variables declared, and its inputs/outputs.

For software testing, SSDM records not only the scenarios/test cases but also the testing processes. The scenarios and test cases may be generated based on the information captured in the software requirements and design model or the software implementation model.

Finally, the software maintenance model consists of a set of fix, bug, and modification objects that record the information generated from modifications.

SSDM Annotations

In SSDM, different kinds of information are modeled using a set of related objects. The basic structure of the annotations for an object is:

```
Object_Name {
        [Object Identity]
        [Identities of Parent Objects] (To specify the objects it belongs to in higher layers)
        [Attributes for this object] (To annotate the name, type and properties for this object)
        [Identities of Child Objects] (To specify the objects it owns in lower layers, such as the
statements for a class file object, etc.)
}
```

For each type of object, we may specify its parent and child objects. A parent-child relationship between two objects can be represented by the "[Identities of Child Objects]" attribute in the parent object or the "[Identities of Parent Objects]" attribute in the child object. In this way, objects with different types at different levels can be integrated to a group, and it is easy to infer the relationships among them.

Relationships in SSDM

According to this annotation structure, a number of relationships among the objects within SSDM can be addressed. These relationships organize the objects at different levels to make it a tightly coupled data model. In this section, we describe the details of some relationships in SSDM.

1. The relationship between a "use case diagram" and a set of "dynamic UML diagrams" (sequence/collaboration, activity, and statechart diagrams) in the behavioral model:

    *   A use case in a "use case diagram" is illustrated by several dynamic UML diagrams.

2. The relationship between a "class diagram" and a set of "dynamic UML diagrams" (sequence/collaboration, activity, and statechart diagrams) in the behavioral model:

    *   The objects in a sequence/collaboration diagram and the objects described by a statechart diagram are the instances of the classes in the corresponding class diagram.

    *   For a stimulus in a sequence diagram, a message in a collaboration diagram, an activity in an activity diagram or a transition in a statechart diagram, if its type (stimulus_Type, message_Type, activity_Type or transition_Type) is the "behavior" of an object, then the "behavior" should be a declared operation for the corresponding class.

3.   The relationship between a "class diagram" and "implementation":
   •   Each class in a class diagram corresponds to a class file in Implementation.
   •   All the attributes and operations of a class are consistent between a "class diagram" and "implementation" respectively.

4.   The relationship between "software measurements" and "implementation":
   •   Each class file in "implementation" is measured by a set of software metrics in "software measurement".

5.   The function call relationships among the operations of different classes:
   •   An operation is called by many other operations.

For a software system, a set of function call relationship trees can be derived to represent the relationships among all the operations of the classes. Each operation may be called by a set of operations, and these operations may be further called by another set of operations. For each operation, we specify all the operations it calls, and we can infer the function call relationships among these operations.

6.   The relationships between a "class declaration" and "statements":
   •   A class file consists of a set of statements.
   •   An attribute is declared by a statement.
   •   An operation is composed of a set of statements.
   •   An object or variable is declared by a statement.
   •   An attribute/behavior of an object is modified or used in a statement.
   •   A system output or user input is implemented in a statement.

SSDM Construction

We have constructed some tools to help construct the SSDM.

Software Requirements and Design Information Generation

Figure 3 shows an implementation that extracts information from the software requirements and design phases.

The software requirements and design information extraction process consists of the following steps:

1.   Generate UML diagrams using ArgoUML.
2.   Export the UML diagrams from ArgoUML to XML-formatted UML diagrams.
3.   Check in XML-formatted UML diagrams.

Figure 3. An implementation for extracting requirements and design information

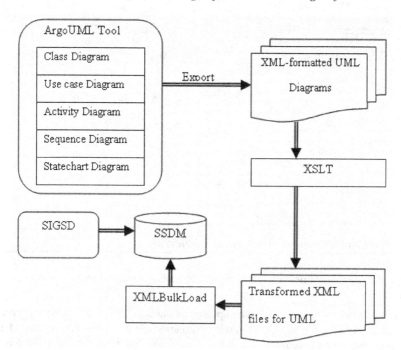

4.   Input related information about the XML files checked-in (e.g., diagram type, system name, use case name, etc.).

5.   Based on a specific XSLT, an XML file checked in is transformed into a new XML file as we want.

6.   Based on a specific XSD, load the new XML file into the database.

7.   Input the following additional information through the supplemental information generator for software development (SIGSD):

   a.   For use case diagrams, the include/extend/generation relationships between use cases, and the "act on" relationships between the actor and use cases;

   b.   For class diagrams, the extend/implement relationships between classes;

   c.   For sequence diagrams, the time-sequence, source object and destination object for a stimulus between objects;

   d.   For statechart diagrams, the source and destination states for a transition;

   e.   For activity diagrams, the transitions for this activity diagram in terms of source activities, destination activities and conditions.

Figure 4. An implementation to retrieve implementation information

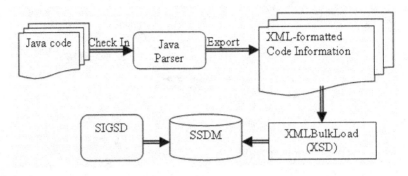

Software Implementation Information Generation

Figure 4 shows an implementation to extract information from the software implementation phase.

The finished Java files are checked in and parsed by our Java Parser that generates certain XML-formatted code information. The code information can be loaded into SSDM. Meanwhile, users can input any supplemental information through the supplemental information generator for software development (SIGSD).

In order to parse Java code to get the detailed code information in the format we designed, we use the Java Compiler Compiler (JavaCC™) to generate our own parser. JavaCC is the most popular parser generator for use with Java applications. A parser generator is a tool that reads a grammar specification and converts it to a Java program that can recognize the grammar.

Semantic Project Management Model (SPMM)

The semantic project management model (SPMM) is another model of DPSSEE via which the information generated from the project management and version control modules is integrated.

SPMM Construction

In this section, we describe the details of the construction of SPMM based on the information obtained from MS Project 2002 and Visual SourceSafe 6.0 (VSS). We suppose all MS

Figure 5. SPMM construction

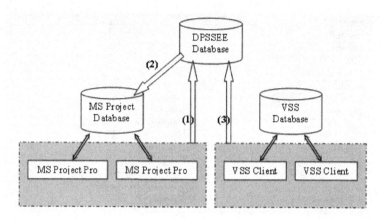

Project clients store their data in a single MS Project database, and also all the VSS clients access the same VSS database, and DPSSEE always extracts the up-to-day data from the MS Project database and VSS database.

At present, we allow users to modify any MS Project data extracted from DPSSEE; the approved modifications to MS Project data from DPSSEE include Update and Delete, which are propagated back to the MS Project database.

In the following, we will discuss the issue of data transformation among MS Project, VSS and DPSSEE in terms of three directions (as marked in Figure5), and introduce two rules that need to be followed for integration.

Information Extraction from MS Project

The information extraction process from MS Project to DPSSEE is implemented by the automation interface provided by MS Project. The MS Project object module is depicted in Figure 6.

We employed a macro written in *vbscript* to retrieve certain data based on the earlier-mentioned object module. As soon as the user opens a project, the macro is run to trap all the events of interest. Currently the following events can be detected:

> ProjectBeforeAssignmentDelete: before an assignment is deleted;
> ProjectBeforeClose: before a project is closed;
> ProjectBeforeResourceDelete: before a resource is deleted;
> ProjectBeforeTaskDelete: before a task is deleted.

Figure 6. MS project object module (MS project help)

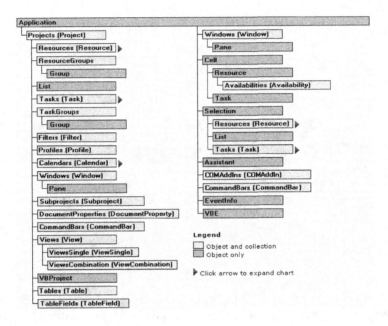

We do not catch all possible types of events to avoid frequent communications with the DPSSEE database. It should be straight forward, however, to extend the macro to capture more events.

Modifications from DPSSEE to MS Project

To keep the data consistent between DPSSEE and MS Project, we defined a set of triggers in the DPSSEE database. These triggers modify the corresponding MS Project database when the user updates or deletes the project data stored (Project, Task, Assignment, and Resource data) in the DPSSEE database.

In contrast, we cannot modify any file version control data from DPSSEE. This is because the data of VSS cannot be stored into the SQL server (so far as we know), therefore we cannot modify them through triggers.

Information Extraction from Visual SourceSafe

We used the automation interface exposed by Visual SourceSafe version 6.0 to capture the information from VSS. This interface allows the user to hook into and control certain events within a SourceSafe session. The Visual SourceSafe object module is shown in Figure7.

Figure 7. Visual SourceSafe object module (Felder, 1995)

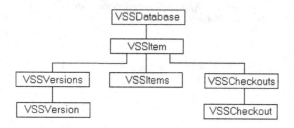

During the information extraction process, we can detect the following events:

> AfterAdd: after a new file is added into Visual SourceSafe.
>
> AfterCheckIn: after a file is checked in.
>
> AfterCheckOut: after a file is checked out.
>
> AfterRename: after a file or project is renamed.
>
> AfterUndoCheckOut: after a user undo the check out action for a checked out file.

In DPSSEE, we retrieve all the file-related information about these events. With such, the user can check the history of any specific file.

Model-Based Testing and Maintenance

Based on SSDM, information can be acquired for testing and maintenance with four different levels of abstractions: algorithmic-level, class-level, use-case-level, and system-level. The algorithmic level information includes the code for each operation in a class. The class level information consists of the interactions of methods and data that are declared within a class. The use case level information contains the interactions among a set of cooperating classes, which work together to accomplish some use cases. The system level information is composed of all the use cases.

Different strategies can be developed in terms of the information and relationships provided by SSDM. In this section, we will discuss the model-based test case generation and regression test selection techniques.

Test Case Generation for All-Branch Testing

Given an activity diagram, we can generate a set of test scenarios to cover all the branches in the diagram. This can be accomplished by tracing all the possible next activities for each activity to cover all the activity execution paths using the following "Activity_Tracing" function recursively:

Test_Case_Generation (system_Name, use_Case_Name)
{

    Initial_Activity = (Select initial_Activity from Activity_Diagram where system_Name = system and use_Cases = Use_Case_Name)

    If (Initial_Activity <> Null)
    (
      Generate a new empty Test Case: Initial_Test_Case
      Activity_Tracing (Initial_Activity, Initial_Test_Case)
    }
    Else
    {
      Message ("No any test cases can be generated for" & use_Case_Name& "use case in"& system_Name & "system!")
    }
}

Activity_Tracing (Current_Activity, Current_Test_Case)
{

    Num_of_Next_Activities= 0
    Next_Activities [] = Select transition_Desitination_Activity from Transition_For_Activities where transition_Source_Activity = Current_Activity

    Num_of_Next_Activities = Select COUNT (transition_Desitination_Activity) from Transition_ For_Activities where transition_Source_Activity = Current_Activity

    // the ending activity and return point
    If (Num_of_Next_Activities = 0)
    {
      Based on "Current_Activity", Generate a new test case step for the Current_Test_Case.

      Message (Current_Test_Case & "has been ended by" & Current_Activity)

      Return
    }

    Test_Case [0] = Current_Test_Case

    //Generate new test cases for all the other possible activity paths
    For (i = 1; i < Num_of_Next_Activities; i++)
    {
      Generate a new Test Case: Test_Case[i], copy all the set of Test_Case_Steps from Test_Case [0]
    }

    //Generate new test cases steps, the test case step should perform the activity of "Current_ Activity" and can cause the "Next_Activity[i]", and go on tracing the next activities
    For (i = 0; i < Num_of_Next_Activities; i++)
    {
      Based on "Current_Activity" and Next_Activities [i], Generate a new Test Case Step for Test_Case [i]. This test case step will cause the Next_Activity[i] and perform the "Current_Activity".

      Activity_Tracing (Next_Activity[i], Test_Case [i])

    }
}

Test Case Generation for Boundary Testing and Faulty Testing

If an attribute or a variable is not a string, it may be bounded by a minimum value (attribute_Min_Value/ Variable_Min_Value) and a maximum value (attribute_Max_Value/ Variable_Max_Value). Based on these, we can obtain the testing scenarios for boundary testing. In addition, based on the value ranges, we can obtain the testing scenarios for faulty testing.

```
Activity_Tracing (Current_Activity, Current_Test_Case)
{
//Get the activity Type
Activity_Type = Select activity_Type From Activity where activity_ID = Current_Activity

//If the type of an activity is user_input, and then we may generate different new test cases for
Boundary testing and Faulty testing.
If (Activity_Type = 'user_input')
{

//Suppose we know the corresponding attribute or variable for this user input, here we give an
example for "Attribute" input.
If (input_Type = 'Attribute')
{
Attribute_Type = Select attribute_Type from Attribute_In_Class_File where attribute_ID = '*****'

Attribute_Min_Value = Select attribute_Min_Value from Attribute_In_Class_File where attribute_ID =
'*****'

Attribute_Max_Value = Select attribute_Max_Value from Attribute_In_Class_File where attribute_ID =
'*****'

//Boundary Testing
If (Attribute_Min_Value<>Null)
{
Generate a new test case: New_Test_Case that copies all the set of Test_Case_Steps from the
Current_Test_Case.

Based on the Current_Activity, a new test step for New_Test_Case can be generated, where the
"Attribute_Min_Value" is assigned as the user input, and it will cause the "Next_Activity".

Activity_Tracing (Next_Activity, New_Test_Case)

}

If (Attribute_Max_Value<>Null)
{
Generate a new test case: New_Test_Case that copies all the set of Test_Case_Steps from the
Current_Test_Case

Based on the Current_Activity, a new test step for New_Test_Case can be generated, where the
"Attribute_Max_Value" is assigned as the user input, and it will cause the "Next_Activity".
```

Activity_Tracing (Next_Activity, New_Test_Case)

}

//Faulty Testing
//Out of range
If (Attribute_Min_Value<>Null)
{
Generate a new test case: New_Test_Case that copies all the set of Test_Case_Step of Current_ Test_Case

Based on the "Current_Activity", a new test step for New_Test_Case can be generated, where a value **smaller than** "Attribute_Min_Value" is assigned as the user input, and it will cause the "Next_Activity".

Activity_Tracing (Next_Activity, New_Test_Case)
}

If (Attribute_Max_Value<>Null)
{
Generate a new test case: New_Test_Case that copies all the set of Test_Case_Step of Current_ Test_Case

Based on the "Current_Activity", a new test step for New_Test_Case can be generated, where a value **larger than** "Attribute_Max_Value" is assigned as the user input, and it will cause the "Next_Activity".

Activity_Tracing (Next_Activity, New_Test_Case)
}
. . . .
}
}

Regression Test Selection

According to SSDM, for each modification made to the source code, we can find all the related use cases that need to be tested.

For example, based on the relationships between a use case diagram and a set of dynamic UML diagrams, between a class diagram and a set of dynamic UML diagrams, and the function call relationships among different operations of the classes, if an operation is modified, then all the use cases affected (i.e., whose corresponding operation has called this operation) should be tested based on the following steps:

1. Find all the operations called this operation.

2. Find all the dynamic UML diagrams that include the corresponding "behaviors" for these related operations.

3. Find all the use cases that are described by these dynamic UML diagrams.

4. Test these use cases.

Rule Generation and Applications

In addition to system-derived rules, the DPSSEE rule generator (shown in Figure 8) allows the user to define constraint and proactive rules.

Basic Syntax

RuleName: [Rule name]
Event:
      [Event type] [Event object]
Condition:
      IF EXISTS [Target objects (a set of)]
      FROM [Involved tables (a set of)]
      WHERE [Conditions (a set of)]
Actions:
      [Actions (a set of)]

In this, as soon as the event happens, if the conditions are fulfilled, then the actions will be performed. Note that the condition part can be empty, which means the actions will be performed anyway.

Rule Applications

The integration of constraint and proactive rules based on the information provided by SSDM and SPMM allows users to further capture the semantics of a software development

Figure 8. Rule generator UI

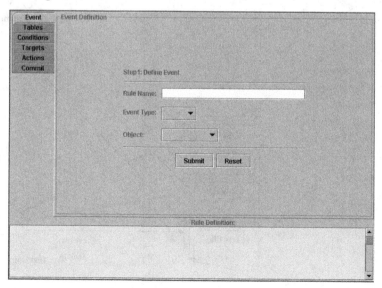

process and project management. The flowing applications are introduced as example usages of rules asserted on top of SSDM and SPMM.

Software Development Workflow Control

For software development tools, these rules allow the workflow of a software project to be coordinated automatically, timely, and efficiently. Figure 9 shows some typical interactions among the managers, programmers, and test engineers. A manager can create a new project and new tasks, assign the tasks to the developers or test engineers, and receive periodical work reports. A programmer can get his assignments, check in his finished modules, check out the test results provided by the test engineers, and create daily and monthly reports. A test engineer can check out the source codes uploaded from programmers, check in test files, and create daily and monthly reports.

The semantics implicated in the programming objects or generated by the developers can automate these interactions in a timely fashion. The proactive agent in DPSSEE can employ a set of rules to control the workflows of the software development and testing processes.

Proactive rules can be defined to link specific actions with the concerned situations, such as send notifications, assignment and test a file, or update the properties of programming objects under some specific situations. The following two rules (Rule 1 and Rule 2) are examples.

Figure 9. Software development interactions

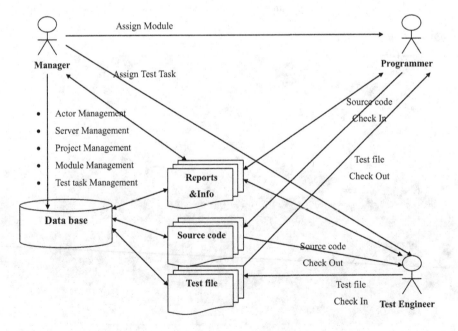

[Rule 1] As soon as a new assignment is made to a programmer, the programmer will be sent an email before time t_3.

NewAssignment(a, t_1, t_2) ∧ Module(m, t_1, t_2) ∧ Employee (e, t_1, t_2) ∧ eq(a.ModuleID, m.ModuleID) ∧ eq(e. EmployeeID, a.Programmer) → Notify(e.Email, t_3)

[Rule 2] If the deadline of a module is just one week later, the system will insert a new record into "RemindInfo" to remind the test engineer of this module before time t_3.

Module(m, t_1, t_2) ∧ TestTask(k, t_1, t_2) ∧ Employee(e, t_1, t_2) ∧ eq(k.ModuleID, m.ModuleID) ∧ eq(e.Employee-eID, k.Tester) ∧ After(Today, m.Deadline, '00:00:07:00:00:00') → Insert(RemindInfo, e.name, 'Deadline reminding information', t_3)

On the other hand, constraint rules can be defined to check the consistency and integrity in the programming database, to guarantee the matching of situations at any time. Rule 3 and Rule 4 shown next are constraints rules to check the constraints on deadlines and the matching between the testing time and the completion date for a single module.

[Rule 3] The deadline of a project should be after the deadline of all the modules of this project.

Project(p, t_1, t_2) ∧ Module(m, t_3, t_4) ∧eq(p.ProjectID, m.ProjectID) ∧ During((t_3, t_4), (t_1, t_2)) → Before(m. Deadline, p.Deadline)

[Rule 4] The testing time of a module should be before the module completion date.

TestTask(k, t_1, t_2) ∧ Module(m, t_1, t_2) ∧ eq(k.ModuleID, m.ModuleID) → Before(k.TestDate, m.CompletedDate)

By applying constraint and proactive rules, DPSSEE can do a better job to support software development workflows, ease the work of managers, programmers and test engineers, and allow them to cooperate with each other more conveniently and timely.

Maintaining the Consistency of Software Design

When different people work together on a large software system, it is easy to have inconsistency among different models. In the following, we will introduce some rules, based on the information extracted from the UML diagrams, to maintain the consistency of a software design.

Suppose, for simplicity, the information extracted from UML diagrams is represented in terms of the following predicates:

1.   ClassDiagram(Classes, Attributes, Operations, ...)
   *   Class(classID, name,...)
   *   Attribute(attributeID, name, allowedValues,...)
   *   Operation(operationID, name, argument, ...)

2.   UseCaseDiagram(UseCases, Actors, …)
- UseCase(useCaseID, name,…)

3.   ObjectDiagram(Objects, Associations, …)
- ODObject(objectID, type, …)

4.   StatechartDiagram(object, States, Stimulus,…)
- State(stateID, Attributes,…)
- SDAttribute(attributeID, name, value,…)
- Stimulus(stimulusID, annotation, …)

5.   SequenceDiagram(scenario, Objects, Messages,…)
- SDObject(objectID, type, …)
- SDMessage(messageID, timeSequence, annotation, …)

6.   ColloborationDiagram(scenario, Objects, Messages, …)
- CDObject(objectID, type, …)
- CDMessage(messageID, sequenceNum, annotation, …)

7.   ActivityDiagram(scenario, Activities, Conditions,…)
- Activity(activityID, annotation, …)

Based on the class diagram that provides the basic elements (*classes, operations,* and *attributes*), we can obtain the following:

1.   For each *object* in an object diagram, sequence diagram, and collaboration diagram, there should exist a corresponding declaration of a *class* in the class diagram.

[Rule1] Each object in the object diagram should be declared in the corresponding class diagram.
ObjectDiagram(od) ∧ ODObject(o) ∧ includes(od.Objects, o.ObjectID) → ClassDiagram(cd) ∧ Class(c) ∧ includes(cd.Classes, c.ClassID) ∧ eq(c.Name, o.Type)

[Rule2] If one class in the class diagram is deleted, then the corresponding object in the object diagram should also be deleted.
ClassDiagram(cd) ∧ Class(c) ∧includes(cd.Classes, c.ClassID) ∧ObjectDiagram(od) ∧ODObject(o) ∧includes(od.Objects, o.ObjectID) ∧eq(c.Name, o.Type) ∧Delete (c) →Delete(o)

2.   For each massage in the sequence/collaboration diagram, each stimulus in the statechart diagram and each activity in the activity diagram, there should exist a corresponding declaration of an operation in the class diagram.

[Rule1] Each message in the sequence diagram should be declared in the class diagram.
SequenceDiagram(sd) ∧ SDMessage(m) ∧ includes(sd.Messages, m.MessageID) →ClassDiagram(cd) ∧ Operation(op) ∧ includes(cd.Operations, op.OperationID) ∧ eq(m.Annotation, op.Name)

3. For each *object* illustrated by a statechart diagram, there should exist a corresponding declaration of a *class* in the class diagram. Also a *state* represents a summary of the values that the *attributes* of a class can take.

[Rule1] For each *object* illustrated by a statechart diagram, there should exist a corresponding declaration of a *class* in the class diagram.

StatechartDiagram(scd) → ClassDiagram(cd) ∧ Class(c) ∧ includes(cd.Classes, c.ClassID) ∧ eq(c.Name, scd.Object)

[Rule2] A *state* represents a summary of the values that the *attributes* of a class can take.

Statechart-Diagram(scd) ∧ State(s) ∧ includes(scd.States, s.StateID) ∧ Attribute(a1) ∧ includes(s.Attributes, a1.AttributeID) ∧ ClassDiagram(cd) ∧ Attribute(a2) ∧ includes(cd.Attributes, a2.AttributeID) ∧ eq(a2.Name, a1.Name) → includes(a2.AllowedValues, a1.Value)

4. For each *scenario* illustrated by a sequence diagram, collaboration diagram, and activity diagram, there should exist a corresponding *use case* in the use case diagram.

[Rule1] For each *scenario* illustrated by a sequence diagram, there should exist a corresponding *use case* in the use case diagram.

SequenceDiagram(sd) → UseCaseDiagram(ucd) ∧ UseCase(uc) ∧ includes(ucd.UseCases, uc.UseCaseID) ∧ eq(uc.Name, sd.Scenario)

5. For the same use case, the sequence diagram and collaboration diagram provide the identical information, that is, the same *objects* should be included, the same *messages* should be sent from one object to another, and the same *sequence* should be defined among these messages.

[Rule1] The objects in a sequence diagram should be consistent with the objects in the corresponding collaboration diagram.

SequenceDiagram(sd) ∧ SDObject(o1) ∧ includes(sd.Objects, o1.ObjectID) → CollaborationDiagram(cbd) ∧ CDObject(o2) ∧ includes(cdb.Objects, o2.ObjectID) ∧ eq(sd.Scenario, cbd.Scenario) ∧ eq(o1.Type, o2.Type)

[Rule2] These two diagrams should have the same number of messages and objects.

SequenceDiagram(sd) ∧ Collaboration-Diagram(cbd) ∧ eq(sd.Scenario, cbd.Scenario) → eq(Count(sd.Objects), Count(cbd.Objects)) ∧ eq(Count(sd.Messages), Count(cbd.Messages))

[Rule3] The messages in these two diagrams should be in the same sequence.

SequenceDiagram(sd) ∧ SDMessage(m1) ∧ SDMessage(m2) ∧ includes(sd.Messages, m1.MessageID) ∧ includes(sd.Messages, m2.MessageID) ∧ Before(m1.TimeSequence, m2.TimeSequence) → CollaborationDiagram(cbd) ∧ CDMessage(m3) ∧ CDMessage(m4) ∧ includes(cbd.Messages, m3.MessageID) ∧ includes(cbd.Messages, m4.MessageID) ∧ eq(sd. Scenario, cbd.Scenario) ∧ eq(m1.Annotation, m3.Annotation) ∧ eq(m2.Annotation, m4.Annotation) ∧ Before(m3.SequenceNum, m 4.SequenceNum)

6.   For the same use case, each message in the sequence/collaboration diagram and each activity in the activity diagram should always be consistent. In addition, each stimulus in the statechart diagram should correspond to a message/activity in the corresponding sequence diagram, collaboration diagram, and activity diagram. Such as,

[Rule1] For the same use case, each message in the sequence diagram and each activity in the activity diagram should always be consistent.

SequenceDiagram(sd) ∧ SDMessage(m) ∧ includes(sd.Messages, m.MessageID) → ActivityDiagram(ad) ∧ Activity(a) ∧ includes(ad.Activities, a.ActivityID) ∧ eq(sd.Scenario, ad.Scenario) ∧ eq(m.Annotation, a.Annotation)

These rules can be used to maintain the consistency and completeness of a set of UML diagrams. If any modification is made to one of these diagrams, some corresponding updates should be made to all the related UML diagrams to avoid any inconsistencies.

Proactive Rules for Testing and Maintenance

The integration of proactive rules based on the information provided by SSDM allows users to further capture the semantics of a testing and maintenance process.

For software testing, users can define proactive rules to specify the test cases needed to be executed under specific events or conditions. For examples,

[Rule1] If Tests T34 and T36 are successful, there is no need to apply test case T67.

Test_Process_Doc(p1) ∧ Test_Process_Doc(p2) ∧ Test_Case(t) ∧ eq(p1.test_Case_ID, 'T34') ∧ eq(p2. test_Case_ID, 'T36') ∧ eq(t.test_Case_ID, 'T67') ∧ eq(p1.verification_Flag, 'True') ∧ eq(p2.verification_Flag, 'True') → Message("No need to apply test case T67")

[Rule 2] If the range of a variable "a" is changed from "x" to something larger, it is suggested to rerun test cases T34 and T36.

Variable_In_Operation(v) ∧ eq(v.variable_ID, 'a') ∧ Test_Case(t1) ∧ eq(t1.test_Case_ID, 'T34') ∧ Test_Case(t2) ∧ eq(t2.test_Case_ID, 'T36') ∧ gt(v.variable_Max_Value, 'x') → Message("run T34 and T36")

[Rule 3] If the operation Op1 is modified after 12/12/2003, it is suggested to rerun test cases T34 and T36.

Operation_In_Class_File(o1) ∧ eq(o.operation_ID, 'Op1') ∧ after (o1.last_Modified_Date, '12/12/2003') → Message("run T34 and T36")

For software maintenance, proactive rules can be defined to notify any modifications, make changes, or select test case for regression testing, and so forth. For examples,

[Rule 1] If a new use case for a system is added after 12/12/2003, then notify the system maintainer.

Use_Case(uc) ∧ gt(uc.creation_Date, '12/12/2003') ∧ Use_Case_Diagram(ucd) ∧ eq(uc.diagram_ID, ucd.diagram_ID) ∧ eq(ucd.system_Name, 'banking system') → Notify (software maintainer)

[Rule 2] If a new behavior is added into a sequence diagram after 12/12/2003, then notify the system maintainer.

Stimulus(s) ∧ gt(s.creation_Date, '12/12/2003') ∧ Sequence_Diagram(sqd) ∧ eq(sq.diagram_ID, s.diagram_ID) ∧ eq(sqd.system_Name, 'banking system') → Notify (software maintainer)

[Rule 3] If the range of a variable "*a*" is changed from "*x*" to something larger, it is suggested to change statements R12 and R13 to ....

Variable_In_Operation(v) ∧ eq(v.variable_ID, 'a') ∧ Statement(s1) ∧ eq(s1.statementID, 'R12') ∧ Statement(s2) ∧ eq(s2.statementID, 'R13') ∧ gt(v.variable_Max_Value, 'x') → Message("change statements R12 and R13 to...")

[Rule 4] If the class A1 was deleted from the class diagram, it is suggested to delete operations Op1 and Op2 ....

Class_File(a1) ∧ eq(a1.class_ID, 'A1') ∧ Delete(a1) → Message (Delete op1 and op2)

[Rule 5] If the attribute "balance" is deleted, test case T1 and T2 are suggested to be tested again.

Item(it) ∧ eq(it.item_Type, 'Attribute') ∧ eq(it.item_Name, 'Balance') ∧ Modification(m) ∧ includes (m.delete_Items, it.item_ID) → Message ("Test case T1 and T2 need to be tested.")

Conclusions

In this chapter we have described a distributed proactive semantic software engineering environment (DPSSEE). The goal of DPSSEE is to introduce semantic rules into a software development and project management process. It encodes and utilizes additional semantics to all levels of the software life cycle to make software development and project management more efficient and intelligent.

The extensibility in DPSSEE allows us to incorporate more software tools to extract information from a software project that, in turn, allows us to express more semantics about the project.

References

Alur, R., & Yannakakis, M. (1998). Model checking of hierarchical state machines. In the *Proceedings of the 6th ACM Symposium on Foundations of Software Engineering,* Lake Buena Vista, FL, November 3-5 (pp. 175-188). New York: ACM Press.

Boyapati, C., Khurshid, S., & Marinov, D. (2002). Korat: Automated testing based on Java predicates. In the *Proceedings of the International Symposium on Software Testing and Analysis (ISSTA),* Rome, Italy, July 22-24 (pp. 123-133). New York: ACM Press.

Carver, R. H., & Tai, K.-C. (1998). Use of sequencing constraints for specification-based testing of concurrent programs. *IEEE Transaction on Software Engineering, 24*(6), 471-490.

Chen, H. Y., Tse, T. H., & Chen, T. Y. (2001). TACCLE: A methodology for object-oriented software testing at the class and cluster levels. *ACM Transactions on Software Engineering and Methodology, 10*(1), 56-109.

Chen, Y.-F., Rosenblum, D., & Vo, K.-P. (1994). Testtube: A system for selective regression testing. In the *Proceedings of the 16th International Conference on Software Engineering,* Sorrento, Italy, May 16-21 (pp. 211-220). Los Alamitos, CA: IEEE Computer Society Press.

Devanbu, P. et al. (1991). LASSIE: A knowledge-based software information system. *Communications of the ACM, 34*(5), 34-49.

Devlin, K. (1991). *Logic and information.* Cambridge, UK: Cambridge University Press.

Felder, K. (1995). *Visual SourceSafe OLE Automation.* MSDN Library. Microsoft Corporation. Retrieved September 2006, from http://msdn.microsoft.com/library/en-us/dnvss/html/msdn_vssole.asp?frame=true&_r=1

Gery, E., Harel, D., & Palatshy, E. (2002). A complete lifecycle model-based development system. In the *Proceedings of the 3rd International Conference on Integrated Formal Methods (IFM 2002),* Turku, Finland, May 15-18 (pp. 1-10). London, UK: Springer-Verlag.

Glinz, M., Berner, S., Joos, S., Ryser, J., Schett, N., & Xia, Y. (2001). The ADORA approach to object-oriented modeling of software. In *Proceedings of the 13th International Conference (CAiSE),* Interlaken, Switzerland, June 4-8 (pp. 76-92). London, UK: Springer.

Graham, T. C. N., Morton, C. A., & Urnes, T. (1996). ClockWorks: Visual programming of component-based software architecture. *Journal of Visual Languages and Computing, 7*(2), 175-196.

Grundy, J. (2000). Software architecture modelling, analysis and implementation with SoftArch. In the *Proceedings of the 34th Annual Hawaii International Conference on System Sciences (HICSS-34),* Maui, Hawaii, January 3-6 (Volume 9, pp. 9051). Washington, D.C.: IEEE Computer Society.

Grundy, J. C., Mugridge, W. B., & Hosking, J. G. (1998). Static and dynamic visualisation of component-based software architectures. In the *Proceedings of 10th International Conference on Software Engineering and Knowledge Engineering,* San Francisco, CA, June 18-20 (pp. 426-433). Skokie, IL: KSI Press.

Harel, D., & Gery, E. (1997). Executable object modeling with statecharts. *IEEE Computer, 30*(7), 31-42.

Jones, B. F., Eyres, D. E., & Sthamer, H.-H. (1998). A strategy for using genetic algorithms to automate branch and fault-based testing. *The Computer Journal, 41*, 98-107.

Kelly, V. E., & Jones, M. A. (1993). KITSS: A knowledge-based translation system for test scenarios. In the *Proceedings of the 11th National Conference on Artificial Intelligence*, Washington, D.C., July 11-15 (pp. 804-810). Menlo Park, CA: AAAI Press.

Lin, J.-C., & Yeh, P.-L. (2000). Using genetic algorithms for test case generation in path testing. *Test Symposium, 2000 (ATS2000). Proceedings of the Ninth Asian,* Taipei, Taiwan, December 4-6 (pp. 241-246). Washington, D.C.: IEEE Computer Society.

Liu, A. (1998). Dynamic distributed software architecture design with PARSE-DAT. In the *Proceedings of the 1998 Australasian Workshop on Software Architectures*, Melbourne, Australia, November 6-9 (pp. 199-207). Clayton, Australia: Monash University Press.

Lüer, C., & Rosenblum, D. S. (2001). WREN—An environment for component-based development. *ACM SIGSOFT Software Engineering Notes, 26*(5), 207-217.

Mark, W., Tyler, S., McGuire, J., & Schossberg, J. (1992). Commitment-based software development. *IEEE Transactions on Software Engineering, 18*(10), 870-884.

Maurer, F., & Bowen, S. (2002). Process support and knowledge management for virtual teams. In the *Proceedings of the 26th International Computer Software and Applications Conference on Prolonging Software Life: Development and Redevelopment*, Oxford, England, August 26-29 (pp. 1118-1122). Washington, D.C.: IEEE Computer Society.

Microsoft Project Objects. Retrieved September 2006, from http://msdn.microsoft.com/library/en-us/dnpom/html/pjtocobjectmodelapplication.asp?frame=true&_r=1

Polo, M., Piattini, M., Ruiz, F., & Calero, C. (1999). MANTEMA: A software maintenance methodology based on the ISO/IEC 12207 standard. In the *Proceedings of 3rd European Conference on Software Maintenance and Reengineering (CSMR),* Amsterdam, The Netherlands, March 3-5 (pp. 76-81). Washington, D.C.: IEEE Computer Society.

Rayadurgam, S. (2001). Automated test-data generation from formal models of software. In the *Proceedings of the 16th IEEE International Conference on Automated Software Engineering,* Coronado Island, San Diego, CA, November 26-29 (p. 438). Washington, D.C.: IEEE Computer Society.

Robbins, J., Hilbert, D. M., & Redmiles, D. F. (1998). Extending design environments to software architecture design. *Automated Software Engineering, 5*(3), 261-390.

Ryser, J. (2000). *SCENT: A method employing scenarios to systematically derive test cases for system test.* Technical report 2000.03, University of Zurich, Institut fr Informatik.

Smith, D. R. (1990). KIDS: A semi-automatic program development system. *IEEE Transactions on Software Engineering, 16*(9), 1024-1043.

Tahat, L. H., Vaysburg, B., Korel, B., & Bader, A. J. (2001). Requirement-based automated black-box test generation. In the *Proceedings of the 25th International Computer Software and Applications Conference on Invigorating Software Development,* Chicago, IL, October 8-12 (pp. 489-495). Washington, D.C.: IEEE Computer Society.

Tsai, W.-T., Bai, X., & Yu, L. (2001). Scenario-based functional regression testing. *25th Annual International Computer Software and Applications Conference,* Chicago, IL, October 8-12 (pp. 496-501). Washington, D.C.: IEEE Computer Society.

Wegener, J., Sthamer, H., Jones, B. F., & Eyres, D. E. (1997). Testing real-time systems using genetic algorithms. *Software Quality Journal, 6*(2), 127-135.

Endnote

[1]   This research is supported in part by NSF under grant number IDM-0236409.

Chapter XVI

Adding Context into an Access Control Model for Computer Security Policy

Shangping Ren, Illinois Institute of Technology, USA

Jeffrey J. P. Tsai, University of Illinois at Chicago, USA

Ophir Frieder, Illinois Institute of Technology, USA

Abstract

In this chapter, we present the role-based context constrained access control (RBCC) model. The model integrates contextual constraints specified in first-order logic with the standard role-based access control (RBAC). In the RBCC access control model, the permission assignment functions are constrained by the user's current accessing contexts. The accessing contests are further categorized in two classes, that is, system contexts and application contexts. System contexts may contain accessing time, accessing location, and other security-related system information; while application contexts are abstractions of relationships among different types of entities (i.e., subjects, roles, and objects) as well as implicit relationships derived from protected information content and external information. The ability to integrate contextual information allows the RBCC model to be flexible and capable of specifying a variety of complex access policies and providing tight and just-in-time permission activations. A set of medical domain examples will be used to demonstrate the expressiveness of the RBCC model.

Introduction

Networked computers reside at the heart of systems on which people now rely, both in critical national infrastructures and in private enterprises. Today, many of these systems are far too vulnerable to cyber-attacks that can inhibit their functioning, corrupt important data, or expose private information. For instance, more and more medical facilities are digitizing their records daily. This trend necessitates security protocols that protect patient privacy and at the same time provide convenient timely access. To provide security constraints, often a role-based access control (RBAC) model-based approach is used. In such an approach, user roles define access rights. However, as we later show, these measures are insufficient in medical applications, and thus, we present the role-based context constrained (RBCC) model that integrates constraints with the traditional RBAC model using first-order logic. In addition to assigning access rights based on roles as in an RBAC approach, context constraints also play an important role in assigning access rights in the RBCC model.

In RBAC based approaches, individuals are associated with roles, and the security policy is based only on roles. In particular, once the individual assumes a role in a given session, the role becomes the only factor in deciding the individual's access rights, and the individual's own identity is ignored in such decision process. Hence, the access control in the RBAC model is very coarse-grained and at the role level only.

Unfortunately, in many commercial applications such as the healthcare domain, role level coarse-grained access control is not sufficient to enforce individual-based privacy rules. Consider a security rule: *a head nurse is allowed to view all patient medical files if the patient's doctors are in the same department as the head nurse and the patients are not under the supervision of the head nurse.* In this example, although the policy defines access privilege for the head nurse role, a different head nurse in the same department may have a different set of records that he/she can view. More specifically, the user's identity and the relationship between the user (the head nurse) and the owner of the records (patient's records) as well as the role decide the access rights. As RBAC only provides coarse-grained and role level control, it is difficult to model such fine-grained security policy if not impossible.

The example has also shown other characteristics of access control in healthcare applications. For instance, the accessing context (such as time, location, relationships among entities) has impact factors in deciding access rights. Unfortunately, such factors are not considered in current RBAC model and existing extension-based solutions.

We present a model that integrates a traditional RBAC model with context constraints. The presented RBCC model can dynamically constrain the role-permission relationship based on the current accessing context. The accessing context may contain current user, role, object, and system properties, relationships among these entities, and implicit external information. With the RBCC model, the traditional static role-permission assignment function in the RBAC model becomes dynamic and state dependent, and hence allows for fine-grained access control.

Related Work

Role-Based Access Control

Sandhu, Coyne, Feinstein, and Youman (1996) have defined a family of role-based access control models. In their RBAC family, roles are the focusing point. Permission assignments are based on the roles that users assume during each session. The RBAC model suits well for large, structured organization with coarse-grained security policies for the following reasons. First, roles and role hierarchies can mirror an organization's structure quite easily. Second, RBAC policies change very little over time, as transaction permissions are associated with roles, not users. Third, RBAC naturally supports delegation of access permissions (Moyer & Ahamad, 2001). The higher models of the RBAC family (such as RBAC2) define mutually exclusive sets of roles and enforce that the mutually exclusive roles cannot be assigned to the same user at the same time. In other words, certain types of role centered access constraints are defined in higher RBAC models.

However, despite its advantages, the RBAC model is fundamentally limited by its *role-centric* nature. In particular, temporal constraints, object specific constraints, locality constraints, and so forth, are not modeled in the RBAC family and hence are difficult to specify if not impossible. Several extensions to the family have been proposed, such as temporal role-based access control model (Bertino, Bonatti, & Ferrari, 2001), environment role-based access control model (Covington, Long, Srinivasan, Dev, Ahamad, & Abowd, 2001), generalized role-based access control model (Moyer et al., 2001), and team-based access control model (Thomas, 1997), to name a few. All these extensions aim to maximize the benefits derived from traditional RBAC models, mainly, its simplicity, scalability, and policy-neutral nature (Sandhu, 1996), and at the same time, support different types of constraints on role activations.

Temporal Role-Based Access Control

A temporal role-based access control model developed by Bertino et al. (2001) extends the traditional RBAC model by adding timing constraints into role activations. The main features of TRBAC are to support both periodic activations and deactivation of roles, and temporal dependencies among such actions are expressed by means of *role triggers*, whose actions may be either executed immediately, or be deferred by an explicitly specified amount of time. Both triggers and periodic activations/deactivation have a priority associated with them to resolve conflicting actions. In the RBAC model, role activation is session based. For each given session, a set of roles are activated for the session owner. These sets of roles remain activated until the session finishes. TRBAC extends the RBAC model and provides dynamic role activation based on time, or in more general term, based on events. However, TRBAC is also role-centric and focuses on *when* a specific type of role can be activated based on time and other role activation events. Other possible events, such as emergency events, which could also cause roles' permission change, are not modeled in the TRBAC model.

Environment Role-Based Access Control

Environment roles are proposed to capture security-relevant aspects of the environment in which an application executes. In the ERBAC model (Covington et al., 2001), an environment role is an abstraction for a system state that the system can accurately collect. For example, an environment role can be defined to correspond to the locations of subjects, time of the day, and so forth. These environment roles are defined by environment conditions and can be used in policy rule specifications. When the environment conditions become true, the corresponding environment roles are activated. By adding the environment roles into traditional RBAC model, we can easily specify access constraints which are based on system states. This approach is more generic than TRBAC in the sense that timing constraints in TRBAC model can be captured by an environment role that represents time and a corresponding environment condition which constrains the activation of the environment roles. However, it still endures role-centric disadvantages—security-related relationships among entities (including roles, subjects, objects, and environments) are ignored. Hence, fine-grained security policies which may depend on individual instances of the subjects and objects are difficult to model and specify.

Generalized Role-Based Access Control

Generalized role-based access control (GRBAC) is a new paradigm for creating and maintaining rich access control policies (Moyer et al., 2001). The GRBAC model defines three different types of roles—namely, subject roles, object roles, and environment roles. The subject roles abstract the security-relevant characteristics of subjects into categories, while object roles abstract characteristics of objects, such as object types (text file, executable file) or sensitivity level (e.g., classified, non-classified) into categories. Environment roles capture environment information, such as time of day, or access location, or system load. All of these three different types of roles together decide a user's access rights. The GRBAC model uses the *role* grouping primitive to capture security-relevant commonalities among subjects, objects, and environmental states and to uniformly handle access controls. The GRBAC *object roles* are similar to subject roles in RBAC model. Their purposes are to classify the objects in a system based on those objects' security-relevant properties, such as the class of readable-files. Similar to the ERBAC model, *environment roles* in the GRBAC model are used to capture security-relevant information about the environment for use in the GRBAC policies.

Different from the TRBAC and ERBAC models, the GRBAC model further abstracts subject, object, and environment into different types of roles. On the other hand, all three models share the same characteristic—control decisions are based on roles which are classified into subjects, objects, or environment. The environment that captured in the model is anything that system can accurately measure, such as time, location, CPU load, network load, and so forth. However, there are other types of contexts which are not be quantitatively measurable, but may affect access decisions. For instance, the relationships between entities associated with an access decision are often very important. Unfortunately, these types of contexts are not considered in the model.

Relationships in Role-Based Access Control

Barkley, Beznosov, and Uppal (1999) demonstrated how relationship information can be included in access decisions by using the Object Management Group's Resource Access Decision (RAD) facility. The work is done from an implementation and systems point of view. However, other than user/role and role/role relationships, how relationships among entities are defined and specified in a formal way is missing from the work.

Context Constraints in an RBAC Environment

Instead of constraining when a role can be activated by a user, Neumann and Strembeck (2003) presented another approach that associates constraints with permissions. Permissions are conditional—role is granted with a permission only when the associated context constraints are satisfied. A context constraint is defined using context attribute which represents a certain property of the environment whose actual value might change, or vary for different instances of the same abstract entity. As context attribute can be defined to capture fine-grained properties of the environment, and hence provides a mechanism to specify fine-grained security policies while still maintaining the advantages of RBAC. However, in Neumann et al.'s work, the context constraints are based on individual properties of the environment or individual properties of the related entities, for example, subjects, objects, and roles. The relationships among entities which represent a large category of constraints are not addressed.

UCON

Recently, Park and Sandhu (2004) and Zhang, Park, and Parisi-Presicce (2004) have proposed a generalized usage control model UCON. The authorization predicates are based on the attributes of objects and subjects. However, objects and subjects themselves are independent in the model. Their relationships are not considered. Our work is motivated by the observation that in the healthcare domain, not only the access environment, such as accessing time, location, but also the profiles of individual entities, the relationships among users, roles and objects, implicit relationships between users, and the content of objects play an important role in making access decisions.

Role-Based Context Constrained Access Control Model

As discussed, the RBAC mode and its extensions have limitations which prevent them from being able to fully specify all the security requirements in healthcare domains. The root cause of the limitations is that the models try to simplify the complex access control problems by focusing on roles only, and omit factors which can often be safely ignored, but become critical elements in deciding access permissions in healthcare domains.

We introduce our role-based context constrained access control (RBCC) model, in which the constraints are based on contexts. There are two different categories of contexts, namely, application context and system context. Application context in security access control domain involves security control entities, namely, subjects, roles, objects, permissions; while system context is an abstraction of data that can be obtained by the system, such as time of the day, access IP address, network load, and so forth. We first use an example to present relationship-oriented constraints in medical information access control. We then formally define the RBCC model, and discuss its properties. At the end, we exam the model's express power by revisiting the examples most referenced in the literature.

A Nurse Can Only View Her Doctor's Patients' Medical Records

Consider a typical security policy in a healthcare domain—*a nurse can only view his/her doctor's patients' medical records*. As we know, different nurses may work for different doctors. Therefore, although nurse A and nurse B have the same title and play the same role in a healthcare organization as a role NURSE, they may have different access rights to different patients' records. Hence, the purely role-based permission assignment is too coarse to differentiate such discrepancy. This example further reveals that other than the *role* that the individual subject assumes, the individual's own identity, or in more general terms, the individual's profile, and the relationship between the individual subject, who requests the access rights, and the individual object, which is to be accessed, has crucial impact in making the final access control decision. Such relationships sometimes are neither direct nor straightforward, and may need to be inferred through a third party. As shown in this example, a doctor is the mediator who relates the nurse with the patient's records.

In most enterprises, the access rights to secure information can be assigned based on the individual's responsibilities, or roles that the individual plays in the organization. In these organizations, the organizational hierarchy is quite stable, and the relationships between individuals are also quite static (meaning if John works for Jason within the organization, the manager-engineer relationship will not change on a daily basis). Hence, the role-based access control provides a scalable and efficient security model for protecting organizational information. However, in the healthcare domain, although the organizational hierarchy does not often change, responsibilities of individual care-givers could change on a daily basis. For example, Dr. A may work in emergency room as an ER doctor every Monday, as a family doctor for the rest of the week; nurse B works for Dr. A every Monday and Tuesday; for Dr. C every Wednesday and Thursday; and in the emergency room every Friday. Furthermore, because of the information privacy act, the owner of a medical record has the rights to protect his/her medical information from being released to some individuals. Both the highly dynamic individual responsibilities and the involvement of individuals (individuals who are to access information and individuals who own the information) in the healthcare information access control call for a new model that not only provides scalable and efficient access control, but also provide sufficiently fine granularity to ensure the rigid access control.

The RBCC Model

The role-based context constrained access control model is an extension of the role-based access control model in which the role-permission assignments are dynamically constrained by current accessing contexts. The accessing contexts are abstractions of characteristics of individual entities (such as users or subjects, information or objects, and roles), relationships among the entities, and relationships between entity and system environment. To control the complex contextual information itself, we limit our context to the healthcare domain. In other words, the range of contextual information with which we are concerned is tailored to healthcare applications. However, the model itself is generic and can be applied to other areas where fine-grained access control to secure information is needed.

In the RBCC access control model, there are six types of basic elements. They are *Entity*, *Operation*, *Permission*, *Context*, *Context Constraint*, and *Assignment Function*.

Entity

Entity generalizes different types of individual elements involved in role-based access control systems. More specifically, in a role-based access control system, there are three different types of entities, namely, *users*, *roles* and protected resources called secure objects *SObj*.

Operation

Operations are actions that are to be performed on secured objects. For instances, for computer data, *read*, *write*, *create*, and *delete* are possible operations.

Permissions and Assignment Functions

Permissions are approvals to perform operations on protected resources. Permissions are assigned to roles and constrained by current requesting context. Permission assignment is an example of assignment functions in the RBCC model.

Context and Context Constraints

Contexts are collections of information in the healthcare domain that may impact security decisions. There are different types of contexts that can influence the security rulings. For instance, location and time where an access request comes from are one type of context, while Doctor A is Patient B's neighbor is another type of context. More specifically, context in RBCC model is categorized into two classes: system context and application context. Context constraints are the restrictions on context values.

Context Model—Context Predicate

Similar to the approach used by Ranganathan and Campbell (2003), we define the contexts in the RBCC model as context predicates and use first-order context predicate to specify context constraints. A context predicate is a first-order predicate in which the name of the predicate is the type of context that is being described. The context predicates describe the properties and structures of the context information and the kinds of operations that can be performed on the context. The operation within a context predicate may be relational operations (such as "=", "≠"), or containment operations, to name a few. A few context predicate examples are:

- Location(Doctor A's office, 192.169.10.100)
- Time(CurrentTime, "=", 8:00)
- Time(BusinessHour, "within", [8:00, 17:00])
- DoctorPatient(Doctor A, Patient B)
- Neighbor(Doctor A, Patient B)

The *location* context predicate indicates that from Doctor A's office an access request from the IP address of 192.169.10.100 was generated; the first *time* context predicate symbolize that the current time is 8:00am, while the second *time* context predicate implies the business hours are from 8:00am to 5:00pm. The *doctor patient* and *neighbor* predicates define the type of relationships.

The context predicates define the context types. For instance, the *location* predicate defines the location context type for which the first argument must be a physical location and the second argument must be a valid IP address. The *time* predicate requires that the time context must have a name as its first parameter, "<", "=", "within", and so on, as a second parameter, and a valid time duration as the third parameter. The neighborhood context predicate decides that the context involves two persons. The structures of different context predicates and their required argument types are predefined and pre-specified in an ontology which checks the validity of context predicates.

As argued in Ranganathan et al. (2003), and as shown in the previous examples, this representation of context is expressive and can be used to present various kinds of contexts in a simple, concise, and uniform way. Furthermore, the model supports operations on contexts like conjunction, disjunction, negation, and quantification. It thus allows the creation of complex first-order logic expressions of contexts and hence provides a very powerful tool to not only write rules and constraints about contexts, but also to reason about consistencies of the contexts and prove context properties. The context constraints are defined by the first-order logic context predicate expressions. Many formal method efforts focus on the power, expressiveness, and decidability of first-order logic (Chandra et al., 1985; Shmueli, 1987) and a number of reasoning tools, such as theorem provers and software verification tools, are also available for reasoning about logic. Therefore, one of the key advantages of using this formal model for context is that we can directly use these research results and tools to design our security access control systems.

System Context

System context is an abstraction for system measurable data. Current time, access location, current cpu/network load, and so forth, are examples of system context. In the healthcare domain, the most frequently used security related contexts include accessing time and accessing locations. For instance, the location predicate and the first time predicate in the previous examples give the system context about the request location which is 192.169.10.100 and the current time which is 8:00 in the morning. Other environment-related information may be inferred from the obtained data. In particular, if a request time happens at 2:00am, we know it is not during regular business hours. Similarly, a set of IP addresses may be allocated to emergency rooms. Therefore, according to the IP address, we may conclude whether a request comes from an emergency room. Depending on the accessing time and where an access request originates, a user's access rights may differ.

Time and location are system explicit and measurable data. They are obtained dynamically for each request. The implicit knowledge, such as "2:00am is not a regular business hour", "124.14.08.8 is allocated to the emergency room for network connection", is defined statically using relationship predicates. The system context is defined by the dynamic system data, static relationships among the data, and the application execution environment.

Application Context

Similar to system context, application context contains dynamic data which are individual users and object profiles, and statically-defined relationships among users, objects, and roles. For instance, user's identification belongs to user profile. Different users have different profiles. Although to each entity, its corresponding profile remains relatively static, different access requests might come from different individuals, and hence, the profiles associated with an access request may vary.

There are also a set of statically-defined relationships among users, roles, and objects. For instance, each doctor may have a group of his/her own patients; a medical record (object) is owned by its patient; nurses works for doctors; user A is user B's parent, and so forth. Because of the sensitivity of medical data, the user and the relationship between the user and the requested data are determining factors on whether the user has the access rights to the data. The previous *DoctorPatient* and *Neighbor* predicates are examples of the application contexts.

Context Constraints

Context constraints are first-order logic expressions of contexts. The operations that can be performed on the contexts are Boolean operations and quantifications. The syntactic definition of context constraints is:

Definition 1 (Context Constraints)

Given context predicate C, context constraints Φ *are expressions of the form:*

$$\Phi := C \mid C \wedge C \mid C \vee C \mid \neg C \mid \exists x\, C \mid \forall x\, C$$

The quantification operations allow us to parameterize contexts and hence allow us to represent a much richer set of contexts. To illustrate the simplicity and expressiveness of our context and context constraint model, we present a few examples. Given a scenario that *"Nurse A requests an access to Patient B's record at 10:00am from Nurse A's office. The patient's doctor is the one whom Nurse A is currently working for"*, we can use the following context predicates to define the context:

1. $\exists_{Doctor}x(\text{NurseDoctor}(NurseA, x) \land \text{DoctorPatient}(x, PatientB))$

2.   Location(Nurse A's office, 192.169.10.100)

3.   Time(requestTime, "=", 10:00)

If an access security policy states that *a nurse can only access those patients' records whose doctors are the doctors the nurse works for. Furthermore, a nurse can only access the records during business hours.* The constraints on the context are given by the following first order expression of context predicates:

$$\Phi = \forall_{Nurse}n\forall_{Record}r\exists_{Doctor}d\exists_{Patient}p(\text{NurseDoctor}(n, d)$$
$$\land \text{PatientRecord}(p, r)$$
$$\land \text{DoctorPatient}(d, p))$$
$$\land \text{Time}(requestTime, within, [8:00, 17:00])$$

Given the constraint, a nurse can access a patient's record only when the earlier-noted first-order logic expression evaluates to true.

Formal Definition of RBCC Access Control Model

With the understanding of context and context constraints, we are able to give a formal definition for role-based context constrained access control model.

Definition 2 (RBCC Access Control Model)

The RBCC Access Control Model consists of the following components:
- *Entity $E = (U \cup R \cup O \cup S)$*
  - *a set of subjects, or users U*
  - *a set of roles R (which inherit their characteristics from the RABC model)*
  - *a set of secured objects O*
  - *a set of sessions S*

- *Operation(Op)*
- *Context(C)*
- *Context Constraints (Φ) first order logic expression based on context*
- *Permission Assignment Function $F_A : R \times O \times \Phi \rightarrow 2^{Op}$.*

We use the notation $r \xrightarrow[\Phi=true]{o} \{op\}$ to denote that a role r has a permission to perform the operation op on the object o if the protected object is bounded to o and the context constraint Φ is satisfied.

Figure 1 is a graphical representation of the model. As the figure illustrates, constraints are based on two types of contexts—namely, system context and application context. System contexts represent security-relevant system data; while the application contexts provide information about individual entities and their relationships among themselves and with the environment. Notice that, in the RBCC model, permission assignment function is the only assignment function that is defined in the model. The role assignment function in the traditional RBAC model and its families becomes one of application contexts in the RBCC model. Furthermore, although the permission assignment function is statically-defined, the mapping results are dynamic. More specifically, given the same user, role and protected objects, different contexts may result in different access rights.

Next, we first use RBCC constraint to specify a set of separation of duty examples given in RCL2000 (Ahn & Sandhu, 2000) and hence show the expressiveness of the RBCC model. We further present a few examples in healthcare applications for which RBAC family does not provide sufficient control granularity to guarantee accurate and tight permissions while RBCC does.

Figure 1. Role-based context constrained access control model

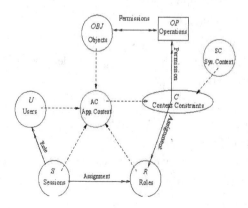

Expressiveness and Tightness of RBCC Access Control Model

We now use a set of examples to illustrate the expressiveness and tightness of the RBCC access control model. In particular, a set of separation of duty properties that are often cited in the literature (Ahn et al., 2000) are expressed with RBCC model. In addition, we list a set of security rules that are common in medical applications, but hard to specify with traditional RBAC model or its existing extensions to show the expressive power of the RBCC model.

Static Separation of Duty

Separation of duty can be categorized into two classes depending on when we enforce such properties: static separation of duty and dynamic separation of duty. As the name states, static SOD specifies the rules statically, while DSOD is more session based. Researchers have defined several forms of static separation of duty (Ahn et al., 2000; Kuhn, 1997; Sandhu, 1996). The most straightforward one is that *no user should be assigned to two roles which are in conflict with each other*. Other forms include *a user can have at most one conflicting permission acquired through roles assigned to the user*, as well as *each role can have at most one conflicting permission without consideration of user-role assignment*. We use the second form as an example to illustrate how we can use our model to present the property.

Example 1

A user can have at most one conflicting permission acquired through roles assigned to the user:

- Predefined application contexts (C_{pre}): conjunction of the following predicates:
  - User(x): x is a valid user of the system
  - Role(x): x is a valid role
  - Permission(p): p is a permission
  - Conflict(x, y): x conflicts with y
  - UserRole(x, y): user x assumes role y
  - RolePermission(r, p): role r has permission p under any context
- Constraint policy (SSOD) P

  $P = \forall_{User} u \forall_{Role} r \forall_{Permission} p, q\ UserRole(u, r)$
  $\quad \land RolePermission(r, p) \land RolePermission(r, q)$
  $\quad \land \neg Conflict(p, q)$

- Current application contexts (C_{curr}): conjunction of the following predicates:
  - UserRole(Mary, HNURSE);

- Time(requestTime, "within", (8:00, 17:00))
- Context constraint: Φ

$$\Phi = C_{pre} \wedge C_{curr} \wedge P$$

Dynamic Separation of Duty

Different from static separation of duty, dynamic separation of duty is session based. A typical DSOD property is given in the following example.

Example 2

No user can activate conflicting rules within the same session (Ahn & Sandhu, 2000).

With the similar predicates defined in SSOD, the constraint policy for DSOD P is as following:

$$P = \forall_{User} u \forall_{Role} r_{1}, r_{2} \, \mathrm{UserRole}(u, r_{1})$$
$$\wedge \, \mathrm{UserRole}(u, r_{2})$$
$$\wedge \, \neg \mathrm{Conflict}(r_{1}, r_{2})$$

Context Dependent Healthcare Examples

Here, we present a few healthcare applications that require knowledge of context in deciding access permissions.

Example 3

Head nurses can view all their department doctors' patients' medical records during business hours, except the medical records of their colleague's in the same department.

This example constrains role *HNurse*'s access permission on patients' records. The individual relationships between a user who assumes the *HNurse* role and a patient whose medical record is being requested plays an important role in deciding access permissions for a *HNurse*. This example is formalized as the following:

- Operations: $op = \{\text{view}\}$
- Predefined application contexts (C_{pre}): conjunction of the following predicates:
  - User(x): x is a valid user
  - Patient(x): x is a patient
  - Record(x): x is a patient record

- Doctor(x): x is a doctor
- DoctorPatient(x, y): x is y's patient
- Affiliation(x, y): x and y have the same affiliation
- PatientRecord(x, y): record y is about patient x
- UserRole(x, y): user x assumes role y
- RequestTime(x): x is the request time
- BusinessHour(x): x is between 8:00 to 17:00

- Constraint policy P

$$P = \forall_{User} u \forall_{Record} o \forall_{RequestTime} t \; UserRole(u, HNURSE)$$
$$\wedge \; \exists_{Patient} p \; PatientRecord(p, o)$$
$$\wedge \; \exists_{Doctor} d \; DoctorRecord(d, p)$$
$$\wedge \; Affiliation(u, d) \wedge \neg Affiliation(u, p)$$
$$\wedge \; BusinessHour(x)$$

- Current application contexts (C_{curr}): conjunction of the following predicates:
  - UserRole(Mary, HNURSE)
  - RequestTime(SysTime(x)): SysTime is a system function that returns the current system time
- Context constraint: Φ

$$\Phi = C_{pre} \wedge C_{curr} \wedge P$$

The current context includes a system context, that is, time. Hence, in addition to other application context, depending on the request time, the value of Φ could be different. For Mary to be able to view a patient's record, the context constraint Φ as defined earlier must be satisfied. In other words, the permission assignment function is constrained by the following:

$$UserRole(Mary, HNURSE) \xrightarrow[\Phi=true]{o} \{view\}$$

This example indicates the importance of the relationship among individual entities in making access control decisions. With traditional RBAC model, as soon as a user assumes the rule HNURSE, his/her own identity is cast away. By casting away user information and focus on roles only, the model is more scalable. However, the drawback is that it becomes difficult to specify such fine-grained access controls. Different from information access control in enterprises where the subject's position and responsibility is generally the only fact in deciding their information access privileges, in the healthcare domain, because of the information privacy law, and complicated relationship among individuals (who may be caregivers, researchers, social workers, patients, to name a few), not only the individual's responsibility, but also their identities, or in more general term, their profiles, and the profile of the accessed object all play an important role in making access decisions. Here is another example to illustrate the importance of individual profile and data profile in deciding user's access privilege.

Example 4

Pharmaceutical medicine researchers can only view records of patients who have taken the medicines that are the result of the researchers' study.

This example requires patients' medical records be characterized by their contents, such as records of cancer patients who have taken the newly-developed drug. Furthermore, the profile of the user as a research subject is also important, and it must match the profile of the data. In other words, the individual user must be involved in the medicine research for which the patient has taken. We formalize the example as following:

- Operations: $op = \{view\}$
- Predefined application contexts (C_{pre}): conjunction of the following predicates
  - User(x): x is a valid user
  - Researcher(x): x is a pharmaceutical researcher
  - UserRole(x, y): user x assumes role y
  - Record(x): x is a patient record
  - RecordContent(x, y): record x has content about y
  - Medicine(x): x is a medicine
  - ResearcherMedicine(x, y): x is a pharmaceutical researcher on medicine y
  - UserRole(x, y): user x assumes role y
  - Constraint policy P

$$P = \forall_{User} u \forall_{Record} o \; UserRole(u, Researcher)$$
$$\wedge \exists_{Medicine} m \; ResearcherMedicine(u, m)$$
$$\wedge \exists_{RecordContent} d \; RecordContent(o, m)$$

- Current application contexts (C_{curr}): conjunction of the following predicates
  - UserRole(Mary, RESEARCHER)
  - ResearcherMedicine(Mary, CancerDrugA)
- Context constraint: Φ

$$\Phi = C_{pre} \wedge C_{curr} \wedge P$$

The permission assignment function is given in the following:

$$UserRole(\textit{Mary, RESEARCHER}) \xrightarrow[\Phi=true]{o} \{view\}$$

These examples have shown that constraints based on subject's and object's profiles, and system environment are important in making tight security access decisions. These concerns are not addressed in existing RBAC-based models.

Implementation Architecture

We use an aspect-oriented approach to prototype the RBCC model. In particular, we consider the context gathering and security access checking as two different aspects which are orthogonal to the medical computer system's business logic and orthogonal to each other. In our prototype, we divide the patient information into three different types—namely, *PatientRecord*, *Image*, and *TestResult*. Each type has its own set of operations associated with it, as shown in Figure 2. Validating a client's access right to each operation is clearly a cross-cutting concern. Therefore, instead of repeating and mixing security checking with, for example, the *read* operation (which focuses on how to retrieve data from a data store and present the data in a user friendly format), we use aspects to abstract such a concern. By separating the *read* logic from the process of *check*-ing its validity, or more generally, by separating business logic from security policy, we can easily adapt different security policies. Meanwhile, the security aspects can be re-used by different information systems to enhance security features.

The security control aspect itself has a cross-cutting concern of the management of its own context. We introduce another aspect, *Context*. The context aspect provides advices to the access control aspect about its current context. Figure 2 depicts the relationship between the core logic and two different aspects. The dashed boxes capture the cross-cutting concerns. By separating context management from security policy and security checking from business logic, the system is more modular and easily accommodates individual policy changes and context changes.

Figure 2. Using aspects to separate orthogonal concerns

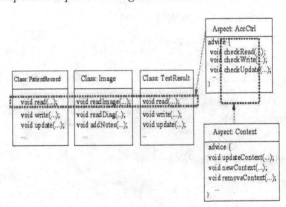

Conclusion

The RBCC model is a dynamic and fine-grained access control model. The model uses statically-defined relationships which may be external to the controlled system to capture the complex relationships among patients, doctors, researchers, medical data, and so forth. We also use entity profiles and dynamically-obtained system data to ensure the awareness of the accessing environment and ensure that accurate access rights are granted in timely fashion. On the other hand, in the RBCC model, the permission assignment is still role-based and hence the advantages of RBAC model, such as scalability, are maintained. As a dynamic control model, RBCC must evaluate the constraints for each request which may result in some performance loss. Nevertheless, in healthcare applications, most of access requests come from human users, instead of processes. Comparing to human beings' process speed, RBCC model's performance issues becomes less important, but the added flexibility provided remains critical.

Future Work

As we have presented, in the RBCC model, role's access permissions are constrained by current accessing contexts. The constraints are specified as a set of logical expressions of current system data, involving party's profiles and statically-defined relationships. For a given set of constraints, checking the satisfiability is an NP-complete problem. However, detecting inconsistencies among the set of policies is nevertheless feasible. Our future work will focus on developing an algorithm to efficiently check consistency of access constraints specified in the RBCC model. Another future research focus is on an implementation framework that utilizes relational database and data mining techniques to represent and retrieve complex and possible implicit relationships that access control depends on. The implementation framework should provide an easy-to-use language abstraction for specifying roles, permissions, and constraints, updating entities profiles and relationships, checking constraint consistencies, and modifying security policies. We will also investigate issues related to allowing dynamic change of access control constraints.

References

Ahn, G.-J., & Sandhu, R. (2000). Role-based authorization constraints specification. *ACM Trans. Information System Security, 3*(4), 207-226.

Barkley, J., Beznosov, K., & Uppal, J. (1999). Supporting relationships in access control using role based access control. In the *Proceedings of the Fourth ACM Workshop on Role-based Access Control,* Fairfax, VA, October 28-29 (pp. 55-65). New York: ACM Press.

Bertino, E., Bonatti, P. A., & Ferrari, E. (2001). Trbac: A temporal role-based access control model. *ACM Trans. Inf. Syst. Secur., 4*(3), 191-233.

Chandra, A. et al. (1985). Horn clauses queries and generalization. *Journal of Logic Program, 1*, 1-15.

Covington, M. J., Long, W., Srinivasan, S., Dev, A. K., Ahamad, M., & Abowd, G. D. (2001). Securing context-aware applications using environment roles. In the *Proceedings of the Sixth ACM Symposium on Access Control Models and Technologies,* Chantilly, VA, May 3-4 (pp. 10-20). New York: ACM Press.

Kuhn, D. R. (1997). Mutual exclusion of roles as a means of implementing separation of duty in role-based access control systems. In the *Proceedings of the Second ACM Workshop on Role-based Access Control,* Fairfax, VA, November 6-7 (pp. 23-30). New York: ACM Press.

Moyer, M. J., & Ahamad, M. (2001). Generalized role-based access control. In the *Proceedings of the 21st International Conference on Distributed Computing Systems,* April 16-19 (pp. 391-398). Washington, D.C.: IEEE Computer Society.

Neumann, G., & Strembeck, M. (2003). An approach to engineer and enforce context constraints in an rbac environment. In the *Proceedings of the Eighth ACM Symposium on Access Control Models and Technologies,* Como, Italy, June 2-3 (pp. 65-79). New York: ACM Press.

Park, J., & Sandhu, R. (2004, February). The UCONabc usage control model. *ACM Transactions on Information and System Security, 7*(1), 128-174.

Ranganathan, A., & Campbell, R. (2003). An infrastructure for context-awareness based on first order logic. *Personal Ubiquitous Comput., 7*(6), 353-364.

Sandhu, R. (1996). Role hierarchies and constraints for lattice-based access controls. In E. Bertino, H. Kurth, G. Martella, & E. Montolivo (Eds.), *Computer Security – Esorics '96, LNCS, 1146,* September 25-27 (pp. 65-97). Rome, Italy: Springer-Verlag.

Sandhu, R., Coyne, E., Feinstein, H., & Youman, C. (1996, February). Role-based access control models. *IEEE Computer, 29*(2), 38-47.

Shmueli, O. (1987). Decidability and expressiveness aspects of logic queries. In the *Proceedings of the Sixth ACM SIGACT-SIGMOD-SIGART Symposium on the Principles of Database Systems,* San Diego, CA, March 23-25 (pp. 23-25). New York: ACM Press.

Thomas, R. (1997). Flexible team-based access control using contexts. In the *Proceedings of the Second ACM Workshop on Role-Based Access Control,* Fairfax, VA, November 6-7 (pp. 13-18). New York: ACM Press.

Zhang, X., Park, J., & Parisi-Presicce, F. (2004). A logical specification for usage control. In the *Proceedings of the Ninth ACM Symposium on Access Control Models and Technologies,* Yorktown Heights, NY, USA, June 2-4 (pp. 1-10). New York: ACM Press.

About the Editors

Du Zhang received his PhD degree in computer science from the University of Illinois. He is a professor and chair of Computer Science Department at California State University, Sacramento. His current research interests include: machine learning and data mining applications in software engineering and bioinformatics, knowledge-based systems, and Internet and Web applications. He has authored or co-authored over 100 publications in journals, conference proceedings, and book chapters in these and other areas. He is a program co-chair for the 2006 IEEE International Conference on Information Reuse and Integration. He was the conference general chair for the 16th IEEE International Conference on Tools with Artificial Intelligence in 2004; the program chair for the 15th IEEE International Conference on Tools with Artificial Intelligence in 2003; and a program co-chair for the 4th IEEE Symposium on Bioinformatics and Bioengineering in 2004, the IEEE International Conference on Information Reuse and Integration in 2004 and 2005, and the 4th IEEE international Conference on Cognitive Informatics in 2005. He is an associate editor for the *International Journal on Artificial Intelligence Tools* and a member of editorial board for the *International Journal of Cognitive Informatics and Natural Intelligence*. He is a senior member of IEEE and a member of ACM.

Jeffrey J. P. Tsai is a professor in the Department of Computer Science at the University of Illinois at Chicago where he is also the director of the Distributed Real-Time Intelligent Systems Laboratory. His current research interests include software engineering, sensor networks, pervasive computing, bioinformatics, software architecture, formal verification, software security, distributed real-time systems, multimedia systems, and agent-based systems. He is a fellow of the IEEE, the AAAS, and the SDPS.

About the Authors

Gary D. Boetticher received his PhD in computer science from West Virginia University and is an associate professor at the University of Houston, Clear Lake. He has been working in advanced machine learning applications in corporate, government, and academia since 1986. He has served on the Executive Board Reuse Interoperability Group and the executive board for the IEEE Reuse Standards Committee. His research interests include data mining, machine learning, bioinformatics, and software metrics. He is a member of the ACM and IEEE.

Michelle Cartwright received a BSc degree (honours) in computer science from the University of Wolverhampton and a PhD from the Bournemouth University, UK. She is a lecturer and researcher at the Brunel Software Engineering Research Centre (B-SERC), in the School of Information Systems, Computing and Mathematics, Brunel University, UK. Her research interests include software metrics for object-oriented systems, empirical software engineering, software prediction, and empirical software engineering for internet technology.

Min Chen received her bachelor's degree in electrical engineering from Zhejiang University in China. She is currently a PhD candidate in the School of Computing and Information Sciences (SCIS) at Florida International University (FIU). Her research interests include distributed multimedia database systems, image and video database retrieval, and multimedia data mining. She has authored and co-authored 17 technical papers published in various prestigious journals, refereed conference/workshop proceedings, and book chapters. She is the recipient of several awards, including a Presidential Fellowship and the Best Graduate Student Research Award from SCIS at FIU.

Shu-Ching Chen received his PhD from the School of Electrical and Computer Engineering at Purdue University, West Lafayette, IN, USA in December, 1998. He also received a master's degrees in computer science, electrical engineering, and civil engineering from Purdue University. He has been an associate professor in the School of Computing and Information Sciences (SCIS), Florida International University (FIU) since August 2004. Prior to that, he was an assistant professor in SCIS at FIU dating from August 1999. His main research interests include distributed multimedia database systems and multimedia data mining. Dr. Chen has authored and co-authored more than 140 research papers in journals, refereed conference/symposium/workshop proceedings, and book chapters. In 2005, he was awarded the IEEE Systems, Man, and Cybernetics Society's Outstanding Contribution Award. He was also awarded a University Outstanding Faculty Research Award from FIU in 2004, Outstanding Faculty Service Award from SCIS in 2004, and Outstanding Faculty Research Award from SCIS in 2002.

J. J. Cuadrado is a lecturer at the University of Alcalá (Madrid). He has a PhD in informatics and his main interests are software estimation, software metrics, and the application of new methods to those areas.

Bojan Cukic is an associate professor in the Lane Department of Computer Science and Electrical Engineering at West Virginia University, where he also serves as the co-director of the Center for Identification Technology Research. His research interests include software engineering for high-assurance systems, fault tolerant computing, information assurance, and biometrics. He received a U.S. National Science Foundation Career award and a Tycho Brahe award for outstanding empirical research from the NASA Office of Safety and Mission Assurance. He is a member of the editorial board of the *Empirical Software Engineering Journal* and served as a guest editor of *IEEE Software Magazine* in November 2005. He received his PhD in computer science from the University of Houston.

Donghua Deng received BS and MS degrees in electronics and information engineering from Huazhong University of Science and Technology, Wuhan, China. She is currently working towards a PhD degree in electrical engineering and computer science at the University of California, Irvine. Her research interests are in the areas of software engineering, knowledge engineering, database applications, business intelligence, query and rule optimizations.

Yi Deng received his PhD in computer science from the University of Pittsburgh in 1992. He is currently the dean and professor of the School of Computing and Information Sciences at Florida International University, the State University of Florida at Miami. Prior to his current appointment, he served as the managing director of the Embedded Software Center at the University of Texas at Dallas. He has been the principal investigator (PI) or Co-PI of fifteen (15) funded research projects total over $10 million, and authored or co-authored over 80 papers in peer-reviewed journals and conference proceedings. He has initiated, led, and managed a number of large-scale and multi-disciplinary research projects; and founded and directed three research centers, including the Center for Advanced Distributed Systems Engineering (CADSE), the NSF CREST Center of Emerging Technologies for Advanced Information Processing and High-Confidence Systems, and the IBM Center for Autonomic and Grid Computing at Florida International University. He has served on the editorial board of the *International Journal on Software Engineering and Knowledge Engineering*, as the conference chair for the International Conference on Distributed Multimedia Systems and the IEEE International Symposium on Multimedia Software Engineering. He co-chairs the Board of Governance for the Latin American Grid (LA Grid), an international alliance co-founded by IBM, Florida International University, University of Puerto Rico, University of Miami, Barcelona Supercomputing Center and Tec de Monterrey, dedicated to collaborative research and education and to the development of an international grid computing infrastructure connecting U.S. and Latin America.

Paul Dietz received his PhD in computer science from Cornell University in 1984. Since then, he has taught at the University of Southern California and the University of Rochester and worked on program transformation at Schlumberger-Doll Research. He has been with Motorola since 1995. His interests include algorithms and data structures, program transformation systems, the lisp family of programming languages, and software testing.

J. J. Dolado is a full professor at the University of the Basque Country. He received a PhD in informatics from that university (1989). His main interests lie in the fields of software engineering, system dynamics, and complex systems. He is the head of the Department of the Computer Languages and Systems of his University. More information at http://www.sc.ehu.es/dolado.

F. Ferrer-Troyano is an assistant professor at the University of Seville. He is working toward his PhD in data mining and software engineering.

Ophir Frieder is the IITRI Chair Professor of Computer Science and the director of the Information Retrieval Laboratory at the Illinois Institute of Technology. His research interests focus on scalable information retrieval systems spanning search and retrieval and communications issues. He is a fellow of the AAAS, ACM, and IEEE.

Tong Gao is a PhD candidate in the Department of Computer Science at the University of Texas at Dallas. He graduated from NanKai University with a bachelor's degree in computer science. His research interests include component-based software engineering, non-functional requirement specification and analysis, and adaptive systems.

Daniele Gunetti received his PhD in computer science from the Universities of Torino and Milano, in 1995. He is currently an associate professor at the Department of Computer Science of the University of Torino, Italy. His main interests are in the field of automatic theorem proving, inductive logic programming with applications to software engineering, biometric measures applied to computer security.

Lan Guo is a research assistant professor in the MBR Cancer Center/Department of Community Medicine at West Virginia University (WVU). She was an assistant professor in the Computer Science Department at the University of Southern Mississippi in 2004/05. Her research interests are bioinformatics, artificial intelligence, information integration, and software engineering. She received a PhD in computer and information science from West Virginia University in 2004. While a graduate student, she was a Lane Fellow. She also received a Microsoft/UPE scholarship in 2001 and a WVU/NASA Outstanding Student Researcher award in 2002.

Xudong He received the BS and MS degrees in computer science from Nanjing University, China, in 1982 and 1984, respectively. He received a PhD degree in computer science from Virginia Polytechnic Institute & State University (Virginia Tech) in 1989. He joined the faculty in the School of Computer Science (now School of Computing and Information Sciences) at Florida International University (FIU) in 2000, and is a professor of the School of Computing and Information Sciences and the Director of the Center for Advanced Distributed System Engineering. Prior to joining FIU, he was an associate professor in the Department of Computer Science at North Dakota State University since 1989. His research interests include formal methods, especially Petri nets, and software testing techniques. He has published about 90 papers in these areas. Dr. He's research has been supported by the NSF, ONR, and NASA. He has been ranked among the top 15 scholars in software and system engineering worldwide during 1999-2003 by the *Journal of System and Software*. He has served on the program committees of numerous international conferences in computer science. He was the organizing chair of the 26th International Conference on Applications and Theory of Petri Nets and Other Models of Concurrency held at FIU in June 2005. Dr. He is a member of the Association for Computing Machinery, and a senior member of the IEEE Computer Society.

Efe Igbide received his BSc degree in computer science from the University of Benin, Nigeria. He then obtained his MSc in computer engineering with interest in data mining from the University of Alberta, Canada. Subsequently, he went on to pursue a BSNA at Union University in Jackson, Tennessee, USA, with a focus on nursing. Currently, he works at the Vanderbilt University Teaching Hospital in Nashville, Tennessee, USA. His research interests lie in combining data mining and nursing in the field of nursing informatics.

Taghi M. Khoshgoftaar is a professor of the Department of Computer Science and Engineering, Florida Atlantic University and the director of the Empirical Software Engineering Laboratory. His research interests are in software engineering, software metrics, software reliability and quality engineering, computational intelligence, computer performance evaluation, data mining, machine learning, and statistical modeling. He has published more than 300 refereed papers in these areas. He is a member of the IEEE, IEEE Computer Society, and IEEE Reliability Society. He was the program chair and general chair of the IEEE International Conference on Tools with Artificial Intelligence in 2004 and 2005, respectively. Khoshgoftaar received an MS in applied mathematics from MIT, an MS in computer science from North Carolina State University, and a PhD in statistics from Virginia Tech.

Timothy C. Lethbridge is a professor of computer science and software engineering at the University of Ottawa, where he received his PhD in 1994. His research is in the areas of software engineering tools, knowledge management, software engineering education, user interface design, and software modeling. He is the author of the textbook, *Object-Oriented Software Engineering: Practical Software Development Using UML and Java*, and has also published over 70 peer-reviewed scientific papers. Dr. Lethbridge is a senior member of the IEEE.

Yi Liu received a PhD degree in the Department of Computer Science and Engineering at Florida Atlantic University in 2003. She is currently an assistant professor in the Department of Information Technology and Marketing at Georgia College and State University. Her research interests include software engineering, software metrics, software reliability and quality engineering, computer performance modeling, genetic programming, and data mining.

Hui Ma is currently a PhD student in the Computer Science Department of the University of Texas at Dallas. He received his bachelor's degree in the Department of Automation at the Tsinghua University, Beijing, China. His research interests include component-based software development methodologies, composition analysis techniques, real-time system design, VoIP systems and security, and evolutionary algorithms.

Yan Ma is a research associate in the Department of Statistics at West Virginia University (WVU). Her research interests are bioinformatics, data mining, microarray data analysis, and information integration. She teaches elementary statistics courses and also works as a consultant in the bioinformatics core facility located in the health science center at WVU. She received her master's degree in statistics and currently is a PhD candidate in the Computational Combinatorics and Discrete Mathematics (CCDM) program at WVU.

Kevin Marth is a PhD candidate at the Illinois Institute of Technology. His research interests include programming paradigms, languages, and compilers, as well as concurrent, distributed, and parallel programming. Since joining Motorola in 1989, Kevin has worked on various cellular infrastructure products and software engineering technologies. He is currently a member of the Motorola Software Design Automation Center, where he has contributed to several components of the Mousetrap program transformation system and is instrumental in deploying automatic code generation technology to Motorola product groups.

Stan Matwin is a professor at the School of Information Technology and Engineering, University of Ottawa, where he directs the Text Analysis and Machine Learning (TAMALE) lab. His research is in machine learning, data mining, and their applications, and is the author and co-author of 150 research papers. He is the former president of the Canadian Society for the Computational Studies of Intelligence (CSCSI) and of the IFIP Working Group 12.2 (Machine Learning), as well as the founding director of the Information Technology Cluster of the Ontario Research Centre for Electronic Commerce. He is a member of the editorial boards of the *Machine Learning Journal*, the *Computational Intelligence Journal*, and the *Intelligent Data Analysis Journal*.

Petr Musilek received his PhD degree in cybernetics from the Military Technical Academy in Brno, Czech Republic, in 1995. In 1997, he was awarded a NATO Science Fellowship and spent two years as a postdoctoral fellow at the Intelligent Systems Research Laboratory, University of Saskatchewan, Canada. In 1999, he joined the Department of Electrical and Computer Engineering at the University of Alberta, Canada, where he serves as an associate professor. In 2005, he was a visiting professor at the Department of Computer Science, University of Carlos III of Madrid, Spain. Currently, he is a visiting scientist at the Institute of Computer Science, Academy of Sciences of the Czech Republic. Dr. Musilek's research includes computational intelligence applied to the areas of autonomous systems, data analysis, and time series prediction. In particular, he conducts research into neural networks, fuzzy systems, evolutionary computing, and artificial immune systems, and applies these computational methods to navigation and control of mobile robots, program generation, and intelligent risk assessment and decision support. He has published a number of journal papers, a textbook, and several book chapters, and contributed to many major conferences.

Chang-Hai Nie received his BS degree in computer science from Southeast University, China in 2004. He is currently an associate professor and a PhD candidate. His research interests are software engineering and software testing, fuzzy information processing, and neutral networks.

Witold Pedrycz is a professor and Canada Research Chair (CRC – Computational Intelligence) in the Department of Electrical and Computer Engineering, University of Alberta, Edmonton, Canada. He is actively pursuing research in computational intelligence, fuzzy modeling, knowledge discovery and data mining, quantitative software engineering, fuzzy control including fuzzy controllers, pattern recognition, knowledge-based neural networks, and relational computing. He has published numerous papers in this area. He is also an author of nine research monographs covering various aspects of computational intelligence and software engineering. Dr. Pedrycz currently serves as an associate editor of *IEEE Transactions on Systems Man and Cybernetics*, *IEEE Transactions on Fuzzy Systems*, and *IEEE Transactions on Neural Networks*. He is an editor-in-chief of *Information Sciences*.

Marek Reformat received his MSc degree from Technical University of Poznan, Poland, and his PhD from University of Manitoba, Canada. His interests were related to simulation and modeling in time-domain, as well as evolutionary computing and its application to optimization problems For three years, he worked for the Manitoba HVDC Research Centre, Canada, where he was a member of a simulation software development team. Currently, Dr. Reformat is with the Department of Electrical and Computer Engineering at University of Alberta. His research interests lay in the areas of application of computational intelligence techniques, such as neuro-fuzzy systems and evolutionary computing, as well as probabilistic and evidence theories to intelligent data analysis leading to translating data into knowledge. He applies these methods to conduct research in the areas of software and knowledge engineering. He has been a member of program committees of several conferences related to computational intelligence and evolutionary computing.

Shangping Ren is an assistant professor at the Computer Science Department, Illinois Institute of Technology. Her research interests include security issues and access control in distributed environment, real-time embedded systems and coordination models for distributed systems with none-algorithmic requirements.

D. Rodriguez is a lecturer in the Department of Computer Science at The University of Reading. He received his BSc degree in computer science from the University of the Basque Country, Spain, in 1995 and his PhD degree from The University of Reading, UK, in 2003. His research interests are in the area of software engineering including empirical software engineering and the application of data mining techniques to software engineering.

J. C. Riquelme Santos was born in Las Palmas de Gran Canarias, Spain, in 1962. He received an MSc degree in Math and a PhD degree in computer science, both from the University of Seville. Since 1987, he has been at the Department of Computer Science, University of Seville, where he is currently an associate professor. His primary areas of interest are data mining and machine learning techniques. His Web page is http://www.lsi.us.es/~riquelme.

Martin Shepperd received a PhD in computer science from the Open University in 1991 for his work in measurement theory and its application to software engineering. He is a professor of software technology at Brunel University, London, UK and the director of the Brunel Software Engineering Research Centre (B-SERC). He has published more than 90 refereed papers and three books in the area of empirical software engineering, machine learning, and statistics. He is the editor-in-chief of the journal *Information & Software Technology* and was an associate editor of *IEEE Transactions on Software Engineering* (2000-4). He has also previously worked for a number of years as a software developer for a major bank.

Phillip C.-Y. Sheu is currently a professor of electrical engineering and computer science at the University of California, Irvine. He received his PhD and MS degrees from the University of California at Berkeley in electrical engineering and computer science in 1986 and 1982, respectively, and his BS degree from National Taiwan University in electrical engineering in 1978. His research interests include complex information systems, information technologies for biology and medicine, semantic software engineering, semantic Web search and services, and large real-time knowledge systems. He is a fellow of IEEE.

Liang Shi received his BS degree in computer science from Southeast University, China in 2001. He is currently a PhD candidate and his research interest is in software analysis and testing.

Jelber Sayyad Shirabad is a research associate with the Text Analysis and Machine Learning Group at the School of Information Technology and Engineering, University of Ottawa. His research interests include mining software repositories with special interest in learning relevance relations and building other predictive software models, and applied machine learning. He worked as a software designer on various business information systems prior to attending Carleton University in Ottawa to obtain his master's in computer science. He received his PhD degree from University of Ottawa in 2003. He was the chair of STEP PSM 2004 and ICSE PROMISE 2005 workshops on predictive software models, as well as a member of the program committee for STEP 2004, PROMISE 2005, and MSR 2005.

Giancarlo Succi is a professor with tenure at the Free University of Bolzano-Bozen, Italy, where he directs the Center for Applied Software Engineering. Before joining the Free University of Bolzano-Bozen, he has been a professor with tenure at the University of Alberta, Edmonton, Alberta, associate professor at the University of Calgary, Alberta, and assistant professor at the University of Trento, Italy. He was also chairman of a small software company, EuTec. Dr. Succi holds a Laurea degree in electrical engineering (Genova, 1988), an MSc in computer science (SUNY Buffalo, 1991) and a PhD in computer and electrical engineering (Genova, 1993). He has been a registered professional engineer in Italy since 1991, and he obtained the full registration also for the province of Alberta, Canada, while residing there. Dr. Succi has written more than 150 papers published in international journals, books, and conferences, and is the editor of four books. He has been the principal investigator for projects amounting more than €5M cash and, overall, he has received more than €10M in research support from private and public granting bodies. He has been chairing and co-chairing several international conferences and workshops, a member of the editorial board of international journals, and a leader of international research networks.

Bhekisipho Twala received a PhD degree in machine learning and statistics from the Department of Statistics, Open University, UK, in 2005. He is currently a research fellow at the Brunel Software Engineering Research Centre (B-SERC), in the School of Information Systems, Computing and Mathematics, Brunel University, London (UK). His research interests include knowledge discovery and reasoning under uncertainty.

Aswin van den Berg received his PhD degree in computer science from Cornell University (1998) in the areas of program transformation and incremental higher-order attribute grammars. He has been with Motorola Labs for five years working on enhancements to the Mousetrap system. He also conducts research in the areas of aspect-oriented modeling and is leading efforts to apply it inside Motorola. He is also interested in software security and how it relates to program transformation and static analysis.

Thomas Weigert is the senior director of software engineering and Dan Noble Fellow with Motorola Global Software Group where he is responsible for the development environment, including processes, methods, tools, and IT infrastructure, deployed in 20 software factories in 13 countries with over 6,000 software engineers. He received a PhD in philosophy from the University of Illinois and an MBA from Northwestern University. He is the author of a textbook as well as over 40 articles on the application of artificial intelligence techniques to the development of product software, in particular for real-time distributed systems. He serves on standards bodies for software design languages with the International Telecommunications Union and the OMG.

Frank Weil received his PhD EE degree from Purdue University and is the manager of the Motorola Software Design Automation Center. He has been working in the area of model-driven engineering for over 15 years. His main work has been in the areas of modeling languages, automatic code generation, and various related technologies such as model checking and feature interaction. Dr. Weil has authored several publications in professional journals and conferences. The publications span a wide range of software engineering topics, including formal analysis and design methods, automatic code generation, object-oriented programming, software and systems development, simulation, and feature interaction.

Xiaoyuan Xie received her BS degree in computer science from Southeast University in China in 2005. She is currently a PhD candidate. Her research area is in software testing.

Baowen Xu received his BS degree in mathematics from Wuhan University, China in 1982. He received an MS degree and a PhD degree in computer science in 1984 and 2002, respectively. He is currently a professor with the Department of Computer Science & Engineering at Southeast University, China. His current research interests include programming language, program analysis, program understanding, software metrics, software testing, Web search engine, and other topics related to software engineering. He has published numerous papers in international conferences and journals and has been a program committee member or chair in several conferences such as SEKE, COMPSAC, QSIC, PRICAI, ICTAI, and FTDCS.

I-Ling Yen received her BS degree from Tsing-Hua University, Taiwan, and her MS and PhD degrees in computer science from the University of Houston. She is currently an associate professor of computer science at the University of Texas at Dallas. Dr. Yen's research interests include fault-tolerant computing, security systems and algorithms, distributed systems, Internet technologies, and QoS analysis for software systems. She had published over 100 technical papers in these research areas and received many research awards from NSF, DOD, NASA, and several industry companies. She has served as a program committee member for many conferences and program chair/co-chair for the IEEE HASE, COMPSAC, ISADS, and so on.

Huiqun Yu received his BS degree from Nanjing University in 1989, MS degree from East China University of Science and Technology (ECUST) in 1992, and PhD degree from Shanghai Jiaotong University in 1995, all in computer science. He has been with the Department of Computer Science and Engineering at ECUST since 1995. He is the director and a professor of the Department of Computer Science and Engineering. From 2001 to 2004, he was a visiting researcher in the School of Computer Science at Florida International University. His research interests include information security, software engineering, and formal methods. He was awarded two National Natural Science Foundation research grants and several grants from the Ministry of Education, China and other sources. He co-authored one text book, and published over 50 papers in research journals and refereed conferences. Dr. Yu is a member of the ACM and the IEEE Computer Society.

Index

Symbols

4cRuleBuilder 29

A

abstract data types 378
ACC 247
access control 439–445, 448, 450, 452,
    454–455
    model 439, 441, 443, 445, 448, 450,
    455
accuracy (ACC) 63, 115, 170, 191, 204, 247
    (see also *performance measure*)
adaptive SOA systems 127
adjusted function points 9
ADORA (analysis and description of require-
    ments and architecture) 411
AI (see *artificial intelligence*)
AID (assess, improve, decide) 277
amorphous slicing 303
analysis 348, 357, 360, 364, 371–372, 381,
    385, 389
    of adaptive SOA systems 127
analytic learning 268
ANN (see *artificial neural networks*)
application context 447
applying rule induction in prediction 268
approximation_level 300–301

architecture of the composition analysis frame-
    work 129
Architecture Research Facility, The (ARF) 28
arithmetical crossover 290
artificial intelligence (AI) 117
artificial neural network-based models 18
artificial neural networks (ANN) 18, 274 (see
    also *neural network*)
assimilation of the results 3
attribute 1–9, 12, 55, 175, 183, 186–191, 193,
    195, 202, 357
    set 187
automated testing 436
automatic code generation 346
    for industrial-strength systems 351
automatic testing 294, 312
automatic test data generation 288, 302

B

background knowledge 77
"backward chaining" 20
bag 108
    of words 188–190
bagging 21, 40, 241, 261
balanced random forest 239, 244, 248, 250,
    254, 257, 259–260
base-level
    data models 29
    model 21, 25, 29, 39

basics of evidence theory 49
basic belief
    assignments 49
    mass (bbm) 22–26, 30–37, 39, 49, 51
basic syntax 429
Bayesian belief network-based models 18
Bayesian belief networks (BBN) 18, 40, 54,
    274, 277
Bayesian network 280
bbm (see *basic belief mass*)
BBN (see *Bayesian belief networks*)
behavioral model 339, 340
behaviors of software architectures 322
belief
    functions 49
    net 18
binary code 289–291
bit mutation 291
black box 101
    models 19
blank lines 60
bloat problem in GP 217
Boolean functions 161
boosting 21, 41, 251
boundary testing 427
BPEL (see *business process execution lan-
    guage*)
branch count 60
branch coverage 294–295, 299, 301, 303, 305
    criterion 294
breeding 216
Breiman observation 6
bug tracking 178
bushing and blossoming techniques 303
business process execution language (BPEL)
    122

C

C4.5 3–4, 13
    algorithm 29
C5.0 190, 197, 206 (see also *decision tree
    learner*)
candidate Web services 128
canonicalization 360, 363–364, 367, 370, 380
CART-LAD 17
CART-LS 17
CART (classification and regression trees) 4,
    17
case-based reasoners (CBR) 54
case-based reasoning (CBR) 18, 273, 279, 281
    (see also *instance-based learning, rule
    induction*)

case-based reasoning models 18
CBDE (see *component-based software develop-
    ment*)
CBIR (see *content-based image retrieval*)
    103–107, 111, 113, 117–118
    feature analysis and similarity measures
    105
    systems, color 113
    systems, initial query 111
    systems, texture 113
CBR (see *case-based reasoners, case-based
    reasoning*)
characteristics of GP 214
class 3
    variable 55–56
classification 3–5, 13, 17–18, 21, 40, 42,
    45–46, 48, 51, 267–268, 270, 272–273,
    276, 279, 281 (see also *data mining,
    prediction*)
    error rate estimation 242
    learning 175–176, 203 (see also *induc-
    tive learning*)
    problems 3
    tree 18, 41, 251
classifier 3, 168, 175–176, 183–185, 191–193,
    195, 197–198, 200, 202–204 (see also
    model)
clause sets 80, 83, 85–86, 89, 91–92, 96, 98,
    100
client-server system 136
cluster 1, 4, 10, 12
    sampling 56
CM1 Project 257
Co-update
    heuristic 180
    relation 175, 178–179, 184, 186, 203
COCOMO I 54
COCOMO II 54
code generation
    details 353
    rules, canonicalization 363
    rules, informational 364
    rules, optimization 367
    rules, semantic analysis 364
    rules, transformational 363
    rules, types 363
    system 346, 348, 350–351, 372
code generator 346, 348, 361, 363 (see also
    program transformation system)
code representation 289–291 (see also *gene
    representation, gene space, search
    space, solution space*)

coding 289–290
    method 289
    scheme 289–290 (see also *gene space, search space, solution space*)
COMET (see *commitment-based software development*)
command control communication system 223
comments 170, 188–189, 195, 197 (see also *source comments, source file comments*)
commitment-based software development (COMET) 412
compiler 351–354, 360, 389, 395
    and platform specifics 353
completeness 77, 79
completion procedure 88
complexity 3
complex software systems 319
component 321–322, 326, 328, 330–333, 336, 338–340
component-based software development (CBDE) 411
components 238, 261
composition analysis 336
    framework 122–123, 129–130
    problem 132
composition correctness 333
composition level specifications 330
computational techniques 3
computational tree logic (CTL) 337
computer security policy 439
concept 169–171, 175, 179, 181, 184, 189 (see also *definition*)
concept of IF-THEN rules 22
confidence
    in results 29
    measure 16, 22, 36, 37, 39 (see also *goodness of rule, rules*)
configurable parameter 126–133, 135, 140–141, 143–144
configuration 129, 142, 299, 312–313
confusion matrix 191, 197
connector 321–322, 328, 330, 332, 336, 339–340
consistency 409, 411–412, 414, 431, 434
    of software design 431
constraints on industrial-strength systems 349
constraint and proactive rules 417
constraint rule 410, 414, 417, 431
constructing models
    empirical approach 54
    machine learning approach 54

constructing the M5 decision tree 5
content-based image retrieval (CBIR) 103–105, 117–118 (see also *image retrieval*)
    system 103
context 439–440, 442–445, 447–455
    and context constraints 445
    constraints 440, 443, 445–449
    constraints in an RBAC environment 443
    dependent healthcare examples 451
    model–context predicate 446
continuous relevance relation 171
control flow graph 300, 303
corrective software maintenance 15
cost 169, 170, 174, 197–198, 200, 202–203
    (see also *error cost*)
    estimation 3
    of misclassification 211, 221
coverability tree 334
coverage-oriented approach 295–297, 299–300
    (see also *fitness function construction, structural evolutionary testing*)
coverage criterion 294–295, 297
credibility assessment of empirical/machine learning models 52
credibility metrics 55
"credibility processes" 55
crossover 44, 290–293 (see also *genetic operation, genetic operator*)
    operator 135
cross validation 55–56, 67–69
CTL (see *computational tree logic*)
cyclomatic complexity 56, 60

D

dataset 2, 4, 6–12, 14, 16, 18, 24, 27–28, 48, 51–52, 237, 239, 241–246, 250–251, 253–255, 257, 259–260
data mining 1–3, 8, 12, 168–169, 178, 202, 206, 239, 263 (see also *knowledge discovery*)
    tool selection 62
data models 14–19, 27, 29–30, 36, 45 (see also *rule-based models*)
data pre-processing 60
data preparation 3
Daubechies wavelet 113
debugging of logic programs 74
decimal code 289, 290, 291
decision rules 54
decision stump 253

decision trees (DTs) 3–5, 13, 16, 21, 29–30,
    41–42, 45–48, 54, 190–191, 195–196,
    267–268, 271, 274, 276, 280 (see also
    *classification tree, classifiers, regression
    tree*)
        as data models 45
        evolutionary-based construction 45
        learner 54, 62, 170, 207
defect 15–18, 28–29, 32, 39, 54, 56, 60–61,
    64–65, 70 (see also *fault, software
    defect*)
        data 58
        datasets, "nasty" experiments 59
        datasets, "nice" experiments 59
        elimination efforts 16
        prediction 54
        prediction model 67
        removal process 15–16
defective 245, 248
        computer systems 54
definition 168–169, 171–175, 182, 188, 206
        of the confusion matrix 63
Dempster's combination rule 24, 50
dependability attributes using SAM 337
dependent variable 55 (see also *class variable*)
derived constraints on transformation systems
    350
designing software architectures 328
design
        information generation 420
        model 346, 360–363, 388
        specification 347–348
development
        and validation of IF-THEN models 23
        characteristics 8
        of the fMUX networks 157
discontinuous 288, 293, 306
discrete
        crossover 290
        relevance relation 171
discriminant analysis 251
distance 295, 297–301, 311
distance-oriented approach 295, 297, 299–300
        (see also *fitness function construction,
        structural evolutionary testing*)
distributed
        mutation 291
        proactive semantic software engineering
        environment (DPSSEE) 409
documentation 178
documents-entity relevance relation 173

domain-specific notation 348
DPSSEE (see *distributed proactive semantic
        software engineering environment*)
drug activity prediction problem 107
dynamic
        code 289
        execution information 295
        semantics of PrT nets 323
        separation of duty 451

E

EAs (see *evolutionary algorithms*)
ease/difficulty of a modeling situation 52
effort 3
        estimation data 58
EFSM (see *extended finite state machine*)
element
        (component/connector) correctness 332
        instances 332
        level specifications 328
        level analysis 333
elimination of defect 30
empirical-based software engineering 54 (see
        also *software engineering*)
empirical/machine
        learning-based models 52
        learning models 52
empirical
        approach 54
        software engineering 52, 54–55, 68, 70
end-to-end latency 337
engineering 409–410, 415–416, 436
ensemble
        method 240–241, 251
        prediction system 15–16
        system 16, 19, 21, 29
ensemble-based
        prediction system 16, 23, 25, 27,
        36–37, 39, 51
        system 21
entity 445
environment role-based access control (ER-
        BAC) 442
ERBAC model (see *environment role-based
        access control*)
error cost 197
essential complexity 60
ET 300–301
Euclidean distance 61
evaluation 215, 290, 292–293, 316
evidence theory 15–16, 21–22, 36, 39, 49, 51

evolution 287–293, 295–296, 298–299,
301–307, 309, 311–314
evolutionary
algorithms (EAs) 43, 131, 146, 315
computing 43
temporal performance testing 309
testing 287–289, 292–293, 295–314
(see also *automatic test data generation,
genetic optimization*)
evolutionary-based construction of decision
trees 46
example 170, 173–175, 179–180, 183, 186,
188, 190–191, 193, 195, 197–198, 200,
202–203 (see also *instance*)
executable lines of code 60
extended finite state machine (EFSM) 413
external
headers 353
libraries 353
extracted knowledge 29
extraction of
IF-THEN rules 14
knowledge 27, 39

F

false positive rate 191, 193, 195, 198, 200
fault 17–19
fault
prediction 262
prone 238, 250, 262
proneness 237, 250, 255, 260
fault-tolerance 338
faulty 238–239, 244–245, 249, 260
testing 427
feature 175, 179, 182, 186, 188–191, 193,
195–197, 202–203 (see also *attribute*)
importance evaluation 243
set 191, 193, 195–197, 200, 203
vector 188–190 (see also *attribute set*)
feed-forward neural network 109, 114 (see also
machine learning, neural network)
FILP (see *functional ILP*)
first order temporal logic 332, 335, 339, 343
fitness function 44, 160, 289–290, 292–293,
295–296, 298–300, 306–307, 310–311,
314 (see also *evaluation, guidance*)
construction 297, 310–311
for classification 220
for module rank 221
for tree size 222
fitness value 290, 292–293, 295–296, 298,

301–302, 307, 310, 313–314
flag 301–304, 315
variable 301–304 (see also *Boolean
functions*)
fMUX (see *fuzzy multiplexers*)
focal element 49
forbidden
clauses 84
conjunctions 84
forecasting 3
formalism 80, 85
for thought processes 269
formal
analysis techniques 332
methods 319–320, 328, 338–340
software architecture analysis 332
specification 309
verification 339
forward chaining 20
frame of discernment 49
functional
evolutionary testing 309
ILP (FILP) 87
testing 288, 292, 309 (see also *specification-based testing*)
function points 4, 54
fuzzy-based models 18
fuzzy clustering 18, 43
fuzzy logic 149, 150
classifiers 148
models 148
fuzzy multiplexers (fMUXs) 148, 150–158,
161, 164, 165–166 (see also *multiplexer*)
fuzzy sets 149, 156–157, 166
and logic 18

G

GAGP 30
GA chromosome 47
GAs (see *genetic algorithms*)
generalized role-based access control (GRBAC)
442
general design scenarios 157
generating code for industrial-strength systems
349
generic processing unit 151
genes and individuals for configuration representation 132
genetics 43

genetic algorithms (GAs) 43–44, 122–123,
        127, 130–134, 142–143, 146, 148, 158,
        160, 162, 166, 274, 280, 287–290,
        292–293, 295, 301, 306, 309, 312–314,
        413 (see also *evolutionary algorithms*)
    for composition analysis 133
    outline 130
genetic algorithm-based
        decision support 130
        QoS analysis tool 121
genetic development of the fMUX networks
        158
genetic operation 289–292, 305, 312
genetic operator 312
genetic optimization 148, 150, 158, 160, 162,
        165
genetic programming (GP) 44, 208–211,
        214–223, 232–233
genetic programs 54
gene
        mapping 142
        representation 292
        space 289
genotypes 44
        representation 158
global
        characterization of a project database 1
        search 288, 293
goodness of
        an empirical model 70
        a model 69
        rule 24, 30
GP (see *genetic programming*)
GP-based model 219
GP modeling process 222
GP optimization 47
GP population 47
gradient-based learning 158
gray code 289
GRBAC (see *generalized role-based access
        control*)
group size 180, 182, 185, 207
guidance 295, 299, 302, 303

H

Halstead
        difficulty 60
        error estimate 60
        intelligent content 60
        length 60
        level 60
        programming effort 60
        programming time 60
        volume 60
Harman, M. 301–303, 313, 315
hazardous condition 310, 311
heuristics 6
hierarchical learning framework 103, 107, 110,
        112, 116, 118 (see also *machine learn-
        ing, MMM_MIL framework*)
    in the MMIR system 110
high-level
        Petri net 339–340
        specification 347–348, 395
human-based estimation 55
hyper pipes 253
hypothesis space 77

I

IBk 252
ID3 4
IF-THEN rules 14, 16, 19–22, 26, 29–30, 34,
        36, 45 (see also *rules*)
IIM (see *inductive inference machine*)
ILP (see *inductive logic programming*)
        problem 77
        system 74
image 108
        representation 113
        retrieval 103–105, 110, 117–118
        segmentation 114
imbalance 182, 186, 191, 193, 195, 203 (see
        also *skewness*)
implementation 388, 346–348, 351–352, 355,
        361, 367, 378–379, 386, 388, 395 (see
        also *realization*)
        of core processes 388
incomplete data 272–273 (see also *missing
        values*)
inconsistent data 272, 280
independent (non-class) variables 55
individual 289, 290–292, 295–296, 301, 306,
        314
induced models 273
induction
        and testing compared 96
        procedure 85–88, 91
inductive bias
        for intersection 82
        for intersection with term sets 83
        of the learning process 80
inductive inference machine (IIM) 79 (see also
        learning system)

inductive learning 175
inductive logic programming (ILP) 74–79, 82,
        85, 87–90, 92–93, 95–97, 99–101
        language 89, 90
inductive program 77, 89–94, 98, 101
        for intersection 92
inductive software process 91
inductive test case generation 97
inference engine 16, 22–23, 25
information extraction
        from MS Project 423
        from Visual SourceSafe 424
initialization 215
input domain 292, 306, 312–314
instance 107–108, 171–173, 175–176, 178,
        181, 183, 185, 202–203, 206
instance-based learning 274
intelligence 266, 281
intelligent analysis of software maintenance
        data 14
International Software Benchmarking Standards
        Group (ISBSG) 2, 7–8, 12
Interprocess Communication 362
Introduction to Testing 95
ISBSG (see *International Software Benchmark-
        ing Standards Group*)

J

J48 251
JM1 Project 255

K

k-nearest neighbor (KNN) 55–56, 61
        algorithm 55–56
KC1 Project 256
KC2 Project 256
kernel density 252
Kestrel interactive development system (KIDS)
        411
KIDS (see *Kestrel interactive development
        system*)
KITSS 412
KNN (see *k-nearest neighbor*)
knowledge-based
        applications 411
        testing 412
knowledge discovery 40, 206
Korat 413
KStar 253

L

LAD (see *least absolute deviation*) 17
language for defining spaces of clauses 80
LASSIE 411
latent semantic indexing (LSI) 107
layered approach 358
learned models 197
learning 148–150, 157–158, 162–163, 166
learning
        intersection 84
        system 76, 77, 79, 91
least absolute deviation (LAD) 17
least median squares (LMS) 2, 7
least squares (LS) 17
linear regression (LR) 2–5, 7, 10, 12
        classifiers 3
lines containing both code and comments 60
lines of comments 60
LMS (see *least median squares*)
local optimal 304
log-based retrieval 106, 116 (see also *image
        retrieval, long-term learning*)
        mechanism 106
logical reasoning 20
logic program 74–77, 80, 85–86, 89–91, 101
        and their examples 76
logic programming 74, 76, 268, 281
logistic regression 250
long-term learning 103, 105–107
low-level Petri net 332, 338
LR (see *linear regression*)
LS (see *least squares*)
LSI (see *latent semantic indexing*)

M

M5 2–6, 10–12
        algorithm 4
        decision tree 5
M5P 2–4, 10–12
machine learner 54, 56
machine learning (ML) 52, 54–55, 62, 68–70,
        74, 105, 107, 117–118, 168–170, 176,
        178, 183–184, 189–191, 204, 265–268,
        271, 278–280 (see also *inductive learn-
        ing, intelligence, supervised learning*)
        algorithm 251, 259–260
        techniques 168
maintainer 18
maintenance 409–410, 412, 414, 417, 419, 425,
        434–435

MANTEMA 414
mapping of the system configurations 143
Markov
        chain model 135
        model for performance analysis 136
        model mediator (MMM) 103, 105–107,
        109–110, 112, 116–117, 120 (see also
        statistical reasoning)
mathematical equations 54
MDP 245
mean magnitude of relative error (MMRE) 7,
        9–10, 12 (see also *Pred(%)*)
measurement 289, 307
memory management 361
meta-heuristic search 287–289, 297, 312 (see
        also *optimization, search problem,
        search technique*)
metrics 54–55, 59–60, 62–63, 70
metric equations 52
MIL (see *multiple instance learning*)
MILOS (see *minimally invasive long term orga-
        nizational support*)
minimally invasive long term organizational
        support 411
MIS 75
misclassification
        cost 169, 197, 198, 200, 203
        error 197
missing values 6, 269, 273, 275
MLR (see *multivariate linear regression*)
MMIR 103
        system 103
MMM (see *Markov mediator model*)
MMM_MIL
        framework 110
        iteration 112
MMRE (see *mean magnitude of relative error*)
model 168–170, 175–176, 179, 183–184, 190,
        197, 200, 202– 204
model-based testing 409–410, 412, 414, 425
        and maintenance 425
model-based test case generation 413
model-driven engineering 346–348, 360–361,
        396
model-level optimizations 372
model checking 333–334, 341
        technique 334
model selection procedure 222
module-order model (MOM) 210–214, 221,
        222–223, 225– 227, 229–233
modules 237–239, 244–245, 247–249, 253,
        255–257, 259–260

module design complexity 60
MOEA (see *multi-objective evolutionary algo-
        rithms*)
MOM (see *module-order model*)
most specific 20
motivation 180
multi-model system 21
multi-objective
        evolutionary algorithms (MOEA) 131,
        146
        optimization 208, 210–211, 218–219,
        232
multilayer feed-forward neural network 109
multiplexer 148, 150–152, 154–156, 161,
        164–165
multiple grammars 357
multiple instance learning (MIL) 103, 105–112,
        116–118 (see also *machine learning*)
multivariate linear regression (MLR) 2
mutation 44, 290–293, 304, 314 (see also *ge-
        netic operation, genetic operator*)
operator 135

N

n-classes 56
n-fold cross validation 55, 56, 69 (see also
        cross validation)
n-tournament selection 305
naive Bayes 252
        classifier 62, 268
NASA 237, 239, 245, 251, 253–254, 257
        datasets 52, 59
        defect repositories 62
        Metrics Data Program (MDP) 59
NASA-based defect
        data 58
        repository dataset 55
"nasty neighbor" test set 61
natural selection 43
Naval Research Laboratories (NRL) 27, 28
nearest-neighbor sampling 60
nearest neighbor-based sampling 68
nearest neighbor
        algorithm 61
        approach 52
        experiments 60
network-interfaces issues 156
network of fMUXs 154
neural net 18
neural networks (NN) 18, 41, 54, 103, 105,
        109, 113–114, 116, 149, 167, 268, 274,
        277, 283

"nice neighbor" test set 61
NN (see *neural networks*)
noise 272–273, 279, 284
    and overfitting 272
nominal attributes 6
non-class
    attributes 55–56
    variable 56
non-consistency mutation 291
non-linear 288, 293, 306
normalized work effort 4, 8
not-fault-prone 249, 250, 260
not relevant heuristic 180
NRL (see *Naval Research Laboratories*)
NSGAII-CAA 133

O

operation 445
optimal solution 287, 288, 292, 304, 313
optimization 317, 347–348, 351, 360, 367, 370,
    372, 378, 380–381, 384–389, 395
outliers 273, 279, 284
output variables 83

P

parameter tuning 184
pareto-optimal
    configuration 129
    front 131–132
    solutions 126, 131
Pargas, R. 295, 296, 315
parse trees 44
path coverage 294, 297
    criterion 294, 297
PC1 Project 255
perceived lack of credibility 52
performance analysis 122, 123, 130, 133,
    135–138, 143
    example 138
    for SOA Systems 137
performance comparison 115
performance measure 184, 191
performance measurement 247
    metric 115
performance requirements 349
performance testing 287–288, 305–306, 309,
    312 (see also *temporal behavior testing,
    temporal performance testing*)
permission 439–441, 443–445, 449–451, 453,
    455

and assignment functions 445
Petri net 321–322, 324, 326, 329, 331–332,
    336–339, 340
    high-level 339–340
    low-level 332, 338
PF (see *probability of a false alarm*)
phenotypes 44
platform 350, 352–353, 360–363, 388
platform-specific interface 360
population 43, 289, 290, 291, 292, 304, 305,
    313
post-pruning 5
pre-processing 182
pre/post conditions 309
precision 169, 191–192, 195, 197, 198, 200,
    202 (see also *accuracy*)
Pred(%) 9, 12 (see also *MMRE*)
predicate 327
    logic 76
    modes 83
    symbols 326
    transition net 322, 337, 339, 342
prediction 15–18, 20–25, 27, 29–30, 33–36,
    265–268, 270, 272, 274–280
    at level 1 7
    of fault-proneness 237, 260
    rate 23, 30, 33, 36–37, 48
    system 16, 22–23, 25, 30, 36–37, 39,
    51 (see also *classification, ensemble-
    based prediction system*)
predictor 171
preferred configurations 129
proactive rule 410, 417, 429–431, 434–435
    for testing and maintenance 434
probability of
    a false alarm (PF) 63, 247
    detection (PD) (or recall) 63, 247
    missing an alarm (NF) 63
problem report 169, 178–179, 188–190, 193,
    195, 197, 200, 202, 207
    attributes 189
    feature 195–197, 202
process of evolution 215
productivity 4
product
    characteristics 7
    metrics 54
programming 409–411, 415–416, 430–431,
    436
program transformation 347–349, 351,
    354–355, 357, 360, 395
    system 348, 351, 354–355, 395

project
    challenged 53
    context 7
    database 1
    effort 281
    failures 53
    management 410–411, 414–415, 422, 430, 435
    metrics 54 (see also *metrics*)
    size data 8
Prolog 75
    notation 80
PROMISE repository 59
property specification 322, 328–333, 335–336, 338, 340
proper interpretation of the results 3
propositional temporal logic 332
protocol data unit (PDU) specifications 353
proximity measurements 244
PrT net 322–330, 332, 334, 336–338

Q

QoS (see quality of service)
QoS-based composition analysis 122, 125, 127, 145
QoS-based composition analysis process 127
QoS analysis 121, 125–126, 129–130, 132–133, 145
    algorithms 133
    process for adaptive SOA systems 128
QoS attribute vector 125
QoS behavior 123, 125, 127, 129, 145
QoS properties of
    individual Web service specification 142
    individual Web dervices 126
QoS property composition 127
    algorithm 127, 129–130
QOS specification model 125
qualifiers 356
qualitative factors 8
quality 350
quality of service (QoS) 122–123, 125–127, 129–130, 132–133, 138, 140, 142–145
quantitative software engineering 148
query-by-example (QBE) 114
query
    center 106
    logs 114
    point 106

R

random forest 237, 239–245, 248–250, 254–257, 259–260 (see also *bagging, balanced random forest, ensemble method*)
    algorithm 241–245, 248–250, 254, 260
random sampling 56
random selection 290–291
random subset selection 217
random testing 288, 293–299, 301–302, 307–309 (see also *automatic testing*)
RBAC 439–443, 449–450, 452, 454–455
RBCC access control model 450
    formal definition of 448
RBCC model 439–440, 444–446, 449–450, 454–455
reachability tree 334–335, 337–338
    technique 334–335, 338
real-world relevance relation 173
realization 347
recall 169, 191–192, 195, 197–198, 200, 202
recombination 290, 293
reconfigurability 121–123
reconfigurable service-oriented systems 121
refinement
    analysis 337
    correctness 333
region 108
region-based
    approaches 106
    learning approach 106
    retrieval 106, 108–109 (see also *content-based image retrieval*)
regression 267
    testing 413, 435, 436
    test selection 414, 425, 428
    tree 17, 18, 51
relationships in role-based access control 443
relationships in SSDM 419
relationship between accuracy and response time 144
relevance feedback (RF) 105–107, 109, 112, 116, 117, 119 (see also *image retrieval*)
relevance relation 169–171, 172–176, 183, 195, 202–203, 207
reliability 338
requirements specification 347
resource
    allocations 128
    specification 127
response time 136–140, 144

RF (see *relevance feedback*)
Rhapsody 412
rigid
    function 326
    variables 326
ROCKY 253
ROC plot 191, 192, 193, 195
role-based access control (RBAC) 439–442,
    444–445
role-based context constrained access control
    model 443
Roper, M. 292, 295, 315
roulette wheel selection 305
rule
    "best" 20
    first applicable 20
    least recently used 20
    most specific 20
    random 20
rule-based modeling (RBM) 19, 273
rule-based models 16, 19–22, 29, 39 (see also
    data models)
rules 15–16, 19–27, 29–39, 265–272, 276–280
ruleset 251
rule applications 429
rule generation and applications 429
rule induction (RI) 265–268, 270–274,
    278–280 (see also *decision trees*)
    in software engineering tasks 274
    in software prediction 265

S

S-PLUS 17
safety
    constraint 310–312 (see also *hazardous*
    condition)
    evolutionary testing 310
    testing 287–288, 292, 309, 311–312
    verification 316
SAM (see *software architecture model*)
    architecture properties 326
    software architecture 321
sampling 55–56, 58, 60–61, 68, 71
    clustered approach 56
    random approach 56
    stratified approach 56
    systematic approach 56
SCENT-Method 412
schedulability 337
SDL (see *Semantic Description Language*)

search
    problem 288, 292, 293, 315
    space 287–289, 292–293, 306, 313 (see
    also *input domain*)
    technique 287–289, 312
security 338
See5/C5 29
    tool 29
selection 215, 289–290, 292–293, 305 (see also
    genetic operation, genetic operator)
    operator 134
    scheme 290
self-adaptation mutation 291
semantic 409–410, 414–417, 422, 429–430,
    434

    Description Language (SDL) 347–348,
    351, 358, 367, 370–372, 378–380,
    384–385, 387–388, 395, 415
    of software engineering 415
    project management model (SPMM)
    422
    software development model (SSDM)
    417
separation of duty (SOD) 449–451
service-oriented architecture (SOA) 121–123,
    125, 129–130, 132–133, 135–138, 143,
    145
service composition 126
set of weights 54
simple object access protocol (SOAP) 123
simple transformation rules 355
single-point crossover 290
singular value decomposition (SVD) 107
size 3
    metrics 60
skewness 193, 195, 197, 200
SLIM 54
Smoothing 7
SOA (see *service-oriented architecture*)
    background 123
SOD (see *separation of duty*)
SoftArch 411
software architecture 319–322, 328–333,
    337–340
    model (SAM) 321–322, 326, 328–330,
    332–333, 336–337, 339–340
    specification 321, 328, 330–331, 333,
    339–340
software attributes 17, 33
software components 14, 29–30, 33, 39, 56,
    340

software configuration systems 178
software cost-estimation techniques 54
software cost estimating 54
software data 163
   models 17
software defect 15, 54, 277, 282
   prediction 54, 277
software design 410–412, 414, 431
software development 75, 89, 92, 95, 266,
   270, 274, 278–280, 409–412, 414–418,
   421–422, 429–431, 435
   process 409–410, 415, 417, 429
   workflow control 430
software effort 267, 274–275, 279 (see *project
   effort*)
   (cost) prediction 274
software engineering 2, 7, 11, 52, 54–55, 58,
   68, 70, 409–410, 415–416, 435
   data 58
   datasets 2, 9
   maintenance data 27
   problems 3
   projects 2
   repository 3
   tasks 274
software entity 171
software fault 209
   tree analysis 311
software intrusion detection 278
software life cycle 54
software maintenance 14–16, 19, 89, 94,
   413–414, 419, 435
   activities 14
   adaptive 15
   corrective 15
   data 14, 16
   data models 16
   effort prediction models 18
   perfective 15
   preventive 15
   process 15
software measurement 256, 261
software metrics 17–18, 40, 54, 211, 223–224,
   228, 233, 238, 245–255, 259–260
   data program (MDP) 245
software modules 17, 18
software prediction 265, 266, 272, 279, 280
   (see also *classification, prediction*)
software processes 149
software process modelling 278
software products 149
   metrics 60

software project management 53
software quality 17, 148–149, 166, 208–213,
   217–218, 220, 222–224, 226, 232–233
   (fault) prediction 275
   classification model 208, 211
   model 238–239 (see also *faulty prediction*)
   prediction 238–239, 249, 255, 259–260
software requirements 417–418, 420
software reuse 74, 89
Software Technology Transfer Finland (STTF)
   2
software testing 418, 434, 436
solution space 289
soundness 79
   and completeness 79
source code 178
source comments 189
source file comments 188, 197
   attributes 189
source lines of code (SLOC) 56, 70 (see also
   size metrics)
specification 319–323, 325–326, 328–333,
   335–336, 338–340
specification-based
   evolutionary testing 309, 311
   testing 287–288, 309, 311–312 (see
   also *functional testing*)
Specification Description Language 413
specification language 347, 359, 370 (see also
   domain-specific notation)
SPMM (see s*emantic project management
   model*)
   construction 422
SSDM (see *semantic software development
   model*)
   annotations 419
   construction 420
   structure 417
Standish Group 53
statement coverage 294, 296, 298, 304–305
   criterion 294
states 326
   functions 327
   variables 326
static
   analysis 311–312, 314 (see also *safety
   verification*)
   separation of duty 450
statistical reasoning 105–106, 109–110
   mechanism 109

Sthamer, H. 289, 292–293, 295, 298–302, 306,
        313, 315
stochastic sampling with replacement 44
stopping condition 290, 292–293, 307, 313
stratified sampling 56, 58, 61
structural
        evolutionary testing 293, 295, 301, 304,
        305
        testing 287–288, 292–295, 297, 301,
        304, 309, 312–313, 315
structures of software architectures 321
subtransformation 356
successful projects 53
summary work effort 8
supervised learning 106, 175, 182, 202,
        267–268 (see also *classification*)
        algorithm 56
        methods 267
support vector machine (SVM) 107
survival 290–292 (see also *genetic operation,
        genetic operator*)
Sustainable Computing Consortium (SCC) 54
syntactic
        attributes 187
        device 82
        features 188, 195, 196, 197
syntax and static semantics of PrT nets 323
systematic sampling 56
system
        architecture 414
        context 447
        life 350
        properties in temporal logic 328
        QoS requirements 126
        QoS specification 140
        relevance graph 171, 172
        relevance subgraph 171, 172
        size 349
        static relevance graph (SSRGR) 172

T

t-conorm 150, 151, 152, 158, 163
t-norm 151, 152, 164
t-test 67
TACCLE 412
target platform interaction 350
task/thread/process management 361
tasks 414, 430
temporal behavior 305–307
        errors 306
        testing 307

temporal error 306, 307
temporal formulas 327
temporal logic 322, 326–329, 332, 334–340
        formula 322, 326–337
temporal performance testing 287–288,
        305–306, 309, 312
temporal role-based access control 441
ten-fold cross validation 52, 55, 67
term sets 81
testability transformation 302–303, 315
testing 74, 80, 89, 91, 94–98, 101, 409–410,
        412–414, 417–418, 425, 427, 430–431,
        434–435
        criterion 294–295 (see also *coverage
        criterion*)
        standard 288
TestTube 413
test aim 293, 299, 312
test case generation 413–414, 425, 427, 437
        for all-branch testing 425
        procedure 97
test data generation 288–289, 292–293, 295,
        299, 301–302, 312
test object 292–293, 295, 299, 301, 306, 311,
        313
test set formulation 60
test suite 413
text-based
        attributes 188
        features 193, 195–197
theorem proving 335
time-critical 307
timer management 362
timing constraints 306–307, 316
total lines of code 60
total operands 60
total operators 60
Tracey, N. 298, 309, 311–312, 316
traditional random forests algorithm 254
training and test set formulation 60
transferable belief model (TBM) 25, 50
transformational implementation 347 (see also
        program transformation)
transformation
        and encoding 183
        of nominal attributes 6
        rules 354
        sets 356
transitions 327
transparency 148–149, 165
transparent model 19
traversal order 356

tree-based models 17
trigger 424
"true" logic programs 74
true negative rate (TNR) 247
true positive rate 191, 193, 198, 200 (see also
        recall)
tuples 56

U

UCON 443
UML 347–348, 351, 368, 370– 372, 378, 388
unadjusted function points 9
uncertainties in data 272
uniform crossover 290
unique
        operands 60
        operators 60
unlabelled data 267
update 174, 175, 178

V

v(g) 56, 57, 58 (see also cyclomatic complex-
        ity)
VAF (see value adjustment factor)
validation dataset 24
validation process of IF-THEN rules 30
values 326
value adjustment factor (VAF) 9
verification 320, 333, 335–339, 341
        technique 336
VF1 252
vocabulary metrics 60
voted perceptron 252
voting 21, 36, 37

W

Waikato environment for knowledge analysis
        (Weka) tool 2–4, 10, 12, 62
Web Ontology Language (OWL) 122
Web service (WS) 122–129, 131–133, 137–141,
        143, 145
Web service-based SOA 123
Web Services Description Language (WSDL)
        123
Web services system model 124
Wegener, J. 288–289, 292–293, 295, 298,
        300–301, 306–307, 309, 311–315
Weichselbaum, R. 295, 317

Weka (see Waikato environment for knowledge
        analysis)
        confusion matrix 63
        toolkit 2, 3
white box 101
        model 19 (see also transparent model)
wireless configurations systems 227
work effort 2
WREN 411

Z

zone regression method 1

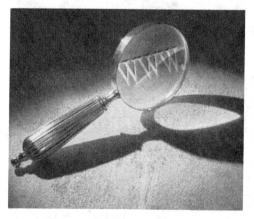